The

BRIHATA JATAKAM

of

Varaha Mihira

Sri Garib Das Oriental Series No.318

BRIHATA JATAKAM

of

Varaha Mihira

Translated by

SWAMI VIJNANANDA

Sri Satguru Publications
A Division of
Indian Books Centre
Delhi, India

Published by
Sri Satguru Publications,
Indological and Oriental Publishers
A Division of
Indian Books Centre
40/5, Shakti Nagar,
Delhi-110007
India

First Edition : Allahabad, 1912
Reprinted : Delhi, 2008

ISBN 81-7030-873-9

Printed at Sachin Printers, Delhi.

CONTENTS

FOREWORD

The Jyotiṣa Śâstra is counted as one of the six aṃgas of the Vedas. All the religious rites and sacrifices of the Hindus are guided by Astronomy and Astrology, both of which are included in the Jyotiṣa Śâstra. Indeed, Astrology is considered as the eye of the Vedas.

Astrology is the oldest of all sciences. Its history is traced back to the Vedas whose wise Ṛiṣis, by the expansion of their consciousness, could reach the Shining Ones. From India the belief in Astrology spread to China, Babylonia and Chaldea ; whence it spread to Egypt, Greece, Rome, and throughout the whole world. Once it taught the people to lift their aspirations by faith, hope, and reverence, through the stars and the planetary spirits to the One and Universal Self.

The hoary saints of the ancient ages, fraught with wisdom, held that "an affinity existed between the stars and the souls of men ; that the ethereal essence is Divine ; that the souls of men are taken from this reservoir and return to it at death ; and that the souls of the more eminent of mankind are converted into stars."

When we come to consider that Astrology was the beginning of nearly all that we hold valuable in art, literature, religion and science ; that the asterisms and the constellations were our first pictures ; and that Astronomy and Astrology sprang from India, we may judge of its value to humanity : nor shall we wonder at its survival amidst the fall of nations and the decline of mighty races.

There are two broad and rational principles on which Astrology is based.

The first principle upon which the science of Astrology rests is that of Vedânta, that the whole Universe is actually what the term implies—a unity ; and that a law which is found in manifestation in one portion of the Universe must also be equally operative throughout the whole. While the Heavens form the macrocosm, man is the microcosm. Each man is a little world exactly representing the Universe. While all seem quiet without, there is an active world within. Such a world is visible to the inner sight of a Yogi. Those laws which are operative among the planetary bodies are also in force amongst ourselves.

The second principle is that, by a study of the motions and relative positions of the planets, the operations of these laws may be observed, measured and determined.

From these two principles, aided by observation and a metaphysical mind, the whole science of Astrology herein expounded can be deduced. Failure in Astrological predictions arises from error in calculation. A well versed and conscientious astrologer is always to be consulted. Error in calculation is as sinful as the murder of a Brâhmiṇ. The best test that can be applied to Astrology, where first-hand knowledge is required, is that of experience.

In Hindu Astronomy the places of the planets and the other heavenly bodies are reckoned from the 1st point of the Nakṣatra Aśvinî, which is constant; whereas in the Western method the places are reckoned from the variable Vernal Equinox, one of the two points where the Ecliptic cuts the Equator. This point is the Western first point of Aries. It has a retrograde motion at the rate of 50″ a year.

Taking entire human life into consideration, the true view is that a man is both a slave of the effects of his *previous karma* in his past incarnations and is a free agent as regards fresh independent deeds, deeds which are in no way directed to thwart, to arrest, to alter, or in any way to modify or remould the effects of his past *karma*. But if he wishes to move along with the natural course of things he may do so and the course will become more easy and more smooth. This view will account for three things:—(1) the many apparently unaccountable failures of attempts, even when the individual tries his best; (2) the easy success on many occasions, even when the individual does not try his best; (3) the success that attends on proportionate labour. In the first case, the attempt was one aimed at moving against the current of fate; in the second case, it was one of moving down with the current; and in the third case, it was an attempt where free human agency can display itself.

Astrology gives us the knowledge of our past *karma*, how to fight against it, as well as how to work out our fresh deeds, so that we can get rid of this wheel of *karma* and be free.

The Bṛihat Jâtaka of Varâha Mihira is generally considered all over India as one of the best and most authoritative treatises on the science of Hindu Horoscopy. In fact, Varâha Mihira is recognised as the greatest of the Indian Astrologers. There are four commentaries on this work. The well-known is that of Bhaṭṭa Utpala; another is known as Subodhini; the third is Mudrâkṣari, and the fourth is known as Srîpatîyam. The commentary of Bhaṭṭa Utpala is followed in this work.

The author has written a smaller work on Astrology known as Laghu Jâtaka. Horoscopy is one of the three sections of Jyotiṣ Śâstra; and Śrî

Varâha Mihirâchârya has treated of all the three branches. The other two branches are Saṃhitâ and Astronomy. On Saṃhitâ, the author's treatise is known as Bṛihat Saṃhitâ, and his Astronomical work is known as Pañcha Siddhântikâ. Varâha Mihira has also written a work on Yoga Yâtrâ. Some say, he lived in the reign of Vikramâditya in the Court of Ujjain and is one of the nine gems (Navaratnas) of the Court. According to this, Varâha Mihira's age would be 24 Vikrama Samvat. Others hold that he lived about the time of 427 Śaka Era, or, 507 A.D, *i.e.*, in the sixth century.

In conclusion, it may be added that Truth can never be destroyed and when we recognise in Astrology the law of the Almighty, we need some courage, as well as mental ability, before we commence the task of learning the harmony of the law of the Almighty. Yet the same energy that is expended in seeking to refute it would, if turned in the direction of learning its first principles, unbar the gate that leads to its understanding.

THE

BRIHAJJATAKAM OF VARAHA MIHIRA

A COMPLETE TREATISE ON HOROSCOPIC ASTROLOGY

FIRST CHAPTER

ON ZODIACAL SIGNS

First Principles and Definitions

शा॰वि॰–मूर्तित्वे परिकल्पितः शशभृतो वर्त्माऽपुनर्जन्मना-
मात्मेत्यात्मविदां क्रतुश्च यजतां भर्तामरज्योतिषाम् ॥
लोकानां प्रलयोद्भवस्थितिविभुश्चानेकधा यः श्रुतौ
वाचं नः स ददात्वनेककिरणस्त्रैलोक्यदीपो रविः ॥१॥

मूर्तित्वे Mûrtitve, to unfold the different phases. परिकल्पितः Parikalpitaḥ, duly arranged; intended entirely. शशभृतः Śaśabhritaḥ, of the moon; of the bearer of spots resembling a hare. Some read शशिभृतः Śaśibhritaḥ, of the god Mahâdeva, who holds moon on his forehead. The Sun is considered to be one of the eight forms of the God Śiva or Mahâdeva. वर्त्मा Vartmâ, the path; the Devayâna or the path of liberation. अपुनर्जन्मनाम् Apunarjanmanâm, of those having no more future births. आत्मा Âtmâ, the Great Self, the Supreme Spîrit. इति Iti, thus. आत्मविदां Âtmavidâm, of the knowers of Self, of those that have realised the Supreme Spirit. क्रतुः Kratuḥ, the Sacrificial Deity. च, Cha. and. यजतां, Jajatâm, of the sacrificers; of those that perform sacrifices. भर्ता Bhartâ, the Chief Supporter; the Supreme. अमरज्योतिषाम् Amarayotiṣâm, amongst the Devas, planets and stars; the Immortal Lights. लोकानाम् Lokânâm, of the (seven) worlds. प्रलयोद्भवस्थितिविभुः Pralayod bhavasthitivibhuḥ, The Creator, Preserver, and Destroyer. च, Cha, and. अनेकधा Anekadhâ, under various names; in various ways. यः yaḥ, who. श्रुतौ Śrutau, in the Vedâs. वाचं Vâcham, the speech. नः Naḥ, unto us. स Sa, he. ददातु Dadâtu, may grant. अनेककिरणः Anekakiraṇaḥ, many-rayed. त्रैलोक्यदीपः Trailokyadîpaḥ, the lamp of the three worlds. रविः Raviḥ, the Sun.

1. May the radiant Sun grant me speech, the Sun who by his light illumines the three worlds and unfolds the different phases of the Moon; who is the Path of those that will have no more incarnations, the Self of the Yogins and the Sacrifice of the Sacrificers; the Up-holder of the Immortal Lights, the gods, planets, and stars; the Creator, Preserver and Destroyer of the seven worlds and who is sung in the Vedas under various names and in various ways.

Note:—The author, Varâhamihirâchârya invokes at the commence ment, the blessings of Sûrya Nârâyaṇa.

The Jyotiṣ (Astronomy, and Astrology, considered as one in ancient times) is counted as one of the six angas or sub-divisions of the Vedas that every Brâhmaṇa must study for his welfare in this and in the other world, inasmuch as it ascertains the exact time when several sacrifices are to be performed and what will be the fruits acquired thereby. Thus the Jyotiṣ is recognised as the eye of the Vedas and as such its superiority is recognised over the other sub-divisions as written in the following verse.

शब्दशास्त्रं मुखं ज्योतिषं चक्षुषी श्रोत्रमुक्तं निरुक्तं च कल्पः करौ ।
या तु शिक्षास्य वेदस्य सा नासिका पादपद्मद्वयं छंद आद्यैर्बुधैः ॥

Thus has been said by the great seer Garga:

"The king who does not honour a scholar accomplished in horoscopy and astronomy, clever in all branches and accessories, comes to grief.

"Even those who, free from egotism and without anything to care for, lead a hermit's life in the wilderness, consult the man that knows the motion of the stars.

"As the night without a light, as the sky without a sun, so is a king without an astrologer; like a blind man, he erreth on the road.

"If there were no astrologer, the hours, dates, asterisms, seasons, and half-years would all be confused.

"Therefore a king should consult a learned and eminent astrologer if he desire victory, glory, fortune, enjoyments, and happiness. —(Chap. II Brihat Saṃhitâ verses 7-11).

N. B.—The earth is being always vitalized by the Immortal Lights from above, by the Sun, Moon, and stars in the ethereal space. All persons born under any particular influence in any particular time will have the characteristics of that particular influence for that particular moment strongly marked in their individual nature. It has been found by a species of inner revelation that the people get their gross material elements mainly from the ethereal space, their desires and personalities from the Moon, their feelings and emotions from the stars, their mental feelings from the planets, and their spirituality from the Sun. So man must learn to rise, till having conquered passion, and having subdued the mind he stands forth free and untrammelled, free from Karma, the idea of fate, the outermost ring of limitation in life, stands in purity, perfect in wisdom, radiant, and in love supreme. Man to effect his liberation from future births must face his way towards the Sun and when he passes through this solar vesture, he reaches the final Goal, merging in the Supreme Spirit.

The word Astrology interpreted means the logic of the stars or " The reason of the stars." There is a general idea that Astrology teaches fatalism. There seem to be many arguments in favour of that idea, but those who have studied the subject from the deeper stand-point, know that it does not teach absolute fatalism. All our mistakes are the results of ignorance. If we had more knowledge there would be less misfortune; therefore it is contended that if we have a knowledge of Astrology --which is a science of life--we should avoid many of our misfortunes. It is shown in the following chapters how that can be done.

शा० वि०--भूयोभिः पटुबुद्धिभिः पटुधियां होराफलज्ञप्तये
शब्दन्यायसमन्वितेषु वहुशः शास्त्रेषु दृष्टेष्वपि ॥
होरातंत्रमहार्णवप्रतरणे भग्नोद्यमानामहं
स्वल्पं वृत्तविचित्रमर्थवहुलं शास्त्रप्लवं प्रारभे ॥ २ ॥

भूयोभिः Bhûyobhiḥ, by many, by numerous. पटुबुद्धिभिः Paṭubuddhibhiḥ, by clever intelligent thinkers. पटुधियां Paṭudhiyâṃ, for clever intelligent persons. होराफलज्ञप्तये Horâphalajñaptaye, to expound the results of past actions (from the rising of a zodiacal sign at a particular moment). शब्दन्यायसमन्वितेषु Śabdanyâyasamanviteṣu, full of deeply reflected reasonable meanings. बहुशः Bahuśaḥ, many a time. शास्त्रेषु Sâstreṣu, astrological works, treatises. दृष्टेषु Dristeṣu, after consulting with अपि Api, even. होरातन्त्रमहार्णवप्रतरणे Horâtantra mahârṇavapratarane, to cross the great ocean of astrological science. भग्नोद्यमानां Bhagnodyamânâm, for the disheartened; for those whose energies have been thwarted. अहम् Aham, I. (Varâhamihirâchârya of Avantika). स्वल्पं Svalpam, concise, not big. वृत्तविचित्रम् Vrittavichitram, ornamented with various metres. अर्थबहुलं, Arthabahulam full of much meaning, complete. शास्त्रप्लवं Sâstraplavam, this sacred book, like a boat. प्रारभे Prârabhe, I begin (to write.)

2. Though many clever thinkers have written various works on Astrology to explain to persons of great intellect this vast science, after pondering over authoritative kindred works full of logic and deep meanings yet the people were disheartened in their attempts to cross this ocean of horoscopy and for such I begin to write this concise yet complete treatise in varied metres and I hope it, like a boat, will safely carry them across.

Note :—There are well-known works of Parâśara, Gárga, Bâdarâyaṇa, Satyâchârya, Yavanâcharya, Maya and others.

इंद्रवज्रा-होरेत्यहोरात्रविकल्पमेके वांछंति पूर्वापरवर्णलोपात् ।
कर्मार्जितं पूर्वभवे सदादि यत्तस्य पक्तिं समभिव्यनक्ति ॥ ३ ॥

होरा Horâ, the word horâ. इति Iti, thus. अहोरात्रविकल्पम् Ahorâtravikalpam, synonym or abbreviation of the word Ahorâtram. एके Eke, some ; others. वांछंति Vânchhanti, are inclined to take. पूर्वापरवर्णलोपात् Pûrvâparavarṇalopât, by dropping the first and last syllables. कर्मार्जितं karmârjitam, earned by deeds. पूर्वभवे Purvabhave. done in previous existences. सदादि Sadádi, good or bad. यत्, Yat, whatever. तस्य Tasya, of which ; whose. पक्तिं Paktim. matured state, fit to bear any fruit. समभिव्यनक्ति, Samabhivyanakti, fully reveals ; clearly manifests.

3. Some persons take the word Horâ as an abbreviated form of Ahorâtram (convenient for frequent usage) ; they drop the first syllable (अ) 'a' and last syllable (त्रं) 'tram' from the word Ahorâtram. (And this they account for by saying that). This day and night makes these twelve zodiacal signs fully visible to us, that represent the matured state of all good and bad actions done in previous existences and now ready to yield their fruits.

Note.—Whatever works, good or bad, we did in our previous births, we get their fruits here in this birth. But we do not know beforehand what these fruits would be : hence we do this grahavichâr, *i. e.*, these astrological calculations. These works are of two kinds, strong and weak (दृढ, अदृढ). The strong works produce दशाफल daśaphala, *i. e.*, periods of fruition given by the several planets ; and when these are auspicious, royal marches, journeys, sacred pilgrimages and any other good works are to be taken in hand ; and if inauspicious, not to be taken in hand. The weak actions bear fruits that are determined by Aṣṭavarga, *i.e.*, by the several positions of the seven planets and the Lagna, as described in Chapter IX. And when these signs are inauspicious, peace-offerings are to be made to the planetary deities to cast off their pernicious influences. In short, the strong are fated to occur and can never be modified; the weak ones can be avoided by proper śântis. The word "horâ" is really a Greek word and the author of this treatise was not ignorant of its origin. Therefore he says "some say horâ is an abbreviation of Ahorâtram" this is not *really* his opinion. Horâ is the same word as the hour in English and "horâśâstram" means the science of calculating time.

शा०वि०–कालांगानि वरांगमाननमुरो हृत्क्रोडवासोभृतो-
बस्तिर्व्यंजनमूरुजानुयुगुले जंघे ततोऽङ्घ्रिद्वयम् ॥
मेषाश्विप्रथमा नवर्क्षचरणाश्चक्रस्थिता राशयो-
राशिक्षेत्रगृहर्क्षभानि भवनं चैकार्थसंप्रत्ययाः ॥ ४ ॥

कालांगानि Kâlângâni, (The several limbs of) the body of the Zodiacal Man (Time represented by zodiacs.) वरांगं Varângam head. आननम् Ânanam, face. उरः uraḥ, the chest. हृत्क्रोडवासोभृतः Hṛitkroḍavâsobhritaḥ, Heart, belly and waist. बस्तिः Bastiḥ, the abdomen, pelvis. व्यंजनं Vyanjanaṃ, the generative organ, the secrets. ऊरुजानुयुगुले Urujânuyugule, the two thighs and knees. जंघे Janghe, the two legs. The two shanks. ततः Tataḥ, from that; afterwards. अंघ्रिद्वयम् Anghridvayam, the two feet. मेषाश्विप्रथमानवर्क्षचरणाः Meṣâśviprathamânavarkṣacharaṇâḥ, sign called Meṣaḥ, the Aries or Ram extending over the nine feet of the asterisms commencing with the asterism Aśvinî (and the successive eleven signs occupying the nine feet at a time of the other asterisms.) चक्रस्थिताराशयः Chakrasthitârâśayaḥ, the signs of the zodiacal circle. राशिक्षेत्रगृहर्क्षभानि Raśikṣetragriharkhṣabhâni, the words râśi (signs), kṣetra (field), griha (house), rikṣa (constellation), and bhaṃ (collection of asterisms). भवनं Bhavanam, mansion. च Cha, and. एकार्थसंप्रत्ययाः Ekârthasaṃpratyâḥ, carrying one and the same meaning; are synonyms.

4. The signs of the zodiac, the Ram, etc., are represented successively by the nine pâdas (feet) of the several stars commencing with Aśvinî. And these signs are (imagined to be the several limbs of the) body of the Zodiacal Man (called Time-Person or Kâlapuruṣa); such as the Ram, etc., are successively represented as the head, face, chest, heart, belly, waist, pelvis, the generative organ, the

thighs, the knees, the legs and the feet. The words Khṣetraṃ, Gṛiham, Rikṣam, bham and bhavanam all denote the same meanings that a Râśi denotes (*i.e.*, a sign of the zodiac); these words are synonymous.

Note.—The twelve signs of the Zodiac are—(1) Meṣa, The Aries or Ram; (2) Vṛiṣa, The Taurus or Bull; (3) Mithuna; The Gemini or Twins; (4) Karkaṭa, The Cancer or Crab; (5) Siṃha, The Leo or Lion; (6) Kanyâ, The Virgo or Virgin; (7) Tulâ, The Librâ or Balance; (8) Vṛiśchika, The Scorpio or Scorpion; (9) Dhanu, The Sagittarius or Archer; (10) Makara, The Capricorn; (11) Kumbha, The Aquarius or Water-carrier; (12) Mîna, The Pisces or Fishes.

The several limbs of the Zodiacal Man are shewn in the annexed diagram:—

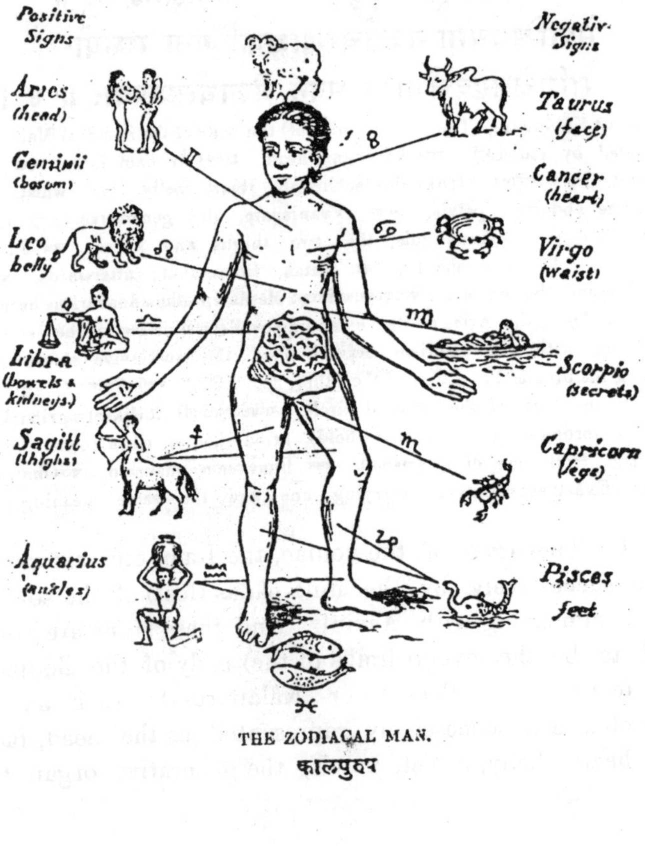

THE ZODIACAL MAN.

कालपुरुष

There are twenty-seven asterisms.—1. Aśvinî. 2. Bharaṇî. 3. Krittikâ. 4. Rohiṇî. 5. Mrigaśirâ. 6. Ârdrâ, 7. Punarvasu. 8. Puṣyâ. 9. Aśleṣâ. 10. Maghâ. 11. Purvaphalgunî. 12. Uttaraphalgunî. 13. Hastâ. 14. Chitrâ. 15. Svâti, 16. Viśâkhâ. 17. Anurâdhâ. 18. Jyeṣṭhâ. 19. Mûlâ. 20. Purvâṣaḍhâ. 21. Uttarâṣaḍhâ. 22. Śravaṇâ. 23 Dhaniṣṭhâ. 24. Śatabhiṣâ. 25. Purvabhâdrapada. 26. Uttarabhâdrapada. 27. Revatî.

Each asterism has got four feet. 27 asterisms have 108 feet. And these are equally divided amongst the twelve signs. So each sign has got nine pâdas. Thus (1) Meṣa is represented by Asvini, Bharaṇî, and one pâda (*i.e.*, one-fourth) of Krittikâ ; (2) Vṛiṣa by 3 pâdas of Krittikâ, Rohiṇî, and 2 pâdas of Mrigaśirâ ; (3) Mithuna by 2 feet of Mrigaśirâ, Ârdrâ and 3 feet of Punarvasu ; (4) Karkaṭa by one foot of Punarvasu, Puṣyâ, Aśleṣâ ; (5) Siṃha by Maghâ, Pûrva Phalgunî, and one foot of Uttara Phalgunî ; (6) Kanyâ by 3 feet of Uttara Phalgunî, Hastâ and 2 feet of Chitrâ ; (7) Tulâ by 2 feet of Chitrâ, Svâti, and 3 feet of Viśâkhâ ; (8) Vṛiśchik by one foot of Viśâkhâ, Anurâdhâ, Jyeṣṭhâ ; (9 Dhanu by Mûlâ, Purvâṣâḍhâ, and one foot of Uttarâṣâḍhâ ; (10) Makara by 3 feet of Uttarâṣâḍhâ, Śravanâ, and two feet of Dhaniṣṭhâ ; (11) Kumbha by 2 feet of Dhaniṣṭhâ, Śatabhiṣâ and 3 feet of P. Bhâdrapada ; and (12) Mîna, is represented by one foot of Pûrva Bhâdrapada, Uttara Bhâdrapada, and Revatî.

Each sign of the zodiac is characterised by a special part of the human body ; thus :—Meṣa is represented by the head ; Vṛiṣa, by the face ; Mithuna, by the breast ; Karkaṭa, by the heart ; Siṃha, by the belly ; Kanyâ, by the hip ; Tulâ, by the abdomen ; Vṛiśchik by the generative organ ; Dhânu, by the thighs ; Makara, by the knees ; Kumbha by the legs, and Mîna, by the feet. See the figure of the Zodiacal Man (Kâla Puruṣa). And therefore when a malefic planet is in any sign, the part of the body characterised by that sign gets afflicted by a scar, or wound or marked by spots like those of a scar ; and when a benefic planet rules any sign then the corresponding part of the body is seen to be fully developed.

Note:—The following table will be useful for purposes of ready reference :—

Râśi.	Sign.	Part of body.
1 Meṣa	Aries	Head.
2 Vṛiṣa	Taurus	Face.
3 Mithuna	Gemini	Chest.
4 Karka·	Cancer	Heart.
5 Siṃha	Leo	Belly,

Rasi.	Sign.	Part of body.
6 Kanyâ	Virgo	Waist.
7 Tulâ	Libra	Pelvis.
8 Vriśchika	Scorpio	The secrets.
9 Dhanu ...	Sagittari	Two thighs.
10 Makara	Capricorn	Two knees.
11 Kumbha	Aquarius	Two legs.
12 Mina	Pisces	Two feet.

The twenty-seven Nakṣatras or asterisms are :—

1 Asvinî (a)	β Arietis.
2 Bharanî (b)	35 Arietis and Musca.
3 Krittikâ (c)	η Tauri. Pleiades.
4 Rohiṇî (d)	α Tauri, Aldebaran.
5 Mrigasirâ (e)	λ Orionis.
6 Ârdrâ (f)	α Orionis.
7 Punarvasu (g)	β Geminū Pollux.
8 Puṣyâ (h)	δ Cancri.
9 Asloṣâ (i)	δ Hydrae 1 & 2 Cancri.
10 Maghâ (j)	α Leonis, Regulus.
11 P. Phalgunî (k)	δ Leonis.
12 U. Phalgunî (l)	β Leonis.
13 Hastâ (m)	ζ Corvi.
14 Chitrâ (n)	α Virginis, Spica.
15 Svati (o)	α Bootis, Arcturus.
16 Viśakhâ (p)	ι Librae.
17 Anurâdhâ (q)	δ Scorpionis.
18 Jyeṣṭhâ (r)	χ Scorpionis, Antares.
19 Mûlâ (s)	λ Scorpionis.
20 P. Âṣâḍhâ (t)	δ Sagittari.
21 U. Âṣâḍhâ (u)	ε Sagittarius.
22 Śravanâ (v)	σ Aquilæ, Altair.
23 Dhaniṣṭhâ (w)	β Delphini.
24 Śatabhiṣâ (x)	λ Aquarii.
25 P. Bhâdrapada (y)	σ Pegasi.
26 U. Bhâdrapada (z)	η Pegasi and Andromedæ.
27 Revatî (a')	ζ Piscium.

The asterisms are denoted in diagrams in this book by a, b, c, d, &c., unless otherwise specified.

वसंततिलका-मत्स्यौ घटी नृमिथुनं सगदं सवीणं
चापी नरोऽश्वजघनो मकरो मृगास्यः ॥
तौली ससस्यदहना प्लवगा च कन्या
शेषाः स्वनामसदृशाः स्वचराश्च सर्वे ॥५॥

मत्स्यौ Matsyau, the two fishes (the tail of each being in the mouth of the other). घटी Ghaṭi, a man carrying on his shoulders an empty water-jar. नृमिथुनं Nrimithunum, man and woman, the couple. सगदं Sagadam, the man with club (in his hand). सवीणं Sabînam, the woman with flute (in her hand.) चापी Châpî, the man with arrow (in his hand). नरः Naraḥ, the man. अश्वजघनः Asvajaghanaḥ, the lower part of the body like that of a horse. मकरः Makaraḥ, (The sign Makara resembling the body of) the shark or crocodile. मृगास्यः Mṛigâsyaḥ, the face like an antelope (or like an elephant). तौली Tauli, the man with a balance in his hand. सस्यदहना Sasasyadahanâ, with ears of corn and fire. प्लवगा Plavagâ, on a boat; resting in a boat. च Cha, and. कन्या Kanyâ, virgin. शेषाः Śeṣaḥ, the others, the remaining signs. स्वनामसदृशाः. Svanâmasadṛiśâḥ, resembling those that are signified by their own names. स्वचराः Svacharâḥ, moving (dwelling) in their own places respectively, (as seen in life). च Cha, and. सर्वे Sarve, all (the signs).

5. The Pisces is represented by the twin fishes (the tail of each in the mouth of the other); the Aquarius, by a man carrying a water-jar; the Geminii, by a couple, man and woman, man with a staff and woman with a harp; the Sagittarius, by an archer with a bow, his upper part resembling a man and lower part a horse; the Capricorn is represented with a face like an elephant (or deer) and body like that of a shark or crocodile. The Libra is represented by a man with a balance (in his hand). The Virgo is represented by a virgin in a boat with ears of corn in one hand and fire in the other. The rest (*i.e.*, the Ram, the Bull, the Cancer, the Leo, the Scorpio) resembling animals that are signified by their own names respectively.[1] And all these twelve signs move in their respective spheres. (The dwelling places of the several signs are places appropriate to the several creatures.)

Notes.—The individual having Meṣa propensities roams and lives in forests; having Vṛiṣa tendencies lives in mountains and villages; with inclinations of Karkaṭa tries to live in water; of Siṃha, roams and lives in forests; of Kanyâ, in particular localities as seen in life; of Tulâ, lives in markets and roads where various businesses are being transacted; of Vṛiśchika, lives in holes and dens; of Dhanu, lives in villages; if of the first half of Makara lives in forests; of the second half of Makara, lives in

[1] The sign Meṣa is of the shape of a ram; Vṛiṣa, of the shape of a bull; Karka, of the shape of a crab; Siṃha, of the shape of a lion; and Vriśchika, of the shape of a scorpion.

water ; of Kumbha, lives in villages ; and the individual with tendencies of Mîna, lives in water.

See the Figure Zodiac, given below :—

THE ZODIAC

राशिचक्र

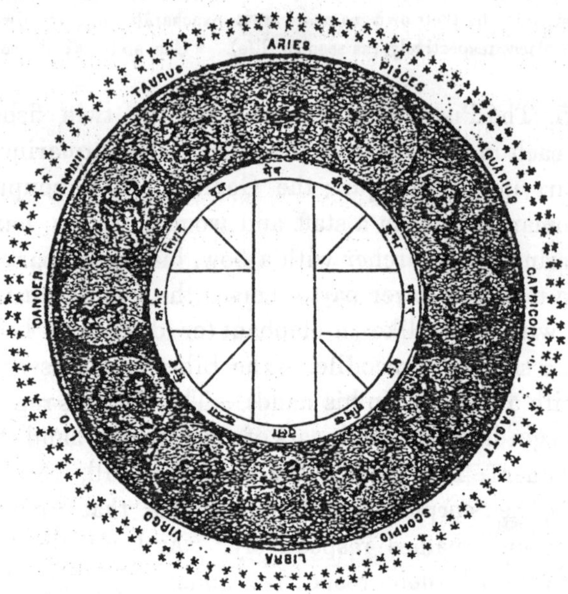

This stanza as well as stanza 4 are chiefly useful in questions connected with horary astrology, in the discovery of stolen property and the like.

त्रोटक ।

क्षितिजसितज्ञचन्द्ररविसौम्यसितावनिजाः ।

सुरगुरुमन्दसौरिगुरवश्च गृहांशकपाः ॥

अजमृगतौलिचन्द्रभवनादिनवांशविधि-

र्भवनसमांशकाधिपतयः स्वगृहात् क्रमशः ॥ ६ ॥

क्षितिजसितज्ञचंद्ररविसौम्यसितावनिजाः: Khṣitija sita jña chandra ravi saumya sitâ vanijâḥ, Mars, Venus, Mercury, the Moon, the Sun, Mercury, Venus, the Mars.

सुरगुरुमन्दसौरिगुरवः Suragurumandasauriguravaḥ, Jupiter, Saturn, Saturn, Jupiter. च Cha, and. गृहांशकपाः gṛihâṃśakapâḥ;(are) the rulers (the lords) of the houses and their several parts. अजमृगतौलिचन्द्रभवनादि नवांशविधिः Aja mriga tauli chandra bhavanâdi navâṃśavidhiḥ, (the rulers of) Meṣa, Makara, Tulâ, Karkaṭa being respectively the rulers of the first ninth part ; this is the ruling. भवनसमांशकाधिपतयः Bhavanasamâṃśakâdhipatayaḥ, the rulers of the twelve parts (respectively). स्वगृहात् Svagrihât, (being counted from the ruler of) its own house. क्रमशः Kramaśaḥ, successively.

6. Mars, Venus, Mercury, the Moon, the Sun, Mercury, Venus, Mars, Jupiter, Saturn, Saturn, Jupiter are successively the rulers of the twelve houses, Meṣa, Vṛiṣa, Mithuna, etc., as well as of the Navâṃśas and Dvâdaśâṃśas of the houses.[1] The rulers of the nine Navâṃśas of Meṣa, Makara, Tulâ, and Karkaṭa are the same who rule the nine houses beginning with Meṣa, Makara, Tulâ and Karkaṭa, respectively. This is the rule about the Navâṃśakaṣ[2] (nine equal parts of a sign.) The rulers of the twelve parts of each house are the rulers of the twelve houses commencing with that house.

(The rulers of the nine Navâṃśas of Meṣa are also the rulers of the nine Navâṃśas of Siṃha and Dhanu ; similarly of Makara are also those of Vṛiṣa and Kanyâ ; of Tulâ, are also of Kumbha and Mithuna ; and of Karkaṭa, are also of Vṛiśchika and Mîna.)

[1] A house is divided into two, three, nine, twelve and thirty equal parts. When it is divided into two equal parts, each part, a space of fifteen degrees, is called a horâ (hour); when divided into three equal parts, each part is called a Drekkân, Decanante, a space of ten degrees ; when divided into nine equal parts each part or space of 3° 20′ is called a Navâṃśaka, ninth part ; when divided into twelve equal parts, each part or space of 2° 30′ is called a Dvâdâśaṃśaka, twelfth part ; when divided into thirty equal parts, each part or space of 1° is called a Triṃśâṃśaka, a thirtieth part.

The rulers of the Navâṃśakas and Dvâdaśâṃśakas are treated of in this verse. The rulers of the Triṃsaṃśakas and Decanates will be mentioned in verses following.

[2] The only thing to be noted here is that the ruler of the first Navâṃśaka of any house is the ruler of the Cardinal sign. If the house be cardinal itself, then its ruler is taken as the ruler of its first Navâṃśaka and if the house be fixed or common then the ruler of the fifth or the ninth house from it which is the ruler of cardinal sign, that is to be taken as the ruler ; *e.g.*, Taurus is a fixed sign ; and the ninth house from Taurus is Capricorn, a cardinal sign ; therefore Saturn, the ruler of Capricorn is the ruler of the first Navâṃśaka of Taurus and so on.

The Rulers of Dvâdaśâṃśakas can be made out easily. See the Tables.

These Navâṃśakas, etc , are dealt with to show that one planet is not to be considered alone, the supreme ruler of any house. Other planets' influences are also felt in that very house.

TABLE I.

THE RULERS OF THE NAVÂMŚAKAS.

Navâṃśakas.	Aries, Leo, Saggit.	Taurus. Virgo Carpricorn.	Libra, Aquarius, Geminii.	Cancer, Scorpio Pisces.	Degrees Minutes.
1st Ruler ...	Mars	Saturn	Venus	Moon	3° 20′
2nd " ...	Venus	Saturn	Mars	Sun	6° 40′
3rd " ...	Mercury	Jupiter	Jupiter	Mercury	10° 0′
4th " ...	Moon	Mars	Saturn	Venus	13° 20′
5th " ...	Sun	Venus	Saturn	Mars	16° 40′
6th " ...	Mercury	Mercury	Jupiter	Jupiter	20° 0′
7th " ...	Venus	Moon	Mars	Saturn	23° 20′
8th " ...	Mars	Sun	Venus	Saturn	26° 40′
9th " ...	Jupiter	Mercury	Mercury	Jupiter	30° 0′

TABLE II.—THE RULERS OF THE DVÂDAŚÂMŚAKAS.

Dvâdaśâmśa.	Aries.	Taurus.	Gemini.	Cancer.	Leo.	Virgo.	Libra.	Scorpio.	Saggittari.	Capricorn.	Aquarius.	Pisces.	° ′
1st Ruler ...	Mars	Venus	Mercury	Moon	Sun	Mercury	Venus	Mars	Jupiter	Saturn	Saturn	Jupiter	2° 30′
2nd „ ...	Venus	Mercury	Moon	Sun	Mercury	Venus	Mars	Jupiter	Saturn	Saturn	Jupiter	Mars	5°
3rd „ ...	Mercury	Moon	Sun	Mercury	Venus	Mars	Jupiter	Saturn	Saturn	Jupiter	Mars	Venus	7° 30′
4th „ ...	Moon	Sun	Mercury	Venus	Mars	Jupiter	Saturn	Saturn	Jupiter	Mars	Venus	Mercury	10°
5th „ ...	Sun	Mercury	Venus	Mars	Jupiter	Saturn	Saturn	Jupiter	Mars	Venus	Mercury	Moon	12° 30′
6 „ ...	Mercury	Venus	Mars	Jupiter	Saturn	Saturn	Jupiter	Mars	Venus	Morcury	Moon	Sun	15°
7th „ ...	Venus	Mars	Jupiter	Saturn	Saturn	Jupiter	Mars	Venus	Mercury	Moon	Sun	Mercury	17°30′
8th „ ...	Mars	Jupiter	Saturn	Saturn	Jupiter	Mars	Venus	Mercury	Moon	Sun	Mercury	Venus	20
...	Jupiter	Saturn	Saturn	Jupitor	Mars	Venus	Mercury	Moon	Sun	Mercury	Venus	Mars	22° 30′
10th „ ...	Saturn	Saturn	Jupiter	Mars	Venus	Mercury	Moon	Sun	Mercury	Venus	Mars	Jupiter	25°
11th „ ...	Saturn	Jupiter	Mars	Venus	Mercury	Moon	Sun	Mercury	Venus	Mars	Jupiter	Saturn	27° 30′
12th „ ...	Jupiter	Mars	Venus	Mercury		Sun	Mercury	Venus	Mars	Jupiter	Saturn	Saturn	30°

Notes.—The Navâṃśas: Each sign being divided into 9 equal parts and there being 12 such signs, there are in all 12×9 or 108 such divisions in the ecliptic. We have already seen that the ecliptic contains 27×4 or 108 Nakṣatrapâdas; it follows therefore that a Navâṃśa is a Nakṣatrapâda, *i.e.*, one-fourth of a lunar mansion. The 108 Navâṃśas beginning from the first point of Meṣa bear the same names as the twelve signs of the Zodiac counted over and over again: the first Navâṃśa of Meṣa is Meṣa itself; that of Vṛiṣa is Makara; that of Mithuna is Tulâ, and that of Karkaṭa is Karkaṭa itself. The same order holds for the 4 signs from Siṃha to Vṛiśchika and for the 4 from Dhanu to Mîna. In other words, the four sets of Trikoṇa or triangular signs begin with the same Navâmsas: that is, the Trikoṇa signs of Meṣa, Siṃha, Dhanu begin with the Navâṃśa of Meṣa. Vṛiṣa, Kanyâ, Makara begin with the Navâṃśa of Makara. Mithuna, Tulâ, Kumbha begin with the Navâṃśa of Tulâ; and Karka, Vṛiśchika, Mîna begin with the Navâṃśa of Karka.

The rulers of the Navâṃśas and Dvâdaśâmśas are the same as the rulers of the signs. These are mentioned in the text in the order of the signs. It will be found that the Sun and Moon have each a house, whilst the other planets have each two houses. These houses are known as the planet's own houses or Svakṣetras; thus :—

Mars is the ruler of Meṣa and Vṛiṣchika.
Venus is the ruler of Vṛiṣa and Tulâ.
Mercury is the ruler of Mithuna and Kanyâ.
Jupiter is the ruler of Mîna and Dhanu.
Saturn is the ruler of Makara and Kumbha.
The moon is the ruler of Karka and the Sun is the ruler of Siṃha.

पुष्पिताग्रा ।

कुजरविजगुरुज्ञशुक्रभागाः पवनसमीरणकौर्पिजूकलेयाः
अयुजि युजि तु भे विपर्ययस्थाः शशिभवनालिझषांतमृच्चसंधिः॥७॥

कुजरविजगुरुज्ञशुक्रभागाः: Kujâravija gurujña-śukrabhâgâḥ, Mars, Saturn, Jupiter, Mercury and Venus successively are the rulers of). पवनसमीरणकौर्पिजूकलेयाः: Pavana-samîraṇa Kaurpijûkaleyâḥ, the five, five, eight, seven and five (triṃśâṃśakas, *i.e.*, the thirty parts in which a sign is divided). अयुजि Ayuji, in the odd sign (*i.e.*, Aries, Geminii, Leo, Libra, Sagittarius, Aquarius signs). युजि तु Yuji tu, but in the even signs (*i.e.*, Taurus, Cancer, Virgo, Scorpio, Capricorn, and Pisces signs). भे Bhe, signs of the Zodiac. विपर्ययस्थाः: Viparyayasthâḥ, in reverse order. शशिभवनालिझषांतम् Śaśibhavanâlijjhaṣântam, the endings (last Navâṃśa) of Cancer, Scorpio, and Pisces. ऋक्षसन्धिः: Rikhśasandhiḥ, the junctions of the asterisms.

7. In the odd signs Mars is the ruler of the first five of the thirty sub-divisions (in which a sign is equally divided); Saturn, the ruler of the next five; Jupiter, the ruler of the next eight; Mercury, the ruler of the next seven; and Venus, the ruler of the last five degrees. But in the even signs these are reversed, *i.e.*, Venus is the ruler of the first five, Mercury is the ruler of the next seven, Jupiter of the next eight, Saturn of the next five and Mars is the ruler of the last five degrees. The endings (last Navâṃśas) of the signs Cancer, Scorpio, and Pisces are also the junctions (Saṃdhis) of the asterisms, *i.e.*, of Aśleṣâ, Jeṣṭhâ, and Revatî stars.

Note.—There are differences of opinion in the divisions and their rulers when the even signs are concerned. Some take both the rulers and the divisions reversed simultaneously; some take the rulers only reversed and the divisions kept the same; some take the divisions reversed and the rulers kept the same. But the meaning stated above and shewn in the following table is the most reasonable.

Table of Triṃśâṃśas.

	1st five parts.	2nd five parts.	3rd eight parts.	4th seven parts.	5th five parts.
Rulers in odd signs.	Mars.	Saturn.	Jupiter.	Mercury.	Venus.

	1st five parts.	2nd seven parts.	3rd eight parts.	4th five parts.	5th five parts.
Rulers in even signs.	Venus.	Mercury.	Jupiter.	Saturn.	Mars.

The junctions of Cancer and Leo, of Scorpio and Sagittarius, and of Pisces and Aries are called Chakrasaṃdhis; and these are also the junctions of the asterisms. These are also called Gaṇḍantas गण्डान्त lasting for a period of one ghaṭi.

The Triṃśâṃśa division is used by the author in his chapter relating to the female horoscopes.

आर्या ।

क्रियतावुरिजितुमकुलीरलेयपाथोनजूककौर्प्याख्याः ॥
तौक्षिक आकोकेरो हृद्रोगश्चांत्यभं चेत्थम् ॥ ८ ॥

क्रियः Kriyaḥ, the name Kriya, Meṣa, Aries. तावुरिः Tâvuriḥ, the name Tâvuri, Vṛiṣa, Taurus. जितुमः Jitumaḥ, the name Jituma, Mithuna, the Geminii. कुलीरः Kulîraḥ, the name Kulira, Karkaṭa, Cancer. लेयः Leyaḥ, the name Leya, Siṃha, Leo. पाथोनः Pathonaḥ, the name Pathona, Kanyâ, Virgo. जूकः Yûkaḥ, the name Yûka, Tulâ, Libra. कौर्प्याख्याः Kaurpyâkṣyâḥ, the name Kaurpyāḥ, Vṛiśchika, the Scorpio. तौक्षिकः Taukṣikaḥ, name Taukṣika, Dhanu, Sagittarius. आकोकेरो Âkokero, name Âkokero, Makara, Capricornus. हृद्रोगः Hṛidrogaḥ, name Hṛidroga, Kumbha, Aquarius. च, Cha, and. अंत्यभं Antyabham, name Antyabham, Mîna, Pisces. च Cha, also. इत्थम् Itthyam, thus.

8. The twelve signs are also termed Kriya, Tâvuri, Jituma, Kulîra, Leya, Pâthona, Jûka, Kaurpyâ, Taukṣika, Âkokero, Hṛidroga and Antyabham.

Note.—These are all Greek names of the twelve signs or houses of the Zodiac—a circumstance clearly indicating that the Greeks were in closer touch with the Hindus some read Pârthona for Pâthona.

इंद्रवज्रा ।

द्रेष्काणहोरानवभागसंज्ञास्त्रिंशांशकद्वादशसंज्ञिताश्च ॥
क्षेत्रं च यद्यस्य स तस्य वर्गो होरेति लग्नं भवनस्य चार्द्धम् ॥ ९ ॥

द्रेष्काणहोरानवभागसंज्ञाः Dreṣkâṇahorâ nava bhâga sanjnâḥ, the three, two, nine equal divisions of a sign termed respectively, Dreṣkâṇa, Horâ, Navâṃśaṣ (space occupying the ninth division) and also termed Vargas. त्रिंशांशकद्वादशसंज्ञिताः Triṃśâṃśaka dvâdaśasangitâḥ, Triṃsâṃśas, and Dvâdaśâṃśa termed also Vargas. च Cha, also. क्षेत्रं Khṣetram, own House. च Cha, also. यत् Yat, whichever. यस्य Yasya, to whichever planet. स Sa, that Navâṃśa, etc. तस्य Tasya, of that planet. वर्गः Vargaḥ, termed Varga (auspicious position) divisions. होरा Horâ, the term Horâ. इति Iti, thus. लग्नं Lagnam, the rising sign. भवनस्य Bhavanasya, of a sign. च Cha, and. अर्द्धम् Ardham, half.

9. A sign (when divided into three equal parts) gets each of its three parts termed Dreṣkâna, Decanate; similarly each of its two equal parts is termed Horâ; each of its nine equal parts is called a Navâṃśa; each of its twelve equal parts is called a Dvâdaśâṃśa; and each of its thirty equal parts is called a Triṃśâṃśa. A planet is said to be in its Varga (position of auspiciousness) if it be in its Decanate,

Horâ, Navâṃśa, Triṃśâṃśa, Dvâdaśâṃśa and own sign (Kṣetra). The term Horâ means both the rising sign and one-half of a sign of the Zodiac.

Note.—A house has six fold divisions :—First, the entire house, called Kṣetra ; second—The semi-house, each half is called Horâ ; a Lagnam ; third, one-third of a house, each position being called a Dreṣkân or Decanate ; fourth, one-ninth of a house called Navâṃśaka ; fifth, one-twelfth of a house, each division being called a Dvâdaśâṃśaka ; sixth, one-thirtieth of a house, each division being called a Triṃśâṃśaka. These six divisions are called the Ṣaḍvargas of a planet.

वसन्ततिलका–गोऽजाश्विकर्किमिथुनाः समृगा निशाख्याः पृष्ठो दया विमिथुनाः कथितास्त एव ॥ शीर्षोदया दिनबलाश्च भवं- ति शेषा लग्नं समेत्युभयतः पृथुरोमयुग्मम् ॥ १० ॥

गोऽजाश्विकर्किमिथुनाः Gojâśvikarkimithunâḥ, the Bull, Ram, Sagittarius, Cancer, the Twins. समृगा Samṛgâ, together with the Capricorn. निशाख्याः Niśakhyâḥ, termed night signs ; potent during the night. पृष्ठोदयाः Pṛṣṭhodyâḥ, rising with their backs facing us. विमिथुनाः. Vimithunâḥ, the Twins excepted. कथिताः Kathitâḥ, are said. ते Te, they. एव Eva, thus. शीर्षोदयाः Śirṣodayâḥ, rising with their heads facing us. दिनबलाः, Dinabalâḥ, day signs ; potent during the day. च Cha, and. भवन्ति Bhavanti, are, become, शेषाः Śeṣâḥ, the remaining (signs). लग्नं Lagnam, the horizon. समेति Sameti, rise. उभयतः Ubhayataḥ, both with their heads and backs facing us. पृथुरोमयुग्मम् Pṛithuromayugmam, the two Fishes ; the sign Pisces.

10. The six signs Aries, Taurus, Geminii, Cancer, Sagittarius, and Capricornus are termed night signs ; these are potent during the night ; they, excepting the Geminii, rise with their backs or rear facing us. The other signs, *i.e.*, the Leo, Virgo, Libra, Scorpio, and Aquarius are called day signs ; these are potent during the day. They rise with their heads facing us. Geminii also rises, with its head facing us. The Pisces rise in the horizon with their heads and backs both facing us at the same time.

Note :—Royal marchings, general marches on any occasion, going out on any important business should be done when the corresponding signs are powerful. Success is then ensured as the result. Otherwise failure and the routing of the forces will be the end.

मंदाक्रान्ता–क्रूरः सौम्यः पुरुषवनिते ते चरागद्विदेहाः प्रागादीशाः क्रियवृषनृयुक्कर्कटाः सत्रिकोणाः ॥ मार्तंडेंद्वोरयुजि समभे चंद्रभान्वोश्च होरे द्रेष्काणाः स्युः स्वभवनसुतत्रि-त्रिकोणांधिपानाम् ॥ ११ ॥

क्रूरः Krûraḥ, cruel, wicked, impulsive, malefic, militant .सौम्यः Saumyaḥ, mild, benefic, pleasing, gentle. पुरुषवनिते Puruṣavanite, male and female (respectively). ते Te, they. चरागद्विदेहाः Charâgadvidehâḥ, cardinal or moveable, fixed and common or mutable. प्रागादीशाः Prâgâdiśâḥ, rulers of the east, south, west, and north directions. क्रियवृषनृयुक्कर्कटाः Kriyavṛiṣanriyukkarkaṭâḥ, Meṣa, Vṛisha, Mithuna and Karka. सत्रिकोणाः Satrikoṇâḥ, with their trines, or triangular houses, *i.e.*, with the rulers of their fifth and ninth houses. मार्तंडेन्द्वोः Mârtaṇḍendvoḥ, appertaining to the Sun and the Moon. अयुजि Ayuji, in the odd signs. समभे Samabhe, in the even signs. चंद्रभान्वोः Chandrabhanvoḥ, to the Moon and the Sun. च Cha, and. होरे Hore, the two halves of a sign. द्रेष्काणाः Dreskâṇâḥ, the Decanates, the three parts of a sign. स्युः Syuḥ, are. स्वभवनसुतत्रित्रिकोणाधिपानाम् Svabhavanasutatritrikoṇâdhipanâm, ruled by the lords of its own, fifth, and ninth houses.

11. The signs (from Meṣa) are alternately malefic and benefic ; male and female ; moveable, fixed and common ; Meṣa, Vṛiṣa, Mithuna, and Karka with their fifth and ninth houses are respectively the rulers of the east, south, west and north sides. The Sun and Moon are respectively the rulers of the two halves of any odd sign ; and the Moon and the Sun become the rulers of the horas of any even sign. The Decanates are ruled by the lords of its own, fifth and ninth houses.

Note.—These classifications of the twelve signs of the zodiac play a most important part in the delineation of nativities, and unless the true nature of each sign is thoroughly understood, a correct judgment cannot be given ; therefore it is necessary that the twelve signs are to be studied as exhaustively as possible. It is impossible to understand the twelve signs as one whole, without perfect knowledge ; but we may know a great deal of the whole by studying the signs in part. Taken in their entirety the signs of the zodiac represent (i) the desire nature, composed of the feelings, passions, and emotions of the world's humanity ; (ii) the whole of the personal consciousness that is dependent upon the senses for its experiences.

These parts are then studied, the twelve signs being separated into pairs of positive and negative ; then into four groups, known as the triplicities ; finally into three distinct divisions, known as qualities.

The divisions of these signs into malefic and benefic, positive and negative, male and female go to shew that the persons born under their influences are of cruel or gentle nature; are of positive or negative characteristics, having male or female principles in preponderance. In making a distinction between positive and negative signs, we may consider the former as more directly concerned with the *life* side of evolution, and the latter with the *form* aspect. The energies and life-giving properties are represented by the positive signs, and the medium or form through which the life works, by the negative signs. The divisions into four trinities cardinal, fixed, and common shew the three qualities of those born under their influences, *i.e.*, their activity, solidity, and indecisiveness or mutability expressed through their several parts governed by their respective signs. Their divisions into four directions give us the clue to the knowledge in what direction a stolen article is carried away by any thief or in what direction the door of a lying-in-chamber is to be located or in what direction a man ought to commence his journey to ensure success. Their divisions into horâs indicate a man energetic, expressive, if born under the Sun horâ; or gentle and recipient, if born under the Moon horâ. Meṣa, Mithuna, Siṃha, Tulâ, Dhanu, and Kumbha are fierce male signs. Vṛiṣa, Karka, Kanyâ, Vṛiśchik, Makara, and Matsya are gentle and feminine signs. Meṣa, Karka, Tulâ, and Makara are cardinal signs. Vṛiṣa, Siṃha, Vṛiśchika and Kumbha are fixed signs. Mithuna, Kanyâ, Dhanu and Mîna are common or mutable signs.

Meṣa, Siṃha, and Dhanu represent east; Vṛiṣa, Kanyâ and Makara represent south; Mithuna, Tulâ, and Kumbha represent west and Karka, Vṛiśchika and Mîna represent north directions.

TABLE OF HORÂS.

Houses.	1	2	3	4	5	6	7	8	9	10	11	12	Degrees.
Ruler of 1st Horâ...	Sun	Moon	Sun	Moon	Sun	Moon	Sun	Moon	Sun	Moon	Sun	Moon	15
Ruler of 2nd Horâ...	Moon	Sun	Moon	Sun	Moon	Sun	Moon	Sun	Moon	Sun	Moon	Sun	30

TABLE OF DREṢKÂNAS.

Houses.	1	2	3	4	5	6	7	8	9	10	11	12	Degrees
Ruler of 1st Dreskana.	Mars ...	Venus...	Mercury	Moon ...	Sun .	Mercury	Venus .	Mars ...	Jupiter	Saturn	Saturn	Jupiter	10
Ruler of 2nd Dreskana.	Sun ..	Mercury	Venus...	Mars ...	Jupiter	Saturn	Saturn	Jupiter	Mars ...	Venus...	Mercury	Moon ...	20
Ruler of 3rd Dreskana.	Jupiter	Saturn	Saturn	Jupiter	Mars ...	Venus...	Mercury	Moon ..	Sun ...	Mercury	Venus...	Mars ...	3

इंद्रवज्रा—केचित्तु होरां प्रथमां भपस्य वांछंति लाभाधिपतेर्द्वितीयाम् ॥ द्रेष्काणसंज्ञामपि वर्णयंति स्वद्वादशैकादशराशिपानाम् ॥१२॥

केचित् Kechit, some, Yavaneśvara and others. होरां Horâm, half of a sign; semi-sign. प्रथमां Prathamâm, first. भपस्य Bhapasya, under the ruler of a sign. वांछंति Vâṃchhanti, are inclined to take, like. लाभाधिपतेः Lâbhâdhipateḥ, under the ruler of the eleventh house (that brings profit). द्वितीयाम् Dvitiyâm, the second half of a sign. द्रेष्काणसंज्ञाम् Dreṣkâṇasaṃgâm, the three parts of a sign termed Dreṣkâṇas, the Decanates. अपि Api, also. वर्णयंति Varṇayanti, describes. स्वद्वादशैकादशराशिपानाम् Svadvâdasaikâ daśarâśipânâm, under the rulers of its own, twelfth, and eleventh signs, respectively.

12. Some astrologers take the first half of a sign under its own lord, and the second half of that sign under the lord of the eleventh house from that sign. They also take the Decanates to be under the rulers of its own, twelfth and eleventh houses, respectively.

Note.—This is the view of Garga and men of his school. But the author's opinion is that expressed in stanza 11 in which he is supported by the opinion of Satyâchârya.

पुष्पिताग्रा—अजवृषभमृगांगनाकुलीरा झषवणिजा च दिवाकरादितुंगाः ॥ दशशिखिमनुयुक्तिथींद्रियांशैस्त्रिनवकविंशतिभिश्च तेऽस्तनीचाः ॥ १३ ॥

अजवृषभमृगांगनाकुलीराः Ajavriṣabhamrigâmganâkulirâḥ, the signs Meṣa, Vriṣa, Makara, Kanyâ, Karkaṭa. झषवणिजा Jhasavaṇijau, the signs Mina and Tulâ. च Cha, and. दिवाकरादिः Divâkarâdiḥ, the Sun, &c., (*i.e.*, the Sun, Moon, Mars, Mercury, Jupiter, Venus, and Saturn). तुंगाः Tuṃgâḥ, get exalted दशशिखिमनुयुक्तिथींद्रियांशैः Daśaśikhimanuyuktithiṃdriyâṃśaiḥ, by the first ten, three, twenty-eight, fifteen, five degrees respectively; these degrees are the highly exalted positions. त्रिनवकविंशतिभिः Trinavakaviṃśatibhiḥ, by the first twenty-seven and twenty degrees. ते Te, those planets. अस्तनीचाः Astanîchâḥ, the seventh (descending) planet considered as debilitated.

13. The Sun, Moon, Mars, Mercury, Jupiter, Venus, and Saturn get exalted in the houses Meṣa, Vriṣa, Makara, Kanyâ, Karka, Mina, and Tulâ, respectively. The Sun gets highly exalted in the first ten degrees of Meṣa; the Moon, in

the first three degrees of Vṛiṣa ; the Mars, in the first twenty-eight degrees of Makara ; the Mercury, in the first fifteen of Kanyâ ; the Jupiter, in the first five of Karka ; the Venus, in the first twenty-seven degrees of Mîna ; and the Saturn, in the first twenty degrees of Tulâ. The seventh houses reckoned from above are the debilitated houses (*i.e.*, houses of detriment). And the highly debilitated degrees are the same as those given above.

Note.—Exalted and highly exalted positions are those when the planets exercise their benefic, and highly benefic influences. The reverse is the case when these are debilitated and highly debilitated positions when the planets are very weak and carry malefic influences. The following table is given for convenience of reference :—

Planets.		Exalted signs.		Debilitated signs.		Highly exalted or debilitated degrees.
Sun	...	Meṣa	...	Tulâ	...	10
Moon	...	Vṛiṣa	...	Vṛiśchika	...	3
Mars	...	Makara	...	Karka	...	28.
Mercury	...	Kanyâ	...	Mîna	...	15
Jupiter	...	Karka	...	Makara	...	5
Venus	...	Mîna	...	Kanyâ	...	27
Saturn	...	Tulâ	...	Meṣa	...	20

वसंततिलका—वर्गोत्तमाश्चरगृहादिषु पूर्वमध्यपर्यन्ततः शुभफला
नवभागसंज्ञाः ॥ सिंहो वृषप्रथमषष्ठहयाङ्गतौलिकुम्भास्त्रि-
कोणभवनानि भवन्ति सूर्यात् ॥ १४ ॥

वर्गोत्तमाः Vargottamâḥ, highly auspicious degrees. चरगृहादिषु Charagṛihâdiṣu, in the cardinal houses, etc. (*i.e.*, in the cardinal or angular, fixed, and mutable houses, respectively.) पूर्वमध्यपर्यन्ततः Purvamadhyaparyaṃtataḥ, the first, middle, and end Spaces of 3° 20′ ; the 1st, 5th and 9th Navâmsas. शुभफलाः Śubhaphalâḥ, bearing auspicious results. नवभागसंज्ञाः Navabhâgasaṃjñâḥ, the ninth part ; a space of 3° 20′, the Navâṃśas. सिंहः Siṃhaḥ, the Leo. वृषप्रथमषष्ठहयाङ्गतौलिकुम्भाः Vṛiṣa-prathamaṣaṣṭhahayâṃgataulikumbhâḥ, Vṛiṣa, first (*i.e.*, Meṣa), sixth (Kanyâ), Dhanu, Tulâ, and Kumbha signs. त्रिकोणभवनानि Trikoṇabhavanâni, the houses termed Mûlatrikoṇa or triplicities. भवन्ति Bhavanti, are considered as. सूर्यात् Suryât, reckoned from the Sun.

14. In the cardinal signs, the first Navâṃśa (space of 3°20′, ninth part) is termed Vargottama or degrees bearing highly auspicious results. In the fixed signs the fifth Navâṃśa (or middle space of 3°20′) is called Vargottama. In the mutable signs the ninth Navâṃśa (or last 3°20′ space) is Vargottama. The Siṃha is considered as the Mûlatrikoṇa house of the Sun; Vṛiṣa, of the Moon; Meṣa, of Mars; Kanyâ, of Mercury; Dhanu, of Jupiter; Tulâ, of Venus; Kumbha, of Saturn (*i.e.*, these planets are considered supremely high benefics when posted in the houses above mentioned.

Note:—The Vargottama places are:—The first Navâṃśas of the 4 moveable signs Meṣa, Karka, Tulâ, and Makara, the 5th Navâṃśas of the four fixed signs Vṛiṣa, Siṃha, Vṛiśchika and Kumbha; and the 9th or last Navâṃśas of the four common signs Mithuna, Kanyâ, Dhanu and Mina. These Navâṃśas will be found to bear the same names as the signs themselves, *e.g.*, the first Navâṃśa of Meṣa is Meṣa, the first of Karka is Karka and so on. The 5th Navâṃśa of Vṛiṣa is Vṛiṣa; of Siṃha is Siṃha and so forth; the 9th Navâṃśa of Mithuna is Mithuna; and so on. The following list contains the Mûla-Trikoṇa signs of the planets.

Planets		Mûla trikoṇa signs.
Planets	Sun—Siṃha.	
„	Moon—Vṛiṣa.	„
„	Mars—Meṣa.	„
„	Mercury—Kanyâ.	„
„	Jupiter—Dhanu.	„
„	Venus—Tulâ.	„
„	Saturn—Kumbha.	„

वसंततिलका—होरादयस्तनुकुटुम्बसहोत्थबन्धुपुत्रारिपत्नि-
मरणानि शुभास्पदायाः ॥ रिःफाख्यमित्युपचयान्यरिकर्मला-
भदुश्चिक्यसंज्ञितगृहाणि न नित्यमेके ॥ १५ ॥

होरादय: Horâdayaḥ, the houses commencing from the Lagna or rising sign. तनुकुटुम्वसहोत्यबंधुपुत्रारिपत्निमरणानि Tanukutuṃbasahottha baṇdhuputtrâripatnimaraṇâni, body, relatives, brothers, friends, sons, enemies, wife, death. शुभास्पदाया: Śubhâspadâyâḥ, auspiciousness, position of rank, financial gain. रि:फाख्यम् Riḥphâkhṣyaṃ, expenditure. इति Iti, thus. उपचयानि Upachayâni, profitable houses. अरिकर्मलाभदुश्चिक्यसंज्ञितगृहाणि । Arikarmalâbhaduśchikyasaṃjñitagrihâṇi, sixth, tenth, eleventh, and third houses. न Na, not. नित्यम्, Nityam, always. एके Eke, some (authors).

15. The nature of the twelve houses commencing with Lagna or the rising sign is thus described :—The Lagna or the first house governs body ; the second house, relatives ; the third house, brothers ; the fourth house, friends ; the fifth house, sons ; the sixth house, enemies ; the seventh house, wives; the eighth house, death or terminus vitæ ; the ninth house, auspicious qualities and the general state of the moral conditions ; the tenth house, profession, honours, dignity ; the eleventh house, income and finance ; the twelfth house indicates expenditure. The sixth, tenth, eleventh, and third houses are called Upachaya (improving) houses ; some authors say that they are not always improving.

Notes.—The remaning houses, *i.e.*, other houses than the sixth, tenth, eleventh and third are called Apachayâni or houses of loss. Profitable houses bring in friends and other desirable things ; houses of loss bring in unfortunate events in the loss of friends and high positions.

The following is a list of the natures of the several houses of the zodiac from the Ascendant.

Ascendant or 1st house —Physique ; Body ; Health.
2nd house—Family relations, wealth, eyes, speech ; truthfulness.
3rd house—Brothers, bravery, meals.
4th house—Friends, education, mother, cows, dwelling places, carriage, comfort.
5th house—Sons, intelligence, previous karma.
6th house—Enemies, kinsmen, diseases.
7th house—Wife, generosity, respect.
8th house—Death, duration of life.
9th house—Deeds of virtue, father, medicine.
10th house—Avocation, knowledge, clothes, income.
11th house—Gain, earning.
12th house—Loss, bad deeds, travels.

Garga and other astrologers are of opinion that the 3rd, 6th, 10th, and 11th houses cease to be Upachaya houses if malefic planets or planets which are unfriendly to the rulers of these four houses should either occupy such houses or aspect the same. But the author does not agree with Garga and he is supported in his views by Satyâchârya and by Yavaneswara.

वसंततिलका—कल्पस्वविक्रमगृहप्रतिभाक्षतानि चित्तोत्थरंध्रगुरुमानभवव्ययानि ॥ लग्नाच्चतुर्थनिधने चतुरस्रसंज्ञे द्यूनं च सप्तमगृहं दशमर्क्षमाज्ञा ॥ १६ ॥

कल्पस्वविक्रमगृहप्रतिभाक्षतानि Kalpasvavikramagrihaprativâkhṣatâni, determinative strength, wealth, heroic valour, residence or home life, sons, injuries. चित्तोत्थरंध्रगुरुमानभवव्ययानि Chittottharandhragurumânabhavavyayâni, wife, weak point, religiousness, high honours, profit and loss. लग्नात् Lagnât, from the Lagnam or the rising sign. चतुर्थनिधने Chaturthanidhane, fourth and eighth (houses). चतुरस्रसंज्ञे Chaturasrasanjñe, termed Chaturasra or square. द्यूनं Dyûnam, known as Dyûnam. सप्तमगृहं Saptamagriham, the seventh house. दशमर्क्षं Daśamarkṣam, the tenth house, *i.e.*, house of command. आज्ञा Âjñâ, termed Âjñâ.

16. The nature of the twelve houses is now described differently :--First the Ascendant or Lagna house denotes determinative strength ; the second house, wealth ; the third house, valour ; the fourth house, residence, home life ; the fifth house, sons ; the sixth house, wounds and injuries ; the seventh house, wife ; the eighth house, weak or assailable point ; the ninth house, religion, father or preceptor ; the tenth house, honor, respectability ; the eleventh house, acquisition, gain ; and the twelfth house, expenditure, loss. The fourth and eighth houses from the Ascendant are termed Chaturasra or square signs ; the seventh house is termed Dyûna ; the tenth house is termed Âjñâ (or command).

Note.—The naming of the 4th, 8th, 9th and 10th houses, should be taken as more convenient words for a sentence.

दोधक—कंटककेंद्रचतुष्टयसंज्ञाः सप्तमलग्नचतुर्थखभानाम् ॥ तेषु यथाभिहितेषु बलाढ्याः कीटनरांबुचराः पशवश्च ॥१७॥

कंटककेंद्रचतुष्टयसंज्ञाः Kantakakendra-chatuṣṭayasamjñâḥ, Kanṭaka, Kendra, (angular) Chatuṣṭaya (quadrants) are the (synonymous) names of. सप्तमलग्नचतुर्थखभानाम् Saptamalagnachaturthakhabhânâm, the seventh, lagna, fourth and tenth houses. तेषु Teṣu, (when) in them; when in these 7th, 1st, 4th and 10th houses, respectively. यथाभिहितेषु Yathâbhihiteṣu, as stated, as fixed. बलाढ्याः Balâḍhyâḥ, (become) strong. कीटनरांबुचराः Kîṭanarâmbucharâḥ, the insect, human, and aquatic signs, called also the centiped, biped, and aquatic signs, respectively. पशवः Paśavaḥ, bestial, quadruped or four-footed signs. च Cha, and.

17. The seventh, rising, fourth, and tenth signs are called Kanṭakas, Kendras (angular), or Chatuṣṭayas (squares). The insect, human, aquatic and bestial signs become strong when they occupy the 7th, 1st, 4th and 10th houses, respectively.

Notes:—Vṛiśchika is an insect or centiped sign and is strong in the seventh house. Mithuna, Kanyâ, Tulâ, and the upper part of Dhanu and Kumbha are biped or human signs and get strengthened when they become the rising sign. Karka, Mîna, the lower part of Makara are aquatic signs and become strong when they become the fourth house. Meṣa, Siṃha, Vṛiśa, the lower part of Dhanu and the first half of Makara are quadruped signs and become strong in the tenth house.

व०ति०—केन्द्रात्परं पणफरं परतस्तु सर्वमापोक्लिमं हिबुकमम्बु सुखं च वेश्म ॥ जामित्रमस्तभवनं सुतभं त्रिकोणं मेषूरणं दशममत्र च कर्म विद्यात् ॥ १८ ॥

केन्द्रात् Kendrât, from the angular houses. परं Param, next. पणफरं Paṇapharam, termed the Panphara or Succedent houses. परतः Parataḥ, next. तु Tu, and again. सर्वम् Sarvam, all. आपोक्लिमं Âpoklimam, termed Âpoklim or cadent houses. हिबुकम् Hibukaṃ, termed Hibukam. अम्बु Ambu, termed Ambu. सुखं Sukhaṃ, known as Sukham; it is the 4th house. वेश्म Veśhma, termed Veśma. जामित्रम् Jâmitram, Jâmitram; this sign indicates the future good luck of one's wife, but the word is obviously connected with the Greek diametron. अस्तभवनं Astabhavanam, the seventh house. सुतभं Sutabham, the fifth house. त्रिकोणं Trikoṇam, Trikoṇam. मेषूरणं Meṣûraṇam, Meṣuraṇam. दशमं Daśamam, the tenth house. अत्र Atra, here, this house. च Cha, also. कर्म Karma, known as Karma. विद्यात् Vidyât, should be understood.

18. The houses next to the angles are known as the Paṇapharas or Succedent houses. The houses next to the Succedent houses are termed the Âpoklims or Cadent houses. The fourth house is known as Hibukam, Ambu, Sukham and Veṣma. The seventh house is known as Jâmitram; the fifth house is called Trikoṇam; and the tenth house is known as Meṣûraṇa and Karma.

Note.—The second, fifth, eighth and eleventh houses are known as the Succedent houses. The third, sixth, ninth and twelfth houses are known as the Cadent house.

Paṇapharas and Apoklims are Greek terms.

शा० वि०—होरा स्वामिगुरुज्ञवीक्षितयुता नान्यैश्च वीर्योत्कटा ।
केन्द्रस्था द्विपदादयोऽह्नि निशि च प्राप्ते च संन्ध्याद्वये॥
पूर्वार्द्धे विषयादयः कृतगुणा मानं प्रतीपं च तद्-
दुश्चिक्यं सहजं तपश्च नवमं त्र्याद्यं त्रिकोणं च तत् ॥१६॥

होरा Horâ, Lagna, the rising sign. स्वामिगुरुज्ञवीक्षितयुता Svamigurujñavîkṣita-yutâ, if well aspected by its own lord, or Jupiter, or Mercury ; or occupied by them. न Na, not. अन्यैः Anyaiḥ, by any other planet (than its lord, Jupiter or Mercury). च Cha, and. वीर्योत्कटा Vîryotkaṭâ, become strong, become powerful. केन्द्रस्थाः Kendrasthâḥ (all the signs when) in the angular houses. द्विपदादयाः Dvipadâdayaḥ, the human signs, etc.; the human, bestial, and insect signs. अह्नि Ahni, during the day. निशि Niśi, during the night. च Cha, and. प्राप्ते Prâpte, on the approach. च Cha, and. संन्ध्याद्वये Sandhyâdvaye, of the morning and evening ; of the twilights. पूर्वार्द्धे Pûrvârdhe, in the first six signs ; in the first half of the Zodiac. विषयादयः Viṣyâdâyaḥ, the numbers five, etc. *i. e.* five, six, seven, eight, nine, and ten. कृतगुणाः Kritaguṇâḥ multiplied by four. मानं Mânam, the measure. प्रतीपं Pratîpam (when) reversed. च Cha, and. तत् Tat, that, those numbers, *i.e.*, those numbers reversed become respectively the measurement in degrees of the six signs, Tulâ, Vṛiśchika, Dhanu, Makara, Kumbha and Mîna. दुश्चिक्यं Duśchikyam, termed Duśchikyam. सहजं Saha-jam, the third house. तपः Tapaḥ, known as Tapaḥ. च Cha, and. नवमं Nav..mam,, the ninth house. त्र्याद्यं Tryâdyam, beginning with Tri ; with Tri prefixed. त्रिकोणं Trikoṇam, termed Trikoṇam (with Tri prefixed.) च तत् Cha tat, and that.

19. The Lagna or the rising sign becomes strong when well aspected or occupied by its own ruler, or Jupiter, or Mercury ; but it is not so, when seen by the other planets than those above mentioned. All the signs become strong, when they are in the Kendras or angles, *i.e.*, (Lagna, fourth, seventh and tenth houses). The human signs are strong during the day ; the quadruped signs during the night, and the insect signs are powerful in the morning and evening (during the twilights). The numbers five, six, seven, eight, nine, and ten each multiplied by four are respectively the (lagna) mânas (measurements in degrees) of the first six signs from Meṣa ; and these reversed become respectively the lagna mânas of the last six signs. The third house is known as Dyuśchikyam ; the ninth house is known as Tapaḥ, Tritrikoṇam.

Note:—The rising sign if not aspected by its Lord, Jupiter, or Mercury, becomes weak.

The signs when in the succedent houses are not so powerful as in the angular houses; they are weaker still in the cadent houses.

Some authors interpret thus:—The human signs are strong in the angular houses, the quadruped signs are strong in the succedent houses and the insect signs are strong in the cadent houses. But this is not approved by the author. By the human signs are meant 3 (Mithuna), 7 (Tulâ), 6 (Kanyâ), the upper half of Dhanu and Kumbha; by the quadruped signs are meant 1 (Meṣa), 2 (Vṛiṣa), 5 (Siṃha), the upper part of Makara and the latter part of Dhanu; and by the insect signs are understood 4 (Karkaṭa), 8 (Vṛiśchik) the latter half of Makara and 12 (Mîna sign).

1. The following table shows the measurements in degrees of the twelve signs that they subtend at the centre:—

	Signs.		Degrees in circular measure.	Chaṣakâs.	Signs.	
The first six signs.	Meṣa ...	...	20	200	Mîna	The second six signs reversed.
	Vṛiṣa ...	...	24	240	Kumbha	
	Mithuna	...	28	280	Makara	
	Karka ...	...	32	320	Dhanu	
	Siṃha ...	...	36	360	Vṛiṣchika	
	Kanyâ ...	...	40	400	Tulâ	
			180°	1800	Chaṣakâs (or 10800 minutes in cir. meas.)	

The six signs cover 180° at the centre in circular measure.

The 360 degrees (circular measure) of the zodiacal circle are described in the course of the day and night, *i.e.*, in 24 hours or 24 × 60 minutes (time. measure)

Therefore we can put—

360° (circ. meas) = 24 × 60′ (in time).

or 360 × 60′ (circ. meas.) = 24 × 60 × 60″ (in time)

or 1′ (circ. meas.) = 4″ in time)

As one Prâna = 4″ (in time) (assumed)

∴ 1′ (circ. meas.) = 1 Prâna (in time.).

60 Ghaṭikâs = 24 hours = 24 × 60 minutes

∴ 1 Ghaṭikâ = 24′ = 24 × 60″ = 24 × 15 Prânas.

= 360 prânas in time = 360′ in circ. meas.)

= 6° in circular measure.

∴ 1 degree (circ. meas.) = ⅙ ghaṭikâ = ⅙ × 24′ = 4′ = 4 × 60.″

= 4 × 15 prânas = 10 × 6 prânas (in time).

Now 1 chaṣakâ = 6 prânas (in time) (assumed.)

= 6 minutes (in circ. meas.)

∴ 1 degree (circ. meas.) = 10 chaṣkâs (in time).

Thus we see that the degrees of Aries, Taurus, &c., (20°, 24°, &c.) multiplied by 10 give chaṣakâs of Aries, Taurus, &c. (200, 240 in time).

The times of rising of the several signs are different at different places; therefore the doubt may be entertained, why are these constant figures inserted here?

The answer is:—these figures are useful in finding out the relative lengths of the several parts of a human body, which is long, which is short, and which is of middle size (see verse 23. Chapter V of this treatise); in case of re-determining lost horoscopes (see stanza 4, Chapter 26 of this treatise); or in similar other questions of horary Astrology of lost articles, whether they are long, short, or of middle size, whether they are square or circular, gross or fine and so forth.

It is to be carefully noted that the times of rising of the several signs in the horizon are to be calculated separately for each place according to the strict rules of Astronomy. See the Surya Siddhânta (stanzas 42-44, Chapter 3), the English rendering of which verses is given below:—

"To find the right ascensions of the first 3 signs of the Ecliptic. Verse 42. (In order to find the right ascensions of the ends of the three first signs of the Ecliptic, *i.e.*, Aries, Taurus and Gemini, find the declinations of the said ends) then multiply the sines of one, two, and three signs by the cosine of the greatest declination of the Sun separately, and divide the products by the cosines of the declinations (above found), respectively: the quotients will be the sines of the arcs; find the arcs in minutes. (These arcs will be the right ascensions of the ends of the three first signs of the Ecliptic.)

"To find the rising periods of those signs at the Equator (43).

The number of minutes contained in the first right ascension (above found) is the number of Prânas which Aries takes in its rising at Lanka (or the Equator); then take the first right ascension from the second and the second from the third; the remainders in minutes will denote the numbers of Prânas in which Taurus and Gemini rise at the Equator. (The numbers of the Prânas, thus found, contained in the rising periods of Aries, Taurus, and Gemini at the Equator are 1670, 1795 and 1935, respectively.

"To find the rising periods of three signs at a given place.

(In order to find the rising periods of the first three signs of the Ecliptic at a given place of North Latitude, find first the ascensional differences of the ends of the said signs at that place and subtract the first ascensional difference from the second and the second from the third. The first ascensional difference and these remainders are severally called the

Charakhaṇḍâs of the said signs for the given place.) Subtract the Charakhaṇḍâ (of the first three signs) for the given place from the rising periods at the Equator: the remainder will be the rising periods in Prâṇas of the said signs at the given place.

" To find the rising periods of the rest.

44. The rising periods of the first three signs of the Ecliptic at the Equator successively increased by their Charakhaṇḍâs give in a contrary order the rising periods of the following three signs (*i.e.*, Cancer, Leo, and Virgo.)

The rising periods of the first six signs, thus found, answer in an inverse order to those of the latt r six signs, Libra, &c, for the given place—(Bapu Deva Śâstri).

मं०क्रां०—रक्तः श्वेतः शुकतनुनिभः पाटलो धूम्रपांडुश्चित्रः कृष्णः कनकसदृशः पिंगलः कर्बुरश्च ॥ बभ्रुः स्वच्छः प्रथमभवनाद्येषु वर्णाः प्लवत्वं स्वाम्याशाख्यं दिनकरयुताद्भाद्द्वितीयं च वेशिः ॥ २० ॥

इति श्रीवराहमिहराचार्यप्रणीते बृहज्जातके राशिप्रभेदोऽध्यायः प्रथमः ॥ १ ॥

रक्तः Raktaḥ, bloody red. श्वेतः Svetaḥ, white. शुकतनुनिभः Śukatanunibhaḥ, yellow, of the colour of the parrot. पाटलः Pâṭalaḥ, pink, pale red, of the colour of Pâṭali (trumpet flower). धूम्रपांडु Dhûmrapâṇḍu, pale, smoke coloured. चित्रः Chitraḥ, variegated in colour. कृष्णः Kriṣṇaḥ, black. कनकसदृशः Kanakasadriśaḥ, golden colour. पिंगलः Pimgalaḥ, tawny colour; auburn colour; yellowish, reddish brown; of the colour of the husk of paddy. कर्बुरः Karburaḥ, gray. च Cha, and. बभ्रुः Babhruḥ, of the colour of the body of mongoose. स्वच्छः Svachchaḥ, of the colour of the body of clear white fishes. प्रथमभवनाद्येषु Prathamabhavanâdyeṣu, Meṣa, etc.; the twelve houses commencing with Meṣa. वर्णाः Varṇâḥ, colours. प्लवत्वं Plavattvam termed Plava (depressed). स्वाम्याशाख्यं Svâmyâśâkhyam, termed after the names north, south, west or east whichever is the direction of their ruler. दिनकरयुताद्भात् Dinakarayutâtbhât, from the sign occupied by the Sun. द्वितीयं Dvitîyam, the second. च Cha, and. वेशिः Veṣiḥ, known as Veṣiḥ.

20. The colours of the twelve signs, Meṣa, Vriṣa, etc., are respectively—(1) blood red (Meṣa), (2) white (of Vriṣa), (3) yellow (of Mithuna), (4) pink (of Karka), (5) smoky (of Siṃha), (6) variegated in colour (of Kanyâ), (7) black

(of Tulâ), (8) golden (of Vṛiśchika), (9) of a tawny colour (of Dhanu), (10) gray (of Makara), (11) of mongoose colour (of Kumbha), and (12) of the colour of fishes, sparkling white (of Mîna). The Plava designations of the several houses or signs are termed after the names of the directions governed by their rulers.[1] The house next to that occupied by the Sun is called Veśi.

End of Chapter I on Zodiacal Sings by Śrî Varâhá Mihira.

Note :—1 The Houses Meṣa or Vṛiśchika are governed by the planet Mars; Mars rules the south; therefore the Plava designation of Meṣa or Vṛiśchika is south. The following table shews the details :—

Signs.	Meṣa, Vṛiśchika.	Vṛiṣa, Tulâ.	Mithuna, Kanyâ.	Karka.	Dhanu, Mîna.	Makara, Kumbha.	Siṃha.
Rulers	Mars	Venus	Mercury	Moon	Jupiter	Saturn	Sun
Plava designation.	South	Agni (south-east)	North	Vâyavya (north-west.)	Îsân (north-east.)	West	East

Râhu is the ruler of South-west or Naiṛita koṇa.

The chief use of these Plava designations is to find out the articles that are lost or stolen; in what direction the thief has fled, or in journeys and marches which direction is auspicious, and so on.

Given below are some synonymous terms, which will be found convenient for reference :—

1. Horâ, Lagna, Ascendant.
2. 3rd House, Duśchikyam.
3. 4th House, Hibukam.
4. 5th House, Trikoṇam.
5. 7th House, Dyunaṃ.
6. 9th House, Trikoṇam.
7. 10th House, Meṣûraṇam.
8. 12th House, Riḥpham.
9. 4th and 8th Houses, Chaturasras.
10. Lagna, 4th, 7th and 10th houses, Kaṇṭaka, Kendra, Chatuṣṭya.
11. 2nd, 5th, 8th, 11th houses, Panpharas succedent houses.
12. 3rd, 6th, 9th, 12th houses, Apoklims, cadent houses.
13. Lagna, Tanu, (Physique). Kalpa (prowess).
14. 2nd House, Kuṭumba, Sva.
15. 3rd House, Sahaja, Vikâma,

16. 4th House, Bandhu (friends), Vesma, Sukha.
17. 5th House, Buddhi, Putra.
18. 6th House, Ari, Kṣata.
19. 7th House, Dārâ (wife), Chittotha, Jâmitra.
20. 8th House, Maraṇa (death), Randhra.
21. 9th House, Śubha, Guru, Tapaḥ.
22. 10th House, Âspada, Karma.
23. 11th House, Bhâva, Âya.
24. 12th House, Vyâya (Expenditure).
25. 3rd, 6th, 10th and 11th and houses are called upachaya houses.
26. 1st, 2nd, 4th, 5th, 7th, 8th, 9th, 12th houses are called Apachaya houses.

The terms up to the number 9 are simply names. Those from 9 to 26 indicate also the effects on the life of the individual born.

Note :—45. How to find the Lagna or the point of the Ecliptic just rising at a given time from sunrise. Rule :—From the Sun's longitude ascertained at the given time, find the Bhukta and Bhogya times in Prânas in the following manner. Find the sign in which the Sun is and find the Bhukta degrees or the degrees which the Sun has passed and the Bhogya degrees or those which he has to pass. Multiply the numbers of the Bhukta and Bhogya degrees (separately) by the rising period of the said sign (at the given place) and divide the products by 30. (The first quotient is the Bhukta time in Prânas in which the Sun has passed the Bhukta degrees, and the latter is the Bhogya time in Prânas in which he has to pass the Bhogya degrees.

46 & 47. From the given time in Prânas (at the end of which the Lagna is to be found) subtract the Bhogya time in Prânas and the rising periods of the next signs (to that in which the Sun is, as long as you can, then at last you will find the sign the rising period of which being greater than the remainder you will not be able to subtract, and which is consequently called the Asuddha sign or the sign incapable of being subtracted, and its rising period the Asuddha rising). Multiply the remainder thus found by 30 and divide the product by the Asuddha rising period : add the quotient, in degrees, to the preceding signs (to the Asuddha sign) reckoned from Aries: (and to the sum apply the amount of the precession of the equinoxes by subtraction or addition according as it will be additive or subtractive) : the result (thus found) will be the place of the Lagna* at the eastern horizon. If the time at the end of which the Lagna is to be found, be given before sunrise, then take the Bhukta time (above found)

* (Thus there are two processes for finding the Lagna, one when the given time is after sunrise and the other when it is before sunrise, and which consequently called Krama or direct and Vyutkrama or indirect process, respectively—B. D.).

and the rising periods of the preceding signs, to that which is occupied by the Sun in a contrary order from the given time ; multiply the remainder by 30 and divide the product by the Asuddha rising period ; subtract the quotient, in degrees, from the signs (reckoned from Aries to the Asuddha sign inclusive) ; the remainder inversely applied with the amount of the precession (of the equinoxes) will be the place of the Lagna at the eastern horizon.

Example :—Find the Lagna at 5 hours 15 minutes (true local time or observed time at the place of question) after the sunrise, the sun's longitude being 8 signs 20 degrees, and the latitude of the place being 22 degrees 30 minutes.

First find the rising times of the several signs at 22°30′ latitude. These are :—Meṣa, 1373 prânas (sidereal) ; Vṛiṣa, 1549 prânas ; Mithuna 1836 prânas ; Karkaṭa 2038 prânas; Siṃha 2037 ; Kanyâ 1967 ; Tulâ 1967 ; Vriṣchika 2037 ; Dhanu, 2038 ; Makara 1836 ; Kumbha 1549 ; Mîna, 1373 prânas. These Pranas (each Prâna=4″ in sidereal measure).

The Sun here is in the sign Dhanu, a Saggitarius 10 degrees of which are yet to be passed over by the Sun.

Now if the 30 degrees of the sign Sagittarius take 2038 prânas to rise, what will 10 degrees take ? Thus the Bhogya time is $679\frac{1}{3}$ prânas. The time after sunrise is 5 hours 15 minutes=315 minutes=4725 prânas (each prâna=4 seconds).

Given prânas = 4725.
Deduct Bhogya time = $679\frac{1}{3}$.
The rising of the 1st point of Makara = $4045\frac{2}{3}$.
Deduct the rising prâna of Makara = 1836.
The rising of the 1st point of Kumbha = $2209\frac{2}{3}$.
Deduct the rising prâna of Kumbha = 1549.
The rising of the 1st point of Mîna = $660\frac{2}{3}$.

Now the rising prâna of Mîna=1373 ; it cannot be deducted from $660\frac{2}{3}$; therefore the sign Mîna is called the Asuddha sign. How much of it has risen above the horizon can be got by the following Rule of Three :—

1373 Prânas are required for 30 degrees to rise ; how many degrees will be required for $660\frac{2}{3}$ prânas. The Mîna risen above$=\frac{660\frac{2}{3}}{1373}\times 30=$ 14° 26′ 8″. Mîna is the Lagna.

Remark.—The Sun's longitude given in our Almanac is reckoned from the first point of the constellation Aries, the Nakṣatra Asvinî, the fixed point (not from the vernal Equinox, the variable). The rising Prânas are always calculated from the vernal Equinox, the variable point. Therefore, first add the Ayanâṃśa (at present) or the amount of the precession of the Equinoxes to the longitude of the Sun. And get the Lagna by the above process. Lastly, subtract the Ayanâmsa from the Lagna and you will get the Nirayaṇa Lagna (from the fixed point Aśvinî). The "Precession of the Equinox" is the slight retrogression of the vernal Equinox of 50" per annum; at present it amounts to about 20 minutes from the 1st point of Aśvinî. If the time given be before sunrise, do the processes as given in the Rule. Draw out the zodiacal circle. Put the Sun in the Hemisphere below the horizon and consider the signs towards the eastern point. You will understand the rule easily.

If the time be given by the clock, apply the equation of time to get the solar local time ("apparent or observed time at the place of question) and then proceed with the operations.

2nd example :—

Required the Lagna Sphutam, that is, the longitude of the Ascendant at 39 gh. 30 v. gh. from sunrise on Friday, the 28th May 1886, for a place whose latitude is 11°.

From the Almanac we find that the Sun entered Taurus at 56 gh., 40 v. gh., on the 12th May, and quits the sign at 12 gh. 27 v. gh. on the 13th June. Therefore time taken by the Sun to move through the sign Taurus

= 3 gh. 20 v. gh. + 31 days + 12 gh. 27 v. gh.
= 31 days 15 gh. 47 v. gh. = 1,12,500 v. ghs.

Time from sunrise on the 28th May to the end of the Sun's course through Taurus = 16 days 12 gh. 27 v. gh.
= 58,327 v. ghs.

Time of oblique ascension of Taurus for latitude 11° = 5 gh. 6 v. gh.
= 306 v. gh.

Therefore time of oblique ascension of the portion of Taurus to be passed over by the Sun on the morning of the 28th

$$= \frac{306 \times 58,327}{1,12,500} = 2 \text{ gh. } 39 \text{ v. gh.}$$

Subtracting this from 39 gh., 30 v. gh. we get time of oblique ascension of signs from Gemini = 39 gh. 30 v. gh.—2 gh. 39 v. gh. = 36 gh. 51 v. gh.

From Tables we find that the time of oblique ascension of signs from Gemini to Scorpio = 31 gh. 36 v. gh.

Therefore the time of oblique ascension of portion Sagittarius that has risen above the horizon

=36 gh. 51 v. gh.—31 gh. 36 v. gh.

=5 gh. 15 v. gh.=315 v. gh.

Time of oblique ascension of the 30 degrees of Sagittarius for latitude 11° is 5 gh. 21 v. gh.=321 v. gh.

Therefore portion of Sagittarius that has risen above the horizon $=\frac{30\times315}{321}=29°26'$, Sagittarius being the 9th sign from Aries.

Lagna sphutam required is 8^s 29°26′.

The other planets' sphutam processes are too complicated to be given here. The reader is referred to the Sûrya Siddhânta or to Siddhânta Śiromaṇi.

How to cast an Horoscope or to construct a map of the Heavens at the time of birth.

Mode I, used in U. P. and Oudh.*

*Remarks :—The Sun is denoted in the diagrams by I ; the Moon, by II ; Mars, by III ; Mercury by IV ; Jupiter by V ; Venus by VI ; Saturn by VII. Râhu (moon's Ascending mode) by VIII ; Ketu (moon's descending mode) by IX.

The 12 Houses or signs beginning with Meṣa (Aries), Vṛiṣa (Taurus), Mithuna (Gemini), etc., are represented in the diagrams by 1,2,3, etc.

The 27 stars or Nakṣatras, or asterisms are denoted in the diagram by *a, b, c, d, e, f, g, h, i, j, k, l, m, n, o, p, q, r, s, t, u, v, w, x, y, z, á,* or in capital letters A, B, C, &c.

Draw the figure I as annexed.

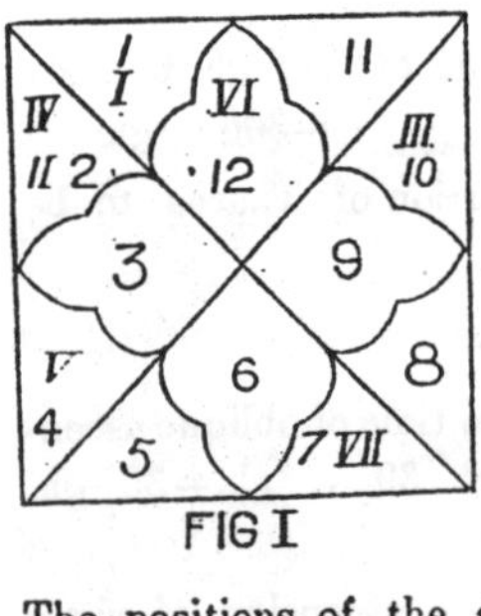

FIG I

The twelve Houses are shewn here. The Ascendant is put on the top House ; and the name of the Ascendant is put in figures ; 1 denoting Meṣa or Aries, 2 Vṛiṣa; 3 Mithuna, 4 Karka, 5 Siṃha, 6 Kanyâ, 7 Tulâ, 8 Vṛiśchika, 9 Dhanu, 10 Makara, 11 Kumbha, and 12 Mîna. The House or sign Mîna is here the Ascendant and its number 12 is put into this House Put down 1, 2, 3, etc., opposite the hands of the watch ; these will represent Meṣa, Vṛiṣa, Mithuna, etc. The positions of the several planets are then inserted in their proper places. The Houses and the signs are identical in the Hindu method.

The details of the planets are shewn separately as in the annexed table.

Planets.	Sun.	Moon.	Mars.	Mercury.	Jupiter.	Venus.	Saturn.	Ascen.
Sign ...	0	1	9	1	3	11	6	11
Degrees	1	2	27	0	4	26	19	29
Minutes	0	0	0	25	0	0	0	59
Seconds	0	0	0	0	0	0	0	0

Mode II, used in Bengal.

See the annexed Figure 2.

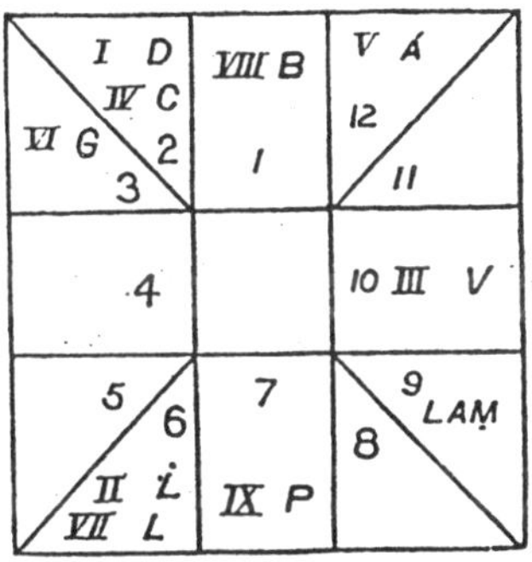

FIG. 2

The figure is square or circular as liked by the astrologer ; but the 12 Houses are marked as here. The sign Meṣa is always at the top ; then the other Houses follow in due order. The Ascendant is indicated by the word "lam" put in the House which is the ascendant at the time of birth. The planets are then inserted in the several Houses, from the Calendar. The Nakṣatras of the planets are inserted in figures in their due order. On either side is written the measure of the day of the birth and the day after or before birth according as the Nakṣatra of the birthday continues the next day or continued the day previous. The measure is 33 Dandas 19 Palas ; and so on.

Day measure : 33-19.	Śakâbdâ 1814.	Day measure : 33-20.
Birthday :	1 21 39 16 30	day next birthday :
6 11 15		7 12 16
8 4 17		9 9 17
4 29 1		7 47 43
2 1 22		43 3 23

The figures in the first vertical row denote the day of the week, the tithi or lunar day, and its measure; *e.g.*, by 6 is denoted the Friday; by 8 is denoted the eighth day of the bright fortnight; and the tithi lasts for 4 dandas and 2 palas. The second vertical row:—11 indicates P. Phalguni Nakṣatra; 4,29 and 1 indicate 4 dandas 29 palas and 1 vipala, the duration of that Nakṣatra. The third vertical row:—15 indicates the Vajra Yoga; 17 and 1 indicate 17 dandas and 1 pala (the duration of the Yoga) 22 represents the 22nd date of the month. The figures at the middle indicate the year 1814 Saka Era; 1 indicates the month of Vaiśâkh; 21 denotes the 21 days of that month passed; 39,16, and 30 indicate 39 dandas 16 palas and 30 vipalas of the 22 Vaiśâkh when the birth took place.

The true positions of the planets are taken from a reliable Calendar (and put in a separate table) thus:—

Planets.				
Sun	1 sign	21 degrees	15 kalâs	and 2 vikalâs.
Moon	5	5	17	4.
Mars	9	16	32	11.

and so for Mercury, Jupiter, Venus, Saturn, and the Moon's Ascending and Descending Nodes called Râhu and Ketu.

Mode III, used in Southern India and recommended by Jaimini, the author of astrological aphorisms. See Fig. III given below:—

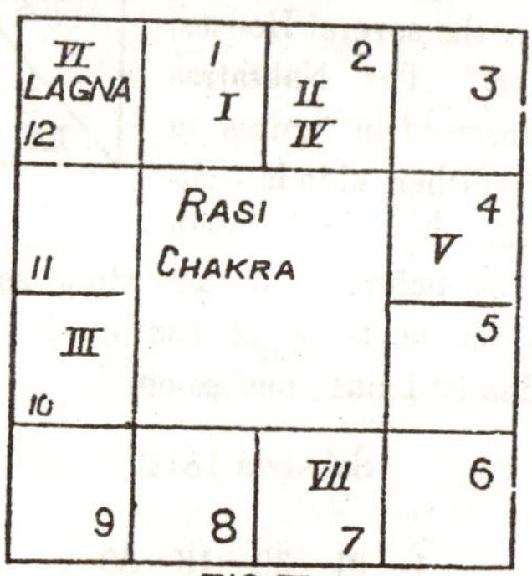

FIG III

The twelve Houses or signs are always written as here. The word Lagna is written in the house which becomes the Ascendant. The several planets are also inserted in the several houses at that time.

ON THE PLANETS.

First Principles and Definitions—(contd.)

शा॰वि॰--कालात्मा दिनकृन्मनस्तुहिनगुः सत्वं कुजो ज्ञो वचो
जीवो ज्ञानसुखे सितश्च मदनो दुःखं दिनेशात्मजः ॥
राजानौ रविशीतगू क्षितसुतो नेता कुमारो बुधः
सूरिर्दानवपूजितश्च सचिवौ प्रेष्यः सहस्रांशुजः ॥ १ ॥

कालात्मा Kâlâtmâ, the soul of the Zodiacal Man or Kâlapuruṣa (Time Person). दिनकृत् Dinakṛit, the Sun. मनः Manaḥ, the mind. तुहिनगुः Tuhinaguḥ, the Moon. सत्वं Satvam, strength, energy, courage, vigour. कुजः Kujaḥ, Mars. ज्ञः Jñaḥ, Mercury. वचः Vachaḥ, the speech. जीवः Jivaḥ, the Jupiter. ज्ञानसुखे Jñânsukhe, knowledge and happiness, knowledge and health. सितः Sitaḥ, the Venus. च Cha, and. मदनः Madanaḥ, the God of love; the love; desires; passion. दुःखं Duḥkham, pain; sorrow. दिनेशात्मजः Dineśâtmajaḥ; Saturn. राजानौ Rajânau, kings; the royal personages. रविशीतगू Raviśitagu, the Sun and Moon. क्षितसुतः Kṣitasutaḥ, the Mars. नेता Netâ, the general commander. कुमारः Kumâraḥ, the prince. बुधः Budhaḥ, the Mercury. सूरिः Sûriḥ, the Jupiter. दानवपूजितः Dânavapûjitaḥ, the Venus, worshipped by the Dânavas. च Cha, and. सचिवौ Sachivau, the ministers, the councillors. प्रेष्यः Preṣyaḥ, the messenger; the servant. सहस्रांशुजः Sahasrânśujaḥ, the Saturn.

1. The Sun is the Soul of the Zodiacal Man (Kâla Puruṣa); the Moon is his mind; Mars, vigour; Mercury, speech; Jupiter, the knowledge and happiness; Venus, the love and desires; Saturn is the sorrow. Of the planets, the Sun and the Moon are the kings; Mars is the commander-in-chief; Mercury, the first prince; Jupiter and Venus are the ministers; and Saturn, the servant.

Notes:—The body of the Zodiacal Man (the Time personified), the outside of it, the outer vesture was represented in the first chapter by the twelve signs (externally), and now the inner aspect or the inside of it, the inner vesture is represented by the several planets (internally). Inasmuch as the planets are the governors of the signs, they are very aptly described as the internal rulers of the body. Thus Time pervades both the outside and inside of this universe. When the planet in any house is afflicted, the inner feeling corresponding to that gets afflicted ; and when the planet is strong, the inner feeling also gets strong. Saturn when under the influence of a benefic planet obeys its orders ; and when under the influence of a malefic planet, obeys again its (contrary) orders ; *i.e.*, does its duty as it is joined with a good or bad planet.

शालिनी—हेलिः सूर्यश्चंद्रमाः शीतरश्मिर्हेम्नो विज्ज्ञो बोध-
नश्चेंदुपुत्रः ॥ आरो वक्रः क्रूरदृक् चावनेयः कोणो
मंदः सूर्यपुत्रोऽसितश्च ॥ २ ॥

हेलि: Helih, termed Helih. सूर्य: Sûryah, the Sun. चंद्रमा Chandramâ, the Moon. शीतरश्मि: Śitaraśmih, named Śitaraśmi, whose rays are cooling. हेम्न: Hemnah, Hemna. वित् Vit, known as Vit. ज्ञ: Jñah, known as Jña. बोधन: Bodhanah, known as Bodhana. च Cha, also. इंदुपुत्र: Induputrah, the son of the Moon ; Mercury. आर: Ârah, named Arah. वक्र: Vakrah, termed Vakra. क्रूरदृक् Krûradrik, Krûradrik. च Cha, also. आवनेय: Avaneyah, Mars, the son of Earth. कोण: Konah, known as Kona. मंद: Mandah, termed Manda. सूर्यपुत्र: Sûryaputrah, Saturn, the son of the Sun. असित: Asitah, termed Asita. च Cha, also.

2. The other names (synonyms) of the several planets. The Sun is named also Helî, the Moon is named Śitaraśmi, Mercury is named Hemna, Vit, Jña, Bodhana, and Chandraputra (the son of the Moon) Mars is named Âra, Vakra, Krûradrik, Âvaneya. Saturn is named Manda, Kona, Suryaputra (the son of the Sun), Asita.

व०ति—जीवोऽङ्गिराः सुरगुरुर्वचसां पतीज्यः शुक्रो भृगुर्भृगु-
सुतः सित आस्फुजिच्च ॥ राहुस्तमोऽगुरसुरश्च शि-
खीति केतुः पर्य्यायमन्यमुपलभ्य वदेच्च लोकात् ॥ ३ ॥

जीव: Jîvah, Jupiter. अङ्गिरा: Angirâh, Angirâh. सुरगुरु: Suraguruh, Suraguru, the guru or the teacher of the Devas. वचसांपति: Vachasâmpatih, Vachasâmpati or Vâchaspati. इज्य: Ijyah, Ijyah. शुक्र: Śukrah, Venus. भृगु: Bhriguh, Bhrigu. भृगुसुत: Bhriguśutah, Bhrigusuta. सित: Sitah, Sita (the white planet). आस्फुजित् Âsphujit, Âsphujit. च Cha, also. राहु: Râhûh, the Dragon's head ; the Moon's Ascending Node. तम: Tamah, Tama. अगु Agu, Agu. असुर: Asurah, Asura. च Cha, also. शिखी Śikhî, Śikhî. इति Iti, thus केतु: Ketuh, the Dragon's tail.

The Moon's Descending Node. पर्यायम् Paryâyam, synonyms. अन्यम् Anyam, other. उपलभ्य Upalabhya, finding out, ascertaining, knowing. वदेत् Vadet, is to be told. च Cha, and. लोकात् Lokât, from other Śastras or authoritative persons.

3. Jupiter is also named Angirâ, Suraguru, Vâchaspati or Îjya; Venus is Bhrigu, Bhrigusuta, Sita, also Âsphujit. The Dragon's Head or the Moon's Ascending Node is Râhu, Tama, Agu, and Asura. The Dragon's tail or the Moon's Descending Node is named Śikhî. There are various other synonyms; one should ascertain them from other Śâstras and accept them.

शालिनी—रक्तश्यामो भास्करो गौर इन्दुर्नात्युच्चांगो रक्तगौरश्च वक्रः ॥ दूर्वाश्यामो ज्ञो गुरुर्गौरगात्रः श्यामः शुक्रो भास्करिः कृष्णदेहः ॥ ४ ॥

रक्तश्यामः Raktaśyâmaḥ, reddish; dusky red; orange; of a red and dark brown colour. भास्करः Bhâskaraḥ, the Sun. गौरः Gauraḥ, white. इंदुः Induḥ, the Moon. नात्युच्चांगः Nâtyuchchâṃgaḥ, not very long. रक्तगौरः Raktagauraḥ, red. च Cha, and. वक्रः Vakraḥ, Mars. दूर्वाश्यामः Dûrvâśyâmaḥ, green like the colour of Dûrvâ grass. ज्ञः Jñaḥ, Mercury. गुरुः Guruḥ, Jupiter. गौरगात्रः Gauragâtraḥ, white, according to some, yellow like molten gold. श्यामः Śyâmaḥ, dark blue. शुक्रः Śukraḥ, Venus. भास्करिः Bhâskariḥ, Saturn. कृष्णदेहः Krisṇadehaḥ, black.

4. (Now the colours of the several planets are described.). The Sun is of a red and dark brown colour; the Moon is of white colour. Mars is red; its stature is not very long. Mercury is green like the colour of Dûrvâ grass and Jupiter is white. Venus is dark blue and Saturn is of black colour.

Note:—The native derives the colour of his body from the planet that is powerful in his nativity.

**शा० वि०—वर्णास्ताम्रसितातिरक्तहरितव्यापीतचित्रासिता ।
वह्न्यम्ब्वग्निजकेशवेन्द्रशचिकाः सूर्यादिनाथाः क्रमात् ॥
प्रागाद्या रविशुक्रलोहिततमः सौरेन्दुवित्सूरयः ।
क्षीणेंद्वर्कमहीसुतार्कतनयाः पापा बुधस्तैर्युतः ॥ ५ ॥**

वर्णाः Varṇâḥ, colours. ताम्रसितातिरक्तहरितव्यापीतचित्रासिताः Tâmrasitâtiraktaharitavyâpîtachitrâsitâḥ, of copper red, white, bloody red, greenish, yellow, variegated, and black colours. वह्न्यम्ब्वग्निजकेशवेन्द्रशचिकाः Vahnyambagnijakeśavendraśachikâḥ, Agni (Fire), Varuṇa (water), Kumâra Kârtikeya, Viṣṇu, Indra, Indrâṇi Śachî and Prajâpati Brahmâ. सूर्यादिनाथाः Sûryâdinâthâḥ, The Sun, the Moon, Mars, Mercury, Jupiter, Venus, Saturn, being successively the lords (of the several colours, etc.) Another meaning is:—Being the lords of the Sun, the Moon, Mars, Mercury, Jupiter, Venus and Saturn. क्रमात् Kramât, successively. प्रागाद्याः Prâgâdyâḥ, Rulers of the east, south-east, south, south-west, west, north-west, north and north-east, respectively. रविशुक्रलोहिततमःसौरेन्दुवित्सूरयः Raviśukralohitatamaḥ saurenduvitsûrayaḥ, the Sun, Venus, Mars, Râhu, Saturn, the Moon, Mercury, Jupiter. क्षीणेन्द्वर्कमहीसुतार्कतनयाः Kṣîṇendvarkamahîsutârkatanayâḥ, the waning Moon, the Sun, Mars, Saturn. पापाः Pâpâḥ, the malefics; the malefic planets. बुधः Budhaḥ, Mercury. तैः युतः Taiḥ yutaḥ, when joined with them.

5. The Sun, Moon, Mars, Mercury, Jupiter, Venus and Saturn preside respectively over the following colours:—copper red; white, bloody red, greenish, yellow, variegated, and black colours.(1) Fire (Agni), Water (Varuṇa) Kârtikeya, Viṣṇu, Indra, Śachî, and Prajâpati Brahmâ are respectively the rulers of the Sun, Moon, Mars, Mercury, Jupiter, Venus and Saturn. (2) The Sun, Venus, Mars, Râhu, Saturn, the Moon, Mercury, and Jupiter are respectively the rulers of east, south-east, south, south-west, west, north-west, north, and north-east directions.(3) The waning Moon, the Sun, Mars, and Saturn are considered as the malefic planets; Mercury when joined with any of these is considered malefic.(4)

Note:—(1) These are useful in ascertaining the colour of stolen articles and in determining the colour of the flowers to be used in the worship of the planets.

(2) From the powerful planet at the time of one's birth, it can be ascertained which particular Deva a person would worship.

(3) These are useful in determining the position of the entrance of the delivery room of a woman and in discovering the direction of the escape of the thieves.

(4) Jupiter, Venus, and Mercury when in conjunction with either of these (*i.e.*, Jupiter or Venus) are benefic planets.

The Moon is called waning from the eighth day of the dark fortnight to the eighth day of the bright fortnight, when she is inauspicious;

after these, the Moon is called waxing or full when she is considered auspicious and benefic.

Yavaneśvarâchârya and others say that the Moon is always considered benefic; though her auspiciousness may be greater or less on certain days.

The native becomes good or bad according as the planets at his birth are benefic or malefic.

त्रोटक—बुधसूर्यसुतौ नपुंसकाख्यौ शशिशुक्रौ युवती नराश्च शेषाः ॥ शिखिभूखपयोमरुद्गणानां वशिनो भूमिसुतादयः क्रमेण ॥ ६ ॥

बुधसूर्यसुतौ Budhasûryasutau, Mercury and Saturn. नपुंसकाख्यौ Napumsakâkhyau, Hermaphrodites, neither male nor female. शशिशुक्रौ Śaśiśukrau, the Moon and Venus. युवती Yuvatî, young women. नराः Narâḥ, men. च Cha, and. शेषाः Śesâḥ, the rest; the others (Sun, Mars, Jupiter). शिखिभूखपयोमरुद्गणानाम् Śikhibhûkhapayomarudganânâm, (the rulers) of fire, earth, ether, water, and air. वशिनः Vaśinaḥ, the rulers. भूमिसुतादयः Bhûmisutâdayaḥ, Mars, Mercury, Jupiter, Venus, and Saturn. क्रमेण Kramena, successively.

6. Mercury and Saturn are considered hermaphrodite planets. The Moon and Venus are considered young female planets. The rest (*i.e.*, the Sun, Jupiter and Márs) are male planets. Mars, Mercury, Jupiter, Venus, and Saturn are respectively the rulers of fire, earth, ether or âkâśa, water, and air (or Vâyu).

Note:—Mercury is a female hermaphrodite and Saturn is a male hermaphrodite.

Also the Sun is fire and the Moon is water.

उपजातिका—विप्रादितः शुक्रगुरू कुजार्कौ शशी बुधश्चेत्यसितोऽन्त्यजानाम् ॥ चंद्रार्कजीवा ज्ञसितौ कुजार्की यथाक्रमं सत्वरजस्तमांसि ॥ ७ ॥

विप्रादितः Viprâditaḥ, of the Brâhmaṇas, Kṣatriyas, Vaiśyas, and Śûdras. शुक्रगुरू Śukragurû, Venus and Jupiter. कुजार्कौ Kujârkau, Mars and the Sun. शशी Śaśi, the Moon. बुधः Budhaḥ, Mercury. च Cha, and. इति Iti, thus. असितः Asitaḥ, Saturn. अन्त्यजानाम् Antyajânâm, of men of the lowest caste. चंद्रार्कजीवाः Chandrârkajîvâḥ, the

Moon, the Sun, and Jupiter. ज्ञसितौ Jñasitau, Mercury and Venus. कुजार्कौ Kujârkî, Mars and Saturn. यथाक्रमं Yathâkramam, in order. सत्वरजस्तमांसि Satvarajastamâṃsi, are of Satva, Rajaḥ, and Tama qualities; represent the qualities of goodness or purity, activity, and inertia.

7. Venus and Jupiter are (the lords of) the Brâhmaṇas, Mars and the Sun are (the lords of) the Kṣatriyas; the Moon (of the) Vaiśyas and Mercury (of the) Śûdras. Saturn is (the lord of the) lowest caste persons, *e.g.*, Chândâlas, Mâgadhas and Niṣâdas. The Sun, the Moon, and Jupiter represent the Satva or the goodness and purity; Mercury and Venus, the Rajas or passionate activity; Mars and Saturn represent the Tamas or darkness and inertia.

Note :—Knowledge is obtained of the caste of persons that have stolen or injured any property on seeing which planet is the most powerful in the querent's nativity.

A man becomes Sâtvik, Râjasik, or Tâmasik according to the nature of the Triṃśâṃśa, which the Sun is found to occupy or according to the nature of the planet that is most powerful in his nativity. Yavaneśwara is of opinion that Mars is Sâtvik.

The nature of the three guṇas or qualities is thus described :—A Sâtvik is kind, steady, truthful, honest and upright, and is devoted to the Brâhmaṇas and Devas. A Râjasic is poetic, of sacrificial spirit, attached to women, and heroic. Persons of Tâmasa quality are illiterate, lazy, wrathful, addicted to much sleep, deceitful, and cunning.

Table showing the colour etc., of the planets.

Planets.	Sun.	Moon.	Mars.	Mercury.	Jupiter.	Venus.	Saturn.	Râhu.
Colours	Dusky red	White	Red	Greenish	White or yellow like molten gold.	Dark blue	Black	Black.
Presides over colours	Copper red	White	Blood red	Green	Yellow	Variegated	Black	Black.
Their Devatâs	Agni	Varuṇa	Kârtikeya	Viṣṇu	Indra	Indra's wife Śachî.	Brahmâ	Demon.
Rulers of the directions.	East	N.-W.	S.	N.	N. E.	S.-E.	W.	S.-W.
Benefic or malefic	Malefic	Benefic, waning Moon malefic.	Malefic	Benefic; united with malefic, malefic.	Benefic	Benefic	Malefic	Malefic.
Male, Female, Hermaphrodite.	Male	Female	Male	Hermaphrodite	Male	Female	Hermaphrodite.	
Rulers of Elements	Fire	Water	Fire	Earth	Âkâśa	Water	Air	
Caste	King	Vaiśya	King	Vaiśya	Brâhmaṇ	Brâhmaṇ	Chândâla	Demon.
Qualities	Sattva	Sattva	Tama	Rajas	Sattva	Rajas	Tama	

Table showing the Gaṇas or classification of the persons born under different Moon-occupied Nakṣatras.

Deva or Gods	Aśvinî (1)	Mṛigaśirâ (5)	Punarvasu (7)	Puṣyâ (8)	Hastâ (13)	Svâtî (15)	Anurâdhâ (17)	Śravaṇâ (22)	Revatî. (27)
Nara or men	Bharaṇî (2)	Rohiṇî (4)	Ârdrâ (6)	P. Phalgunî (11)	U. Phalgunî (12)	P. Âṣâḍhâ (20)	U. Aṣâḍhâ (21)	P. Bhâdra (25)	U. Bhâdra. (26)
Râkṣas or Demons.	Kṛittikâ (3)	Aśleṣâ (9)	Maghâ (10)	Chitrâ (14)	Viśâkhâ (16)	Jyeṣṭhâ (18)	Mûlâ (19)	Dhaniṣṭhâ (23)	Śatabhiṣâ. (24)

N.B.—This Gaṇa table is from the other astrological works.

Table showing the castes of the several signs occupied by the Moon during birth time.

Bráhmaṇas.	Kṣatriyas.	Valśyas.	Śúdras.
Karka	Siṃha	Kumbha	Vṛiṣa.
Mina	Tulā	Meṣa	Mákara.
Vṛiśchika	Dhanu	Mithuna	Kanyá.

त्रोटक—मधुपिङ्गलदृक् चतुरस्रतनुः पित्तप्रकृतिः सवि-ताल्पकचः ॥ तनुवृत्ततनुर्बहुवातकफः प्राज्ञश्च शशी मृदुवाक् शुभदृक् ॥ ८ ॥

मधुपिङ्गलदृक् Madhupiṃgaladṛik, auburn-eyed, having eyes of yellowish colour like that of honey. चतुरस्रतनुः Chaturasratanuḥ, of square body; (*i.e.*, height being equal to the distance between the extremity of one hand to that of the other, both the hands being stretched far and wide); of the length of the two arms stretched out. पित्तप्रकृतिः Pittaprakṛitiḥ, bilious. सविता Savitá, the Sun. अल्पकचः Alpakachaḥ, of scanty hair on one's head. तनुवृत्ततनुः Tanuvṛittatanuḥ, of body, thin and round; round and slender. बहुवातकफः Bahuvâtakaphaḥ, having too much phlegm and wind, much windy and phlegmatic. प्राज्ञः Prâjñaḥ, clever; intelligent; learned. च Cha, and. शशी Śaśí, the Moon. मृदुवाक् Mṛiduvâk, of gentle speech, of soft voice. शुभदृक् Śubhadṛik, of good-looking eyes; of beautiful eyes.

8. The Sun has his eyes somewhat yellow, his height equal to the length of the two arms stretched out, his nature bilious, and very little hair on his head. The Moon has a body round and slender, her temperament much windy and phlegmatic, intelligence great, voice soft and gentle and eyes lovely.

स्वागता—क्रूरदृक् तरुणमूर्तिरुदारः पैत्तिकः सुचपलः कृशमध्यः ॥ श्लिष्टवाक् सततहास्यरुचिर्ज्ञः पित्तमारुतकफ-प्रकृतिश्च ॥ ९ ॥

क्रूरदृक् Krûradṛik, of cruel eyes, of diplomatic eyes. तरुणमूर्तिः Taruṇamûrtiḥ, of young formation; youth. उदारः Udâraḥ, generous. पैत्तिकः Paittikaḥ, bilious. सुचपलः Suchapalaḥ, very restless, very unsteady. कृशमध्यः Kriśamadhyaḥ, of slender waist. श्लिष्टवाक् Śliṣṭavâk, of a tremulous voice, somewhat choked by intense feelings. सततहास्यरुचिः : Satatahâsyaruchiḥ, always humorous and joking. ज्ञः Jñaḥ, Budhaḥ, Mercury. पित्तमारुतकफप्रकृतिः : Pittamârutakaphaprakṛitiḥ, bilious, windy, and phlegmatic. च Cha, and.

9. Mars has cruel and deceitful eyes, is of quite youthful appearance, generous, bilious, versatile, unsteady and of thin waist. Mercury has his voice tremulous, choked by intense feelings, is always humorous and joking and is of bilious, windy and phlegmatic temperaments.

वंशस्थ—बृहत्तनुः पिङ्गलमूर्द्धजेक्षणो बृहस्पतिः श्रेष्ठमतिःकफात्मकः ॥ भृगुः सुखी कान्तवपुः सुलोचनः कफानिलात्मासितवक्रमूर्द्धजः ॥ १० ॥

बृहत्तनुः : Bṛihattanuḥ, corpuscular; having a big body. पिङ्गलमूर्द्धजेक्षणः : Piṅgalamûrddhajekṣaṇaḥ, having yellow eyes and hairs on the head. बृहस्पतिः : Bṛihaspatiḥ, Jupiter. श्रेष्ठमतिः : Sresṭhamatiḥ, of superior intellect; having high intellectual powers. कफात्मकः : Kaphâtmakaḥ, phlegmatic. भृगुः : Bhṛiguḥ, Venus. सुखी Sukhi, happy. कान्तवपुः : Kântavapuḥ, having a beautiful body, सुलोचनः : Sulochanaḥ, with eyes lovely. कफानिलात्मा Kaphânilâtmâ, bilious and windy. असितवक्रमूर्द्धजः : Asitavakramûrddhajaḥ, of black, curling hairs.

10. Jupiter has a big body, yellow hairs and yellow eyes, superior intellect and a phlegmatic nature. Venus is ease-loving and happy, has a body beautiful and eyes lovely, a nature phlegmatic and windy, and hairs black and curling.

Note:—Jupiter is the biggest of all planets. This was known to the Hindus long long ago.

वं०ति०—मंदोऽलसः कपिलदृक् कृशदीर्घगात्रः स्थूलद्विजः परुषरोमकचोऽनिलात्मा ॥ स्नाय्वस्थ्यसृक्त्वगथ शुक्रवसे च मज्जा मन्दार्कचन्द्रबुधशुक्रसुरेज्यभौमाः ॥ ११ ॥

मंदः : Mandaḥ, Saturn. अलसः Alasaḥ, lazy. कपिलदृक् Kapiladṛik, of tawny eyes. कृशदीर्घगात्रः : Kriśadîrghagâtraḥ, lean and tall. स्थूलद्विजः : Sthûladvijaḥ, of long teeth. परुषरोमकचः : Paruṣaromakachaḥ, the hairs of the body and head being coarse and hard. अनिलात्मा Anilâtmâ, of windy temperament. स्नाय्वस्थ्यसृक्त्वक् Snâyvasthyasṛiktvak, of nerves, bones, blood, and skin. अथ Atha, afterwards. शुक्रवसे Śukravase, of spermagenetale and fat. च Cha, and. मज्जा Majjâ, marrow of the bones. मंदार्कचंद्रबुधशुक्रसुरेज्यभौमाः : Mandârkachandrabudhaśukrasurejyabhaumâḥ, Saturn, the Sun, the Moon, Mercury, Venus, Jupiter and Mars.

11. Saturn is lazy, of tawny eyes, slender and tall, of long teeth, the hairs on the head and the body being very coarse and he is of windy temperament.

Saturn presides over muscles, the Sun over bones, the Moon over blood, Mercury over skin, Venus, over semen, Jupiter over flesh, and Mars over the marrow of the bones.

Note:—The physique and the body of the native correspond to the ruler of the rising Navâṃśa or the rising sign, whichever is powerful; he becomes of like figure, and that part of his body becomes hard which corresponds to the powerful planet during birth. These are also useful in questions on Horary Astrology, concerning the nature and the appearance of the thieves or when questions are asked on diseases, the rulers of the rising sign or of the rising Navâṃśa affecting the corresponding parts of the body.

शा० वि०—देवाम्ब्वग्निविहारकोशशयनक्षित्युत्करेशाः
क्रमात् । वस्त्रं स्थूलमभुक्तमाग्निकहतं मध्यं दृढं स्फाटितम् ॥
ताम्रं स्यान्मणिहेमयुक्तिरजतान्यर्काच्च मुक्तायसी । द्रेष्काणैः
शिशिरादयः शशुरुचज्ञग्वादिषूद्यत्सु वा ॥ १२ ॥

देवाम्ब्वग्निविहारकोशशयनक्षित्युत्करेशाः Devâmbvagnivihârakośaśayanakṣityutkareśâḥ, rulers of temples (sacred places or places of pilgrimage), water, fire, amusement, courts, treasury or store-room, bed rooms, and barren places, or lands where sweepings are gathered. क्रमात् Kramât, in due order; successively. वस्त्रं Vastram, cloth; clothes; garment; raiment. स्थूलमभुक्तमग्निकहतं Sthûlamabhuktamagnikahatam, coarse, new, partially burnt (at one corner), and wet (just squeezed out of water). मध्यं Madhyam, tolerably new; not quite new nor quite old. दृढं Dṛiḍham, strong. स्फाटितम् Sphâṭitam, torn. ताम्रं Tâmram, copper. स्यात् Syat, would be considered. मणिहेमयुक्तिरजतानि Maṇihemayuktirajatâni, gem (or jewel or pearl), gold, white copper and silver. (White copper is an amalgam of 25 parts of zinc or tin and 75 parts of copper). अर्कात् Arkât, commencing with the Sun, etc. मुक्तायसी Muktâyasî, pearl and iron. द्रेष्काणैः Dreṣkâṇaiḥ, (or) by their rising Dreṣkâṇs or Decanates (in case there be no planets rising). शिशिरादयः Śiśirâdayaḥ, the six seasons. (1) the Śiśira (the winter), (2) the Vasanta (the spring), (3) the Summer, (4) the Rainy season, (5) the Autumn, and (6) the Hemanta (the cold). The Śiśira is Mâgh and Phâlguna; the Vasanta is Chaitra and Vaiśâkh; the Summer is Jaiṣṭha and Âśâḍha; the Varṣâ is Śrâvaṇa and Bhâdra; the Śarat is Âśvin and Kârtika; the Hemanta is Agrahâyaṇa and Pauṣa. शशुरुचज्ञग्वादिषु Saśuruchajñagvâdiṣu, Saturn,

Venus, Mars, Moon, Mercury, Jupiter, Sun. उद्यत्सु Udyatsu, rising on the horizon. वा Vâ, or.

12 (Now the places over which the several planets preside are being mentioned in due order). The Sun presides over temples and sacred places; The Moon, over wells and water; Mars, over the fiery places (*i.e.*, cooking houses); Mercury, over amusement courts; Jupiter, over the store-room or the treasury; Venus presides over bed rooms, and Saturn over barren places or those places where sweepings are gathered. Now the clothings which the several planets like are being mentioned:—The Sun likes coarse cloth of thick threads; the Moon, quite new cloth; Mars likes cloth partly burnt (at one corner); Mercury, wet cloth (that is just squeezed of water); Jupiter likes cloth not quite new nor quite old; Venus likes strong ones; and Saturn likes torn clothings. Now the metals presided over by the several planets are being mentioned:—The Sun presides over copper; the Moon likes gems; Mars, gold; Mercury white copper; Jupiter likes silver; Venus, pearl and Saturn likes iron.[1] Now the several seasons indicated by the several planets or their Decanates rising in the eastern horizon are being mentioned. Saturn or its Decanate rising on the horizon indicates Sisira (the winter season); Venus indicates the spring; Mars indicates summer; the Moon indicates the rainy seasons; Mercury, autumn; Jupiter indicates Hemanta (the dewy season) and the Sun or his Decanate rising on the horizon indicates summer or very hot season. (If there be no planets rising on the horizon, then the ruler of the rising Decanate indicates the weather).[2]

Note:—(1) The object of this verse is to point our attention to those places where deliveries of children are likely to happen, where articles stolen or missing are carried or where thieves have made good their escapes and also to the clothings that are to be used in the lying-in-room. We infer also what metals are to be kept in the lying-in-room, also what articles are missing or stolen and if the planets are in their upachaya gṛihas or improving signs, those articles would be recovered ; else they would not be recovered.

The rulers of the Rig, Yajur, Sâma and Atharva Vedas are, as stated in the Svalpajâtaka, Jupiter, Venus, Mars, and Mercury. If the thief found be a Brâhmaṇ, then his Śâkhâ or Veda can be determined by this rule.

(2) Attention should be given to the last stanza ; its use is chiefly felt in the re-construction of lost horoscopes ; see Chapter the twenty-sixth. If there be many planets in the rising sign, the most powerful planet will influence the seasonal weather ; some say that the rising Decanate influences the weather ; the planets are not taken into account at all ; but this is not the opinion of the author. If there be no planets in the rising sign then the ruler of the rising Decanate influences the weather, and then only.

The 6 seasons :—(1) The Śiśira or the winter season (15th January to 15th March) comprising the two months when the Sun is in the signs Makâra and Kumbha ; (2) The Vasanta or the spring season (15th March to 15th May) comprising the two months when the Sun is in the signs Mina and Meṣa ; (3) The Gṛiṣma or the summer season (15th May to 15th July) comprising the two months when the Sun is in the signs (Vṛiṣa and Mithuna). (4) The Varṣâ or the rainy season (15th July to 15th September) comprising the two months when the Sun is in the signs Karka and Siṃha ; (5) The Śarat or the autumn (15th September to 15th November) comprising the two months when the Sun is in the signs (Kanyâ and Tulâ) ; and (6) the Hemanta or the cold season (15th November to 15th January) comprising the 2 months when the Sun is in the signs Vṛiśchika and Dhanu.

When Jupiter is in his house, he presides over gold.

प्र० षिं०—त्रिदशत्रिकोणचतुरस्रसप्तमान्यवलोकयन्ति चरणाभिवृद्धितः ॥ रविजामरेज्यरुधिराः परे च ये क्रमशो भवन्ति किल वीक्षणेऽधिकाः ॥ १३ ॥

त्रिदशत्रिकोणचतुरस्रसप्तमानि Tridaśatrikoṇachaturasrasaptamâni, third and tenth, fifth and ninth, fourth and eighth, and seventh houses, (reckoned in the left-hand direction from the exact position of the planet). अवलोकयन्ति Avalokayanti, look ; aspect. चरणाभिवृद्धितः Charaṇâbhivṛiddhitaḥ, with one-fourth, one-half, three-fourth, and full aspects (respectively) ; with one-fourth aspects repeated at every time (successively). रविजामरेज्यरुधिराः Ravijâmarejyarudhirâḥ, Saturn, Jupiter, Mars. परे च ये Pare cha ye, and the other planets that follow (*i.e.*, the Sun, Moon, Mercury and Venus). क्रमशः Kramaśaḥ, regularly, successively; in seriatim. भवन्ति Bhavanti, become. किल Kila, verily; certainly; as they say. वीक्षणे Vikṣaṇe, (on) aspecting. अधिकाः: Adhikâḥ, (yielding) more full results.

13. All the planets (excepting Saturn) aspect the third and tenth houses, (or the planets in these houses) from their positions at that time (reckoned in their left-hand directions) with one-fourth sight (and yield one-fourth results); all the planets (except Jupiter) aspect the fifth and ninth houses (from them in left hand directions) with half sight (and yield one-half results); all the planets (except Mars) aspect the fourth and eighth houses with three-fourth sight (and yield three-fourth results); and all the planets aspect the seventh house with full sight (and yield full results).

Saturn aspects the third and tenth houses with full sight; Jupiter aspects the fifth and ninth houses with full sight; Márs aspects the fourth and eighth houses with full sight; the other planets Sun, Moon, Mercury and Venus aspect the seventh house with full sight.

Note:—Râhu looks on the 5th, 7th, 9th and 12th houses with full aspect; 2nd and 10th houses with three-fourth aspect; 3rd, 4th, 6th and 8th houses with half aspect; 1st and 11th houses with no aspect. Râhu's aspect is counted in a right hand direction.

Ketu has got no aspect at all. See the Table of Aspects.

The above interpretation is supported by Sârâvali and Gârgi and various other authors. But some interpret it a little differently:—all the planets aspect the 3rd and 10th houses with a quarter sight, the 5th and 9th houses with half a sight, the 4th and 8th houses with three-quarters of a sight and the 7th house with a full sight. But the results (fruits of the aspect) given by Saturn are one-fourth (when he aspects well), by Jupiter, one-half, by Mars, three-fourth, and by Sun, Moon, Venus and Mercury, the full amount. But this is not generally accepted.

Notes:—By aspect is meant a certain zodiacal distance intervening between two planets or between one planet and any point of a house. Each aspect corresponds to the relation of one house to another. The aspects of planets are reckoned in the left hand directions from their *the then* position; only the case of Râhu is the opposite. The houses that have no aspect from any planet, do not derive any results, or fruits from these planets.

Suppose A to be a point in the ecliptic occupied by an ascending planet; divide the ecliptic into 12 equal parts of 30° each, beginning from A. So that the 12 points of division will be those respectively marked by A, 30°, 60°, 90°, 120°, 150°, 180°, 210°, 240°, 270°, 300°, and 330° and for purposes of planetary aspects, these points are respectively the middle points of the 1st, 2nd, 3rd, 4th, &c., to 12 houses. So that a planet at A aspects with a quarter sight the middle points of the 3rd and 10th houses, *i.e.*, the points marked 60° and 270° respectively; similarly it aspects with a half sight points marked 120° and 240°; with three-quarters of a sight points marked 90° and 210° and with a full sight the point marked by 180°.

The degree of aspects for other, places may, according to some, be determined by Proportion or Rule of Three, from the degree of aspects of the next points before and behind. As regards the special aspects of Saturn, Jupiter, and Mars, a similar course should be adopted. But if one planet aspects another planet, then subtract the longitude of the former from that of the latter, *i.e.*, take the distance between the two planets in degrees and calculate the degree of aspect as stated above. But others hold that the planets have no aspect at other places than those specified in the text.

वैतालीय–अयनक्षणवासरर्तवो मासोऽर्द्धं च समाश्च भास्करात् ॥ कटुकलवणतिक्तमिश्रिता मधुराम्लौ च कषाय इत्यपि ॥ १४ ॥

अयनक्षणवासरर्तवः Ayanakṣaṇavâsarartavaḥ, six months or Uttarâyaṇa and Dakṣiṇâyana (*i.e.*, Summer and winter solstices), moment (2 ghaṭikâs or 48 minutes), day, season (of two months). मासः Mâsaḥ, month. अर्द्धं Ardham, a fortnight. च Cha, and. समाः Samâḥ, year. च Cha, and. भास्करात् Bhâskarât, commencing with the Sun, *i.e.*, the Sun, Moon, Mars, Mercury, Jupiter, Venus, Saturn. कटुकलवणतिक्तमिश्रिताः Kaṭukalavaṇatiktamiśritâḥ, sharp and pungent taste, salty or acerbity, bitter, and mixed tastes. मधुराम्लौ Madhurâmlau, sweet and sour. च Cha, and. कषाय Kaṣâya, astringent. इति अपि Iti api, and also.

14. The Sun denotes the six months, *i. e.*, the summer and the winter solstices (Uttarâyaṇam and Dakṣiṇâyanam); the Moon denotes moments or two ghaṭikâs or forty-eight

Table of Aspects.

Planets.	Situation.	2nd	3rd	4th	5th	6th	7th	8th	9th	10th	11th	12th
Sun	0	0	¼	¾	½	0	1	¾	½	¼	0	0
Moon	0	0	¼	¾		0	1	¾	½	¼	0	0
Mars	0	0	¼	1	½	0	1	1	½	¼	0	0
Mercury	0	0	¼	¾	½	0	1	¾	½	¼	0	0
Jupiter	0	0	¼	¾	1	0	1	¾	1	¼	0	0
Venus	0	0	¼	¾	½	0	1	¾	½	¼	0	0
Saturn	0	0	1	¾	½	0	1	¾	½	1	0	0
Râhu	0	¾	½	½	1	½	1	½	1	¾	0	1
Ketu	0	0	0	0	0	0	0	0	0	0	0	0

Table of the seasons, metals, &c., of the Planets.

	Sun.	Moon.	Mars.	Mercury.	Jupiter.	Venus.	Saturn.
Situation of Planets.	Temples; and places of worship.	Wells and water.	Fire-places.	Playgrounds.	Store-room and Treasury.	Bed rooms.	Barren lands or places where sweepings are gathered.
Cloths.	Coarse and thick.	New.	Partially burnt.	Wet.	Somewhat used.	Strong.	Torn.
Metals.	Copper.	Gems.	Gold.	Brass.	Silver.	Pearls.	Iron.
Seasons.	Summer.	Rainy.	Summer.	Autumn.	Hemanta.	Spring.	Winter.
Natural aspect.	7	7	4 and 8	7	5 and 9	7	3 and 10

minutes; Mars denotes a day; Mercury denotes a season (of two months); Jupiter, a month; Venus, a fortnight; and Saturn denotes a year. The Sun presides over sharp and pungent taste, the Moon, salty; Mars, bitter, Mercury, on mixture, *i.e.*, on all the six tastes mixed; Jupiter presides over sweet, Venus, sour; and Saturn over astringent tastes.

Note:—On questions of theft, journeys, warfare, profit, and on ceremonies to make the conception a success and on the coming in or going out of any guest from or to distant places, the first stanza of the verse is referred. First find out the ruler of the rising Navâṃśa; then see where this ruler exists, *i. e.*, after how many Navâṃśas this ruler exists; after the same number of ayanas (of six months), the point in question is to take place. Thus when any horoscopic map is missing, it can be recovered by similar calculations. See the Chapter on lost horoscopes.

The mentioning of the six rasas determines which rasa is imbibed by a pregnant woman during her conception; it will correspond to the planet that would be powerful in the horoscope cast at that time.

Or if a question be asked what food is appropriate at any time, then find out which is the rising planet or the rising Navâṃśa at the time of query; this will indicate the taste of the food.

(शा० वि०)—जीवो जीवबुधौ सितेंदुतनयौ व्यर्का विभौमाः क्रमाद्वींद्वर्का विकुजेंद्विनाश्च सुहृदः केषांचिदेवं मतम् ॥ सत्योक्ते सुहृदस्त्रिकोणभवनात्स्वात्स्वांत्यधीधर्मपाः स्वोच्चायुः सुखपाः स्वलक्षणविधेर्नान्यैर्विरोधादिति ॥ १५ ॥

जीवः Jîvaḥ, Jupiter. जीवबुधौ Jîvabudhau, Jupiter and Mercury. सितेंदुतनयौ Sitendutanayau, Venus and Mercury. व्यर्का Vyarkâ, all the planets excepting the Sun. विभौमाः Vibhaumâḥ, all the planets excepting Mars. क्रमात् Kramât, in due order. वींद्वर्काः Vindvarkâh, all the planets excepting the Moon and the Sun. विकुजेंद्विनाः Vikujendvinâḥ, all excepting Mars, the Sun and Moon. च Cha, and. सुहृदः Suhṛidaḥ, friends. केषांचित् Keṣâṃchit, of some. एवं Evam, this. मतम् Matam, the opinion. सत्योक्ते Satyokte, according to the sayings of Satyâchârya (in his Horâśâstra). सुहृदः Suhṛidaḥ, friends. त्रिकोणभवनात् Trikoṇabhavanât, from the Trikoṇa house. स्वात् Svât, from its own. स्वांत्यधीधर्मपाः Svântyadhîdharmapâḥ, the rulers of the second, twelfth, fifth, ninth houses. स्वोच्चायुः सुखपाः Svochchâyuḥsukhapâḥ, the rulers of its exalted house, eighth and fourth houses. स्वलक्षणविधेः Svalakṣaṇavidheḥ, from the rule indicating the friend's houses. न Na, not.

अन्यैः Anyaiḥ, with the other planets (not mentioned in this rule). विरोधात् Virodhât, on account of going against. इति Iti, thus.

15. (Now are being enumerated the planets that are friendly or harmonious and those that are unfriendly towards each other) Jupiter is friendly to the Sun; Jupiter and Mercury, to the Moon; Venus and Mercury to Mars. The planets excepting the Sun are friendly to Mercury; the planets excepting Mars are friendly to Jupiter; the planets excepting the Sun and Moon are friendly to Venus; all the planets but the Sun, Moon and Mars are friendly or harmonious to Saturn. (This is the opinion of one class of authors).(1) According to the opinion of Satyâchârya (in his Horâśâstra) the friends of any planet are the rulers of the second, twelfth, fifth, ninth, eighth, and fourth houses reckoned from the Mûlatrikoṇa house of that planet, as well as the ruler of its exalted house, provided they do not conflict with the rulers of the remaining houses.(2)

Note:—(1) The other planets are the enemies. In the first half of the verse the friends and enemies only are considered; no indifferent planets are considered.

According to Yavaneśwara, Jupiter is friendly to the Sun; the rest are the enemies to the Sun. The planets excepting Mars are friendly to Jupiter. The planets excepting the Sun are friendly to Moon. The planets excepting the Sun and Moon are friendly to Venus. Venus and Mercury are friendly to Mars. Mercury and Jupiter are friendly to Moon; all the planets excepting Mars, Moon and the Sun are friendly to Saturn. The others are enemies.

(2) The same may be expressed otherwise: the rulers of the remaining houses are the enemies of a planet, provided they do not conflict with the rulers of the seven houses described above.

The explanation of the second half of the verse is given thus:—Take the case of Mars. Meṣa is the Mûlatrikoṇa of Mars. The ruler of the fourth house from Mars is Moon, the ruler of the fifth is Sun; of the ninth, twelfth is Jupiter. These are friends to Mars. The ruler of the 3rd and 6th house from Meṣa is Mercury. Not being mentioned in the rule, Mercury is enemy.

The ruler of the second and fifth houses from Meṣa is Venus. Now the second house is mentioned in the rule and the seventh house is not mentioned; hence Venus is indifferent to Mars. Again the 10th and 11th houses from Meṣa are not mentioned but the 10th house is the house of exaltation of Mars and therefore is mentioned; hence Saturn is indifferent. In other words where the planets are found mentioned in two houses, they are friends; where the planets are unmentioned in the two houses, they are enemies; where the planets are mentioned in one house and not mentioned in the second house, they are indifferent. This is the meaning of "Svalakṣaṇavidhiḥ."

TABLE OF THE FRIENDLY, UNFRIENDLY AND INDIFFERENT HOUSES OF THE SEVERAL PLANETS.

	Sun.	Moon.	Mars.	Mercury.	Jupiter.	Venus.	Saturn.	Râhu.	Ketu.
Friends ...	Moon, Mars, Jupiter.	Sun, Mercury.	Moon, Sun, Jupiter.	Sun, Venus.	Moon, Sun, Mars	Mercury, Saturn.	Mercury, Venus.	Venus, Saturn.	Sun, Moon, Mars.
Enemies ...	Saturn, Venus.	...	Mercury.	Moon.	Venus, Mercury.	Sun, Moon.	Moon, Sun, Mars.	Sun, Moon Mars.	Venus, Saturn.
Indifferent	Mercury.	Saturn, Mars, Jupiter, Venus.	Venus, Saturn	Mars, Jupiter, Saturn.	Saturn.	Mars, Jupiter.	Jupiter.	....	Mercury, Jupiter.

शा० वि०—शत्रू मंदसितौ समश्च शशिजो मित्राणि शेषा रवे-
स्तीक्ष्णांशुर्हिमरश्मिजश्च सुहृदौ शेषाः समाः शीतगोः ॥
जीवेंदूष्णकराः कुजस्य सुहृदो ज्ञोऽरिः सितार्की समौ मित्रे
सूर्यसितौ बुधस्य हिमगुः शत्रुः समाश्चापरे ॥ १६ ॥

सूरेः सौम्यसितावरी रविसुतो मध्योऽपरे त्वन्यथा
सौम्यार्की सुहृदौ समौ कुजगुरू शुक्रस्य शेषावरी ॥
शुक्रज्ञौ सुहृदौ समः सुरगुरुः सौरस्य चान्येऽरयो ये प्रोक्ताः
स्वत्रिकोणभादिषु पुनस्तेऽमी मया कीर्तिताः ॥ १७ ॥

शत्रू Ŝatrû, enemies. मंदसितौ Mandasitau, Saturn and Venus. समःच Samaḥ cha, indifferent; neutral. शशिजः Ŝaŝijaḥ, Mercury. मित्राणि Mitrâṇi, friends, allies. शेषाः Ŝesâḥ, the rest (*i.e.,*) Moon, Mars, Jupiter. रवेः Raveḥ the Sun's; to the

Suń. तीक्ष्णांशुः Tîkṣṇâṃśuḥ, the Sun. हिमरश्मिजः Himaraśmijaḥ, Mercury. च Cha, and. सुहृदौ Suhṛidau, friends. शेषाः Śeṣâḥ, the rest, *i.e.*, Mars, Jupiter, Venus, Saturn. समाः Samâḥ, neutral. शीतगोः Śîtagoḥ, to the Moon. जीवेन्दूष्णकराः Jîvendûṣṇakarâḥ, Jupiter, Moon and Sun. कुजस्य Kujasya, of Mars. सुहृदः Suhṛidaḥ, friends. ज्ञः Jñaḥ, Mercury. अरिः Ariḥ, enemy. सितार्कौ Sitârkî, Venus and Saturn. समौ Samau, neutral. मित्रे Mitre, friends. सूर्यसितौ Sûryasitau, the Sun and Venus. बुधस्य Budhasya, of the Mercury. हिमगुः Himaguḥ, Moon. शत्रुः Śatruḥ, enemy. समाः Samâḥ, neutral. च Cha, and. अपरे Apare, the rest *i.e.*, Mars, Jupiter, and Saturn. सूरेः Sûreḥ, of the Jupiter. सौम्यसितौ Saumyasitau, Mercury and Venus. अरी Arî, enemies. रविसुतः Ravisutaḥ, Saturn. मध्यः Madhyaḥ, neutral. अपरे Apare, the rest, *i.e.*, Sun, Moon and Mars. तु Tu, but. अन्यथा Anyathâ, otherwise, *i.e.*, friends. सौम्यार्कौ Saumyârkî, Mercury and Saturn. सुहृदौ Suhṛidau, friends. समौ Samau, neutral. कुजगुरू Kujagurû, Mars and Jupiter. शुक्रस्य Śukrasya, of the Venus. शेषौ Śeṣau, the rest, *i.e.*, the Sun and Moon. अरी Arî, enemies. शुक्रज्ञौ Śukrajñau, Venus and Mercury. सुहृदौ Suhṛidau, friends. समः Samaḥ, neutral. सुरगुरुः Suraguruḥ, Jupiter. सौरस्य Saurasya, of the Saturn. च Cha, and. अन्ये Anye, the rest, *i.e.*, the Sun, Moon, Mars. अरयः Arayaḥ, enemies. ये Ye, these. प्रोक्ताः Proktâḥ, mentioned before. स्वत्रिकोणभादिषु Svatrikoṇabhâdiṣu, in the rule "from its trikoṇa houses, &c.," mentioned in the preceding verse. पुनः Punaḥ, again. ते Te, these. अमी Amî, those rules. मया Mayâ, by me. कीर्तिताः Kîrtitâḥ, mentioned (again now.)

16 & 17. Saturn and Venus are the enemies of the Sun; Mercury is his neutral; and Moon, Mars, and Jupiter are his friends. The Sun and Mercury are the friends of the Moon; the rest, *i.e.*, Mars, Jupiter, Venus, and Saturn are indifferent to the Moon. Jupiter, Moon and the Sun are the friends of Mars; Mercury is his enemy; Venus and Saturn are neutral to Mars. The Sun and Venus are friends to Mercury; Moon, enemy; and Mars, Jupiter and Saturn are indifferent to Mercury. Mercury and Venus are the enemies of Jupiter; Saturn, indifferent, and the Sun, Moon and Mars, friends to Jupiter. Mercury and Saturn are friends to Venus; Mars and Jupiter, indifferent; and the Sun, Moon are enemies to Venus. Venus and Mercury are the friends of Saturn; Jupiter, indifferent; and Sun, Moon and Mars are enemies to Saturn. These have been already mentioned in the preceding verse in the rule "from its own trikoṇa house, &c.," those very things are again cited here as an instance serving a table.

शा० वि०—अन्योन्यस्य धनव्ययायसहजव्यापारबन्धुस्थिता-
स्तत्काले सुहृदः स्वतुंगभवनेऽप्येकेऽरयस्त्वन्यथा ।
द्व्येकानुक्तभपान्सुहृत्समरिपून्संचिन्त्य नैसर्गिकां-
स्तत्काले च पुनस्तु तानधिसुहृन्मित्रादिभिः कल्पयेत् ॥ १८ ॥

अन्योन्यस्य Anyonyasya, amongst one another. धनव्ययायसहजव्यापारबन्धुस्थिताः Dhanavyayâyasahajavyâpâra bandu sthitâḥ, occupying the second, twelfth, eleventh, third, tenth and fourth houses. तत्काले Tatkâle, for the time being; for that time. सुहृदः Suhṛidaḥ, friends. स्वतुंगभवने Svatungabhavane, in its own exalted house. अपि Api, moreover; also. एके Eke, some authors. अरयः Arayaḥ, enemies. तु Tu, but. अन्यथा Anyathâ, otherwise; when seated in other houses then those mentioned above. द्व्येकानुक्तभपान्सुहृत्समरिपून् Dvyekânuktabhapân suhṛitsamaripûn, the friendly, neutral and inimical rulers on account of their occupying the two, one, or unmentioned houses. (As stated in the fifteenth verse). संचिन्त्य Saṃchintya, considering. नैसर्गिकान् Naisargikân, natural. तत्काले Tatkâle, for the time being; at that moment. च Cha, and. पुनः Punaḥ, again, moreover. तु Tu, but. तान् Tân, them. अधिसुहृन्मित्रादिभिः Adhisuhṛinmitrâdibhiḥ, as over-friendly, ' friendly, and neutral rulers etc., (*i.e.*, inimical, over-inimical). कल्पयेत् Kal'payet, are to be considered; consider.

18. Planets occupying the 2nd, 12th, 11th, 3rd, 10th and 4th houses from a particular planet are *the then* friends of that planet and the rest are his *the then* enemies. Some authors are of opinion that the planets occupying the exalted sign of a particular planet are also *the then* friends of that planet. Combining together the three *permanent* relations as given in stanzas 16 and 17 with the two relations *for the time* now given, we may determine the five following relations existing between planets: Atimitra (very friendly), Mitra (friendly), Sama (neutral), Śatru (inimical) and Atiśatru (very inimical).

Note.—Stanzas 16 and 17 relate to the three relations of *permanent* friendship, neutrality and enmity. Stanza 18 relates to the two relations of *temporary* friendship. Combining the two together, we get the following results :—

Under stanzas 16 and 17.		Under stanza 18.	Result.
(Friend) Mitra	+	Mitra (friend)	Atimitra (over friendly).
(Enemy) Śatru	+	Śatru (enemy)	Ati Śatru (over inimical).
(Neutral) Sama	+	Mitra (friend)	Mitra (friendly).
(Neutral) Sama	+	Śatru (enemy)	Śatru (enemy).
(Friend) Mitra	+	Śatru (enemy)	Sama (neutral).

Remark:—These points are useful in questions on birth time, journeys, marriage, or any query.

(दोधक) स्वोच्चसुहृत्स्वत्रिकोणनवांशैः स्थानबलं स्वगृहोपगतैश्च ।
दिक्षु बुधांगिरसौ रविभौमौ सूर्यसुतः सितशीतकरौ च ॥ १९ ॥

स्वोच्चसुहृत्स्वत्रिकोणनवांशैः Svochchasuhritsvatrikoṇanavâṃśaiḥ, by virtue of their being posited in their exalted house, in their friends' house, in their own mûla-trikoṇa house, in their own Navâṃśas. स्थानबलं Sthânabalam, strength due to position; local or positional strength. स्वगृहोपगतैः Svagrihopagataiḥ, by virtue of their being located in their own houses. च Cha, and. दिक्षु Dikṣu, (are powerful) in the east, south, west, and north directions respectively. बुधांगिरसौ Budhâṃgirasau, Mercury and Jupiter. रविभौमौ Ravibhaumau, Sun and Mars. सूर्यसुतः Sûryasutaḥ, Saturn. सितशीतकरौ च Sitaśîtakarau cha, and Venus and Moon.

19. Any planet when stationed in its exalted house, or in its (*the then*) friend's house, or in its mûla-trikoṇa house, or in its Navâṃśa or in its own sign becomes powerful by virtue of its position or location (Sthânabala). In the four cardinal directions East, South, West and North, Mercury and Jupiter, Sun and Mars, Saturn, Venus and Moon are successively powerful. (Dikbalî) (1).

Note.—Here it should be noted that the house Siṃha which is called the mûla-trikoṇa of the Sun is also the house of the Sun; the house Meṣa is the mûla-trikoṇa as well as the proper house of Mars; the Kanyâ is the exalted, mûla-trikoṇa, as well as the proper house of Mercury; the Dhanu is the trikoṇa as well as the proper house of Jupiter; the Tulâ is the trikoṇa as well as the proper house of Venus. These specialities are not mentioned in the verse.

Mercury and Jupiter get power in the Eastern direction, *i.e.*, when they are situated in the Ascendant or Lagna. The Sun and Mars are powerful in the Southern direction, *i.e.*, when situated in the tenth house. Saturn is powerful in the West, *i.e.*, in the seventh house. Venus and Moon are powerful in the North, *i.e.*, in the fourth house. The planet in the house seventh from that in which it is powerful, is weak; and in the intermediate house its strength goes on decreasing in due proportion.

See the annexed Figure. V, IV represent Jupiter, Mercury; I, III represent Sun, Mars; VII represents Saturn; VI, II represent Venus, Moon.

(1) That is: they then possess Dikbala. According to some commentators, Mercury and Jupiter are powerful when in the Eastern triangular signs of Aries, Leo, and Sagittari. The Sun and Mars are powerful when in the Southern triangular signs of Taurus, Virgo and Capricorn. Saturn is powerful when in the Western triangular signs of Gemini, Libra, and Aquarius; and the Moon and Venus are powerful when in the Northern triangular signs of Cancer, Scorpio and Pisces.

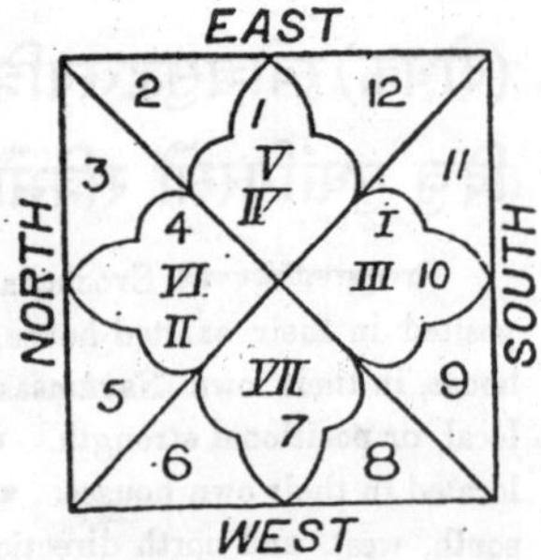

FIG 4

दोधक–उदगयने रविशीतमयूखौ वक्रसमागमगाः परिशेषाः ॥
विपुलकरा युधि चोत्तरसंस्थाश्चेष्टितवीर्ययुता परिकल्प्याः २०॥

उदगयने Udagayane, in the northern path of the Sun; *i.e.*, in any of the six signs beginning with Makara, in any of the signs Makara, Kumbha, Mina, Mesa, Vrisa, and Mithuna. रविशीतमयूखौ Raviśîtamayûkhau, the Sun and Moon. वक्रसमागमगाः Vakrasamâgamagâḥ, when the planets are retrograde or united with the Moon. परिशेषाः Pariśeṣâḥ, the rest, *i.e.*, Mars, Mercury, Jupiter, Venus and Saturn. विपुलकराः Vipulakarâḥ, brilliant; highly lustrous. युधि Yudhi, in the battle; in the planetary conjunction. च Cha, and. उत्तरसंस्थाः Uttarasamsthâḥ, when they happen to be northward. चेष्टितवीर्ययुताः Cheṣṭitavîryayutâḥ, endowed with vigorous effort; victorious or powerful by virtue of effort or motional strength. परिकल्प्याः Parikalpyâḥ, are to be considered. Consider.

20. The Sun and the Moon possess Cheṣṭâbala or strength by virtue of their motion when they are in the Northern path, *i.e.*, in any of the 6 signs—10th, 11th, 12th, 1st, 2nd and 3rd signs. The other five planets Mars, Mercury, Jupiter, Venus and Saturn possess it when retrograde or when conjoined with the Moon; or when they are very brilliant or when they happen to go northward in planetary conjunction (which is called here the fight amongst the planets).

Note.—When the five planets Mars, Mercury, Jupiter, Venus and Saturn are in the second quadrant of their orbits, the Śighra Kendra being taken into account, they generally become highly lustrous. Then they are about to take a retrograde direction. Here the battle referred to is this:—When two or three planets are seen in the sky near one other, one of them happens to be so placed in connection with the two luminaries, the Sun or the Moon, that it reflects the greatest light and thus is seen very brilliant; then this brilliant planet is called victorious in the battle over the other planets which get dwindled in their lustre and generally go towards the south. It is the Venus only that is always victorious, even when she goes to the south.

मालिनी-निशि शशिकुजसौराः सर्वदा ज्ञोऽह्नि चान्ये ।
बहुलसितगताः स्युः क्रूरसौम्याः क्रमेण ॥
द्व्ययनदिवसहोरा मासपैः कालवीर्यं ।
शरुबुगुशुचसाद्या वृद्धितो वीर्यवन्तः ॥ २१ ॥

इत्यवन्तिकाचार्यवराहमिहिरविरचिते बृहज्जातके
ग्रहभेदाध्यायो द्वितीयः ॥ २ ॥

निशि Niśi, during the night. शशिकुजसौराः Śaśikujasaurâḥ, Moon, Mars and Saturn. सर्वदा Śarvadâ, always; during the day as well as during the night. ज्ञः Jñaḥ, Mercury. अह्नि Ahni, during the day. च अन्ये Cha Anye, and the rest, *i. e.*, the Sun, Jupiter, and Venus. बहुलसितगताः Bahulasitagatâḥ, during the dark and bright fortnights (respectively). स्युः Syuḥ, become. क्रूरसौम्याः Krûrasaumyâḥ, the malefic and benefic planets. क्रमेण Kramena, successively; in due order. द्व्ययनदिवसहोरामासपैः Dvyayana divasa horâ mâsapaiḥ, by the rulers of the 2 ayanas, *i.e.*, two summer and winter solstices (years), days, hours and months. कालवीर्यं Kâlavîryam, power by virtue of time; temporal strength. शरुबुगुशुचसाद्याः Śarubuguśuchasâdyâḥ, Saturn, Mars, Mercury, Jupiter, Venus, Moon and the Sun. वृद्धितः Vṛiddhitaḥ, more and more. वीर्यवन्तः Vîryavantaḥ, become powerful.

21. The Moon, Mars, and Saturn possess Kâlabala, *i.e.*, become (temporarily) powerful during the night; Mercury is always powerful whether during the day or during the night; the Sun, Jupiter and Venus are powerful during the day. The malefic planets, *i.e.*, the Sun, Mars, and Saturn, are powerful during the dark half of the month and the benefic planets, *i.e.*, Moon, Mercury, Jupiter, and Venus, are powerful during the bright half of the month. The ruler of the years, days, hours, and months are powerful in their own years, days, hours and months, respectively.

Saturn, Mars, Mercury, Jupiter, Venus, the Moon and the Sun are each naturally more powerful than the immediately preceding planet in the order stated, *i.e.*, Saturn is the weakest or least powerful; greater than Saturn is Mars powerful and so on and the Sun is the strongest (1).

Thus ends the Second Chapter on the First Principles and Definitions regarding the Planets in Bṛihajjâtakam by Sree Varâhamihirâchârya.

Notes:—(1) Such strength is known as Naisargikbala or natural strength. Some authors maintain that the Moon is malefic and powerful during the dark fortnight. Yavaneśwara says thus:—"Before the commencement of the first day of the bright half of the month, on the tenth day of the dark fortnight the Moon is half strong; on the second of the dark half is fully strong and most auspicious; on the third day is less strong and when viewed by Mercury, is always strong."

From the last stanza of the verse we infer that when many planets are equally strong on other considerations, then the casting vote of their superiority is given by their superiority in the order of their natural strength.

Here the fruits or the results arising from the four kinds of strength of the planets are not mentioned by the author. They are thus stated in Sârâvalî: "Planets when exalted give glory and superhuman power; when in their mûla-trikoṇa houses give ambassadorship or the post of a Commander-in-chief; when in their own houses give wealth, grains, prosperity and happiness; when in their friends' houses give fame and valour, happiness, fire, and wealth from the king; and when in their own Navâṃśas make a person famous."

The Sûkṣma Jâtaka says thus :—

The Moon and Venus are strong in the female signs; the Sun, Mars, Jupiter, Mercury and Saturn become strong when they occupy the male signs. These become strong also when viewed auspiciously by the benefic planets, when they occupy their friends' houses, their own exalted houses or their Navâṃśas.

The fruits (phala) obtained by any individual born under the various benefic aspects of a planet are stated thus :—

(1) The benefic aspect of a strong planet makes a man obtain name, fame, wealth, health, prominence, good look, gentleness, prosperity and happiness.

(2) Planets when in their proper male or female signs bring to a native honour and respect from the public; make him skilled in fine arts, music, sculpture and painting; make him tranquil, vigorous, energetic, religious, and mindful of his after-life.

(3) Planets when powerful by Dikbala make a man go out hopeful to the proper direction where he gets clothings, ornaments, conveyances and friends.

(4) Planets when powerful by Cheṣṭâbala give a man sometimes kingdom, sometimes worship, sometimes fame and sometimes various useful articles.

(5) Planets when retrograde, powerful, and auspicious give kingdoms; when they are inauspicious make a person idle, of ill-luck, wander about fruitlessly and fall under various calamities and disasters.

(6) The Sun being auspicious makes a man healthy and comfortable, victorious in battles, gives him kingdoms, all his foes being vanquished.

(7) Planets when powerful by day or by night give one lands, elephants, and make one powerful over one's enemies and enjoy one's kingdom with subjects.

(8) Planets ruling the corresponding years, months and days give a man four times what is his due, and in their Daśâ periods, give him friends, wealth and fame.

(9) Planets that are the rulers of the corresponding fortnights make a man the destroyer of his enemies, give him jewels, clothings, elephants, and prosperity; give him wives, wealth, lands and spotless fame.

(10) Planets when they are powerful in all respects make a man always a hero of spotless fame and lustre, give him kingdoms, friends and all his desires and objects beyond their expectations.

(11) The benefic planets being auspicious make a man observe good conduct, his family rites, customs and practices; make him courteous, friendly, pure and clean, of handsome features, energetic, learned, devoted to the Brâhmaṇas and Devas and fond of good clothings, garlands, ornaments, and a favourite amongst his people.

(12) The malefic planets becoming powerful make a man covetous, addicted to vile actions, selfish, vicious, quarrelsome, lazy, cruel, deceitful, dirty, prone to do mischief and kill others, and treacherous.

(13) A male planet in a male sign makes a man resolute and self-possessed, fond of wars and battle, powerful, heartless, harsh, cruel and illiterate.

(14) A female planet in a female sign makes a man womanish, coward in battles, fond of water, flowers, and clothings, gentle and endowed with sweet jingling voice and loving smiles.

Remark: — Before applying the astrological truths contained in the subsequent pages, the reader must consider the strength or weakness of each house of its ruler, and of the planets occupying or aspecting such house. For these various other purposes it will not do to have a mere Râśi chakra or Navâṃśa chakra to represent roughly the planetary positions. The actual longitudes (sphuṭa) of the planets and of the Ascendant from the 1st point of the Nakṣatra Aśvinî should be known.

CHAPTER THE THIRD.

ON THE MANIFOLD BIRTHS,

i.e., On animal and Vegetable Horoscopy.

व० ति०–क्रूरग्रहैः सुबलिभिर्विबलैश्च सौम्यैः क्लीबे चतुष्टयगते तदवेक्षणाद्वा ॥ चंद्रोपगद्विरसभागसमानरूपं सत्वं वदेद्यदि भवेत्स वियोनिसंज्ञः ॥ १ ॥

क्रूरग्रहैः: Krûragrahaiḥ, by the malefic planets, *i.e.*, by the Sun, Mars, or Saturn, Mercury joined with any of the above, or waning Moon. सुबलिभिः: Subalibhiḥ, endowed with power; when powerful (*i.e.*, when situated in their own houses, or exaltation degrees, or in their friends' houses, or aspected by their friends). विबलैः: Vibalaiḥ, deprived of power; when weak, *i.e.*, when stationed in their enemy's houses, or in their detriment signs or aspected by their enemies. च Cha, and. सौम्यैः: Saumyaiḥ, by the benefic planets; *i.e.*, the waxing Moon, Jupiter, Venus, or Mercury not joined with the Sun, Mars and Saturn. क्लीबे Klîbe, the natural eunuchs (*i.e.*, Mercury or Saturn). चतुष्टयगते Chatuṣṭayagate, situated in the four cardinal centres or angles. तदवेक्षणात् वा Tadavekṣṇât vâ, or when (the Lagna is) aspected by Mercury or Saturn. चंद्रोपगद्विरसभागसमानरूपं Chandropagadvirasa bhâgasamânarûpam, the manifold births of insects, birds, fixed trees, &c., resembling what is indicated by the Dvâdaśâṃśa, where the Moon exists. सत्वं Satvam, a living being; animal, beast, or plant or trees. वदेत् Vadet, one is to ascertain. यदि Yadi, if. भवेत् Bhavet, be. स Sa, that. वियोनिसंज्ञः: Viyonisaṃjñaḥ, coming under the term Viyoniyoga, *i.e.*, conjunctions of planets suited to produce manifold births as enumerated above.

1. When, at the time of birth or query, the malefic planets become powerful and the benefic planets weak and if the eunuch Saturn or Mercury be stationed in any of the four angular houses, there is the first case of Viyoniyoga; or when the Lagna or Ascendant is aspected by Saturn or Mercury (the malefic planets being powerful and the benefic planets weak) there is the second case of Viyoniyoga. In

either of these two cases, when the Moon is situated in any Dvâdaśâṃśa (indicative of manifold birth) the birth of any insect, bird, or animals or trees, &c., will be that indicated by the particular Dvâdaśâṃśa.

Note.—If the Moon be in Meṣa Dvâdaśâṃśa, the birth of a goat, sheep etc., is to be inferred; if the Moon be in Vṛiṣa Dvâdaśâṃśa, cow, buffalo etc., are to be born; if in Karka, tortoise etc., are to be inferred; if in Siṃha, then lions, tigers, dogs, cats, etc., are to be inferred; if in Vṛischik, then snakes, scorpions etc., are to be inferred; if in the latter half of Dhanu, then horses, asses etc., are to be inferred; if in the first half of Makara, deer, elephants are to be inferred; if in the latter half of Makara, frogs and aquatic animals are to be inferred; if in the Mîna Dvâdaśâṃśa, then fishes and others of like nature are to be inferred. These judgments are to be then and then only given when there is in the horoscopic map during the birth time or during the time of enquiry either of the two cases of Viyoniyoga mentioned in the verse.

If the Moon be in human signs, then the birth of a human being is to be inferred.

In the second yoga, the planets Mercury and Saturn may remain in any of the houses; it is not necessary that they should be situated in the four cardinal houses; what is required that they are to aspect any of the 4 Kendras, especially the Lagna.

Suppose, for instance, at the time of birth the Moon occupies the 20° of the sign Siṃha. As a Dvâdaśâṃśa contains 2½° degrees, the 21° of Siṃha is the ninth Dvâdaśâṃśa of Siṃha. As the names of the Dvâdaśâṃśas of Siṃha begin from Siṃha, the ninth Dvâdaśâṃśa is that of the sign Mîna. The creature born will therefore be a fish.

Besides, the number of the offspring will be that represented by the number of Dvâdaśâṃśas passed over by the Moon. Of these the number of odd Dvâdaśâṃśas will represent the male issues, and the number of even Dvâdaśâṃśas will represent the female issues, the number that will die shortly after birth will be that of the number of the Dvâdaśâṃśas that might be occupied by the malefic planets or that might otherwise become weak.

वै॰ली॰—पापा बलिनः स्वभागगाः पारक्ये विबलाश्च शोभनाः ॥
लग्नं च वियोनिसंज्ञकं दृष्ट्वात्रापि वियोनिमादिशेत् ॥ २ ॥

पापाः Pâpâḥ, malefic planets. बलिनः Balinaḥ, powerful. स्वभागगाः Svabhâgagâḥ, in their own Navâṃśas. पारक्ये Pârakye, in the enemy's Navâṃśas. विबलाः Vibalâḥ, weak. च Cha, and. शोभना: Śobhanâḥ, the benefic planets. लग्नं Lagnam, the Ascendant, the rising sign. च Cha, and. वियोनिसंज्ञकं Viyonisaṃjñakam, as understood by Viyonisanjñâ ; the rising sign should be other than Mithuna, Kanyâ, Tulâ, the second half of Dhanu and Kumbha. दृष्ट्वा Dṛistvâ, on finding. अत्र अपि Atra api, in this case also. वियोनिम् Viyonim, the manifold births of animals or vegetables as stated above. आदिशेत् Âdiśet, the astrologer is to pronounce (his judgment).

2. When the malefic planets are powerful in their own Navâṃśas, and when the benefic planets are weak, due to their being in the malefic planet's Navâṃśas, and when the Lagna is other than the human signs (1) then there is the third case of Viyoniyoga ; and the astrologer is to pronounce his judgment of manifold births of animals, &c., according to the nature of the Dvâdaśâṃśa that the Moon then occupies.

Note :—(1) The rising sign should be Meṣa, Vṛisa, Karka, Siṃha, Vṛiśchika, the 2nd half of Dhanu, Makara or Mîna.

By the Viyonisañjñak Lagna is meant the Lagna or Ascendant when it is not any human sign.

उ०जा०—क्रियः शिरो वक्त्रगले वृषोऽन्ये पादांशकं पृष्ठमुरोऽथ पार्श्वे ॥ कुक्षिस्त्वपानांघ्र्यथ मेढ्रमुष्कौ स्फिक्पुच्छमित्याह चतुष्पदाङ्गे ॥ ३ ॥

क्रियः Kriyaḥ, the sign Meṣa. शिरः Śiraḥ, the head. वक्त्रगले Vaktragale, mouth and neck. वृषः Vṛiṣaḥ, the sign Vṛiṣa. अन्ये Anye, the other signs. पादांशकं Pâdâṃśakam, the two feet and the two shoulders. पृष्ठं Priṣṭham, the back. उरः Uraḥ, the breast, the bosom. अथ Atha, thus in order. पार्श्वे Pârśve, the two sides. कुक्षिः Kukṣiḥ, the belly, the abdomen, the womb. तु Tu, so. अपानांघ्री Apânâṃghrî, the anus and the feet. अथ Atha, thus. मेढ्रमुष्कौ Medhramuṣkau, the generative organ and the testicle. स्फिक्पुच्छम् Sphikpuchcham, the buttocks and the tail. इति Iti, thus. आह Âha, say. चतुष्पदांगे Chatuṣpadâṃge, the body of a quadruped.

3. (Now the several parts of the body of a quadruped are represented by the several signs of the zodiac.) The sign Meṣa represents the head ; the sign Vṛiṣa represents the face and the neck ; the sign Mithuna represents the forelegs and the shoulders ; the sign Karka represents the back ; the sign Siṃha represents the breast ; Kanyâ, the

two sides; Tulâ, the belly; Vriśchika represents the anus; Dhanu, the hind legs; Makara represents the generative organ and the testicles; Kumbha, the buttocks; and the Mîna represents the tail.

Note.—In the case of bipeds everything resembles that of a quadruped; only the front legs are to be substituted for the wings on those portions of the body whence come out the two wings.

This stanza will also enable us to ascertain the colour or wounds of particular parts of the creature's body from the nature of the powerful planet.

वैश्वदेवी–लग्नांशकाद् ग्रहयोगेक्षणाद्वा वर्णान्वदेद्बल-
युक्ताद्वियोनौ ॥ दृष्ट्वा समानान्प्रवदेत्स्वसंख्यया रेखां वदेत्स्मर-
संस्थैश्च पृष्ठे ॥ ४ ॥

लग्नांशकात् Lagnâmśakât, from the rising Navâṃśa of the Ascendant. ग्रहयोगे Grahayoge, the planets in the rising sign. ईक्षणात् Ikṣaṇât, by the planets aspecting the rising sign. वा Vâ, or. वर्णान् Varṇân, colours (of the animals born at a particular time or of the articles stolen or missing). वदेत् Vadet, one should judge. बलयुक्तात् Balayuktât, by the rising Navâṃśa of the Ascendant when strong, *i.e.*, joined with its ruler or when aspected by its ruler. वियोनौ Viyonau, of the animals born. दृष्ट्वा Dṛiṣṭyâ, on looking, or counting. समानान् Samânân, the number of colours according to the number of planets that are seen in the Ascendant, (and the preponderance of the colour of the most powerful planet). प्रवदेत् Pravadet, one is to say. स्वसंख्यया Svasaṃkhyayâ, according to its numbers. रेखां Rekhâm, marks such as lines, etc. वदेत् Vadet, should declare. स्मरसंस्थैः Smarasaṃsthaiḥ, from the planets in the seventh house from the Ascendant. च Cha, and. पृष्ठे Pṛiṣthe, on the back.

4. (Now the colours and marks or stripes on the bodies of the animals born are being mentioned). Colours (*e. g.*, copper, white, red, etc., as mentioned in verse 5, Chapter 2) of the animals born are to be ascertained from the colour of the planets occupying the Ascendant; if not, from the colour of the planets aspecting the Ascendant, or from the rising Navâṃśa (1) in case there be no planet in the Ascendant or aspecting the Ascendant. In case there be many planets in the Ascendant, many colours are to be ascertained and the preponderance of the colour of the

most powerful planet amongst them is to be inferred. If the rising Navâṃśa be occupied by its ruling planet or be aspected by its ruling planet, then that colour is to be given preference over all others. The number of stripes on the back of the creature will be according to the number of the planets in the 7th house.

Notes:—(1) The colour will be that of the sign whose Navâṃśa is the rising Navâṃśa.

Sârâvali says:—Jupiter gives yellow colours; Moon, white; Venus, variegated; the Sun and Mars, red; Saturn, black; Mercury, spotted.

वंशस्थ—खगे दृकाणे बलसंयुतेन वा ग्रहेण युक्ते चरभांशकोदये ॥ बुधांशके वा विहगाः स्थलांबुजाः शनैश्चरेंद्वीक्षणयोगसंभवाः ॥५॥

खगे दृकाणे Khage Dṛikâṇe, (on the rising of) the bird Decanate. The second Dreṣkâṇa of the sign Mithuna, the first of Siṃha, the second of Tulâ, the first Dreṣkâṇa of Kumbha, any one of these is called the bird Dreṣkâṇa. The first Navâṃśa, *i.e.*, first space of 3°20′ (three degrees and twenty minutes) of the rising sign or Lagna, is called the first Dreṣkâṇa; the next space of 3°20′ (three degrees and twenty minutes) is called the second Dreṣkâṇa; the next or third space of 3°20′ (three degrees and twenty minutes), is called the third Dreṣkâṇa. बलसंयुतेन Balasaṃyutena, occupied by the powerful planets. वा Vâ, or. ग्रहेण Graheṇa, by the planets. युक्ते Yukte, united with. चरभांशकोदये Charabhâṃśakodaye, on the rising of the Navâṃśa of the moveable signs. बुधांशके Budhaṃśake, on the rising in the horizon of the Navâṃśa of the planet, Mercury; *i.e.*, on the rising of the Navâṃśas of any of the two signs Mithuna or Kanyâ. वा Vâ, or. विहगाः Vihagâḥ, birds. स्थलांबुजाः Sthalâmbujâḥ, land birds or water birds. शनैश्चरेंद्वीक्षणयोगसंभवाः Śanaiścharendvîkṣaṇayogasaṃbhavâḥ, united with or aspected by Saturn or Moon.

5. If either a bird Decanate (1) or a Chara Navâṃśa (2) or a Navâṃśa of Mercury (3) rise in the horizon and be occupied by powerful planets, the creature born would be a land bird, provided that the rising Decanate or Navâṃśa be either occupied or aspected by Saturn; and a water bird, if it be occupied or aspected by the Moon.

Notes :—(1) The second Decanate of the sign Mithuna, the first Decanate of the sign Siṃha, the second Decanate of Tulâ, and the first Decanate of Kumbha are bird Decanates.

(2) The Chara Navâṃśa is the Navâṃśa of the moveable signs.

(3) The Navâṃśas of Mercury are those of the signs Mithuna and Kanyâ.

व० ति०—होरेन्दुसूरिरविभिर्विबलैस्तरूणां तोये स्थले तरुभवोंशकृतः प्रभेदः ॥ लग्नाद् ग्रहः स्थलजलर्क्षपतिस्तु यावांस्तावन्त एव तरवः स्थलतोयजाताः ॥ ६ ॥

होरेन्दुसूरिरविभिः: Horendusûriravibhiḥ, the Lagna, Moon, Jupiter and the Sun. विबलैः: Vibalaiḥ, being weak. तरूणां Taruṇâm, of the trees. तोये स्थले Toye Sthale, growing in water or land. तरुभव: Tarubhavaḥ, the growing of trees (in land or water depends on the nature of the rising Navâṃśa). अंशकृत: Aṃśakṛitaḥ, depending on the nature of the rising Navâṃśa ; (if the rising Navâṃśa be one of land, trees will grow on land, and if it be one of water, trees will grow in water). प्रभेद: Pravedaḥ, difference. लग्नात् Lagnât, from the Lagna. ग्रह: Grahaḥ, planet. स्थलजलर्क्षपति: Sthalajalarkṣapatiḥ, the ruler of the rising Navâṃśa. तु Tu, but. यावान् Yâvân, distant by as many number of signs. तावन्त: Tâvantaḥ, so many in number. तरव: Taravaḥ, trees. स्थलतोयजाता: Sthalatoyajâtâḥ, growing on land or water.

6. (On a query being asked, one is to infer that) it is the birth of a tree, if the Ascendant, Moon, Jupiter, and the Sun be all weak at that moment ; and if the rising Navâṃśa be watery, then such trees would grow in water ; if earthy (1) then such trees would grow on land. The number of trees on land or in water is to be inferred from the number of houses that the ruler of the rising Navâṃśa is separated from the Ascendant.(2)

Notes.—(1) The watery Navâṃśas are those of Karka, the second half of the Navâṃśa of Makara, and the Navâṃśa of the sign Mîna. The other Navâṃśas are those of land.

(2) For instance: Suppose the 20° of the Karka sign is rising ; the rising Navâṃśa is the 6th and therefore that of Jupiter or of the sign Dhanu ; it is a land Navâṃśa. The trees will therefore be one growing on dry land. The lord of Dhanu is Jupiter. Suppose Jupiter to occupy Kumbha at the time. From Karka to Kumbha are 8 signs. The number of trees will therefore be 8.

Again from Sârâvali we get this :—If the ruler of the rising Nâvâmśa be either in his exalted sign or retrograde in his motion, the number already obtained should be trebled; but if the ruler be in his Vargottama or in his own Navâmśa or sign or Decanate, such number should be doubled. For instance, in the above example if Jupiter should either be retrograde in motion or occupy his exalted sign Karka, the number, *viz.*, 1 from Karka should be trebled. This will give us 3. But if Jupiter would occupy the 6th Navâmśa of Mithuna (one of his Navâmśas) the number is 12 × 2 = 24. And so on.

मंदाक्रांता—अंतःसाराञ्जनयति रविर्दुर्भगान्सूर्यसूनुः क्षीरोपेतांस्तुहिनकिरणः कंटकाढ्यांश्च भौमः॥ वागीशज्ञौ सफलविफलान्पुष्पवृक्षांश्च शुक्रः स्निग्धानिंदुः कटुकविटपान्भूमिपुत्रश्च भूयः ॥ ७ ॥

अंतःसारान् Antaḥsârân, solid, strong, heavy. जनयति Janayati, gives rise to, bears. रविः Raviḥ, the Sun. दुर्भगान् Durbhagân, ugly. सूर्यसूनुः Sûryasûnuḥ, Saturn. क्षीरोपेतान् Kṣîropetân, sweet, full of sweet juice. तुहिनकिरणः Tuhinakiraṇaḥ, the Moon. कंटकाढ्यान् Kanṭakâdhyân, thorny. च Cha, and. भौमः Bhaumaḥ, Mars. वागीशज्ञौ Vâgîśajñau, Jupiter and Mercury. सफलविफलान् Saphalaviphalân, with fruits or without any fruit, fruitful and fruitless, productive and fruitless. पुष्पवृक्षान् Puṣpavrikṣân, flowery trees. शुक्रः Śukraḥ, Venus. स्निग्धान् Snigdhân, juicy ; gummy, *e. g.*, Chir, Deodar, &c. इंदुः Induḥ, Moon. कटुकविटपान् Kaṭukaviṭapân, bitter, such as, Nim trees, &c. च Cha, and. भूयः Bhûyaḥ, also ; moreover.

7. When the ruler of the rising Navâmśa is the Sun, solid trees (such as Seesum, &c.) are produced ; if the ruler be Saturn, ugly and useless trees (such as Kuśa, &c.) are produced ; if it be Moon, trees of sweet juice, such as, sugar-cane &c., are produced ; if it be Mars, thorny trees, such as, Bâbul are produced ; if it be Jupiter, trees bearing fruits such as mango, etc., are produced ; if it be Mercury, fruitless trees bearing only flowers are produced ; if it be Venus, the ruler of the rising Navâmśa, flowery trees are inferred ; moreover Moon gives rise to gummy trees, such as, Chir, Deodar ; and Mars to bitter trees, such as Nim, &c. (The conditions given in the preceding verse remaining the same.)

वंशस्थ–शुभो शुभर्क्षे रुचिरं कुभूमिजं करोति वृक्षं विपरीत-
मन्यथा ॥ परांशके यावति विच्युतः स्वकाद्भवंति तुल्यास्तर-
वस्तथाविधाः ॥ ८ ॥

इति श्रीवराहमिहिराचार्यप्रणीते बृहज्जातके वियोनिजन्मा-
ध्यायस्तृतीयः ॥ ३ ॥

शुभः Śubhaḥ, the benefic planet, the ruler of the rising Navâṃśa. अशुभर्क्षे Aśubharkse, in a malefic planet's sign. रुचिरं Ruchiram, beautiful. कुभूमिजं Kubhûmijam, the trees growing on a bad soil. करोति Karoti, makes. वृक्षं Vṛikṣam, the tree. विपरीतं Viparitam, contrary. अन्यथा Anyathâ, otherwise. परांशके Parâṃśake, in another's Navâṃśa. यावति Yâvati, as much; by as many Navâṃśas. विच्युतः Vichyutaḥ, moved; shifted. स्वकात् Svakât, from its own Navâṃśa. भवंति Bhavanti, become; are. तुल्याः Tulyâḥ, so many; equal in number. तरवः Taravaḥ, trees. तथाविधाः Tathâvidhâḥ, of that sort.

8. If the ruler of the rising Navâṃśa be a benefic planet occupying a malefic sign(1) the tree will be a superior one growing on a bad soil, the reverse being the case, *i.e.*, when the ruler of the rising Navâṃśa is a malefic planet occupying a benefic sign, inferior trees are produced on a good soil. The number (and quality) of trees are also the number (and the nature) of Navâṃśas by which the ruler of the rising Navâṃśa is displaced from his Navâṃśa.

Notes—(1). The other conditions given in stanza 6 remaining the same.

Thus ends the third Chapter on Animal and Vegetable Horoscopy by Śri Varâha Mihira of Avantika.

CHAPTER FOURTH.

ON IMPREGNATION.

Or on the time of Conception.

वंशस्थ–कुजेन्दुहेतुः प्रतिमासमार्तवं गते तु पीडर्क्षमनुष्णदीधितौ ॥ अतोन्यथास्थे शुभपुंग्रहेक्षिते नरेण संयोगमुपैति कामिनी ॥ १ ॥

कुजेन्दुहेतुः Kujenduhetuḥ. Mars and Moon are the causes. प्रतिमासमार्तवं Pratimâsamârtavam, of the monthly menses. गते Gate, when situated. तु Tu, but. पीडर्क्षं Pîḍarkśam, in the houses of no profit; in the Anupachaya houses; in the signs 1, 2, 4, 5, 7, 8, 9, 12 from the house where the Moon was situated at the time of birth. अनुष्णदीधितौ Anuśṇadîdhitau, Moon. अतः Atah, from this. अन्यथास्थे Anyathâsthe, otherwise situated. शुभपुंग्रहेक्षिते Śubhapuṃgrahekṣite, aspected by benefic masculine planets, (*i.e.*, Jupiter). नरेण Nareṇa, by man. संयोगम् Saṃyogâm, intercourse. उपैति. Upaiti, gets, is to have. कामिनी Kâminî, the woman.

1. Mars and the Moon are the causes of the monthly menses.(1) And if during any menstruation period the Moon occupy any Anupachaya houses (*i.e.*, 1, 2, 4, 5, 7, 8, 9, 12, houses from the woman's Janma Râśi, *i.e.*, the Moon-occupied sign during her birth time) and be aspected by Mars, the *conception* will take place. (2) If the Moon occupy the Upachaya houses, (*i.e.*, 3, 6, 10, 11 houses) from the husband's Janma Râśi and if she be aspected by a benefic male planet (Jupiter) in his horoscope, the conception will take place from intercourse with her husband (3) (4).

Remarks.—The more literal translation of this verse would be as follows :—

The menses that appear as monthly, because of Mars and the Moon(1) (bring about conception when the Moon is in one of the Anupachaya signs.(2) If the Moon be otherwise and be aspected by a benefic male planet,(3) there will be sexual union between a woman and her husband.

Notes.—(1) Menses appear in women whenever the Moon is aspected by Mars, that is especially when the Moon occupies the 4th, 7th, or the

8th house from Mars. In connection with this subject, the author of Sârâvali says:

"The Moon is water: Mars is fire, a mixture of water and fire is bile; when the bile mixes with the blood, menstrual discharge occurs."

(2) If, when aspected by Mars, the Moon happens to occupy one of the Anupachaya signs in the horoscope, or nativity of the woman, at the time of the appearance of the menses, conception will follow. The Upachaya signs are the 3rd, 6th, 10th and 11th house from the Ascendant; and the other signs are known as Anupachaya signs.

(3) That is from the time the woman bathes on the 4th day, when the Moon reaches one of the Upachaya houses in the horoscope or nativity of the husband. And then there will be the sexual union between the husband and wife if the Moon be aspected by powerful Jupiter.

(4) The Commentator adds as follows:

"If the Moon be aspected by the Sun, the woman will have sexual union with a royal officer; if aspected by Mars, then with a sensualist; if aspected by Mercury, then with a person of fickle mind; if aspected by Venus, then with a beautiful person; if aspected by Saturn, then with a servant; and if aspected by several malefic planets, the woman will become a harlot."

इंद्रवज्रा—यथास्तराशिर्मिथुनं समेति तथैव वाच्यो मिथुनप्रयोगः ॥ असद्ग्रहालोकितसंयुतेऽस्ते सरोष इष्टैः सविलासहासः ॥ २ ॥

यथा Yathâ, in the way; in whichever manner. अस्तराशिः Astarâśiḥ, the seventh sign from the Ascendant (during the time of cohabitation or when a question is made). मिथुनं Mithunam, male and female. समेति Sameti, have their mutual intercourse; cohabit with each other. तथा Tathâ, in the same manner. एव Eva, certainly. वाच्यः Vâchyaḥ, should be judged, spoken of. मिथुनप्रयोगः Mithunaprayogaḥ, the application of the couple; cohabitation; impregnation. असद्ग्रहालोकितसंयुते Asadgrahâlokiâtasaṃyute, when united with or aspected by an evil planet. अस्ते Aste, the seventh sign. सरोषः Saroṣaḥ, angrily; quarrelling. इष्टैः Iṣṭaiḥ, when united with or aspected by a good planet. सविलासहासः Savilâsahâsaḥ, with amorous playfulness and laughter.

2. The nature of cohabitation of a male and a female will be according to the nature of seventh sign from the Ascendant during the time of impregnation or enquiry. If the seventh sign be occupied or aspected by an evil planet,

cohabitation takes place in an angry and a quarrelsome state; if the 7th sign be aspected by a benefic planet, the cohabitation takes place with amorous playfulness and smiles.

Note.—The commentator adds that if the setting sign be occupied or aspected by both malefic and benefic planets the union will be attended with both joy and displeasure.

वंशस्थ–रवींदुशुक्रावनिजैः स्वभागगैर्गुरौ त्रिकोणोदयसंस्थितेऽपिवा । भवत्यपत्यं हि विबीजिनामिमे करा हिमांशोर्विदृशामिवाफलाः ॥ ३ ॥

रवींदुशुक्रावनिजैः Ravîndusukrâvanijiaḥ, Sun, Moon, Venus, and Mars(being situated). स्वभागगैः Svabhâgagaiḥ, in their own Navâṃśas. गुरौ Gurau, Jupiter being situated in. त्रिकोणोदयसंस्थिते Trikoṇodayasaṃsthite, being situated in any of these houses, *i. e.*, the fifth, ninth, houses from the Lagna or in the Lagna. अपि Api, also; even. वा Vâ, or. भवति Bhavati, is produced; is successful. अपत्यं Apatyaṃ, child conception. हि Hi, certainly. विबीजिनाम् Vibîjinâm, of impotent persons, male or female. इमे Ime, these circumstances. कराः Karâḥ, beams. हिमांशोः Himâṃśoḥ, of the Moon. विदृशां Vidriśâṃ, to the blind persons. इव Iva, like. अफलाः Aphalâḥ, useless; of no use; ineffective.

3. If at the time of cohabitation or during the time of query, the Sun, Moon, Venus and Mars occupy their Navâṃśas, (1) or if Jupiter be in the Lagna or in the 5th or the 9th house from it, the conception will turn out a successful one. To persons of no virility, the above Yoga (planetary combination) will be of no use as the Moon's rays are to the blind.

Note.—The commentater Bhattotpala remarks that there would also be conception even when these four planets are not in their Navâṃśas, provided the Sun and Venus would occupy the Upachaya signs in the horoscope of the man and at the same time be in their Navâṃśas, or if Mars and Moon would occupy the Upachaya signs in the horoscope of the woman and at the same time be in their Navâṃśas.

वंशस्थ–दिवाकरेन्द्वोः स्मरगौ कुजार्कजौ गदप्रदा पुङ्गलयोषितोस्तदा । व्ययस्वगौ मृत्युकरौ युतौ तथा तदेकदृष्ट्या मरणाय कल्पितौ ॥ ४ ॥

दिवाकरेन्द्वोः Divâkarendvoḥ, from Sun and Moon respectively. स्मरगौ Smaragau, situated in the seventh house. कुजार्कजौ Kujârkajau, Mars and Saturn. गदप्रदौ Gadapradau, cause (to the persons) disease and suffering (in their own months.) पुङ्गलयोषितः Puṅgalayoṣitaḥ, to the males and females respectively. तदा Tadâ, then (in their own months.) व्ययस्वगौ Vyayasvagau, in the second and twelfth houses. मृत्युकरौ Mṛityukarau, cause death. युतौ Yutau, united with one. तथा Tathâ, and. तदेकदृष्ट्या Tadeka dṛiṣṭyâ, and being aspected by another. मरणाय Maraṇâya, for death. कल्पितौ Kalpitau, intended.

4. If there be in the seventh house from the Sun during the time of impregnation or enquiry Mars or Saturn, then disease and suffering come to the male (in the months of Mars and Saturn); and if there be Mars or Saturn, in the 7th house from the Moon then disease comes to the female (in their months). Again if there be Mars and Saturn one in the second and another in the twelfth house from the Sun, then death comes to the male (in their own months); and if there be Mars and Saturn, one in the second and another in the twelfth house from the Moon, then death comes to the female (at that time). Again if the Sun be in conjunction with any of the two, Mars or Saturn, and be aspected by the other, then death comes to the male and if the Moon be in conjunction with one (of Mars or Saturn) and aspected by the other, then death comes to the female. (1)

Note:—(1). In the month of either Saturn or Mars, whichever is powerful.

वंशस्थ–दिवार्कशुक्रौ पितृमातृसंज्ञितौ शनैश्चरेन्दू निशि तद्विपर्ययात् । पितृव्यमातृष्वसृसंज्ञितौ च तावथौजयुग्मर्क्षगतौ तयोः शुभौ ॥ ५ ॥

दिवा Divâ, during the day; to persons born after impregnation during the day. अर्कशुक्रौ Arkaśukrau, Sun and Venus. पितृमातृसंज्ञितौ Pitṛimâtṛisaṃjñitau, termed father and mother. शनैश्चरेन्दू Śanaiścharendu, Saturn and Moon. निशि Niśi, during the night; to persons born after nocturnal intercourse. तद्विपर्ययात् Tadviparyayât, in the reverse cases, *i.e.*, during the nocturnal and diurnal conceptions instead of the diurnal and nocturnal as mentioned before. पितृव्यमातृष्वसृसंज्ञितौ Pitṛivyamâtṛi ṣvasṛisaṃjñitau, termed paternal uncle and mother's sister (maternal aunt). च Cha, and. तौ Tau, they; the Sun, Venus or Saturn, Moon. अथ Atha, thus.

ओजयुग्मर्क्षगतौ Oja yugmarkṣagatau, when situated in the odd and even signs respectively. तयोः Tayoḥ, to them ; to the father, mother, or to the paternal uncle, maternal aunt as the case may be. शुभौ Śubhau, benefic, producing good results ; making them happy.

5. In the case of the conception (1) by day, the Sun represents the father and Venus the mother. During nocturnal conception, Saturn represents the father and Moon the mother. During the night conception the Sun represents the paternal uncle, and Venus the mother's sister (maternal aunt); and during the day conception Saturn represents the paternal uncle, and Moon the mother's sister (maternal aunt). If the planets representing the father and the paternal uncle occupy the odd signs, or if the planets representing the mother and the maternal aunt occupy the even signs at the time, then the father and paternal uncle, or the mother and maternal aunt would be happy. (2).

Notes :—(1) Or birth, according to the commentator Bhaṭṭoji.

(2) In the odd signs during the conception by day the Sun is benefic to the father ; during the night conception, benefic to paternal uncle.

In the even signs during the day conception the Sun is benefic to mother ; during the night conception, to maternal aunt.

In the odd signs during the night conception Saturn is benefic to father ; during the day conception, to paternal uncle.

In the even signs during the night conception, the Moon is benefic to mother ; during the day conception, to maternal aunt.

In the even signs during the day conception Venus is benefic to mother ; and during the night conception, to maternal aunt.

वंशस्थ—अभिलषद्भिरुदयर्क्षमसद्भिर्मरणमेति शुभदृष्टिमयाते । उदयराशिसहिते च यमे स्त्री विगलितोडुपतिभूसुतदृष्टे ॥६॥

अभिलषद्भिः Abhilaṣadbhiḥ, about to enter the Ascendant, wishing. उदयर्क्षम् Udayarkṣam, the Lagna or Ascendant : some say the 12th house ; some say the 2nd house. असद्भिः Asadbhiḥ, by the evil planet. मरणम् Maraṇam, death. एति Eti, encounters. शुभदृष्टिम् Śubhadriṣṭim, good aspect of a benefic planet. अयाते Ayâte, not coming. उदयराशिसहिते Udayarâśisahite, when in the Ascendant. च Cha, and. यमे Yame, Saturn. स्त्री Strî, female ; wife ; the pregnant woman. विगलितोडुपतिभूसुतदृष्टे, Vigalitoḍupati bhûsuta driṣṭe, on being aspected by the waning Moon and Mars.

6. When an evil planet is about to enter the Ascendant (*i. e.*, when it is in the second house from the Ascendant) (1) and when the Ascendant is not well aspected by any benefic planet, then the pregnant woman is to meet with her death. Another case is this when Saturn is in the Ascendant and it is aspected by the waning Moon and Mars, then also the wife will die.(2).

Notes:—(1) The twelfth house is meant here according to some commentators.

(2) Before delivery time according to commentator.

These planetary combinations are here referred to according to the commentator during the conception time or the time of enquiry, or time of birth.

वै० ली०—पापद्वयमध्यसंस्थितौ लग्नेन्दू न च सौम्यवीक्षितौ ।
युगपत्पृथगेव वा वदेन्नारी गर्भयुता विपद्यते ॥ ७ ॥

पापद्वयमध्यसंस्थितौ Pâpadavaya madhya saṃsthitau, situated betwixt two evil planets (whether by signs or by Navâṃśas). लग्नेन्दू Lagnendû, the Ascendant and Moon (both or any one of them.) न च Na cha, and not. सौम्यवीक्षितौ Saumyavîkṣitau, aspected by a benefic planet. युगपत् Yugapat, both at the same time. पृथक् एव Pṛithak eva, any one of them separately. वा Vâ, or. वदेत् Vadet, should be judged. नारी Nâri, the female; the wife. गर्भयुता Garbhayutâ, with child in the womb. विपद्यते Vipadyate, dies; comes to danger.

7. If the Ascendant and the Moon, both or any one of them, be situated between the evil planets and not aspected by any benefic planet, then the pregnant woman with the child in her womb encounters death (before delivery and in the month of the powerful malefic planet).

Note:—As the malefic planets in the present case can only be three, *viz.*, the Sun, Mars, and Saturn, both the rising sign and the Moon can be between them at the same time, either when they are together or occupy two alternate houses. The Commentator adds that malefic planets might occupy either the 12th and the 2nd houses from the Ascendant or the Moon or both, or they might occupy the Navâṃśas on either side.

These planetary combinations are referred to during conception time or the time of query.

वैतालिया—क्रूरे शशिनश्चतुर्थगे लग्नाद्वा निधनाश्रिते कुजे।
बंध्वंत्यगयोः कुजार्कयोः क्षीणेंदौ निधनाय पूर्ववत् ॥ ८ ॥

क्रूरे Krûre, evil planets. शशिनः Śaśinaḥ, from the Moon. चतुर्थगे Chaturthage, situated in the fourth house. लग्नात् Lagnât, from the Ascendant. वा Vâ, or. निधनाश्रिते Nidhanâśrite, situated in the eighth house. कुजे Kuje, Mars. बंध्वंत्यगयोः Bandhvaṇtyagayoḥ, situated in the fourth and twelfth houses respectively. कुजार्कयोः Kujârkayoḥ, Mars and the Sun. क्षीणेंदौ Kṣiṇendau, and the Moon waning. निधनाय Nidhanâya, for death. पूर्ववत् Pûrvavat, as before.

8. If any evil planet be seen in the fourth house and Mars in the 8th house from the Moon or from the Ascendant or if there be from the Ascendant, Mars in the fourth and the Sun in the twelfth and the Moon be waning, then in these (three) cases, the pregnant woman dies with child in her womb.

Note:—These are the planetary positions at the time of conception or at the time of enquiry.

वै० ली०—उदयास्तगयोः कुजार्कयोर्निधनं शस्त्रकृतं वदे-
त्तथा । मासाधिपतौ निपीडिते तत्काले स्रवणं समादिशेत् ॥९॥

उदयास्तगयोः Udayâstagayoḥ, in the Ascendant and Descendant. कुजार्कयोः Kujârkayoḥ, Mars and the Sun. निधनं Nidhanam, death. शस्त्रकृतं Śastrakṛitam, from the weapons. वदेत् Vadet, should declare. तथा Tathâ, in the manner (as before). मासाधिपतौ Mâsâdhipatau, the planet, the ruler of any month. निपीडिते Nipiḍite, afflicted. तत्काले Tatkâle, in that corresponding month. स्रवणं Sravaṇam, abortion; miscarriage. समादिशेत् Samâdiśet, should pass his opinion.

9. If there be Mars in the Ascendant and Sun in the Descendant, then the pregnant woman is to meet with her death from weapons and the abortion takes place in that month when the ruler (1) of that month is afflicted.(2)

Notes:—(1) For the rulers of the several months of pregnancy see stanza 16 of this Chapter.

(2) The planet is said to be afflicted when it is defeated by any other planet in its lustre and brightness when they come together as it were for fight (in planetary conjunction) or when it is obscured by Dragon's Tail or Ketu, or when it is united with meteors, or when it is united with the Sun, the waning Moon, or united with them during solar or lunar eclipses.

वंशस्थ—शशांकलग्नोपगतैः शुभग्रहैस्त्रिकोणजायाऽर्थसुखास्पदस्थितैः । तृतीयलाभर्क्षगतैश्च पापकैः सुखी तु गर्भो रविणा निरीक्षितः ॥ १० ॥

शशांकलग्नोपगतैः Sasâṃkalagnopagataiḥ, situated in the Ascendant or with the Moon. शुभग्रहैः Subhagrahaiḥ, by the benefic planets, *i.e.*, Mercury, Jupiter and Venus. त्रिकोणजायाऽर्थसुखास्पदस्थितैः Trikoṇajâyârthasukhâspadasthitaiḥ, situated in the fifth, ninth, seventh, second, fourth, and tenth houses (from the Ascendant or from the Moon or from both). तृतीयलाभर्क्षगतैः Tṛitiyalâbharkṣagataiḥ, in the third, eleventh houses. च Cha, and. पापकैः Pâpakaiḥ, by the evil planets. सुखी Sukhî, fully developed. तु Tu, but. गर्भो Garbho, the fœtus. रविणा Raviṇâ, by the Sun. Some say गुरुणा Guruṇa, by the Jupiter. The second version is not proper. निरीक्षितः Nirikṣitaḥ, aspected by.

10. If there be benefic planets (Mercury, Jupiter or Venus) in the Ascendant or with the Moon or if the benefics exist in the fifth, ninth, seventh, second, tenth and fourth houses from the Lagna or the Moon,(1) the fœtus in the womb gets fully developed and there will be safe delivery, provided there be evil planets in the third and eleventh houses (from the Moon or the Lagna) and the Moon or the Ascendant be also aspected by the Sun.(2)

Notes:—(1) Or if some benefics be in the Ascendant and some benefics be with the Moon. According to the commentator.

(2) Some say "by the Jupiter" and not by the Sun; but this is opposed to Sârâvali.

शा॰ वि॰—ओजर्क्षे पुरुषांशकेषु बलिभिर्लग्नार्कगुर्विंदुभिः । पुंजन्म प्रवदेत्समांशकगतैर्युग्मेषु तैर्योषितः । गुर्वर्कौ विषमे नरं शशिसितौ वक्रश्च युग्मे स्त्रियं । द्व्यंगस्था बुधवीक्षणाच्च यमलौ कुर्वंति पक्षे स्वके ॥ ११ ॥

ओजर्क्षे Ojarkṣe, in the odd signs. पुरुषांशकेषु Puruṣâṃsakeṣu, in the odd Navâṃsas. बलिभिः Balibhiḥ, by the powerful. लग्नार्कगुर्विंदुभिः Lagnârkagurvindubhiḥ, by the Lagna, the Sun, Jupiter, and Moon. पुंजन्म Puṃjanma, male birth. प्रवदेत् Pravadet, should declare. समांशकगतैः Samâṃsakagataiḥ, in the even Navâṃsas. युग्मेषु Yugmeṣu, in the even signs. तैः Taiḥ, by them, *i.e.*, the powerful Ascendant, Sun, Jupiter, and Moon. योषितः Yoṣitaḥ, female birth. गुर्वर्कौ Gurvarkau, Jupiter and the Sun. विषमे Viṣame, in the odd signs. नरं Naram, male. शशिसितौ Sasisitau, Moon and Venus. वक्रः Vakraḥ, Mars. च Cha, and. युग्मे Yugme, in the even signs. स्त्रियं Striyam, female. द्व्यंगस्थः Dvyaṃgasthaḥ, in the common signs, *i.e.*, Mithuna, Kanyâ, Dhanu and Mîna. बुधवीक्षणात् Budhavikṣaṇât, on being aspected by Mercury. च Cha, and. यमलौ Yamalau, the twins. कुर्वंति Kurvanti, produce. पक्षे Pakṣe, towards the side. स्वके Svake, in their own, male or female Navâṃśas as the case may be.

11. (Now from the impregnation time, birth time or questioning time male or female or twin births are being ascertained). If there be seen during the map of the impregnation, birth, or questioning times the Ascendant, Sun, Jupiter and Moon all powerful and in the odd signs in their odd Navâṃśas, then male birth is to be inferred; if there be the Ascendant, Sun, Jupiter and Moon all powerful and in the even signs and in the even Navâṃśas, the female child is to be inferred. (1). Or if there be Jupiter and the Sun powerful in the odd signs (only) then the male issue is to be judged; and if there be seen Moon, Venus, and Mars powerful in the even signs, female birth is to be inferred. Again if there be Jupiter, Sun, Venus and Mars in the common signs (*i.e.*, Mithuna, Kanyâ, Dhanu, or Mîna), and in the odd or even Navâṃśas, as the case may be, and these again be aspected by Mercury, then twin birth is to be inferred. If the Sun and Jupiter be in Mithuna and Dhanu in the odd Navâṃśas and if the Sun and Jupiter be aspected by Mercury, then the two males are to be born; again if the Moon, Venus and Mars be in Kanyâ or Mîna signs in the even Navâṃśas, and Moon, Venus, Mars be aspected by Mercury then the two females are to be born. And if there be both the influences by parts, then one male and another female are to be inferred (2).

Note.—(1) If some of the planets be in the male and some in the female signs or Navâṃśas, then the sex of the issue will be that which predominates.

(2) The issue will be male twins as well as female twins if all the four common Navâṃśas be so occupied. This is the opinion of some authors.

(उपेंद्रवज्रा)—विहाय लग्नं विषमर्क्षसंस्थः सौरोऽपि पुंजन्मकरो विलग्नात् । प्रोक्तग्रहाणामवलोक्य वीर्यं वाच्यः प्रसूतौ पुरुषोंऽगना वा ॥ १२ ॥

विहाय Vihâya, avoiding, not taking into account. लग्नं Lagnam, the Ascendant. विषमर्क्षसंस्थः Viṣamarkṣasamsthaḥ, situated in the odd signs, *i.e.*, third; fifth, seventh, ninth and eleventh houses. सौरः Sauraḥ, the Saturn. अपि Api, also. पुंजन्मकरः Puṃjanmakaraḥ, the cause of male birth. विलग्नात् Vilagnât, counted from the Lagna or Ascendant. प्रोक्तग्रहाणाम् Proktagrahâṇâm, of the planets, previously stated. अवलोक्य Avalokya, on looking; on judging. वीर्यं Viryam, the strength. वाच्यः Vâchyaḥ, should be decided. प्रसूतौ Prasutau, during the birth time. पुरुषः Puruṣaḥ, male. अंगना Amganâ, female. वा Vâ, or.

12. Leaving aside the Ascendant, if there be seen Saturn in any of the odd signs (*i.e.*, the third, fifth, seventh, ninth, eleventh house) from the Lagna, then male birth, otherwise female birth is to be inferred. Now if the case be that males or females both are likely to be born, on looking at a nativity, then judge which planet is strongest and pass your verdict accordingly, whether a male or a female will be born.

Note.—This verse is to be considered when the conditions of the preceding verse are not applicable.

शा० वि०—अन्योन्यं यदि पश्यतः शशिरवी यद्यार्किसौम्यावपि वक्रो वा समगं दिनेशमसमे चन्द्रोदयौ चेत् स्थितौ । युग्मौजर्क्षगतावपींदुशशिजौ भूम्यात्मजेनेक्षितौ पुम्भावे सितलग्नशीतकिरणाः षट्क्लीबयोगाः स्मृताः ॥ १३ ॥

अन्योन्यं Anyonyam, each other. यदि Yadi, if. पश्यतः Pasyataḥ, looking. शशिरवी Śasiravî, the Moon and the Sun. यदि Yadi, if. आर्किसौम्यौ Arkisaumyau, Saturn and Mercury. अपि Api, also. वक्रः Vakraḥ, Mars. वा Vâ, or. समगं Samagam, situated in the even signs. दिनेशं Dineśam, the Sun. असमे Asame, in the odd signs. चंद्रोदयौ Chandrodayau, the Moon and the Lagna. चेत् Chet, if. स्थितौ Sthitau, situated. युग्मौजर्क्षगतौ Yugmaujarkṣagatau, occupying the even and odd signs respectively. अपि Api, also. इंदुशशिजौ Induśaśijau, Moon and Mercury. भूम्यात्मजेन Bhûmyâtmajena, by the Mars. ईक्षितौ Ikṣitau, on being aspected. पुंभागे Puṃbhâge, in the odd Navâmśas. सितलग्नशीतकिरणः Sitalagnaśîtakiraṇaḥ, Venus, Ascendant, and

Moon. स्युः Syuḥ, be. क्लीबयोगाः Klibayogâḥ, conditions of being impotent or eunuch. च Cha, and.' षट् Ṣat, six. स्मृताः Smṛitâḥ, remembered

13. (Now the six conditions of the birth of an eunuch are being stated). The Moon in the even signs and the Sun in the odd signs fully aspecting each other (1). Saturn in the even signs and Mercury in the odd signs aspecting each other (2). Mars in the odd signs and aspecting the Sun in the even signs (3). If the Moon and the Lagna be in the odd signs and be aspected by Mars in any even signs (4). The Moon in the even signs and Mercury in the odd signs and these be aspected by Mars (5). Venus, Ascendant, and Moon be in the odd Navâṃśas in the odd signs (6). Then eunuchs will be born.

Note.—These Napuṃsaka Yogas take effect only in the absence of male and female Yogas.

शा०वि०—युग्मे चंद्रसितौ तथौजभवने स्युर्ज्ञारजीवोदया लग्नेंदू नृनिरीक्षितौ च समगौ युग्मेषु वा प्राणिनः। कुर्युस्ते मिथुनं ग्रहोदयगतान्द्व्यंगांशकान्पश्यति स्वांशे ज्ञे त्रितयं ज्ञगांशकवशाद्युग्मं त्वमिश्रैः समम् ॥ १४ ॥

युग्मे Yugme, in the even signs. चंद्रसितौ Chandrasitau, Moon and Venus. तथा Tathâ, so, as. ओजभवने Ojabhavane, in the odd signs. स्युः Syuḥ, exist. ज्ञारजीवोदयाः Jñârajîvodayâḥ, Mercury, Mars, Jupiter and the Ascendant. लग्नेंदू Lagnendû, the Ascendant and Moon. नृनिरीक्षितौ Nṛinirikṣitau, aspected by a male planet. च Cha, and. समगौ Samagau, in the even signs. युग्मेषु Yugmeṣu, in the even signs, *i.e.*, Mercury, Mars, Jupiter and the Ascendant being in the even signs. वा Vâ, or. प्राणिनः Prâṇinaḥ, being powerful. कुर्युः Kuryuḥ, produce. ते Te, they. मिथुनं Mithunam, couple. ग्रहोदयगतान् Grahodayagatân, the planets, Mercury, Mars, Jupiter and the Ascendant being situated in. द्व्यंगांशकान् Dvyaṃgâṃśakân, in the common signs in the corresponding Navâṃśas. पश्यति Paśyati, aspecting. स्वांशे Svâṃśe, situated in its own Navâṃśa. ज्ञे Jñe, Mercury. त्रितयं Tritayam, three births at the same time. ज्ञगांशकवशात् Jñagâṃśakavaśât, on account of the Mercury being situated in any particular Navâṃśa. युग्मं Yugmam, two births, two males or two females corresponding to the particular Navâṃśa. तु Tu, but. अमिश्रैः Amiśraiḥ, being situated in the common signs of the same nature. समम् Samam, all of one nature, *i.e.*, three male or three female births.

11

14. (Now two, three births are being stated). If there be in the even signs Moon and Venus, and in the odd signs be Mercury, Mars, Jupiter, and the Ascendant, then a couple, one boy and the other girl, are to be stated; again if there be in the even signs the Ascendant and Moon and these be aspected by a male planet, then also a couple as before is stated. This also is to be the case, *i.e.*, a couple is to be born, if Mercury, Mars, Jupiter and the Ascendant be powerful in the even signs. Now three births will take place when Mercury, Mars, Jupiter and the Ascendant be in the common signs in the corresponding Navâṃsas, and these again are aspected by Mercury in his Navâṃsa; and in this last case the following particulars are to be noted:—in whichever Navâṃsa Mercury is situated, two male or two female births will take place, according as the particular Navâṃsa occupied by Mercury is indicative of male or female characteristics; and the third will be of the opposite sex. Again three male or three female births are to be judged when the planets Mercury, Mars, Jupiter and the Ascendant are situated in the common signs, all of one characteristic mark, either male or female (1).

Note.—(1) If Lagna and all the planets occupy the common Navâṃśas and be aspected by Mercury in his Navâṃśa, the issue will be three children: of these two will be male children if the Navâṃśa occupied by Mercury be that of Mithuna, and two will be female children if such Navâṃśa be that of Kanyâ. Again, if when Mercury occupies the Navâṃśa of Mithuna, the other planets and Lagna occupy the Navâṃśas of Mithuna and Dhanu, all the three will be male children; and if, when Mercury occupies the Navâṃśa of Kanya, the other planets and Lagna occupy the Navâmśas of Kanyâ and Mina, all the three will be female children.

These are stated more clearly in the following:—

If Mercury, situated in the Mithuna Navâṃśa, aspect the Ascendant, Mars, Jupiter situated in the common signs, then two boys and one girl are to be judged. If Mercury situated in Kanyâ Navâṃśa aspect the planets and Lagna as before, then two female and one male births are to be stated.

If Mercury, situated in the Mithuna Navâmśa aspect the Ascendant, Mars and Jupiter situated in Mithuna or Dhanu Navâmśas, then 3 male births are signified. If Mercury situated in Kanyâ Navamśa aspect the Ascendant etc. in Kanyá or Mina Navâmśas, then 3 female births are signified.

उपजातिका–धनुर्धरस्यांत्यगते विलग्ने ग्रहैस्तदंशोपगतैर्बलिष्ठैः । ज्ञेनार्किणा वीर्ययुतेन दृष्टैः संति प्रभूता अपि कोशसंस्थाः ॥ १५ ॥

धनुर्धरस्य Dhanurdharasya, of the sign Dhanu. अंत्यगते Antyagate, the last Navâmśa. विलग्ने Vilagne, being the Ascendant. ग्रहैः Grahaiḥ, the planets as in the preceding verse ; Mercury, Mars, Jupiter. तदंशोपगतैः Tadamśopagataiḥ, situated in the last Navâmśa, or Dwâdaśâmśa of the sign Dhanu. बलिष्ठैः Balisthaiḥ, being powerful. ज्ञेनार्किणा Jñenârkiṇâ, by Mercury and Saturn. वीर्ययुतेन Viryayutena, getting powerful. दृष्टैः Dristaiḥ, being aspected. संति Santi, are produced. प्रभूता Prabhûtâ, many, *i.e.* seven, ten. अपि Api, also. कोशसंस्थाः Kośasamsthâḥ, situated in the womb.

15. If the last Navâmśa of the sign Dhanu begin to rise, if all the planets Mercury, Mars, Jupiter occupy the Navâmśa of the sign Dhanu and be powerful (together with the Ascendant), and if the rising sign be aspected by strong Mercury and Saturn, the conception will be of more than three children (five, seven, or ten).

कुटक–कललघनाङ्कुरास्थिचर्मांगजचेतनताः सितकुजजीवसूर्यचन्द्रार्किबुधाः परतः ॥ उदयपचन्द्रसूर्यनाथाः क्रमशो गदिता भवंति शुभाशुभं च मासाधिपतेः सदृशम् ॥ १६ ॥

कललघनाङ्कुरास्थिचर्मांगचेतनतः Kalalaghanâm-kurâsthicharmâmgachetanataḥ, of the first month, the beginning, the period of embryo formation, *i.e.*, mixing of the blood and spermagenetale ; the second month, the formation of flesh, *i.e.*, when the two things get solidified ; the third month, the formation of limbs, when hands etc., come out ; the fourth month, when bones are formed : the fifth month when skin is formed ; the sixth month, when hairs begin to grow ; and the seventh month, intelligence or conciousnesss is infused. सितकुजजीवसूर्यचंद्रार्किबुधाः Sitakujajîvasûryachandrârkibudhâḥ, Venus, Mars, Jupiter, the Sun, Moon, Saturn and

Mercury. परतः Paratah, and of the following. उदयपचंद्रसूर्यनाथाः Udayapachandrasûrya-nâthâh, the ruler of the Ascendant, at the time of the conception, Moon, and the Sun are, the rulers. क्रमशः Kramaśah, successively. गदिता Gaditâ, are said. भवंति Bhavanti, become. शुभाशुभं Śubhâśubham, good and bad results; the suffering, or development of the fœtus in the womb. च Cha, and. मासाधिपतेः Mâsâdhipateh, according as the rulers of each month (were ill or well at the conception time.) सदृशम् Sadriśam, like, resembling.

16. Venus is the ruler of the first month after the conception when the embryo in formed, *i.e.*, when spermagenetale and blood mix with each other; Mars is the ruler of the second month, when the above things are solidified into flesh; Jupiter is the ruler of the third month when limbs, *i.e.*, hands, mouth &c., are formed; the Sun is the ruler of the fourth month when bones are formed; the Moon is the ruler of the fifth month when the skin is formed; Saturn is the ruler of the sixth month when hairs begin to grow; Mercury is the ruler of the seventh month when consciousness is infused into the child; the ruler of the Ascendant during the conception time, is the ruler of the eighth month (when food is being taken through the navel chord); the Moon is the ruler of the ninth month (when motion is produced, movements are felt in the womb): and the Sun is the ruler of the tenth month (when delivery takes place). The fœtus in the womb fares well or ill as the then ruler was well or ill at the conception time. If the ruler of any month be afflicted at the time of conception (in the fight with other planets &c.), then miscarriage takes place in that month; if any ruler be weak then the fœtus suffers in his month and if the ruler be strong, the fœtus gets fully developed.

Note:—According to Yavaneśwara the ruler of the first month is Mars and that of the second month is Venus. If the Sun be powerful the child would resemble its father, and if the Moon be powerful, the child would resemble its mother. The health and disposition of the child follow those of its parents at the time of conception.

वंशस्थ—त्रिकोणगे ज्ञे विबलैस्तथा परैर्मुखांघ्रिहस्तैर्द्विगुण-स्तदा भवेत् । अवाग्गवींदावशुभैर्भसंधिगैः शुभेक्षितश्चेत्कुरुते गिरं चिरात् ॥ १७ ॥

त्रिकोणगे Trikoṇage, posted in the fifth and ninth house from the Lagna or Ascendant. ज्ञे Jñe, on Mercury being. विबलैः Vibalaiḥ, on becoming weak. तथा Tathâ, again; and. परैः Paraiḥ, the other planets. मुखांघ्रिहस्तैः Mukhâṃghrihastaiḥ, face, feet and hands. द्विगुणः Dviguṇaḥ doubled. तदा Tadâ, then. भवेत् Bhavet, get; become. अवाक् Avâk, mute; void of the power of speech. गवि Gavi, in the sign Vṛiṣa. इंदौ Indau, on Moon being. अशुभैः Aśubhaiḥ, malefic. भसंधिगैः Bhasandhigaiḥ, in the last Navâṃśas of Karka, Vṛiśchika, and Mîna signs. शुभेक्षितः Śubhekṣitaḥ, aspected by benefic planets. चेत् Chet, if. कुरुते Kurute, produce. गिरं Giram, speech. चिरात् Chirât, after a long time.

17. If there be Mercury in the fifth and ninth houses (1) from the Ascendant and all the other planets be weak then 2 heads, 4 hands 4 feet are produced. If there be Moon in the sign Vṛiṣa. and if malefic planets be in the last Navâṃśas of Karka, Vṛiśchik and Mîna then the issue will be mute from his birth; and if the Moon be aspected by benefic planets, then there will be speech after a long time (2).

Notes:—(1) According to some commentators, the word Trikoṇa in the text is Mûla Trikoṇa, *i.e.*, in the sign Kanyâ here. But this is not the opinion of Garga.

(2) But if malefic planets aspect the Moon, the child will never speak; if both malefic and benefic planets aspect the Moon, the effects will follow the powerful planets.

मदांक्रान्ता—सौम्यर्क्षांशे रविजरुधिरौ चेत्सदंतोऽत्र जातः कुब्जः स्वर्क्षे शशिनि तनुगे मंदमाहेयदृष्टे । पंगुर्मीने यमशशि-कुजैर्वीक्षिते लग्नसंस्थे संधौ पापे शशिनि च जडः स्यान्न चेत्सौम्यदृष्टः ॥ १८ ॥

सौम्यर्क्षांशे Saumyarkṣâṃśe, in the signs Mithuna or Kanyâ: there is another meaning:— in the Navâṃśas of the signs Mithuna or Kanyâ. रविजरुधिरौ Ravijarudhirau, Saturn and Mars. चेत् Chet, if. सदंतः Sadantaḥ, with teeth. अत्र Atra, in these circumstances. जातः Jâtaḥ, is born. कुब्जः Kubjaḥ, hump-backed. स्वर्क्षे

Svarkṣe, in its own house; in the sign Karka. शशिनि Śaśini, on the Moon being. तनुगे Tanuge, in the Lagna or Ascendant. मंदमाहेयदृष्टे Mandamâheya driṣṭe, aspected by Saturn and Mars. पंगुः Pangnḥ, lame, crippled. मीने Mîne, in the sign Mîna or Pisces. यमशशिकुजैः Yamaśaśikujaiḥ, by Saturn, Moon and Mars. वीक्षिते Vîkṣite, being aspected by. लग्नसंस्थे Lagnasaṃsthe, situated in the Ascendant. संधौ Saṃdhau, in the last Navâṃśa of Karka, Vṛiśchika and Mîna. पापे Pâpe, evil planets, *i.e.*, one of the planets Sun, Mars, and Saturn. शशिनि Śaśini, Moon. च Cha, and. जड़ः Jaḍaḥ, deaf. स्यात Syât, become. न Na, not. चेत् Cheṭ, if. सौम्यदृष्टः Saumya-driṣṭaḥ, aspected by benefic planets.

18. If there be Saturn and Mars in the Navâṃśakas of Mercury or in his signs, *i.e.*, Mithuna and Kanyâ (1) then the child comes out of the womb with teeth. If there be Moon in the rising sign Karka and if she be fully aspected by Saturn and Mars, hump-backed child comes out of the womb. If there be Moon in the sign Mîna or Pisces rising in the horizon, and if it be aspected by Saturn, Moon, and Mars then lame, crippled child is born. If there be a malefic planet (2) and the Moon, in the last Navâṃśas of Karka, Vṛischika and Mîna, then deaf child is born. In all these four cases, if there be benefic aspect of good planets (3) then the result is somewhat modified for the better; nay, if aspected by strong Jupiter, the effects will not occur.

Note:—(1) Or both the signs and Navâṃśas according to some commentators.

(2) One of the three planets, the Sun, Mars and Saturn.

(3) If aspected by Jupiter, the effect will not occur.

दोधक—सौरशशांकदिवाकरदृष्टे वामनको मकरांत्यविलग्ने ।
धीनवमोदयगैश्च दृकाणैः पापयुतैरभुजांघ्रिशिराः स्यात् ॥ १९ ॥

सौरशशांकदिवाकरदृष्टे Sauraśaśâṃkadivâkaradṛiṣṭe, on being aspected by Saturn, Moon and Sun. वामनकः Vâmanakaḥ, dwarfish; of low stature, of 52 Aṅgulas high. मकरांत्यविलग्ने Makarâṇtyavilagne, the Ascendant being the last (*i.e.*, ninth) Navâṃśa of the Makara (Capricornus) sign. धीनवमोदयगैः दृकाणैः Dhînavamodayagaiḥ Dṛikâṇaiḥ, on the rising of the second, third and first Dreṣkâṇa in the horizon; or it may mean on the (rising) Decanate of the fifth, ninth, and the first house successively. पापयुतैः Pâpayutaiḥ, united with (here, aspected by) evil planets Saturn, Moon and the Sun as before. According to some, occupied by the malefic Mars. अभुजांघ्रिशिराः Abhujâṃghriśirâḥ, without arms, legs, and head. स्यात् Syât, become; are produced; are born.

19. If the last Navâṃśa of the sign Makara (Capricornus) begin to rise and if it be aspected by Saturn, the Moon and the Sun, then the issue will be a dwarf. If, during the time of impregnation or the questioning-time, the (rising) Dreṣkâṇa of the fifth house from Lagna be occupied by Mars and again aspected by Saturn, Moon and the Sun then handless (armless) beings are born; if the (rising) Dreṣkâṇa of the ninth house from the Lagna be occupied by Mars and if it be aspected by Saturn, Moon, and Sun then beings without legs are born; if the (rising) Dreṣkána of the Lagna or the Ascendant be occupied by Mars and it be aspected by Saturn, Moon and the Sun then headless beings are born. (This is the most reasonable interpretation and agrees with the opinion of Garga).

Another meaning:—If the first Dreṣkâṇa rises and second, third Dreṣkâṇas be united with an evil planet then no arms are seen; if the second Dreṣkâṇa rises, and the first and third Dreṣkâṇas be united with evil planets then no legs are seen; and if the third Dreṣkâṇa be the Ascendant and the first, second Dreṣkâṇas be united with or aspected by evil planets then no head is visible.

A third meaning:—

If the second Dreṣkâṇa rises in the horizon and it be aspected by Saturn, Moon and the Sun then the native is without hands; if the third Dreṣkâna rises and it be aspected by Saturn, Moon and the Sun, then the native is without legs; if the first Dreṣkâṇa rises with the above mentioned conditions then the native is without a head.

Note:—The second and the third meanings are to be taken of the 2nd half of this stanza, a fourth meaning is sometimes given as follows:—

If Mars occupy the 2nd or the 3rd or the 1st Decanate of a rising sign, then no arms, no legs, no head are successively visible. But this is opposed to the opinion of Gârgî.

हरिणी—रविशशियुते सिंहे लग्ने कुजार्किनिरीक्षिते नयन-रहितः सौम्यासौम्यैः सबुद्बुदलोचनः। व्ययगृहगतश्चंद्रो वामं हिनस्त्यपरं रविर्न शुभगदिता योगा याप्या भवंति शुभेक्षिताः ॥ २० ॥

रविशशियुते Raviśaśiyute, united with the Sun and the Moon. सिंहे Siṃhe, the sign Siṃha (Leo). लग्ने Lagne, in the Ascendant. कुजार्किनिरीक्षिते Kujârkinirîkṣite, aspected by Mars and Saturn. नयनरहितः Nayanarahitaḥ, totally blind. सौम्यासौम्यैः Saumyâsaumyaiḥ, by the good and evil planets. सबुद्बुदलोचनः Sabudbudalochanaḥ, with swollen eyes. व्ययगृहगतः Vyayagṛihagataḥ, in the twelfth house. चंद्रः Chandraḥ, the Moon. वामं Vâmam, left eye. हिनस्ति Hinasti, deprives of. अपरं Aparam, the other *i.e.*, the right eye. रविः Raviḥ, the Sun. न Na, no ; not. शुभगदिता Śubhagaditâ, good as mentioned before. योगाः Yogâḥ, conditions; circumstances ; planetary positions. याप्याः Yâpyâḥ, not fully; partially. भवंति Bhavanti, produce. शुभेक्षिताः Śubhekṣitâḥ, aspected by good planets.

20. If Leo be the rising sign occupied by the Sun and Moon and if it be aspected by Saturn and Mars, then totally blind child will be born. (If there be in the above case the Sun only in the Ascendant, then right eye only is deprived ; and if there be Moon only, then left eye is deprived (1). And if the rising sign, in the above case, be aspected by benefic planets, then swollen eyes (2) are seen. Again if there be in the twelfth house the Moon (aspected by the evil planets Mars and Saturn) (3) then the left eye is deprived ; and if, in the above case, the Sun exist instead of the Moon, then the right eye is deprived. All the bad planetary influences mentioned in this and the preceding verses from 17th stanza, when aspected by benefic planets, are somewhat moderated ; not entirely removed. (If proper precautionary measures are taken, then bad influences may be almost averted).

Notes :—(1) According to commentator.

(2) Or with a mote in its eyes ; or with one eye smaller.

(3) According to Subodhini Commentator.

वसंततिलका—तत्कालमिंदुसहितो द्विरसांशको यस्तत्तुल्यराशिसहिते पुरतः शशांके। यावानुदेति दिनरात्रिसमानभागस्तावद्गते दिननिशोः प्रवदंति जन्म ॥ २१ ॥

तत्कालमिंदुसहितः Tatkâlamindusahitaḥ, occupied by the Moon during the impregnation period or during the time of query. द्विरसांशकः Dvirasâṃśakaḥ, the Dvâdaśaṃśa (of the sign occupied by the Moon existing during the impregnation period or enquiry). यः Yaḥ, whichever (Dvâdaśâṃśa); the number of the Dvâdasâṃśa in question. तत्तुल्यराशिसहिते Tattulyarâśisahite, by so many signs distant (from the sign Meṣa or Aries, or from the sign whose Dvâdasâṃśa is occupied by the Moon at the time). पुरतः Purataḥ, onwards in the order of the signs; (some say in the tenth month from the time of conception when the Moon will occupy the required sign). शशांके Saśâṃke, on the Moon occupying. यावान् Yâvân, whichever position of the rising sign (the night sign or the day sign as the case may be); some authors take the rising Navâṃśa instead of the rising sign. उदेति Udeti, rises (above the horizon at the time of query or conception). दिनरात्रिसमानभागः Dinarâtrisamânabhâgaḥ, the corresponding part of the day or night (as the case may be). तावत् Tâvat, that portion. गते Gate, being passed. दिननिशोः Dinaniśoḥ, of the day or the night as the case may be. प्रवदंति Pravadanti, tell; declare (the author of Sârâvali and others). जन्म Janma, the delivery time; the birth time.

21. Find out the number of the particular Dvâdaśâṃśa occupied by the Moon at the time of conception or query in any zodiacal sign. Note this sign. Count from this (noted) sign (1) as many signs onward as the number of Dvâdaśâṃśas already found. When the Moon comes to such (last obtained) sign (2) the birth of the child will occur.

Again, the birth will occur by day or by night according as the rising sign (3) at the time is a day or a night sign. The hour of birth from sunrise or sunset may be calculated from the portion of the rising sign (4) that may have arisen above the horizon (at the time of query or conception). Thus it is said by different authors (the author of Sârâvali and others).

Note.—(1) The meaning given above is also favoured by Gârgi.

Different authors have expressed different opinions on this point. Some render the meaning thus:—(*a*) Find out the number of the particular Dvâdaśâṃśa occupied by the Moon at the time in any zodiacal sign. Note the zodiacal sign whose name the Dvâdaśâṃśa bears. Count from the next sign as many signs as the number of Dvâdaśâṃśas by which the Moon may have advanced in any particular sign. When the Moon comes to such last sign the birth of the child will occur. Some render the meaning thus:—(b) Count from the sign Meṣa or Aries as many signs as the number of Dvâdaśâṃśas already found. When the Moon comes to such sign, the birth of the child will occur.

(2) In the tenth month from the time of conception. The ninth month is also by some taken into account.

(3) and (4) Some authors take the Navâṃśa instead of the sign.

Remarks.—In this stanza the author proposes to discover the time of child birth from the time of conception or query.

Suppose the Moon to occupy, say, the 8th Dvâdaśaṃśa of the sign Kumbha. This Dvâdaśâṃśa is known as the Dvâdaśâṃśa of Kanyâ. According to the meaning given in the text the 8th sign from Kumbha is Kanyâ. The child will therefore be born when the Moon passes through the sign Kanyâ.

According to Note (1)a. The 8th Dvâdaśâṃśa of the sign Kumbha is known as the Dvâdaśâṃśa of Kanyâ. The sign next to the sign Kanyâ in the Zodiac is the sign Tulâ. As the Moon occupies the 8th Dvâdaśâṃśa in Kumbha, the 8th sign from Tulâ is the sign Vṛiṣa. The child will therefore be born when the Moon passes through the sign Vṛiṣa.

The Commentator adds that the particular star which the Moon would occupy at the time of birth might be discovered from the advance made by her in the particular Dvâdaśâṃśa occupied by her. For instance, suppose the Moon to occupy the middle of the 8th Dvâdaśâṃśa in Kumbha. The middle of the sign Vṛiṣa is the 2nd quarter of the star Rohinî; so that at the time of birth of the child the Moon will occupy the asterism Rohinî.

Again, if the rising sign for instance be the sign Dhanu, a night sign, the birth will occur at night. The time of birth from sunset should be calculated by proportion from the time by which the portion of Dhanu may have risen above the horizon, the period of oblique ascension of the sign representing the period of the whole night.

Remarks.—The signs Siṃha (Leo), Kanyâ (Virgo), Tulâ (Libra), Vṛiśchik (Scorpio) or Kumbha (Aquarius) are strong during the day; so if the impregnation Ascendant be any of these signs, then birth will take place during the day. And by how many degrees in time of this Ascendant that have passed the horizon, by so many corresponding degrees of day or night having been passed, the delivery will take place.

The signs Meṣa (Aries), Vṛiṣa (Taurus), Mithuna (the Gemini), Karka (Cancer), Dhanu (the Sagittarius) or Makara (Capricornus) are strong during the night.

The sign Mîna (Pisces) is strong during the day or during the night. Here the delivery may take place during the day or during the night.

मालिनी—उदयति मृदुभांशे सप्तमस्थे च मंदे यदि भवति निषेकः सूतिरब्दत्रयेण ॥ शशिनि तु विधिरेष द्वादशेऽब्दे प्रकुर्यान्निगदितमिह चिंत्यं सूतिकालेऽपि युक्त्या ॥ २२ ॥

इति श्रीवराहमिहिराचार्यप्रणीते बृहज्जातके निषेकाऽध्यायश्चतुर्थः ॥ ४ ॥

उदयति Udayati, rises in the horizon. मृदुभांशे Mridubhâmśe, the Navâmśa of Saturn. सप्तमस्थे Saptamasthe, in the seventh house from the Ascendant, *i.e.*, in the Descendant. च Cha, also. मंदे Mande, Saturn. यदि Yadi, if. भवति Bhavati, be. निषेकः Niṣekaḥ, impregnation, conception. सूतिः Sûtiḥ, the delivery of the child; the pregnant woman. अब्दत्रयेण Abdatrayeṇa, in three years; after three years. शशिनि Śaśini, Moon. तु Tu, but. विधिः Vidhiḥ, rule. एषः Eṣaḥ, this. द्वादशे अब्दे Dvâdaśe abde, in twelve years. प्रकुर्यात् Prakuryât, gets (delivery). निगदितं Nigaditam, what has been said. इह Iha, in this (chapter). चिंत्यं Chintyam, should be thought over. सूतिकाले Sûtikâle, delivery time. अपि Api, also. युक्त्या Yuktyâ, with discretion and judgment.

22. If during the impregnation time, there begin to rise the Navâmśa of Saturn(1) and if Saturn be in the Descendant, then delivery will take place after three years. If there be rising the Karka Navâmśa and Moon be in the Descendant, then delivery will take place after twelve years. Whatever have been stated in this chapter are to be thought over and judgment should be given with discretion(2).

Notes.—(1) That is, the Navâmśa of Makara or Kumbha.

(2) *e. g.*, Yogas relating to the birth of children with extra or defective organs are to be taken to refer as much to the time of birth as to the time of conception. As regards such Yogas as those relating to the miscarriage of pregnancy and the like, they are to be taken to refer to the time of conception above. As regards the happiness of the father, mother, paternal uncle, maternal aunt, they are to be taken to refer to the Lagna, &c., at the time of birth and also after the time of birth. Whatever seems impossible is not to be told.

Thus ends the Fourth Chapter on Impregnation in Śrî Bṛihat Jâtaka by Śree Varâha Mihirâchârya.

CHAPTER FIFTH.

ON BIRTH MATTERS.

(On women recently delivered ; or laid in confinement.)

अनुष्टुभ्–पितुर्जातः परोक्षस्य लग्नमिंदावपश्यति ॥
विदेशस्थस्य चरभे मध्याद् भ्रष्टे दिवाकरे ॥ १ ॥

पितु: Pituḥ, father's. **जातः** Jâtaḥ, is produced ; is born. **परोक्षस्य** Parokṣyasya, absence. **लग्नम्** Lagnam, the Ascendant. **इंदौ** Indau, the Moon. **अपश्यति** Apaśyati, not seeing ; not aspecting. **विदेशस्थस्य** Videśasthasya, gone to another (different) place ; not at home ; gone to a foreign or distant country. **चरभे** Charabhe, situated in cardinal or moveable sign. **मध्यात्** Madhyât, from the tenth sign ; from the zenith or m. c. **भ्रष्टे** Bhraṣṭe, fallen from (*i.e.*, when in the 11th, 12th or 9th, 8th signs). **दिवाकरे** Divâkare, the Sun

1. If, at the time of the birth of a child, the Ascendant be not aspected by the Moon, then the child is born when the father is away from the house ; if, moreover, the Sun be in the eleventh or twelfth house or ninth or eighth house and be situated in a moveable sign, then the father is away in distant land.

Note :—If the Sun were in a fixed sign, all the other conditions remaining the same as before, the father was in his own native town but not where the child was born. If the Sun be in common signs, then the father was not in his native town, nor in foreign place, but in a place somewhere between the two, might be returning to his country.

अनुष्टुभ्–उदयस्थेऽपि वा मंदे कुजे वास्तं समागते ॥
स्थिते वांतः क्षपानाथे शशांकसुतशुक्रयोः ॥ २ ॥

उदयस्थे Udayasthe, in the Ascendant. **अपि** Api, even. **वा** Vâ, or. **मंदे** Mande, Saturn. **कुजे** Kuje, Mars. **वा** Vâ, or. **अस्तं** Astam, in the Descendant. **समागते** Samâgate, gone towards. **स्थिते** Sthite, situated in. **वा** Vâ, or. **अंतः** Antaḥ, between. **क्षपानाथे** Kṣapânâthe, the Moon. **शशांकसुतशुक्रयोः** Saśâṃkasutaśukrayoḥ, between Mercury and Venus.

2. On the Saturn being situated (at the time of birth) in the Ascendant, or on the Mars being in the Descendant, or

on the Moon lying between Mercury and Venus, one should infer that the father was away when the child was born.

Note :—If, Mercury or Venus, ono be in the 12th house from the Moon, and the other be in the second house, then the Moon is said to be lying between Venus and Mercury. If in one sign Moon lies between Venus and Mercury, she is also taken as lying between Venus and Mercury.

शशांके पापलग्ने वा वृश्चिकेशत्रिभागगे ॥
शुभैः स्वायस्थितैर्जातः सर्पस्तद्वेष्टितोऽपि वा ॥ ३ ॥

शशांके Sasâṃke, on Moon being. पापलग्ने Pâpalagne, in the evil Ascendant. वा Vâ, or. वृश्चिकेशत्रिभागगे Vriśchikeśatribhâgage, in the Dreṣkâṇa of Mars. शुभैः Subhaiḥ, on the benefic planets being. स्वायस्थितैः Svâyasthitaiḥ, in the second and eleventh house. जातः Jâtaḥ, the one born. सर्पः Sarpaḥ, the serpent; or like the serpent in form. तद्वेष्टितः Tadveṣṭitaḥ, surrounded by snakes. अपि Api, also. वा Vâ, or.

3. If, at the time of birth, the Moon be in the Dreṣkâṇa of Mars and if there be benefic planets in the second and eleventh house from the rising sign then the native will be a serpent. Again if in the evil Ascendant, be rising the Dreṣkâṇa of Mars and if there be benefic planets in the second or eleventh houses, then the native is born with a snake coiled round his body (1).

Notes :—Another meaning—If there be Moon in the evil Ascendant or in the Dreṣkâṇa of Mars, and if there be benefic planets in the second or eleventh house then the native is a snake or one coiled by a snake.

(1) This meaning is proper and is supported by Garga and Sârâvali. The Dreṣkâṇas of Mars are the 1st Dreṣkaṇa of Meṣa, the 2nd of the Karka, the 3rd of Siṃha, the 1st of Vriśchika, the 2nd of Dhanu, and the 3rd of Mîna. The evil Ascendant or the sign of a malefic planet:—Meṣa, Karka (when it is waning Moon), Siṃha, Vriśchika, Makara and Kumbha; Kanyâ and Mithuna, when occupied by an evil planet, are also taken as evil Ascendants.

अनुष्टुभ्—चतुष्पादगते भानौ शेषैर्वीर्यसमन्वितैः ॥
द्वितनुस्थैश्च यमलौ भवतः कोशवेष्टितौ ॥ ४ ॥

चतुष्पादगते Chatuṣpâdagate, in the quadruped signs, *i.e.*, Meṣa, Vriṣa, Siṃha, latter half of Dhanu and first half of Makara. भानौ Bhânau, on the Sun being. शेषैः Śeṣaiḥ, the remaining planets; all the other planets. वीर्यसमन्वितैः Vîryasamanvitaiḥ, strong. द्वितनुस्थैः Dvitanusthaiḥ, in the common signs. च Cha, and. यमलौ

Yamalau, twins. भवतः Bhavataḥ, be born. कोशवेष्टितौ Kośaveṣṭitau, surrounded by the womb.

4. If there be Sun in the quadruped signs (Meṣa, Vṛiṣa, Siṃha, latter half of Dhanu or upper half of Makara) and the other planets all powerful and in the common signs then the issue will be twins.

छागे सिंहे वृषे लग्ने तत्स्थे सौरेऽथवा कुजे ॥
राश्यंशसदृशे गात्रे जायते नालवेष्टितः ॥ ५ ॥

छागे Chhâge, in the sign Meṣa. सिंहे Siṃhe, in the sign Siṃha. वृषे Vṛiṣe, in the sign Vṛiṣa. लग्ने Lagne, being the Ascendant. तत्स्थे Tatsthe, if there be. सौरे Saure, Saturn. अथवा Athavâ, or. कुजे Kuje, Mars. राश्यंशसदृशे Râśyaṃśasadṛiśe, corresponding to the rising Navâṃśa, *i.e.*, corresponding to that part of the body of Kâla Puruṣa (Zodiacal Man) denoted by the rising Navâṃśa. गात्रे Gâtre, in that part of the body. जायते Jâyate, is born. नालवेष्टितः Nâlaveṣṭitaḥ, with the umbilical cord twined round.

5. If, at the time of birth, the sign Meṣa, Vṛiṣa, or Siṃha be the rising sign, and if it be occupied by Mars or Saturn, then the child born will be coiled round by the umbilical cord on that part of its body corresponding to that of the Zodiacal Man indicated by the rising Navâṃśa (1).

Note:—(1) If the Navâṃśa of Meṣa be the rising Navâṃśa at the time, then round his head; if it be that of Vṛiṣa, then round the face, and so on, following the division of the body referred to in stanza 4, Chapter I.

वंशस्थ—न लग्नमिंदुं च गुरुर्निरीक्षते न वा शशांकं
रविणा समागतम् ॥ सपापकोऽर्केण युतोऽथ वा शशी परेण
जातं प्रवदंति निश्चयात् ॥ ६ ॥

न Na, not. लग्नम् Lagnam, the Ascendant. इंदुं Indum, the Moon. च Cha, and. गुरुः Guruḥ, Jupiter. निरीक्षते Nirîkṣate, aspects, sees. न Na, not. वा Vâ, or. शशांकं Śaśaṃkam, the Moon. रविणा Raviṇâ, by the Sun. समागतम् Samâgatam, approached by; united with. सपापकः Sapâpakaḥ, united with the evil planet, Mars or Saturn, अर्केण Arkeṇa, with the Sun; by the Sun. युतः Yutaḥ, united; conjoined. अथ Atha. and. वा Vâ, or. शशी Śaśî, Moon. परेण Pareṇa, by another person; not by the proper father. जातं Jâtam, produced. प्रवदंति Pravadanti, declare. निश्चयात् Niśchayât, with certainty.

6. If, at the time of birth, the Ascendant and the Moon be not aspected by Jupiter, then the child born is

certainly illegitimate (bastard); (1) or if there be together the Sun and Moon (in conjunction) and if they be not aspected by Jupiter, then also illegitimate child is born; or if the Sun be in conjunction with the Moon and they also be united with Saturn or Mars, then also the illegitimate child is born.

Note:—(1) If the Ascendant and Moon be in the Navâmśaka, ruled by Jupiter, then the child is not illegitimate.

If Jupiter aspect either the one or the other, the child will not be illegitimate.

According to YAVANESWARA, if either the Ascendant Navâmśa or the Navâmśa occupied by the Moon be that of Jupiter, the child will not be illegitimate.

According to Gârgî, if the Moon occupy a sign of Jupiter, or if she be in conjunction with Jupiter in any other sign, or if the Moon be in the Dreṣkâṇa or Navâmśa of Jupiter, the child will not be illegitimate.

वैतालीया—क्रूरर्क्षगतावशोभनौ सूर्याद्द्यूननवात्मजस्थितौ ॥
बद्धस्तु पिता विदेशगः स्वे वा राशिवशादथो पथि ॥ ७ ॥

क्रूरर्क्षगतौ Krûrarkṣagatau, when in the evil signs; when in the signs ruled by evil planets, *i. e.*, Meṣa, Simha, Vriśchika, Makara, Kumbha, Karkaṭa during the waning Moon, Kanyâ and Mithuna when Mercury is united with evil planets. अशोभनौ Aśobhanau, evil; malefic. सूर्यात् Sûryât, from the Sun. द्यूननवात्मजस्थितौ Dyuna-navâtmajasthitau, when situated in the seventh, ninth, and fifth houses. बद्धः Baddhaḥ, bound up, tied, confined in jail. तु Tu, but. पिता Pitâ, father. विदेशगः Videśagaḥ, in a foreign place, when gone to a foreign place. स्वे Sve, in his own land or place, native place. वा Vâ, or. राशिवशात् Râśivaśât, according as the sign where the Sun is, is moveable, fixed, or common. अथः Athaḥ, or. पथि Pathi, while on his way.

7. If, at the time of birth, there be in the evil signs, *i.e.*, 1, 5, 8, 10, 11 signs, Saturn and Mars, and again these planets be situated in the seventh, ninth, or fifth houses from the Sun, then the father of the child will be in custody at the time. This state will take place in a foreign place if the Sun be in a moveable sign; in his native place if the Sun be in a fixed sign; and on his way if the Sun exist in a common sign.

वैतालीया—पूर्णे शशिनि स्वराशिगे सौम्ये लग्नगते शुभे सुखे ॥ लग्ने जलजेऽस्तगेऽपि वा चंद्रे पोतगता प्रसूयते ॥८॥

पूर्णे Pûrṇe, full. शशिनि Śaśini, Moon. स्वराशिगे Svarâśige, in her own sign, *i.e.*, in the sign Karka. सौम्ये Saumye, on Mercury being. लग्नगते Lagnagate, being the Ascendant. शुभे Śubhe, Jupiter. सुखे Sukhe, in the fourth house from the Ascendant. लग्ने Lagne, the Ascendant. जलजे Jalaje, watery ; Karka ; Makara, latter half of Mîna. अस्तगते Astagate, the Descendant. अपि Api, also. वा Vâ, or. चंद्रे Chandre, the Moon. पोतगता Potagatâ, in a boat. प्रसूयते Prasûyate, is delivered ; the delivery takes place.

8. The full Moon being in Karka sign, Mercury being the Ascendant, and Jupiter in the 4th house from the Ascendant, the delivery takes place in a boat. Such will be the case also if the Ascendant be watery and Moon in the Descendant.

वैतालीया—आप्योदयमाप्यगः शशी सम्पूर्णः समवेक्षतेऽथ वा ॥ मेषूरणबन्धुलग्नगः स्यात्सूतिः सलिले न संशयः ॥९॥

आप्योदयम् Apyodayam, the Ascendant being one of the watery signs, *i.e.*, latter half of Makara, Karka, Mîna signs. आप्यगः Âpyagaḥ, situated in one of the watery signs. शशी Śaśi, the Moon, सम्पूर्णः : Sampûrṇaḥ, fully. समवेक्षते Samavekṣate, aspects. अथ Atha, thus. वा Vâ, or. मेषूरणबन्धुलग्नगः : Meṣûraṇabandhulagnagaḥ, situated in the 10th, 4th, or 1st house. स्यात् Syât, takes place. सूतिः : Sûtiḥ, birth. सलिले Salile, in water. न संशयः Na Saṃśayaḥ, no doubt.

9. If a watery sign begin to rise, the birth will certainly occur on the banks of waters, if (1) the Moon be also in a watery sign, or (2) if the Moon be full and aspect the rising sign, or (3) if the Moon be in the 10th or 4th house or in Lagna.

वैतालीया—उदयोडुपयोर्व्ययस्थिते गुप्त्यां पापनिरीक्षिते यमे ॥ अलिकर्किंयुते विलग्नगे सौरे शीतकरोक्षिते वटे ॥ १० ॥

उदयोडुपयोः : Udayoḍupayoḥ, from the Ascendant or the Moon. व्ययस्थिते Vyayasthite, in the twelfth house. गुप्त्यां Guptyâm, in jail. पापनिरीक्षिते Pâpanirîkṣite, on being aspected by evil planet. यमे Yame, Saturn. अलिकर्किंयुते Alikarkiyute, in Vriśchika or Karka signs. विलग्नगे Vilagnage, in the Ascendant. सौरे, Saure, Saturn. शीतकरोक्षिते Śîtakarekṣite, aspected by the Moon. वटे Vaṭe, under the banyan tree ; in excavated places, moats or ditches.

10. If the Moon be in the Ascendant and if Saturn occupy the 12th house from the Lagna and be aspected by a malefic planet, then delivery will take place in a jail. Again if either the sign Vṛiśchika or Karka begin to rise and be occupied by Saturn and aspected by the Moon, the birth will occur in a ditch.

वैतालीया–मंदेऽब्जगते विलग्नगे बुधसूर्येंदुनिरीक्षिते क्रमात्॥
क्रीडाभवने सुरालये सोखरभूमिषु च प्रसूयते ॥ ११ ॥

मंदे Mande, on Saturn (occupying). अब्जगते Abjagate, a watery sign (beginning to rise). विलग्नगे Vilagnage, beginning to rise. बुधसूर्येंदुनिरीक्षिते Budhasûryendunirîkṣite, aspected by Mercury, the Sun, or the Moon. क्रमात् Kramât, in due order; successively. क्रीडाभवने Krîḍâbhavane, in a dancing house; in a pleasure house. सुरालये Surâlaye, in temples. सोखरभूमिषु Sokharabhûmiṣu, in sterile soil; in sandy places. च Cha, and. प्रसूयते Prasûyate, is born.

11. If Saturn be in the watery Ascendant and if it be aspected by Mercury, then delivery takes place in dancing halls; if aspected by the Sun, in temples; if aspected by Moon, delivery takes places in sterile or sandy soils.

उपजाती–नृलग्नगं प्रेक्ष्य कुजः श्मशाने रम्ये सितेंदू गुरुरग्निहोत्रे ॥ रविर्नरेंद्रामरगोकुलेषु शिल्पालये ज्ञः प्रसवं करोति ॥ १२ ॥

नृलग्नगं Nṛilagnagam, situated in the Ascendant that is one of the human signs, *i. e.*, in Mithuna, Kanyâ, Tulâ, first half of Dhanu, and Kumbha; anyone of these being the Ascendant; the Ascendant, being any of the human signs. प्रेक्ष्य Prekṣya, when aspected by. कुजः Kujaḥ, Mars. श्मशाने Smaśâne, in a burning ground; in a place for burning the dead. रम्ये Ramye, in beautiful houses. सितेंदु Sitendu, Venus and Moon. गुरुः Guruḥ, Jupiter. अग्निहोत्रे Agnihotre, in those places where sacred fires are perpetually maintained; in the cook rooms; where *havanas* are conducted. रविः Raviḥ, the Sun. नरेंद्रामरगोकुलेषु Narendrâmaragokuleṣu, in palaces, temples, or cowsheds. शिल्पालये Silpâlaye, in workshops. ज्ञः Jñaḥ, Mercury. प्रसवं Prasavam, delivery. करोति Karoti, effects; produces.

12. If a human sign be rising and if Saturn remains there, and Mars aspecting it, delivery will take place in burning ground; Venus and Moon aspecting, delivery will take place in beautiful spots or houses; Jupiter aspecting,

in sacred places of fires; Sun aspecting, in palaces, temples or cowsheds; and Mercury aspecting, delivery takes place in workshops.

वैतालीया–राश्यंशसमानगोचरे मार्गे जन्म चरे स्थिरे गृहे ॥ स्वर्क्षांशगते स्वमंदिरे बलयोगात्फलमंशकर्क्षयोः ॥१३॥

राश्यंशसमानगोचरे Râśyaṃśasamânagochare, corresponding to the Ascendant, and the rising Navâṃśa, *i.e.*, corresponding to what is indicated as liked by the Ascendant or Navâṃśa in the verse 5, Chapter I, Khacharâścha Sarve. मार्गे Mârge, on the way. जन्म Janma, birth. चरे Chare, moveable; the Ascendant being one of the moveable signs. स्थिरे Sthire, fixed; the Ascendant being one of the fixed signs. गृहे Gṛihe, houses. स्वर्क्षांशगते Svarkṣâṃśagate, when situated in the rising Navâṃśa of the Ascendant. स्वमंदिरे Svamandire, in their own houses. बलयोगात् Balayogât, according to the strength of the Ascendant or the rising Navâṃśa. फलम् Phalam, result; *i.e.*, delivery. अंशकर्क्षयोः Aṃśakarkṣayoḥ, between the Ascendant and its rising Navâṃśa.

13. The birth will occur in places (1) represented by the rising sign or Navâṃśas, whichever is powerful. If such sign or Navâṃśa be a moveable one, the birth will occur in roads; if fixed, then, within a building (2). If the rising Navâṃśa be a Vargottama one, the house will be one's own property.

Notes:—(1) These places are those referred to in stanza 5, Chapter I. We will give here the several places appropriate to the several signs of the zodiac.

Meṣa represents the sheds of the sheep, mountains, the residence of an army, a fire place, metal mines, and mines where precious stones are found.

Vṛiṣa represents forests, bottom of hills, places frequented by the elephants and cattle and dwelling places of the farmer.

Mithuna represents places frequented by women learned in music and painting for purpose of either play or to carry love messages to lovers.

Karka represents rice-fields, tanks, sand-banks, and places frequented by the nymphs.

Siṃha represents forests, inaccessible places, caves, mountains covered with forests, and places frequented by forestmen.

Kanyâ represents places overgrown with grass, women's sleeping apartments, and female schools.

Tulâ represents custom houses, middle streets, bazaars, roads leading to towns, market-places, high ground and places where crops grow.

Vṛiśchika represents caves, fortified towns, ditches, places where there are poisonous stones, hills, snake holes and scorpion holes.

Dhanu represents good and even places where there are horses or cavalry men or armed men, places of sacrificial fire or where vehicles are kept.

Makara represents rivers, gardens, forests, tanks, water-banks and ditches.

Kumbha represents places frequented by birds, by women, by dealers in liquor or by gamblers.

Mîna represents temples, places frequented by the Brâhmiṇs, holy waters, rivers, and seas.

(2) If both fixed and moveable, the birth would occur in the outer verandah of the house.

वैतालीया—आरार्कजयोस्त्रिकोणगे चंद्रेऽस्ते च विसृज्यतेंऽबया ॥ दृष्टेऽमरराजमंत्रिणा दीर्घायुः सुखभाक्च स स्मृतः ॥१४॥

आरार्कजयोः Ârârkajayoḥ, Mars and Saturn being in one sign. त्रिकोणगे Trikoṇage, in the fifth and ninth houses. चंद्रे Chandre, the Moon. अस्ते Aste, in the seventh house ; in the Descendant. च Cha, and. विसृज्यते Visṛijyate, left ; forsaken ; deserted. अंबया Ambayâ, by its mother. दृष्टे Drişṭe, aspected. अमरराजमंत्रिणा Amararâjamantriṇâ, by the Jupiter. दीर्घायुः Dîrghâyuḥ, long-lived. सुखभाक् Sukhabhâk, happy. च Cha, and. स्मृतः Smṛitaḥ, should be remembered or considered.

14. Mars and Saturn being in one sign and the Moon (1) in the fifth, ninth or seventh house from them, the child will be forsaken by its mother; but if Jupiter aspects the Moon, then the child, though abandoned by its mother, will enjoy happiness and long life.

Note:—(1) According to some other reading "if the Moon or the Sun occupy the 5th or the 9th house."

वसंततिलका—पापेक्षिते तुहिनगावुदये कुजेऽस्ते त्यक्तो विनश्यति कुजार्कजयोस्तथाये ॥ सौम्येऽपि पश्यति तथाविधहस्तमेति सौम्येतरेषुपरहस्तगतोऽप्यनायुः ॥ १५ ॥

पापेक्षिते Pâpekşite, aspected by evil planets, *i.e.*, Sun or Saturn. तुहिनगौ Tuhinagau, the Moon (occupying). उदये Udaye, in the Ascendant ; in the rising sign. कुजे Kuje, Mars (being). अस्ते Aste, in the Descendant. त्यक्तः Tyaktaḥ, forsaken.

विनश्यति Vinaśyati, dies. कुजार्कजयोः Kujârkajayoḥ, Mars and Saturn. तथा Tathâ, similarly. आये Âye, in the eleventh house. सौम्ये Saumye, or benefic planets (aspecting). अपि Api, also. पश्यति Paśyati, aspecting. तथाविधहस्तं Tathâvidhahastam, to the hands of one of the same caste as indicated by the corresponding planets. एति Eti, comes; falls into the hands of. सौम्येतरेषु Saumyetareṣu, other than the good planets, *i.e.*, malefic planets aspecting (and also being more powerful). परहस्तगतः Parahastagataḥ, even when sheltered by the persons. अपि Api, even. अनायुः Anâyuḥ, ceases to have any life; will die.

15. If the Moon occupy the Ascendant and be aspected by a malefic planet (Mars or Saturn), Mars at the same time occupying the Descendant, the child deserted by its mother will die.

Again if the Moon occupy the Ascendant and be aspected by a malefic planet (the Sun), Mars and Saturn at the same time occupying the 11th house from the Moon, the child deserted by its mother will die.

In the above two cases, if the Moon be also aspected by a powerful benefic planet (Jupiter), the deserted child will fall into the hands of the class of men represented by the aspecting benefic planet and will live; in this latter case, if the aspecting malefic planet be powerful, the deserted child will fall into the hands of others and will perish.

वैतालीय–पितृमातृगृहेषु तद्बलात्तरुशालादिषु नीचगैः शुभैः ॥ यदि नैकगतैस्तु वीक्षितौ लग्नेदू विजने प्रसूयते ॥ १६ ॥

पितृमातृगृहेषु. Pitṛimâtṛigṛiheṣu, in the house of one's father and mother. तद्बलात् Tadbalât, by virtue of their superior strength. तरुशालादिषु Taruśâlâdiṣu, under a tree, or in a wooden house. नीचगैः Nîchagaiḥ, when in their detrimental houses. शुभैः Śubhaiḥ, all the benefic planets. यदि Yadi, if. न Na, not. एकगतैः Ekagataiḥ, situated in the same house. तु Tu, but. वीक्षितौ Vîkṣitau, aspected. लग्नेदू Lagnendû, the Ascendant and the Moon. विजने Vijane, where there are no persons; in deserted places. प्रसूयते Prasûyate, is produced; is born.

16. Birth will take place in one's father's or uncle's house if a paternal planet (Sun or Saturn) be powerful; in one's mother's or maternal aunt's house if the maternal planets (Moon or Venus) be powerful. If all the benefic planets be in their detrimental houses, then delivery will

take place under trees, in wooden houses ; and if the Ascendant and the Moon be not aspected by at least three benefic planets in one sign, then delivery will take place in deserted places where there are no bodies ; (and if aspected by many good planets in one house, then birth will take place in places where there are many persons).

मंदाक्रांता—मन्दर्क्षांशे शशिनि हिबुके मन्ददृष्टेऽब्जगे वा ।
तद्युक्ते वा तमसि शयने नीचसंस्थैश्च भूमौ ॥ यद्वद्राशिर्व्रजति
हरिजं गर्भमोक्षस्तु तद्वत्पापैश्चन्द्रात् स्मरसुखगतैः क्लेशमाहुर्जनन्याः ॥ १७ ॥

मन्दर्क्षांशे Mandarkṣâṃśe, in Saturn's Navâṃśa. शशिनि Śaśini, the Moon. हिबुके Hibuke, the fourth house from the Ascendant. मंददृष्टे Mandadriṣṭe, aspected by Saturn. अब्जगे Abjage, in the water signs (Karka and Mina.) वा Vâ, or. तद्युक्ते Tadyuke, united with the Saturn. वा Vâ, or. तमसि Tamasi, in dark places; in places without any lamp. शयने Śayane, in the bed room ; in the room where delivery takes place ; in lying-in-room. नीचसंस्थैः Nîchasaṃsthaiḥ, when more than three benefic planets are situated in their detrimental houses. भूमौ Bhûmau, on the ground ; on the ground covered over with leaves. यद्वत् Yadbat, in whatever manner. राशिः Râśiḥ, sign. व्रजति Vrajati, moves ; rises. हरिजं Harijam, in the horizon. गर्भमोक्षः Garbhamokṣaḥ, delivery ; birth. तु Tu, but. तद्वत् Tadvat, in the same manner. पापैः Pâpaiḥ, by the evil planets (with the Moon.) चंद्रात् Chandrât, from the Moon. स्मरसुखगतैः Smarasukhagataiḥ, in the seventh, and fourth houses from the Ascendant. क्लेशं Kleśam, birth-pain ; travail. आहुः Áhuḥ, say. जनन्याः Jananyâḥ, of the mother.

17. There will be darkness, no lamp (*a*) in the delivery place if the following conditions prevail :—(1) if the Moon be in Saturn's Navâṃśa, (2) or if the Moon be in the fourth house (*b*) from the Ascendant, (3) or if the Moon be aspected by Saturn, (4) or if the Moon be in the Navâṃśas of watery signs, (*c*) or (5) if the Moon be united with Saturn.

The delivery will take place on ground covered with leaves of trees, if three benefic planets occupy their detrimental houses (*d*). The child will come out of the womb in the manner in which the rising sign reaches the horizon (*e*).

The mother will suffer much from travail if Saturn (or malefic planet) and the Moon occupy the same sign or if malefics occupy the 4th or the 7th house from the Ascendant.

Notes :—(*a*) If the Sun be powerful and be aspected by Mars, there will be no darkness; or if the Moon be aspected by the Sun, there will be no darkness. These are respectively the opinions of Sârâvali and Yavaneśwara.

(*b*) Yavaneśwara used the word *kendra*, meaning the 1st, 4th, 7th, and 10th houses.

(*c*) Water Navâṃśas are those of Karka and Mîna (here).

(*d*) Sârâvali has the word " Neecha Saṃsthe, *i.e.*, if the Moon be in her Neecha sign, *viz.*, Scorpio.

(*e*) That is, if the sign be one that rises with its head, then the head of the child will appear first; if the sign be one that rises with its back, the leg of the child will appear first; and if it be one that rises with both its head and leg, as the sign Mîna, the hands will appear first. According to certain commentators this part of the text is interpreted as follows :—If the body of the rising sign be in his direct course,. the birth will be a natural one; and if in his retrograde motion, the birth will be an irregular one. This meaning has the support of Manittha.

इंद्रवज्रा—स्नेहः शशांकादुदयाच्च वर्तिर्दीपोऽर्कयुक्तर्क्ष-
वशाच्चराद्यः ॥ द्वारं च तद्वास्तुनि केंद्रसंस्थैर्ज्ञेयं ग्रहैर्वीर्यसम-
न्वितैर्वा ॥ १८ ॥

स्नेहः Snehaḥ, oil in a lamp. शशांकात् Śaśâṃkâṭ, from the position of the Moon in the sign which she occupies, *i.e.*, according as the Moon is in the beginning, the middle, or the end of the sign, so the oil is full, half full or empty. उदयात् Udayât, from the Ascendant. च Cha, and. वर्तिः Vartiḥ, the wick of a lamp. दीपः Dîpaḥ, lamp. अर्कयुक्तर्क्षवशात् Arkayuktarkṣavaśâṭ, according to the sign where the Sun exists. चराद्यः Charâdyaḥ, moveable, fixed or common. (If moveable sign, then the lamp was being removed from one place to another; if fixed, the lamp was fixed in a corner; if common, the lamp was just placed in a corner after its removal.) Some are of opinion that the lamp is faced to the direction that is denoted by the sign where the Sun exists, some again say that the lamp is faced to the direction which the Sun in his diurnal revolution at present indicates. The Sun faces towards 8 directions respectively during the eight *praharas*, one *praharà* being equal to 3 hours. Some again say, that the colour of the wick of the lamp resembles the colour of the Ascendant. द्वारं Dvâram, the door. च Cha, and.

तद्वास्तुनि Tadvâstuni, in the lying-in chamber. केन्द्रसंस्थैः Kendrasaṃsthaiḥ, in the angles. ज्ञेयं Jñeyam, to be known. ग्रहैः Grahaiḥ, by the planets. वीर्यसमन्वितैः Vîryasamanvitaiḥ, according to its strength. वा Vâ, or.

18. The oil in the lamp of a lying-in room will be full, half-full, or nearly empty if the Moon be at the beginning, middle or end of any sign (1). The wick will be full, half, or nearly exhausted according as the Ascendant is just rising, half risen or nearly wholly risen (2). The lamp is being moved, or stationary or just being fixed according as the sign where the Sun exists is cardinal, fixed, or common. The lamp will be fixed to that direction where the Sun points in the course of his diurnal revolution (the Sun points successively to eight directions in eight *praharas.*) The entrance door to a lying-in chamber will be in the direction of the powerful planets occupying an angle or *kendra* and if there be many planets, then in the direction of the most powerful planets (3).

Notes :—(1) According to Sârâvali, if the Moon be full, the oil will be full and the quantity of the oil varies with the illuminated portion of the Moon's disc. Bhatta Utpala, the commentator, objects to this view, for he says that if such were the case, children born on new Moon days should always be born in the dark—this cannot be.

(2) The length of the wick varies with the position of the point of the rising sign in contact with the horizon. The wick is of the colour of the rising sign.

(3) If there are no planets in the kendras, the entrance will be in the direction of the Ascendant or its Dvâdaśâṃśa.

शाः वि०—जीर्णं संस्कृतमर्कजे क्षितिसुते दग्धं नवं शीतगौ काष्ठाढ्यं न दृढं रवौ शशिसुते तन्नैकशिल्प्युद्भवम् ॥ रम्यं चित्रयुतं नवं च भृगुजे जीवे दृढं मंदिरं चक्रस्थैश्च यथोपदेशरचनां सामंतपूर्वां वदेत् ॥ १९ ॥

जीर्णं Jirṇam, old; used as such, on many previous occasions as such. संस्कृतं Saṃskṛitam, thoroughly repaired. अर्कजे Arkaje, Saturn. क्षितिसुते Kṣtisute, Mars. दग्धं Dagdham, burnt by fire. नवं Navam, new. शीतगौ Śîtagau, Moon. काष्ठाढ्यं Kâṣṭhâḍhyam, of wood. न दृढं Na Dṛiḍham, not strong. रवौ Ravau, the Sun. शशिसुते

Śaśisute, Mercury. तत् Tat, that lying-in chamber. नैकशिल्प्युद्भवम् Naikaśilpyudbhavam, of varied workmanship. रम्यं Ramyam, pleasant and delightful. चित्रयुतं Chitrayutam, of various ornamentations. नवं Navam, new. च Cha, and. भृगुजे Bhṛiguje, Venus. जीवे Jîve, Jupiter. दृढं Dṛiḍham, solid, lasting for many years. मन्दिरं Mandiraṃ, the lying-in room. चक्रस्थैः Chakrasthaiḥ, in the horoscope. By the other planets near the most powerful planet in the horoscope that fixes the lying in room. च Cha, and. यथोपदेशरचनां Yathopadeśarachanâm, the arrangement of the rooms as deduced from the directions given above. सामन्तपूर्वां Sâmantapûrvâm, on all the four sides of the lying-in room, the other rooms adjoining the lying-in chamber, in due order. वदेत् Vadet, say.

19. If Saturn be the most powerful in one's nativity, the delivery takes place in a chamber that is old but thoroughly repaired. If Mars be powerful, the lying-in chamber will be partly burnt; if the Moon be powerful, then it is a newly-built chamber; if the Sun be powerful, the birth will occur in a chamber built of wood but weak and fragile; if Mercury be powerful, then in a chamber of nice workmanship of various workmen; if Venus be powerful, then in a beautiful chamber newly built and adorned with pictures; and if Jupiter be powerful, the delivery takes place in a strong durable chamber. The other rooms on all the four sides of the lying-in chamber are also judged from the other planet's positions in one's nativity (from the most powerful one in due order).

Notes:—According to Sârâvali, if the Sun occupy the sign occupied by the most powerful planet as given in the text, the delivery will occur in the room set apart for the worship of the Devas; if the Moon occupy the sign occupied by the most powerful planet, the birth will occur in the bath room or where water is kept; if Mars, then in the kitchen or where sacred fires are kept; if Mercury, in the bed room; if Jupiter, in the treasure-room or store-house; if Venus, then in the playground; and if Saturn, the birth will occur in the place where all sweepings are gathered.

The commentator adds if there be 3 or more planets in the 3 signs beginning from that occupied by the most powerful planet, there will be rooms on the eastern side of the nature of the planet; if in the next 3 signs, there will be rooms on the south-eastern side; if in the next three, there will be rooms on the western side; and so on; and if in the last three, there will be rooms on the northern side.

Again, according to Laghu Jâtaka, if Jupiter at the same time be in the 10th house from the Ascendant and at the same time exalted having passed over the exaltation degree, the birth will occur in a two-storied house; if he be under the exaltation degree, the birth will occur in a three-storied house, and if in the exaltation degree, then in a four-storied house.

Again, if the sign Dhanu be powerful, the birth will occur in a house consisting of 3 inner verandahs; if Jupiter occupy the 10th house from the Ascendant or one of the signs, Mithuna, Kanyâ and Mîna, the house will be one with two inner verandahs.

दोधक—मेषकुलीरतुलालिघटैः प्रागुत्तरतो गुरुसौम्य गृहेषु ॥
पश्चिमतश्च वृषेण निवासो दक्षिणभागकरौ मृगसिंहौ ॥ २० ॥

मेषकुलीरतुलालिघटैः Meṣa Kulîratulâlighaṭaiḥ, by the signs Meṣa, Karka, Tulâ, Vṛiśchika, and Kumbha (or their Navâṃśas, whichever is powerful). प्राक् Prâk, eastern, towards the eastern portion of the house. उत्तरतः Uttarataḥ, northern, towards the north side of house. गुरुसौम्यगृहेषु Gurusaumyagṛiheṣu, in the houses of Jupiter and Mercury, *i.e.*, the signs Dhanu, Mîna, Mithuna, and Kanyâ (becoming the Ascendant). पश्चिमतः Paśchimataḥ, towards the western side of the house. वृषेण Vṛiṣeṇa, the sign Vṛiṣa (rising). निवासः Nivâsaḥ, the position of the lying-in chamber. दक्षिणभागकरौ Dakṣiṇabhâgakarau, towards the southern side of the house. मृगसिंहौ Mrigasiṃhau, the signs Makara and Siṃha (rising).

20. The Ascendant being Meṣa, Karka, Tulâ, Vṛiśchika, or Kumbha or any of its Navâṃśas (1) the lying-in chamber will be situated towards the east, (2); the Ascendant being one of the signs Dhanu, Mîna, Mithuna or Kanyâ, towards the north; the Ascendant being Vṛiṣa, towards the west; the Ascendant being Makara or Siṃha, towards the south.

(1) Whichever is powerful.
(2) The eastern portion of the house.

वैतालीय—प्राच्यादिगृहे क्रियादयो द्वौ द्वौ कोणगता द्विमूर्तयः ॥ शय्यास्वपि वास्तुवद्वदेत्पादैः षट्त्रिनवान्त्यसंस्थितैः ॥ २१ ॥

प्राच्यादिगृहे Prâchyâdigṛihe, the eastern, etc., directions of the lying-in chamber in the dwelling house, *i.e.*, the directions (east, east-south, south, south-west, west, north-west, north, or north-east of the dwelling house,) where the lying-in chamber is situated. क्रियाद्य: Kriyâdayaḥ, the twelve signs, Meṣa, etc. द्वौ द्वौ Dvau Dvau, two and two. कोणगता: Koṇagatâḥ, towards the corners, *i. e.*, south-east, south-west, north-west, and north-east corners. द्विमूर्तय: Dvimûrtayaḥ, the common signs. शय्यासु Śayyâsu, the cot on which slept the child with the mother. अपि Api, also. वास्तुवत् Vâstuvat, like the dwelling house. वदेत् Vadet, is to say. पादैः Pâdaiḥ, the four legs of the cot. षट्त्रिनवान्त्यसंस्थितै: Ṣaṭtrinavântyasaṃsthitaiḥ, considered as the sixth, third, ninth, and twelth houses from the Ascendant.

21. The sign Meṣa or Vṛiṣa being the Ascendant, the bed of the mother will be towards the east of the lying-in chamber; Mithuna being the Ascendant, towards the south-east; Karka or Siṃha being the Ascendant, towards the south; Kanyâ being the Ascendant, towards the south-west; Tulâ, or Vṛiśchika being the Ascendant, towards the west; Dhanu indicate the north-west; Makara or Kumbha, the north; and Mîna towards the north-east. The same rule holds good for the place in the bed or cot where the mother might lie. As regards the cot again, its two front legs will point towards the directions indicated by the 12th and 3rd houses from the Ascendant, and its two hind legs towards the quarters indicated by the 6th and 9th houses (1).

Notes:—(1) In other words, the 12th and the 3rd houses indicate the position of the fore legs; the 9th and 6th houses indicate the hind legs; the 3rd and 6th houses indicate the two right legs and the 12th and the 9th houses indicate the two left legs. Also the Ascendant at birth time and the 2nd house represent the head of the cot, the 4th and 5th house represent the right side; the 7th and 8th houses represent the part between the two hind legs, and the 10th and 11th houses represent the left side. Now whatever portion of the cot may be represented by the common signs, there the côt will be bent down a little, and this will not be the case if such sign is either occupied or aspected by its ruler or by a benefic planet.

Again, there will be defects, knots, cracks, holes, etc., in those parts of the cot which are represented by signs occupied by malefic planets and this will not be the case if such malefic planets be in their exaltation signs, in their Mûla Trikoṇa signs, in friendly signs or in their own houses.

अनुष्टुभ्—चन्द्रलग्नान्तरगतैर्ग्रहैः स्युरुपसूतिकाः ॥
बहिरन्तरचक्रार्द्धे दृश्यादृश्येऽन्यथा परैः ॥ २२ ॥

चन्द्रलग्नान्तरगतैः Chandralagnântargataiḥ, found between the Lagna at birth time and the Moon. ग्रहैः Grahaiḥ, by the planets. स्युः Syuḥ, existed. उपसूतिकाः Upasûtikâḥ, the woman near to the woman recently delivered of child; the midwives and others close by. बहिः Bahiḥ, outside the lying-in room. अन्तः Antaḥ, inside the room. च Cha, and. चक्रार्द्धे Chakrârdhe, in the same zodiac. दृश्यादृश्ये Dṛiśyâdṛiśye, the visible and invisible; the upper and the lower. अन्यथा Anyathâ, otherwise; reversed. परैः Paraiḥ, different writers; other writers.

22. The number of women close by the woman recently delivered (including midwives) is as many as there are planets in the houses between the Lagna at birth time and the house occupied by the Moon. Of these, outside the lying-in room would be as many women as there are planets in the visible half of the Zodiac; and inside would be as many as there are planets in the invisible (*i.e.*, the lower) half of the Zodiac. Some writers are inclined to take just the reverse.

Note:—The age, caste and colour of the women are similar to the corresponding planets; if the benefic planets occupy the signs from the Lagna to the Moon, the midwives and other women will all be beautiful, well dressed and adorned; if malefic planets occupy the signs, the women will be dirty, ugly and with no ornaments. Some writers say that the women inside correspond to the planets in the visible Zodiac and the outside women correspond to the planets in the lower port of the Zodiac. Varâha Mihira does not concur to this. If any of the planets be in its exalted portion or retrograde position then the number of women is to be trebled; if any of the planets be in its Dreşkâṇas, or in its own Navâṃśas or in its own sign then the number of females is it to doubled.

दोधक—लग्ननवांशपतुल्यतनुः स्याद्वीर्ययुतग्रहतुल्यवपुर्वा ॥
चंद्रसमेतनवांशपवर्णः कादिविलग्नविभक्तभगात्रः ॥ २३ ॥

लग्ननवांशपतुल्यतनुः Lagnanavâṃśaepatulyatanuḥ, resembling the ruler of the rising Navâṃśa, verse 8, Chapter II in form and appearance. स्यात् Syât, becomes. वीर्ययुतग्रहतुल्यवपुः Vîryautagrahatulyavapuḥ, of a body resembling that of the strongest planet in one's nativity. चंद्रसमेतनवांशपवर्णः Chandrasametanavâṃśapavarṇaḥ, colour resembling the ruler of the Navâṃśa where Moon exists. (See verse 4, Chap. II.)

कादिविलग्नविभक्तभगात्रः: Kâdivilagnavibhaktabhagâtraḥ, the separate limbs of the body resembling their corresponding signs and their rulers and the planets in them as stated in the verse beginning with the letter Kâ.

23. The child resembles, in structure and other peculiarities of the body, the ruler of the rising Navâṃśa or the Ascendant (whichever is powerful, *vide* verse 8, Chapter II) or, if these be weak, resembles the most powerful planet in its nativity. The colour of the child is similar to the ruler of the Navâṃśa occupied by the Moon (verse 4, Chapter II). And the separate limbs would be according to the corresponding parts of the body of the Zodiacal Man (verse 4, Chapter I). (1) the Ascendant representing the head.)

Note:- (1) The Lagna represents the head; the 2nd, the face; the 3rd, the chest; the 4th, the heart; the 5th, the belly; the 6th, the waist; the 7th, the abdomen; the eighth, the private parts; the ninth, the scrotum; the 10th, the thighs; the 11th, the knees; the 12th, the legs and feet. If the ruler of a long sign exists in a long sign, the part corresponding will be long; if the ruler of a long sign exists in a short sign, the part will be of middle size and so on (*vide* stanza 19 of Chapter I).

In stanza 19 of Chapter I, the relative magnitudes of the several signs of the Zodiac were given as follows :—

I	Meṣa	20 Mina.
	Vṛiṣa	24 Kumbha.
II	Mithuna	28 Makara.
	Karka	32 Dhanu.
III	Siṃha	36 Vṛiśchika.
	Kanyâ	40 Tulâ.

Of these the 4 signs referred to in Division I are known as short signs. The 4 of Division II are known as signs of middle length and the 4 of Division III are known as long signs. So that the part of the body will be long or short according as the sign representing it is long or short. If the ruler of a short sign occupy a long sign, or if the ruler of a long sign occupy a short sign, the size of the part of body represented will be of middle length. If several planets occupy a sign, the most powerful of them shall be taken into account, and if no planets occupy a sign the size of the part of body will simply follow that of the sign.

According to some the colour must be determined from the sign occupied by the Moon, *vide* stanza 20, Chapter I. To this the commentator objects. For he says there are no people of the colour of the parrot. In determining the colour, the country, the climate, occupation, the colour of the father, mother and the like should be taken into account.

शा० वि०—कं दृक्श्रोत्रनसाकपोलहनवो वक्त्रं च होरादयस्ते कंठांसकबाहुपार्श्वहृदयक्रोडानि नाभिस्ततः ॥ बस्तिः शिश्नगुदे ततश्च वृषणावूरू ततो जानुनी । जंघांघ्रीत्युभयत्र वाममुदितैर्द्रेष्काणभागैस्त्रिधा ॥ २४ ॥

कंदृक्श्रोत्रनसाकपोलहनवः Kamdrikśrotranasâkapolhanavaḥ, head, eyes, ears, nostrils, cheek, and jaws. वक्त्रं Vaktram, face. Cha, and. होरादयः Horâdayaḥ, the signs beginning with the Ascendant as the first house. ते Te, they; the signs. कंठांसकबाहुपार्श्वहृदयक्रोडानि Kanṭhâmsakabâhupârśvahṛidayakroḍâni, neck, shoulders, arms, sides, heart, belly. नाभिः Nâbhiḥ, the navel. ततः Tataḥ, after that in the rising of the second Dreṣkâṇâ. बस्तिः Vastiḥ, the abdomen. शिश्नगुदे Śiśnagude, the generative organ and the anus. ततः Tataḥ, after that; on the rising of the third Dreṣkâṇa. च Cha, and. वृषणौ Vṛiṣaṇau, the testicles. ऊरू Urû, the thighs. ततः Tataḥ after that. जानुनी Jânunî, the knees. जंघा Jamghâ, the shanks. अंघ्री Amghrî, the feet. इति Iti, thus. उभयत्र Ubhayatra, where the two things are mentioned. वामम् Vâmam, the left (is indicated). उदितैः Uditaiḥ, by the upper half of the Zodiac that has risen above. द्रेष्काणभागैः Dreṣkâṇbhâgaiḥ, according to the division into Dreṣkâṇas. त्रिधा Tridhâ, three-fold division of the body beginning with the head, the neck, and the abdomen according as the three Dreṣkâṇas of any Ascendant begin to rise.

24. (Now the different parts of the body are represented according to the rising in the horizon of the three Dreṣkâṇas of any sign). When the first Decanate rises in the horizon, the Ascendant represents the head, the second and twelfth sign representing right and left eyes; 3 and 11, the ears; 4 and 10, nostrils; 5 and 9, cheek; 6 and 8, jaws; 7, face. When the second Decanate rises in the horizon, the Ascendant indicates the neck; 2 and 12, the shoulders; 3 and 11, arms; 4 and 10, the sides; 5 and 9, the breasts;

6 and 8, belly; 7, navel. When the third Decanate rises in the horizon, the Ascendant represents the abdomen: 2, and 12, the generative organs and anus; 3 and 11, the right and left testicles; 4 and 10, the right and left thighs; 5 and 9, the knees; 6 and 8, shankles; 7, feet. In all these cases the right part of the body is denoted by the signs from the Lagna to the seventh sign and the left part of the body is denoted by the signs from the 7th to the 12th, respectively.

Note:—The object of the verse is to fix the scars or marks in any part of the body of the new-born child.

शा० वि०—तस्मिन् पापयुतं व्रणे शुभयुते दृष्टे च लक्ष्मादिशेत्
स्वर्क्षांशे स्थिरसंयुतेषु सहजः स्यादन्यथागंतुकः ॥
मंदेश्मानिलजोऽग्निशस्त्रविषजो भौमे बुधे भूभवः
सूर्ये काष्ठचतुष्पदेन हिमगौ शृंग्यब्जजोऽन्यैः शुभम् ॥ २५ ॥

तस्मिन् Tasmin, in any of the Decanates rising in the horizon. पापयुतं Pâpayutam, united with the evil planets. व्रणे Vraṇe, sign of a boil, a tumour, sore or an ulcer. शुभयुते Śubhayute, united with the benefic planets. दृष्टे Driṣṭe, aspected by. च Cha, and. लक्ष्मादिशेत् Lakṣmâdiśet, should declare that there are spots, marks of sesamum, moles, &c. स्वर्क्षांशे Svarkṣâmśe, in its own sign on Navâmśa. स्थिरसंयुतेषु Sthirasamyuteṣu, in a fixed sign. सहजः Sahajaḥ, natural; from birth. स्यात् Syât, produced. अन्यथा Anyathâ, otherwise. आगंतुकः Âgantukaḥ, after birth due to some causes. मंदेश्मानिलजः Mandesmânilajaḥ, Saturn being the cause of wound, scars are due to the falling of stones or due to illness Vâtavyâdhi. अग्निशस्त्रविषजः Agniśastraviṣajaḥ, arising from fire, weapons or poisons. भौमे Bhaume, Mars being the cause of wound. बुधे Budhe, Mercury being the cause of wound. भूभवः Bhûbhavaḥ, caused by falls on the ground. सूर्ये Sûrye, the Sun being the cause. काष्ठचतुष्पदेन Kâṣṭhachatuṣpadena, from wood, or from the quadruped animals. हिमगौ Himagau, the (waning) Moon being the cause. शृंग्यब्जजः Śringabjajaḥ, arising from the wounds inflicted by the horned animals or by aquatic animals. अन्यैः Anyaiḥ, by other signs occupied by the benefic planets. शुभम् Śubham, auspicious.

25. The rising Decanate, if united with evil planets, produces scars due to hurts, wounds in the corresponding parts of the body as determined in the preceding verse; if united with benefic planets or aspected by them, produces moles,

black marks or clots of hair such as til, &c. If the planets be in their own houses or Navâṃśas or in the Navâṃśas of fixed signs, then the marks are natural, seen from birth; otherwise, the marks are produced subsequently due to some wounds or other causes (1). If Saturn be the cause, the mark arises out of hurts from stones or by the wind. If Mars be the cause, the mark arises out of hurts from fire, weapons or poisons. If malefic Mercury be the cause, then falls on the earth are the causes of marks. If the Sun be the cause, marks arise from hurts by wooden materials or quadruped animals. If the waning Moon be the cause, then horned animals or aquatic animals are the sources of marks. There will be no wound in those parts of the body which are represented by signs occupied by the benefic planets.

Note:—(1) That is, in the Daśâ periods of the several planets.

हरिणी—समनुपतिता यस्मिन्भागे त्रयः सबुधा ग्रहा भवति नियमात्तस्यावाप्तिः शुभेष्वशुभेषु वा। व्रणकृदशुभः षष्ठे देहे तनोर्भसमाश्रिते तिलकमशकृद्दृष्टः सौम्यैर्युतश्च स लक्ष्मवान्॥ २६॥

इति श्रीवराहमिहिराचार्यप्रणीते बृहज्जातके जन्मविधिर्नामाध्यायः पञ्चमः॥ ५॥

समनुपतिताः Samanupatitâḥ, are seen; exist. यस्मिन् Yasmin, in whatever. भागे Bhâge, portions; right or left sides. त्रयः Trayaḥ, the three. सबुधाः Sabudhâḥ, with Mercury. ग्रहाः Grahâḥ, planets. भवति Bhavati, arises. नियमात् Niyamât, according to rule, certainly; with all certainty, surely. तस्य Tasya, their; of them; the marks due to scars or other wounds as described before. अवाप्तिः Avâptiḥ, receiving; getting; having; on being endowed with; possessing. शुभेषु Śubheṣu, benefic (planets). अशुभेषु Aśubheṣu, malefic. वा Vâ, or. व्रणकृत् Vraṇakṛit, scar-producing cause; agent causing marks, *e. g.*, black spots, &c. अशुभः Aśubhaḥ, malefic planet. षष्ठे Ṣaṣṭhe, the sixth house from the Ascendant. देहे Dehe, on the body. तनोः Tanoḥ, from the Ascendant. भसमाश्रिते Bhasamâśrite, on the portion of the body indicated by the corresponding sign as inferred from verse 4, Kâlângâni, Chapter I. तिलकमशककृत् Tilakamaśakakṛit, producer of black mark, Tila,

Maśaka, &c. दृष्टः Driṣtaḥ, is seen. सौम्यैः Saumyaiḥ, with benefic planets. युतः Yutaḥ, united. च Cha, and. स Sa, that ; evil planet. लक्ष्मवान् Lakṣmavân, producing marks, such as clots of hair termed Lakṣmâ.

26. On whichever part of the body (represented by the sign, see stanza 24, of this Chapter) right or left, is seen the planet Mercury joined by the three other planets, benefic or malefic, there will surely be seen marks caused by wounds or moles, etc. If the malefic planet causing marks, be situated in the sixth house from the Ascendant, then on that part of the body as denoted by verse 4, Chapter I, will be seen scars (1). But if a benefic planet aspects the malefic one then a dark and a white mole will be seen ; but if the sixth house be occupied by benefics, then will be seen simply a clot of hair.

Note:—(1) In the Daśâ period of the most powerful planet.

Thus ends the Fifth Chapter of Brihajjâtaka on Rules regarding births by Śrî Varâha Mihira of Avantika.

CHAPTER VI.

ON BÂLÂRIṢṬA OR EARLY DEATH.

विद्युन्माला—संध्यायां हिमदीधितिहोरापापैर्भांतगतैर्निध-
नाय । प्रत्येकं शशिपापसमेतैः केंद्रैर्वा स विनाशमुपैति ॥ १ ॥

संध्यायां Saṃdhyâyâm, in the twilight period, *i.e.*, in the morning or evening, that period which precedes the moment ($1\frac{1}{2}$ ghaṭis earlier) when the Sun has just half risen and that which succeeds the moment when the Sun has just half set during which the stars are invisible. हिमदीधितिहोरा Himadîdhitihorâ, the lunar horâ rising; the second halves in the odd signs, and the first halves in the even signs, are known as lunar horâs. पापैः Pâpaiḥ, the evil planets (occupying). भांतगतैः Bhâṃtagataiḥ, the last Navâṃśas of signs. निधनाय Nidhanâya, for death (soon after birth). प्रत्येकं Pratyekam, one in every angle. शशिपापसमेतैः Śaśipâpasametaiḥ, the Moon and the three other malefic planets (occupying). केंद्रैः Kendraiḥ, situated in the angular houses. वा Vâ, or. स Sa, he; the child born. विनाशम् उपैति Vinâśam Upaiti, meets with death; dies.

1. The new-born child will die soon after birth, if he be born in the twilights in the morning or evening, when there is rising the horâ of the Moon (1) and when the evil planets are situated in the last Navâṃśas of the signs. Similar will be the result if at the time of birth, the Moon exists in one angle and 3 evil planets in the three other angles, respectively.

Note:—(1) In the odd signs the second horâs, and in the even signs the first halves are known as lunar horâs.

इं० व०—चक्रस्य पूर्वापरभागगेषु क्रूरेषु सौम्येषु च
कीटलग्ने । क्षिप्रं विनाशं समुपैति जातः पापैर्विलग्नास्तमया-
भितश्च ॥ २ ॥

चक्रस्य Chakrasya, of the Zodiacal circle. पूर्वापरभागगेषु Pûrvâparabhâgageṣu, situated in the first or eastern and second or western halves (of the Zodiac) respectively. The second half begins with the 4th house from the Ascendant and ends with the 10th house. The remainder is the first half. How many degrees of the Ascendant have risen above the horizon so many degrees should be deducted from the fourth sign and corresponding corrections made in the 10th sign. Some again remark that the first half is counted from the Ascendant to the seventh house and the second half, the remainder. क्रूरेषु Krûreṣu, the malefic planets occupying. सौम्येषु Saumyesu, the benefic planets occupying. च Cha, and. कीटलग्ने Kiṭalagne, on the rising in the horizon of Vṛiśchika and Karka signs (these are the two meant here according to Bâdarâyaṇa). क्षिप्रं Kṣipram, soon. विनाशं Vinâśam, death. समुपैति Samupaiti, will meet with. जातः Jâtaḥ, the new-born child. पापैः Pâpaiḥ, the malefic planets occupying. विलग्नास्तमयाभितः Vilagnâsta-mayâbhitaḥ, situated (अभितः) in the Ascendant and in the Descendant. Some say, situated in the Ascendant or in the Descendant. Some say, when the malefic planets are on the two sides (अभितः) of the Lagna or of the Descendant, respectively, *i.e.*, when there are the malefic planets in the second and twelfth houses in one case; and where there are evil planets in the sixth and eighth houses in another case; in both these cases respectively the child will die soon. Some give a third meaning :—When all the evil planets occupy the second house and are about to rise (अभितः) in the horizon or when all the evil planets occupy the eighth house and are about to disappear in the horizon. Some say again, when all the evil planets occupy the twelfth or the sixth houses respectively from the Lagna, for those are about to appear and disappear in the horizon respectively. These different interpretations hang on the several meanings of the word अभितः Abhitaḥ. च Cha, and.

2. If there be malefic planets in the first or eastern half of the Zodiac (*i. e.*, from the 10th sign to the 4th sign from the Lagna) and if there be benefic planets in the second or western half of the Zodiac (*i.e.*, from 4th sign to the 10th sign from the Lagna) while the Ascendant is Karka or Vṛiśchika sign, then the child born will soon die. Again, if there be evil planets in the twelfth and in the seventh houses, from the Ascendant, the child will soon die (1).

Notes:—(1) Some commentators take "If there be evil planets in the twelfth house or in the seventh house from the Ascendant, there will be early death. Again some commentators take " If malefic planets occupy the 12th and 2nd houses or the 6th and 8th houses from the rising sign, the child would die. Some again write " If malefics occupy the 2nd, 12th, 6th and 8th houses, the child will die early." According to Gârgî, the child will die in each of the following cases, (1) all the malefic planets occupying the 6th and the 12th houses, (2) the 8th and 2nd houses, (3) the 12th and 2nd houses; (4) the 8th and 6th houses.

अनुष्टुभ्—पापावुदयास्तगतौ क्रूरेण युतश्च शशी। दृष्टश्च शुभैर्न यदा मृत्युश्च भवेदचिरात् ॥ ३ ॥

पापौ Pâpau, the malefic planets being situated. उदयास्तगतौ Udayâstagatau, in the Ascendant and Descendant. क्रूरेण Krûreṇa, with a malefic planet. युतः च Yutaḥ cha, and united with. शशी Sasi, the Moon (being). दृष्टः Dristaḥ, aspected by. च Cha, and. शुभैः Subhaiḥ, by the benefic planets. न Na, not. यदा Yadâ, when. मृत्युः Mrityuḥ, death. च Cha, and. भवेत् Bhavet, will overtake. अचिरात् Achirât, soon.

3. Death will soon overtake the new-born child if there be a malefic planet each in the Ascendant and the Descendant and if the Moon be at the same time attended by an evil planet and not aspected by benefic planets.

अनुष्टुभ्—क्षीणे हिमगौ व्ययगे पापैरुदयाष्टमगैः। केन्द्रेषु शुभाश्च न चेत् क्षिप्रं निधनं प्रवदेत् ॥ ४ ॥

क्षीणे Ksîṇe, waning. हिमगौ Himagau, the Moon. व्ययगे Vyayage, occupying the twelfth house from the Ascendant. पापैः Pâpaiḥ, the evil planet occupying. उदयाष्टमगैः Udayâṣṭamagaih, the Ascendant and the eighth house. केन्द्रेषु Kendreṣu, in the angles. शुभाः Śubhâḥ, the benefic planet. च Cha, and. न Na, not. चेत् Chet, if. क्षिप्रं Ksipram, soon. निधनं Nidhanam, death. प्रवदेत् Pravadet, declare.

4. If there be in the twelfth house from the Ascendant the waning Moon and the evil planets be seen in the Ascendant and the eighth house and if there be no benefic planets in the angles, the child will die soon.

अनुष्टुभ्—क्रूरेण संयुतः शशी स्मरान्त्यमृत्युलग्नगः। कण्टकाद्बहिः शुभैरवीक्षितश्च मृत्युदः ॥ ५ ॥

क्रूरेण Krûreṇa, by the evil planets. संयुतः Saṃyutaḥ, be attended by. शशी Śaśî, the Moon. स्मरान्त्यमृत्युलग्नगः Smarântyamrityulagnagaḥ, occupying the seventh, twelfth, eighth and first houses. कण्टकात् Kaṇṭakât, the angles. बहिः Bahiḥ, outside. शुभैः Śubhaiḥ, by the benefic planets. अवीक्षितः Avîkṣitaḥ, not aspected. च Cha, and. मृत्युदः Mrityudaḥ, causing death.

5. If the Moon be joined with an evil planet and if she exist in the seventh, twelfth, eighth or in the first house, and if she be not aspected by the benefic planets, also if there be no benefic planets in the angles, the child will die soon.

N. B.—If there be good planets in the angles, then the child survives.

पृथ्वी–शशिन्यरिविनाशगे निधनमाशु पापेक्षिते शुभैरथ समाष्टकन्दलमतश्च मिश्रैः स्थितिः । असद्भिरवलोकिते बलिभिरत्र मासं शुभे कलत्रसहिते च पापविजिते विलग्नाधिपे ॥ ६ ॥

शशिनि Śaśini, the Moon occupying. अरिविनाशगे Arivināśage, the sixth and eighth houses from the Ascendant. निधनम् Nidhanam, death. आशु Âśu, soon. पापेक्षिते Pâpekṣite, aspected by an evil planet. शुभैः Śubhaiḥ, by the benefic planets. अथ Atha, thus. समाष्टकं Samáṣṭakam, for eight years. दलं Dalam, the half. अतः Ataḥ, from this; of this (*i.e.*, eight years). च Cha, and. मिश्रैः Miśraiḥ, both by the good and bad planets. स्थितिः Sthitiḥ, life in this world. असद्भिः Asadbhiḥ, by the evil planets. अवलोकिते Avalokite, aspected by. बलिभिः Balibhiḥ, by the powerful planets. अत्र Atra, in the sixth or eighth house. मासं Mâsam, one month. शुभे Śubhe, the good planets, Mercury, Jupiter or Venus. कलत्रसहिते Kalatrasahite, in the seventh house. च Cha, and. पापविजिते Pâpavijite, defeated in the battle with other planets. विलग्नाधिपे Vilagnâdhipe, the ruler of the Ascendant at birth time.

6. If the Moon occupy the sixth or the eighth house from the Ascendant and be aspected by any of the evil planets the child will die soon; if the Moon be aspected by the benefic planets when she is in the sixth or in the eighth house, the child lives for eight years and then dies. If the Moon in the above case be aspected by both the good and the evil planets, the child lives half the period of eight years (*i.e.*, 4 years) and then dies. If in the sixth or eighth house there be any benefic planet Mercury, Jupiter or Venus aspected by powerful evil planets the child lives for one month only. If the ruler of one's Ascendant be in the seventh house and be defeated in battle (by an evil planet), the child lives for one month and then dies.

N. B.—Note should be here made that if the Moon in the sixth or eighth house be not aspected by any evil or good planet then there is wanting that union of circumstances which causes death; the child does not die. Also if the Moon, in the above case be in the house of a benefic planet or united with good planets, the child does not die. If a child be born in the dark fortnight during day time, the child (according to Mândavya) does not die; if a child be born in the bright fortnight and in the night time, the child does not die even if the Moon be in the 6th or 8th house and aspected by both the good and evil planets.

The battle of the planets, *i.e.*, the planetary conjunction, takes place in the sky; when two or more planets come near each other, that planet is said to be defeated whose lustre is diminished and which goes towards the south, is retrograde in motion, or of small size. Venus is always victorious, even if she be in the south.

मं०क्रा०—लग्ने क्षीणे शशिनि निधनं रन्ध्रकेन्द्रेषु पापैः। पापान्तस्थे निधनहिबुकद्यूनसंस्थे च चन्द्रे ॥ एवं लग्ने भवति मदनच्छिद्रसंस्थैश्च पापैर्मात्रा सार्द्धं यदि न च शुभैर्वीक्षितः शक्तिभृद्भिः ॥ ७ ॥

लग्ने Lagne, occupying the Ascendant. क्षीणे Kṣîṇe, the waning crescent. शशिनि Śaśini, the Moon occupying. निधनं Nidhanam, death. रन्ध्रकेन्द्रेषु Randhra Kendreṣu, in the eighth house and in the four angles. पापैः Pâpaiḥ, by the malefic planets. पापान्तस्थे Pâpântyasthe, between the malefic planets. निधनहिबुकद्यूनसंस्थे Nidhanahibuka-dyunasaṃsthe, situated in the eighth, fourth or the seventh houses. च चन्द्रे Cha Chandre, and the Moon. एवं Evam, thus. लग्ने Lagne, occupying the Ascendant. भवति Bhavati, be. मदनच्छिद्रसंस्थैः Madanachhidrasaṃsthaiḥ, occupying the seventh and eighth houses. च Cha, and. पापैः Pâpaiḥ, the malefic planets occupying. मात्रा सार्द्धं Mâtrâ sârdham, with the mother. यदि Yadi, if. न Na, no. च Cha, and. शुभैः Śubhaiḥ, by the benefic planets. वीक्षितः Vikṣitaḥ, aspected. शक्तिभृद्भिः Śaktibhṛidbhiḥ, the powerful planets (failing to aspect.)

7. If the waning Moon be in the Ascendant and the malefic planets exist in the eighth, and the angles, the child soon dies. Again, if Moon exists between the evil planets and occupies the eighth, fourth or the seventh houses, the child dies. Again, if Moon exists in the Ascendant between the two evil planets and if the malefic planets occupy the seventh or eighth house and the Moon be not aspected by powerful benefic planets, the child dies with its mother (if aspected by the powerful good planets, the child dies, the mother is saved.)

इं०व्र—राश्यंतगे सद्भिरवीक्ष्यमाणे चंद्रे त्रिकोणोपगतैश्च पापैः ॥ प्राणैः प्रयात्याशु शिशुर्वियोगमस्ते च पापैस्तुहिनांशुलग्ने ॥ ८ ॥

राश्यंतगे Râśyantage, occupying the last Navâṃśas of any sign. सद्भिः Sadbhiḥ, by the benefic planets. अवीक्ष्यमाणे Avîkṣyamâṇe, not being aspected. चंद्रे Chandre, the Moon (occupying). त्रिकोणोपगतैः Trikoṇopagataiḥ, occupying the fifth and ninth houses from the Ascendant. च Cha, and. पापैः Pâpaih, the malefic planets (occupying.) प्राणैः Prâṇaiḥ, with life. प्रयाति Prayâti, departs. आशु Âśu, soon. शिशुः Śiśuḥ, the child. वियोगम् Viyogam, separation. अस्ते Aste, occupying the Descendant. च Cha, and. पापैः Pâpaiḥ, by the malefic planets. तुहिनांशु Tuhinâmṣu, the Moon. लग्ने Lagne, in the Ascendant.

8. If the Moon occupy, at the birth time, the last Navâmṣa of any sign, and be not aspected by any benefic planet and also the malefic planets exist in the 5th and 9th houses, the child soon dies. Again the Moon being in the Ascendant and the malefic planets in the Descendant, death ensues of the child.

हरिणी—अशुभसहिते ग्रस्ते चंद्रे कुजे निधनाश्रिते जननिसुतयोर्मृत्युर्लग्ने रवौ तु सशस्त्रजः ॥ उदयति रवौ शीतांशौ वा त्रिकोणविनाशगैर्निधनमशुभैर्वीर्योपेतैः शुभैर्न युतेक्षिते ॥ ९ ॥

अशुभसहिते Aśubhasahite, united with evil planets; united with Saturn. ग्रस्ते Graste, with Râhu; eclipsed. Râhu=the Moon's Ascending Node. चंद्रे Chandre, the Moon occupying. कुजे Kuje, Mars occupying. निधनाश्रिते Nidhanâśrite, the eighth house (being occupied.) जननिसुतयोः Jananisutayoḥ, of the child and the mother both. मृत्युः Mrityuḥ, death. लग्ने Lagne, in the Ascendant. रवौ Ravau, the Sun. तु Tu, but. सशस्त्रजः Saśastrajaḥ, caused by weapons. उदयति Udayati, rises; in the Ascendant. रवौ Ravau, the Sun. शीतांशौ Sitamśau, the Moon. वा Vâ, or. त्रिकोणविनाशगैः Trikoṇavinâśagaih, situated in the 5th, 9th and 8th house. निधनं Nidhanam, death. अशुभैः Aśubhaiḥ, the evil planets occupying. वीर्योपेतैः Vîryopetaiḥ, by the powerful planets. शुभैः Śubhaiḥ, by the benefic planets. न Na, not. युते Yute, united with. ईक्षिते Ikṣite, aspected by.

9. If, during birth, the Ascendant be occupied by the eclipsed Moon and a malefic planet (Saturn) and the 8th house be occupied by Mars, the mother and child both will die. If instead of the Moon, there be Sun in the above case, death will occur by weapons. Again, if the Ascendant be occupied by either the Sun or the Moon, and there exist in the 5th, 8th and 9th houses all the malefic planets, and if the Sun or the Moon be not aspected nor attended by any powerful benefic planet, the above result will take place (1).

Note:—(1) Some take there the death of the child only and not of the mother.

अपरवक्त्र—असितरविशशांकभूमिजैर्व्ययनवमोदयनैधनाश्रितैः ॥
भवति मरणमाशु देहिनां यदि बलिना गुरुणा न वीक्षिताः ॥१०॥

असितरविशशांकभूमिजैः Asitaraviśaśâṃkabhuûmjaiḥ, Saturn, the Sun, the Moon, and Mars occupying respectively. व्ययनव मोदयनैधनाश्रितैः Vyayanavamodayanaidhanâśritaiḥ, the twelfth, ninth, first, and eighth houses respectively. भवति Bhavati, arises. मरणम् Maraṇam, death. आशु Âśu, soon. देहिनां Dehinâm, of the child. यदि Yadi, if. बलिना Balinâ, by the powerful. गुरुणा Guruṇâ, by Jupiter. न Na, not. वीक्षिताः Vîkṣitâḥ, aspected.

10. If there be, at the birth time, Saturn in the twelfth house, the Sun in the ninth house, the Moon in the Ascendant and Mars in the eighth house respectively and powerful Jupiter does not aspect these, the child soon dies. (If Jupiter aspects some and does not aspect others or if weak Jupiter aspects all, then the child meets with death but not so soon. To aspect all the four planets Jupiter must occupy the 5th house) (1).

Notes:—(1) If powerful Jupiter aspect all the four planets, then the child will be saved.

पुष्पिताग्रा—सुतमदननवांत्यलग्नरंध्रेष्वशुभयुतो मरणाय शीतरश्मिः ॥ भृगुसुतशशिपुत्रदेवपूज्यैर्यदि बलिभिर्न युतोऽवलोकितो वा ॥ ११ ॥

सुतमदननवांत्यलग्नरंध्रेषु Sutamadananavâutyalagnarandhreṣu, in the fifth, seventh, ninth, twelfth houses, Ascendant or the eighth house. अशुभयुतः Aśubhayutaḥ, united with an evil planet. मरणाय Maraṇâya, intended for death. शीतरश्मिः Śîtaraśmiḥ, the Moon; here the waning Moon is intended. भृगुसुतशशिपुत्रदेवपूज्यैः Bhṛigusutaśaśiputradevapûjyaiḥ, by Venus, Mercury and Jupiter. यदि Yadi, if. बलिभिः Balibhiḥ, by the powerful. न Na, not. युतः Yutaḥ, united with, attended by. अवलोकितः Avalokitaḥ, aspected by. वा Vâ, or.

11. If at the time of birth, the (waning) Moon be in the Ascendant or fifth, seventh, ninth, eighth or twelfth house and united with an evil planet and be not united with nor aspected by any of the powerful planets Mercury, Venus or Jupiter, then death ensues soon after birth.

भ्रमर विलसिता—योगे स्थानं गतवति बलिनश्चंद्रे स्वं वा तनुग्रहमथ वा ॥ पापैर्दृष्टे बलवति मरणं वर्षस्यांतः किल मुनिगदितम् ॥ १२ ॥

इति श्रीवराहमिहिराचार्यप्रणीते बृहज्जातकेऽरिष्टाध्यायः षष्ठः ॥ ६ ॥

योगे Yoge, the combination of planets by which death of the child is forecast. स्थानं Sthânam, the sign or house where the most powerful planet (causing death of the child) exists during the time of birth. गतवति Gatavati, when reaching (in the course of her revolutions in a year). बलिनः Balinaḥ, of the most powerful planet at the birth time (causing death to the child). चंद्रे Chandre, the Moon. स्वं Svam, her own, the sign where the Moon existed during the birth time. वा Vâ, or. तनुगृहम् Tanugriham, the Ascendant during the birth time. अथ Atha, thus. वा Vâ, or. पापैः Pâpaiḥ, by the malefic planets. दृष्टे Driṣṭe, being aspected by. बलवति Balavati, becoming powerful when the Moon becomes powerful on entering any of the three houses above stated. मरणं Maraṇam, death. वर्षस्य Varṣasya, of one year. अंतः Antaḥ, the end. किल Kila, certainly. मुनिगदितम् Munigaditam, spoken of by sages.

12. (In the above planetary combinations) death overtakes the child within one year after birth, when the Moon goes to the house which was occupied by the most powerful planet at birth time causing such death, or when she goes again to the sign which she herself occupied at birth, or to the rising sign at the time, provided she becomes powerful and aspected by powerful malefic planets (1). So the sages say. (This verse is stated with an object to fix the exact period of death, that was not stated in the preceding 11 verses predicting the death of the child.

Notes :—(1) The Moon makes about 13 revolutions in the course of a year. Whenever the Moon in the course of motion becomes powerful and is aspected by powerful malefic planets on reaching one of the three places mentioned in the text, death will occur.

The conditions, rather planetary positions, that counteract the early death combinations stated in this Chaper, are now being stated by the commentators (taken from other authoritative sources).

1st Jupiter in the Ascendant and also very powerful averts early death.

2nd. If the ruler of the Ascendant during birth time be very powerful, be aspected by benefic planets in the angles and be not aspected by any malefic planet, early death ceases.

3rd. Though the Moon occupy the 8th house, early death is averted if the Moon occupy the Decanates of Venus, Jupiter, or Mercury.

4th. There will be no early death if the full Moon exist in a benefic house, between the benefic planets and if she be aspected by Venus.

5th. If Mercury, Venus or Jupiter occupy any angle and be very powerful, there will be no early death even if any of these be accompanied by a malefic planet.

6th. Though the Moon occupy the 6th house, the death is averted if the Moon occupy the Decanates of Jupiter, Venus or Mercury.

7th. If the full Moon exist between two benefic signs or planets, early death is averted.

8th. The full Moon (in a bright fortnight) averts early death. If, during the waning Moon the birth occur by day or during the waxing Moon the birth occur by night, then there will be no early death even if the Moon occupy the 6th or the 8th house.

9th. Powerful Jupiter in the angles and aspecting the full Moon averts death.

10th. Jupiter, Moon, Venus and Mercury, all being situated in the benefic's house, in the benefic Navâṃśas or in their Decanates the danger is averted.

11th. The ruler of the Moon-occupied sign or a benefic planet occupying any of the angles, averts early death.

12th. The malefic planets, if seen in benefic Vargas and at the same time if aspected by benefic planets occupying also their benefic Vargas, early death ceases.

13th. If Râhu (the Moon's Ascending Node) occupy the 3rd, 6th or 11th house and be aspected by the benefics, early death ceases.

14th. If all the planets occupy the signs that rise with their faces in front, there will be no early death.

15th. If, during the birth time, the victorious benefic planet (in planetary fight) be aspected by other benefics, then the danger is averted.

16th. If the full Moon be favourably aspected by all the planets in the Zodiac, then the death is averted and the child gets influence like that of a king.

Thus ends the Sixth Chapter on Symptoms of the approaching Death of a child by Śrî Varâha Mihirâchârya.

CHAPTER VII.

ON THE LENGTH OF LIFE OF A CHILD.

i.e., on Âyurdâya.

पुष्पिताग्रा—मयवनमणित्य शक्तिपूर्वैर्दिवसकरादिषु वत्सराः प्रदिष्टाः ॥ नवतिथिविषयाश्विभूतरुद्रदशसहिता दशभिःस्वतुंगभेषु ॥ १ ॥

मययवनमणित्थशक्तिपूर्वैः Mayayavanamaṇittha Śaktipûrvaiḥ, by Maya, Yavana, Manittha and Saktipûrva. Maya, the Asura, got the knowledge of Astronomy revealed to him by the God Sûrya himself. Yavana is a foreign Astrologer. Manittha is an Âchârya in Astrology. Śaktipûrva is Parâśara, whose father is Śakti. दिवसकरादिषु Divasakarâdiṣu, to the planets, the Sun, etc. *i.e.*, the Sun, Moon, Mars, Mercury, Jupiter, Venus, and Saturn. वत्सराः Vatsarâḥ, the maximum number of years ordained to the above planets. प्रदिष्टाः Pradiṣṭâḥ, are stated. नवतिथिविषयाश्विभूतरुद्रदशसहिताः Navatithiviṣayâśvibhûtarudradaśasahitâḥ, nine, fifteen, five, two, five, eleven, ten together with. दशभिः Daśabhiḥ, ten. स्वतुंगभेषु Svatuṅgaveṣu, in the exalted degrees of their own signs, respectively.

1. The maximum number of years ordained to an individual by the Sun, Moon, Mars, Mercury, Jupiter, Venus and Saturn, when they are in their exalted degrees, are respectively, nineteen (19), twenty-five (25), fifteen (15), twelve (12), fifteen (15), twenty-one (21), and twenty (20), as stated by Maya, Yavana, Manittha, Śaktipûrva and other Âchâryas on Astrology.

Notes:—There are three systems as to how the length of the human and the other animal lives are determined from the planetary position at the time of birth; these are called Amśâyu, Pindâyu, and Nisargâyu. The author here tries to establish the Amśâyu, rejecting the other two. But as the rules of proportion are clearly shown in the Pindâyu and Nisargâyu systems, the author first explains these and then he deals with the Amśâyu system. These Pindâyu and Nisargâyu systems are advocated by the ancient authors Mayâchârya, Yavanâchârya, Manitthâchârya, Parâśara, the son of Śakti Âchârya and others.

The years ordained by the Sun in his exalted degrees are					...	19
„	„	Moon	„	„	...	25
„	„	Mars	„	„	...	15
„	„	Mercury	„	„	...	12
„	„	Jupiter	„	„	...	15
„	„	Venus	„	„	...	21
„	„	Saturn	„	„	...	20

The exalted signs with the exalted degrees of the several planets are given in stanza 13, Ch. I.

Before the length of life can be ascertained, the years given above have to be subjected to various reductions.

मं०क्रां०—नीचेऽतोऽर्द्धं ह्रसति हि ततश्चांतरस्थेऽनुपातो होरा
त्वंशप्रतिममपरे राशितुल्यं वदंति ॥ हित्वा वक्रं रिपुग्रहगतैर्हीयते
स्वत्रिभागः सूर्योच्छिन्नद्युतिषु च दलं प्रोज्झ्य शुक्रार्कपुत्रौ ॥ २ ॥

नीचे Niche, in their detrimental degrees. When the planets, the Sun, etc. go to their lowest detrimental degrees in their houses of detriment (six signs distant from their exalted degrees). अतः Ataḥ, of this; of the maximum number of years stated before. अर्द्धं Ardham, the half. ह्रसति Hrasati, is diminished. हि Hi, certainly. ततः Tataḥ, then. च Cha, and. अंतरस्थे Aṃtarasthe, situated within (anywhere in the six signs from the exalted to the debilitated house). अनुपातः Anupâtaḥ, according to proportion; according to the Rule of Three. होरा Horâ, the Ascendant, the life granted by the Ascendant. तु Tu, but. अंशप्रतिमम् Aṃśa-pratimam, according to the rule of Navâṃśas, *i.e.*, as many Navâṃśas of the Ascendant have risen above the horizon, so many years, months, etc., are the life granted by the Ascendant. अपरे Apare, others; Maṇittha and men of his school. राशितुल्यं Râśitulyam, equal to the number of signs, *i.e.*, as many signs, degrees, minutes have risen above the horizon, so many years, months, days, etc., are the life granted by the Ascendant. वदंति Vadanti, say. हित्वा Hitvâ, leaving out of account. वक्रं Vakram, the planets while in their retrograde position. रिपुगृहगतैः Ripugṛihagataiḥ, owing to their being in their enemies' houses. हीयते Hîyate, loses. स्वत्रिभागः Svatribhâgaḥ, the third part of its fixed period of life. सूर्योच्छिन्नद्युतिषु Sûryochhinnadyutiṣu, while in the Descendant, when one's lustre is overpowered by that of the Sun, *i. e.*, when one is descending below the horizon. च Cha, and. दलं Dalam, the half. प्रोज्झ्य Projjhya, leaving out of account; not considering. शुक्रार्कपुत्रौ Śukrârkaputrau, Venus and Saturn.

2. The planets, when they run to their lowest detrimental degrees, grant only half the period of life mentioned in the preceding verse; and at places intermediate, grant

the number of years proportionately (1). The number of years granted by the Ascendant is the same as the number of Navâṃśas of the Ascendant that have risen above the horizon (2); according to others (Maṇitṭha and men of his school) it is the same as the number of signs from the beginning of Meṣa to the Ascendant on the horizon (3). When the planets are in their inimical houses, they lose a third of their period save those that are then retrograde (4); the planets descending and when their lustre is obscured by the light of the Sun, lose half their period, except Venus and Saturn.

Notes:—(1) Suppose for instance, Mars to occupy 4^s-9°-0-$0''$ *i.e.* the ninth degree of Siṃha. Required the number of years granted by him to the individual born. The exalted degree of Mars is the 28th degree of Makara and his detrimental degree is the 28th degree of Karka. When in the detrimental degrees, Mars grants half of what he grants in the exalted degrees, *i.e.*, $\frac{1}{2} \times 15 = 7\frac{1}{2}$ years. From the 28th degree of Karka to the 9th degree of Siṃha is 11th degrees. From the 28th degree of Makara to the 28th degree of Karka is 180 degrees. So that every degree gives us $\frac{7\frac{1}{2}}{180}$ years. What will 11 degrees give? 11 degrees give us $11 \times \frac{7\frac{1}{2}}{180} = 5$ months 15 days. Adding this to $7\frac{1}{2}$ years, we get 7 years 11 months and 15 days as the life granted by Mars. The years of the other planets may be similarly ascertained. These years are subject to certain reductions as will be seen further on.

(2) The author gives here what is known as Lagnâyurdáya, *i.e.*, the number of years granted by the rising sign, as if it were another planet. A sign of the Zodiac consists of nine Navâṃśas and therefore gives us 9 years. So that if the 10th degree of Siṃha is rising, the number of years granted by the Ascendant is derived from the following proportion:—

$3^\circ 20' : 10^\circ :: 1$ year : x (number of years granted by the Ascendant)

$\therefore x = \frac{10 + 60}{200} = 3$ years.

(3) In other words each sign of the Zodiac gives a year; so that if the 10th degree of Siṃha, the 5th sign from Meṣa be rising, the number of years given by the Ascendant $= 4\frac{10}{30}$ years $= 4$ years 4 months. The commentator adds that in the case of the life granted by the Ascendant, the rule given in note (2) should be followed, if the rule of the

rising Navâmsa be powerful; and that given in this note should be followed if the ruler of the rising sign be powerful.

(4) The period here referred to is that granted by the planet after being corrected according to note (1).

A planet is said to be descending and his light overpowered by that of the Sun when it is within the degrees from the Sun as per following table :—

Mars	when	within	17	degrees	from the Sun.
Mercury	,,	,,	14	,,	,,
Mercury retrograde	,,	,,	12	,,	,,
Jupiter	,,	,,	11	,,	,,
Venus	,,	,,	10	,,	,,
Venus retrograde	,,	,,	8	,,	,,
Saturn	,,	,,	15	,,	,,
Moon	,,	,,	12	,,	,,

Remarks :—The word *vakra* is used to mean here the planets when retrograde. Some, *e. g.*, Bâdarâyaṇa and others take it to mean the planet Mars, *i e.*, Mars in the inimical house does not lose any number of years. But this view is not favoured by Varâha Mihira.

प्रहर्षिणी—सर्वार्द्धत्रिचरणपंचषष्टभागाः क्षीयंते व्ययभवना-दसत्सु वामम् ॥ सत्स्वर्द्धं ह्रसति तथैकराशिगानामेकोंऽशं हरति बली तथाह सत्यः ॥ ३ ॥

सर्वार्द्धत्रिचरणपंचषष्ठभागाः Sarvârdhatricharaṇapañchaṣaṣṭha bhâgâḥ, the full, the half, the third, the fourth, the fifth, and the sixth part of the life periods. क्षीयंते Kṣîyante, are lost, are diminished. व्ययभवनात् Vyayabhavanât, commencing from the twelfth house, *i.e.*, from the twelfth, eleventh, tenth, ninth, eighth, and seventh houses, respectively. असत्सु Asatsu, of the malefic planets. वामम् Vâmam, counted in the left-hand direction. सत्सु Satsu, of the benefic planets. अर्द्धं Ardham, half of the periods (as stated above with regard to the malefic planets) will be lost. ह्रसति Hrasati, are diminished. तथा Tathâ, similarly (in cases where). एकराशिगानां Ekarâsigânâm, of the planets when they are all situated in one sign. एकोंशं Ekomsam, the portion (*i.e.*, the fractional part) that was previously assigned to one of the planets (that is the most powerful). हरति Harati, disappears, loses. बली Balî, the most powerful. तथा Tathâ, thus. आह Âha, said. सत्यः Satyaḥ, Satyâchârya, the famous Astrologer.

3. Of the malefic planets the whole of their life periods is lost when any of them is situated in the twelfth house ; of the malefic in the eleventh house, half ; in the tenth house, one-third ; in the ninth house, one-fourth, ; in the eighth house, one-fifth ; and in the seventh house, one-sixth of their life periods is lost. Of the benefic planets, they lose half in the twelfth, one-fourth in the eleventh, one-sixth in the tenth house ; one-eighth in the ninth ; one-tenth in the eighth house ; and one-twelfth in the seventh house (*i. e.*, half of the above periods) (1). If many planets exist in one sign, only the most powerful planet loses its due portion as assigned before. Thus says Satyâchârya. (This is also the opinion of Varâha Mihira).

Note :—Where the amount of reduction was stated to be full in the case of a malefic planet, it is only half of that in the case of a benefic planet ; where it was stated to be one-half in the former case, it is only one-fourth in the latter case, and so forth.

व० ति०—सार्द्धोदितोदितनवांशहतात्समस्ताद्भागोऽष्टयुक्त-शतसंख्यमुपैति नाशम् । क्रूरे विलग्नसहिते विधिना त्वनेन सौम्येक्षिते दलमतः प्रलयं प्रयाति ॥ ४ ॥

सार्द्धोदितोदितनवांशहतात् Sârdhoditoditanavâṃśahatât, by multiplying the total number of years already obtained by the number of the Navâṃśas between the commencement of Meṣa and the rising Navâṃśa of the Ascendant. (The rising Navâṃśa though not risen fully is to be taken into account). समस्तात् Samastât, the full life periods, the total number of years granted by all the planets. भागः Bhâgaḥ, divided by. अष्टयुक्तशतसंख्यं Aṣṭayuktaśatasaṃkhyam, one hundred and eight (108) (the total number of Navâṃśas of the Zodiac). उपैति Upaiti, gets. नाशम् Nâśam, removal; decrease ; subtraction. क्रूरे Krûre, any of the malefic planets, Sun, Mars, Saturn (here the waning Moon is not taken into account). विलग्नसहिते Vilagnasahite, when in the Ascendant during the time of birth. विधिना Vidhinâ, by (this) rule. तु Tu but. अनेन Anena, this. सौम्येक्षिते Saumyekṣite, if aspected by benefics. दलम् Dalam, half. अतः Ataḥ, of this. प्रलयं प्रयाति Pralayam prayâti, is lost ; is subtracted.

4. If the Ascendant be occupied by a malefic planet, then multiply the total number of years (of all the planets)

already obtained by the number of Navâṃśas between the beginning of the sign Meṣa and the rising Navâṃśa of the Ascendant (1); divide the product by 108 (the total number of the Navâṃśas in the Zodiac). The quotient will be the number of years to be deducted from the total number of years already obtained. But if a benefic planet aspects the malefic above-mentioned, only one-half of what was stated above is to be deducted.

Notes:—This reduction is a very important one; it is called Sârdhodita reduction or Krûrodayaharaṇa, or the reduction due to the malefic planet being in the Ascendant.

(1) According to some the number of years of reduction is obtained by multiplying the total number of years already obtained by the number of Navâṃśas of the rising sign that have risen above the horizon and dividing the product by 108, the total number of the Navâṃśas of the Zodiac.

When both the benefic and the malefic are in the Ascendant, then the planet that is nearer to the eastern horizon is to be considered and not the others. If the malefic planet is nearer, then correction is to be made; if there be benefic, then no correction is to be made. This is the opinion of the commentator.

Example:—The position of the planets and the Ascendant during the birth time is given in the following table; find how long will the individual live?

Planets.	Sun.	Moon.	Mars.	Mercury.	Jupiter.	Venus.	Saturn.	Ascendant.
Sign ...	0	1	10	11	9	11	0	10
Degree ...	9	2	28	24	4	26	19	0
Minute ...	0	0	0	0	0	0	7	1

Here the first Navâṃśa of the sign Kumbha is the Ascendant. The Sun, the Moon, and Venus occupy the exalted degrees; Mercury, Jupiter and Saturn occupy their debilitated degrees and Mars occupies the 28th degree of the sign Kumbha.

Now as the Sun, the Moon and Venus are in their exalted degrees, their years are respectively 19, 25, and 21; and as Mercury, Jupiter and Saturn occupy their debilitated degrees, their years are one-half of their maximum years, *i.e.*, one-half of 12, 15 and 20 or 6, 7½, and 10 respectively. Now the 28th degree of the sign Makara is the exalted degree of Mars, and as he occupies the 28th degree of Kumbha, he is removed from the exalted degree by exactly 30 degrees. His maximum number of years when in the 28th degree of Makara being 15 ; 30 degrees or a sign gives us $\frac{15}{2} \times \frac{1}{6}$ or 1 year 3 months. Subtracting this from 15 years we get 13 years and 9 months as the years of Mars. As the Ascendant Kumbha was just rising, it gives us no years ; so that, at this stage, the planetary years stand as follows :—

The Sun—19 years.	**Mercury—6 years.**
Moon—25 years.	**Jupiter—7 years 6 months.**
Venus—21 years.	**Saturn—10 years.**

and Mars 13 years 9 months. Now as Jupiter, a benefic planet, occupies the 12th house from the Ascendant, his years suffer a reduction of one-half of their length ; so that after the reduction he gives us only 3 years and 9 months ; again, as all the planets occupy friendly signs, no reductions for enemies' houses need be made. Saturn being within 10 degrees from the Sun is a Descending planet and therefore his years suffer no reduction. So that Saturn gives us 10 years. Thus we have the following :—

The Sun—19 years.	**Jupiter—3 years 9 months.**
Moon—25 years.	**Saturn—10 years.**
Venus—21 years.	**Mars—13 years 9 months.**
Mercury—6 years.	
Total	**98 years 6 months.**

Now as Mars, a malefic planet, occupies the rising sign, the total number of 98 years and 6 months have to be subjected to a reduction known as malefic planet's rising reduction. In other words, the 108 Navâṃśas of the ecliptic represent the total number of years. Now there are $10 \times 9 + 1 = 91$ Navâṃśas between the first point of Meṣa and the last point of the rising Navâṃśa of Kumbha. The quantity of reduction therefore is $\frac{91}{108} \times 98\frac{1}{2}$. Therefore the years remaining after the reduction$=\frac{17}{108} \times \frac{197}{2}=$ 15 years 6 months and 10 days = the length of life required. (This is evidently less than 20 years).

Remarks.—When any number of degrees, minutes are to be converted into the number of Navâṃśas, reduce to minutes and divide by 200 (the number of minutes in the Navâṃśa 3°20′). The result of division will give the number of Navâṃśas.

This reduction system that has been applied to the number of years of all the planets, is to be applied to the number of years of each planet to get the corrected number of years granted by each planet.

शिखरिणी—समाषष्टिर्द्विघ्ना मनुजकरिणां पंच च निशा हयानां द्वात्रिंशित्खरकरभयोः पंचकृतिः। विरूपा साऽप्यायुर्वृष-महिषयोर्द्वादशशुनां स्मृतं छागादीनां दशकसहिताः षट् च परमम् ॥ ५ ॥

समाषष्टिः Samâsastih, sixty years. द्विघ्ना Dvighnâ, doubled. मनुजकरिणां Manuja-karinâm, of men and elephants. पंच च निशा Pañcha cha niśâ, five days more. हयानां Hayânâm, of horses. द्वात्रिंशत् Dvâtrimśat, thirty-two. खरकरभयोः Kharakarabhayoh, of asses and camels. पंचकृतिः Pañchakakritih, five square, *i.e.*, twenty-five. विरूपा Virûpâ, diminished by one. सा Sâ, that, *i.e.*, the number twenty-five. अपि Api, also. आयुः Âyuh, life. वृषमहिषयोः Vrisamahisayoh, of bullocks and buffaloes. द्वादश शुनां Dvâdaśa śunâm, twelve years of dogs and others having claws, *e.g.*, lions, cats, &c. छागादीनां Chhâgâdinâm, of goats etc. (deer and other animals like these). दशकसहिताः Daśakasahitâh, plus ten ; added to ten. षट् Sat, six. च Cha, and. परमम् Paramam, the maximum longevity ; the maximum length of life that is possible.

5. Now the maximum lengths of lives of different creatures are being stated :—Men and elephants live highest up to 120 years and 5 days ; horses, thirty-two years ; camels and asses, twenty-five years ; bullocks and buffaloes, twenty-four years ; dogs (and animals with claws), twelve years ; goats, rams and deer etc., sixteen years.

N.B.—These animals seldom live to such an extent. These figures are mentioned for the sake of calculation. Whatever calculations are done with regard to men, their highest lives being taken as 120 years 5 days, the same calculations are to be done with regard to the lives of other animals by Rule of Three thus :—if 120 years 5 days represent so many for men, what will 32 years represent for horses ; and so on.

पुष्पिताग्रा—अनिमिषपरमांशके विलग्ने शशितनये गवि पंचवर्गलिप्ते। भवति हि परमायुषः प्रमाणं यदि सकलाः सहिताः स्वतुंगभेषु ॥ ६ ॥

अनिमिषपरमांशके Animisaparamâmśake, the ninth (last) Navâmśa of the sign Mîna (the Pisces). विलग्ने Vilagne, being the Ascendant at birth time. शशितनये Saśitanaye, Mercury. गवि Gavi, in the sign Vrisa. पंचवर्गलिप्ते Pañchavargalipte, twenty-five minutes. भवति Bhavati, comes out. हि Hi, certainly. परमायुषः Paramâ-yusah, full life ; highest longevity. प्रमाणं Pramânam, measure. यदि Yadi, if,

सकलः: Sakalaḥ, all the planets. सहिताः: Sahitâḥ, are found together with ; exist in. स्वतुंगगेषु Svataṃgaveṣu, their highest exaltation degree ; in their exalted signs.

6. The person born under the ninth Navâṃśa of the sign Mîna (the Pisces) as the Ascendant, when Mercury is situated within the twenty-fifth minute of the sign Vṛiṣa, and when all the remaining planets are in their exalted houses, attains the maximum length of life, *i.e.*, lives up to 120 years and 5 days.

Note.—The planetary positions are shewn here under which a man born attains the maximum life, *i.e.*, 120 years and 5 months. How this is obtained is shewn in the following :—

Planets.	Sun.	Moon.	Mars.	Mercury.	Jupiter.	Venus.	Saturn.	Ascendant.
Sign ...	0	1	9	1	3	11	6	11
Degrees ...	9	2	27	0	4	26	19	29
Minutes ...	0	0	0	25	0	0	0	59

The positions of the planets, the Sun etc. and the Ascendant are shewn in the above table. All of them are in their highly exalted degrees except Mercury. Now to find the life of Mercury :—

	s	°	′	″
Mercury's position	1	0	25	0
Mercury's detrimental degrees	11	15	0	0
Difference	1	15	25	0

=2725 minutes.

Now by Rule of Proportion,

$$\overset{s}{6} : 2725' :: \overset{\text{years.}}{6} : x$$

or $10800' : 2725' :: 6 : x$

or x = 1 year 6 months 5 days.

This is to be added to the minimum life of Mercury, six years. We get, then, 7 years 6 months 5 days as the life of Murcury.

Now a reduction known as Chakrapâtaharaṇa is to be made from the years of Mars and Saturn, these two malefic planets occupying respectively the 11th and the 8th houses from the Ascendant.

Thus :—Mars being in the eleventh house from the Ascendant, half of his full life 15 years is lost (see verse 3).

∴ The life of Mars = 7 years 6 months.

Saturn being in the eighth house, one-fifth of its life is lost.

∴ the life of Saturn = 16 years.

The life of the Ascendant in years equals the number of the Navâṃśas, *i.e.*, = 9 years.

Now sum up the lives of all :—

		Years	months	days.
Sun	... ...	19	0	0
Moon	... ...	25	0	0
Mars	... ...	7	6	0
Mercury	... ...	7	6	5
Jupiter	... ...	15	0	0
Venus	... ...	21	0	0
Saturn	... ...	16	0	0
Lagna	... ...	9	0	0
Total	...	120	0	5, the highest life that a human being can attain.

Here the corrections due to enemies' houses (Śatrukṣetraharaṇa) Descending planets, (Aṣṭangataharaṇa) and malefic planet rising reductions (Krûodayaharaṇa) are not to be made.

It should be noted here that Mercury cannot exist in the sign Kanyâ, its exalted house. For Mercury is seen close to the Sun ; hence its position is assumed in the twenty-five minutes of the sign Vṛiṣa.

If Mercury's position be 1-4-0-0, then following the above calculations we get 7 years 7 months 18 days as the life of Mercury. In this case the highest life comes to 120 years 1 month 23 days.

Some authors say that all the planets are to be taken in their highly exalted degrees: but this cannot be possible.

Remarks :—Some authors urge that the Moon occupies the Venus' house (Vṛiṣa); Moon being the enemy of Venus, ⅓ reduction is to be made from the life of the Moon. Thus the maximum longevity is not attained. Venus is not also the then friend of Moon. This is one defect in the Piṇḍâyu system. This is not valid ; as the houses occupied are certainly friendly.

शालिनी—आयुर्दायं विष्णुगुप्तोऽपि चैवं देवस्वामी सिद्धसेनश्च चक्रे। दोषश्चैषां जायतेऽष्टावरिष्टं हित्वा नायुर्विंशतेः स्यादधस्तात् ॥ ७ ॥

आयुर्दायं Âyurdâyam, this sum total longevity called Piṇḍâyu; This Piṇḍâyurdâya method. विष्णुगुप्तः Viṣṇuguptaḥ, the author Visṇugupta. अपि Api, also. च एवं Cha evam, also in this way. देवस्वामी Devasvâmî, Devasvâmî. सिद्धसेनः Siddhasenaḥ, Siddhasena. च Cha, and. चक्रे Chakre, did; had given out as their opinions. दोषः Doṣaḥ, the fault, error, or discrepancy. च Cha, and. एषां Eṣâm, in this system adopted by these authors. जायते Jâyate, comes out. अष्टावरिष्टं Aṣṭâvariṣṭam, eight years from birth mentioned as the period within which death is forecast of the children. हित्वा Hitvâ, avoiding; rejecting. न Na, not. आयुर्विंशतेः Âyurviṃśateḥ, twenty years as the life period. स्यात् Syât, come out. अधस्तात् Adhastât, below.

7. This maximum length of life is also determined similarly by Viṣṇugupta, Devasvâmî and Siddhasena. The main defect in this system of Piṇḍâyu is that it does not give us in any case years less than 20; the age up to eight, the period of early death being not here taken into account (as none of the Âyurdâya rules are applicable to early death).

Note.—The author here and in the next stanza shows the defect of this Piṇḍâyu system.

The commentator, however, considers that this verse is interpolated; it is not of Varâha Mihira; the commentator shows by example that the Piṇḍâyurdâya does give years below 20. He takes the following horoscope. The first Navâṃśa of Kumbha is the Ascendant. The Sun, Moon and Venus occupy their exaltation degrees; Mercury, Jupiter and Saturn occupy their debilitated degrees and Mars occupies the 28th degree of sign Kumbha.

Mîna Venus, Mercury.	Sun, Meṣa, Saturn.	Vṛiṣa, Moon,	Mithuna.
Kumbha Mars *Lagna.*	Râśi Chakra.		Karka.
Makara Jupiter.			Siṃha.
Dhanu.	Vṛiśchika.	Tulâ.	Kanyâ.

The life of the individual born under this horoscope comes out as 15 years 6 months and 10 days. *Vide* the example worked out under verse 4 of this Chapter. Others argue in the following way against this method of getting the life of an individual as 15 years 6 months and 10 days. It is not proper to put Mars, a malefic planet, in the Ascendant; putting a malefic planet in the Ascendant means reducing the life of an individual to an enormous extent. The object of Varâha Mihira is not so. When he takes for his example, the Mîna sign as the Ascendant in the horoscope given under verse 6, he has taken it without any malefic accompanying it. So you must omit also the malefic planet (Mars) in your example: then the number of years does not come below twenty. Other authors have taken the following horoscope where many planets are in their detrimental houses.

Planets.	Sun.	Moon.	Mars.	Mercury.	Jupitor.	Venus.	Saturn.	Ascendant.
Sign	6	7	3	5	0	5	0	8
Degrees.	9	2	27	20	8	26	19	0

We get the planetary years after all the reductions are done thus:—

Sun	4 years	9 months.
Moon	0 "	0 "
Mars	6 "	0 "
Mercury	5 "	11 "
Jupiter	7 "	6 "
Venus	8 "	9 "
Saturn	10 "	0 "
Lagna	0 "	0 "
The total number ...	42 years	11 months.

Taking all the possible features against the circumstances, when the life of an individual comes to the lowest, we do not get twenty years at the lowest, as mentioned in verse 7 but somewhat more than thirty.

There is another fault of the verse 7. How is the number twenty obtained? Again suppose we get the number twenty as the lowest term of life by the Piṇḍâyu method; now it is very easy to account for the death of persons between the age 8 and between the age 20. There are certain Mṛityu yogas (Planetary combinations on death) when the planets cause death in their Daśâ period or Antardaśâ period as written by Bâdarâyaṇa, which may come any time between the age 8 and between the age 20.

Hence taking all the circumstances into account the commentator thinks that this verse 7 is not written by Varâha Mihira but interpolated here.

शालिनी—यस्मिन्योगे पूर्णमायुः प्रदिष्टं तस्मिन्प्रोक्तं चक्रवर्तित्वमन्यैः। प्रत्यक्षोऽयं तेषु दोषः परोऽपि जीवत्यायुः पूर्णमर्थैर्विनापि ॥ ८ ॥

यस्मिन् Yasmin, in whatever. योगे Yoge, planetary positions. पूर्णम् Pûrṇam, full, highest, maximum. आयुः Âyuḥ, life. प्रदिष्टं Pradiṣṭam, has been ordained; has been declared. तस्मिन् Tasmin, in the very same (planetary positions). प्रोक्तं Proktam, said. चक्रवर्तित्वम् Chakravartitvam, sovereignty, the life of a king. अन्यैः Anyaiḥ, by other authors, *e.g.*, Bâdarâyaṇa and Yavaneśwara. प्रत्यक्षः Pratyakṣaḥ, evident. अयं Ayam, this. तेषु Teṣu, in them. दोषः Doṣaḥ, fault, fallacy, defect in reasoning. परः Paraḥ, others. अपि Api, also. जीवति Jîvati, live. आयुःपूर्णं Âyuḥ Pûrṇam, the maximum period in their lives. अर्थैः Arthaiḥ, wealth. विना Vina, without. अपि Api, also.

8. The planetary positions under which the maximum longevity is said to be attained are the very positions, other authors say, under which a kingdom is attained. Now many persons live to the maximum periods without having any wealth. This then is the defect on the very face of the Piṇḍâu system.

Note:—Look to the horoscope given under verse 6 of this Chapter You will find there six planets exalted. Now Bâdarâyaṇa says :—When six planets are exalted, the individual born becomes the ruler of the three worlds. Now we see many persons living the maximum life and therefore in their horoscope six planets must have been exalted; *i. e.*, they should have obtained kingdom; but they are poor. This is then the second fallacy in this Piṇḍâyu system. This objection is not valid since, the commentator thinks, one set of planetary combinations can give a very long life, though not necessarily giving rulership over a vast dominion. The following horoscope is discussed here :—

Planets.	Sun.	Moon.	Mars	Mercury.	Jupiter.	Venus.	Saturn.	Lagna.
Sign ..	1	2	10	0	4	0	10	8
Degrees ...	10	8	28	15	5	27	20	29
Minutes ...	...	...	...	...	...	20	...	59

The planetary years after the first correction are :—

Sun ...	17 years	5 months.	
Moon ...	22 „	11 „	
Mars ...	13 „	9 „	
Mercury ...	7 „	0 „	
Jupiter ...	13 „	9 „	

	Years.	months.	days.	ghaṭis.
Venus ...	19	2	26	30
Saturn ...	13	4	0	0
Lagna ...	9	0	0	0

Now the other corrections :—

Jupiter in the 9th house from the Ascendant; a reduction of ⅛th the number of years is to be made. Therefore the number of Jupiter's years = 12 years 0 months. 11 days 15 ghaṭis.

Moon being in the 7th house from the Ascendant, ⅙ reduction is to be made. Therefore the number of years for the Moon = 19 years 1 month 5 days. No other corrections need be made here. For Jupiter is Sun's friend; Venus is for the time being friendly, due to its being situated in the Mûla Trikoṇa house; Mars is in the enemy's house (*i.e.*, of Saturn); but being retrograde, no reductions are made and because it is Mars, therefore it is exempted. Mercury is the friend of Jupiter. The Sun is also the friend of Jupiter. Venus is also in the ally's house; for Venus is the friend of Mars. Saturn is in Kumbha, in his own house.

Thus, after all the necessary corrections being made, we get the planetary years as follows :

	Years.	months.	days.	ghaṭis.
Sun	17	5	0	0
Moon	19	1	5	0
Mars	13	9	0	0
Mercury	7	0	0	0
Jupiter	12	0	11	15
Venus	19	2	26	30
Saturn	13	4	0	0
Lagna	9	0	0	0
The total No. of years ...	110	10	12	45

Thus we see that we get in this planetary combination a very long life. But there is Kemadruma Yoga here. (The Kemadruma Yoga will be discussed afterwards in the Nâbhasa yoga Chapter). Those born under Kemadruma Yoga become poor, miserable, mean and doing servile works even if they belong to the royal family. Therefore, the commentator thinks that the seventh and eighth stanzas are not of Varâha Mihira; they are interpolated.

Some may think that this Kemadruma Yoga is not applicable, because the Moon is occupying the angular house; not so; for the Moon is counted with the Ascendant; it is not counted separately. The Moon awards results with the Ascendant; she cannot give a separate result; similarly the Moon cannot give a separate result, due to her being placed in the seventh house from the Ascendant.

उपच्छंदसिका–स्वमतेन किलाह जीवशर्मा ग्रहदायं परमायुषः स्वरांशम् । ग्रहभुक्तनवांशराशितुल्यं बहुसाम्यं समुपैति सत्यवाक्यम् ॥ ९ ॥

स्वमतेन Svamatena, according to his own authority, not according to others' opinions. किल Kila, certainly. आह Âha, said. जीवशर्मा Jîvaśarmâ, the author Jîvaśarmâ. ग्रहदायं Grahadâyam, the life period granted by a planet. परमायुषः Paramâyuṣaḥ, of the maximum length of life, *i. e.*, 120 years 5 days. स्वरांशम् Svarâmśám, one-seventh part. ग्रहभुक्तनवांशराशितुल्यं Grahabhuktanavâmśarâśitulyam, number of years, months the &c., granted by any planet being the same as the number of Navâmśas passed over by that planet from Meṣa Navâmśa up to the planet. बहुसाम्यं Bahusâmyam, the opinions of many Âchâryas. समुपैति Samupaiti, receives the favor of. सत्यवाक्यम् Satyavâkyam, the opinion of Satyâchârya.

9. Jîvâ Śarmâ expresses his opinion that one-seventh of the maximum period of human life (120 years 5 days ÷7=17 years 1 month 22 days 8 ghaṭis, and 34 palas) is the maximum number of years for each planet when in his exalted degrees (1). Satyâchârya holds that the number of years granted by any planet is the same as the number of Navâmśas passed over by that planet from the Meṣa Navâmśa. (2). Satya's view is approved by many authorities.

Notes:—(1) According to Jivaśarmâ the planets, when debilitated, grant half of 17 years 1 month 22 days, 8 ghaṭis and 34 palas. The number of years in the intermediate houses is to be obtained by proportion as shewn in the Piṇḍâyu method.

The other reductions, (*i.e.*, the (1) Śatrukṣetraharaṇa reduction, (2) the Chakrapâtaharaṇa reduction, (3) the Krûrodayaharaṇa reduction, (4) the Aṣṭaṅgataharaṇa reduction), are to be made also as before and then the resulting length of life ascertained. Jiva Śarmâ is not supported by any other Âchârya.

(2 Count from the Meṣa Navâmśa immediately preceding; so that no planet can give more than 12 years. Here the Amśâyu method to ascertain the longevity of any individual is being described. Find out the Navâmśa where any planet (whose life is to be determined) is situated. The whole number of Navâmśas will give the number of years and the fractional part will give the number of months, days and ghaṭis of the planet under question. *e.g.*, The longitude of a planet is 7 signs 25 degrees 10 minutes and 0 seconds. Here leave the signs and take the

degrees, minutes and seconds into account. Of 25° 10′ 0″, the planet has passed the seventh Navâṃśa and is in the eighth Navâṃśa, (each Navâṃśa = 3° 20′). The seven Navâṃśas (23° 20′) give 7 years. The remainder 1° 50′ = 110 minutes; divide it by 200 (the number of minutes in one Navâṃśa); we will get $\frac{11}{20}$ year = 6 months, 18 days. Adding this to 7 years, we get 7 years 6 months and 18 days as the planetary life. See the next stanza and its notes.

आर्या—सत्योक्ते ग्रहमिष्टं लिप्तीकृत्वा शतद्वयेनाप्तम् ।
मंडलभागविशुद्धेऽब्दाः स्युः शेषात्तु मासाद्याः ॥ १० ॥

सत्योक्ते Satyokte, in the method enunciated by Satyâchârya (in the preceding verse). ग्रहम् Graham, the longitude of the planet whose years are to be determined. इष्टं Iṣṭam, desired; under question. लिप्तीकृत्वा Liptîkṛitvâ, converting into minutes. शतद्वयेन Śatadvyaena, by two hundred. आप्तं Âptam, what is obtained by division. मंडलभागविशुद्धे Maṇḍalabhâgaviśuddhe, divided by twelve. अब्दाः Abdâḥ, the number of years (granted by the planet). स्युः Syuḥ, become. शेषात् Śeṣât, from the remainder. तु Tu, also. मासाद्याः Mâsâdyâḥ, months, days, etc.

10. According to Satyâchârya, convert the Sphuṭa or the longitude of the planet into minutes; divide the number of minutes by 200; the quotient will represent the number of Navâṃśas passed over by the planet from the first point of the sign Meṣa. Divide this by 12; the remainder will give the number of Navâṃśas from the Navâṃśa of Aries; this number is the number of years and fraction of a year granted by the planet.

Note.—Suppose the longitude of the Sun to be 115 degrees 13 minutes. This converted into minutes gives 6,913 minutes. Now as a Navâṃśa contains 200 minutes, the number of Navâṃśas passed over by the Sun from the first point of Meṣa $= \frac{6913}{200} = 34\frac{113}{200}$. Dividing, this by 12, we get as remainder 10 $\frac{113}{200}$ Navâṃśas from the next preceding Navâṃśa of Meṣa. This then represents the years of the Sun which will be found to be 10 years 6 months 23 days and 24 ghaṭis; and so on for each planet.

This is the opinion of Varâha Mihra, Yavaneśwara, Satyâchârya, Bâdarâyaṇa, and many other famous astrologers. This is called the Aṃśâyu Method.

वंशस्थ—स्वतुंगवक्रोपगतैस्त्रिसंगुणं द्विरुत्तमस्वांशकभत्रिभागगैः । इयान्विशेषस्तु भदत्तभाषिते समानमन्यत्प्रथमेऽप्युदीरितम् ॥ ११ ॥

स्वतुंगवक्रोपगतैः Svatuṃgavakropagataiḥ, when situated in one's highly exalted degrees, or when in one's retrograde position. त्रिसंगुणं Trisaṃguṇam, the planetary years of the previous verse multiplied by three; thrice. द्विः Dviḥ, twice. उत्तमस्वांशकभत्रिभागगैः Uttamasvâṃśakabhatribhâgagaiḥ, when situated in their own Vargottam Navâṃśas, their own houses, their own Dreṣkâṇas. इयान् Iyân, this. विशेषः Viśeṣaḥ, particularity; point of difference, special feature. तु Tu, but. भदत्तभाषिते Bhadattabhâṣite, according to the statement of Satyâchârya. समानम् Samânam, equal; the same. अन्यत् Anyat, the others (*i.e.*, the other reductions). प्रथमे Prathame, before; according to the opinion of Maya and Yavana, etc. अपि Api, also. उदीरितम् Udîritam, said (in the Piṇḍâyu method.)

11. Again the planets, when highly exalted or retrograde, give thrice the number of years (obtained in the Aṃśâyu method in the preceding stanzas) as their periods; and when in their own Vargottamas, or own Navâṃśas, or own houses, or in their Decanates, give twice the number of years (assigned in the preceding stanza) as their periods. This is the special feature in Satyâchâryaś Aṃśâyu method. In other respects it is the same as the Piṇḍâyurdâya [*i.e.*, the several reductions (1) stated before are to be made here also].

Note:—(1) The reduction known as due to the malefic planets being in the Ascendant (Krûrodayaharaṇa) does not apply to Satyâchârya's method (*vide* stanza 12).

इ०व०–किं त्वत्र भांशप्रतिमं ददाति वीर्यान्विता राशिसमं च होरा । क्रूरोदये चोपचयः स नात्र कार्यं च नाब्दैः प्रथमोपदिष्टैः ॥ १२ ॥

किम् Kim, now. तु Tu, but. अत्र Atra, in this method of finding out the life period granted by planets according to Satyâchârya. भांशप्रतिमं Bhâṃśapratimam, the number of years corresponding to the number of Navâṃśas of the Lagna or Ascendant that have risen above the horizon (calculated from the sign Meṣa). ददाति Dadâti, grants. वीर्यान्विता Vîryânvitâ, very powerful; *i.e.*, if aspected by the ruler of the Ascendant, Jupiter, and Mercury or united with them. राशिसमं Râśisamam, number of years corresponding to the number of signs. च Cha, and. होरा Horâ, the Ascendant. क्रूरोदये Krûrodaye, any evil planet being in the Ascendant. च Cha, and. उपचयः Upachayaḥ, increase; addition (here reduction is referred). स Sa, that; reducing, diminishing. न Na, not. अत्र Atra, in this Satyâchârya's method. कार्यं Kâryam, done. च Cha, also. न Na, not. अब्दैः Abdaiḥ, the years (not being subjected to several reductions). प्रथमोपदिष्टैः Prathamopadiṣṭaiḥ, as before stated in the 1st stanza of this Chapter.

12. Now the life period granted by the Ascendant is being stated according to Satyâchârya's method. If the Ascendant be very strong (on being aspected by its own ruler, Jupiter or Mercury) then it grants so many years as the number of signs that have been passed over from the 1st sign Meṣa, and the months, etc., obtained by the number of Navâṃśas (1). Here if any evil planet be in the Ascendant, no reduction on that account is to be made as had been done in previous cases by the rule Krûrodayaharaṇa in verse 4. The years stated in the first stanza of this Chapter ought not also to be used in other reductions (2).

Notes :—(1) If the rising sign be not powerful, then the number of years, months, etc., is obtained from the number of Navâṃśas of the Ascendant that have risen above the horizon.

(2) Satyâchârya's special years (*vide* stanzas 10, 11) are to be subjected to several reductions.

इ०व०—सत्योपदेशो वरमत्र किन्तु कुर्वन्त्ययोग्यं बहुवर्गणाभिः। आचार्यकत्वं च बहुघ्नतायामेकं तु यद्भूरि तदेव कार्यम् ॥ १३ ॥

सत्योपदेश: Satyopadeśaḥ, Satyâchârya's directions. वरम् Varam, very good ; excellent ; the best of all the three Aṃsâya, Piṇḍâyu and Nisargâyu methods. अत्र Atra, amongst these (three) opinions. किन्तु Kintu, but. कुर्वन्ति Kurvanti, make. अयोग्यं Ayogyam, unworthy ; not fit for acceptance. बहुवर्गणाभि: Bahuvargaṇâbhiḥ, on account of many multiplications. आचार्यकत्वं Âchâryakatvam, the Âchârya's opinion being. च Cha, and. बहुघ्नतायाम् Bahughnatâyâm, in cases of many multiplications. एकं Ekam, once. तु Tu, but. यत् Yat, what. भूरि Bhûri, the highest ; the greatest. तदेव Tadeva, that indeed. कार्यम् Kâryam, is to be done.

13. Amongst these three opinions, that of Satyâchârya is the best ; but the fault of Satyâchârya's method is that it involves many (1) multiplications. (If any planet be in its own house, multiply the planetary years by two ; if that planet be in its own Navâṃśa, multiply the planetary years again by two ; if that planet be in its own Dreṣkâṇa, multiply again by two ; if that planet be in its own Vargottama, multiply again by two ; if that planet be retrograde

or be in its highly exalted degrees, multiply by three; and so on. These cases are settled by the statement in the second half of this verse). This is not so:—In cases of multiplications by several numbers, only one is to be made, that by the highest number. This is also the opinion of Âchârya. (Where many multiplications by two are advised, only one is to be done; where multiplications by two, three are, advised, only multiplication by three is to be made. Similarly where subtractions (2) or divisions are to be made many times; only one is to be done, that which is the highest; *i. e.*, where half, or one-third is to be taken, only one-half is to be taken. In some cases, multiplications, divisions are both advised. In these cases first make the highest division and then make the highest multiplication). (2)

Notes:—(1) Suppose Mercury to occupy the sign Kanyâ, which is his exalted as well as own house. It would seem that under stanza 11 Mercury's years should first be trebled and then doubled. Is this to be done? Again suppose Mercury to occupy the last Navâṃśa of the sign Kanyâ, which is his Vargottama position. His years, it would appear, have to be doubled on that account. Already we found that, for being in his house, his years had to be doubled. The question is, whether the years of Mercury have to be doubled twice. Again, suppose Mercury while occupying the Kanyâ, his exaltation sign, is also retrograde in his motion for which his years have to be trebled. Are his years then to be trebled twice? No.

If any period has to be doubled twice or thrice, it will be enough if it be doubled but once, and where the period has to be trebled twice or thrice, it will be enough if it be trebled but once. Again, if any period has to be both doubled and trebled, it will be enough if it be only trebled.

(2) When a planet is in one's enemy's houses, in the detrimental house, and in the Descending houses, only once the subtraction is to be performed. If there be Chakrapâtaharaṇa also, that is to be made first; and then only one other subtraction is to be made.

Remarks:—Though the author Varâha Mihira is in favour of this Aṃśâyu system, still where the Ascendant is very powerful, the Aṃśâyu method is adopted; and where the Sun is very powerful, there Piṇḍâyu method is adopted. This is the opinion of Manittha and Sârâvalî. Others say the calculations should be made on both the systems; and the Daśâs and the Antardaśâs determined. The commentator prefers the Satyâchârya's method.

पुष्पिताग्रा—गुरुशशिसहिते कुलीरलग्ने शशितनये भृगुजे च केन्द्रयाते। भवरिपुसहजोपगैश्च शेषैरमितमिहायुरनुक्रमाद्विना स्यात् ॥ १४ ॥

इति श्रीवराहमिहिराचार्यप्रणीते बृहज्जातके आयुर्दायाध्यायः सप्तमः ॥ ७ ॥

गुरुशशिसहिते Guruśaśisahite, with Jupiter and Moon. कुलीरलग्ने Kulîralagne, the Ascendant being the sign Karka (Cancer). शशितनये Śaśitanaye, Mercury. भृगुजे Bhṛiguje, Venus. च Cha, and. केन्द्रयाते Kendrayâte, in the angles. भवरिपुसहजोपगैः Bhavaripusahajopagaiḥ, situated in the eleventh, sixth, and third houses. शेषैः Śeṣaiḥ, the remainder; Sun, Mars and Saturn. अमितम् Amitam, not capable of being measured; far exceeding the maximum period of normal human existence. इह Iha, in this world; आयुः Âyuḥ, life. अनुक्रमात् Anukramât, from all the calculations (as stated above). विना Vinâ, without. स्यात् Syât, comes out to be.

14. (Now the planetary combination is being described where the period of life cannot be ascertained by calculations) Jupiter and Moon in the Ascendant Karka; Venus and Mercury in the angles; Sun, Mars, Saturn in the eleventh, sixth and third houses respectively or all in any of them. In this case no calculations can be made. The life of such a man far exceeds the maximum period of normal human existence.

Note:—In other words, the ordinary, Âyurdâya rules for ascertaining the length of a man's life do not apply to the horoscope mentioned in this last stanza.

The whole period of life got by calculations in this chapter is actually seen in cases where the individual lives according to the Śâstric rules and rites. But if the individual lives an immoral, unclean life, this period gets diminished. This is also stated in the Vedas.

End of Chapter VII on Âyurdâya or the length of life of any individual.

Remarks:—The division of life into Daśâs as given by the author is hardly studied by the Indian astrologers, evidently from the difficulties in its application. These astrologers, as a class, employ the exceedingly simple division of life into what is known as Uḍu or Nakṣatra Daśâs. These Nakṣatra Daśâs are again divided under three separate headings:—(1) Triṃśottarî Daśâ, (2) Viṃśottarî Daśâ, and (3) Aṣṭottarî Daśâ. The triṃśottarî Daśâ method is rarely used; the Viṃśottarî system is prevalent in the Deccan and the United Provinces; and the Aṣṭottarî system is prevalent in Bengal. The Viṃśottarî system is now-a-days finding its way in Bengal too.

We will dwell first on the Viṃśottarî system and then on the Aṣṭottarî system.

The Viṃśottarî system:—According to this system the maximum period of human life is 120 years. This period is divided into 9 parts presided over by the seven planets and by Râhu and Ketu, the Ascending and the Descending Nodes of the Moon. They come in the following order and their years are also given below:—

(1) The Sun ...	6 years.	(5) Jupiter ...	16 years.
(2) The Moon ...	10 years.	(6) Saturn ...	19 years.
(3) Mars ...	7 years.	(7) Mercury ...	17 years.
(4) Râhu ...	18 years.	(8) Ketu ...	7 years.

(9) Venus——20 years.

The ruler of the Daśâ period at the time of birth is ascertained from the Nakṣatra which the Moon occupies at that time. If, therefore, at the time of birth, the Moon occupies one of the three asterisms Kṛittikâ, U. Phalguni, and U. Âṣâḍhâ, the Daśâ period is that of the Sun.

Rohiṇî, Hastâ, and Śravaṇâ	... Moon.
Mṛigaśirâ, Chitrâ and Dhaniṣṭhâ	... Mars.
Ârdrâ, Śvâtî and Śatabhiṣâ	... Râhu.
Punarvasu, Viśâkhâ, and P. Bhâdrapada	... Jupiter.
Puṣyâ, Anurâdhâ, and U. Bhâdrapada	... Saturn.
Aśleṣâ, Jyeṣṭhâ, and Revatî	... Mercury.
Aśvinî, Maghâ, and Mûlâ	... Ketu.
Bharaṇî, P. Phalgunî, and P. Âṣâḍhâ	... Venus.

How much of the period of a particular Daśâ has elapsed and how much remains at the time of birth must be ascertained from the portion of the Nakṣatra passed over by the Moon and the portion remaining at the time. This may be roughly ascertained from the time taken by the Moon to go over the *portion* of the Nakṣatra, the whole time in which the Moon passes through a particular Nakṣatra (as given in the calendar) representing the full period of a Daśâ; suppose an individual is born under the Uttara Phalgunî Nakṣatra and suppose the Moon to take 65 daṇḍas 18 palas and 2 vipalas to go over the Nakṣatra Uttara Phalguni and she has already passed over a part of the Nakṣatra denoted by 44 daṇḍas 28 palas and 32 vipalas when the individual was born, required the Daśâ period remaining at the time of birth to be enjoyed by the native. The Daśâ is here that of the Sun, the Nakṣatra being U. Phalgunî.

Now the time in which the Moon will go over the remaining portion of the Uttara Phalgunî Nakṣatra = (65 daṇḍas 18 palas and 2 vipalas)—(44 daṇḍas 28 palas and 32 vipalas) = 20 daṇḍas 43 palas and 30 vipalas.

65 daṇḍas 18 palas and 2 vipalas represent the whole period, *i. e.*, 6 years of the Sun; what will 20d. 43p. 30v. represent?

Therefore the Daśâ period of the

Sun to be enjoyed by the individual $= \frac{6 \text{ years}}{65\text{d. } 18\text{p. } 2\text{v.}} \times$ 20d. 43p. 30v.

= 1 year 10 months and 25 days.

To this must be added in the order stated above, the Daśâ periods of the Moon, Mars, Râhu, &c., till the whole life period granted by the planets is reached, *i.e.*, up to the Daśâ of that planet when the individual's death will occur. The fruits of these Daśâs then will be written in the horoscope.

Again, the nine Daśâ periods are each divided into 9 sub-divisions known as Antardaśâs, the ruler of the first Daśâ being the ruler of the Daśâ period and the rulers of the Antardaśâs which follow are the same as the rulers of the Daśâ periods which follow; so that the Antardaśâs of the Daśâ period of the Moon are those of the Moon, Mars, Râhu, Jupiter, Saturn, Mercury, Ketu, Venus and the Sun. The length or duration of the Antardaśâ periods bears the same proportion to each other as the lengths of the Daśâ periods. For instance, required the length of the Antardaśâ period of the Moon in the Daśâ period of the Sun. The Daśâ period of the Moon is 10 years and the Daśâ period of the Sun is 6 years; that of all the planets is 120 years; then make the proportion :—The maximum life 120 years, give 10 years as the Daśâ of the Moon; what will 6 years, the life period of the Sun, give to Moon?

Years.

120 : 6 :: 10 : x (Moon's. Antardaśâ period).

$x = \frac{6 \times 10}{120} = \frac{1}{2}$ year or 6 months.

Again, each of the Antardaśâ periods is further sub-divided into 9 parts in the same proportion, known as Pratyantara Daśâs or Sûkṣma periods.

The following table is for ready reference when the Antardaśâs are to be found :—

ANTARDAŚÂS.

	Years.	Months.	Days.		Years.	Months.	Days.		Years.	Months.	Days.
Sun, Sun ...	0	3	18	Moon, Moon ...	0	10	0	Mars, Mars ...	0	4	27
„ Moon ...	0	6	0	„ Mars ...	0	7	0	„ Râhu ...	1	0	18
„ Mars ...	0	4	6	„ Rahu ...	1	6	0	„ Jupiter ...	0	11	6
„ Râhu ...	0	10	24	„ Jupiter ...	1	4	0	„ Saturn ...	1	1	9
„ Jupiter ...	0	9	18	„ Saturn ...	1	7	0	„ Mercury ...	0	11	27
„ Saturn ...	0	11	12	„ Mercury ...	1	5	0	„ Ketu ...	0	4	27
„ Mercury ...	0	10	6	„ Ketu ...	0	7	0	„ Venus ...	1	2	0
„ Ketu ...	0	4	6	„ Venus ...	1	8	0	„ Sun ...	0	4	6
„ Venus ...	1	0	0	„ Sun ...	0	6	0	„ Moon ...	0	7	0
...	6	0	0		10	0	0		7	0	0
Râhu, Râhu ...	2	8	12	Jupiter, Jupiter ...	2	1	18	Saturn, Saturn ...	3	0	3
„ Jupiter ...	2	4	24	„ Saturn ...	2	6	12	„ Mercury ...	2	8	9
„ Saturn ...	2	10	6	„ Mercury	2	3	6	„ Ketu ...	1	1	9
„ Mercury ...	2	6	18	„ Ketu ...	0	11	6	„ Venus ...	3	2	0
„ Ketu ...	1	0	18	„ Venus ...	2	8	0	„ Sun ...	0	11	12
„ Venus ...	3	0	0	„ Sun ...	0	9	18	„ Moon ...	1	7	0
„ Sun ...	0	10	24	„ Moon ...	1	4	0	„ Mars ...	1	1	9
„ Moon ...	1	6	0	„ Mars ...	0	11	6	„ Râhu ...	2	10	6
„ Mars ...	1	0	18	„ Râhu ...	2	4	24	„ Jupiter ...	2	6	12
	18	0	0		16	0	0		19	0	0
Mercury, Mercury	2	4	27	Ketu, Ketu ...	0	4	27	Venus, Venus ...	3	4	0
„ Ketu ...	0	11	27	„ Venus ...	1	2	0	„ Sun ...	1	0	0
„ Venus ...	2	10	0	„ Sun ...	0	4	6	„ Moon ...	1	8	0
„ Sun ...	0	10	6	„ Moon ...	0	7	0	„ Mars ...	1	2	0
„ Moon ...	1	5	0	„ Mars ...	0	4	27	„ Râhu ...	3	0	0
„ Mars ...	0	11	27	„ Râhu ...	1	0	18	„ Jupiter ...	2	8	0
„ Râhu ...	2	6	18	„ Jupiter ...	0	11	6	„ Saturn ...	3	2	0
„ Jupiter	2	3	6	„ Saturn ...	1	1	9	„ Mercury ...	2	10	0
„ Saturn	2	8	9	„ Mercury ...	0	11	27	„ Ketu ...	1	2	0
	17	0	0		7	0	0		20	0	0

THE AṢṬOTTARÎ DAŚÂ SYSTEM.

According to this system the maximum period of human-life is 108 years; this period divided into 8 parts (instead of 9 as in the Vimśottari system) presided over by 7 planets and by Râhu (Ketu is not taken into account).

They come in the following order and their years are given below :—

The Sun ...	... 6 years.	Saturn ...	... 10 years.
The Moon ...	... 15 years.	Jupiter ...	... 19 years.
Mars ...	... 8 years.	Râhu ...	... 12 years.
Mercury ...	... 17 years.	Venus ...	... 21 years.

The ruler of the Daśâ period, at the time of birth, is ascertained from the asterism which the Moon occupies at the time. If, therefore, at the time of birth, the Moon occupy any of the three asterisms Kṛittikâ, Rohiṇî, Mṛigaśirâ, the Daśâ period is that of the Sun.

Ârdrâ, Punarvasu, Puṣyâ, Aśleṣâ	... Moon.
Maghâ, P. Phalgunî, U. Phalgunî	... Mars.
Hastâ, Chitrâ, Svâtî, Viśâkhâ	... Mercury.
Anurâdhâ, Jyeṣṭhâ, Mûlâ	... Saturn.
Pûrvâṣâḍhâ, U. Âṣâḍhâ, Śravaṇâ	... Jupiter.
Dhaniṣṭhâ, Śatabhiṣâ, Pûrva Bhâdrapada	... Râhu.
U. Bhâdrapadâ, Revatî, Aśvinî, Bharaṇî	... Venus.

Now if there be any of the three Nakṣatras, Kṛittikâ, Rohiṇî or Mṛigaśirâ occupied by the Moon during the birth time of any individual, the Sun's Daśâ is prevalent; 6 years is the Sun's Daśâ; therefore each Nakṣatra enjoys 2 years for the Sun's Daśâ. So on for the other Nakṣatras; as :—

$$\frac{\text{Planet's Daśâ period}}{\text{The number of Nakṣatras covering that period}} = \text{each Nakṣatra's Daśâ.}$$

$$e.\,g.,\quad \frac{\text{Moon's Daśâ 15 years}}{\text{Ârdrâ, Punarvasu, Puṣyâ, and Aśleṣâ (the moon-occupied Nakṣatras)}} = \frac{15}{4} = \text{3 years 9 months,}$$

as the Daśâ of Ârdrâ or Punarvasu, or Puṣyâ or Aśleṣâ.

How much of the period of a particular Daśâ has elapsed and how much remains to be enjoyed at the time of birth by the native must be ascertained from the asterism and portion of the asterism passed over by the Moon and the asterism and portion of the asterism remaining to be passed over at the time. This may be roughly ascertained, thus :—

Suppose a child is born on the 22nd Jaiṣṭha—39 daṇḍas 16 palas and 30 vipalas in the year 1814 Saka era under Uttara Phalgunî. Find out how much Daśâ and which planet's Daśâ has to be enjoyed yet by the child. Referring to the above list of the Daśâs of the planets we find the three asterisms Maghâ, P. Phalgunî, and U. Phalgunî are under the Daśâ period of Mars. So the Daśâ under question is that of Mars. On the date 22nd Jaiṣṭha, the duration of P. Phalgunî was 4 daṇḍas 29 palas and 1 vipala, the duration of U. Phalgunî on that date was therefore (60 daṇḍas—4 daṇḍas 29 palas 1 vipala=) 55 daṇḍas 30 palas and 59 vipalas, and its duration next day was 9 daṇḍas 47 palas 30 vipalas, the whole duration of U. Phalgunî being 55 daṇḍas 30 palas 59 vipalas+9 daṇḍas 47 palas and 3 vipalas=64 daṇḍas 35 palas 2 vipalas, the time taken by the Moon to pass over the Nakṣatra U. Phalgunî. The birth took place at 39 daṇḍas 16 palas and 30 vipalas. Therefore the portion of the Nakṣatra U. Phalgunî yet to be enjoyed by the child is (64 daṇḍas 35 palas 2 vipalas) – (39 daṇḍas 16 palas 30 vipalas—4 daṇḍas 29 palas 1 vipala = (64 daṇḍas 35 palas 2 vipalas)—(34 daṇḍas 47 palas 29 vipalas) = 29 daṇḍas 47 palas 33 vipalas.

Now 64 daṇḍas 35 palas 2 vipalas, the measure of U. Phalgunî represent 2 years 8 months ($\frac{1}{3} \times 8$ years), how many years will 29 daṇḍas 47 palas and 33 vipalas represent; the answer is 1 year 2 months 22 days 50 daṇḍas and 50 palas the Daśâ period of Mars. Then ascertain the period of death; under whose Daśâ period death will occur. See Mṛityu Yogas. Then write down the fruits of the Daśâs of the several planets.

Again the eight Daśâ periods are each sub-divided into 8 sub-divisions known as Antardaśâs, the ruler of the first Antardaśâ being the ruler of the Daśâ period and those of the Antardaśâs which follow are the same as the rulers of the Daśâ periods which follow. The length of the Antardaśâ periods bear the same proportion to each other as the lengths of the Daśâ periods, *e.g.*, determine the Antardaśâ of Mercury in Sun's Daśâ.

108 years represent the Sun's Daśâ period 6 years; how much will 17 years the Daśâ period of Mercury represent?—$\frac{8 \times 17}{108}$ years or 11 months and 10 days will represent the Antardaśâ of Mercury.

Again each of the Antardaśâ period is further sub-divided into 8 parts in the same proportion known as Pratyantardaśâ periods or Sûkṣma periods.

The following table represents the Antardaśâ periods.

The Antardaśâs of	The Daśâs.							
	Sun.	Moon.	Mars.	Mercury.	Saturn.	Jupiter.	Râhu.	Venus.
	y. m. d.	y. m. d.	y. m. d. d.	y. m. d. d.	y. m. d. d.	y. m. d. d.	y. m. d. d.	y. m. d. d
Sun ...	0 4 0	0 10 0	0 5 10 0	0 0 11 10	0 6 20 0	1 0 20 0	0 8 0 0	1 2 0 0
Moon ...	0 10 0	2 1 0	1 1 10 0	0 2 4 10	0 1 .4 20	2 7 20 0	1 8 0 0	2 11 0 0
Mars ...	0 5 10	1 1 10	0 7 3 20	1 3 3 20	0 8 26 40	1 4 26 40	0 10 20 0	1 6 20 0
Mercury.	0 11 10	2 4 10	1 3 3 20	2 8 3 20	1 6 26 40	2 11 26 40	1 10 20 0	3 3 20 0
Saturn ...	0 6 20	1 4 20	0 8 26 40	1 6 26 40	0 11 3 20	1 9 3 20	1 1 10 0	1 11 10 0
Jupiter ...	1 0 20	2 7 20	1 4 26 40	2 11 26 40	1 9 3 20	3 4 3 20	2 1 10 0	3 8 10 0
Râhu ...	0 8 0	1 8 0	0 10 20 0	0 1 10 20	0 1 1 10	2 1 10 0	1 4 0 0	2 4 0 0
Venus ..	1 2 0	2 11 0	1 6 20 0	0 3 3 20	1 11 10 0	3 8 10 0	2 4 0 0	4 1 0 0
	6 years	15 years	8 years.	17 years.	10 years.	19 years.	12 years.	21 years.

Under Râhu's Daśâ period the individual is liable to quarrel with his friends for his wife and her ornaments. There is fear from being struck with weapons; the individual becomes fearful, powerless, deprived of friends, wealth, health and his life is in danger.

CHAPTER VIII.

ON PLANETARY DIVISIONS AND SUB-DIVISIONS OF LIFE, KNOWN AS DAŚÂS AND ANTARDAŚÂS.

मालिनी—उदयरविशशांकप्राणिकेंद्रादिसंस्थाः प्रथमवयसि मध्येंऽत्ये च दद्युः फलानि । न हि न फलविपाकः केंन्द्रसंस्थाद्य भावे भवति हि फलपक्तिः पूर्वमापोक्लिमेऽपि ॥ १ ॥

उदयरविशशांकप्राणिकेंद्रादिसंस्थाः Udayaraviśaśâmkaprâṇikendrâdisaṃsthâḥ, the Ascendant, the Sun or the Moon, (whichever of these three is most powerful); then the planets residing in the angles; then those in the succedent or fixed houses (2, 5, 8, 11); then those in the cadent or mutable houses (3, 6, 9, 12), all reckoned. प्रथमवयसि Prathamavayasi, in the first part of life. मध्ये Madhye, in the middle part of life. अंत्ये Antye, in the latter part of life. च Cha, and. दद्युः Dadyuḥ, give; grant. फलानि Phalâni, effects; results; fruits. न Na, not. हि Hi, certainly. न Na, no. फलविपाकः Phalavipâkaḥ, period when the planets are ready to yield fruits. केंद्रसंस्थाद्यभावे Kendrasaṃsthâdyabhâve, on there being no planets in the angles (from the strongest planet). भवति Bhavati, arise; accrue. हि Hi, certainly. फलपक्तिः Phalapaktiḥ, ripening of fruits, becoming ready to yield fruits. पूर्वम् Pûrvam, results like the preceding ones, fruits similar to those in the earlier period. आपोक्लिमेऽपि Apoklime Api, even if the planets be situated in the cadent houses (3, 6, 9, 12). If the planets be not situated in the angles, the fruits will be given by the planets in the succedent houses; if they are not found in the succedent, the fruits will be given by the planets in the cadente houses.

1. The Ascendant, the Sun, or the Moon whichever of these three is the strongest, first acts on the life of any individual (and continues to act for a period equal to the number of years obtained in the preceding Chapter as his planetary years) and yields fruits according to its nature; this period is known as the Daśâ of that planet. Then act the planets in the angular houses (1, 4, 7, 10 houses reckoned from the house of the strongest) (according to their superiority in strength, *vide* next stanza) in the middle part of his life and award fruits proper to their natures respectively; next come the planets in the succedent houses

(2, 5, 8, 11 from the house of the strongest); and lastly work the planets in the cadent houses (3, 6, 9, 12 from the house of the strongest) in the latter part of the life of that individual. (These several periods of the several planets are called the Daśâs or the planetary Divisions of life). In case there be no planets in the angles, the planets in the succedent houses will act in their places and award fruits; and if there be no planets in the succedent houses, the planets in the cadent houses will act in their places and award appropriate results).

Notes.—The first point to determine is which planet's Daśâ period comes first; which planet's Daśâ comes second; which planet's Daśâ comes third and so on.

Determine first which of the following three is most powerful—the Rising sign, the Sun or the Moon. His Daśâ comes first. Second comes the most powerful of the planets that are occupying the Kendra houses, from such powerful rising sign or the Sun or the Moon. Then the other planets of the Kendra houses come in their seniority of strength; but if the planets be all of equal power, the Daśâ period of the planet, whose period is the longest comes first; and if the planets be of equal power and period, then the period of the planet which rises first, *i.e.*, reappears after its conjunction with the Sun, comes first. Then comes the periods or Daśâs of the planets occuping the succedent or Panphara houses in the order above stated; and lastly, these of the Apoklima or cadent houses come.

Remarks:—If there be no planets in the angles, will this part of life be void of any planetary influences? No, the planets in the succedent (and if their house be without any planets) or cadent house will at once come in and exert their influences. If there be planets in the angles and no planets in the succedent or cadent houses, the planets in the angles will exert their influence throughtout the remaining part; so that no period of life will be void of any planet's influence. If there be no planet in the angles or succedent houses, then the planets in the cadent houses work throughout the remaining part of life. If there be no planets in the cadent houses, the planets in the succedent houses will go on working throughout the remaining part of life.

This is also the opinion of Yavaneswara and others.

General Remarks:—The first thing to be noted is that during the working period (Daśâ period) of any planet other planets also work. The ruling planet of the period works first for a part of its period; then the other planets as mentioned in the 2nd verse work during the remaining part. These periods are called Antardaśâs. The Antardaśâ of the ruling planet is called the Mûla or Primary Antardaśâ and the Antardaśâs of the other planets are called the subsidiary Antardaśâs.

It is owing to these Antardaśâs that the period of working (Daśâ) of any planet is not one of continuous pleasure or of continuous pain; other planets intervene and thus make the period bright or dark at intervals as the case may be.

इ० व०—आयुः कृतं येन हि यत्तदेव कल्प्या दशा सा प्रबलस्य पूर्वाम् । साम्ये बहूनां बहुवर्षदस्य तेषां च साम्ये प्रथमोदितस्य ॥ २ ॥

आयुः Âyuḥ, life; number of years granted by a planet after corrections (according to the rules in the preceding Chapter.) कृतं Kritam, granted; ordained. येन Yena, by whichever planet. हि Hi, certainly. यत् Yat, whatever (number of years.) तत् Tat, the same number of years. एव Eva, certainly. कल्प्या Kalpyâ, are to be reckoned; are to be considered. दशा Daśâ, the period of working; the Planetary Division of life. सा Sâ, the period; the Daśâ. प्रबलस्य Prabalasya, of the strongest planet, of the planet that is very powerful. पूर्वाम् Pûrvam, first (acts and produces results.) साम्ये Sâmye, on being equally strong. बहूनां Bahûnâm, of many planets. बहुवर्षदस्य Bahuvarṣadasya, of that planet which ordains the greatest number of years as life. तेषां Teṣâm, of these. च Cha, and. साम्ये Sâmye, on being equal on account of their granting the same number of years as the life period. प्रथमोदितस्य Prathamoditasya, of that planet which rises first in the horizon.

2. The periods of the several Planetary Divisions known as Daśâs are the same as the planetary years found in the last Chapter. Again, of the several planets occupying the angular, succedent, or cadent houses, the Daśâ period of the strongest planet appears first, next appears that of the planet next in power and so on; but if the planets be all equally strong, the Daśâ period of the planet whose period is the longest comes first; and if the planets be equally strong and lasting, then the period of the planet which rises first (*i. e.*, reappears after its conjunction with the Sun) comes first.

Note:—The planets are to be reckoned equally strong when their position in their friends' houses, fifth and ninth houses, their houses of exaltation, their favourable aspects, when their strength as regards position, direction, energy and time, all taken together are equal. Some planets are naturally strong; and in that case when all planets are equally strong as far as the above considerations are made, still by virtue of the natural strength one is superior. Suppose one, for instance, Saturn is strengthened by three other favourable positions and Mars is strengthened by only two other favourable positions, yet Mars being naturally stronger than Saturn, Mars in this case is equal to Saturn.

The planets are said to rise on the horizon either when they rise first naturally in the east above the horizon or when they rise in the west just after sunset.

व० तिं०—एकर्क्षगोऽर्द्धमपहृत्य ददाति तु स्वं त्र्यंशं त्रिकोणगृहगः स्मरगः स्वरांशम् । पादं फलस्य चतुरस्रगतः सहोरास्त्वेवं परस्परगताः परिपाचयंति ॥ ३ ॥

एकर्क्षगः Ekarkşagah, the planet that is situated in the same sign (with the Daśâpati or the then ruler of the Daśâ period. अर्द्धं Arddham, half of Antardaśâ of the Daśâpati. अपहृत्य Apahritya, taking; appropriating for its own purpose. ददाति Dadâti, grants. तु Tu, but. स्वं Svam, its own; (the Antardaśâ period) of the planet that is in the same sign as the ruler of the Daśâ period. त्र्यंशं Tryamśam, one-third (of the Antardaśâ period of the Daśâpati). त्रिकोणगृहगः Trikoņagrihagaḥ, when the planet is in the fifth and ninth houses from the house of the Daśâpati. स्मरगः Smaragaḥ, when in the seventh house from the Daśâpati. स्मरांशम् Smaramśam, one-seventh part (of the Antardaśâ period of the Daśâpati). पादं Pâdam, one-fourth (of the Antardaśâ period of the Daśâpati). फलस्य Phalasya, of the fruits; of the result; of the period of the Daśâpati. चतुरस्रगतः Chaturasragatah, when the planet is in the eighth and the fourth house from the Daśâpati. सहोराः Sahorâḥ, the planets that are with Ascendant, here the Ascendant is considered as the Daśâpati. तु Tu, but. एवं Evam, in this way; in the manner mentioned above. परस्परगताः Paramparagatâḥ, situated in houses in the order stated above. परिपाचयंति Paripâchayanti, award results according to their natures respectively; bears fruits according to their own natures.

3. The Daśâ period (*i.e.*, the planetary division of a life) of any planet is divided into sub-periods. These sub-periods, called Antardaśâs, belong first to the Daśâ-pati itself or the ruling planet; then to the planet occupying the same house as the Daśâpati; then to the planet occupying the 5th or 9th house from the Daśâpati; then to the planet occupying the seventh house; and lastly to the planet

occupying the 4th or 8th house from the Daśâpati. If there be several planets in the same house with the Daśâpati, the most powerful amongst them will only have the Antardaśâ period. Similarly, if several planets occupy the 5th or 9th houses, or the 7th house, or the 4th or 8th house from the sign occupied by the Daśâpati, the ruler of the Antardaśâ in each of the houses is the most powerful planet. If there be no planets in one or two of these houses, the Antardaśâ period of the planets in the remaining houses only should be taken.

Now, the Antardaśâ period of the planet that is in the same sign with the Daśâpati is half of the Antardaśâ period of the Daśâpati; the Antardaśâ period of the planet that is in the 5th and 9th house is one third the Antardaśâ period of the Daśâpati; in the 7th house, one-seventh; in the 4th and 8th houses from that of the Daśâpati, one-fourth of the Antardaśâ period of the Daśâpati. When the Ascendant is the Daśâpati, the planet with the Ascendant or situated in the order above stated, will award its Antardaśâ results (as specified).

Note:—The several Antardaśâ periods are in the proportion $1 : \frac{1}{2} : \frac{1}{3} : \frac{1}{7} : \frac{1}{4}$; 1 representing the Antardaśâ period of the Daśâpati. If there be many planets in the houses under consideration, the strongest one in each house awards its Antardaśâ results for a period as stated; not the others. This is also the opinion of many other authors and is the correct one. There are some authors who advocate that all the planets in the same sign should share the number of years due to them; not the strongest only; others there are who say that one share is to be taken only, but that should be proportionately distributed to all. These views are not correct.

इ० व०—स्थानान्यथैतानि सवर्णयित्वा सर्वाण्यधश्छेदविवर्जितानि। दशाब्दपिंडे गुणका यथांशं छेदस्तदैक्येन दशाप्रभेदः ॥४॥

स्थानानि Sthânâni, the numbers corresponding to the houses, *e. g.*, half, one-third, one-seventh and one fourth. अथ Atha, and; afterwards; then. एतानि Etâni, these. सवर्णयित्वा Savarṇaitvâ, converting them so as to have the same denominators.

सर्वाणि Sarvâṇi, all the numbers corresponding to the planets' situations. अधश्छेदविवर्जितानि Adhaśchhedavivarjitâni, depriving their fractions of their denominators, *i. e.*, taking the numerators only. दशाब्दपिण्डे Daśâbdapiṇḍe, on the life period granted by any Daśâpati or the ruling planet. गुणकाः Guṇakâḥ, the multipliers. यथांशं Yathâṃśam, the numbers in the numerators (being respectively the multipliers). छेदः Chhedaḥ, the divisor being. तदैक्येन Tadaikyena, their sum; the sum of the numerators (being the divisor). दशाप्रभेदः Daśâpravedaḥ, the number of years, the Antardaśâs of each planet respectively.

4. The fractions (1, $\frac{1}{2}$, $\frac{1}{3}$, $\frac{1}{7}$, and $\frac{1}{4}$), should all be reduced to have a common denominator with different numerators. The Daśâ period of the Daśâpati should be divided by the sum of the numerators and the quotient when multiplied by the several numerators will give the periods of the Antardaśâs of the other planets.

Notes:—Suppose, for instance, there are planets in the several places referred to in the last stanzas, excepting say, the 7th house from the sign occupied by the Daśâ ruler. The periods of the four Antardaśâs—those of (1) the Daśâ ruler; (2) the planet with it; (3) the planet occupying the 5th or the 9th house from it; and (4) the planet occupying the 4th or the 8th house from it are in the porportion of $\frac{1}{1}$, $\frac{1}{2}$, $\frac{1}{3}$, $\frac{1}{4}$. Reducing these fractions to those with a common denominator, we get $\frac{12}{12}$, $\frac{6}{12}$, $\frac{4}{12}$, $\frac{3}{12}$; in other words, the Antardaśâ periods are in the proportions of 12 : 6 : 4 : 3. The sum of these numbers is 25; if therefore the Daśâ period of the Daśâpati be divided by 25, and the quotient multiplied 12, 6, 4, and, 3, we shall obtain the periods of the four Antardaśâs respectively.

Remarks.—Each case is now separately dealt with:—

Example.—(1) Suppose there is only one planet with the planet Daśâpati and there are no other planets in the houses above mentioned. In this case proceed as follows. Put for Daśapati $\frac{1}{1}$. Put for the other planet which absorbs half the period of the Antardâśâ of the Daśâpati $\frac{1}{2}$. Thus put $\frac{1}{1}$, $\frac{1}{2}$. Convert these fractions to have the same denominators. Thus we get $\frac{2}{2}$, $\frac{1}{2}$. Take away the denominators, and we get the numerators, 2 and 1 as the multiplier and their sum (2+1=3) 3 as the divisor. Here suppose the life period granted by the Daśâ ruler is 3. Now multiply 3 by 2 and 1 respectively and divide by 3 we get $\frac{3\times2}{3}$ and $\frac{3\times1}{3}$ equal to 2 and 1 thus 2 (two years) are the Antardaśâ of the Daśâpati and 1 year 0 months 0 days and 0 ghatis represents the Antardaśâ of the planet that is with the Daśâpati. Thus it is evident that the secondary planet absorbs half the Antardaśâ ($\frac{1}{2}\times2=1$) of the Daśâpati.

(2) Suppose there is one planet in the 5th or 9th house from the Daśâpati and there are no other planets in the 4th, 8th or 7th house or with the Daśâpati. Put for Daśâpati $\frac{1}{1}$ and for the other planet $\frac{1}{3}$. Bring these to a common denominator $\frac{3}{3}$, $\frac{1}{3}$. Three and one are respectively the multipliers and 4 is the divisor. Suppose years months days, 4-0-0-0, ghaṭis is the life period granted by the ruling planet. Multiply it by 3 and 1 divide by 4. We get 3 and 1. Thus 3 years 0 months 0 days 0 ghaṭis are the Antardaśâ of the ruling planet and 1 year, 0 month, 0 days, 0 ghaṭis are Antardaśâ of the subsidiary planet.

(3) Suppose there is a planet in the fourth or eighth house from the Daśâpati and there is no other planet with the principal planet or in any of the other houses above mentioned. Proceed as follows. Put for the Daśâpati $\frac{1}{1}$; and for the subsidiary planet $\frac{1}{4}$; make these have a common denominator $\frac{4}{4}$, $\frac{1}{4}$. 4 and 1 are the multipliers and 5 is the divisor. Suppose 5 to be the Daśâ, *i. e.*, the life period granted by the ruling planet. Then $\frac{5\times4}{5}$ and $\frac{5\times1}{5}=4$ and 1. Thus 4 years, 0 months, 0 days, 0 ghaṭis, = the Antardaśâ of the ruling planet and 1 year 0 months 0 days, 0 ghaṭis = the Antardaśâ of the subsidiary planet.

(4) Suppose there is a planet in the seventh house from the ruling planet and no other planet with the ruler or in the 9th, 5th, 4th, 8th house. Proceed as follows $\frac{1}{1}$, $\frac{1}{7}$; make these a common denominator thus:—$\frac{7}{7}$, $\frac{1}{7}$. Then 7 and 1 are the multipliers and 8 is the divisor. Suppose 8 years 0 months 0 days 0 ghaṭis = Mûla Dâśâ. Then $\frac{8\times7}{8}$ and $\frac{8\times1}{8}=7$ and 1. Thus 7 yearsare the Antardaśâ of the ruling planet and 1 year is the Antardaśâ of the subsidiary planet.

(5) Suppose there is one planet with the ruler (Daśâpati) and another planet in the fifth or ninth house and no other planet in 4th, 8th, or 7th house. Proceed as follows. Put $\frac{1}{1}$, $\frac{1}{2}$, $\frac{1}{3}$; make these of a common denominator, $\frac{6}{6}$, $\frac{3}{6}$, $\frac{2}{6}$; then 6, 3, and 2 are the multipliers and their sum 11 is the divisor. Suppose 11 years as the life or Daśâ of the ruler. Then $\frac{11\times6}{11}$, $\frac{11\times3}{11}$ and $\frac{11\times2}{11}=6$, 3, and 2, representing the Antardaśâs of the ruler, the planet with the ruler and the planet in the 5th or 9th house respectively.

(6) Suppose there is a planet with the ruler and there is a planet in the 4th or 8th house from the ruler and there are no other planets in the 9th, 5th or 7th house. Proceed as follows:—Put the fractions thus $\frac{1}{1}$, $\frac{1}{2}$, $\frac{1}{4}$; make these of a common denominator $\frac{8}{8}$, $\frac{4}{8}$, $\frac{2}{8}$. Thus8, 4 and 2 are the multipliers and 14 is the divisor. Then suppose 14 as the life period of the ruler. Now $\frac{14\times8}{14}$, $\frac{14\times4}{14}$, $\frac{14\times2}{14}=8$, 4 2 representing the Antardaśâs in

years of the ruler, the planets with the ruler, and of the planet in the 4th or 8th house respectively.

(7) Suppose there is a planet with the ruler and there is another planet in the seventh house from the ruler and no other planets in the other houses above mentioned. Put the fractions thus, $\frac{1}{1}, \frac{1}{2}, \frac{1}{7}$; make them of a common denominator $\frac{14}{14}, \frac{7}{14}, \frac{2}{14}$. Thus 14, 7 and 2 become the multipliers; and their sum 23 is the divisor. Suppose 23 is the Daśâ of the ruler; then $\frac{23\times14}{23}, \frac{23\times7}{23}, \frac{23\times2}{23}$ or 14, 7, and 2 are the Antardaśâs of the ruler, of the planet with the ruler, and of the planet in the 7th house from the ruler.

8. Suppose there is a planet in the 5th house and there is another planet in the ninth house from the ruler and no other planets anywhere in the aforesaid other houses. Put the fractions thus $\frac{1}{1}, \frac{1}{3}, \frac{1}{3}$; make these of a common denominator $(3\times3=9)$ 9 thus $\frac{9}{9}, \frac{3}{9}, \frac{3}{9}$. Thus 9, 3 and 3 are the multipliers; and 15 is the divisor. Supposing 5 the life period of the ruler, we get $\frac{5\times9}{15}, \frac{5\times3}{15}, \frac{5\times3}{15}$, or 3, 1, 1 as the Antardaśâs of the ruler, and the two other planets.

9. Suppose there is a planet in the 5th or 9th house from the ruler, and also another planet in the 4th or 8th house from the ruler and no other planets in the other houses of reference. Put the fractions thus:— $\frac{1}{1}, \frac{1}{3}, \frac{1}{4}$; make them of a common denominator, $\frac{12}{12}, \frac{4}{12}, \frac{3}{12}$. Thus 12, 4, 3 are the multipliers; and 19 is the divisor. Supposing 19 years the Daśâ of the ruler, we get $\frac{19\times12}{19}, \frac{19\times4}{19}, \frac{19\times3}{19}$ or 12, 4 and 3 as the Antardaśâs of the ruler, and the planet in the Trikoṇa and of the planet in the 4th or 8th house respectively.

10. Suppose there is a planet in the 5th or 9th house from the ruler and another planet in the 7th house. Put the fractions thus:—$\frac{1}{1}, \frac{1}{3}, \frac{1}{7}$; make them of a common denominator, $\frac{21}{21}, \frac{7}{21}, \frac{3}{21}$; the numerators 21, 7, and 3 are the multipliers and their sum 31 is the divisor. Supposing 31 years to be the life period granted by the ruler we get $\frac{31\times21}{31}, \frac{31\times7}{31}$ and $\frac{31\times3}{31}$ or 21, 7, 3 as the number of years, the Antardaśâ of the ruler and the subsidiary planets respectively.

11. Suppose there is a planet in the 4th and also a planet in the 8th house from the ruler. Put the fractions thus, $\frac{1}{1}, \frac{1}{4}, \frac{1}{4}$; make them of a common denominator 16 thus $\frac{16}{16}, \frac{4}{16}, \frac{4}{16}$. Then 16, 4, 4 are the multipliers and 24 is the divisor. Supposing 6 to be the life period granted by the ruler, we get $\frac{6\times16}{24}, \frac{6\times4}{24}, \frac{6\times4}{24}$, or 4, 1, 1, as the Antardaśâs of the ruler and the two other planets, respectively.

12. Suppose there is a planet in the 4th or 8th house from the ruler and also one planet in the 7th house from the ruler. Put the fractions thus :—$\frac{1}{1}$, $\frac{1}{4}$, $\frac{1}{7}$; make them of a common denominator $\frac{28}{28}$, $\frac{7}{28}$, $\frac{4}{28}$. Thus 28, 7, 4 are the multipliers and their sum 39 is the divisor. Supposing 36 years the life period granted by the ruler we get $\frac{36\times28}{39}$, $\frac{36\times7}{39}$, $\frac{36\times4}{39}$ or 25 years 10 months 4 days and 36 ghaṭis ; 6 years 5 months 16 days and 9 ghaṭis ; 3 years 8 months 9 days and 15 ghaṭis, as the Antardaśâs of the ruler and the other planets respectively. Thus far 3 planets are taken on supposition.

13. Suppose there is one planet with the ruler or Daśâpati and there is one planet in the 5th and another planet in the ninth house. Put the fractions thus $\frac{1}{1}$, $\frac{1}{2}$, $\frac{1}{3}$, $\frac{1}{3}$; make them of a common denominator $\frac{18}{18}$, $\frac{9}{18}$, $\frac{6}{18}$, $\frac{6}{18}$; The numerators 18, 9, 6, 6 are respectively the multipliers and their sum 39 is the divisor. Supposing 13 years as the Daśâ of the Daśâpati we get $\frac{13\times18}{39}=6$ years as the Antardaśâ of the ruler. Similarly $\frac{13\times9}{39}$, $\frac{13\times6}{39}$, $\frac{13\times6}{39}$ or 3, 2, 2 years are respectively the Antardaśâs of the other planets.

14. Suppose there is one planet with the ruler, one planet in the 5th or 9th house, and one other planet in 4th or 8th house. Put the fractions thus $\frac{1}{1}$, $\frac{1}{2}$, $\frac{1}{3}$, $\frac{1}{4}$; make them of a common denominator thus :—$\frac{24}{24}$, $\frac{12}{24}$, $\frac{8}{24}$, $\frac{6}{24}$. Thus 24, 12, 8, 6 are the multipliers and their sum 50 is the divisor. Supposing 36 years as the Mûla Daśâ or the life period granted by the ruler, we get $\frac{36\times24}{50}$, $\frac{36\times12}{50}$, $\frac{36\times8}{50}$, $\frac{36\times6}{50}$ or 17 years 3 months 10 days 48 ghaṭis ; 8 years 7 months 20 days 28 ghaṭis ; 5 years 9 months 3 days and 36 ghaṭis ; 4 years 3 months 25 days and 12 ghaṭis as the Antardaśâs of the ruler and the subsidiary planets.

15. Suppose there is one planet with the ruler, and one planet in the 5th or 9th house, and one other planet in the 7th house. Put the fractions thus $\frac{1}{1}$, $\frac{1}{2}$, $\frac{1}{3}$, $\frac{1}{7}$; make these of a common denominator $\frac{42}{42}$, $\frac{21}{42}$, $\frac{14}{42}$, $\frac{6}{42}$; thus 42, 21, 14 and 6 are the multipliers and 83 is the divisor. Suppose 16 years as the Mûladaśâ of the ruler. We get $\frac{16\times42}{83}$, $\frac{16\times21}{83}$, $\frac{16\times14}{83}$, $\frac{16\times6}{83}$ or 8 years 1 month 4 days 42 ghaṭis ; 4 years 0 months 17 days and 21 ghaṭis ; 2 years 8 months 11 days and 34 ghaṭis ; 1 year 1 month 26 days 23 ghaṭis as respective Antardaśâs.

16. Suppose there is one planet with the ruler and one planet in the 4th and another planet in the 8th house. Put the fractions thus $\frac{1}{1}$, $\frac{1}{2}$, $\frac{1}{4}$, $\frac{1}{4}$; make these of a common denominator $\frac{32}{32}$, $\frac{16}{32}$, $\frac{8}{32}$, $\frac{8}{32}$. Thus 32, 16, 8, 8 are the multipliers and 64 is the divisor. Suppose the life

period of the ruler is 36. Then by the above mentioned processes 18 years, 9 years, 4½ years, 4½ years are the Antardaśâs of the ruler and planets respectively.

17. Suppose there is one planet with the ruling planet, one in the 4th or 8th house, another planet in the 7th house. Put the fractions thus $\frac{1}{1}, \frac{1}{2}, \frac{1}{4}, \frac{1}{7}$: or $\frac{56}{56}, \frac{28}{56}, \frac{14}{56}, \frac{8}{56}$. Thus 56, 28, 14 and 8 are the multipliers and their sum 106 the divisor. Supposing 36 years the life period of the ruler, we get by the above process, 19 years 0 months 6 days 48 ghaṭis; 9 years 6 months 3 days and 24 ghaṭis; 4 years 9 months 1 day 42 ghaṭis; 2 years 8 months 18 days 6 ghaṭis as the respective Antardaśâs.

18. Suppose there is one planet in the 5th, one planet in the 9th and another planet in 4th or 8th house. Put the fractions thus, $\frac{1}{1}, \frac{1}{3}, \frac{1}{3}, \frac{1}{4}$, or $\frac{36}{36}, \frac{12}{36}, \frac{12}{36}, \frac{9}{36}$. Thus 36, 12, 12, and 9 are the multipliers and 69 is the divisor. Supposing 23 as the life period of the ruler, we get 12, 4, 4, 3 years as the respective Antardaśâs.

19. Suppose there is one planet in the 5th or 9th house and one planet in the 4th and another planet in the 8th house. Put thus $\frac{1}{1}, \frac{1}{3}, \frac{1}{4}, \frac{1}{4}$ or $\frac{48}{48}, \frac{16}{48}, \frac{12}{48}, \frac{12}{48}$; we get 48, 16, 12, 12, as the multipliers and 88 as the divisor. Suppose 22 years the life period of the ruler; we get 12, 4, 3, 3, as the Antardaśâs of the ruler and the other planets.

20. Suppose there is one planet in the 5th or 9th, one planet in the 4th or 8th, another planet in the seventh house. Put thus :—$\frac{1}{1}, \frac{1}{3}, \frac{1}{4}, \frac{1}{7}$ or $\frac{84}{84}, \frac{28}{84}, \frac{21}{84}, \frac{12}{84}$. We get 84, 28, 21, 12 as the multipliers and 145 as the divisor. Take 36 as the life of the ruler. We get 20-10-7-51, 6-11-12-38, 5-2-16-58, 2-11-22-33 as the respective Antardśâs.

21. Suppose there is one planet in the 4th, one planet in the 8th and one planet in the 7th house. Put thus $\frac{1}{1}, \frac{1}{4}, \frac{1}{4}, \frac{1}{7}$; or $\frac{112}{112}, \frac{28}{112}, \frac{28}{112}, \frac{16}{112}$. We get 112, 28, 28, 16 as the multipliers and their sum 184 as the divisor. Suppose 36 years as the life of the ruler. We get 21-10-28-42 ; 5-5-22-10 ; 5-5-22-10 ; 3-1-16-8 as the Antardaśâs respectively.

22. Now 5 planets are being taken. Here only the fractions are put. From the fractions one is to infer the positions of the planets $\frac{1}{1}, \frac{1}{2}, \frac{1}{3}, \frac{1}{3}, \frac{1}{4}$; multipliers 24, 12, 8, 8, 6 and divisor 58.

23. Fractions $\frac{1}{1}, \frac{1}{2}, \frac{1}{3}, \frac{1}{3}. \frac{1}{7}$; multipliers 42, 21, 14, 14, 6 ; divisor 97

24. Fractions $\frac{1}{1}, \frac{1}{2}, \frac{1}{3}, \frac{1}{4}, \frac{1}{4}$; multipliers 24, 12, 8, 6, 6 ; divisor 56

25. Fractions $\frac{1}{1}, \frac{1}{2}, \frac{1}{4}, \frac{1}{4}, \frac{1}{7}$; multipliers 56, 28, 14, 14, 8 ; diviso 120.

26. Fractions $\frac{1}{1}, \frac{1}{2}, \frac{1}{3}, \frac{1}{4}, \frac{1}{7}$; multipliers 84, 42, 28, 21, 12 ; diviso 187.

27. Fractions $\frac{1}{1}$, $\frac{1}{3}$, $\frac{1}{3}$, $\frac{1}{4}$, $\frac{1}{4}$; multipliers 144, 48, 48, 36, 36; divisor 312.

28. Fractions $\frac{1}{1}$, $\frac{1}{3}$, $\frac{1}{3}$, $\frac{1}{4}$, $\frac{1}{7}$; multipliers 84, 28, 28, 21, 12; divisor 173.

29. Now six planets are taken. Fractions $\frac{1}{1}$, $\frac{1}{2}$, $\frac{1}{3}$, $\frac{1}{3}$, $\frac{1}{4}$, $\frac{1}{7}$; multipliers 252, 126, 84, 84, 63, 36; divisor 645.

30. Fractions $\frac{1}{1}$, $\frac{1}{2}$, $\frac{1}{3}$, $\frac{1}{4}$, $\frac{1}{4}$, $\frac{1}{7}$; multipliers 168, 84, 56, 42, 42, 24; divisor 416.

31. Fractions $\frac{1}{1}$, $\frac{1}{2}$, $\frac{1}{3}$, $\frac{1}{3}$, $\frac{1}{4}$, $\frac{1}{4}$; multipliers 96, 48, 32, 32, 24, 24; divisor 256.

32. Fractions $\frac{1}{1}$, $\frac{1}{3}$, $\frac{1}{3}$, $\frac{1}{4}$, $\frac{1}{4}$, $\frac{1}{7}$; multipliers 84, 28, 28, 21, 21, 12; divisor 194.

32. Now 7 planets are taken. Fractions $\frac{1}{1}$, $\frac{1}{2}$, $\frac{1}{3}$, $\frac{1}{3}$, $\frac{1}{4}$, $\frac{1}{4}$, $\frac{1}{7}$; multipliers 168, 84, 56, 56, 42, 42, 24; divisor 472.

Thus there arise 32 cases in all. There are 4 cases of two planets; 7 of three; 9 of four; 7 of five; 4 of six and 1 of seven.

Thus all the possible cases have been discussed.

वैतालीय–सम्यग्बलिनः स्वतुंगभागे संपूर्णा बलवर्जितस्य रिक्ता । नीचांशगतस्य शत्रुभागे ज्ञेयानिष्टफला दशा प्रसूतौ ॥ ५ ॥

सम्यग्बलिनः Samyagbalinaḥ, the period of the planet that is all powerful, (occupying the exaltation degree of its exalted sign). स्वतुंगभागे Svatuṃgabhâge, when the planet is in its highly exalted degrees. संपूर्णा Sampûrṇâ, named "Sampûrṇâ," *i. e.*, All-complete. बलवर्जितस्य Balavarjitasya, the period of that planet which is without any strength; the period of a very weak planet. रिक्ता Riktâ, is termed "riktâ", *i. e.*, All-empty.

नीचांशगतस्य Nîchâṃśagatasya, the period of the planet when situated in the degrees of detriment or in the Navâṃśas of detrimental sign. शत्रुभागे Śatrubhâge, in the houses of enemies or in the enemies' Navâṃśas. ज्ञेया Jñeyâ, is known. अनिष्टफला Aniṣṭaphalâ, bearing evil results in the shape of loss of wealth or loss of health. दशा Daśâ the Daśâ period (as well as the Antardaśâ period). प्रसूतौ Prasûtau, during any man's birth time.

5. The Daśâ (and the Antardaśâ) of the strongest planet when exalted and in its exalted degrees is termed Sampûrṇâ. The Daśâ of the weak planet when debilitated and in detrimental degrees is termed Riktâ. The Daśâ of the planet when in its enemy's Navâṃśa and also

in its debilitated house and in detrimental degrees is termed Anisṭa.

Note.—When the Daśâ or Antardaśâ is Sampûrṇâ, one gets wealth, health, happiness, and prosperity.

The Daśâ period of a planet occupying simply its exaltation sign and not very powerful is known as Pûrṇa. The person will get health, wealth, in due time.

The Daśâ period of a weak planet occupying simply its detrimental sign is known as Riktâ. During this period one will suffer the loss of wealth and the loss of health. So in Anisṭa Daśâ also; but to a greater degree.

इंद्रवज्रा-भ्रष्टस्य तुंगादवरोहिसंज्ञा मध्या भवेत्सा सुहृदुच्च भागे । अरोहिणी निम्नपरिच्युतस्य नीचारिभांशेष्वधमा भवेत्सा ॥ ६ ॥

भ्रष्टस्य—Bhrasṭasya, when going away from; when descending. तुंगात् Tuṅgât, from the highest exaltation; अवरोहिसंज्ञा Avarohisanjñâ, termed 'descending.' मध्या Madhyâ, middling; fair; average. भवेत् Bhavet, becomes. सा Sâ, that. सुहृदुच्चभागे Suhṛiduchchabhâge, when in its friend's quarters, when in its own Navâṃśakas or when in its own house. आरोहिणी Ârohiṇî, ascending. निम्नपरिच्युतस्य Nimnaparichyutasya, when quitting the lowest degrees of detriment (towards the exaltation). नीचारिभांशेषु Nîchâribhâṃśeṣu, in the detrimental degrees, in its enemies' quarters or Navâṃśas. अधमा Adhamâ, worst. भवेत् Bhavet, becomes. सा Sâ, that; the then Daśâ period is called).

6. When a planet is in its descent from the highest degrees of exaltation, its Daśâ period is known as 'descending,' (till it reaches the lowest degrees of detriment). When in course of its descent, it comes to its ally's quarters or in its own or ally's Navâṃśas, the Daśâ is called 'fair or average.' When a planet is in its ascent from its lowest degrees of detriment, it is termed 'Ascending' and when in course of its ascent, it comes to its enemies' quarters or enemies' Navâṃśas, its state is termed the 'Adhama.'

N. B.—The planet yields bad results in its 'descending' Daśâ and good results in its 'ascending' Daśâ. The planet is somewhat better in its average Daśâ. The results in the Aniṣṭâ Daśâ in the preceding verse are to be considered as more painful than the results in 'Adhamâ' as stated in this verse.

उपजातिका–नीचारिभांशे समवस्थितस्य शस्ते गृहे मिश्रफला प्रदिष्टा । संज्ञानुरूपाणि फलान्यथैषां दशासु वक्ष्यामि यथोपयोगम् ॥ ७ ॥

नीचारिभांशे Nîchâribhâmśê, in the houses of detriment, in the enemies' houses, or in the enemies' Navâmśas, or in the Navâmśas of its detrimental sign. समवस्थितस्य Samavasthitasya, the Daśâ as well as the Antardaśâs of the planet that is situated. शस्ते Śaste, in the auspicious houses, *i.e.*, in its exalted, Mûlatrikoṇa, own house, or the ally's house. गृहे Grihe, houses. मिश्रफला Miśraphalâ, mixed results; fruits partly good and partly bad. संज्ञानुरूपाणि Saṃjñânurûpâni, according to their names or designations. फलानि Phalâni, result; fruits. अथ Atha, and afterwards. एषां Eṣâm, of these; their. दशासु Daśâsu, in their Daśâs or planetary life periods. वक्ष्यामि Vakṣyâmi, will narrate. यथोपयोगम् Yathopyogam, duly; in proper order; in a befitting way.

7. The planet situated in the exalted portion, Mûlatrikoṇa, own house, or ally's house, if found to occupy the detrimental Navâṃśa or the enemy's Navâṃśa will yield in his Daśâ or Antardaśâ period mixed results, *e.g.*, will give wealth but at the same time will inflict diseases. Similarly if the planet be situated in an enemy's house or in the house of detriment, and also occupies the exalted Navâṃśas or ally's Navâṃśas or his own Navâṃśas then, too, mixed results will be awarded. The results will be highly auspicious, in auspicious, mixed, and worst according to their designations respectively. Now will be stated in their proper order the Daśâ and the Antardaśâ results.

Notes.—The name "Saṃpûrṇâ" indicates vast prosperity. Pûrṇâ indicates prosperity. Adhamâ indicates misery or destruction and very little prosperity. Riktâ indicates misery and poverty. And Miśraphala indicates mixture of both good and evil.

वैतालीय–उभयेऽधममध्यपूजिता द्रेष्काणैश्चरभेषु चोत्क्रमात् ॥ अशुभेष्टसमाः स्थिरे क्रमाद्धोरायाः परिकल्पिता दशा ॥ ८ ॥

उभये Ubhaye, in the common signs; in the dual signs; when the Ascendant is a common sign. अधममध्यपूजिता Adhamamadhyapûjitâ, worst, fair and best. द्रेष्काणैः;

Dreṣkâṇaiḥ, by the three Decanates. चरभेषु च Charabheṣu Cha, when the Ascendant is a cardinal sign. च उत्क्रमात् Cha Utkramât, and inversely. अशुभेष्टसमाः Aśubheṣṭasamâḥ, bad, best and fair. स्थिरे Sthire, when the Ascendant is a fixed sign. क्रमात् Kramât, in due order; respectively. होरायाः Horâyâh, of the Ascendant. परिकल्पिताः Parikalpitâḥ, are considered; are told. दशा Daśâ, the fruits in the life of any planet.

8. The Daśâpati being the Ascendant, what will be its Daśâ? When the Ascendant is a common sign, the first Dreṣkâṇa is worst; the second Dreṣkâṇa is mixed, partly good and partly bad; and the third Dreṣkâṇa is good. If the Ascendant be a cardinal sign, the first Dreṣkâṇa is good, the second is mixed, and the third Dreṣkâṇa is worst. If the Ascendant be a fixed sign, the first Dreṣkâṇa is inauspicious, the second is good, the third is mixed.

Note :—In other words, if the rising sign be one of the common signs, Gemini, Virgo, Sagittari, and Pisces, the Lagna Daśâ is known as Adhamâ if the rising Decanate be the 1st; Madhyamâ if it be the 2nd; and Uttamâ or Pûjitâ if it be 3rd. Again, if the rising sign be one of the moveable signs Aries, Cancer, Libra, and Capricorn, the Lagna Daśâ is known as Uttamâ if the rising Decanate be the 1st; Madhyamâ, if it be the 2nd; and Adhamâ, if it be 3rd. Lastly, if the rising sign be one of the fixed signs Taurus, Leo, Scorpio, and Aquarius, the Lagna Daśâ is known as Adhamâ or Aśubha if the rising Dreṣkâṇa be the first; Uttamâ or Iṣṭa if it be the 2nd; and Madhyamâ or Samâ if it be the 3rd. These names indicate the nature of the Daśâ period, *e.g.*, Adhamâ indicates misery, Madhyamâ, indicates partly good and partly evil; Uttamâ indicates prosperity.

शा० वि०—एकं द्वौ नवविंशतिर्धृतिकृती पंचाशदेषां क्रमा-
च्चंद्रारेंदुजशुक्रजीवदिनकृद्दैवाकरीणां समाः। स्वैः स्वैः पुष्टफ-
लानि सर्गजनितैः पक्तिर्दशायाः क्रमादंते लग्नदशा शुभेति यवना
नेच्छंति केचित्तथा ॥ ९ ॥

एकं Ekam, one. द्वौ Dvau, two. नवविंशतिः Navaviṃśatiḥ, nine and twenty. धृतिकृती Dhritikritî, eighteen and twenty. पंचाशत् Panchâśat, fifty. एषां Eśâm, of these planets. क्रमात् Kramât, in regular order, successively. चंद्रारेंदुजशुक्रजीवदिनकृद्दैवाकरीणां Chandrârendujaśukrajîvadinakriddaivâkarîṇâm, Moon, Mars, Mercury, Venus, Jupiter, Sun and Saturn. समाः Samâḥ, years. स्वैः Svaiḥ, their own. स्वैः Svaiḥ, their own. पुष्टफलाः Puṣṭaphalâḥ, with prosperous results; with ally's benefic results. निसर्गजनितैः Nisargajanitaiḥ, when coinciding with the natural Daśâs. पक्तिः Paktiḥ, maturity. दशायाः Daśâyâḥ, of the Daśâs or the planetary periods as stated in the previous Chapter. क्रमात् Kramât, regularly; in seriatim. अन्ते Ante, the period that is over 120 years. लग्नदशा Lagna Daśâ, the natural Daśâ of the Ascendant, the Ascendant's natural period. शुभा Śubhâ, auspicious. इति Iti, thus (is the opinion). यवना Yavanâ, (of) the author Yavanâchârya. न Na, not. इच्छन्ति Ichhanti, wish. केचित् Kechit, some authors, Śrutikîrti and others. तथा Tathâ, in the same light; auspicious.

9. Now the natural Daśâs or life periods of the planets are being stated. The first year after birth belong to the Moon; next two years belong to Mars; next nine years to Mercury; next twenty years belong to Venus; next eighteen years to Jupiter; next twenty years to the Sun; and next fifty years belong to Saturn. Thus one hundred and twenty years are the sum total of the natural Daśâs of the several planets. If the planetary periods or Daśâs as determined in the preceding Chapter (1) coincide with these natural Daśâs regularly, then the period gets full advantages and becomes prosperous. The closing period and that over 120 years belong to the Ascendant's natural Daśâ and it is auspicious; this is the opinion of Yavanâchârya. Other authors do not like this.

N.B.—When a natural ruler is strong and situated in Upachaya houses, the results are auspicious and when the natural ruler is weak and in Apachaya house, the results are inauspicious. This is true with all the natural rulers.

(1) A similar remark applies to the Antardaśâ periods.

शा० वि०—पाकस्वामिनि लग्नगे सुहृदि वा वर्गेऽस्य सौ-
म्येऽपि वा प्रारब्धा शुभदा दशा त्रिदशषड्लाभेषु वा पाकपे ।
मित्रोच्चोपचयत्रिकोणमदने पाकेश्वरस्य स्थितश्चंद्रः सत्फलबोध-
नानि कुरुते पापानि चातोऽन्यथा ॥ १० ॥

पाकस्वामिनि Pâkasvâmini, the ruler whose Daśâ or Antardaśâ has commenced. लग्नगे Lagnage, when in the Ascendant. सुहृदि Suhṛidi, the ally (of the ruler, whose Daśâ has commenced). वा Vâ, or. वर्गे Varge, the Varga (of the ruler, whose Antardaśâ has commenced). अस्य Asya, of the ruler whose Antardaśâ has commenced. सौम्ये Saumye, the benefic planet. अपि Api, even. वा Vâ, or. प्रारब्धा Prârabdhâ, the beginning of the period, Antardaśâ. शुभदा Subhadâ, auspicious, producing beneficial effects. दशा Daśâ, the Daśâ or Antardaśâ period. त्रिदशषड्लाभेषु Tridaśaṣaḍlâbheṣu, in the third, tenth, sixth and eleventh houses. वा Vâ, or. पाकपे Pâkape, the ruler, whose Daśâ or Antardaśâ has begun. मित्रोच्चोपचयत्रिकोणमदने Mitrochchopachayastrikoṇamadane, in the ally's house, or in the exalted house, or in the Upachaya house, or in the fifth, ninth or seventh houses. पाकेश्वरस्य Pâkeśvarasya, the ruler of the Antardaśâ. स्थितः Sthitaḥ, when situated. चंद्रः Chandraḥ, the Moon. सत्फलबोधनानि Satphalabodhanâni, auspicious results. कुरुते Kurute, manifests. पापानि Pâpâni, inauspicious results. च Cha, and. अतः Ataḥ, from this. अन्यथा Anyathâ, differing, *i.e.*, when the Moon is in the ruler's detrimental or enemy's house or in the same house with the ruler or in the 2nd, 4th, 8th and 12th houses, then the results are bad, even when the commencement of the Daśâ is lucky.

10. The Daśâ period (*a*) is an auspicious one when the Daśâpati (1) is in the Ascendant or when its ally or any of its Vargas (2) or any benefic planet is in the Ascendant; or when the Daśâpati occupies the third, tenth, sixth, or eleventh houses from the then Ascendant.

If the Moon resides in the Daśâpati's the then houses of friendship, in its exalted or in its Upachayas houses or in the fifth, ninth and seventh houses from the Daśâpati then happiness and prosperity are markedly manifested (3). Contrary effects, *i.e.*, misery and suffering are visible when the Moon resides in houses other than those mentioned above.

Notes :—(*a*) Or the Antardaśâ period.

(1) This is interpreted to mean the rising sign at the moment of the commencement of the Daśâ period; so that the hour of commencement of a Daśâ period must first be ascertained and a figure of the heavens drawn up for the hours.

(2) Varga: If, for instance, the Ascendant be the sign, Horâ, Decanate, Navâṃśa, Dvâdaśâṃśa, or Triṃsâṃśa of the Daśâ ruler.

(3) If either the friendly planet or the benefic planet occupying the Ascendant be an Atimitra planet to the Daśâ ruler, such period will be a very prosperous one. If such benefic planet be an Atiśatru planet, the period will not be a prosperous one; but if the planet be a neutral one, just the effects of the Daśâ period will occur.

The Commentator says :—

When the ruler of the Antardaśâ is in its enemy's houses or in the detrimental houses, then the evil effects are produced when the Moon resides in the Daśâpati's enemies' houses, or in the detrimental houses, or lives in the same house with the ruler or in the 2nd, 4th, 8th, or 12th houses from the Ascendant then bad effects are visible though the beginning is auspicious.

Time is measured in four ways :—(1) Solar, (2) Sâvana, (3) Nâkṣatra, and (4) Lunar. By Solar day is meant the period when one degree is passed over by the Sun. When the Sun makes a complete circuit of the Zodiac, it is called a Solar year of 365 days. By Sâvana day is meant the period from one rising of the Sun to the next rising. It is sixty ghaṭis. And 360 such days make one Sâvana year. Here in this verse Sâvana time is the standard according to which astrological calculations are made. Thus from the Khaṇḍâs during the birth time of any individual, prepare the Daśâ periods ; next is to be ascertained when the period of a Daśâ or Antardaśâ commences.

शा० वि०—प्रारब्धा हिमगौ दशा स्वगृहगे मानार्थसौख्यावहा कौजे दूषयति स्त्रियं बुधगृहे विद्यासुहृद्वित्तदा । दुर्गारण्यपथालये कृषिकरी सिंहे सितर्क्षेऽन्नदा कुस्त्रीदा मृगकुंभयोर्गुरुगृहे मानार्थसौख्यावहा ॥ ११ ॥

प्रारब्धा Prârabdhâ, just commenced ; just entered (if at the commencement of the Daśâ period of a planet). हिमगौ Himagau, Moon. दशा Daśâ, the life period. स्वगृहगे Svagrihage, in her own house ; *i.e.*, in the sign Karka (Cancer). मानार्थसौख्यावहा Mânârthasaukhyâvahâ, giving honour, wealth and happiness. कौजे Kauje, Mars' houses, *i.e.*, in the signs Meṣa and Vriśchika. दूषयति Dûṣayati, makes one vicious. स्त्रियं Striyam, wife. बुधगृहे Budhagrihe. in the houses of Mercury, *i.e.*, in the house Mithuna and Kanyâ. विद्यासुहृद्वित्तदा Vidyâsuhridvittadâ, giving learning, friends and wealth. दुर्गारण्यपथालये Durgâraṇyapathâlaye, close to forts, forests, roads, and houses. कृषिकरी Kriṣi karî, cultivating lands. सिंहे Simhe, in the sign Simha. सितर्क्षे Sitarkṣe, in the signs of Venus, *i.e.*, in the signs Vriṣa and Libra. अन्नदा Annadâ, giving articles of food, sweets and delicious eatables. कुस्त्रीदा Kustridâ, giving ugly wife. मृगकुंभयोः Mrigakumbhayoḥ, in the houses Mriga and Kumbha, *i.e.*, Capricorn and Aquarius. गुरुगृहे Gurugrihe, in the houses of Jupiter, *i.e.*, in the houses (Sagittarius) Dhanu and (Pisces) Mîna. मानार्थसौख्यावहा Mânârthasaukhyâbahâ, carrying honour, wealth and happiness.

11. If, at the commencement of any planet's Daśâ period (or Antardaśâ periyd), the Moon be situated in the

house Karka (Cancer), she brings honour, wealth and happiness ; if at the time, the Moon be in the houses Meṣa (Aries) and Vṛiśchika (Scorpio), the wife of the individual will become unchaste ; if in the houses Kanyâ (Virgo) and Mithuna (the Geminni) she gives learning, friends and wealth ; if in the sign Siṃha (Leo), makes one cultivate land near fortified places, forests, road, and dwelling houses ; if in the houses Vṛiṣa (Taurus) and Tulâ (the Libra), gives sweet articles of food; if in the signs Mṛiga (Capricorn) and Kumbha (Aquarius) gives bad ugly wife and if in the houses Dhanu (Sagittarius) and Mîna (Pisces), carries honour, wealth and happiness.

Note :—When this auspicious beginning of the Antardaśâ happens in an auspicious moment, the effects are better and far excellent, and when the inauspicious beginning happens in an unlucky moment the bad effects are rendered far worse ; and mixed results follow when they follow a middle course.

शा०वि०—सौर्यां स्वन्नखदंतचर्मकनकक्रौर्याध्वभूपाहवैस्तैक्ष्ण्यं धैर्यमजस्रमुद्यमरतिः ख्यातिः प्रतापोन्नतिः । भार्यापुत्रधनारिशस्त्रहुतभुग्भूपोद्भवा व्यापदस्त्यागी पापरतिः स्वभृत्यकलहो हृत्क्रोडपीडामयाः ॥ १२ ॥

सौर्यां Sauryâm, during the Sun's Daśâ or Antardaśâ period. स्वं Svam, wealth. नखदंतचर्मकनकक्रौर्याध्वभूपाहवैः Nakhadantacharmakanakakrauryâdhvabhûpâhavaiḥ, arising from the sale of fragrant scents, nails, elephant's tusks, tigers' or other animals' skins, gold, wicked actions, or from roads, kings, or battles. तैक्ष्ण्यं Taiksṇyam, hot temper. धैर्यमजस्रमुद्यमरतिः Dhairyamayasramudyamaratiḥ, persevering, courageous, and always active. ख्यातिः Khyâtiḥ, a man of fame. प्रतापोन्नतिः Pratâponnatiḥ, prosperity on one's own exertion. भार्यापुत्रधनारिशस्त्रहुतभुग्भूपोद्भवाः Bhâryâputtradhanâriśastrahutabhugbhûpodbhavâḥ, arising from wife, son, wealth, enemies, weapons, fire, kings. व्यापदः Vyâpadaḥ, dangers, serious calamities. त्यागी Tyâgî, generous ; charitable ; when the auspicious Daśâ prevails, then one gives in good causes and under good circumstances. When the unlucky Daśâ prevails, then one gives away things in bad causes and under bad circumstances. पापरतिः Pâparatiḥ, addicted to vices. स्वभृत्यकलहः : Svavṛityakalahaḥ, quarrels with one's own servants. हृत्क्रोडपीडामयाः Hṛitkroḍapîḍâmayâḥ, diseases of heart and abdomen or belly.

12. During the Sun's auspicious Daśâ or Antardaśâ period, one acquires wealth by dealing in fragrant scents, nails, ivory articles, hides, (*e.g.*, tigers' and other hides) and gold; or one will get wealth by cruel deeds, (by exacting taxes from) thoroughfares, through kings, or battles. One becomes cruel, of firm and patient disposition, incessantly active and enterprising, gets fame and prosperity by one's own exertion and valour.

During the Sun's inauspicious Daśâ or Antardaśâ one gets calamities through one's wife, children, one's own wealth, enemies, weapons, fire, or kings. One is also prone to be munificent for a good cause in auspicious Daśâs and for bad purposes in case of inauspicious Daśâs; one is addicted to vices, quarrels with one's own servants, and will become afflicted in mind and will be liable to be attacked with chest diseases and those of belly.

Notes:—Mixed results, partly good and partly bad, will follow where there is a mingling of auspicious and inauspicious causes. Discretion is to be used in judging of the effects.

**शा० वि–इंदोः प्राप्य दशां फलानि लभते मंत्रद्विजात्यु-
द्भवानीक्षुक्षीरविकारवस्त्रकुसुमक्रीडातिलान्नश्रमैः । निद्रालस्य-
मृदुद्विजामररतिः स्त्रीजन्म मेधाविता कीर्त्यर्थोपचयक्षयौ च बलि-
भिर्वैरं स्वपक्षेण च ॥ १३ ॥**

इंदोः Indoḥ, of the Moon. प्राप्य Prâpya, on having. दशां Daśâm, the Daśâ or the Antardaśâ. फलानि Phalâni, the results. लभते Labhate, gets. मंत्रद्विजात्युद्भवानि Mantradvijâtyudbhavâni, the sacred Mantras from the Brâhmaṇas. इक्षुक्षीरविकारवस्त्रकुसुमक्रीडातिलान्नश्रमैः Ikṣukṣîravikâravastrakusumkrîḍâtilânnaśramaiḥ, good profits from molasses, curds, clothings, flowers, amusement, sesamum, food, and strength. निद्रालस्यमृदुद्विजामररतिः Nidrâlasyamṛdudvijâmararatiḥ, sleep, idleness, forbearing nature, attachment towards Devas and Brâhmaṇas. स्त्रीजन्म Strîjanma, daughters. मेधाविता कीर्त्यर्थोपचयक्षयौ Medhâvitâkîrtyarthopachayakṣyayau, the loss of intellect, fame, and wealth, even when these are increasing. च Cha, and. बलिभिः Balibhiḥ, with the strong. वैरं Vairam, enmity. स्वपक्षेण Svapakṣeṇa, with one's own relations. Cha, and.

13. During the Moon's auspicious Daśâ or Antardaśâ, the individual will be blessed with the Mantrams from the twice-born (the Brâhmaṇas) and will derive profits by dealing in molasses, curds, butter, clothings, flowers, amusements, sesamum seed, food and his personal strength; he will respect the virtuous Brâhmaṇas and Devas; he will acquire an increase of wisdom, wealth and renown.

During the Moon's inauspicious Daśâ or Antardaśâ one will indulge in laziness and sleep; will be of a forbearing nature; will get daughters and lose his quick intelligence, wealth and renown; and will be involved in enmity with the strong and with his own relations.

**शा० वि०—भौमस्यारिविमर्दभूपसहजक्षित्याविकाजैर्धनं प्र-
द्वेषः सुतमित्रदारसहजैर्विद्वद्गुरुद्वेष्टृता । तृष्णासृग्ज्वरपित्तभंग-
जनिता रोगाः परस्त्रीकृताः प्रीतिः पापरतैरधर्मनिरतिः पारुष्यतै-
क्ष्ण्यानि च ॥ १४ ॥**

भौमस्य Bhaumasya, of Mars; during Mars's Daśâ, auspicious and inauspicious, respectively. अरिविमर्दभूपसहजक्षित्याविकाजैः Arivimardabhûpasahajakṣityâvikâjaiḥ, by crushing enemies: from kings, brothers, earth, and woollen things obtained from sheep's wool. धनं Dhanam, wealth. प्रद्वेषः Pradveṣaḥ, enmity. सुतमित्रदारसहजैः Sutamitradârasahajaiḥ, with sons, friends, wives, and brothers. विद्वद्गुरुद्वेष्टृता Vidvadgurudveṣṭṛitâ, disagreement with literary persons and religious teachers. तृष्णासृग्ज्वरपित्तभंगजनिताः Tṛiṣṇâsṛigjvarapittabhaṅgajanitâḥ, arising out of hunger and thirst, fever from spoilt blood, bilious disaffections, and boils. रोगाः Rogâḥ, diseases. परस्त्रीकृताः Parastrîkṛitâḥ, arising out of illegitimate intercourses. प्रीतिः Prîtiḥ, love, affection; friendship; intimacy. पापरतैः Pâparataiḥ, with vicious persons. अधर्मनिरतिः Adharmaniratiḥ, pleasure in committing sins. पारुष्यतैक्ष्ण्यानि Pâruṣyataikṣṇâni, of harsh speech and cruel temper.

14. During Mars's auspicious Daśâ or Antardaśâ, one gets wealth through defeated enemies, kings, brothers, lands and woollen articles and goats.

During Mars's inauspicious Daśâ or Antardaśâ one hates one's own sons, friends, wives, brothers, literary persons and religious teachers; will suffer from diseases caused by hunger and thirst, spoilt blood, bilious disaffections; fevers and boils, from illegitimate intercourses and friendship with wicked persons and vicious acts. One will become harsh in speech and cruel.

शा० वि०—बौध्यां दौत्यसुहृद्गुरुद्विजधनं विद्वत्प्रशंसा यशो युक्तिद्रव्यसुवर्णवेसरमहीसौभाग्यसौख्याप्तयः । हास्योपासनकौशलं मतिचयो धर्मक्रियासिद्धयः पारुष्यं श्रमबंधमानसशुचः पीडा च धातुत्रयात् ॥ १५ ॥

बौध्यां Baudhyâṃ, during Mercury's Daśâ or Antardaśâ, auspicious and inauspicious. दौत्यसुहृद्गुरुद्विजधनं Dautyasuhṛidgurudvijadhanam, wealth from ambassadorship, friends, preceptors and Brâhmaṇas. विद्वत्प्रशंसा Vidvatpraśaṃsâ, praises from literary persons. यशः Yaśaḥ, fame. युक्तिद्रव्यसुवर्णवेसरमहीसौभाग्यसौख्याप्तयः Yuktidravyasuvarṇavesaramahîsaubhâgyasaukhyâptayaḥ, attainment of brass and other mixed metal utensils, gold, mules, lands, good fortune, and happiness. हास्योपासनकौशलं Hâsyopâsanakauśalam, cleverness in witty talks and serving others. मतिचयः Matichayaḥ, much intellect. धर्मक्रियासिद्धयः Dharmakriyâsiddhayaḥ, success in religious duties. पारुष्यं Pârushyam, harsh words. श्रमबंधमानसशुचः Śramabandhamânasaśuchaḥ, suffering from grief, imprisonment, and mental pain. पीडा Pîḍâ, diseases. च Cha, and. धातुत्रयात् Dhâtutrayât, (diseases) out of the three humours of the body, *viz.*, bile, phlegm, and wind (disordered).

15. During Mercury's auspicious Daśâ or Antardaśâ one gets wealth from ambassadorship, from friends, preceptors, and Brâhmaṇas; acquires name and fame amongst literary persons and obtains brass utensils, gold, mules, lands, good fortune and happiness. One is also very witty, serviceable, of much intellectual power, and attains success in doing religious deeds.

During Mercury's inauspicious Daśâ or Antardaśâ, one becomes rough in speech, suffers from grief, imprisonment, pain of mind and diseases due to the disorders in bile, phlegm, and wind.

शा० वि०—जैव्यां मानगुणोदयो मतिचयः कान्तिः प्रतापोन्नतिर्माहात्म्योद्यममन्त्रनीतिनृपतिस्वाध्यायमन्त्रैर्धनम् । हेमा-

श्वात्मजकुञ्जराम्बरचयः प्रीतिश्च सद्भूमिपैः । सूक्ष्म्योहागहनाश्रमः श्रवणरुग्वैरं विधर्माश्रितैः ॥ १६ ॥

जैव्यां Jaivyâm, during Jupiter's Daśâ or Antardaśâ, auspicious, or inauspicious. मानगुणोदयः Mânagunodayaḥ, worship, learning, prowess and similar good qualifications. मतिचयः Matichayaḥ, much intellectual power. कान्तिप्रतापोन्नतिः Kântiḥpratâponnatiḥ, beauty and riśe on one's own prowess (in putting enemies under control). माहात्म्योद्यममन्त्रनीतिनृपतिस्वाध्यायमन्त्रैः Mâhâtmyodyamamantranîtinripatisvâdhyâyamantraiḥ, by means of one's greatness, energy, or by means of Vaidik mantras, politics, or from kings, studies, or by reciting sacred formulæ of prayer to any deity. धनम् Dhanam, wealth. हेमाश्वात्मजकुञ्जराम्बरचयः Hemâśvâtmajakuñjarâmbarachayaḥ, increment of gold, horses, sons, elephants, raiments. प्रीतिः च Prîtiḥ cha, and friendly feelings. सद्भूमिपैः Sadbhûmipaiḥ, with good and talented kings. सूक्ष्म्योहागहनाश्रमः Sûkṣmyohâgahanâśramaḥ, labour in solving subtle problems. श्रवणरुक् Śravaṇaruk, eye diseases. वैरं Vairam, enmity. विधर्माश्रितैः Vidharmâśritaiḥ, with the religious disbelievers.

16. During Jupiter's auspicious Daśâ or Antardaśâ one acquires reverential feelings, learning, prowess, intellect and beauty. One gets wealth through one's own power; by being beneficial to others, energetic; from Vaidik mantras; from kings, studies, and recitation of sacred formulæ. One gets gold, horses, sons, elephants, and raiments, and becomes friendly to great kings.

During Jupiter's inauspicious Daśâ or Antardaśâ, one gets mental pain in solving subtle problems, eye diseases and enmity with religious disbelievers.

शा० वि०—शौक्र्यां गीतरतिः प्रमोदसुरभिद्रव्यान्नपानाम्बरस्त्रीरत्नद्युतिमन्मथोपकरणज्ञानेष्टमित्रागमाः । कौशल्यं क्रयविक्रये कृषिनिधिप्राप्तिर्धनस्यागमो । वृन्दोर्वीशनिषादधर्मरहितैर्वैरं शुचः स्नेहतः ॥ १७ ॥

शौक्र्यां Saukryâm, during Venus' Daśâ or Antardaśâ, auspicious or inauspicious. गीतरतिः Gîtaratiḥ, taste for music; pleasure in music. प्रमोदसुरभिद्रव्यान्नपानाम्बरस्त्रीरत्नद्युतिमन्मथोपकरणज्ञानेष्टमित्रागमाः Pramodasurabhidravyânnapânâmbarastrîratnadyutimanmathopakaraṇajñaneṣṭamitrâgamâḥ, attainment of pleasures and amusements, fragrant articles, sumptuous fooding, drinking, clothings, fine appearance, valour and women, jewels, gems, nice beddings, etc., to increase one's passion, knowledg desires, and friends. कौशल्यं Kauśalyam, cleverness in actions. क्रयविक्रये Krayavikraye, in buying and selling. कृषिनिधिप्राप्तिः Kriṣinidhiprâptiḥ, tilling, and attainment of hidden treasures and wealth. धनस्य Dhanasya, of wealth. आगमः Âgamaḥ, getting. वृन्दोर्वीशनिषादधर्मरहितैः Vrindorvîśaniṣâdadharmarahitaiḥ, with the crowd, with the king, with the hunter, and irreligious persons. वैरं Vairam, enmity. शुचः Śuchaḥ, suffering pain. स्नेहतः Snehataḥ, out of too much affection, love.

17. During Venus' auspicious Daśâ or Antardaśâ, one is fond of music, will enjoy pleasures and amusements, obtain fragrant articles, fooding, drinking, clothing, women, gems and jewels, acquirements (*e.g.*, fine appearance, valour, *i.e.*, tending to incite lust), knowledge, objects of desires and friends. One becomes clever in buying and selling, tilling and attains hidden treasures and wealth.

During Venus' inauspicious Daśâ or Antardaśâ one is involved in quarrels with the public, king, hunter and irreligious folks and suffers pains from undue feeling of love.

शा०वि०—सौरीं प्राप्य खरोष्ट्रपक्षिमहिषीवृद्धाङ्गनावाप्तयः । श्रेणीग्रामपुराधिकारजनिता पूजा कुधान्यागमः ॥ श्लेष्मेर्ष्यानिलकोपमोह- मलिनव्यापत्तितन्द्राश्रमान् । भृत्यापत्यकलत्रभर्त्सनमपि प्राप्नोति च व्यङ्गताम् ॥ १८ ॥

सौरीं Saurîm, during Saturn's Daśâ and Antardaśâs, auspicious and inauspicious. प्राप्य Prâpya, on getting. खरोष्ट्रपक्षिमहिषीवृद्धाङ्गनावाप्तयः : Kharoṣṭrapakṣimahiṣîvṛidhâmganâvâptayaḥ, acquiring of asses, camels, hawks, buffaloes and old wife. श्रेणीग्रामपुराधिकारजनितापूजा Sreṇîgrâmapurâdhikârajanitâpûjâ, worship from villagers and townsmen where many people of the same caste reside. कुधान्यागमः : Kudhânyâgamaḥ, obtaining of grains, *e.g.*, of jowâri and bâjra that are usually taken by poorer classes. श्लेष्मेर्ष्यानिलकोपमोहमलिनव्यापत्तितन्द्राश्रमात् Śleṣmerṣyânilakopamohamalinavyâpattitandrâśramât, arising from cold and cough, jealousy, wind, anger, delusion, miserableness, calamities, sleep, or fatigue. भृत्यापत्यकलत्रभर्त्सनं Bhrityâpatyakalatrabhartsanam, revilings and threats from servants, children, and wife. अपि Api, also. प्राप्नोति Prâpnoti, gets. च Cha, also. व्यङ्गताम् Vyangatâm, from the cutting of some parts of the body or from diseases of defective limbs; from some defective organs.

18. During Saturn's auspicious Daśâ or Antardaśâ, one gains asses, camels, hawks and other birds, old wife and

worship from villagers or townsmen where many people of the same caste reside, and also coarse grains such as jowâr and bâjrâ, &c.

During Saturn's inauspicious Daśâ or Antardaśâ, one gets calamities from cough, jealousy, wind, anger, delusion, miserableness, idleness, and fatigue (1); one also gets reproaches from servants, children and wife, and suffers from defective organs.

Note:—(1) The individual will suffer from phlegmatic and windy complaints; will be jealous, angry, distracted in mind, dirty, exposed to danger, idle, suffer from grief, and be much troubled.

उपजातिका—दशासु शस्तासु शुभानि कुर्वंत्यनिष्टसंज्ञा स्वशुभानि चैवम् । मिश्रासु मिश्राणि दशाफलानि होराफलं लग्नपतेः समानम् ॥ १६ ॥

दशासु Daśâsu, during the Daśâ period. शस्तासु Śastâsu, auspicious. शुभानि Śubhâni, good, beneficial. कुर्वंति Kurvanti, do; effect; produce. अनिष्टसंज्ञासु Aniṣṭasaṃjñâsu, when inauspicious. अशुभानि Aśubhâni, bad. च एवम् Cha evam, and thus. मिश्रासु Miśrâsu, mixed, of the nature of good and bad mixed. मिश्राणि Miśrâṇi, mixed. दशाफलानि Daśâphalâni, results; fruition; fruits in Daśâ periods. होराफलं Horâphalaṃ, the result of the Ascendant. लग्नपतेः Lagnapateḥ, of the ruler of the Ascendant. समानम् Samânam, equal, similar.

19. The planets in their auspicious Daśâs when in the auspicious houses, *e.g.*, Upachaya houses, when not descendant, in the exalted houses, and in their auspicious Vargas, produce good and beneficial effects.

The planets in their inauspicious Daśâ or Antardaśâ periods, *i.e.*, when in the inauspicious houses, *e.g.*, when defeated, or when descendant, or when in the detrimental houses produce bad effects in their Daśâs. When the causes are good as well as bad, the effects are also mixed. The effects of the Ascendant Daśâ are the same as those of its ruler's Daśâ.

शालिनी—संज्ञाध्याये यस्य यद्द्रव्यमुक्तं कर्माजीवो यश्च यस्योपदिष्टः । भावस्थानालोकयोगोद्भवं च तत्तत्सर्वं तस्य योज्यं दशायाम् ॥ २० ॥

संज्ञाध्याये Sanjñâdhyâye, in the Chapter on Sanjñâ, where technical names and their designations are stated. यस्य Yasya, of whichever planet. यद्द्रव्यं Yaddravyam, whichever things, copper, etc. उक्तं Uktam, are mentioned. कर्माजीवः Karmâjîvaḥ, the occupation of a man in his life. यः च Yaḥ cha, and who. यस्य Yasya, of whichever planet. उपदिष्टः Upadiṣṭaḥ, are advised; are stated. भावस्थानालोकयोगोद्भवं Bhâvasthânâlokayogodbhavam, fruits arising from the natures of the twelve houses or signs and the aspects and combinations. तत् तत्सर्वं Tat tat sarvam, all these. तस्य Tasya, to that. योज्यं Yojyam, to be considered; to be taken in account. दशायाम् Daśâyâm, during the Daśâ period; when the Daśâ or fruition period of planets are taken into account.

20. The materials, copper, etc., favourite to any planet, mentioned already in the Chapter on Sanjñâ or designations or whatever occupations advised under each planet (in the following chapters), the natures of the 12 houses, the mutual aspects of planets and their combinations, all these are to be reckoned into account, when judging of the effects, of the Daśâ, *i.e.*, fruition period of any planet. If the Daśâ period be auspicious, these materials will be gained by the native; else they will be lost. When the combinations are of a mixed character, the result will be mixed.

Notes:—As stated already, the character, whether benefic or malefic of a Daśâ period is to be determined from the technical names given to the ruler of the period. *Vide* stanzas 6 and 7. Again, if, at the time of birth, any of the planets occupy the Upachaya houses, be of bright discs and of distinct motion, the effects will be good in their Daśâ periods. But if the planets suffer defeat in conjunction, be of disagreeable appearance or of small disc, the effects will be bad in their Daśâ periods. The planets which, at the time of the commencement of their Antardaśâ periods, might be aspected by benefic planets or occupy the Vargas of benefic or very friendly planets, are powerful and will not cause death; if they be situated otherwise they will cause death.

इ० व०—छायां महाभूतकृतां च सर्वेऽभिव्यंजयन्ति स्वदशामवाप्य । कंत्वग्निवाय्वंबरजान्गुणांश्च नासास्यदृक्त्वक्छ्रवणानुमेयात् ॥ २१ ॥

छायां Chhâyâm, the light, the reflection in this body. महाभूतकृतां Mahâbhûtakṛtâm, caused by the primary elements, earth, water, fire, air, and Âkâśa. च Cha, and. सर्वे Sarve, all the planets. अभिव्यंजयंति Abhivyamjayanti, manifest, make visible.

स्वदशां Svadasâm, their Daśâs. अवाप्य Avâpya, on having. क्ष्मांब्वग्निवाय्वंबरजान् Kkambvagnivâyavambarajân, derived from earth, water, fire, air and Âkâśa respectively. गुणान् Guṇân, the properties ; the qualities, smell, taste, appearance, touch and sound respectively. च Cha, and. नासास्यदृक्त्वक्श्रवणानुमेयान् Nâsâsyadṛiktvakśravaṇânumeyân, inferred by nose, tongue, sight, skin, and ears respectively.

21. All the planets on attaining their Daśâs reflect in our bodies their respective qualities smell, taste, appearance, touch, and sound generated out of the primary elements, earth, water, fire, air and Âkâśa and that can be perceived by nose, tongue, sight, skin and ears.

Note.—If the reflection caused by a planet be good, the results will be good ; otherwise, bad ; and if the combination of planets be of a mixed character, the result will also be mixed. This verse is specially intended to find out the Daśâpatis where the Daśâs of planets are unknown during the birth time. They can be inferred indirectly by the reflections caused by the planets as described above. The quality of earth is smell and this can be perceived by nose ; similarly the quality of water is taste and can be perceived by tongue ; the quality of fire is appearance, form and can be recognised by sight ; the quality of air is touch and can be perceived by touch and the quality of Âkâśa is sound and can be perceived by ears. Now the question is :—Find out which planet's Daśâ is working at any time. The Answer is :—Find out which element is working predominantly and the planet corresponding to that element has its Daśâ at that time. Suppose nice smell is perceived, then the planet Mercury is working. If one likes sweet things at any moment, then the Moon or Venus is working. If the appearance of the body be beautiful and of good complexion, know that it is caused by fire and the Sun or Mars is working then. If the touch be gentle, then Saturn's Daśâ is working, and if the voice of any person be sweet at any time, Jupiter is working. If these reflections be good, then the Daśâ is good ; otherwise, of a bad or mixed character as the case may be.

Remarks.—Physical man is a composition of the five elementary principles—earth, water, fire, air and Âkâsa (ether) ; Mercury presides over earth ; Venus and the Moon over water ; Mars and the Sun over fire ; Saturn over air ; and Jupiter over Âkâśa. In the Daśâ period of a particular planet, his elementary principle will predominate and the complexion of the person during such period will be that due to the particular elementary principle. Varâha Mihira in Chapter 68 of his Bṛihat Saṃhitâ (stanzas 90 to 93) has thus stated in detail the complexion due to each of the seven planets.

"The complexion discernible in shining teeth, skin, nails and hairs of the body and of the head will be attended with prosperity; it is caused by the element of earth; it makes the person happy, rich and virtuous."

"The complexion which is glossy, white, clear, green and agreeable to look at is caused by the element of water; it will make all creatures possessing it happy and successful in all their attempts and will produce wealth, comfort, luxury and prosperity."

"The complexion which is fearful, unbearable, of the colour of the lotus, gold, or fire and indicating strength, power, and valour, is caused by the element of fire, and it brings success to a person and enables him to gain his desired object."

"The complexion which is dirty, not glossy, black and and of bad scent, is caused by the element of air, it will cause to the person death or imprisonment, disease, ruin, and loss of wealth."

"The complexion which is of the colour of crystal, noble, clear and indicating wealth, and generosity, is caused by the element of ether; it gives a person all that he desires."

Now suppose the Daśâ period to be that of Mars, his element is fire; the complexion caused by the elementary principle of fire described above, will be the complexion of a person in the Daśâ period of Mars and so for the other planets.

Again, the property of earth is smell, discernible by the nose; that of water is taste, discernible by the tongue; that of fire or light is shape or appearance, discernible by the eye; that of air is touch, discernible by the body; and that of Âkâśa is sound, discernible by the ear. Suppose the Daśâ period to be that of Venus; his element is water; the quality belonging to water is taste, discernible by the tongue. Therefore in the Daśâ period of Venus, the person will eat juicy meals according to his desire, In the Daśâ period of Jupiter (Âkâśa-sound) the person's speech will be sweet and agreeable to the ear; in the period of Mercury (earth-smell) the person's body will be with an agreeable odour; in that of Mars (fire-shape) he will be of agreeable appearance; and in that of Saturn (air-touch) he will be of soft body. From a careful observation of these qualities the particular Daśâ period of a person may also be determined.

मालिनी–शुभफलददशाया तादृगेवान्तरात्मा । बहु जनयति पुंसां सौख्यमर्थागमं च ॥ कथितफलविपाकैस्तर्कयेद्वर्तमानां । परिणमति फलाप्तिः स्वप्नचिन्तास्ववीर्यैः ॥ २२ ॥

शुभफलददशायां Subhaphaladadaśâyâm, in the auspicious Daśâ time of any planet. तादृगेव Tâdṛik eva, certainly of the same nature. अन्तरात्मा Antarâtmâ, the inner self. बहु Bahu, all sorts. जनयति Janayati, bring forth. पुंसां Puṃsâm, to any person. सौख्यम Saukhyam, pleasurable, happy feelings. अर्थागमं Arthâgamam, the gaining of wealth. च Cha, and. कथितफलविपाकैः Kathitaphalavipâkaiḥ, on knowing the results aforesaid. तर्कयेत् Tarkayet, one is to argue; one should get information. वर्तमानां Vartamânâm, the present Daśâ; the Daśâ that is being experienced at the time in question. परिणमति Pariṇamati, become experienced; become perceived. फलाप्तिः Phalâptiḥ, the results; the fruits obtained. स्वप्नचिंतासु Svapnachintâsu, during the dreaming or mental state. अवीर्यैः Avîrjaiḥ, by the planets, by the Daśâpatis when they are weak; by the weak planets.

22. As the Daśâ of a planet is auspicious, so the inner self of the person is also pleased and happy, and all sorts of pleasure and wealth are incoming at that time (1). Therefore when one knows the present state of one's mind or the results that are being experienced at that time, one can at once tell what the Daśâ is and which planet is working. If the planet be not sufficiently strong, then its Daśâ is also weak and can be perceived while in a dreamy state or in mind only, not actually carried out in practice.

Note.—In all these cases it should be remembered that when the planetary combinations are partly good and partly bad, the results also become so.

(1) If the Daśâ period be inauspicious, the inner self also feels itself weak and unhappy; and if the Daśâ period be of a mixed nature, the inner self also feels itself so.

व० ति०—एकग्रहस्य सदृशे फलयोर्विरोधे । नाशं वदेद्यदधिकं परिपच्यते तत् ॥ नान्यो ग्रहः सदृशमन्यफलं हिनस्ति । स्वां स्वां दशामुपगताः सफलप्रदास्युः ॥ २३ ॥

इति श्रीवराहमिहिरविरचिते बृहज्जातके दशान्तर्दशाध्यायोऽष्टमः ॥ ८ ॥

एकग्रहस्य Ekagrahasya, of one and the same planet. सदृशे Sadṛiśe, equal; of the same strength. फलयोः Phalayoḥ, of the fruits. विरोधे Virodhe, being contradictory. नाशं Nâśam, non-effective. वदेत् Vadet, should say; is to declare or pass his judgment. यत् Yat, whichever of the two fruits. अधिकं Adhikam, of the greater strength; stronger. परिपच्यते Paripachyate, comes into effect; bears fruit.

तत् Tat, that. न Na, not. अन्य: Anyaḥ, other planet. ग्रह: Grahaḥ, planet. सदृशं Sadṛiśam, of the same power, similarly strong. अन्यफलं Anyaphalam, opposite results. हिनस्ति Hinasti, destroys. स्वां स्वां Svâm svâm, their own (respectively). दशां Daśâm, Dasâs ; fruition periods. उपगता: Upagatâḥ, on getting. स्वफलप्रदा: Saphala-pradâḥ, bestower of their own fruits. स्यु: Syuḥ, become.

23. When one plànet gives two equal contradictory results, then no results are carried into effect. When two contradictory results are not of the same strength, the more powerful one is carried into effect. One planet does not destroy another planet's effect, though one is equal and contradictory to the other. Both these bear fruits in their own Daśâs or fruition periods respectively.

Note:—Suppose one planet gives wealth by one sort of reasoning (under one set of planetary combinations) and this very planet takes away wealth by another sort of reasoning (under another set of planetary combinations) and both the reasonings are equally strong; in this case, no coming of wealth nor loss will take place. But if one reasoning be stronger, then gain or loss as the case may be will take place. Suppose one planet gives wealth; another planet takes it with equal force; in this case fruits will not be nullified. Wealth will come and go respectively in each planet's fruition period (Daśâ).

Thus ends the Eighth Chapter in Bṛihat Jâtakam dealing on Daśâs and Antardaśâs by Śrî Varâha Mihirâchârya of Avantika.

CHAPTER IX

ON AṢṬAKA VARGA.

शा० वि०—स्वादर्कः प्रथमायबंधुनिधनद्व्याज्ञातपोद्यूनगो
वक्रास्स्वादिव तद्वदेव रविजाच्छुक्रात्स्मरांत्यारिषु । जीवाद्धर्मसु-
तायशत्रुषु दशत्र्यायारिगः शीतगोरेष्वेवांत्यतपः सुतषु च बुधाल्ल-
ग्नात्सबंधव्त्यगः ॥ १ ॥

स्वात् Svât, from its own (position). The sign where any planet resides during the time of birth is called that planet's own position. Here the Sun's position (*i.e.*, the sign occupied by the Sun) is meant. अर्कः Arkaḥ, the Sun. प्रथमायबंधुनिधनद्व्याज्ञातपोद्यूनगः Prathamâyabandhunidhanadvyâjñâtapodvyunagaḥ, in the first, eleventh, fourth, eighth, second, tenth, ninth and seventh houses reckoned from the Sun's own position, (it is auspicious). वक्रात् Vakrât, from the Mars. स्वात् Svât, own position. इव Iva, like. तद्वत् Tadvat, similar to that (the Sun.) एव Eva, certainly. रविजात् Ravijât, from Saturn. शुक्रात् Śukrât, from Venus. स्मरांत्यारिषु Smarâmtyâriṣu, in the seventh, twelfth and sixth houses. जीवात् Jîvât, from Jupiter. धर्मसुतायशत्रुषु Dharmasutâyaśatruṣu, in the ninth, fifth, eleventh, and sixth houses. दशत्र्यायारिगः Daśatryâyârigaḥ, in the tenth, third, eleventh and sixth houses. शीतगोः Śîtagoḥ, from the Moon. एषु एव Eṣu eva, in these also. अंत्यतपःसुतेषु Antyatapaḥsuteṣu, in the twelfth, ninth, and fifth houses. च Cha, and ; in the case of Mercury also. बुधात् Budhât, from Mercury. लग्नात् Lagnât, from the Ascendant. सबंधव्त्यगः Sabandhvantyagaḥ, with the fourth and twelfth houses in addition ; (in addition to the houses from the Moon).

Now the benefic and malefic places of a planet with reference to the eight positions (the positions occupied by the seven planets and the Ascendant at the time of birth) are being described. The sign where any planet exists during the birth time is called that planet's own position.

The benefic or malefic results arising from the positions of the seven planets with respect to each other or with respect to the Ascendant as described here, are called the *Gochara* results.

As the eight positions are considered in this Chapter, *i.e.*, the seven positions of the seven planets and the Ascendant, this Chapter is called the Chapter on Aṣṭaka Varga (the eight positions)

1. The Sun in the 1st, 2nd, 4th, 7th, 8th, 9th, 10th and 11th houses from his position (*i.e.*, the sign occupied by

him at birth time) produces auspicious results; if in the remaining houses, produces inauspicious results. The Sun in the same places (*i.e.*, 1st, 2nd, 4th, 7th, 8th, 9th, 10th and 11th) from Mars and Saturn produces good, benefic results; if in the other houses, evil results. When the Sun is in the 6th, 7th and 12th houses from Venus, the results are auspicious; elsewhere inauspicious. When the Sun is in the 5th, 6th, 9th and 11th houses from Jupiter, the results are auspicious. When the Sun is in the 3rd, 6th, 10th and 11th houses from the Moon, the results are auspicious. When the Sun is in the 3rd, 5th, 6th, 9th, 10th, 11th and 12th houses from Mercury, the results are auspicious. And when the Sun is in the 3rd, 4th, 6th, 10th, 11th and 12th houses from the Ascendant, the auspicious results are produced; in the houses other than those mentioned, evil results are produced.

Note:—This is the Aṣṭaka Varga of the Sun. This is also the opinion of Satyâchârya. The auspicious houses of a planet are known as the benefic places and the inauspicious houses as the malefic places of a planet.

शा० वि०—लग्नात्षट्त्रिदशायगः सधनधीधर्मेषु चारा-
च्छशी स्वात्सास्तादिषु साष्टसप्तसु रवेः षट्त्र्यायधीस्थो यमात् ।
धीत्र्यायाष्टमकंटकेषु शशिजाज्जीवाद्व्ययायाष्टगः केंद्रस्थश्च
सितात्तु धर्मसुखधीत्र्यायास्पदानंगगः ॥ २ ॥

लग्नात् Lagnât, from the Ascendant. षट्त्रिदशायगः Saṭtridaśâyagaḥ, in the 6th, 3rd, 10th, and eleventh houses. सधनधीधर्मेषु Sadhanadhîdharmeṣu, in the 2nd, 5th, and 9th houses in addition to those mentioned above. च Cha, and. आरात् Ârât, from the Mars. शशी Śaśî, the Moon. स्वात् Svât, from her own position. सास्तादिषु Sâstâdiṣu, in the 7th and 1st houses in addition. साष्टसप्तसु, Sâṣṭasaptasu, in the 8th and 7th houses in addition. रवेः Raveḥ, from the Sun. षट्त्र्यायधीस्थः Ṣaṭtryâyadhîsthaḥ, in the 6th, 3rd, 11th and 5th houses. यमात् Yamât, from Saturn. धीत्र्यायाष्टमकंटकेषु Dhîtryâyâṣṭamakamṭakeṣu, in the 5th, 3rd, 11th, 8th, 1st, 4th, 7th and 10th houses. शशिजात् Śaśijât, from the Mercury. जीवात् Jîvât, from Jupiter. व्ययायाष्टगः Vyayâyâṣṭagaḥ, in the 12th, 11th and 8th houses. केन्द्रस्थः Kendrasthaḥ, in the 1st, 4th, 7th and 10th houses. च Cha, and. सितात् Sitât, from Venus. तु

Tu, but. धर्मसुखधीत्र्यायास्पदानंगगः Dharmasukhadhîtryâyâspadânaṃgagaḥ, in the 9th, 4th, 5th, 3rd, 11th, 10th and 7th houses.

2. The auspicious results are produced when the Moon lies in the 6th, 3rd, 10th and 11th houses from the Ascendant; or in the 6th, 3rd, 10th, 11th, 2nd, 5th and 9th houses from Mars; or in the 6th, 3rd, 10th, 11th, 7th and 1st houses from her own position; or in the 6th, 3rd, 10th, 11th, 8th and 7th houses from the Sun; or in the 6th, 3rd, 11th and 5th houses from Saturn; or in the 5th, 3rd, 11th 8th, 1st, 4th, 7th and 10th houses from Mercury; or in the 12th, 11th, 8th, 1st, 4th, 7th and 10th houses from Jupiter; or in the 9th, 4th, 5th, 3rd, 11th, 10th and 7th houses from Venus.

Notes:—This is also the opinion of Satyâchârya. This is the Aṣṭaka Varga of the Moon. When the Moon lies in houses other than those mentioned above, inauspicious results are seen.

शा० वि०—वक्रस्तूपचयेष्विनात् सतनयेष्वाद्याधिकेषूदया- । चन्द्राद्दिग्विफलेषु केन्द्रनिधनप्राप्त्यर्थगः स्वाच्छुभः ॥ धर्मायाष्ट- मकेन्द्रगोऽर्कतनयाज्ज्ञात् षट्त्रिधीलाभगः । शुक्रात् षड्व्ययलाभ- मृत्युषु गुरोः कर्मान्त्यलाभारिषु ॥ ३ ॥

वक्रः Vakraḥ, Mars. तु Tu, but. उपचयेषु Upachayeṣu, in the Upachaya houses, *i.e.*, 3rd, 6th, 11th and 10th houses. इनात् Inât, from the Sun. सतनयेषु Satanayeṣu, in the 5th house in addition. आद्याधिकेषु Âdyâdhikeṣu, with the 1st house also. उदयात् Udayât, from the Ascendant. चन्द्रात् Chandrât, from the Moon. दिग्विफलेषु Digviphaleṣu, excepting the 10th house. केन्द्रनिधनप्राप्त्यर्थगः Kendranidhanaprâptyarthagaḥ, in the 1st, 4th, 7th, 10th, 8th, 11th and 2nd houses. स्वात् Svât, from its own sign. शुभः Śubhaḥ, auspicious. धर्मायाष्टमकेन्द्रगोः Dharmâyâṣṭamakendragoḥ, in the 9th, 11th, 8th, 1st, 4th, 7th and 10th houses. अर्कतनयात् Arkatanayât, from Saturn. ज्ञात् Jñât, from Mercury. षट्त्रिधीलाभगः Saṭtridhîlâbhagaḥ, in the 6th, 3rd, 5th, 11th houses. शुक्रात् Śukrât, from Venus. षड्व्ययलाभमृत्युषु Saḍvyayalâbhamṛityuṣu, in the 6th, 12th, 11th and 8th houses. गुरोः Guroḥ, from Jupiter. कर्मान्त्यलाभारिषु Karmântyalâbhâriṣu, in the 10th, 12th, 11th and 6th houses.

3. The auspicious results are produced in the following cases. When Mars is the 3rd, 6th, 10th, 11th and 5th houses from the Sun; or in the 3rd, 6th, 10th, 11th

and 1st houses from the Ascendant; or in the 3rd, 6th and 11th houses from the Moon; or in the 1st, 4th, 7th, 10th, 8th, 11th and 2nd houses from his own position; or in the 9th, 11th, 8th, 1st, 4th, 7th, and 10th houses from Saturn; or in the 6th, 3rd, 5th, 11th houses from Mercury; or in the 6th, 12th, 11th, and 8th houses from Venus; or in the 10th, 12th, 11th, and 6th houses from Jupiter.

Note:—This is also the opinion of Satyâchârya. Thus is the Aṣṭaka Varga of Mars.

शा॰ वि॰—द्व्याद्यायाष्टतपः सुखेषु भृगुजात्सत्र्यात्मजेष्विदुजः साज्ञास्तेषु यमारयोर्व्ययरिपुप्राप्त्यष्टगो वाक्पतेः। धर्मायारिसुतव्ययेषु सवितुः स्वात्साद्यकर्मत्रिगः षट्स्वायाष्टसुखास्पदेषु हिमगोः साद्येषु लग्नाच्छुभः ॥ ४ ॥

द्व्याद्यायाष्टतपःसुखेषु Dvyâdyâyâṣṭatapaḥsukheṣu, in the 2nd, 1st, 11th, 8th, 9th, 4th houses. भृगुजात् Bhrigujât, from Venus. सत्र्यात्मजेषु Satryâtmajeṣu, with the 3rd and 5th houses in addition. इन्दुजः Indujaḥ, from the Moon. साज्ञास्तेषु Sâjñâsteṣu, with the 10th and 7th houses in addition. यमारयोः Yamârayoḥ, from Saturn and Mars. व्ययारिपुप्राप्त्यष्टगोः Vyayaripuprâptyaṣṭagoḥ, in the 12th, 6th, 11th, and 8th houses. वाक्पतेः Vâkpateḥ, from Jupiter. धर्मायारिसुतव्ययेषु Dharmâyârisûtavyaeṣu, in the 9th, 11th, 6th, 5th, and 12th houses. सवितुः Savituḥ, from the Sun. स्वात् Svât, from its own sign. साद्यकर्मत्रिगः Sâdyakarmatrigaḥ, with the 1st, 10th, 3rd houses in addition. षट्स्वायाष्टसुखास्पदेषु Ṣaṭsvâyâṣṭasukhâspadeṣu, in the 6th, 2nd, 11th, 8th, 4th and 10th houses. हिमगोः Himagoḥ, from the Moon. साद्येषु Sâdyeṣu, with the 1st house in addition. लग्नात् Lagnât, from the Ascendant. शुभः Śubhaḥ, auspicious.

4. The auspicious results of Mercury are produced in the following cases.

When Mercury is in the 2nd, 1st, 11th, 8th, 9th, 4th, 3rd and 5th houses from Venus; or in the 2nd, 1st, 11th, 8th, 9th, 4th, 10th, and 7th houses from Saturn or from Mars; or in 12th, 6th, 11th and 8th houses from Jupiter; or in the 9th, 11th, 6th, 5th, and 12th houses from the Sun; or in the 9th, 11th, 6th, 5th, 12th, 1st, 10th and 3rd houses from its own position ; or in the 6th, 2nd, 11th, 8th, 4th, and 10th houses from the Moon ; or in the 6th, 2nd, 11th, 8th, 4th, 10th, and 1st houses from the Ascendant.

Note :—This is also the opinion of Satyâchârya. This is the Aṣṭaka Varga of Mercury

शा० वि०—दिक्स्वाद्याष्टमदायबंधुषु कुजात्स्वात्संत्रिकेष्वं गिराः सूर्यात्सत्रिनवेषुधीस्वनवदिग्लाभारिगो भार्गवात् । जाया-यार्थनवात्मजेषु हिमगोर्मंदात्रिषड्धीव्यये दिग्धीषट्स्वसुखायपूर्व-नवगो ज्ञात्ससमरश्चोदयात् ॥ ५ ॥

दिक्स्वाद्याष्टमदायबंधुषु Diksvâdyâṣṭamadâyabandhuṣu, in the 10th, 2nd, 1st, 8th, 7th 11th and 4th houses. कुजात् Kujât, from Mars. स्वात् Svât, from his (Jupiter's) own position. सत्रिकेषु Satrikeṣu, with the 3rd house in addition. अंगिराः Aṃgirâḥ, Jupiter. सूर्यात् Sûryât, from the Sun. सत्रिनवेषु Satrinaveṣu, with the 3rd and 9th houses in addition. धीस्वनवदिग्लाभारिगः : Dhisvanavadiglâbhârigaḥ, in the 5th, 2nd, 9th, 10th, 11th and 6th houses. भार्गवात् Bhârgavât, from Venus. जायायार्थनवात्मजेषु Jâyâyârthanavâtmajeṣu, in the 7th, 11th, 2nd, 9th and 5th houses. हिमगोः Himagoḥ, from the Moon. मंदात् Mandât, from Saturn. त्रिषड्धीव्यये Triṣaḍdhîvyae, in the 3rd, 6th, 5th, and 12th houses. दिग्धीषट्स्वसुखायपूर्वनवगः : Dighdhîṣaṭsvasukhâya-pûrvanavagaḥ, in the 10th, 5th, 6th, 2nd, 4th, 11th, 1st and 9th houses. ज्ञात् Jñât, from Mercury. ससमरः : Sasmaraḥ, with the 7th house in addition. च Cha, and. उदयात् Udayât, from the Ascendant.

5. The auspicious results are produced in the following cases :—When Jupiter is in the 10th, 2nd, 1st, 8th, 7th, 11th, and 4th houses from Mars ; or in the 10th, 2nd, 1st, 8th, 7th, 11th, 4th and 3rd houses from his own position ; or in the 10th, 2nd, 1st, 8th, 7th, 11th, 4th, 3rd, and 9th houses from the Sun ; or in the 5th, 2nd, 9th, 10th, 11th, and 6th houses from Venus ; or in the 7th, 11th, 2nd, 9th and 5th houses from the Moon ; or in the 3rd, 6th, 5th and 12th houses from Saturn ; or in the 10th, 5th, 6th, 2nd, 4th, 11th, 1st and 9th houses from Mercury ; or in the 10th, 5th, 6th, 2nd, 4th, 11th, 1st, 9th, and 7th houses from the Ascendant.

Note.—There are some differences here with Satyâchârya. This is the Aṣṭakavarga of Jupiter.

शा० वि०—लग्नादासुतलाभरंध्रनवगः सांत्यः शशांकात्सितः स्वात्साज्ञेषु सुखत्रिधीनवदशच्छिद्राप्तिगः सूर्यजात् । रंध्रायव्ययगो रवेर्नवदशप्राप्त्यष्टधीस्थो गुरोर्ज्ञाद्धीत्र्यायनवारिगस्त्रिनवषट्पुत्राय-सांत्यः कुजात् ॥ ६ ॥

लग्नात् Lagnât, from the Ascendant. आसुतलाभरंध्रनवगः Âsutalâbharandhranavagaḥ, in the 1st, 2nd, 3rd, 4th, 5th, 11th, 8th and 9th houses. सांत्यः Sântyaḥ, with the 12th houses in addition. शशांकात् Saśâṃkât, from the Moon. सितः Sitaḥ, Venus. स्वात् Svât, from her own position. साज्ञेषु Sâjñeṣu, with the 10th house in addition. सुखत्रिधीनवदशच्छिद्राप्तिगः Sukhatridhînavadaśachhidrâptigaḥ, in the 4th, 3rd, 5th, 9th, 10th, 8th and 11th houses. सूर्यजात् Sûryajât, from Saturn. रंध्रायव्ययगः Randhrâyavyayagaḥ, in the 8th, 11th and 12th houses. रवेः Raveḥ, from the Sun. नवदशप्राप्त्यष्टधीस्थः Navadaśaprâptyaṣṭadhîsthaḥ, in the 9th, 10th, 11th, 8th and 5th houses. गुरोः Guroḥ, from Jupiter. ज्ञात् Jñât, from Mercury. धीत्र्यायनवारिगः Dhîtryâyanavârigaḥ, in the 5th, 3rd, 11th, 9th and 6th houses. त्रिनवषट्पुत्रायसांत्यः Trinavaṣaṭ putrâysântyaḥ, in the 3rd, 9th, 6th, 5th, 11th, 12th houses. कुजात् Kujât, from Mars.

6. These are the following auspicious cases :—When Venus is in the 1st, 2nd, 3rd, 4th, 5th, 11th, 8th, and 9th houses from the Ascendant, or in the 1st, 2nd, 3rd, 4th, 5th, 11th, 8th, 9th and 12th houses from the Moon; or in the 1st, 2nd, 3rd, 4th, 5th, 11th, 8th, 9th, 10th houses from her own position; or in the 4th, 3rd, 5th, 9th, 10th, 8th, 11th houses from Saturn; or in the 8th, 11th, 12th houses from the Sun; or in the 9th, 10th, 11th, 8th, 5th houses from Jupiter; or in the 5th, 3rd, 11th 9th, and 6th houses from Mercury; or in the 3rd, 9th, 6th, 5th, 11th and 12th houses from Mars.

Note.—This is in accordance with Satyâchârya, and is the Aṣṭakavarga (*i.e.*, the benefic places) of Venus.

शा० वि०—मंदस्वात्त्रिसुतायशत्रुषु शुभः साज्ञांत्यगो भूमिजात् केंद्रायाष्टधनेष्विनादुपचयेष्वाद्ये सुखे चोदयात् । धर्मायारिदशांत्यमृत्युषु बुधाच्चंद्रात्त्रीषड्लाभगः षष्ठायांत्यगतः सितात्सुरगुरोः प्राप्त्यंत्यधीशत्रुषु ॥ ७ ॥

मंद: Mandaḥ, Saturn. स्वात् Svât, from its own position. त्रिसुतायशत्रुषु Trisutâyaśatruṣu, in the 3rd, 5th, 11th and 6th houses. शुभ: Śubhaḥ, auspicious. साज्ञांत्यगः Sâjñântyagaḥ, with the 10th and 12th houses in addition, *i.e.*, in 3rd, 5th, 11th, 6th, 10th, and 12th houses. भूमिजात् Bhûmijât, from Mars. केन्द्रायाष्टधनेषु Kendrâyâṣṭadhaneṣu, in the 1st, 4th, 7th, 10th, 11th, 8th and 2nd houses. इनात् Inât, from the Sun. उपचयेषु Upachayeṣu, in the 3rd, 6th, 10th and 11th houses. आद्ये Âdye, in the 1st house (also). सुखे Sukhe, in the 4th house (also). च Cha, also. उदयात् Udayât, from the Ascendant. धर्मायारिदशांत्यमृत्युषु Dharmâyâridaśântyamrityuṣu, in the 9th, 11th, 6th, 10th, 12th, and 8th houses. बुधात् Budhât, from Mercury. चंद्रात् Chandrât, from the Moon. त्रिषड्लाभगः Triṣaḍlâbhagaḥ, in the 3rd, 6th, 11th houses. षष्ठायांत्यगतः Saṣṭhâyântyagataḥ, in the 6th, 11th, 12th houses. सितात् Sitât, from Venus. सुरगुरोः Suraguroḥ, from Jupiter. प्राप्त्यन्त्यधीशत्रुषु Prâptyantyadhîśatruṣu, in the 11th, 12th, 5th, and 6th houses.

7. The following are the auspicious cases :—When Saturn is in the 3rd, 5th, 11th, and 6th houses from its own position; or in the 3rd, 5th, 11th, 6th, 10th, and 12th houses from Mars; or in the 1st, 4th, 7th, 10th, 11th, 8th and 2nd houses from the Sun; or in the 3rd, 6th, 10th, 11th, 1st, and 4th houses from the Ascendant; or in the 9th, 11th, 6th, 10th, 12th, and 8th houses from Mercury; or in the 3rd, 6th, and 11th houses from the Moon; or in the 6th, 11th, and 12th houses from Venus; or in the 11th, 112th, 5th, and 6th houses from Jupiter.

Note.—This is the Aṣṭakavarga of Saturn.

मालिनी–इति निगदितमिष्टं नेष्टमन्यद्विशेषादधिकफल-
विपाकं जन्मभात्तत्व दद्युः । उपचयगृहमित्रस्वोच्चगैः पुष्टमिष्टं
त्वपचयगृहनीचारातिगैर्नेष्टसम्पत् ॥ ८ ॥

इति श्रीवराहमिहिरविरचिते बृहज्जातके
अष्टकवर्गाध्यायो नवमः ॥ ९ ॥

इति Iti, thus. निगदितं Nigaditam, said. इष्टं Iṣṭam, whatever is auspicious; the auspicious cases. न Na, not. इष्टं Iṣṭam, auspicious. अन्यत् Anyat, not mentioned. विशेषात् Viśeṣât, after the required correction; what remains as net balance, especially after correcting the auspicious and inauspicious results; the sum total that is left as balance whether auspicious or inauspicious or neutral. अधिकफलविपाकं Adhikaphalavipâkam, the excess in the good and bad results, all considered together; the net result, whether good, bad, or neutral. जन्मभात् Janmabhât, from the signs where the planets were found during birth time. तत्र Tatra, at any sign in question. दद्युः Dadyuḥ, produced; gave; yielded. उपचयगृहमित्रस्वोच्चगैः Upachayagṛihamitrasvochchagaiḥ, in the Upachaya houses (from the Ascendant or the Moon) or in the allies' houses, or in the houses of exaltation. पुष्टं Puṣṭam, get very much increased. इष्टं Iṣṭam, the auspicious result. तु Tu, but. अपचयगृहनीचारातिगैः Apachayagṛihanîchârâtigaiḥ, in the Apachaya houses, (from the Ascendant or the Moon) enemies' houses, or houses of detriment. न Na, not. इष्टसम्पत् Iṣṭasampat, good auspicious results as desired. The auspicious results here are not of the best order as might be desired; they are rather of inferior or bad order.

8. Those that are mentioned above are productive of auspicious results; and those that are not mentioned, are full of inauspicious results. Thus at any sign, of all the good or evils taken collectively as indicated by the planets at birth time, only so much of either as remains after cancellation is seen to bear fruit. The net good results, when in the Upachaya houses (houses of profit, *i.e.*, 3rd, 6th, 10th, and 11th), in the allies' houses, and in the houses of exaltation, are rendered successively auspicious whereas those in the Apachaya houses (houses of loss), in the enemies' houses and in the houses of detriment are much weakened. (The net bad results are rendered more malefic in the Apachaya houses and somewhat improved in the Upachaya houses etc.).

Note:—The manner in which cancellation of good or evil is done is shown thus:—The good results are indicated by dots (o) and the bad results are indicated by vertical lines (1). Deduct the number of dots from the number of lines, if the number of lines exceed; or the reverse, if the number of dots exceed. The balance will indicate the good or bad that will actually come to pass. If the number of dots be eight then the fullest amount of good will come to pass. If the number of dots be six after cancellation, then three fourths good will be visible; if the number of dots be four, half the good results will come to pass; if the number of dots be two, one-fourth good will be seen. Thus is calculated about the lines also. Now let us take an example. The horoscope here referred to is given in the annexed diagram ; and here the Aṣṭakavarga of Mars has been exemplified. Thus :—

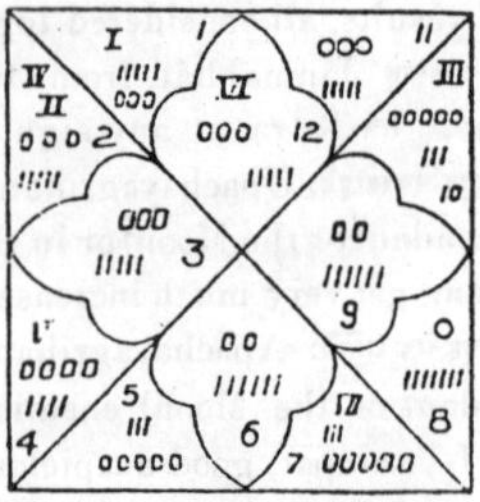

FIG. 5

In the 1 house of Meṣa, 5 lines and 3 dots are seen. Cancel three lines with three dots. There remain two lines. Thus the native suffers always one-fourth evil whenever Mars happens to move through the sign Meṣa or Aries. And so with other signs. Wherever the dots and lines are equal, *i.e.*, four in number, then neither good nor evil is visible. Apart from the Aṣṭakavarga, whenever there is contradiction in the similar results, (by other yogas) then no results will be visible; this is to be understood. For instance, by one sort of planetary combination, one is to acquire gold ; and by another sort of combination, one is to lose gold ; in this case no gold will be obtained by the native.

The Aṣṭakavarga tables are generally prepared with the number of benefic dots alone marked in them, the number representing the malefic lines being the difference between the number 8 and the number of dots.

The A. V. (Aṣṭaka Varga) tables are useful in the prediction of most of the important events of life. Regular treatises by Parâśara and others exist on this branch of horoscopy, which should be consulted for full particulars.

In predicting the length of life, Antardaśâs, and all other benefic or malefic results, these Aṣṭakavarga results are first determined to ascertain which planets are benefic (or malefic) in which houses, as they pass round the heavens ; and then ultimate results are judged.

CHAPTER X.

ON AVOCATION

Or Means of Livelihood.

प्रहर्षिणी—अर्थाप्तिः पितृपितृपत्निशत्रुमित्रभ्रातृस्त्रीभृतकजनाद्दिवाकराद्यैः । होरेंद्वोर्दशमगतैर्विकल्पनीया भेंद्वर्कास्पदपतिगांशनाथवृत्त्या ॥ १ ॥

अर्थाप्तिः Arthâptiḥ, the acquisition of wealth. पितृपितृपत्निशत्रुमित्रभ्रातृस्त्रीभृतकजनात् Pitṛipitṛipatniśatrumitrabhrâtṛistrîbhṛitakajanât, from father, father's wife (mother), foe, friend, brothers, wife, and servant. दिवाकराद्यैः: Divâkarâdyaiḥ, under the influence of the Sun, etc.; *i.e.*, of the Sun, Moon, Mars, Mercury, Jupiter, Venus, and Saturn. होरेंद्वोः: Horendvoḥ, from the Ascendant and the Moon. दशमगतैः: Daśamagataiḥ, in the tenth house. विकल्पनीया: Vikalpanîyâḥ, to be considered. भेंद्वर्कास्पदपतिगांशनाथवृत्त्या Bhendvarkâspadapatigâṃśanâthavṛityâ, under the influence of the rulers of the Navâṃśakas where the rulers of the tenth houses from the Ascendant, the Moon and the Sun severally are residing.

Now the Chapter on the means of acquiring money is commenced. Here the planets are described as the bestowers of wealth in two ways. The planet in the tenth house from the Ascendant or the Moon bestows wealth. In case there be no planet in the tenth house, the ruler of the Navâṃśaka where the lord of the tenth house from the Ascendant, the Moon or the Sun resides, is the bestower of wealth.

1. If there be Sun in the tenth house from the Ascendant or the Moon during one's nativity, then wealth comes from father; if there be Moon, then wealth is obtained from mother; if Mars, then wealth is got from enemy; if Mercury, friends give wealth; if Jupiter, brothers; if Venus, wife; if Saturn, servants give wealth. In case there be no planets in the tenth house, then the ruler of the Navâṃśaka which is governed by the lord of the tenth house

from the Ascendant, the Moon or the Sun bestows wealth in the way above described(1).

Note:—If there be one planet in the tenth house from the Ascendant and if there be another planet in the tenth house from the Moon, then it should be understood that both the planets bestow wealth in their respective Daśâs. If there be many planets, then all of them give wealth in their respective Antardaśâs. It is also to be noted that the meaning that the most powerful of the planets bestow wealth and not the other planets, is not tenable here, since there are various ways of acquiring money and the planets are so many sources whereby money can be had. Besides one planet overpowering another and making it ineffective is not meant here.

(1) Suppose the sign Karka is the Ascendant; the 10th house from Karka is Meṣa; the ruler of Meṣa is Mars; suppose Mars to occupy the Navâṃśa of Dhanu; the ruler of Dhanu is Jupiter and the avocation stated for Jupiter (see 3rd stanza) will be the avocation of a person. It also follows that a person's avocation will be all the three stated for the rulers of the Navâṃśas occupied by the rulers of the 10th houses from the Ascendant, the Moon and the Sun.

प्रहर्षिणी—अर्कांशे तृणकनकोर्णभेषजाद्यैश्चंद्रांशे कृषिजल-
जांगनाश्रयाच्च । धात्वग्निप्रहरणसाहसैः कुजांशे सौम्यांशे लिपि-
गणितादिकाव्यशिल्पैः ॥ २ ॥

अर्कांशे Arkâṃśe, on the Sun being the ruler of the Navâṃśa where the ruler of the tenth house from the Ascendant, Moon, and the Sun resides. तृणकनकोर्णभेषजाद्यैः: Tṛiṇakanakorṇabheṣajâdyaiḥ, by means of scents, gold, woollen articles, drugs and practice of medicines. चंद्रांशे Chandrâṃśe, on the Moon being the ruler of the Navâṃṣa. कृषिजलजांगनाश्रयात् Kṛiṣijalajâṃganâśrayât, by means of cultivation, trade in conchshells; pearls &c., things of the sea; or from women; or by giving shelter to women and others. च Cha, and. धात्वग्निप्रहरणसाहसैः: Dhâtvagnipraharaṇasâhasaiḥ, by dealing with metals, earthen pots or orpiment and other mineral ores, by cooking or other acts in contact with fire, by acts of bravery or warfare with swords and other weapons. कुजांशे Kujâṃśe, on Mars' Navâṃśa, *i.e.*, on Mars being the ruler of the Navâṃśa where the ruler of the tenth house from the Ascendant, the Moon, or the Sun resides. सौम्यांशे Saumyâṃśe, on Mercury being the ruler of the Navâṃsa where the ruler of the tenth house from the Ascendant the Moon and the Sun resides. लिपिगणितादिकाव्यशिल्पैः: Lipigaṇitâdikâvyaśilpaiḥ, by means of writing, mathematical knowledge, poetry, or fine and mechanical arts.

Now is described the second way how wealth is acquired, *i.e.*, when the planet is the ruler of the Navâṃśaka where the ruler of the tenth house from the Sun, Moon and the Ascendant resides.

2. On Sun being the ruler of the Navâṃśa, (1) the native earns money from scents, dealings with gold, woollen materials, drugs; on Moon being so, money is got from cultivation, selling conch shells, whalebones, pearls, &c. (articles of the sea), from women, and from protecting others. On Mars being such, from metals, cooking and all sorts of action in connection with fire (2) from bravery and using weapons. On Mercury being such, from reading and writing arithmetic, poetry and fine or mechanical arts (3).

Notes:—(1) That is, the ruler of the Navâṃśa occupied by the ruler of the 10th house from the Ascendant, the Moon, and the Sun.

(2) The native may be the driver of a fire engine or a dealer in matches and the like.

(3) *e. g.*, painting, bookbinding, arrow-making or the making of flower wreaths, sandal paste, perfumes, and the like.

प्रहर्षिणी—जीवांशे द्विजविबुधाकरादिधर्मैः काव्यांशे मणि-रजतादिगोमहिष्यैः । सौरांशे श्रमवधभारनीचशिल्पैः कर्मेशाध्यु-षितनवांशकर्मसिद्धिः ॥ ३ ॥

जीवांशे, Jivâmśe, on Jupiter being such, *i.e.*, the ruler of the Navâṃśa. द्विजविबुधाकरादिधर्मैः Dvijavibudhâkarâdidharmaiḥ, from the Brâhmaṇas, Devas, or learned men, from dealings with material sderived from ores, or from religious practices, *i.e.*, sacrifices, gifts, austerities, pilgrimages, or serving religious preceptors. काव्यांशे Kâvyâṃśe, on Venus being such. मणिरजतादिगोमहिष्यैः Maṇirajatâdigomahiṣyaiḥ, from dealing with jewels, silver, etc., cows and also from queens. सौरांशे Saurâṃśe, on Saturn being such. श्रमवधभारनीचशिल्पैः Śramavadhabhâranîchaśilpaiḥ, by hard labour, marching on roads, or by hunting, or by carrying heavy loads, or by lower arts. कर्मेशाध्युषितनवांशकर्मसिद्धिः Karmeśâdhyuṣitanavâṃśakarmasidhhiḥ, according to the nature of the ruler of the Navâṃśaka where the ruler of the tenth house from the Ascendant, Sun or Moon resides.

3. On Jupiter being the ruler of the Navâṃśaka where the ruler of the tenth house from the Ascendant, the Moon and the Sun resides, one earns money from the Brâhmaṇas,

Devas, or learned men; from mines or dealings with substances from ores; or from religious sacrifices, gifts, austerities, pilgrimages or serving religious preceptors; on Venus being such, money is obtained from dealing with jewels, silver, etc., from cows and also from buffaloes (1); on Saturn being such, from hard labour, marching on roads, or by hunting and acts of torture (2) or by lower acts unsuited to his rank. Thus persons acquire wealth by avocation stated for the rulers of the Navâṃśas occupied by the rulers of the 10th house.

Notes:—(1) Some take the word to mean "queens"

(2) Either by self-torture or by torturing others.

प्रहर्षिणी—मित्रारिस्वगृहगतैर्ग्रहैस्ततोऽर्थं तुंगस्थे वलिनि च भास्करे स्ववीर्यात् । आयस्थैरुदयधनाश्रितैश्च सौम्यैः संचिंत्यं वलसहितैरनेकधा स्वम् ॥ ४ ॥

इति श्रीवराहमिहिराचार्यप्रणीते वृहज्जातके कर्माजीवाध्यायो दशमः ॥ १० ॥

मित्रारिस्वगृहगतैः Mitrârisvagṛihagataiḥ, when found in friend's, foe's, or in one's own house. ग्रहैः Grahaiḥ, by the planets (in the Navâṃśaka where the ruler of the tenth house from the Ascendant, Sun or Moon) resides. ततः Tataḥ, from those friend's, foe's or one's own house respectively. अर्थं Artham, wealth; money; livelihood. तुंगस्थे Tuṃgasthe, in one's exalted position. बलिनि Balini, becoming powerful; well aspected by other powerful planets. च Cha, and. भास्करे Bhâskare, the Sun. स्ववीर्यात् Svavîryât, by one's own efforts; by one's own prowess. आयस्थैः Âyasthaiḥ, when in the eleventh house. उदयधनाश्रितैः Udayadhanâśritaiḥ, in the Ascendant or the second house. सौम्यैः Saumyaiḥ, by the benefic planets. संचिन्त्यं Saṃchintyam, to be thought. बलसहितैः Balasahitaiḥ, well aspected by the other powerful planets. अनेकधा Anekadhâ, from various sources. स्वम् Svam, wealth; the money.

4. When the ruler of the Navâṃśaka where the ruler of the tenth house from the Ascendant, the sun and Moon (1) resides in friend's house, wealth is obtained from friends; if in enemy's house, enemies give wealth; if in one's own house,

then wealth is got from one's own house ; when the above-mentioned ruler is Sun and it resides in the exalted house, *i.e.*, in the sign Meṣa and favourably aspected by other benefics, then wealth is got by one's own prowess. If there be, during his birth time, in the eleventh, second houses, or in the Ascendant the powerful benefic planets (*i.e.*, well aspected by strong planets) then one gets wealth easily from various sources, (*i.e.*, in any avocation he chooses to follow).

Notes:—(1) Or the planet which occupies the 10th house from the Ascendant or the Moon.

Thus ends the tenth Chapter on Avocation by Varâha Mihira.

CHAPTER XI.

ON RÂJA YOGÂDHÂYA

Or on the Birth of Kings.

वैतालीय–प्राहुर्यवनाः स्वतुंगगैः क्रूरैः क्रूरमतिर्महीपतिः ।
क्रूरैस्तु न जीवशर्मणः पक्षे क्षित्यधिपः प्रजायते ॥ १ ॥

प्राहुः: Prâhuḥ, said; declared. यवनाः: Yavanâḥ, Yavanâchârya, the famous astrologer Yavanâchârya and others. स्वतुंगगैः: Svatuṃgagaiḥ, when in their own exalted houses. क्रूरैः: Krûraiḥ, by three or more malefic planets. क्रूरमतिः: Krûra-matiḥ, cruel; tyrannical; wicked; hot tempered; impetuous. महीपतिः: Mahîpatiḥ, king; lord of the earth; sovereign. क्रूरैः: Krûraiḥ, by the three or more malefic planets. तु Tu, but. न Na, not. जीवशर्मणः: Jîvaśarmaṇaḥ, according to Jîvaśarmâ, the astrologer. पक्षे Pakṣe, opinion. क्षित्यधिपः: Kṣityadhipaḥ, kings. प्रजायते Prajâyate, are born.

When the planets three or more are in their respective exalted houses, then sovereignty is obtained. This is in all Jâtaka (astrological) works. Now the point of difference according to Yavanâchârya is being stated.

1. Yavanâchârya and others are of opinion that when three or more malefic planets are in their own respective exalted houses, then the cruel and tyrannical kings are born(1).

But according to Jîvaśarmâ, no kings at all are born by such malefic planets(2).

Note:—(1) According to Yavanâchârya and others, when the three or more malefics are in their exalted positions, sovereigns are born but cruel; when the three benefics are exalted, sovereigns become virtuous; and when both benefic and malefics are exalted, sovereigns partly virtuous and partly wicked are born. But (2) according to Jîvaśarmâ, no kings are born; they become wealthy like the kings; and they are also angry, quarrelsome, and cruel. Varâha Mihira is of the opinion of the Yavanas.

व०ति०—वक्रार्कजार्कगुरुभिः सकलैस्त्रिभिश्च स्वोच्चेषु षोडश नृपाः कथितैकलग्ने ॥ द्व्येकाश्रितेषु च तथैकतमे विलग्ने स्वक्षेत्रगे शशिनि षोडश भूमिपाः स्युः ॥ २ ॥

वक्रार्कजार्कगुरुभिः Vakrârkajârkagurûbhih, by the Mars, Saturn, Sun, and Jupiter. सकलैः Śakalaih, by all of them; by all the four. त्रिभिः Tribhih, by the three (of the above mentioned planets); by any three of the above mentioned planets. च Cha, and. स्वोच्चेषु Svochcheṣu, in their own respective exalted houses. षोडशनृपाः Sodaśanripâh, sixteen cases of the birth of kings; 16 Râjayogas. कथितैकलग्ने Kathitaikalagne, one of the aforesaid planets being the Ascendant. द्व्येकाश्रितेषु Dyekâśriteṣu, when any two of the above mentioned planets, or when any one of them are exalted. च Cha, and. तथा Tathâ, similarly. एकतमे Ekatame, one of the two exalted, or one exalted. विलग्ने Vilagne, the Ascendant. स्वक्षेत्रगे Svakṣetrage, in their own houses. शशिनि Śaśini, the Moon. षोडशभूमिपाः Sodaśabhûmipâh, sixteen (cases) of Râjayogas. स्युः Syuh, arise.

2. Sixteen cases of Râjayogas or kingships arise when the four planets Mars, Saturn, Sun and Jupiter are all exalted or when any three of them are exalted, one of the four or three above mentioned being then the Ascendant. Any two or one of the aforesaid planets when exalted, one of these two being the Ascendant at the same time, bring out also sixteen cases of kingships provided the Moon occupy her own house Karka.

Note:—The first sixteen cases are being enumerated :—

FOUR PLANETS EXALTED AND ONE ASCENDANT.

1. Sun in Meṣa (Ascendant); Jupiter in Karka, Saturn in Tulâ, Makara in Mars.

2. Jupiter in Karka (Ascendant), Saturn in Tulâ, Mars in Makara, Sun in Meṣa.

3. Saturn in Tulâ (Ascendant), Mars in Makara, Sun in Meṣa, Jupiter in Karka.

4. Mars in Makara (Ascendant), Sun in Meṣa, Jupiter in Karka, Saturn in Tulâ.

THREE PLANETS EXALTED, AND ONE OF THESE THE ASCENDANT.

5. Sun in Meṣa (Lagna); Jupiter in Karka, Saturn in Tulâ.

6. Sun in Meṣa (Lagna); Jupiter in Karka, Mars in Makara.

7. Sun in Meṣa (Lagna); Saturn in Tulâ, Mars in Makara.

8. Jupiter in Karka (Lagna); Saturn in Tulâ, Mars in Makara.
9. Jupiter in Karka (Lagna); Saturn in Tulâ, Sun in Meṣa.
10. Jupiter in Karka (Lagna); Mars in Makara, Sun in Meṣa.
11. Saturn in Tulâ (Lagna); Mars in Makara, Sun in Meṣa.
12. Saturn in Tulâ (Lagna); Mars in Makara, Jupiter in Karka.
13. Saturn in Tulâ (Lagna); Jupiter in Karka, Sun in Meṣa.
14. Mars in Makara (Lagna); Sun in Meṣa, Jupiter in Karka.
15. Mars in Makara (Lagna); Sun in Meṣa, Saturn in Tulâ.
16. Mars in Makara (Lagna); Saturn in Tulâ, Jupiter in Karka.

The second sixteen cases are being enumerated, thus:—

(a) MOON IN KARKA; TWO PLANETS EXALTED; ONE BEING THE ASCENDANT.

1. Sun in Meṣa, (Lagna), Jupiter in Karka, Moon in Karka.
2. Sun in Meṣa, Jupiter and Moon in Karka (Lagna).
3. Sun in Meṣa, (Lagna), Moon in Karka, Saturn in Tulâ.
4. Sun in Meṣa, Moon in Karka, Saturn in Tulâ (Ascendant).
5. Sun in Meṣa, (Lagna), Moon in Karka, Mars in Makara.
6. Sun in Meṣa, Moon in Karka, Mars in Makara (Ascendant).
7. Saturn in Tulâ, Moon in Karka, Jupiter in Karka (Ascendant).
8. Saturn in Tulâ (Ascendant), Moon in Karka, Jupiter in Karka.
9. Mars in Makara, Moon in Karka, Jupiter in Karka (Ascendant).
10. Mars in Makara (Ascendant), Moon in Karka, Jupiter in Karka.
11. Saturn in Tulâ, Moon in Karka, Mars in Makara (Ascendant).
12. Saturn in Tulâ (Ascendant), Moon in Karka, Mars in Makara.

(b) MOON IN KARKA; ONE PLANET EXALTED AND ASCENDANT.

13. Sun in Meṣa (Ascendant); Moon in Karka.
14. Jupiter in Karka (Ascendant); Moon in Karka.
15. Saturn in Tulâ (Ascendant); Moon in Karka.
16. Mars in Makara (Ascendant); Moon in Karka.

अनुष्टुभ्—वर्गोत्तमगते लग्ने चंद्रे वा चन्द्रवार्जितैः ॥
चतुराद्यैर्ग्रहैर्दृष्टे नृपा द्वाविंशतिः स्मृताः ॥ ३ ॥

वर्गोत्तमगते Vargottamagate, posted in Vargottama. The first Navâṃśa of Meṣa, Karka, Tulâ or Makara is their Vargothama respectively; the fifth Navâṃśa of Vṛiṣa, Siṃha, Vṛiśchika and Kumbha is their Vargottama respectively and the last (*i.e.*, the ninth Navâṃśa) of Mithuna, Kanyâ, Dhanu and Mîna is their Vargottama respectively. लग्ने Lagne, in the Ascendant. चंद्रे Chandre, on the Moon being. वा Vâ, or. चंद्रवर्जितैः Chandravarjitaiḥ, on the absence of the Moon. चतुराद्यैः Chaturâdyaiḥ, by the four, five, six, planets. ग्रहैः Grahaiḥ, by the planets. दृष्टे Driṣṭe, aspected. नृपाः Nṛipâḥ, kings. द्वाविंशतिः Dvâviṃśatiḥ, twenty-two. स्मृताः Smṛitâḥ, considered.

3. If the Ascendant or the Moon be in Vargottama position (in the Navâṃśakas where the sign Ascendant or the Moon in her Navâṃśas give most auspicious results) and if these be at the same time aspected by 4, 5, or 6 planets excepting the Moon, then twenty-two cases of Râjayogas arise in each case (forty-four cases arise when both the Lagna and the Moon are considered).

Note :—15 cases arise when four planets aspect the Ascendant or Moon Vargottama, six cases arise when five planets aspect, and one case only when six planets aspect. These are now being mentioned :—

FOUR PLANETS ASPECTING ; MOON NOT IN THE ASCENDANT.

1.	Sun,	Mars,	Mercury,	Jupiter.
2.	Sun,	Mars,	Mercury,	Venus.
3.	Sun,	Mars,	Mercury,	Saturn.
4.	Sun,	Mars,	Jupiter,	Venus.
5.	Sun,	Mars,	Jupiter,	Saturn.
6.	Sun,	Mars,	Venus,	Saturn.
7.	Sun,	Mercury,	Jupiter,	Venus.
8.	Sun,	Mercury,	Jupiter,	Saturn.
9.	Sun,	Mercury,	Venus,	Saturn.
10.	Sun,	Jupiter,	Venus,	Saturn.
11.	Mars,	Mercury,	Jupiter,	Venus.
12.	Mars,	Mercury,	Jupiter,	Saturn.
13.	Mars,	Mercury,	Venus,	Saturn.
14.	Mars,	Jupiter,	Venus,	Saturn.
15.	Mercury	Jupiter,	Venus,	Saturn.

5 PLANETS ASPECTING.

16.	Sun,	Mars,	Mercury,	Jupiter,	Venus.
17.	Sun,	Mars,	Mercury,	Jupiter,	Saturn.
18.	Sun,	Mars,	Mercury,	Venus,	Saturn.
19.	Sun,	Mars,	Jupiter,	Venus,	Saturn.
20.	Sun,	Mercury,	Jupiter,	Venus,	Saturn.
21.	Mars,	Mercury,	Jupiter,	Venus,	Saturn.

6 PLANETS.

22.	Sun,	Mars,	Mercury,	Jupiter,	Venus,	Saturn.

Similarly these 22 cases also arise when there is Moon in the Ascendant. Thus 44 cases in all. If each of the twelve houses be taken in succession, then 22 × 12 cases arise in one, *i. e.*, 264 cases ; and so 264 cases in the other, making in all 528 cases.

शिखरिणी—यमे कुम्भेऽर्केऽजे गवि शशिनि तैरेव तनुगैर्नृयुक्सिंहालिस्थैः शशिजगुरुवक्रैर्नृपतयः ॥ यमेन्दूतुङ्गेऽङ्गे सवितृशशिजौ षष्ठभवने तुलाजेन्दुक्षेत्रैः ससितकुजजीवैश्च नरपौ ॥ ४ ॥

यमे Yama, Saturn occupying. कुम्भे Kumbhe, the sign Kumbha. अर्के Arke, the Sun occupying. अजे Aje, the sign Meṣa. गवि Gavi, the sign Vṛiṣa. शशिनि Śaśini, the Moon occupying. तैः Taiḥ, by them ; by any one of them. एव Eva, certainly. तनुगैः Tanugaiḥ, in the Ascendant. नृयुक्सिंहालिस्थैः Nṛiyuksiṃhâlisthaiḥ, posted in Mithuna, Simha, and Vṛiśchik. शशिजगुरुवक्रैः Śaśijagurûvakraiḥ, Mercury, Jupiter, and Mars (being posted in). नृपतयः Nṛipatayaḥ, kings ; three cases of kingship. यमेन्दू Yamendû, Saturn and the Moon being. तुङ्गे Tuṅge, exalted. अङ्गे Aṅge, the Ascendant. सवितृशशिजौ Savitṛiśaśijau, Sun and Mercury being. षष्ठभवने Ṣaṣṭhabhavane, in the sixth house Kanyâ. तुलाजेन्दुक्षेत्रैः Tulâjenduksetraiḥ, in the signs Tulâ, Meṣa, and Karka. ससितकुजजीवैः Sasitakujajîvaiḥ, with Venus, Mars, and Jupiter. नरपौ Narapau, two cases of kingship.

4. Saturn in Kumbha sign, Sun in Meṣa, Moon in Vṛiṣa and one of these three being the Ascendants also, Mercury in Mithuna, Jupiter in Siṃha, and Mars in Vṛiśchika, (3) three cases of king-making combinations arise. Saturn and Moon being exalted and one of these being the Ascendant, Sun and Mercury in the sign Kanyâ, the sixth sign, Venus in Tulâ, Mars in Meṣa, and Jupiter in Karka, two cases of king-making combinations arise.

Note:—Some take the sixth sign as the one from the Ascendant and not the sign Kanyâ as the sixth sign. But this is not reasonable. For Venus being in the Ascendant Tulâ, the Sun cannot be taken as residing in the sixth house from Tulâ, *i.e.*, Mîna. The author Bâdarâyaṇa takes the sixth sign to mean Kanyâ.

शिखरिणी—कुजे तुंगेऽर्केन्द्वोर्द्धनुषि यमलग्ने च कुपतिः पतिर्भूमेश्चान्यः क्षितिसुतविलग्ने सशशिनि ॥ सचंद्रे सौरेऽस्ते सुरपतिगुरौ चापधरगे स्वतुंगस्थे भानावुदयमुपयाते क्षितिपतिः ॥ ५ ॥

कुजे Kuje, Mars occupying. तुंगे Tuṅge, the exalted sign. अर्केन्द्वोः Arkendoḥ, the Sun and Moon being situtated. धनुषि Dhanuṣi, in the sign Dhanu. यमलग्ने

Yamalagne, Saturn in the Ascendant Makara. Others hold one of the two signs Makara and Kumbha as the Ascendant. च Cha, and. कुपतिः Kupatiḥ, king. पतिः Patiḥ, lord. भुवेः Bhûmeḥ, of the earth. च Cha, and. अन्यः Anyaḥ, the second case of Râjayoga. क्षितिसुतविलग्ने Kṣitisutavilagne, Mars being the Ascendant. सशशिनि Saśaśini, together with the Moon. सचंद्रे Sachandre, with the Moon. सौरे Saure, Saturn being. अस्ते Aste, in the Descendant. सुरपतिगुरौ Surapatigurau, Jupiter being. चापधरगे Châpadharage, in the sign Dhanu. स्वतुंगस्थे Svatuṅgasthe, being exalted. भानौ Bhânau, the Sun being. उदयम् Udayam, rising in the horizon. उपयाते Upayâte, on or about to commence. क्षितिपतिः Kṣitipatiḥ, lord of the earth, a king.

5. Mars exalted in Makara, the Sun and Moon in Dhanu, and Saturn being in the Ascendant Makara, the lord of the earth is born. Second case :—Makara being the Ascendant, the Moon and Mars being in Makara, Sun in Dhanu, a king also is born. Third case :—Meṣa being the Ascendant and the Sun being in Meṣa, Jupiter in Dhanu, the Moon and Saturn in Tulâ, a king again is born.

शिखरिणी—वृषे सेंदौ लग्ने सवितृगुरुतीक्ष्णांशुतनयैः सुहृज्जायाखस्थैर्भवति नियमान्मानवपतिः ॥ मृगे मंदे लग्ने सहजरिपुधर्मव्ययगतैः शशांकाद्यैः ख्यातः पृथुगुणयशाः पुंगलपतिः ॥ ६ ॥

वृषे Vriṣe, the sign Vriṣa being. सेंदौ Sendau, with the Moon. लग्ने Lagne, being the Ascendant. सवितृगुरुतीक्ष्णांशुतनयैः Savitrigurutîkṣṇâṃśutanaiḥ, Sun, Jupiter and Saturn being respectively. सुहृज्जायाखस्थैः Surhijjâyâkhasthaiḥ, posted in the fourth, seventh and tenth houses, i.e., in the signs Siṃha, Vriśchika, Kumbha. भवति Bhavati, becomes. नियमात् Niyamât, certainly; undoubtedly. मानवपतिः Mânavapatiḥ, ruler of men. मृगे Mrige, the sign Makara. मंदे Mande, Saturn occupying. लग्ने Lagne, becoming the Ascendant. सहजरिपुधर्मव्ययगतैः Sahajaripudharmavyayagataiḥ, in the third, sixth, ninth, and twelfth houses. शशांकाद्यैः Saśâṃkâdyaiḥ, the Moon, Mars, Mercury, Jupiter occupying respectively. ख्यातः Khyâtaḥ, famous; far-famed. पृथुगुणयशाः Prithuguṇayaśâḥ, whose goodness and prowess are spread far and wide. पुंगलपतिः Puṅgalapatiḥ, lord of men.

Two cases of Râjayoga are being described here.

6. The Ascendant being the sign Vriṣa and the Moon occupying it, the Sun being in the sign Siṃha, Jupiter in Vriśchika, and Saturn in Kumbha, the ruler of men is

certainly born. The second case is mentioned in the following:—The Ascendant being Makara and Saturn in it, also Moon, Mars Mercury, and Jupiter in Mîna, Mithuna, Kanyâ, and Dhanu respectively, the world renowned lord of men whose prowess and goodness have spread far and wide, is born unto this earth.

शिखरिणी—हये सेंदौ जीवे मृगमुखगते भूमितनये स्वतुं-
गस्थौ लग्ने भृगुजशशिजावत्र नृपती ॥ सुतस्थौ वक्रार्कौ गु-
रुशशिसिताश्चापि हिबुके बुधे कन्यालग्ने भवति हि नृपोऽन्योऽपि
गुणवान् ॥ ७ ॥

हये Haye, the sign Dhanu. सेंदौ Sendau, with the Moon. जीवे Jîve, Jupiter being. मृगमुखगते Mrigamukhagate, in the first half of Makara. भूमितनये Bhûmitanaye, Mars being. स्वतुंगस्थौ Svatumgasthau, exalted in their own houses respectively. लग्ने Lagne, the Ascendant, *i.e.*, Venus or Mercury in their exalted houses and becoming the Ascendant. भृगुजशशिजौ Bhrigujaśaśijau, Venus or Mercury becoming. अत्र Atra, in this. नृपती Nripatî, two cases of Râjayogas. सुतस्थौ Sutasthau, in the fifth house (from Kanyâ; *i.e.*, in Mîna). वक्रार्कौ Vakrârkau, Mars and Saturn. गुरुशशिसिताः Guruśaśisitâh, Jupiter, Moon and Venus. च अपि Cha api, also. हिबुके Hivuke, in the 4th house, *i.e.*, in the sign Dhanu. बुधे Budhe, Mercury being. कन्यालग्ने Kanyâlagne, in the Ascendant Kanyâ. भवति Bhavati, gets born. हि Hi, certainly. नृपः Nripah, king. अन्यः Anyah, second. अपि Api, also. गुणवान् Gunavân, well qualified.

7. Jupiter in Dhanu, and the Moon being in it, Mars in the first half of Makara, Mercury or Venus being exalted in their own houses, two cases of kingship arise, one when the sign Mîna is the Ascendant, and second when the sign Kanyâ is the Ascendant. Third case:—Kanyâ, the Ascendant and Mercury in it, Saturn and Mars in Makara; and Jupiter, Moon and Venus in the sign Dhanu, then in this case a well qualified king is born.

शिखरिणी—झषे सेंदौ लग्ने घटमृगमृगेन्द्रेषु सहितै-
र्यमारार्कैर्योऽभूत्स खलु मनुजः शास्ति वसुधाम् ॥
अजे सारे मूर्तौ शशिगृहगते चामरगुरौ ।
सुरेज्ये वा लग्ने धरणिपतिरन्योऽपि गुणवान् ॥ ८ ॥

झषे Jjhaṣe, the sign Mîna becoming सेन्दौ Sendau, with the Moon. लग्ने Lagne, the Ascendant. घटमृगमृगेन्द्रेषु Ghaṭamṛigamṛigendreśu, in the signs Kumbha, Makara, and Siṃha. सहितैः Sahitaiḥ, with. यमारार्कैः Yâmârârkaiḥ, by Saturn, Mars and the Sun respectively. यः Yaḥ, He. अभूत् Abhût, who is born. खलु Khalu, certainly. मनुजः Manujaḥ, men. शास्ति Śâsti, rules. वसुधाम् Vasudhâm, the earth. अजे Aje, in the sign Meṣa. आरे Âre, Mars being. मूर्तौ Mûrtau, (Meṣa) becoming the Ascendant. शशिगृहगते Śaśigṛihagate, the sign Karka (also rising.) च अमरगुरौ Cha Amaraguru, and Jupiter occupying. सुरेज्ये Surejye, Jupiter being. वा Vâ, or. लग्ने Lagne, in the Ascendant. धरणिपतिः Dharaṇipatiḥ, lord of the earth. अन्यः Anyaḥ, another; third case. अपि Api, also. गुणवान् Guṇavân, well qualified.

8. The Ascendant being the sign Mîna with the Moon in it, Saturn in Kumbha, Mars in Makara and the Sun in Siṃha produce rulers of the earth. This is the first case. Mars in Meṣa the Ascendant, Jupiter in Karka produce powerful kings. This is the second case. Jupiter in Karka the Ascendant and Mars in Meṣa produce also rulers of the earth. This is the third case.

विद्युन्माला—कर्किणि लग्ने तत्स्थे जीवे चंद्रसितज्ञैराय-प्राप्तैः ॥ मेषगतेऽर्के जातं विंद्याद्विक्रमयुक्तं पृथ्वीनाथम् ॥ ९ ॥

कर्किणि Karkiṇi, Karka being. लग्ने Lagne, the Ascendant. तत्स्थे Tatsthe, in that. जीवे Jîve, Jupiter. चंद्रसितज्ञैः Chandrasitajñaiḥ, the Moon, Venus, and Mercury occupying. आयप्राप्तैः Âyaprâptaiḥ, the eleventh house, the sign Vṛiṣa. मेषगते Meṣagate, in the sign Meṣa. अर्के Arke, the Sun being. जातं Jâtam, born. Vidyât, know. विक्रमयुक्तम् Vikramayuktam, powerful. पृथ्वीनाथम्. Pṛithvînâtham, ruler of the earth.

9. Jupiter in the Ascendant Karka and the eleventh house, the sign Vṛiṣa, being occupied by the Moon, Venus and Mercury, and the Sun being in the sign Meṣa produce powerful kings.

द्रुतविलंबिता—मृगमुखेऽर्कतनयस्तनुसंस्थः क्रियकुलीरहरयोऽधिपयुक्ताः ॥ मिथुनतौलिसहितौ बुधशुक्रौ यदि तदा पृथुयशाः पृथिवीशः ॥ १० ॥

मृगमुखे Mṛigamukhe, in the sign Makara. अर्कतनयः Arkatanayaḥ, Saturn being. तनुसंस्थः Tanusaṃsthaḥ, being the Ascendant. क्रियकुलीरहरयोः Kriyakulîraharayoḥ, in the signs Meṣa, Karka, and Siṃha. अधिपयुक्ताः Adhipayuktâḥ, with their rulers, *i.e.*, Mars, Moon and the Sun being respectively. मिथुनतौलिसहितौ Mithunataulisahitau, in the signs Mithuna and Tulâ. बुधशुक्रौ Budhaśukrau, Mercury and Venus being respectively. यदि Yadi, if. तदा Tadâ then. पृथुयशाः Pṛithuyaśâḥ, far-famed; world-renowned. पृथिवीशः Pṛithivîśaḥ, lord of the earth.

10. Saturn in the Ascendant Makara, Mars in Meṣa, Moon in Karka, the Sun in Simha, Mercury in Mithuna and Venus in Tulâ produce famous rulers of the soil.

अनुष्टुभ्–स्वोच्चसंस्थे बुधे लग्ने भृगौ मेषूरणाश्रिते ॥
सजीवेऽस्ते निशानाथे राजा मंदारयोः सुते ॥ ११ ॥

स्वोच्चसंस्थे Svochchasamsthe, in its own exalted house, *i. e.*, in the sign Kanyâ. बुधे Budhe, Mercury being. लग्ने Lagne, the Ascendant. भृगौ Bhṛigau, Venus. मेषूरणाश्रिते Meṣûraṇâśrite, in the tenth house, the sign Mithuna. सजीवे Sajîve, with Jupiter. अस्ते Aste, in the seventh house; the sign Mîna. निशानाथे Niśânâthe, the Moon. राजा Râjâ, king. मंदारयोः Mandârayoḥ, Saturn and Mars. सुते Sute, in the fifth house, the Sign Makara.

11. Mercury in the Ascendant Kanyâ, Venus in the sign Mithuna, Jupiter and the Moon in the sign Mîna, Saturn and Mars in Makara, a person born becomes a king.

मालिनी–अपि खलकुलजाता मानवा राज्यभाजः किमुत नृपकुलोत्थाः प्रोक्तभूपालयोगैः ॥ नृपतिकुलसमुत्थाः पार्थिवा वक्ष्यमाणैर्भवति नृपतितुल्यस्तेष्वभूपालपुत्रः ॥ १२ ॥

अपि Api, even. खलकुलजाताः Khalakulajâtâḥ, born in low families. मानवाः Mânavâḥ, persons. राज्यभाजः Râjyabhâjaḥ, become kings. किमुत Kimuta, what to say; there is nothing to be said against. नृपकुलोत्थाः Nṛipakulotthâḥ, (those) born of a royal family. प्रोक्तभूपालयोगैः Proktabhûpâlayogaiḥ, under the planetary combinations already stated (indicating future kingships). नृपतिकुलसमुत्थाः Nṛipatikulasamutthâḥ, born of a royal family. पार्थिवाः Pârthivâḥ, kings. वक्ष्यमाणैः Vakṣyamâṇaiḥ, now to be described. भवति Bhavati, become. नृपतितुल्यः Nṛipatitulyaḥ, rich like kings. तेषु Teṣu, in them. अभूपालपुत्रः Abhûpâlaputraḥ, persons otherwise than the sons of kings.

12. Persons born under the various Yogas above stated will become kings, though they come out of low families. If such persons are born of a royal family they will doubtless be kings. We shall now proceed to describe certain Yogas, persons born under which will become kings if they belong to a royal family; otherwise they will become immensely rich like kings.

श्रौपच्छंदसिक–उच्चस्वत्रिकोणगैर्बलस्थैस्त्र्याद्यैर्भूपतिवंशजा नरेंद्राः ॥ पंचादिभिरन्यवंशजाता हीनैर्वित्तयुता न भूमिपालाः ॥ १३ ॥

उच्चस्वत्रिकोणगैः : Uchchasvatrikoṇagaiḥ, in their exalted house or in their Mûlatrikoṇa houses, or in their own houses. बलस्थैः: Balasthaiḥ, when strong by virtue of time, effort, and one's natural strength, (see the end of Chapter II). त्र्याद्यैः: Tryâddaiḥ, three or more planets. भूपतिवंशजाः: Bhûpativaṃśajâḥ, born of a royal family. नरेंद्राः: Narendrâḥ, kings. पंचादिभिः: Pañchâdibhiḥ, the five, six, or seven planets (being). अन्यवंशजाताः: Anyvaṃśajâtâḥ, born of other than royal family. हीनैः: Hînaiḥ, deprived of strength by virtue of time, &c. Some authors take it to mean, if the number of powerful planets be less than three or five. वित्तयुताः: Vittayutâḥ, wealthy; immensely rich. न Na, not. भूमिपालाः: Bhûmipâlâḥ, kings.

13. Three or more planets when exalted or in their own houses or in their Mûlatrikoṇa houses and also endowed with power (by virtue of time, &c.), persons born of a royal family become kings, and others become wealthy. If these three or more be devoid of strength (by virtue of time, &c.) then persons of the royal family do not become kings but wealthy. If 5, 6, or 7 planets be exalted or in their own houses or in their Mûlatrikoṇa houses, then others also, even if they do not come out of the royal family, become kings. (If in either case the number of powerful planets be less than three or five, the persons described above will not become kings but will become only rich.)

विद्युन्माला–लेखास्थेऽर्केऽजेंदौ लग्ने भौमे स्वोच्चे कुंभे मंदे ॥ चापप्राप्ते जीवे राज्ञः पुत्रं विंद्यात्पृथ्वीनाथम ॥ १४ ॥

लेखास्थे Lekhâsthe, the Ascendant. Some read लेयस्थे Leyasthe, in the sign Siṃha. अर्के Arke, the Sun becoming. अजे Aje, in the sign Meṣa. इंदौ Indau, the Moon being. लग्ने Lagne, the Ascendant. भौमे Bhaume, Mars being. स्वोच्चे Svochche, in their exalted houses. कुंभे Kumbhe, in Kumbha sign. मंदे Mande, Saturn being. चापप्राप्ते Châpaprâpte, in the sign Dhanu. जीवे Jîve, Jupiter. राज्ञः: Râjñaḥ, of kings. पुत्रं Puttram, son. विंद्यात् Vindyât, know. पृथ्वीनाथम् Prithvînâtham, lord of the earth.

14. The Sun and Moon being in the Ascendant Meṣa, Mars in Makara, Saturn in Kumbha, and Jupiter in Dhanu, make kings the persons born of a royal family only.

Note :—Some read सेव instead of सेव. Then the Sun enters in the sign Simha and Moon in Meṣa becomes the Ascendant. This is also correct.

विद्युन्माला—स्वर्क्षे शुक्रे पातालस्थे धर्मस्थानं प्राप्ते चंद्रे ॥
दुश्चिक्यांगप्राप्तिप्राप्तैः शेषैर्जातः स्वामी भूमेः ॥ १५ ॥

स्वर्क्षे Svarkṣe, in her own sign ; in the sign Vṛiṣa or Tulâ. शुक्रे Sukre, Venus being. पातालस्थे Pâtâlasthe, in the fourth house from the Ascendant. धर्मस्थानं Dharmasthânam, the ninth house. प्राप्ते Prâpte, seen. चंद्रे Chandre, the Moon occupying. दुश्चिक्यांगप्राप्तिप्राप्तैः Duśchikyâṅgaprâptiprâptaiḥ, in the 3rd, the Ascendant, and eleventh houses. शेषैः Śeṣaiḥ, by the remaining planets, *i.e.*, Sun, Mars, Mercury, Jupiter, Saturn. जातः Jâtaḥ, person born ; native. स्वामी Svâmî, lord. भूमेः Bhûmeḥ, of the earth.

15. Venus in her own sign (Vṛiṣa or Tulâ) and in the fourth house from the Ascendant; the Moon in the ninth house ; the other planets, *viz.*, the Sun, Mars, Mercury, Jupiter, and Saturn being in the 3rd, 1st, and 11th houses, persons of royal family become kings ; others become wealthy like kings.

Note :—Kumbha may be the Ascendant, or Karka may be the Ascendant. These are the two cases.

नवमालिका—सौम्ये वीर्ययुते तनुयुक्ते वीर्याढ्ये च शुभे शुभयाते ॥ धर्मार्थोपचयेष्ववशेषैर्धर्मात्मा नृपजः पृथिवीशः ॥१६॥

सौम्ये Saumye, on Mercury becoming. वीर्ययुते Vîryayute, strong (by virtue of time, &c.). तनुयुक्ते Tanuyukte, in the Ascendant. वीर्याढ्ये Vîrâḍhye, strong. च Cha, and. शुभे Śubhe, the benefic planet Jupiter or Venus occupying. शुभयाते Śubhayâte, in auspicious signs ; in religious signs ; in the 9th sign. Some read सुखयाते Sukhayâte, *i.e.*, benefics in the 4th house. धर्मार्थोपचयेषु Dharmârthopachayeṣu, in the 9th, 2nd, 3rd, 6th, 10th, and 11th signs. अवशेषैः Avaśeṣaiḥ, the remaining planets. धर्मात्मा Dharmâtmâ, virtuous. नृपजः Nṛipajaḥ, prince. पृथिवीशः Pṛithivîśaḥ, lord of the earth.

16. Mercury becoming strong and occupying the Ascendant (1) and a benefic planet Venus or Jupiter being also strong and occupying the ninth sign (2) and the other planets (3) occupying as far as possible the 9th, 2nd, 3rd, 6th 10th and 11th houses (4), princes become virtuous rulers of the earth.

Notes :—(1) This may be any one of the 12 signs. (2) Some read सुखयाते instead of शुभयाते, *i.e.*, the benefic planets being in the 4th house. (3) When one or more of the other planets according to the Commentator. (4) One of these houses according to the Commentator.

वंशस्थ–वृषोदये मूर्तिधनारिलाभगैः शशांकजीवार्कसुता-परैर्नृपः ॥ सुखे गुरौ खे शशितीक्ष्णदीधिती यमोदये लाभगतै-र्नृपोऽपरैः ॥ १७ ॥

वृषोदये Vrisodaye, the Ascendant being Vrisa. मूर्तिधनारिलाभगैः Mûrtidhanâri-lâbhagaih, in the Ascendant, second, sixth and eleventh houses. शशांकजीवार्कसुतापरैः Saśâmkajîvârkasutâparaih, the Moon, Jupiter, Saturn, and also others, *i.e.*, Sun, Mars, Mercury, Venus. नृपः Nripah, king. सुखे Sukhe, in the fourth sign. गुरौ Gurau, Jupiter being. खे Khe, in the tenth house. शशितीक्ष्णदीधिती Saśitîksnadîdhitî, Moon and the Sun. यमोदये Yamodaye, Saturn in the Ascendant. लाभगतैः Lâbhagataih, in the eleventh house. नृपः Nripah, king. अपरैः Aparaih, the remaining planets, *i.e.*, Mars, Mercury, and Venus.

17. The Ascendant Vrisa with the Moon, Jupiter in Mithuna, Saturn in Tulâ, Sun, Mars, Mercury and Venus in Mîna, make princes kings. Others become wealthy like a king. Second case :—Saturn in the Ascendant, (1) Jupiter in the fourth house, the Sun and Moon in the tenth house, Mars, Mercury and Venus in the eleventh house make also princes kings.

Note :—(1) This may be any one of the 12 signs according to Commentator.

वसन्ततिलका–मेषूरणायतनुगाः शशिमंदजीवा ज्ञारौ धने सितरवी हिबुके नरेंद्रम् । वक्रासितौ शशिसुरेज्यसितार्कसौम्या होरासुखास्तशुभखाप्तिगताः प्रजेशम् ॥ १८ ॥

मेषूरणायतनुगाः Mesuranâyatanugâh, in the tenth and eleventh houses and in the Ascendant. शशिमंदजीवाः Saśimandajîvâh, the Moon, Saturn and Jupiter respectively occupying. ज्ञारौ Jñârau, Mercury and Mars being. धने Dhane, in the second house. सितरवी Sitaravî, Venus and the Sun being. हिबुके Hibuke, in the fourth house. नरेंद्रम् Narendram, king. वक्रासितौ Vakrâsitau, Mars, and Saturn being. शशिसुरेज्यसितार्कसौम्याः Saśisureyyasitârkasaumyâh, the Moon, Jupiter, Venus, the Sun, and Mercury being. होरासुखास्तशुभखाप्तिगताः Horâsukhâstaśubhakhâptigatâh, in the Ascendant, fourth, seventh, ninth, tenth, and eleventh houses, respectively. प्रजेशम् Prajeśam, ruler of subjects.

18. The Moon in the tenth house, Saturn in the eleventh house, Jupiter in the Ascendant; Mercury and Mars in the second house, Venus and the Sun in the 4th house make princes kings. Second Case :—Mars and Saturn in the Ascendant, the Moon in the fourth house, Jupiter in the seventh house, Venus in the ninth house, the Sun in the tenth, Mercury in the eleventh house make also princes kings. Others become wealthy like kings.

स्वागता—कर्मलग्नयुतपाकदशायां राज्यलब्धिरथवा प्रब-
लस्य । शत्रुनीचगृहयातदशायां छिद्रसंश्रयदशा परिकल्प्या ॥१६॥

कर्मलग्नयुतपाकदशायां Karmalagnayutapâkadaśâyâm, during the Daśâ or the Antardaśâ of the planet that is in the Ascendant or during the Daśâ or the Antardasâ of the planet in the 10th house from the Ascendant. राज्यलब्धिः Râjyalabdhiḥ, the acquisition of sovereignty or kingdom. अथवा Athavâ, or. प्रबलस्य Pravalasya, during the Daśâ of the planet that is most powerful. शत्रुनीचगृहयातदशायां Śatrunîchagrihayâtadaśâyâm, during the Daśâ or the Antardaśâ of the planet residing in the house of the enemy of the king-making planet or in its detrimental house. छिद्रसंश्रयदशा Chhidrasaṃśrayadaśâ, the weak period during the Daśâ when kingdom might be lost and when making friendship or taking refuge under other powerful victorious kings is advisable. परिकल्प्या Parikalpyâ, to be considered over.

19. The kingdom will be obtained when the Daśâ or the Antardasâ comes of the planet that is in the Ascendant, (1) or in the 10th house from the Ascendant, or in that of the most powerful planet (2). The kingdom might be lost also during the Daśâ or the Antardaśâ of the planet that is in the enemies' houses or in the detrimental houses (3); if it be not powerful then resort to other just and powerful kings should be had recourse to.

Notes :—(1) If there be planets both in the Ascendant and in the 10th house or if there be several planets in either, then in the Antardaśâ period of the most powerful of them.

(2) If there be no planets both in the Lagna and in the 10th house.

(3) If such planets be powerful, the king will lose his kingdom permanently ; and if they be not powerful, he will recover it by the help of his allies.

मालिनी–गुरुसितबुधलग्ने सप्तमस्थेऽर्कपुत्रे वियति दिवस-
नाथे भोगिनां जन्म विंद्यात् । शुभबलयुतकेन्द्रैः क्रूरसंस्थैश्च
पापैर्व्रजति शबरदस्युस्वामितामर्थभाक्च ॥ २० ॥
इति श्रीवराहमिहिरविरचिते बृहज्जातके राज-
योगाध्यायः एकादशः ॥११॥

गुरुसितबुधलग्ने Gurusitabudhalagne, on Jupiter, Venus or Mercury being in the Ascendant. सप्तमस्थे Saptamasthe, in the 7th house. अर्कपुत्रे Arkaputre, Saturn being. वियति Viyati, in the tenth house. दिवसनाथे Divasanâthe, on the Sun going. भोगिनां Bhoginâm, of those that are devoted to enjoyments ; the enjoyers of the senses ; of the epicures. जन्म Janma, the birth of. विंद्यात् Vindyât, know. शुभबलयुतकेन्द्रैः Śubhabalayutakendraiḥ, when the powerful, auspicious signs are in the angular houses. क्रूरसंस्थैः च Krûrasaṃsthaiḥ cha, and in the malefic signs. पापैः Pâpaiḥ, when the malefic planets reside in. व्रजति Vrajati, gets ; goes into. शबरदस्युस्वामिताम् Śabaradasyusvâmitâm, the chief of hunters and dacoits. अर्थभाक् च Arthabhâk cha, and becomes wealthy.

20. Jupiter, Venus or Mercury in the Ascendant, (1) Saturn in the seventh house, the Sun in the tenth give birth to epicures (*i.e.*, men of enjoyments). When the powerful benefic signs form the angular houses (Kendras) (2) and the malefic planets occupy the malignant signs, persons born become rich and turn out the chiefs of the hunters and dacoits.

Notes :—(1) The interpretation given of this portion of the text is objected by some on the ground that when Venus and Mercury (the inferior planets) occupy the rising sign, the Sun cannot occupy the 10th house, a place more than 60 degrees removed from them. Accordingly the following interpretation is proposed :—"If the rising sign be the house of Jupiter, Venus, or Mercury." Bhattautpala, the Commentator, while granting the validity of the objection, says that the interpretation has the support of Gârgî whom he quotes. Varâha Mihira, while admitting the impossibility of the Yoga, says that his task is simply to state the views of the ancient writers and nothing more.

(2) This portion of the text is interpreted by some as follows :—

"When powerful benefic planets occupy the Kendras." But this interpretation is opposed to Gârgi whom the Commentator quotes.

Thus ends the eleventh Chapter on Râjayoga by Śrî Varâha Mihira of Avantika.

CHAPTER XII.

ON NÂBHASA YOGAS.

Or on Particular Heavenly Combination.

औपच्छंदसिक—नवदिग्वसवस्त्रिकाग्निवेदैर्गुणिता द्वित्रिचतुर्विकल्पजाः स्युः । यवनैस्त्रिगुणा हि षट्शती सा कथिता विस्तरतोऽत्र तत्समाः स्युः ॥ १ ॥

नवदिग्वसवः Navadigvasavaḥ, the numbers nine, ten, and eight, respectively; 9, 10, 8. त्रिकाग्निवेदैः Trikâgnivedaiḥ, by three, three and four respectively; by 3, 3, 4. गुणिताः Guṇitâḥ, multiplied by. द्वित्रिचतुर्विकल्पजाः Dvitrichaturvikalpajâḥ, arising out of the combinations of the first two, first three, and first four numbers (indicating the number of the four varieties of heavenly combinations). The first variety is called Âkṛiti Yoga or the combination consequent on a specific form; and its number is 20. The second variety is called the Saṃkhyâ Yoga or the combination consequent on numbering; and its number is seven. The third variety is called Âśraya Yoga or the combination consequent on dependence on another; and its number is three. The fourth variety is called Dala Yoga or the combination consequent on the troop of planets all being arranged so as to produce good or bad effects; and its number is two. Now it will be seen easily that the number 27 is got by adding 20 and 7; the number 30 is got by adding 20, 7, and 3; and the number 32 is got by adding 20, 7, 3, and 2 respectively. यवनैः Yavanaiḥ, by the astrologer Yavanâchârya and other ancient astrologers. त्रिगुणा Triguṇâ, thrice. हि Hi. षट्शती Ṣaṭśatî, six hundred. सा Sâ, the Nâvasa Yogas. कथिता Kathitâ, said; mentioned. विस्तरतः Vistarataḥ, in detail; extensively. अत्र Atra, here; in this treatise. तत्समाः Tatsmâḥ, those in brief. स्युः Syuḥ, are (described).

1. The numbers nine, ten and eight (9, 10, 8), multiplied respectively by three, three, and four (3, 3, 4), give rise to the numbers (*i.e.*, 27, 30, 32) indicating the sums of the first two, first three and the first four combinations. Yavanâchârya and others treat extensively of 1,800 varieties of various such combinations. What is described in this treatise is a summary of them, (but containing the essence of 1,800 varieties).

Note.—The heavenly combinations (Nâvasa Yogas) are conceived to be of four kinds:—The first kind is called Âkṛiti Yoga; the second kind is called Saṃkhyà Yoga ; the third kind is called Âśraya Yoga ; the fourth kind is called Dala Yoga. The first one has twenty sub-divisions, the second one, seven sub-divisions ; the third one, three ; and the fourth one has got two sub-divisions. These will be described in details shortly ; their fruits too will be described. Yavanâchârya's 1,800 varieties will also be dealt with in the Notes at the end of this Chapter.

श्रौपच्छंदसिक–रज्जुर्मुशलं नलश्चराद्यैः सत्यश्चाश्रयजाञ्ज-
गाद योगान् ॥ केंद्रैः सदसद्युतैर्दलाख्यौ स्रक्सर्पौ कथितौ
पराशरेण ॥ २ ॥

रज्जुः Rajjuḥ, named Rajju, (*i. e.*, rope, cord, tie). मुशलं Muśalaṃ, named Muśalam (club). नलः Nalaḥ, termed Nala (a tube). चराद्यैः Charâdyaiḥ, according as the planets are in the moveable, fixed, or common signs. सत्यः Satyaḥ, Satyâchârya, the astrologer. च Cha, and. आश्रयजान् Âśrayajân, arising out of Âsraya, or of dependent position. जगाद Jagâda, said ; mentioned. योगान् Yogân, combinations. केन्द्रैः Kendraiḥ, the angles. सदसद्युतैः Sadasadyutaiḥ, when occupied by benefics or malefics. दलाख्यौ Dalâkṣyau, termed Dala Yoga. स्रक्सर्पौ Sraksarpau, named otherwise Garland Yoga or Serpent Yoga. कथितौ Kathitau, said. पराशरेण Parâśareṇa, by Parâśara, the Astrologer.

2. Satyâchârya says :—The Âśraya Yoga is termed Rajju (rope), Muśalam (club), or Nala (tube) according as all the planets (1) are found in the moveable, fixed or common signs. Again, Parâśara says that Dala Yoga is then formed when the planets reside in the angles. The Dala Yoga is termed Srak Yoga (combinations looking like a garland) when the *benefic* planets (2) reside in the angles and it is also named Sarpa Yoga (combinations looking like a Serpent) when the *malefic* planets (3) reside in the angles.

Notes.—The author here begins with Âśraya and Dala Yogas, the 3rd and the 4th variety of Nâbhasa Yoga.

(1) When all the planets are found in one, two, three or four moveable signs, it is called Rajju or Rope combination ; similarly, when all the planets are found in one, two, three, or four fixed signs, it is termed Muśalam (club) combination ; and when all the planets are found in one, two, three, or four common signs, it is named Nala (tube) combination. Some say when all the planets are found in all the 4 moveable signs it is called Rajju and so on ; but this is not proper, as not being countenanced by higher authorities Gârgî and others. Persons born under **Rajju Yoga**

are fond of gambling and residing in foreign or distant lands and get wealth ; those under Muśala Yoga get honor and wealth ; those under Nala Yoga get lean or fat bodies; they become clever, amass wealth and derive enjoyments.

(2) When the benefic planets Mercury, Jupiter, and Venus are in any three angles, it is termed Garland combination ; and (3) when the malefic planets Sun, Mars and Saturn reside in any three angles, it is termed Serpent combination. Here any three angles are taken into account and not all the angles for this reason : the Moon is considered benefic in the light half and malefic in the dark half of the lunar month. And when the benefics reside in the three angles and the waning Moon in the fourth angle, it is known as Serpent Yoga ; or when the *malefics* reside in the three angles and the waning Moon in the fourth angle, even then it is known as Serpent Yoga. And this is countenanced by higher authorities Gârgi, Parâśara, etc.

Srak-Yoga or Garland-Yoga produces auspicious good effect and Serpent Yoga evil effects.

उपजातिका—योगा व्रजंत्याश्रयजाः समत्वं यवाब्जवज्रांडजगोलकाद्यैः ॥ केंद्रोपगैः प्रोक्तफलौ दलाख्यावित्याहुरन्ये न पृथक्फलौ तौ ॥ ३ ॥

योगाः Yogâḥ, combinations. व्रजंति Vrajanti, go to. आश्रयजाः Âśrayajâḥ, Aśraya Yoga, called Rajju, Musalam, and Nala Yogas. समत्वं Samatvam, equality ; sameness. यवाब्जवज्रांडजगोलकाद्यैः : Yavâbjavajrâṇḍajagolakâdyaiḥ, with Yava (barley), Abja (lotus), Vajra (the thunderbolt), Aṇḍaja (birds), Golaka (globe) combinations, etc. केन्द्रोपगैः: Kendropagaiḥ, due to the planets being stationed in the angles. प्रोक्तफलौ Proktaphalau, the effects, auspicious or inauspicious as the case may be, already mentioned. दलाख्यौ Dalâkṣau, termed Dala Yoga. इति Iti, thus. आहुः: Âhuḥ, said ; mentioned. अन्ये Anye, other astrologers. न Na, not. पृथक्फलौ Prithakphalau, producing separate effects. तौ Tau, they.

3. Other astrologers say that the Âśraya Yogas (the Rope, Club, and tubular combinations) do not differ at all from the Yava (barley), Abja (lotus), Vajra (thunderbolt), Aṇḍaja (bird), Golaka (globe) and the like Yogas (see the next stanzas), and that when the effects of planets occupying the Kendras (or angles) are described, the effects of Dala Yogas are also described and they produce no separate effects.

Notes :—In this stanza the author states the reason why certain astrologers have not mentioned at all in their works, the Âśraya and the Dala Yogas. It may be asked why then Varâha Mihîra has mentioned these in his treatise? The reply is, there are special reasons for their being mentioned separately here. The Âśraya Yogas may be these and may not be these; hence the author has deemed it advisable to treat them separately. For instance, if all the planets occupy the signs Mithuna and Dhanu—2 of the common signs—when one of these is also the rising sign, the Yoga is known both as Vajra and Nala; but if any other sign be the rising sign, it is not a Vajra Yoga but only a Nala Yoga.

As regards the Dala Yogas, it is said that other writers have described the effects of benefic and of malefic planets occupying the Kendras and as these are also the effects of the two Dala Yogas they have omitted to treat them separately; the author here treats of these separately in order to make it known that the two are Nâbhasa Yogas and as such their effects are felt throughout life (*i.e.*, in all the Daśâs). The other Yogas produce effects in their respective Daśâ or Antardaśâ period and do not produce any effect when that Daśâ period is over.

The special reasons for taking the Âśraya and Dala Yogas separately will be further discussed in the notes at the end of this Chapter.

व०ति०—आसन्नकेंद्रभवनद्वयगैर्गदाख्यस्तन्वस्तगेषु शकटं विहगः खबंध्वोः ॥ शृंगाटकं नवमपंचमलग्नसंस्थैर्लग्नान्यगैर्हलमिति प्रवदंति तज्ज्ञाः ॥ ४ ॥

आसन्नकेन्द्रभवनद्वयगैः: Âsannakendrabhavanadvayagaiḥ, when in the two adjacent angular houses, (all the planets occupy). गदाख्यः: Gadâksyaḥ, Yoga termed Gadâ (club). तन्वस्तगेषु Tanvastageṣu, when in the Ascendant and Descendant, (all the planets occupy). शकटं Śakaṭaṃ, Yoga termed Śakaṭam (cart). विहगः: Vihagaḥ, Yoga termed Vihaga (bird). खबंध्वोः: Khabandoḥ, when in the tenth and fourth houses, (all the planets reside). शृंगाटकं Śringâṭakam, Yoga termed Śringâṭakam; नवमपंचमलग्नसंस्थैः: Navamapañchamalagnasaṃsthaiḥ, in the ninth, fifth, and the first houses, (all the planets reside). लग्नान्यगैः: Lagnânyagaiḥ, in the other triangular houses, *i.e.*, the other ninth and fifth houses than those counted from the Ascendant. This may be in 3 ways :—(1) the 2nd, 6th and 10th houses, (2) the 3rd, 7th and 11th houses, (3) the 4th, 8th and 12th houses. हलं Halam, Yoga termed Halam. इति Iti, thus. प्रवदंति Pravadanti, say. तज्ज्ञाः: Tajjñâḥ, astrologers well versed in their sciences.

4. The Yoga is known as Gadâ when all the planets are in the two adjacent angular houses; (1) termed Śakaṭam

when all the planets are in the Ascendant and the Descendant ; known as Vihaga when all the planets are in the tenth and fourth houses ; termed Sriṅgâṭakaṁ when all the planets are in the fifth, ninth houses and in the Ascendant ; and the Yoga is known as Halam when all the planets are in the other triangular houses, *i.e.*, other fifth and ninth houses, than those stated above (2). Thus say the well-versed astrologers.

Notes :—(1) The author now proceeds to describe the 20 Âkṛiti Yogas ; 5 of them are described in this stanza. There are 4 varieties in the Gadâ Yoga. (1) Gadâ (Lagna, fourth) ; (2) Saṃkha (fourth and seventh) ; (3) Bavruka (seventh and tenth) ; (4) Dhvajâ, (tenth and Lagna). The Yavanas consider these 4 as 4 distinct Yogas and call them respectively as Gadâ, Saṃkha, Bavruka and Dhvajâ.

(2) This may be in 3 ways.

All the planets may occupy.

(1) the 2nd, 6th and 10th houses.

(2) the 3rd, 7th and 11th houses.

(3) the 4th, 8th and 12th houses.

वैतालीया–शकटांडजवच्छुभाशुभैर्वज्रं तद्विपरीतगैर्यवः ॥
कमलं तु विमिश्रसंस्थितैर्वापि तद्यदि केंद्रवाह्यतः ॥ ५ ॥

शकटांडजवत् Sakaṭâṇḍajavat, like Śakaṭa and Aṇḍaja (as described in the preceding verse). शुभाशुभैः Śubhâśubhaiḥ, by the benefic and malefic planets respectively. वज्रं Vajram, Yoga termed Vajra (thunderbolt). तद्विपरीतगैः Tadviparîtagaiḥ, when posted in the reverse order (from the Vajra yoga). यवः Yavaḥ, Yoga known as Yavaḥ. कमलं Kamalaṃ, Yoga termed Kamala (lotus). विमिश्रसंस्थितैः Vimiśrasaṃsthitaiḥ, when all the planets, benefics and malefics, are stationed (without any restriction) in all the angular houses. वापी Vâpî, Yoga termed Vâpî. तत् Tat, all the planets. यदि Yadi, if. केंद्रवाह्यतः Kendravâhyataḥ, in the other houses than the angles ; in the four succedent or in the 4 cadent houses.

5. The Vajra Yoga takes place when the benefic planets are in the Ascendant and Descendant and the malefic planets are in the fourth and tenth houses (no planets being in the other houses); the reverse of this is Yava Yoga, *i.e.*, when the malefics are in the Ascendant and Descendant and the benefics are in the fourth and tenth houses. The Yoga is known as Kamala or Avja, when all the planets are scattered

without any restriction in all the angles and nowhere else; and the Yoga is termed Vâpî when all the planets are interspersed in houses other than the angles (*i.e.*, in the four succedent or in the 4 cadent houses.)

Note:—Four Âkṛiti Yogas are described in this verse. Thus far nine (5 + 4) Âkṛiti Yogas are described.

अनुष्टुभ्—पूर्वशास्त्रानुसारेण मया वज्रादयः कृताः ॥
चतुर्थे भवने सूर्याज्ज्ञसितौ भवतः कथम् ॥ ६ ॥

पूर्वशास्त्रानुसारेण Pûrvaśâstrânusâreṇa, according to the ancient treatises (by Maya, Yavana, Gârga and others). मया Mayâ, by me (VarâhaMihirâchârya). वज्रादयः Vajrâdayaḥ, these Yogas, Vajra, etc., (and the yoga mentioned in the beginning of stanza 20 of the Chapter on Râja Yoga). कृताः Kritâḥ, done. चतुर्थे Chaturthe, in the fourth. भवने Bhavane, house. सूर्यात् Sûryât, from the Sun. ज्ञसितौ Jñasitau, Mercury and Venus. कथम् Katham, how.

6. These Vajra and other Yogas I have taken from the ancient Śâstras by Maya, Yavana and others. The discrepancy arises thus:—when the Sun is in the 4th (or 10th) house (with the malefics) how can Venus and Mercury be in the 1st or 7th house? (*i.e.*, this is impossible, as Venus and Mercury cannot be so distant from the Sun) (1).

Note:—(1) According to Mr. Sundareswara Srouty of Trivadi, the Vajra and Yava Yogas refer to the positions of the planets in the Bhâva Chakra and not to their position in their Râśi Chakra as supposed by Varâha Mihira. He is therefore of opinion that Garga and other writers have not erred in treating of these Yogas as possible ones.

अनुष्टुभ–कंटकादिप्रवृत्तैस्तु चतुर्गृहगतैर्ग्रहैः। यूपेषु शक्तिदंडाख्या होराद्यैः कंटकैः क्रमात् ॥ ७ ॥

कंटकादिप्रवृत्तैः Kanṭakâdipravrittaiḥ, commencing first from the angular house. तु Tu, but. चतुर्गृहगतैः Chaturgrihagataiḥ, when posted in the four houses consecutively. ग्रहैः Grahaiḥ, the planets occupying. यूपेषु शक्तिदंडाख्याः Yupeṣu Śaktidaṇḍâkhyâḥ, the Yogas named Yûpa and Iṣu, Śakti and Daṇḍa. होराद्यैः Horâdyaiḥ, taking first the Ascendant. कंटकैः Kanṭakaiḥ, the angles. क्रमात् Kramât, successively.

7. When all the planets are found in the four houses consecutively from the Ascendant, the fourth, the seventh

and the tenth, the angular houses, respectively, the Yogas are termed Yûpa, Iṣu, Śakti, and Danda one after another (1).

Note.—Four Âkṛiti Yogas are described in this verse. Thus (5 + 4 + 4) thirteen Âkṛiti Yogas in all are described.

(1) If all the planets occupy the four signs 1st, 2nd, 3rd and 4th, the Yoga is known as Yupa. If they occupy the 4th, 5th, 6th, and 7th houses, the Yoga is known as Iṣu; if they occupy the 7th, 8th, 9th and 10th houses, the Yoga is known as Śakti; and if they occupy the 4 signs 10th, 11th, 12th and the Ascendant, the Yoga is known as Daṇḍa.

अनुष्टुभ्–नौकूटच्छत्रचापानि तद्वत्सप्तर्क्षसंस्थितैः । अर्द्ध-चंद्रस्तु नावाद्यैः प्रोक्तस्त्वन्यर्क्षसंस्थितैः ॥ ८ ॥

नौकूटच्छत्रचापानि Naukûṭachhatrachâpâni, the Yogas termed Nau (boat), Kûṭa (mountain peak), Chhatra (umbrella) and Châpa (arrow). तद्वत् Tadvat, like what have been described in the preceding verse, from the Ascendant, the 4th, the 7th, and the 10th houses. सप्तर्क्षसंस्थितैः Saptarkṣasaṃsthitaiḥ, situated in the seven signs. अर्द्धचंद्रः Ardhachandraḥ, the Yoga known as Ardhachandra (semi-lunar). तु Tu, but. नावाद्यैः Nâvâdyaiḥ, the Nau Yoga, etc., that have been already mentioned. प्रोक्तः Proktaḥ, mentioned. तु Tu, but. अन्यर्क्षसंस्थितैः Anyarkṣasaṃsthitaiḥ, situated in the signs not according to the previous arrangement, *i.e.*, in the signs not commencing with the Ascendant, but with the cadent or succedent houses.

8. If, as before, the seven planets reside in the seven houses consecutively, starting from the Ascendant, the fourth, the seventh, and the tenth houses respectively, we will have Nau (boat) Yoga, Kûṭa (mountain peak) Yoga, Chhatra (umbrella) Yoga, and Châpa (arrow) Yoga. And if these seven planets be situated in the seven houses consecutively not starting from the Ascendant or the angles but from the succedent or cadent houses, we get the Ardhachandra (semi-lunar) Yoga.

Notes.—Here five Âkṛiti Yogas (so far 18 Âkṛiti Yogas) are described. Ardhachandra Yoga is of eight sub-divisions, and these can be easily traced out. As there are 4 succedent and 4 cadent houses, the Ardhachandra Yogas are of 8 kinds :—*viz.*, all the planets may occupy (1) from the 2nd to the 8th houses, (2) from the 3rd to the 9th house, (3) from the

5th to the 11th house, (4) from the 6th to the 12th house, (5) from the 8th to the 2nd house, (6) from the 9th to the 3rd house, (7) from the 11th to the 5th house, (8) from the 12th to the 6th house.

अनुष्टुभ्—एकांतरगतैरर्थात्समुद्रः षड्गृहाश्रितैः । विलग्नादिस्थितैश्चक्रमित्याकृतिजसंग्रहः ॥ ६ ॥

एकांतरगतैः Ekântaragataiḥ, when situated in every alternate houses. अर्थात् Arthâṭ, (beginning) from the second house. समुद्रः Samudraḥ, the Yoga known as Samudra Yoga (ocean). षड्गृहाश्रितैः Ṣaḍgrihâśritaiḥ, situated in the six alternate houses. विलग्नादिस्थितैः Vilagnâdisthitaiḥ, situated in the houses commencing from the Ascendant. चक्रम् Chakram, termed Chakra (wheel) Yoga. इति Iti, thus. आकृतिजसंग्रहः Âkṛitijasaṃgrahaḥ, all the Âkṛiti Yogas thus described briefly.

9. When all the planets are found in the six (*i.e.*, 2nd, 4th, 6th, 8th, 10th, and 12th) (1) houses, it is known as Samudra Yoga; when all the planets are found in the six (*i.e.*, 1st, 3rd, 5th, 7th, 9th, and 11th) (2) houses, it is termed Chakra Yoga. Thus all the Âkṛiti Yogas are described briefly.

Note.—Here 2 Âkṛiti Yogas are described. Thus twenty Âkṛiti Yogas in all are dealt with.

(1) Six alternate signs beginning from the 2nd house.

(2) Six alternate houses beginning from the Ascendant.

शालिनी—संख्यायोगाः स्युः सप्तसप्तर्क्षसंस्थैरेकापायाद्वल्लकी दामिनी च । पाशः केदारः शूलयोगो युगं च गोलश्चान्यान्पूर्वमुक्तान्विहाय ॥ १० ॥

संख्यायोगाः Sankhyâyogâḥ, all the Sankhyâ Yogas. स्युः Syuḥ, are these ; are the following. सप्तसप्तर्क्षसंस्थैः Saptasaptarkṣasaṃsthaiḥ, the seven planets being situated in the seven signs. एकापायात् Ekâpâyât, removing one (from the seven houses ; six houses, five, four, three, and two one house, successively.) वल्लकी Vallakî, named Vallakî Yoga. दामिनी Dâminî, known as Dâminî Yoga. च Cha, and. पाशः Pâśaḥ, Pâśa Yoga. केदारः Kedâraḥ, Kedâra Yoga. शूलयोगः Śûlayogaḥ, Śûla Yoga. युगं Yugam, Yuga Yoga. च Cha, and. गोलः Golaḥ, Gola Yoga. च Cha, and. अन्यान् Anyân, others. पूर्वमुक्तान् Pûrvamuktân, already mentioned. विहाय Vihâya, avoiding ; not taking into account.

10. Now the seven Sankhyâ Yogas are being described. When the seven planets are in any seven signs, it is known as Vallakî Yoga. When the seven planets are in any six

signs, it is Dâminî; in any five, Pâśa; in any four, Kedâra; in any three, Śûla Yoga; in any two, Yuga Yoga; and when all the planets are in any one sign, it is known as Gola Yoga. The Yogas already described, if they look like Saṃkhyâ Yoga, are not to be taken into account under Saṃkhyâ Yogas. (1)

Note:—(1) For instance, the Gadâ, Śakaṭa, and Vihaga Yogas described in stanza 4 are to be treated only as such and not as Yuga yoga described in this stanza; the Śṛiṅgaṭaka and Hala Yogas described in stanza 4 are to be treated only as such and not as Śûla Yoga described in this stanza. Again the Vajra, Yava, Kamala, and Vâpî Yogas described in stanza 5 as well the Yûpa, Iśu, Śakti, and Daṇḍa Yogas described in stanza 7 shall not be confounded with the Kedâra Yogas described in this stazna. And so on.

वं० ति०—ईर्ष्युर्विदेशनिरतोऽध्वरुचिश्च रज्ज्वां मानी धनी च मुशले बहुकृत्यसक्तः। व्यंगः स्थिराढ्यनिपुणो नलजः स्रगुत्थो भोगान्वितो भुजगजो बहुदुःखभाक्स्यात् ॥ ११ ॥

ईर्ष्युः Îrṣyuḥ, envious; jealous of the wealth of others. विदेशनिरतः–Videśaniratah, living in foreign or distant lands. अध्वरुचिः Adhvaruchiḥ, fond of travelling. च Cha, and. रज्ज्वां Rajjvâm, in the Rajju Yoga, (coming under Âśraya Yoga). मानी Mânî, proud; respectable. धनी Dhanî, wealthy. च Cha, and. मुशले Muśale, in the Muśala Yoga. बहुकृत्यसक्तः Bahukṛithyasaktaḥ, capable of doing great works. व्यंगः Vyaṃgaḥ, of defective body; of defective organs. स्थिराढ्यनिपुणः Sthirḍâhyanipuṇaḥ, steady and clever. नलजः Nalajaḥ, arising out of Nala Yoga. स्रगुत्थः Sragutthaḥ, arising out of Srak or Garland Yoga. भोगान्वितः Bhogânvitaḥ, possessed of all enjoyments, living in comfort and luxury. भुजगजः Bhujagajaḥ, arising out of Serpent Yoga. बहुदुःखभाक् Bahudḥukhabhâk, very miserable. स्यात् Syât, become.

11. Those born under Rajju Yoga are envious, fond of travelling, and live in foreign or distant lands; those born under Muśala Yoga are respectable and wealthy; and capable of doing great works. Those born under Nala Yoga are defective in body, steady and clever. People born under Srak or Garland Yoga are possessed of many enjoyments and those born under Serpent Yoga get many afflictions and miseries.

Note:—In this stanza, the author describes the effects of the three Âśraya Yogas and of the two Dala Yogas.

अनुष्टुभ्—आश्रयोक्तास्तु विफला भवन्त्यन्यैर्विमिश्रिताः ।
मिश्रा यैस्ते फलं दद्युरमिश्राः स्वफलप्रदाः ॥ १२ ॥

आश्रयोक्ताः Âśrayoktâḥ, what have been already described as to the effects of Âśraya Yoga. तु Tu, but. विफलाः Viphalâḥ, not producing any result; ineffective. भवन्ति Vabanti, are. अन्यैः Anyaiḥ, with other Yogas. विमिश्रिताः Vimiśritâḥ, resembling in form. मिश्राः Miśrâḥ, like; resembling; similar in appearance. यैः Yaiḥ, with whatever other Yogas. ते Te, those other Yogas. फलं Phalam, fruits. दद्युः Dadyuḥ, bear. अमिश्राः Amiśrâḥ, not resembling with any other Yoga. स्वफलप्रदाः Svaphalapradâḥ, productive of its own consequences.

12. The Âśraya Yogas become ineffective, when they look like other Yogas. The other Yogas, with which the Âśraya Yogas happen to resemble, those other Yogas become operative and bear fruits. When the Âśraya Yogas do not bear any resemblance with other Yogas, it is then that the Âśraya Yogas produce results.

Note:—For instance, if a Rajju Yoga or a Muśala Yoga or a Nala Yoga partake of the nature of a Kamala Yoga (see Stanza 5) it should be treated as the latter.

व० ति०—यज्वार्थभाक्सततमर्थरुचिर्गदायां तद्वृत्तिभुक् शकटजः सरुजः कुदारः । दूतोऽटनः कलहकृद्विहगे प्रदिष्टः शृङ्गाटके चिरसुखी कृषिकृद्धलाख्ये ॥ १३ ॥

यज्वार्थभाक् Yajvârthabhâk, will perform sacrificial rites, and will become rich. सततं Satatam, always. अर्थरुचिः Artharuchiḥ, eager to amass wealth; eager to collect money. गदायां Gadâyâm, under Gadâ Yoga. तद्वृत्तिभुक् Tadvṛittibhuk, earning one's livelihood by business in carts, hackney carriages, etc. शकटजः Śakaṭajaḥ, of those born under Śakaṭa Yoga. सरुजः Sarujaḥ, having always one bodily complaint or other; of diseased body. कुदारः Kudâraḥ, having ugly and blameable wife; having a mean wife. दूतः Dûtaḥ, messenger; envoy; ambassador. अटनः Aṭanaḥ, of wandering habits; fond of travels. कलहकृत् Kalahakṛit, querulous; quarrelsome. विहगे Vihage, under Vihaga Yoga. प्रदिष्टः Pradiṣṭaḥ, mentioned. शृङ्गाटके Śriṃgâṭake, under Śriṃgâṭaka Yoga. चिरसुखी Chirasukhî, always happy; happy throughout their lives. कृषिकृत् Kriṣikrit, earning one's livelihood by agriculture. हलाख्ये Halâkṣye, under Hala Yoga.

13. Persons born under Gadâ Yoga perform religious sacrifices, are always eager to collect wealth and they amass also much wealth; those under Sakaṭa Yoga earn their livelihood by means of trade in carts or hackney carriages, are always sickly, and possess ugly mean wives; those born under Vihaga Yoga become messengers, travellers, and are quarrelsome; those under Sṛiṃgâṭaka Yoga are happy throughout their lives and those born under Hala Yoga are agriculturists.

Note:—In this stanza the author describes the effects of 5 Âkṛiti Yogas.

व०ति०—वज्रेऽन्त्यपूर्वसुखिनः सुभगोऽतिशूरो वीर्यान्वितोऽप्यथ यवे सुखितो वयोऽन्तः ॥ विख्यातकीर्त्यमितसौख्यगुणश्च पद्मे वाप्यां तनुस्थिरसुखो निधिकृन्न दाता ॥ १४ ॥

वज्रे Vajre, under Vajra Yoga. अन्त्यपूर्वसुखिनः Antyapûrvasukhinaḥ, happy in the early and in the old age; at the beginning and end of life. सुभगः Subhagaḥ, lovely; liked by all; a general favourite. अतिशूरः Atiśûraḥ, very powerful; much endowed with strength; bold in fight. वीर्यान्वितः Vîryânvitaḥ, powerful; vigorous; full of energy. अपि Api, also. अथ Atha, and. यवे Yave, under Yava Yoga. सुखितः Sukhitaḥ, happy. वयोऽन्तः Vayontaḥ, in their middle age. विख्यातकीर्त्यमितसौख्यगुणः Vikhyâtakîrtyamitasaukhyaguṇaḥ, of world-renowned fame; of deep friendship and inestimable good qualities. च Cha, and. पद्मे Padme, under Padma Yoga. वाप्यां Vâpyâm, under Vâpî Yoga. तनुस्थिरसुखः Tanusthirasukhaḥ, always tolerably happy; possessing bodily enjoyments throughout their life; of good physique. निधिकृत् Nidhikṛit, hiding their wealth underground. न Na, not. दाता Dâtâ, giver; donor; generous man.

14. Persons born under Vajra Yoga are happy in their young and old ages, become very lovely and great warriors; those born under Yava Yoga are vigorous and happy in their middle ages; those born under Padma Yoga acquire glory on all sides and their friendship and good qualities are unsurpassed; those born under Vâpi Yoga are somewhat rich, of good physique, keep their wealth hidden safely underground and do not subscribe any money in any cause (are misers).

Note.—In this stanza, the author describes the effects of 4 more Âkṛiti Yogas.

व०ति०—त्यागात्मवान्क्रतुवरैर्यजते च यूपे हिंस्रोऽथ गुप्त्यधिकृतः शरकृच्छराख्ये ॥ नीचोऽलसः सुखधनैर्वियुतश्च शक्तौ दंडे प्रियैर्विरहितः पुरुषोंऽत्यवृत्तिः ॥ १५ ॥

त्यागात्मवान्क्रतुवरैः Tyâgâtmavânkratuvaraiḥ, generous, self-controlled, and ranked as best sacrificer. यजते Yajate, performs sacrifices. च Cha, and. यूपे Yûpe, under Yupa Yoga. हिंस्रः Himsraḥ, mischievous; murderous. अथ Atha, and. गुप्त्यधिकृतः Guptyadhikṛitaḥ, jailor; making prisoners; master of prisons. शरकृत् Sarakṛit, maker of arrows. शराख्ये Sarâkṣye, under Sara Yoga. नीचः Nîchaḥ, mean; doing acts unworthy of one's position. अलसः Alasaḥ, idle, lazy. सुखधनैः Sukhadhanaiḥ, of pleasure and wealth. वियुतः च Viyutaḥ cha, and bereft of. शक्तौ Saktau, under Sakti Yoga. दंडे Daṇḍe, under Daṇḍa Yoga. प्रियैः Priyaiḥ, with those that are nearest and dearest. विरहितः Virahiath, devoid, bereft of. पुरुषः Puruṣaḥ, the person born. अंत्यवृत्तिः Antyavṛittiḥ; of servile disposition.

15. Persons born under Yûpa Yoga are generous, self-controlled and great sacrificers; those under Sara Yoga are mischievous, murderous, masters of prisons and makers of bows and arrows; those under Sakti Yoga are of low disposition, indolent, poor and unhappy; those born under Daṇḍa Yoga suffer bereavements from their nearest and dearest relations, and pass their days in servile works.

Note.—In this stanza the author describes the effects of 4 more Âkṛiti Yogas.

व०ति०—कीर्त्या युतश्चलसुखः कृपणश्च नौजः कूटेऽनृतप्लवनबंधनपश्च जातः ॥ छत्रोद्भवः स्वजनसौख्यकरोंऽत्यसौख्यः शूरश्च कार्मुकभवः प्रथमांत्यसौख्यः ॥ १६ ॥

कीर्त्या Kîrtyâ, with fame. युतः Yutaḥ, endowed. चलसुखः Chalasukhaḥ, of varying happiness. कृपणः च Kṛipaṇaḥ cha, and misers. नौजः च Naujaḥ, of persons born under Nau Yoga. कूटे Kûṭe, under Kûta Yoga. अनृतप्लवनबंधनपः च Anṛitaplavanabandhanapaḥ cha, and meditating and telling lies, and preserving or guarding the jails. जातः Jâtaḥ, born; persons born. छत्रोद्भवः Chhatrodbhavaḥ, persons born under Chhatra Yoga. स्वजनसौख्यकरः Svajanasaukhyakaraḥ, giver of happiness to one's own relations. अन्त्यसौख्यः Antyasaukhyaḥ, happy in their old age. शूरः च Sûraḥ cha, and powerful hero in battle. कार्मुकभवः Kârmukabhavaḥ, persons born under Châpa Yoga. प्रथमान्त्यसौख्यः Prathamântyasaukhyaḥ, happy in their childhood and in their old age.

16. Persons born under Nau Yoga get name and fame, sometimes happy, sometimes miserable, and they are misers; those born under Kûṭa Yoga meditate and tell lies and are the jail keepers; those born under Chhatra Yoga keep their relations happy and they themselves become happy in their old age; those born under Châpa Yoga are great warriors and are happy in their childhood and in their old age.

Note.—The effects of four more Âkṛiti Yogas are described in this stanza.

व० ति०—अर्धेंदुजः सुभगकांतवपुः प्रधानस्तोयालये नरपतिप्रतिमस्तु भोगी । चक्रे नरेंद्रमुकुटद्युतिरंजितांघ्रिर्वीणोद्भवश्च निपुणः प्रियगीतनृत्यः ॥ १७ ॥

अर्धेंदुजः Ardhendujaḥ, persons born under Ardhendu Yoga. सुभगकांतवपुः Subhagakântavapuḥ, lovely and of fine appearance. प्रधानः Pradhânaḥ, worshipped by all; the chief amongst men; superior. तोयालये Toyâlaye, under Samudra Yoga. नरपतिप्रतिमः: Narapatipratimaḥ, like a king, enjoying like a king. भोगी Bhogi, enjoying; an epicure. चक्रे Chakre, under Chakra Yoga. नरेंद्रमुकुटद्युतिरंजितांघ्रिः: Narendramukuṭadyutiranjitâṃghriḥ, whose feet are worshipped by the kings bowing with their heads ornamented with jewels; become Mahârâjâdhirajâs (due to their performing austerities and attaining knowledge). वीणोद्भवः: Vîṇodbhavaḥ, persons born under Vîṇâ Yoga. निपुणः: Nipuṇaḥ, of subtle vision and judgment. प्रियगीतनृत्यः: Priyagîtanṛityaḥ, fond of music and dancing.

17. Persons born under Ardhachandra Yoga are lovely and of fine appearance and superior to all persons; those born under Samudra Yoga become king-like and great epicures; those born under Chakra Yoga become Mahârâjâdhirâjas and their feet are worshipped by kings, wearing lustrous jewels on their crowns; and those born under Vîṇâ Yoga are discriminating and fond of dancing and music.

Note:—In this stanza the author describes the effects of the three Âkṛiti Yogas and of the first Saṅkhyâ Yoga.

व० ति०—दातान्यकार्यनिरतः पशुपश्च दाम्नि पाशे धनार्जनविशीलसभृत्यवन्धुः । केदारजः कृषिकरः सुवहूपयो-यः शूरःक्षतो धनरुचिर्विधनश्च शूले ॥ १८ ॥

दाता Dâtâ, generous; kind-hearted. अन्यकार्यनियतः Anyakâryaniyataḥ, doing good to others; of philanthropic disposition. पशुपः च Paśupaḥ cha, and the protector of cattle; and the master of cattle. दाम्नि Dâmni, under Dâm or Rajju Yoga. पाशे Pâśe, under Pâsa Yoga. धनार्जनविशीलसभृत्यबंधुः Dhanârjanaviśîlasabhṛitya-bandhuḥ, earning money by honest means and doing good works with friends and servants. केदारजाः Kedârajâḥ, persons born under Kedâra Yoga. कृषिकरः Kṛiṣikaraḥ, agriculturist. सुबहूपयोज्यः Subahûpayojyaḥ, doing good to many people. शूरः Śûraḥ, hero in battle. क्षतः Kṣataḥ, bearing marks of warfare in body. धनरुचिः Dhanaruchiḥ, very eager to get money. विधनः च Vidhanaḥ cha, and poor; having no money. शूले Śûle, under Śûla Yoga.

18. Persons born under Rajju (Dâminî) Yoga are generous, philanthropic, and warders of many cattle; those under Pâśa Yoga earn money with honest endeavours and are surrounded by friends and servants; those born under Kedâra Yoga are agriculturists and do good to many people; and those born under Śûla Yoga are great warriors, get marks of wounds on their bodies, eager to acquire money but they are without any money.

Note:—In this stanza the author describes the effects of 4 more Saṃkhyâ Yogas.

हरिणी—धनविरहितः पाखंडी वा युगे त्वथ गोलके विध-नमलिनो ज्ञानोपेतः कुशिल्प्यलसोऽटनः । इति निगदिता योगाः सार्द्धं फलैरिह नाभसा नियतफलदाश्चिंत्या ह्येते समस्तदशा-स्वपि ॥ १९ ॥

इति श्रीवराहमिहिराचार्यप्रणीते बृहज्जातके नाभसयोगा-ध्यायो द्वादशः ॥ १२ ॥

धनविरहितः Dhanavirahitaḥ, void of money. पाखंडी Pâkhandî, an heretic; a hypocrite; one not following the tenets of Veda; one acting in contravention of Vedic rules. वा Vâ, or. युगे Yuge, under Yuga Yoga. तु Tu, but. अथ Atha, and. गोलके Golake, under Golaka Yoga. विधनमलिनः Vidhanamalinaḥ, poor, dirty, and gloomy. अज्ञानोपेतः Ajñânopetaḥ, illiterate. कुशिल्पी Kuśil possessing knowledge of bad workmanship; bad workman. अलसः Alasaḥ, idle, lazy; not capable of doing any work. अटनः Aṭanaḥ, of wandering habits. इति Iti, thus. निगदिताः Nigaditâḥ, said. योगाः Yogâḥ, the different combinations. सार्द्धं Sârdham, with. फलं Phalam, effects. इह Iha, in this Chapter. नाभसाः Nâ-

vasâḥ, heavenly. नियतफलदाः Niyataphaladâḥ, always effective. हि एते Hi ete, these certainly. समस्तदशासु Samastadaśâsu, in all the Daśâs throughout one's life. अपि Api, even.

19. Persons born under Yuga Yoga are void of money, irreligious and not the abider of the Vedas; those born under Gola Yoga are poor, dirty and gloomy, illiterate, bad workmen, indolent and of wandering habits (1). Thus have been described the several Nâvasa Yogas with their effects. These bear fruits throughout one's life, in all the Daśâs of human beings (2).

Notes ;—In this stanza the effects of the remaining two Saṃkhyâ Yogas are described.

(1) For bare subsistence.

(2) Except in case of Vajra and other Yogas (see stanza 14) whose effects will be felt, as stated in certain periods of a person's life. So that wherever no periods are mentioned the effects will be felt throughout life.

Thus ends the twelfth Chapter on Nâvasa Yoga (miscellaneous heavenly combinations), by Śrî Varâha Mihirâchârya of Avantika.

Note:—It is to be remembered that this Nâvasa Yoga, as a rule, yields results throughout all the periods of life. Now the doubt arises:—in Vajra Yoga it has been mentioned that people are happy in their young and old age; how then this rule is applicable to the whole period of life? The answer is that the rule will be applicable there only where no definite periods of time are expressly stated. Again the doubt arises:—there are cases where it has been stated that the person will be happy throughout all the periods of their lives; now a person, in the midst of all sorts of happy circumstances, feels some mental pain and becomes miserable; or a person in the midst of all distressing circumstances, feels happiness in his mind; how is that possible? The answer is that this Nâvasa Yoga does not nullify the effect of Aṣṭaka Varga or other planetary combinations and therefore a man feels happiness in the midst of all contrary circumstances indicated in this Chapter.

In the 3rd Śloka of this Chapter, it has been mentioned that there are special reasons for mentioning Âśraya Yoga and Dala Yoga separate from Âkṛita Yoga and Saṃkhyâ Yoga. Now these reasons are being explained. When the Dala Yoga resembles the Saṃkhyâ Yoga the effects of the Dala Yoga are visible and not those of the Saṃkhyâ Yoga (see verse 10). This accounts for taking the Dala Yoga separate.

The Dala Yogas do neither coincide with Âśraya Yogas nor with Âkṛiti Yogas. Where the Âkṛiti Yoga resembles the Âśraya Yoga, there the effects of the Âkṛiti Yoga are visible. Where the Âkṛiti Yoga resembles the Saṃkhyâ Yoga, even there the Âkṛiti Yoga bears fruits (see verse 12). Here then one can argue that the Saṃkhyâ Yoga should not also be taken separately. As Saṃkhyâ Yoga has been counted separate, so Âśraya Yoga may also be taken separately.

Now the meaning of the statement "Âśraya Yoga becomes inoperative when it resembles other Yogas" should be made clear. Here it means that the Saṃkhyâ Yogas and the Âśraya Yogas both are inoperative when these two resemble Âkṛiti Yogas. Now suppose Âśraya and Saṃkhyâ Yogas to coincide with each other. Are they to be treated as the former or as the latter? The Commentator says that if the coincidence refers to the Kedâra, Śûla, and Yuga Yogas, the Yogas are to be treated as Âśraya Yogas only; but if it refers to the Gola Yoga it is to be treated as such, and not as an Âśraya Yoga—otherwise there will be no room for Gola Yoga at all. Thus there is sufficient reason for taking the Âśraya Yogas separately.

Now the 1,800 sub-divisions of Nâvasa Yogas as enunciated by the ancient Yavanâchârya, are being described. Taking any sign as the Ascendant, there are 150 sub-divisions (will be explained further on); then taking the twelve signs as Ascendants consecutively, there are $12 \times 150 = 1800$ sub-divisions. According to Yavana, there are 23 sub-divisions in the Âkṛiti Yogas; and 127 sub-divisions in the Saṃkhyâ Yogas; thus giving the number 150 (127+23). The Yavanas do not take Âśraya and Dala Yogas into account. Varâha Mihira has mentioned 20 Âkṛiti Yogas; but the Gadâ Yoga in it has 4 sub-divisions (as already stated). Thus (19+4) 23 Âkṛiti Yogas of Yavana are easily understood. One hundred and twenty-seven Saṃkhyâ Yogas are thus made out:—Taking one planet we get 7 cases: two planets we get 21 cases; three planets we get 35 cases; four planets 35 cases: five planets, 21 cases; six planets, 7 cases; seven planets, one case; thus making up the total $(7+21+35+35+21+7+1)=127$ cases. These numbers are thus obtained.

The first Saṃkhyâ Yoga treated of by Varâha Mihira is known as Vallakî Yoga; according to which the 7 planets might occupy any seven signs. This may be in many ways; but the Yavanas select only a few; as each of the seven planets might occupy the Lagna, the number of Yogas under this division is 7. Again the 2nd Saṃkhyâ Yoga treated of by the author is one according to which the 7 planets are said to occupy any six signs. This may be in many ways; but the Yavanas select the following few: of the seven planets, five may occupy five houses and two more may occupy the Lagna. These two may be any two of the seven planets. The number of Yogas under this head will be the number of combinations of seven things taken two at a time$=\frac{7\times 6}{1\times 2}=21$.

Again, the 3rd Saṃkhyā Yoga is one in which the seven planets occupy 5 houses. This may be in many ways; but the following are selected :—4 planets occupying 4 houses and 3 more occupying the Lagna. These three may be any three out of the 7 planets. The number of cases under this head is the number of combinations of 7 things taken 3 at a time$=\frac{7\times 6\times 5}{1\times 2\times 3}=35$. And so on.

6, 7, thus:— $\frac{7}{1}\Big|\frac{6}{2}\Big|\frac{5}{3}\Big|\frac{4}{4}\Big|\frac{3}{5}\Big|\frac{2}{6}\Big|\frac{1}{7}$.

Put 7, 6, 5, 4. 3, 2, 1, in one line; and below that line put 1, 2, 3, 4, 5.

When one planet is taken into account, take 7 and divide by 1, the number underneath; when two planets are taken into account, take 7, 6; and multiply; divide the product by the product of the figures underneath; thus $\frac{7\times 6}{1\times 2}=21$; thus we get 21. And so on; $\frac{7\times 6\times 5}{1\times 2\times 3}=35$; and so on. In other words, take the combinations of seven things taken one at a time take two at a time and so on. These are now shewn by the positions of the planets.

First case; one planet.

1. Sun.
2. Moon.
3. Mars.
4. Mercury.
5. Jupiter.
6. Venus.
7. Saturn.

Second case; two planets.

1. Sun, Moon.
2. Sun, Mars.
3. Sun, Mercury.
4. Sun, Jupiter.
5. Sun, Venus.
6. Sun, Saturn.

Second case; two planets.

7. Moon, Mars.
8. Moon, Mercury.
9. Moon, Jupiter.
10. Moon, Venus.
11. Moon, Saturn.
12. Mars, Mercury.
13. Mars, Jupiter.
14. Mars, Venus.
15. Mars, Saturn.
16. Mercury, Jupiter.
17. Mercury Venus.
18. Mercury, Saturn.
19. Jupiter, Venus.
20. Jupiter, Saturn.
21. Venus, Saturn.

Third case ; three planets.

1. Sun, Moon, Mars.
2. Sun, Moon, Mercury.
3. Sun, Moon, Jupiter.
4. Sun, Moon, Venus.
5. Sun, Moon, Saturn.
6. Sun, Mars, Mercury.
7. Sun, Mars, Jupiter.
8. Sun, Mars, Venus.
9. Sun, Mars, Saturn.
10. Sun, Mercury, Jupiter.
11. Sun, Mercury, Venus.
12. Sun, Mercury, Saturn.
13. Sun, Jupiter, Venus.
14. Sun, Jupiter, Saturn.
15. Sun, Venus, Saturn.
16. Moon, Mars, Mercury.
17. Moon, Mars, Jupiter.
18. Moon, Mars, Venus.
19. Moon, Mars, Saturn.
20. Moon, Mercury, Jupiter.
21. Moon, Mercury, Venus.
22. Moon, Mercury, Saturn.
23. Moon, Jupiter, Venus.
24. Moon, Jupiter, Saturn.
25. Moon, Venus, Saturn,
26. Mars, Mercury, Jupiter.
27. Mars, Mercury, Venus.
28. Mars, Mercury, Saturn.
29. Mars, Jupiter, Venus.
30. Mars, Jupiter, Saturn.
31. Mars, Venus, Saturn.
32. Mercury, Jupiter, Venus.
33. Mercury, Jupiter, Saturn.
34. Mercury, Venus, Saturn.
35. Jupiter, Venus, Saturn.

Fourth case, 4 planets.

1. Sun, Moon, Mars, Mercury.
2. Sun, Moon, Mars, Jupiter.
3. Sun, Moon, Mars, Venus.
4. Sun, Moon, Mars, Saturn.
5. Sun, Moon, Mercury, Jupiter.
6. Sun, Moon, Mercury, Venus.
7. Sun, Moon, Mercury, Saturn.
8. Sun, Moon, Jupiter, Venus.
9. Sun, Moon, Jupiter, Saturn.
10. Sun, Moon, Venus, Saturn.
11. Sun, Mercury, Jupiter, Venus.
12. Sun, Mercury, Jupiter, Saturn.
13. Sun, Mars, Mercury, Jupiter.
14. Sun, Mars, Mercury, Venus.
15. Sun, Mars, Mercury, Saturn.
16. Sun, Jupiter, Venus, Saturn.
17. Sun, Mars, Jupiter, Venus.
18. Sun, Mars, Jupiter, Saturn.
19. Sun, Mars, Venus, Saturn.
20. Sun, Mercury, Venus, Saturn.
21. Moon, Mars, Mercury, Jupiter.
22. Moon, Mars, Mercury, Venus.
23. Moon, Mars, Mercury, Saturn.
24. Moon, Mars, Jupiter, Venus.
25. Moon, Mars, Jupiter, Saturn.
26. Moon, Mercury, Jupiter, Venus.
27. Moon, Mercury, Jupiter, Saturn.
28. Moon, Jupiter, Venus, Saturn.
29. Moon, Mars, Venus, Saturn.
30. Moon, Mercury, Venus, Saturn.
31. Mars, Mercury, Jupiter, Venus.
32. Mars, Mercury, Jupiter, Saturn.
33. Mars, Mercury, Venus, Saturn.
34. Mars, Jupiter, Venus, Saturn.
35. Mercury, Jupiter, Venus, Saturn.

Fifth case, 5 planets.

1. Sun, Moon, Mars, Mercury, Jupiter.
2. Sun, Moon, Mars, Mercury, Venus.
3. Sun, Moon, Mars, Mercury, Saturn.
4. Sun, Moon, Mars, Jupiter, Venus.
5. Sun, Moon, Mars, Jupiter, Saturn.
6. Sun, Moon, Mars, Venus, Saturn.
7. Sun, Moon, Mercury, Jupiter, Venus.
8. Sun, Moon, Mercury, Jupiter, Saturn.
9. Sun, Moon, Mercury, Venus, Saturn.
10. Sun, Moon, Jupiter, Venus, Saturn.
11. Sun, Mars, Mercury, Jupiter, Venus.
12. Sun, Mars, Mercury, Jupiter, Saturn.
13. Sun, Mars, Mercury, Venus, Saturn.
14. Sun, Mars, Jupiter, Venus, Saturn.
15. Sun, Mercury, Jupiter, Venus, Saturn.
16. Moon, Mars, Mercury, Jupiter, Venus.
17. Moon, Mars, Mercury, Jupiter, Saturn.
18. Moon, Mars, Mercury, Venus, Saturn.
19. Moon, Mars, Jupiter, Venus, Saturn.
20. Moon, Mercury, Jupiter, Venus, Saturn.
21. Mars, Mercury, Jupiter, Venus, Saturn.

Sixth case, 6 planets.

1. Sun, Moon, Mars, Mercury, Jupiter, Venus.
2. Sun, Moon, Mars, Mercury, Jupiter, Saturn.

3. Sun, Moon, Mars, Jupiter, Venus, Saturn.
4. Moon, Mars, Mercury, Jupiter, Venus, Saturn.
5. Sun, Moon, Mercury, Jupiter, Venus, Saturn.
6. Sun, Mars, Mercury, Jupiter, Venus, Saturn.
7. Sun, Moon, Mars, Mercury, Venus, Saturn.

Seventh case, 7 planets.

1. Sun, Moon, Mars, Mercury, Jupiter, Venus, Saturn.

The following table shews the Divisions and Sub-divisions of the Nâvasa Yogas:—

Nâvasa Yogas...	(1) Âkṛiti Yoga ...	1. Gadâ Yoga, all the planets in any two adjacent angles.
		2. Śakaṭa Yoga, all the planets in the 1st and 7th houses.
		3. Vihaga Yoga, all the planets in the 10th and 4th houses.
		4. Śṛingâṭaka Yoga, all the planets in the 1st, 5th and 9th houses.
		5. Hala Yoga, all the planets (a) in 2nd, 6th, 10th houses. (b) in 3rd, 7th, 11th houses. (c) in 4th, 8th, 12th houses.
		6. Vajra Yoga, auspicious planets in the 1st and 7th and malefics in 4th and 10th houses.
		7. Yava Yoga, benefics in 4th and 10th and malefics in 1st and 7th houses.
		8. Kamala Yoga, all the planets promiscuously in 4 angles.
		9. Vâpî Yoga, all the planets promiscuously in all the 4 succedent or 4 cadent houses.
		10. Yûpa Yoga, all the planets in the 1st, 2nd, 3rd and 4th houses.
		11. Śara (Iṣu) Yoga, all the planets in the 4th, 5th, 6th and 7th houses.
		12. Śakti Yoga, all the planets in the 7th, 8th, 9th and 10th houses.
		13. Daṇḍa Yoga, all the planets in the 10th, 11th, 12th, and 1st houses.
		14. Nau Yoga, all the planets in the 1st, 2nd, 3rd, 4th, 5th, 6th and 7th houses.
		15. Kûṭa Yoga, all the planets in the 4th, 5th, 6th, 7th, 8th, 9th and 10th houses.
		16. Chhatra Yoga, all the planets in the 7th, 8th, 9th, 10th, 11th, 12th and 1st houses.
		17. Châpa Yoga, all the planets in the 10th, 11th, 12th, 1st, 2nd, 3rd and 4th houses.
		18. Ardhachandra Yoga, all the planets in the 7 houses beginning from the 4 Panaphara and 4 Âpoklîma houses.
		19. Samudra Yoga, all planets in the 2nd, 4th, 6th 8th, 10th, and 12th houses.
		20. Chakra Yoga, all planets in the 1st, 3rd, 5th, 7th, 9th and 11th houses.
	(2) Saṃkhyâ Yoga ...	1. Vallakî Yoga, all the planets in any 7 houses
		2. Dâminî Yoga " " 6 "
		3. Pâśa Yoga " " 5 "
		4. Kedâra Yoga " " 4 "
		5. Sûla Yoga " " 3 "
		6. Yuga Yoga " " 2 "
		7. Gola Yoga " " 1 "
	(3) Âśraya Yoga ...	1. Rajju Yoga, all the planets in 1, 2, 3 or 4 moveable signs.
		2. Musala Yoga, all the planets in 1, 2, 3 or 4 fixed signs.
		3. Nala Yoga, all the planets in 1, 2, 3 or 4 common signs.
	(4) Dala Yoga ...	1. Srak Yoga, all the benefics in 1, 2, 3 or 4 angles and no malefic in the angles.
		2. Sarpa Yoga, all the malefics in 1, 2, 3 or 4 angles and no benefic in the angles.

CHAPTER XIII.

ON CHANDRA YOGA, OR LUNAR COMBINATIONS.

मालिनी—अधमसमवरिष्ठान्यर्ककेंद्रादिसंस्थे शशिनि विनयवित्तज्ञानधीनैपुणानि ॥ अहनि निशि च चंद्रे स्वेऽधिमित्रांशके वां सुरगुरुसितदृष्टे वित्तवान्स्यात्सुखी च ॥ १ ॥

अधमसमवरिष्ठानि Adhamasamavariṣṭhâni, worst, middling and best; poor, moderate or excellent. अर्ककेंद्रादिसंस्थे Arkakendrâdisaṃsthe, situated in the angles, etc. (*i. e.*, in the angles, succedent or cadent houses, respectively) from the Sun. शशिनि Śaśini, the Moon occupying. विनयवित्तज्ञानधीनैपुणानि Vinayavittajñânadhînaipuṇâni, modesty, politeness, wealth, knowledge, intelligence, and cleverness. अहनि Ahani, during the day. निशि च Niśi cha, and during the night (successively). चंद्रे Chandre, the Moon being. स्वे Sve, in her own Navâṃśaka. अधिमित्रांशके Adhimitrâṃśake, or in the Navâṃśas of her Adhimitra (or a very friendly planet). वा Vâ, or. सुरगुरुसितदृष्टे Suragurusitadṛiṣṭe, aspected by Jupiter and Venus respectively. वित्तवान् Vittavân, wealthy. स्यात् Syât, becomes. सुखी च Sukhî cha, and happy.

1. When the Moon is in any of the angular houses from the Sun, the native is wanting in modesty, politeness, wealth, knowledge, intelligence, and cleverness; if the Moon be in the succedent houses (2, 5, 8, 11) from the Sun, the native is possessed of the above qualities in a moderate degree; and if the Moon be in the cadent houses (3, 6, 9, 12) from the Sun, the native possesses the above qualities pre-eminently. Again if the Moon be in her own Navâṃśaka or in the Navâṃśas of her Adhimitra, the native, if born during the day, becomes wealthy and happy provided the Moon be aspected by Jupiter; or if the Moon be in her Navâṃśaka or in her Adhimitra's Navâṃśas and if she be aspected by Venus, then the native becomes wealthy and happy, if the birth take place during the night.

Note:—This meaning is supported by Yavana, Gârgî and others; hence this meaning is correct. A man will have very little of the above qualities if the Moon occupy either the sign occupied by the Sun, or the

4th, 7th, or 10th sign from it. He will have these qualities in a moderate degree if the Moon occupy the 2nd, 5th, 8th or 11th sign from the sign occupied by the Sun; and he will have these qualities in a greater degree if the Moon occupy the 3rd, 6th, 9th or 12th sign from the sign occupied by the Sun.

व०ति०—सौम्यैः स्मरारिनिधनेष्वधियोग इंदोस्तस्मिंश्चमूपसचिवक्षितिपालजन्म ॥ संपन्नसौख्यविभवा हतशत्रवश्च दीर्घायुषो विगतरोगभयाश्च जाताः ॥ २ ॥

सौम्यैः Saumyaiḥ, the benefic planets Mercury, Jupiter and Venus (being situated in). स्मरारिनिधनेषु Smarârinidhaneṣu, in the sixth, seventh and eighth houses. अधियोग Adhiyoga, is known as Adhiyoga. इन्दोः Indoḥ, from the Moon. तस्मिन् च Tasmin cha, and in this Adhiyoga; and the results of this Adhiyoga. चमूपसचिवक्षितिपालजन्म Chamûpasachivakṣitipâlajanma, indicating the birth of a commander of an army, a minister of a king, or a king. सम्पन्नसौख्यविभवाः Sampannasaukhyavibhabâḥ, and having close intimacy with friends and enjoying great pleasures, power and property. हतशत्रवः Hataśatravaḥ, whose enemies are killed or crushed or subdued. च Cha, and. दीर्घायुषः Dîrghâyuṣaḥ, of long life; long-lived. विगतरोगभयाः च Vigatarogabhayâḥ cha, and free from diseases or fear.

2. When the benefics Mercury, Jupiter, and Venus are in the sixth, seventh and eighth houses from the Moon, the Yoga is known as Adhiyoga. Persons born under this Yoga become commanders of armies, king's ministers, or kings (1); they will get intimate friends, great pleasures and wealth, will have their enemies crushed, will live long, free from diseases and fear.

Note:—(1) If the benefics are all very powerful by virtue of time, position, &c., then persons born will become kings; if the benefics be fairly powerful, then they become councillors, and if they be tolerably powerful, they become commanders.

There are seven sub-divisions, rather seven different combinations in this Yoga:—(1) When the benefics are all in the sixth house, (2) when all are in the seventh house, (3) when all are in the eighth house, (4) when all are in the sixth and seventh, (5) when all are in the sixth and eighth, (6) when all are in the seventh and eighth, and (7) when all are distributed in the sixth, seventh, and eighth.

In the astrological work known as Sârâvalî, the Adhiyoga is classed with Râjayoga when the planets Mercury, Jupiter, and Venus are not

Astangata or setting planets, nor aspected by malefic planets. Mandâvya is of the same opinion.

शा०वि०–हित्वार्कं सुनफानफादुरुधुराः स्वांत्योभयस्थै-
र्ग्रहैः शीतांशोः कथितोऽन्यथा तु बहुभिः केमद्रुमोऽन्यैस्त्वसौ ॥
केंद्रे शीतकरेऽथवा ग्रहयुते केमद्रुमो नेष्यते केचित्केंद्रनवांशकेषु
च वदंत्युक्तिः प्रसिद्धा न ते ॥ ३ ॥

हित्वार्कं Hitvârkam, not taking the Sun into account; excepting the Sun. सुनफानफादुरुधुराः Sunaphânaphâdurudhurâḥ, known as Sunaphâ Yoga, Anaphâ Yoga, and Durudhurâ Yoga, respectively. स्वांत्योभयस्थैः Svântyobhayasthaiḥ, in the second or twelfth houses or in both of them. ग्रहैः Grahaiḥ, the other planets (excepting the Sun) occupying. शीतांशोः Śitamśoḥ, from the Moon. कथितः Kathitaḥ, said. अन्यथा Anyathâ, otherwise; if there be no planets in the second and twelfth houses from the Moon. तु Tu, again. बहुभिः Bahuviḥ, by many astrologers. केमद्रुमः Kemadrumaḥ, known as Kemadruma Yoga. अन्यैः Anyaiḥ, according to other astrologers, Gârgi, Parâśara, &c. तु Tu, again. असौ Asau, this (Kemadruma-yoga). केंद्रे Kendre, in the angles from the Ascendant, *i.e.*, in the 4th, or 10th house from the Ascendant. शीतकरे Śitakare, the Moon occupying. अथवा Athavâ, or. ग्रहयुते Grahayute, accompanied by any of the above mentioned planets, Mars, &c. केमद्रुमः Kemadrumaḥ, the Yoga Kemadruma. न इष्यते Na iṣyate, not approved of; not liked, *i. e.*, the Kemadruma Yoga is not formed; it ceases to exist. केचित् Kechit, some authors, Śrutakîrtiḥ, Jîvaśarmâ. केंद्रनवांशकेषु Kendranavâmśakeṣu, in the houses on both sides of the sign, whose Navâmśa is occupied by the Moon. च Cha, and. वदंति Vadanti, say. उक्तिः Uktiḥ, these views. प्रसिद्धाः Prasiddhâḥ, authoritative. न Na, not. ते Te, these.

3. If the planets other than the Sun (*i.e.*, Mars, Mercury, Jupiter, Venus or Saturn) occupy the second house from the Moon, the Yoga is known as Sunaphâ Yoga; if the planets above mentioned (*i.e.*, excepting the Sun) occupy the twelfth house from the Moon, the Yoga is known as Anaphâ Yoga; again if these planets (excepting the Sun) be in the second as well as in the twelfth house from the Moon, the Yoga is known as Durudhurâ Yoga (1). But if there be no planets (above mentioned) in the second as well as in the twelfth houses from the Moon, it is known by numerous writers as Kemadruma Yoga.

According to some astrologers (Garga and Parâśara) if the Moon occupy the Kendra house (the angular house) from the Ascendant or if the Moon be accompanied by any of the above mentioned planets, the Yoga ceases to be a Kemadruma Yoga.

According to others (Śrutakîrti and others) these three Yogas take place when the above planets Mars, &c., occupy the Kendra houses (the angular houses, fourth, tenth, or both) from the Moon (2); while, again, according to some (Jîvaśarmâ and others) these three Yogas take place when the above mentioned planets occupy the second and the twelfth houses from the sign whose Navâṃśa is occupied by the Moon (3). But these views are not considered as authoritative.

Notes:—(1) If the Sun be found with any of the other planets in these houses, there is no harm; the only thing to be remembered is that the Sun here is not at all the agent.

(2) That is, if the planets excepting the Sun occupy the 4th house from the Moon, the Yoga is known as Sunaphâ; if they occupy the 10th house from the Moon, the Yoga is known as Anaphâ, and if they occupy both the 4th and the 10th house from the Moon, it is known as Durudhura and if the 4th and 10th houses from the Moon be not occupied by planets the Yoga is known as Kemadruma.

(3) Suppose the Moon to occupy the Navâmśa of Dhanu in Meṣa sign. Now if the planets excepting the Sun and the Moon occupy the 2nd or the 12th or both the 2nd and the 12th houses from the Dhanu sign, the Yoga is respectively known as Sunaphâ, Anaphâ and Durudhurâ; but if these two houses be not so occupied the Yoga is known as Kemadruma.

इंद्रवज्रा—त्रिंशत्सरूपाः सुनफानफाख्याः षष्टित्रयं दौरुधुरे प्रभेदाः ॥ इच्छाविकल्पैः क्रमशोऽभिनीय नीते निवृत्तिः पुनरन्यनीतिः ॥ ४ ॥

त्रिंशत्सरूपाः: Trimśatsarûpâḥ, thirty-one 31 (each.) सुनफानफाख्याः: Sunaphânaphâkhyâḥ, the Sunaphâ Yoga and the Anaphâ Yoga. षष्टित्रयं Saṣṭitrayam, one hundred and eighty (180). दौरुधुरे Daûrudhure, in Durûdhura Yoga. प्रभेदाः: Prabhedâḥ, varieties; differences. इच्छाविकल्पैः: Ichhâvikalpaiḥ, by the various combinations as desired amongst the 1, 2, 3, 4, 5 planets. क्रमशः: Kramaśaḥ, successively; one after another. अभिनीय Âbhinîya, representing or exhibiting; by forming the series of combinations according to mathematical rule. नीते Nîte, when the combinations are arrived at according to the rule. निवृत्तिः: Nivrittiḥ, it is finished; it is satisfied; it is diminished one by one (*i.e.*, 5, 4, 3, 2, 1). पुनः:

Punaḥ, again. अन्यानि: Anyaniti, forming another series of combinations, either representing on paper another set of combinations or working out according to the rule.

4. There are thirty-one (31) varieties of Sunaphâ and thirty-one (31) varieties of Anaphâ Yoga and there are one hundred and eighty (180) varieties of Durudhurâ Yoga. These varieties are to be taken one by one and represented actually on paper or worked out according to mathematical rule (for finding the number of combinations of a given number of things taken *r* at a time).

Notes:—The three Yogas are formed by (1) Mars, (2) Mercury, (3) Jupiter, (4) Venus, and (5) Saturn. Now the 31 varieties of Sunaphâ Yoga and 31 varieties of Anaphâ Yoga are being shewn in the following table.

Put the numbers 5, 4, 3, 2, and 1 in one row; underneath another row of the same numbers reversed (1, 2, 3, 4, 5) thus:—

5	4	3	2	1
1	2	3	4	5

Then when one planet is taken into account, the number of combinations is $\frac{5}{1} = 5$; when two planets are taken in account, the number of combinations is $\frac{5 \times 4}{1 \times 2} = 10$. When three planets are taken in account, the number is $\frac{5 \times 4 \times 3}{1 \times 2 \times 3} = 10$. When four planets are taken, the number is $\frac{5 \times 4 \times 3 \times 2}{1 \times 2 \times 3 \times 4} = 5$. When five planets are taken, the number is $\frac{5 \times 4 \times 3 \times 2 \times 1}{1 \times 2 \times 3 \times 4 \times 5} = 1$. Thus the total combinations $= 5 + 10 + 10 + 5 + 1 = 31$. Graphically thus:—

Different combinations of Sunaphâ Yoga.

1. Mars.
2. Mercury.
3. Jupiter.
4. Venus.
5. Saturn.
6. Mars, Mercury.
7. Mars, Jupiter.
8. Mars, Venus.
9. Mars, Saturn.
10. Mercury, Jupiter.
11. Mercury, Venus.
12. Mercury, Saturn.
13. Jupiter, Venus.
14. Jupiter, Saturn.
15. Venus, Saturn.
16. Mars, Mercury, Jupiter.
17. Mars, Mercury, Venus.
18. Mars, Mercury, Saturn.
19. Mars, Jupiter, Venus.
20. Mars, Jupiter, Saturn.
21. Mars, Venus, Saturn.
22. Mercury, Jupiter, Venus.
23. Mercury, Jupiter, Saturn.
24. Jupiter, Venus, Saturn.
25. Mercury, Venus, Saturn.
26. Mars, Mercury, Jupiter, Venus.
27. Mars, Mercury, Jupiter, Saturn.
28. Mars, Jupiter, Venus, Saturn.
29. Mercury, Jupiter, Venus, Saturn.
30. Mars, Mercury, Venus, Saturn.
31. Mars, Mercury, Jupiter, Venus, Saturn.

Different combinations of Anaphâ Yoga—Same as Sunaphâ Yoga.

Now about 180 varieties of the Durudhurâ Yoga:—

Take the case in which the 2nd house from the Moon is occupied by a single planet; while it does so, the remaining four planets may occupy the 12th house from the Moon 1, 2, 3, and 4 at a time. The number of these will be the sum of the number of combinations of four things taken 1, 2, 3, and 4 together. This will be found to be $4 + 6 + 4 + 1 = 15$. So that for one of the five Sunaphâ Yogas we get 15 Durudhurâ Yogas. The five Sunaphâ Yogas of one planet will therefore give us $5 \times 15 = 75$ Durudhurâ Yogas. Take one of the 10 Sunaphâ Yogas of two planets from Mars to Saturn; the remaining 3 planets may occupy the 12th house from the Moon, 1, 2, and 3 at a time. The number required is the sum of the number of combinations of three things taken 1, 2, and 3 at a time. This will be found to be $3 + 3 + 1 = 7$. Combining these with the 10 Sunaphâ Yogas of two planets we shall get $10 \times 7 = 70$ Durudhurâ Yogas. Similarly the 10 Sunaphâ Yogas of three planets will give $10 \times 3 = 30$ Durudhurâ Yogas; and the five Sunaphâ Yogas of 4 planets will give us $5 \times 1 = 5$ Durudhurâ Yogas. So that the number of possible Durudhurâ Yogas $= 75 + 70 + 30 + 5 = 180$.

Now 180 varieties of Durudhurâ Yoga are being mentioned graphically. M=Mercury; J=Jupiter; V=Venus; S=Saturn; Mr.=Mars.

1. Mr, M.
2. M, Mr.
3. Mr, J.
4. J, Mr.
5. Mr, V.
6. V, Mr.
7. Mr, S.
8. S, Mr.
9. M, J.
10. J, M.
11. M, V.
12. V, M.
13. M, S.
14. S, M.
15. J, V.
16. V, J.
17. J, S.
18. S, J.
19. V, S.
20. S, V.
1. Mr, M, J.
2. M, J, Mr.
3. J, V, M.
4. M, Mr, V.
5. Mr, M, S.
6. M, S, Mr.
7. Mr, J, V.
8. J, V, Mr.
9. Mr, J, S.
10. Mr, S, M.
11. Mr, V, S.
12. V, S, Mr.
13. M, Mr, J.
14. J, Mr, M.
15. M, Mr, V.
16. Mr, V, M.
17. M, Mr, S.
18. Mr, S, M.
19. M, J, V.
20. J, V, M.
21. M, J, S.
22. J, S, M.
23. M, V, S.
24. V, S, M.
25. J, Mr, M.
26. Mr, M, J.
27. J, Mr, V.
28. Mr, V, J.
29. J, Mr, S.
30. Mr, S, J.
31. J, M, V.
32. M, V, J.
33. J, M, S.
34. M, S. J.
35. J, V, S.
36. V, S, J.
37. V, Mr, M.
38. Mr, M, V.
39. V, Mr, J.
40. Mr, J, V.
41. V, Mr, S.
42. Mr, S, V.
43. V, M, J.
44. M, J, V.
45. V, M, S.
46. M, S, V.
47. V, J, S.
48. J, S, V.
49. S, Mr, M.
56. Mr. M, S.
51. S, Mr, J.
52. Mr, J, S.
53. S, Mr, V.
54. Mr. V, S.
55. S. M, J.
56. M, J, S.
57. S, M, V.
58. M, V, S.
59. S, J, V.
60. J, V, S.
61. Mr, M, J, V.
62. M, J, V. Mr.
63. Mr, M, J, S.
64. M, J, S, Mr.
65. Mr, M, V. S.
66. M, V, S, Mr.
67. Mr, J, V, S.
68. J, V, S, Mr.
69. M, Mr, J, V.
70. Mr, J, V, M.
71. M, Mr, J, S.
72. Mr, J, S, M.
73. M, Mr, V, S.
74. Mr, V, S, M.
75. M, J, V, S.
76. J, V, S, M.

77. J, Mr, M, V.
78. Mr, M, V, J.
79. J, Mr, M, S.
80. Mr, M, S, J.
81. J, Mr, V, S.
82. Mr, V, S, J.
83. J, M, V, S.
84. M, V, S, J.
85. V, Mr, M, J.
86. Mr, M, J, V.
87. V, Mr, M, S.
88. Mr, M, S, V.
89. V, Mr, J, S.
90. Mr, J, S, V.
91. V, M, J, S.
92. M, J, V, S.
93. S, Mr, M, J.
94. Mr, M, J, S.
95. S, Mr, M, V.
96. Mr, M, V, S.
97. S, Mr, J, V.
98. Mr, J, V, S.
99. S, M, J, V.
100. M, J, V, S.
101. Mr, M, J, V, S.
102. M, J, V, S, Mr.
103. M, Mr, J, V, S.
104. Mr, J, V, S, M.
105. J, Mr, M, V, S.
106. Mr, M, V, S, J.
107. V, Mr, M, J, S.
108. Mr, M, J, S, V.
109. S, Mr, M, J, V.
110. Mr, M, J, V, S.
111. Mr, M, J, V.
112. J, V, Mr, M.
113. Mr, M, J, S.
114. J, S, Mr, M.
115. Mr, M, V, S.
116. V, S, Mr, M.
117. Mr, J, V, M.
118. V, M, Mr, J.
119. Mr, J, M, S.
120. M, S, Mr, J.
121. Mr, J, V, S.
122. V, S, Mr, J.
123. Mr, V, M, J.
124. M, J, Mr, V.
125. Mr, V, M, S.
126. M, S, Mr, V.
127. Mr, V, J, S.
128. J, S, Mr, V.
129. M, J, Mr, S.
130. Mr, S, M, J.
131. Mr, S, M, V.
132. M, V, Mr, S.
133. Mr, S, J, V.
134. J, V, Mr, S.
135. M, J, V, S.
136. V, S, M, J.
137. M, V, J, S.
138. J, S, M, V.
139. J, V, M, S.
140. M, S, J, V.
141. Mr, M, J, V, S.
142. J, V, S, Mr, M.
143. Mr, J, M, V, S.
144. M, V, S, Mr, J.
145. Mr, V, M, J, S.
146. M, J, S, Mr, V.
147. Mr, S, M, J, V.
148. M, J, V, Mr, S.
149. M, J, Mr, V, S.
150. Mr, V, S, M, J.
151. M, V, Mr, J, S.
152. Mr, J, S, M, V.
153. M, S, Mr, J, V.
154. Mr, J, V, M, S.
155. J, V, Mr, M, S.
156. Mr, M, S, J, V.
157. J, S, Mr, M, V.
158. Mr, M, V, J, S.
159. V, S, Mr, M, J.
160. Mr, M, J, V, S.

160+20=180.

मालिनी–स्वयमधिगतवित्तः पार्थिवस्तत्समो वा भवति हि सुनफायां धीधनख्यातिमांश्च ॥ प्रभुरगदशरीरः शीलवान्ख्यातकीर्तिर्विषयसुखसुवेषो निर्वृतश्चानफायाम् ॥ ५ ॥

स्वयमधिगतवित्तः Svayamadhigatavittaḥ, acquiring wealth by one's own exertion. पार्थिवः Pârthivaḥ, king. तत्समः Tatsamaḥ, like a king. वा Vâ, or. भवति Bhavati, becomes. हि Hi, certainly. सुनफायां Sunaphâyâm, under the Sunaphâ Yoga. धीधनख्यातिमां Dhîdhanakhyâtimâm, endowed with intelligence, wealth, and fame. च Cha, and. प्रभुः Prabhuḥ, master whose commands are obeyed. अगदशरीरः Agadaśarîraḥ, free from diseases. शीलवान् Śîlavân, good-natured; well behaved. ख्यातकीर्तिः Khyâtakîrtiḥ, famous. विषयसुखसुवेषः Viṣayasukhasuveśaḥ, enjoying pleasures of the senses and having decent dresses, &c. निर्वृतः Nirvṛitaḥ, mind undisturbed by the passions; calm; serene. च Cha, and. अनफायाम् Anaphâyâm, under Anaphâ Yoga.

5. Persons, born under the Sunaphâ Yoga, acquire wealth by their own exertions, become kings or like kings and are endowed with intelligence, fame and wealth. Persons, born under the Anaphâ Yoga, are men of influence and authority, good natured, healthy, far-famed, enjoying pleasures of the senses, dressing well, and enjoying peace of mind.

व०ति०—उत्पन्नभोगसुखभुग्धनवाहनाढ्यस्त्यागान्वितो दुरुधुराप्रभवः सुभृत्यः ॥ केमद्रुमे मलिनदुःखितनीचनिःस्वाः प्रेष्याः खलाश्च नृपतेरपि वंशजाताः ॥ ६ ॥

उत्पन्नभोगसुखभुक् Utpannabhogasukhabhuk, enjoying all manner of pleasures. धनवाहनाढ्यः Dhanavâhanâḍhyaḥ, having wealth, horses, and conveyances, etc. त्यागान्वितः Tyâgânvitaḥ, generous; liberal-minded. दुरुधुराप्रभवः Durudhurâpravabaḥ, under the influence of Durudhurâ Yoga. सुभृत्यः Subhṛityaḥ, posessing faithful servants. केमद्रुमे Kemadrume, under Kemadruma Yoga. मलिनदुःखितनीचनिःस्वाः Malinaduḥkhitanîchaniḥsvâḥ, dirty, miserable, morose, mean, and poor. प्रेष्याः Preṣyâḥ, doing servant's works. खलाः च Khalâḥ cha, and wicked. नृपतेः Nṛipateḥ, of kings. अपि Api, even. वंशजाताः Vaṃśajâtâḥ, born out of the families.

6. Persons born under Durudhurâ Yoga enjoy various pleasures arising from the possession of the produced articles, get wealth, horses, conveyances and faithful servants. Persons born under Kemadruma Yoga are dirty, miserable, morose, mean, poor, fond of doing servile works unsuited to their ranks and are wicked, even born of a royal family.

व०ति०—उत्साहशौर्यधनसाहसवान्महीजः सौम्यः पटुः सुवचनो निपुणः कलासु ॥ जीवोऽर्थधर्मसुखभाङ् नृपपूजितश्च कामी भृगुर्बहुधनो विषयोपभोक्ता ॥ ७ ॥

उत्साहशौर्यधनसाहसवान् Utsâhaśauryadhanaśâhasavân, always energetic, heroic, wealthy, and daring (not minding the consequences). महीजः Mahîjaḥ, born under the abiding influence of Mars: born when Mars is supreme in the Yoga. When Mars is the Yoga planet. सौम्यः Saumyaḥ, when Mercury is supreme; when Mercury is the Yoga planet. पटुः Paṭuḥ, clever; skilled in work. सुवचनः Suvachanaḥ, speaking good words, polite in speech; smooth-tongued. निपुणः Nipuṇaḥ, expert. कलासु Kalâsu, in music and fine arts. जीवः Jîvaḥ, when Jupiter presides. अर्थधर्मसुखभाक् Arthadharmasukhabhâk, possessing wealth, religion and happiness; wealthy, religious and happy. नृपपूजितः Nṛipapûjitaḥ, honoured by kings. कामी Kâmî, passionate; liking women. भृगुः Bhṛiguḥ, when Venus presides. बहुधनः Bahudhanaḥ, very wealthy. विषयोपभोक्ता Viṣayopabhoktâ, epicures; enjoying sexual pleasures.

7. In the three Yogas above described if Mars be supreme, then persons born become energetic, heroic, wealthy and daring; if Mercury be supreme, people become clever,

polite in speech, and expert in fine arts. When Jupiter reigns, people enjoy religion, wealth, happiness and are honoured by kings ; Venus reigning, people become addicted to women, get very much wealth and enjoy the senses verily.

पुष्पिताग्रा—परविभवपरिच्छदोपभोक्ता रवितनयो बहुकार्यकृद्गणेशः ॥ अशुभकृदुडुपोऽह्नि दृश्यमूर्तिर्गलिततनुश्च शुभोऽन्यथान्यदूह्यम् ॥ ८ ॥

परविभवपरिच्छदोपभोक्ता Paravibhavaparichhadopabhoktâ, enjoying other's wealth and property. रवितनयः Ravitanayaḥ, Saturn; when Saturn is the chief in the planetary combination. बहुकार्यकृत् Bahukâryakṛit, doing various works. गणेशः Gaṇeśaḥ, lord of many people; the chief of parties of men. अशुभकृत् Aśubhakṛit, producing bad results, *e. g.*, poverty, &c.; bringing in misery. उडुपः Uḍupaḥ, the Moon. अह्नि Ahni, during the day. दृश्यमूर्तिः Driśyamûrtiḥ, above the horizon (when the moon is visible). गलिततनुः Galitatanuḥ, below the horizon (when the moon is invisible). च Cha, and. शुभः Śubhaḥ, auspicious; producing prosperity; bringing in prosperity. अन्यथा Anyathâ, otherwise. अन्यत् Anyat, the reverse effects. ऊह्यम् Uhyam, are understood.

8. When Saturn is the ruler in the above Yoga, persons born enjoy others' wealth, property, and servants, do many works and get the leadership of lots of persons, (1). Under the Moon's sway, if she be above the horizon persons born during the day become miserable; but if she be below, people become prosperous and happy ; the reverse effect is to be understood in the opposite case (*i.e.*, persons born during the night become prosperous and happy if the Moon be above the horizon and miserable if she be below the horizon).

Note:—(1) If two or more planets be Yoga planets, the effects described for them all will come to pass.

व०ति०—लग्नादतीव वसुमान्वसुमाञ्छशांकात्सौम्यग्रहैरुपचयोपगतैः समस्तैः ॥ द्वाभ्यां समोऽल्पवसुमांश्च तदूनतायामन्येष्वसत्स्वपि फलेष्विदमुत्कटेन ॥ ९ ॥

इति श्रीवराहमिहिराचार्यप्रणीते बृहज्जातके चंद्रयोगाऽध्यायस्त्रयोदशः ॥ १३ ॥

लग्नात् Lagnât, from the Ascendant. **अतीव** Atîva, very. **वसुमान्** Vasumân, wealthy. **वसुमान्** Vasuman, wealthy. **शशांकात्** Śaśâṃkât, from the Moon. **सौम्यग्रहैः** Saumyagrahaiḥ, benefic planets, Mercury, Jupiter and Venus (occupying). **उपचयोपगतैः** Upachayopagataiḥ, situated in the Upachaya (3, 6, 10, and 11) houses. **समस्तैः** Samastaiḥ, all (the three planets Mercury, Jupiter and Venus). **द्वाभ्यां** Dvâbhyâṃ, the two planets occupying. **समः** Samaḥ, mean; middling; fairly wealthy. **अल्पवसुमान्** Alpavasumân, very little wealthy. **च** Cha, and. **तदूनतायां** Tadûnatâyâm, when there is less; *i. e.*, when there is only one benefic planet in the 3, 6, 10, and 11 houses. **अन्येषु** Anyeṣu, other. **असत्सु** Asatsu, inauspicious results. **अपि** Api, even. **फलेषु** Phaleṣu, results. **इदम्** Idam, this, *i.e.*, the auspicious results described above takes place. **उत्कटेन** Utkaṭena, owing to its being more powerful (than any inauspicious combination, such as Kemadruma Yoga, &c.)

9. If all the benefic planets Mercury, Jupiter and Venus occupy the Upachaya houses from the Ascendant at the time of birth, a person will become exceedingly wealthy; if the benefic planets Mercury, Jupiter and Venus be all found in the third, sixth, tenth and eleventh houses (the Upachaya houses) from the Moon, then the people become wealthy; if two benefics be in these houses, less wealthy; if one, then very little wealthy (1). These effects take place in the face of other inauspicious results to be brought about by other combinations (2) (Kemadruma Yoga, for instance). So the result in this verse is very strong.

Notes:—(1) Or poor. If benefic planets occupy the Upachaya houses both from the Ascendant and from the Moon, a person will be exceedingly rich. (2) That is, suppose a person to be born in a Kemadruma Yoga and suppose the benefic planets to occupy the Upachaya houses from the Ascendant or from the Moon or from both, the person will become rich and not poor.

Thus ends the Thirteenth Chapter on the Chandra Yoga in the Bṛihajjâtaka by Śrî Varâha Mihirâchârya.

CHAPTER XIV.

ANY TWO PLANETS IN ANY ONE SIGN.

शा०वि०—तिग्मांशुर्जनयत्युषेशसहितो यंत्राश्मकारं नरं
भौमेनाघरतं बुधेन निपुणं धीकीर्तिसौख्यान्वितम् ॥
क्रूरं वाक्पतिनान्यकार्यनिरतं शुक्रेण रंगायुधै-
र्लब्धस्वं रविजेन धातुकुशलं भांडप्रकारेषु वा ॥ १ ॥

तिग्मांशुः Tigmâṃśuḥ, the Sun. जनयति Janayati, produces. उषेशसहितः Uṣeśasahitaḥ, when residing with the Moon. यंत्राश्मकारं Yantrâśmakâram, maker of various machines, fire engines, &c., and clever in stone-work. नरं Naram, the man (born). भौमेन Bhaumena, when residing with Mars. अघरतं Aghartam, vicious; addicted to sinful deeds. बुधेन Budhena, when with Mercury. निपुणं Nipuṇam, clever. धीकीर्तिसौख्यान्वितम् Dhîkîrtisaukhvyânvitam, endowed with intelligence, fame, comfort and friends. क्रूरं Krûram, cruel; wicked. वाक्पतिना Vâkpatinâ, when with Jupiter. अन्यकार्यनिरतं Anyakâryaniratam, engaged in doing other's (unprofitable) works. शुक्रेण Śukreṇa, with Venus. रंगायुधैः Rangâyudhaiḥ, by wrestling and fighting with weapons. लब्धस्वं Labdhasvam, getting money. रविजेन Ravijena, with Saturn. धातुकुशलं Dhâtukuśalam, clever in dealing with various metals; skilled in metal-work. भांडप्रकारेषु वा Bhâṇḍaprakâreṣu vâ, or in making various potteries; or clever in earthenware works.

1. When the Sun is in the same sign with the Moon, persons born at that time become makers of fire-engines and various other machines (1) and they are clever in stone works; when the Sun is with Mars, persons become vicious; when with Mercury, men become clever and intelligent; famous and get comfort and aptitude to make friends with others; when the Sun is with Jupiter, persons become cruel and do other men's works; when with Venus, people gain wealth by wrestling and fighting with weapons and when the Sun is in the same sign with Saturn, people are clever in metal-work and in earthenware works, *i.e.*, in dealing with various metals and pottery work.

Note.—(1) Engines of destruction according to Commentator.

शा० वि०—कूटस्त्र्यासवकुम्भपण्यमशिवं मातुः सवक्रः शशी । सज्ञः प्रश्रितवाक्यमर्थनिपुणं सौभाग्यकीर्त्यान्वितम् । विक्रान्तं कुलमुख्यमास्थिरमतिं वित्तेश्वरं सांगिरा । वस्त्राणां ससितः क्रियादिकुशलं सार्किः पुनर्भूसुतम् ॥ २ ॥

कूटस्त्र्यासवकुम्भपण्यं Kûtastryâsavakumbhapaṇyam, pimps and publicans, and sellers of rough instruments; sellers of works of art, wives, wines and bottles. By works of art are meant hammer, ploughshare, concealed weapons, &c. अशिवं Asivam, an evil; harmful; giving trouble to one's mother. मातुः Mâtûḥ, to one's mother. सवक्रः Savakraḥ, when united with Mars. शशी Sasî, the Moon. सज्ञः Sajñyaḥ, when united with Mercury. प्रश्रितवाक्यम् Prasritavâkyam, polite; graceful in speech. अर्थनिपुणं Arthnipuṇam, clever in earning wealth or skilled in literary interpretation. सौभाग्यकीर्त्यान्वितम् Saubhâgyakîrtyânvitam, endearing to all, and praised by all. विक्रान्तं Vikrântam, powerful; heroic. कुलमुख्यं Kulamukhyam, illustrious in one's family. अस्थिरमतिं Asthiramatim, fickle; irresolute. वित्तेश्वरं Vithesvaram, very wealthy. सांगिरा Sâmgirâ, when united with Jupiter. वस्त्राणां Vastrâṇam, skilled in cloth-work, ससितः Sasitaḥ, with Venus. क्रियादिकुशलं Kriyâdikusalam, clever in buying and selling cloths, in weaving, stitching, dyeing. सार्किः Sârkiḥ, with Saturn. पुनर्भूसुतम् Punarbhûsutam, son of mother who has married a second time; the son of a remarried woman.

2. When the Moon is in the same house with Mars, persons born at that time become pimps and publicans, sellers of many implements, *e.g.*, hammer, &c., and troublesome to their mothers; when the Moon is in conjunction with Mercury, persons become graceful in their speech, clever in acquiring money or in making literary interpretation, endearing and praised by all; when with Jupiter, people become heroic and powerful, illustrious scions, fickle, and get much wealth; when she is with Venus, people are clever in weaving, stitching, dyeing, &c., and buying and selling clothes; and if the Moon be with Saturn, people are born of twice-married women.

शा०वि०—मूलादिस्नेहकूटैर्व्यवहरति वणिग्बाहुयोद्धा ससौम्ये । पुर्यध्यक्षः सजीवे भवति नरपतिः प्राप्तवित्तो द्विजो वा ॥ गोपो मल्लोऽथ दक्षः परयुवतिरतो द्यूतकृत्सासुरेज्ये दुःखार्तोऽसत्यसंधः ससवितृतनये भूमिजे निंदितश्च ॥ ३ ॥

मूलादिस्नेहकूटैः Mûlâdisnehakuṭaiḥ, with roots of various plants, &c. (leaves, flowers, gums, barks) and various sorts of (sweet scented or ordinary) oils. व्यवहरति Vyavaharati, deals; practises trade with. वणिक् Vaṇik, a trader. बाहुयोद्धा Bâhuyoddhâ, a wrestler. ससौम्ये Sasaumye, when united with Mercury. पुर्याध्यक्षः Puryadhyakṣyaḥ, ruler; a custodian of cities. सजीवे Sajîve, when united with Jupiter. भवति Bhavati, becomes. नरपतिः Narapatiḥ, king. प्राप्तवित्तः Prâptavittaḥ, will acquire money. द्विजः Dvijaḥ, a Brahmin. वा Vâ, or. गोपः Gopaḥ, cow-herd. मल्लः Mallaḥ, a wrestler. अथ Atha, thus. दक्षः Dakṣaḥ, clever. परयुवतिरतः Parayuvatirataḥ, addicted to others' wives. द्यूतकृत् Dyûtakṛit, gambler and cheat. सासुरेज्ये Sâsurejye, with Venus. दुःखार्तः Duḥkhârtaḥ, afflicted with grief, miserable sufferer of pains. असत्यसन्धः Asatyasandaḥ, untruthful; liars of the first water, ससवितृतनये Sasavitṛitanaye, with Saturn. भूमिजे Bhûmije, Mars. निन्दितः Ninditaḥ, cursed by all; reproached by all; low; vile. च Cha, and.

3. When Mars and Mercury are in one sign, persons born become wrestlers and merchants, deal in roots of plants, leaves, flowers, gums, barks and in various sorts of ordinary or sweet-scented oils; when Mars is in the same sign with Jupiter, they are custodians of cities or kings or Brâhmaṇs, and get money; when Mars is with Venus in one sign, persons become wrestlers, cowherds, clever, addicted to others' wives, gamblers, and cheats; and when Mars is with Saturn, people are afflicted with grief, full of miseries, untruthful, and reproached by all.

शा० वि०—सौम्ये रंगचरो बृहस्पतियुते गीतप्रियो नृत्यवि-
द्वाग्मी भूगणपः सितेन मृदुना मायापटुर्लंघकः । सद्विद्यो
धनदारवान्बहुगुणः शुक्रेण युक्ते गुरौ ज्ञेयः श्मश्रुकरोऽसितेन
घटकृज्जातोऽन्नकारोऽपि वा ॥ ४ ॥

सौम्ये Saumye, Mercury being. रंगचरः Ramgacharaḥ, a wrestler; a boxer. बृहस्पतियुते Vṛihaspatiyute, united with Jupiter. गीतप्रियः Gîtapriyaḥ, fond of music. नृत्यवित् Nṛityavit, skilled in dancing. वाग्मी Vâgmî, eloquent speaker; orator. भूगणपः Bhûgaṇapaḥ, owners of lands and chief amongst a number of followers. सितेन Sitena, with Venus. मृदुना Mṛidunâ, with Saturn. मायापटुः Mâyâpaṭuḥ, clever in cheating; a great cheat. लंघकः Laṃghakaḥ, disobeying the religious preceptors; disobedient. सद्विद्यः Sadvidyaḥ, having higher knowledge; learned in various good subjects. धनदारवान् Dhanadârvân, having wife and riches. बहुगुणः Bahuguṇaḥ, well qualified in many subjects; variously qualified. शुक्रेण Śukreṇa, with Venus. युक्ते Yukte, united with. गुरौ Gurau, with Jupiter. ज्ञेयः Jñyeaḥ, to be learnt; to be understood. श्मश्रुकरः Smaśrukaraḥ, a barber. असितेन Asitena, with Saturn. घटकृत् Ghaṭakrit, a potter. जातः Jâtaḥ, born; the person born. अन्नकारः Annakâraḥ, a cook. अपि Api, even. वा Vâ, or.

4. When Mercury is in the same sign with Jupiter, persons born become great athletes, are fond of music, and well skilled in dancing. When Mercury is with Venus, persons born become eloquent, landlords and chief amongst great assemblages; when Mercury is with Saturn, a man becomes a great cheat, disobedient to elders and superiors. When Venus and Jupiter are in one sign, a man gets knowledge in some respectable department, possesses wife and wealth and many good qualities. When Jupiter and Saturn are in one sign, a man becomes a barber, a potter or a cook.

पुष्पिताग्रा—असितसितसमागमेऽल्पचक्षुर्युवतिसमाश्रयसम्प्रवृद्धवित्तः । भवति च लिपिपुस्तकचित्रवेत्ता कथितफलैः परतो विकल्पनीयाः ॥ ५ ॥

इति श्रीवराहमिहिरविरचिते बृहज्जातके द्विग्रहयोगाध्यायश्चतुर्दशः ॥ १४ ॥

असितसितसमागमे Asitasitasamâgame, when Venus is united with Saturn. अल्पचक्षुः Alpachakṣuḥ, short-sighted. युवतिसमाश्रयसम्प्रवृद्धवित्तः Yuvatisamâśrayasampravriddhavittaḥ, increasing their wealth under the influence of one's wife or a young woman. भवति Bhavati, becomes. च Cha, and. लिपिपुस्तकचित्रवेत्ता Lipipustakachitravettâ, authors of books, paintings and pictures. कथितफलैः Kathitaphalaiḥ, by the effects already described; by means of the aforesaid fruits. परतः Parataḥ, after two; when three planets are united. विकल्पनीयाः Vikalpanîyâḥ, ought to be applied and determined.

5. When Venus and Saturn are in one sign, persons born become short-sighted, earn money and increase it through their wives or young women, are authors and painters. When more than two planets are united, the results will also be according to the aforesaid results. (For instance, if there be three planets, three results are to be

mentioned, *e.g.*, if the Sun, Moon and Mars be in one sign; here (1) the results of the Sun and the Moon, (2) the results of the Sun and Mars, and (3) the results of the Moon and Mars are to be taken into account. And so on.

Thus ends the fourteenth Chapter on the two Planetary Combinations by Varâha Mihira in Bṛihajjâtakam.

CHAPTER XV.

ON PRAVRAJYÂDHYÂYA

Or on Ascetic Yogas.

एकस्थैश्चतुरादिभिर्बलयुतैर्जाताः पृथग्वीर्यगैः ।
शाक्याजीविकभिक्षुवृद्धचरका निर्ग्रन्थवन्याशनाः । माहे-
यज्ञगुरुक्षपाकरसितप्राभाकरीनैः क्रमात् । प्रव्रज्या बलिभिः
समा परजितैस्तत्स्वामिभिः प्रच्युतिः ॥ १ ॥

एकस्थैः: Ekasthaiḥ, situated in one sign. चतुरादिभिः: Chaturâdibhiḥ, by four, five, six or seven planets; by the planets, whose number commences with four (*i.e.*, four, five, six, or seven planets). बलयुतैः: Balayutaiḥ, strong by virtue of time, position, &c. जाताः: Jâtâḥ, persons born. पृथग्वीर्यगैः: Pṛithagvîryagaiḥ, different (sorts of asceticism) according to the nature of the most powerful planet. शाक्याजीविकभिक्षु-वृद्धचरकाः निर्ग्रन्थवन्याशनाः: Śâkyâjîvikabhikṣuvṛiddhacharakâḥ nirgranthavanyâśanâḥ, (1) Śâkya (a class of Buddhist ascetics, wearing red coloured cloths), (2) Âjîvika (a class of Jaina mendicants), (3) Bhikṣu, (a class of Brâhmiṇ ascetics, holding one staff, called Ekadaṇḍîs, these abandoning their homes and families and subsisting on alms). (4) Vṛiddha (Vṛiddha Śrâvaka, a class of Buddhist saints or votaries or otherwise called Kâpâlikas, a class of Śakti followers.) (5) Charaka, a class of devotees wearing circular discus, (6) Nirgranthas or Nâgâs, a class of devotees, quite naked and (7) Vanyâśanâḥ, a class of devotees or ascetics, living on fruits and roots only and engaged in Divine meditation. माहेयज्ञगुरुक्षपाकरसितप्राभाकरीनैः: Mâheyajñagurukṣapâkarasitaprâbhâkarînaiḥ, under the presiding influence of Mars, Mercury, Jupiter, Moon, Venus, Saturn and the Sun, respectively. क्रमात् Kramât, successively; in seriatim. प्रव्रज्याः: Pravrajyâḥ, asceticisms. बलिभिः: Balibhiḥ, to the most powerful planet that decides the fate of asceticism. समाः: Samâḥ, corresponding to. पराजितैः: Parajitaiḥ, when defeated (by other strong planets in planetary conjunction). तत्स्वामिभिः: Tatsvâmibhiḥ, by the lord of any other form of asceticism. प्रच्युतिः: Prachyutiḥ, fall; renouncing the order of asceticism that was first accepted and reverting to his former condition.

1. When not less than four planets (4, 5, 6, or 7 planets) occupy any one sign at the time of birth, know that Pravrajyâ Yoga (the planetary combination indicating asceticism) is to take place, as indicated by the strongest in the

group in that sign. (If the Pravrajyâ-making planets be all weak, the Pravrajyâ Yoga ceases. If one planet be found the strongest, the corresponding order of asceticism will be adopted; if two planets be equally strong, the two corresponding orders will be taken, one after another and so on) (1).

If Mars be the strongest of all the planets in the group, a person born becomes a Śâkya ascetic (a class of Buddhist monks wearing Bhâguâ or red-coloured cloth); if Mercury be the most powerful in one's nativity, a person becomes an Âjîvika (a class of Jaina ascetics or class of Vaiṣṇavites); if Jupiter be the most powerful, persons become Ekadaṇḍis, (a class of the Brâhmaṇ Sannyâsins, leaving their homes and families and always engaged in Divine communion); if Moon be so, persons become Kâpâlikas (a certain class of Śâktas or worshippers of Śakti); if Venus reigns supreme, then Charakas or Chakradharas wearing circular discus are born; if Saturn be the strongest, then Nâgâs or naked ascetics are indicated, and if the Sun be the most powerful, then persons born become ascetics living on roots and fruits, engaged in Divine meditation. If such lord of one order of asceticism be defeated at the time of birth in planetary conjunction by the lord of another order of asceticism, then the person born will accept the first order, renounce it and adopt the second order and so on or revert to his former condition, if all the planets be defeated (2).

Notes:—(1) If all the Yoga planets be equally strong, the person born will take up each corresponding order during the Antardaśâs of the corresponding ruler and renounce the previous order.

(2) The person will take first the ascetic life indicated by the most powerful planets in its Daśâ and Antardaśâ period, then that indicated by the next in power and so on, in the Antardasâ periods of the respective planets. If the most powerful planet be one only and if that does not encounter any defeat in the battle of planetary conjunction, the native will continue to be an ascetic of one order till the moment of his death;

otherwise he will revert to his former state by a single powerful planet which does not suffer defeat in conjunction ; the ascetic life assumed will continue till death.

वैतालीय–रविलुप्तकरैरदीक्षिता बलिभिस्तद्गतभक्तयो
नराः। अभियाचितमात्रदीक्षिता निहतैरन्यनिरीक्षितैरपि ॥ २ ॥

रविलुप्तकरैः: Raviluptakaraiḥ, on the strongest planet descending ; by the planet whose lustre has been overpowered by the Sun (1). अदीक्षिताः: Adiksitâḥ, not initiated. बलिभिः: Balibhiḥ, by the powerful planet. तद्गतभक्तयः: Tadgatabhaktayaḥ, votaries to those who have entered the ascetic order. नराः: Narâḥ, persons. अभियाचितमात्रदीक्षिताः: Abhiyâchitamtâradikṣitâḥ, wanting to be initiated ; desirous of being initiated. निहतैः: Nihatai, when defeated (by other planets) in conjunction. अन्यनिरीक्षितैः: Anyanirîkṣitaiḥ, when aspected by other planets. अपि Api, even ; and meanwhile.

2. Persons born under the most powerful but descending (1) (ascetic-producing) planet do not become initiated Ascetics (2) but they become the votaries (Bhaktas) of those who have entered into an ascetic order. Again, if the strongest planet be defeated in planetary battle (*i.e.*, planetary conjunction) but if it be aspected by other planets (3), then a native becomes very desirous to get initiation into the holy mantrams but they do not find themselves initiated (4).

Notes:—(1) In the verse the planet that has been overpowered by the lustre of the Sun is mentioned ; this may occur at sunrise or at sunset ; nay, even some hours before that. But here the sunset is meant according to the Commentator.

(2) It may be that he may lead an outward appearance of asceticism without being initiated.

(3) The doubt here may arise, when the most powerful planet is stated to be defeated by other planets, it may be taken to mean (*vide* preceding stanza), that the native becomes an initiated ascetic and then renounces his order. But not so :—In this verse it has been specially stated "that when the strongest planet is defeated but aspected by another planet." This state of being aspected by another planet nullifies the meaning of the 1st stanza ; and it should be taken to mean that the native becomes very eager to get initiation but he does not become successful. If the powerful planet were not aspected he would have been initiated, and after a time reverted to his former state, as mentioned in the 1st stanza.

(4) It may be that the person might lead outwardly an ascetic life but he will not get initiation.

मालिनी–जन्मेशोऽन्यैर्यद्यदृष्टोऽर्कपुत्रं पश्यत्यार्किर्जन्मपं वा बलोनम् । दीक्षां प्राप्नोत्यार्किदृक्काणसंस्थे भौमार्क्यंशे सौरदृष्टे च चंद्रे ॥ ३ ॥

जन्मेश: Janmeśaḥ, the ruler of the sign which the Moon occupies during the time of birth. अन्यै: Anyaiḥ, by other planets. यदि Yadi, if. अदृष्ट: Adṛiṣṭaḥ, not aspected. अर्कपुत्रं Arkaputtram, Saturn. पश्यति Paśyati, aspects. आर्कि: Arkiḥ, Saturn. जन्मपं Janmapam, the ruler of the sign where the Moon resides during birth time. वा Vâ, or. बलोनम् Balonam, weak. दीक्षां Dîkṣâm, initiation. प्राप्नोति Prâpnoti, gets. आर्किदृक्काणसंस्थे Arkidṛikkâṇasaṃsthe, situated in the Decanate of Saturn. भौमार्क्यंशे Bhaumârkyaṃśe, and occupying the Navâṃśa of Mars or that of Saturn. सौरदृष्टे Sauradṛiṣṭe, aspected by Saturn (only and not by other planets). च Cha, and. चन्द्रे Chandre, Moon.

3. If the ruler of the sign which the Moon occupies during the birth be not aspected by others and if it aspects Saturn, then the order of asceticism indicated by Saturn (1) will be entered into; or when Saturn aspects the above mentioned ruler and if that ruler be weak, then also the order of Saturn will be entered into. The same result also takes place if the Moon occupy the Saturn Decanate and the Navâṃśa of Mars or that of Saturn, and if she be aspected by Saturn (only and not by other planets).

Note:—(1) And it will take place in the Antardaśâ of Saturn or the ruler, whichever is powerful.

मालिनी–सुरगुरुशशिहोरास्वार्किदृष्टासु धर्मे गुरुरथ नृपतीनां योगजस्तीर्थकृत्स्यात् । नवमभवनसंस्थे मंदगेऽन्यैरदृष्टे भवति नरपयोगे दीक्षितः पार्थिवेंद्रः ॥ ४ ॥

इति श्रीवराहमिहिराचार्यप्रणीते बृहज्जातके प्रव्रज्यायोगाध्यायः पंचदशः ॥ १५ ॥

सुरगुरुशशिहोरासु Suraguruśaśihorâsu, on Jupiter, Moon and the Ascendant. आर्किदृष्टासु Arkidṛiṣṭâsu, being aspected by Saturn. धर्मे Dharme, in the ninth house. गुरु: Guruḥ, Jupiter. अथ Atha, thus. नृपतीनां Nṛipatînâm, of kings. योगज: Yogajaḥ, person born under any one King-making combination. तीर्थकृत् Tîrthakṛit, pilgrim and compiler of Śâstras and Darsanas (*i.e.*, philosophy, etc.); pilgrim going from one sacred place to another. स्यात् Syât, becomes. नवमभवनसंस्थे Navamabhavanasaṃsthe, situated in the ninth house. मन्दगे Mandage, Saturn. अन्यैः Anyaiḥ, by other planets. अदृष्टे Adṛiṣṭe, not aspected. भवति Bhavati, becomes. नरपयोगे Narapayoge, born under the combinations indicating kingship. दीक्षितः Dîkṣitaḥ, initiated in the ascetic order. पार्थिवेन्द्रः Pârthivendraḥ, king.

4. If Jupiter, Moon and the Ascendant be aspected by Saturn and if Jupiter be in the ninth house from the Ascendant, and if there be one Râja Yoga, then the person born will roam about in places of pilgrimage and will read and write Śâstras and will not become a king in spite there be the combinations tending to make him a king. If Saturn be in the ninth house from the Ascendant and if it be not aspected by any other planet, and if there be any king-making planetary combination then the person born will become a king and will also take the order of asceticism; if there be no king-making combination, then simply the ascetic life will be lead.

Note:—Some render the meaning of the first half of the verse thus:—if Dhanu, Mîna or Karkaṭa be the Ascendant and be aspected by Saturn, then the person born under a Râja Yoga will not be a king but he will be a Śâstrakâra or author of sacred scriptures. But this is not generally approved.

Persons born under the first case will become like Kaṇâda, Buddha, Pâñcha Śikha, Varâha Mihira, Brahmagupta, and others; persons born under the second case will become like Janaka, Kâśîrâja, Śuchidhavaja and others. If there be two Râja Yogas and one ascetic Yoga, the person will become a king.

Thus ends the fifteenth Chapter on Asceticism in Bṛihajjâtaka by Śrî Varâha Mihirâchârya.

CHAPTER XVI.

ON THE MOON AND STARS.

**आर्या—प्रियभूषणः सुरूपः सुभगो दक्षोऽश्विनीषु मति-
मांश्च । कृतनिश्चयसत्यारुग्दक्षः सुखितश्च भरणीषु ॥ १ ॥**

प्रियभूषण : Priyabhûṣaṇaḥ, fond of dressing and decorating one's body. सुरूपः Surûpaḥ, handsome. सुभग : Subhagaḥ, lovely; endearing. दक्ष: Dakṣaḥ, clever. अश्विनीषु Aśvinîṣu, under Aśvinî asterism; when Moon is in the star Aśvinî. मतिमान् Matimân, intelligent. च Cha, and. कृतनिश्चय: Kritaniśchayaḥ, firmly resolved (to do a thing thoroughly); resolute; determinate. सत्य: Satyaḥ, truthful. अरुक् Aruk, healthy. दक्ष : Dakṣaḥ, clever; skilful. सुखित : Sukhitaḥ, happy. च Cha and. भरणीषु Bharaṇîṣu, in Bharaṇî star; when the Moon is in the Bharaṇî star.

The Moon and the star Aśvinî (Arietis.)

1. The combination of the Moon with the star Aśvinî (Arietis) during the birth time of any individual makes the character a lover of show, fine clothes and ornaments, an attractive personality, handsome and lovely; clever, skilful and intelligent.

The Moon and the star Bharaṇî (Musca). The combination of Moon with the star Bharaṇî (Musca) makes one firm in one's resolves, truthful, healthy, dexterous, free from grief and happy.

Note:--This Chapter gives the results when the Moon is found in each of the twenty-seven (27) Asterisms successively. In this verse the results are stated when the Moon lies in Arietis and Musca, (Aśvinî and Bharaṇî.)

**आर्या—बहुभुक्परदाररतस्तेजस्वी कृत्तिकासु विख्यातः ।
रोहिण्यां सत्यशुचिः प्रियंवदः स्थिरमतिः सुरूपश्च ॥ २ ॥**

बहुभुक् Bahubhuk, eating much; voracious eater; glutton. परदाररत : Paradâra-rataḥ, addicted to other's wives. तेजस्वी Tejasvî, energetic; spirited; mighty; mettled; splendid. कृत्तिकासु Krittikâsu, in Krittikâ star. When the Moon passes through Pleiades. विख्यात : Vikhyâtaḥ, famous. रोहिण्यां Rohiṇyâm, under the Rohiṇî star; when the Moon passes through Rohiṇî. सत्यशुचि : Satyaśuchiḥ, truthful and pure; truthful and uncovetous. प्रियंवद: Priyamvadaḥ, sweet tongued; of smooth and persuasive tongue. स्थिरमति: Sthiramatiḥ, constant; not fickle; resolute. सुरूप: Surûpaḥ, of good appearance; handsome; lovely; elegant. च Cha, and.

2. The Moon and the Pleiade (or the star Krittikâ). This combination makes one a voracious eater, holding illicit intercourse with others' wives, very spirited and intolerant, and of wide celebrity.

The Moon and the star Rohinî (Aldebaran). This makes one truthful, pure, uncovetous, clean, of smooth and persuasive tongue, of steady mind and heart, and of excellent appearance.

आर्या—चपलश्चतुरो भीरुः पटुरुत्साही धनी मृगे भोगी ।
शठगर्वितः कृतघ्नो हिंस्रः पापश्च रौद्रर्क्षे ॥ ३ ॥

चपल: Chapalaḥ, fickle; unsteady; wavering. चतुर: Chaturaḥ, ingenious; crafty; shrewd. भीरु: Bhîruḥ, timid; afraid; shy; cowardly. पटु: Paṭuḥ, clever; skilful; expert. उत्साही Utsâhî, energetic; encouraging. धनी Dhanî, wealthy. मृगे Mrige, under Mriga asterism; when the Moon passes through Mrigaśirâ. भोगी Bhogî, enjoyer; an epicure. शठगर्वितः Saṭhagarvitaḥ, deceitful and haughty. कृतघ्न: Kritaghnaḥ, traitor; treacherous; ungrateful. हिंस्र: Himsraḥ, cruel; mischievous; murderous. पाप: Pâpaḥ, vicious. रौद्रर्क्षे Raudrarkṣe, when the Moon passes through Ârdrâ star.

3. The Moon and λ Orionis (the star Mrigaśirâ). This combination makes one flying and quick, like a deer, *i.e.*, unsteady and ingenious, timid and shy, skilful, hopeful and energetic, rich, and a great epicure.

The Moon and α Orionis (the star Ârdrâ). The native will be vain and deceitful, treacherous, harmful, and vicious.

आर्या—दांतः सुखी सुशीलो दुर्मेधा रोगभाक्पिपासुश्च ।
अल्पेन च संतुष्टः पुनर्वसौ जायते मनुजः ॥ ४ ॥

दांत: Dântaḥ, forbearing; whose passions are subdued. सुखी Sukhî, happy. सुशील: Suśîlaḥ, courteous; modest; polite; humble. दुर्मेधा: Durmedhâḥ, stupid; of a dull intellect; of wrong views. रोगभाक् Rogabhâk, sickly; diseased; ill. पिपासु: Pipâsuḥ, thirsty. च Cha, and. अल्पेन च Alpena cha, and with very little. संतुष्ट: Santuṣṭaḥ, satisfied. पुनर्वसौ Punarvasau, when the Moon passes through the Punarvasu star. जायते Jâyate, is born. मनुज: Manujaḥ, person.

4. The Moon and the star Punarvasu (β Geminorum). The individual born under this combination will draw the mind away from evil deeds, will be happy, good-natured and humble but rather of dull intellect, sickly, thirsty and contented with very little.

आर्या—शान्तात्मा सुभगः पण्डितो धनी धर्मसंस्तृतः पुष्ये।
शठः सर्वभक्षपापः कृतघ्नधूर्त्तश्च भौजङ्गे ॥ ५ ॥

शान्तात्मा Sântâtmâ, of a calm temper; one whose passions are subdued. सुभगः Subhagaḥ, lovely. पण्डितः Panditaḥ, well versed in Sâstras; learned; scholar. धनी Dhani, wealthy. धर्मसंस्तृतः Dharmasamsritaḥ, virtuous. पुष्ये Pusye, when the Moon passes through the Pusyâ star. शठः Sathaḥ, a cheat. सर्वभक्षपापः Sarvabhaksapâpaḥ, hoarding money and vicious; it may mean also, eating every thing and doing evil deeds. कृतघ्नधूर्त्तः Kritghna dhûrtaḥ, ungrateful and wily. च Cha, and. भौजङ्गे Bhaujamge, under the Aslesâ star.

5. The Moon and the Star Pusyâ (Cancri). The native enjoys mental quietness on account of the restraint of his passions, is of lovely figure, well versed in his Sâstras, wealthy, religious and observes religious rites and ceremonies.

The Moon and the Star Aslesâ (α 1 and 2 Cancri). The man becomes wanting in honesty of purpose, eats all sorts of food and does evil deeds, is wily and treacherous.

आर्या—बहुभृत्यधनो भोगी सुरपितृभक्तो महोद्यमः पित्र्ये।
प्रियवाग्दाता द्युतिमानटनो नृपसेवको भाग्ये ॥ ६ ॥

बहुभृत्यधनः Bahubhrityadhanaḥ, having very many servants and much wealth. भोगी Bhogî, enjoyer; epicure. सुरपितृभक्तः Surapitribhaktaḥ, devotee of the Devas and Pitris. महोद्यमः Mahodyamaḥ, very energetic; a great enthusiast. पित्र्ये Pitrye, under the Star Regulus or Maghâ. प्रियवाक् Priyavâk, of smooth and persuasive tongue; sweet-speaking; affable; agreeable. दाता Dâtâ, generous; charitable. द्युतिमान् Dyutimân, handsome; majestic; beautiful. अटनः Aṭanaḥ, sojourner; one of a travelling disposition. नृपसेवकः Nripasevakaḥ, devoted to the service of kings; loyal. भाग्ये Bhâgye, under Pûrva Phalguni Star.

6. The Moon and the Star Maghâ (α Leonis, Regulus). The man born under this combination will become a great enthusiast, a great devotee of the Devas

and the Pitris (the Fathers), a thorough enjoyer of the sexual pleasures and will be attended by numerous servants and will possess immense wealth.

The Moon and the Star Pûrva Phalgunî (δ Leonis). This combination makes one affable, charitable, illustrious and beautiful. One will be very prone to travel and will be a walker and engaged in honouring and paying one's service to kings.

आर्या—सुभगो विद्याप्तधनो भोगी सुखभाक् द्वितीयफाल्गुन्याम् । उत्साही धृष्टः पानपो घृणी तस्करो हस्ते ॥ ७ ॥

सुभगः Subhagaḥ, lovely and handsome. विद्याप्तधनः Vidyâptadhanaḥ, obtaining wealth by one's literary merits. भोगी Bhogî, an enjoyer of the senses; an epicure. सुखभाक् Sukhabhâk, happy. द्वितीयफाल्गुन्याम् Dvitîyaphâlgunyâm, under the Uttara Phâlgunî star. उत्साही Utsâhî, energetic; liable to be intensely excited. धृष्टः Dhriṣṭaḥ, bold; rude; insolent. पानपः Pânapaḥ, addicted to drinking. घृणी Aghriṇî, heartless; cruel; hateful. तस्करः Taskaraḥ, thief. हस्ते Haste, under the Hastâ star.

7. The Moon and the star Uttara Phalgunî (β Leonis). The native will be beautiful and lovely, earn money by his literary merits, will be an enjoyer of the senses, and happy.

The Moon and the star Hastâ (γ or δ Corvi). This combination makes one liable to be very easily and intensely excited, bold and insolent, addicted to drinking habits, heartless and lastly a thief.

आर्या—चित्राम्बरमाल्यधरः सुलोचनाङ्गश्च भवति चित्रायाम् । दान्तो वणिक् कृपालुः प्रियवाग्धर्माश्रितः स्वातौ ॥८॥

चित्राम्बरमाल्यधरः Chitrâmbaramâlyadharaḥ, wearing variegated clothes and garlands. सुलोचनाङ्गः च Sulochanâmgaḥ cha, and possessing beautiful eyes and limbs. भवति Bhavati, becomes. चित्रायाम् Chitrâyâm, under the Chitrâ or Spicâ star. दान्तः Dântaḥ, of subdued passions. वणिक् Vaṇik, merchant; trader. कृपालुः Kripâluḥ, generous; merciful. प्रियवाक् Priyavâk, sweet tongued. धर्माश्रितः Dharmâśritaḥ, virtuous. स्वातौ Svâtau, under the star Svâtî.

8. The Moon and the star Chitrâ (Spica). This combination makes one fond of wearing variously coloured garments and garlands and makes the eyes and limbs well proportioned and elegant.

The Moon and the star Svâtî (α Bootes; Arcturus). This makes one practise self-retraint, a merchant, generous-hearted, sweet speaking, and religious in spirit and actions.

आर्या—ईर्ष्युर्लुब्धो द्युतिमान्वचनपटुः कलहकृद्विशाखासु।
आढ्यो विदेशवासी क्षुधालुरटनोऽनुराधासु ॥ ६ ॥

ईर्ष्युः Irṣuḥ, envious; jealous. लुब्धः Lubdhaḥ, avaricious; greedy. द्युतिमान् Dyutimân, fair complexioned; lustrous. वचनपटुः Vachanapaṭuḥ, clever in speaking; some read it अर्थपटुः Arthapaṭuḥ, clever in earning money. कलहकृत् Kalahakṛit, quarrelsome. विशाखासु Viśakhâsu, under the star Viśâkhâ. आढ्यः Âḍhyaḥ, wealthy. विदेशवासी Videśavâsî, living in foreign or distant lands. क्षुधालुः Kṣudhâluḥ, unable to bear hunger. अटनः Aṭanaḥ, vagrant; wandering. अनुराधासु Anurâdhâsu, under the star Anurâdhâ.

9. The Moon and the star Viśâkhâ (α or x Libra). This combination makes one jealous, avaricious, fair complexioned; one will speak nicely and persuasively to gain one's ends, and will bring about quarrels among men.

The Moon and the star Anurâdhâ (δ Scorpionis). This combination brings forth wealthy persons living in foreign countries, and of travelling habits These are unable to bear hunger.

आर्या—ज्येष्ठासु न बहुमित्रः संतुष्टो धर्मकृत्प्रचुरकोपः।
मूले मानी धनवान्सुखी न हिंस्रः स्थिरो भोगी ॥ १० ॥

ज्येष्ठासु Jyeṣthâsu, under the star Jyeṣthâ. न Na, no; not. बहुमित्रः Bahumitraḥ, having many friends. संतुष्टः Saṃtuṣṭaḥ, contented; happy. धर्मकृत् Dharmakṛit, virtuous. प्रचुरकोपः Prachurakopaḥ, very angry. मूले Mûle, under the star Mûlâ. मानी Mânî, proud; haughty; respectable. धनवान् Dhanavân, wealthy. सुखी Sukhî, happy. न Na, not. हिंस्रः Hiṃsraḥ, mischievous. स्थिरः Sthiraḥ, steady. भोगी Bhogî, enjoyer; one living in luxury; epicure.

10. The Moon and the star Jyeṣthâ (α Scorpionis; Antares).

Persons born under the star Jyeṣthâ have a few friends, are well contented, virtuous, but very angry.

The Moon and the star Mûlâ (ν Scorpionis). Persons under the star Mûlâ are haughty, respectable, wealthy, happy, not mischievous, one-minded; and these live in luxury.

आर्या–इष्टानंदकलत्रो मानी दृढसौहृदश्च जलदैवे। वैश्वे
विनीतधार्मिकवहुमित्रकृतज्ञसुभगश्च ॥ ११ ॥

इष्टानंदकलत्रः Iṣtânandakalatraḥ, getting an agreeable wife who gives comfort and happiness. मानी Mânî, respectable; honourable; proud. दृढसौहृदः च Dṛiḍhasauhṛidaḥ cha, and a staunch friend. जलदैवे Jaladaive, under the star Pûrvâṣâḍhâ. वैश्वे Vaiśve, under the star Uttarâṣâḍhâ. विनीतधार्मिकवहुमित्रकृतज्ञसुभगः Vinîtadhârmikabahu-mitrakṛitajñasubhagaḥ, humble and obedient; virtuous; having many friends; grateful and lovely. च Cha, and

11. The Moon and the star Pûrvâṣâḍhâ (δ Sagittarii). This combination gives one an agreeable wife giving comfort and happiness, makes one proud, honourable and a staunch friend.

The Moon and the star Uttarâṣâḍhâ (Sagittarii). One born under this combination becomes gentlemanly, obedient, religious, gets himself surrounded by many friends, becomes grateful, and he is beautiful and general y liked.

आर्या–श्रीमाञ्छ्रवणे श्रुतवानुदारदारो धनान्वितः ख्यातः।
दाता आढ्यः शूरो गीतप्रियो धनिष्ठासु धनलुब्धः ॥ १२ ॥

श्रीमान् Śrimân, fortunate; prosperous; beautiful. श्रवणे Śravaṇe, under the star Śravaṇâ. श्रुतवान् Śrutavân, versed in Vedas; learned. उदारदारः Udâradâraḥ, having a liberal minded wife. धनान्वितः Dhanânvitaḥ, wealthy. ख्यातः Khyâtaḥ, well known; celebrated. दाता Dâtâ, generous; charitable. आढ्यः Âḍhyaḥ, wealthy. शूरः Sûraḥ, hero. गीतप्रियः Gîtapriyaḥ, fond of music. धनिष्ठासु Dhaniṣṭhâsu, under the star Dhaniṣṭhâ. धनलुब्धः Dhanalubdhaḥ, covetuous; eager to acquire money; desirous of wealth.

12. The Moon and the star Śravaṇâ (α Aquilae). This combination makes one prosperous and fortunate, versed in the Vedas, gives one a noble and distinguished wife, wealth and fame.

The Moon and the star Dhaniṣṭhâ (δ Delphini). This combination makes one charitable, wealthy, hero, fond of music and desirous of wealth.

आर्या—स्फुटवाग्व्यसनी रिपुहा साहसिकः शतभिषजि
दुर्ग्राह्यः ॥ भाद्रपदासूद्विग्नः स्त्रीजितधनी पटुरदाता च ॥ १३ ॥

स्फुटवाक् Sphuṭavâk, truthful; frank; plain speaking. व्यसनी Vyasanî, addicted to evil practices; vicious. रिपुहा Ripuhâ, the killer of enemies; crushing one's enemies. साहसिकः Sâhasikaḥ; daring, adventurous. शतभिषजि Śatabhiṣaji, under the star Śatabhiṣâ. दुर्ग्राह्यः Durgrâhyaḥ, not liking to be subordinate, bearing no subordination. भाद्रपदासु Bhâdrapadâsu, under the star Pûrvabhâdrapada; उद्विग्नः Udvignaḥ, thinking of some inauspicious circumstances; anxious; sorrowful. स्त्रीजितः Strîjitaḥ, under one's wife's control; henpecked. धनी Dhanî, wealthy. पटुः Paṭuḥ, clever. अदाता Adâtâ, ungenerous; uncharitable.

13. The Moon and the star Śatabhiṣâ (λ Aquarie). This combination makes one truthful, harsh in one's speech, vicious, the conqueror of one's enemies, bold and daring, very difficult of subordination, somewhat of an independent character.

The Moon and the star Pûrvabhâdrapada (Pegasi). This combination makes one anxious and sorrowful; look on one's wife as one's master; one will also be wealthy, clever and uncharitable.

आर्या—वक्ता सुखी प्रजावान् जितशत्रुर्धार्मिको द्विती-
यासु। सम्पूर्णाङ्गः सुभगः शूरः शुचिरर्थवान् पौष्णे ॥ १४ ॥
इति—श्रीवराहमिहिरकृते बृहज्जातके नक्षत्रफलाध्यायः
षोडशः ॥ १६ ॥

वक्ता Vaktâ, eloquent speaker; eloquent in Śâstras. सुखी Sukhî, happy. प्रजावान् Prajâvân, having many sons and grandsons. जितशत्रुः Jitaśatruḥ, victorious over one's enemies. धार्मिकः Dhârmikaḥ, virtuous द्वितीयासु Dvitîyâsu, under the star second or Uttarabhâdrapada. सम्पूर्णाङ्गः Sampûrṇâṃgaḥ, of a fully developed body or limbs; well-proportioned. सुभगः Subhagaḥ, lovely; graceful. शूरः Śûraḥ, hero; valiant. शुचिः Śuchiḥ, pure. अर्थवान् Arthavân, wealthy. पौष्णे Pauṣṇe, under the star Revatî.

14. The Moon and the stars Uttarabhâdrapada (α Andromedo) and Revatî (ε Piscium). Persons born under the star Uttarabhâdrapada can speak on Śâstras or religious books fluently, are happy and blessed with many sons and grandsons, conquerors of enemies and are religious.

Persons born under the star Revatî get all their limbs fully developed, look lovely and graceful, become heroes, pure and wealthy.

Note.—It should be borne in mind that the above described results will fully take place only when the Moon is powerful.

Thus ends the sixteenth Chapter on the Moon and Stars in Brihajjâtaka by Śrî Varaha Mihirâchârya.

CHAPTER THE XVII.

ON THE MOON AND THE ZODIAC.

शा० वि–वृत्तातामहगुष्णशाकलघुभुक् च्छिप्रप्रसादोऽटनः । कामी दुर्बलजानुरस्थिरधनः शूरोऽङ्गनावल्लभः । सेवाज्ञः कुनखी व्रणाङ्कितशिरा मानी सहोत्थाग्रजः । शक्त्या पाणितलेऽङ्कितोऽतिचपलस्तोयेऽतिभीरुः क्रिये ॥ १ ॥

वृत्ताताम्रदृक् Vrittâtâmradrik, eyes round and ruddy. उष्णशाकलघुभुक् Usna sâkalaghubhuk, eating vegetables warm and fresh but moderately. An abstemious vegetarian, taking fresh and warm things. क्षिप्रप्रसादः Kṣipraprasâdaḥ, very easily satisfied; feeling compassion too easily. अटनः: Aṭanaḥ, wandering; vagrant. कामी Kâmî, lustful; sensual. दुर्बलजानुः: Durbalajânuḥ, of weak knees; of meagre knees. अस्थिरधनः: Asthiradhanaḥ, of fluctuating wealth; at times wealthy, at times poor. शूरः: Sûraḥ, hero; brave warrior. अंगनावल्लभः: Amganâvallabhaḥ, cynosure of women; liked by women. सेवाज्ञः: Sevâjñaḥ, serviceable; knowing how to do service to others. कुनखी Kunakhî, with ugly nails. व्रणाङ्कितशिराः: Vraṇâmkitaśirâḥ, having scars on one's head. मानी Mânî, haughty, arrogant; respectable. सहोत्थाग्रजः: Sahotthâgrajaḥ, the eldest amongst brothers; superior amongst them. शक्त्या Saktyâ, with peculiar marks indicative of strength. पाणितले Pâṇitaḥ, on one's palm. अंकितः: Aṃkitaḥ, marked. अतिचपलः: Atichapalaḥ, very fickle. तोये च Toye cha, and in water. भीरुः: Bhîruḥ, afraid; fearful; timid. क्रिये Kriye, in the sign Meṣa, *i. e.*, when Moon is in the sign Aries.

1. The Moon in the sign Meṣa or Aries during the birth time.

This combination gives the native eyes round and ruddy, makes him a vegetarian and eat moderately fresh and hot things; and his nature is easily relenting. It keeps him very frequently out of doors, making him knock about here and there, prone to travel, and makes him lustful. His knees are meagre and weak; his wealth is not steady; he is a militant and a great hero and he is very much loved by the opposite sex. He knows very well how to serve others; his nails are ugly and there are many scars or marks of great wounds on his head. He is honourable, eldest amongst his brothers and there are marks indicative of strength on the palm of his hand; he is very fickle and timid of water.

शा॰वि॰—कांतः खेलगतिः पृथूरुवदनः पृष्ठास्यपार्श्वांकित-
स्त्यागी क्लेशसहः प्रभुः ककुदवान्कन्याप्रजः श्लेष्मलः ॥
पूर्वैर्बंधुधनात्मजैर्विरहितः सौभाग्ययुक्तः क्षमी
दीप्ताग्निः प्रमदाप्रियः स्थिरसुहृन्मध्यांत्यसौख्यो गवि ॥ २ ॥

कांतः Kântaḥ, lovely; beautiful. खेलगतिः Khelagatiḥ, of playful motions and gestures. पृथु Prithû, broad; wide; large. ऊरुवदनः Urûvadanaḥ, thighs and face. पृष्ठास्यपार्श्वांकितः Priṣṭhâsyapârśvâṅkitaḥ, having some marks on the back, face, and sides. त्यागी Tyâgî, generous; liberal hearted. क्लेशसहः Kleśasahaḥ, patient; enduring. प्रभुः Prabhuḥ, master. ककुद्वान् Kakudvân, having one's neck raised like that of a bull. कन्याप्रजः Kanyâprajaḥ, having many daughters. श्लेष्मलः Śleṣmalaḥ, phlegmatic. पूर्वैः Pûrvaiḥ, first. बंधुधनात्मजैः Bandhudhanâtmajaiḥ, friends, wealth and sons. विरहितः Virahitaḥ, deprived of. सौभाग्ययुक्तः Saubhâgyayuktaḥ, prosperous. क्षमी Kṣamî, forgiving. दीप्ताग्निः Dîptâgniḥ, of strong appetites; voracious; greedy. प्रमदाप्रियः Pramadâpriyaḥ, liked by women. स्थिरसुहृत् Sthirasuhṛit, staunch friend. मध्यांत्यसौख्यः Madhyântasaukhyaḥ, happy in the middle (*i.e.*, youth) and old age. गवि Gavi, in the sign Vṛiṣa, *i.e.*, when the Moon is in Taurus.

2. The Moon in the sign Taurus or Vṛiṣa during the birth time.

This combination makes one fine and lovely and of a beautiful gait, the thighs and face being broad, rather fleshy and heavy. His back, face and sides get marked with some signs; the individual becomes unselfish and generous, capable to endure pain and suffering, can command and authorise over others; his neck is raised; he gives birth to many daughters and is phlegmatic. He will be separated from his former friends, from the money that he first earns and from his first born sons. He will be, however, a fortunate man, forgiving. His appetites will be strong; he will be liked by the other sex; he will become a staunch friend; and the middle and the latter part of his days will be spent happily.

शा०वि०—स्त्रीलोलः सुरतोपचारकुशलस्ताम्रेक्षणः शास्त्रवि-
द्दूतः कुंचितमूर्द्धजः पटुमतिर्हास्येंगितद्यूतवित् ॥
चार्वंगः प्रियवाक्प्रभक्षणरुचिर्गीतप्रियो नृत्यवित्
क्लीबैर्याति रतिं समुन्नतनसश्चंद्रे तृतीयर्क्षगे ॥ ३ ॥

स्त्रीलोलः Strilolaḥ, amative ; fond of women. सुरतोपचारकुशलः Suratopachâra-kuśalaḥ, skilled in the art of lust; clever in sexual union. ताम्रेक्षणः Tâmrekṣaṇaḥ, eyes red. शास्त्रवित् Śâstravit, versed in the Śâstras, दूतः Dûtaḥ, envoy; messenger; an ambassadar. कुंचितमूर्द्धजः Kuñchitamûrdhajaḥ, of curling hair. पटुमतिः Paṭumatiḥ, of sharp intellect. हास्येंगितद्यूतवित् Hâsyengitadyutavit, witty; jolly; doing many gestures and skilled in gambling. चार्वंगः Chârvaṅgaḥ, of graceful limbs. प्रियवाक् Priyavâk, sweet tongued. प्रभक्षणरुचिः Prabhakṣaṇaruchiḥ, voracious; a great eater. गीतप्रियः Gitapriyaḥ, fond of music. नृत्यवित् Nṛityavit, skilled in dancing. क्लीबैः Klibaiḥ, with eunuchs; with timid persons. रतिं Ratim, friendship; intercourse. समुन्नतनसः Samunnatanssaḥ, with an elevated nose (like the beak of some birds). चन्द्रे Chandre, Moon. तृतीयर्क्षगे Tṛitiyarkṣage; in the third sign, *i.e.*, Mithuna or Gemini.

3. The Moon in Gemini or Mithuna.

The native is greatly fond of women and clever in sexual union. His eyes are reddish; he knows Śâstras and can play the part of a messenger. The hairs on his head are curling; he becomes very clever and intelligent; he becomes very witty, a joker and a thorough gambler. His limbs are graceful; he is of smooth and persuasive speech; can eat much, is fond of music; knows well how to dance and joins in coxual union or friendship with eunuchs or timid persons; his nose is tolerably elevated.

शा०वि०—आवक्रद्रुतगः समुन्नतकटिः स्त्रीनिर्जितः सत्सुहृ-
दैवज्ञः प्रचुरालयक्षयधनैः संयुज्यते चन्द्रवत् ॥
ह्रस्वः पीनगलः समेति च वशं साम्ना सुहृद्वत्सल- ।
स्तोयोद्यानरतः स्ववेश्मसहिते जातः शशाङ्के नरः ॥ ४ ॥

आवक्रद्रुतगः Âvakradrutagaḥ, body crooked and going fast. समुन्नतकटिः Samun-natakaṭiḥ, hips raised or elevated, having high hips. स्त्रीनिर्जितः Strinirjitaḥ, under one's wife; subject to the influence of women. सत्सुहृत् Satsuhṛit, an excellent friend. दैवज्ञः Daivajñaḥ, an astrologer. प्रचुरालयः Prachurâlayaḥ, owner of lots of houses. क्षयधनैः Kṣyayadhanaiḥ, with changing (sometimes increasing, sometimes decreasing) wealth. संयुज्यते Saṃyujyate, united. चन्द्रवत् Chandravat, like the (waning or waxing) moon. ह्रस्वः Hrasvaḥ, of short stature. पीनगलः Pînagalaḥ, broad or thick-necked. समेति Sameti, comes ; gets. च Cha, and. वशं Vaśam, capable of being won over. साम्ना Sâmnâ, by sweet and loving words. सुहृद्वत्सलः Suhṛidvatsalaḥ, loving his friends. तोयद्यानरतः Toyadyânarataḥ, liking tanks and gardens. स्ववेश्मसहिते Svaveśmasahite, united with one's own house ; in Karka sign. जातः Jatâḥ, born शशाङ्के Saśâṃke, Moon. नरः Naraḥ, person.

4. The Moon in Cancer.

The individual is in the habit of going fast and his body is not straight; (his body being somewhat crooked); his hips are elevated ; he is completely under the grasp of his wife and other women. He is a good friend and astrologer. He possesses good many houses and there are many ups and downs in his wealth like the wanings and waxings of the Moon. He is of short stature, his neck is broad ; he can be brought over by sweet words ; loves his friends very much ; and is found engaged in making tanks and gardens that he likes.

शा०वि०—तीक्ष्णः स्थूलहनुर्विशालवदनः पिङ्गेक्षणोऽल्पात्मजः । स्त्रीद्वेषी प्रियमांसकाननगः कुप्यत्यकार्ये चिरम् ॥
क्षुत्तृष्णोदरदन्तमानसरुजा सम्पीडितस्त्यागवान् ।
विक्रान्तः स्थिरधीःसुगर्वितमना मातुर्विधेयोऽर्कभे ॥ ५ ॥

तीक्ष्णः Tîkṣṇaḥ, angry ; easily affected. स्थूलहनुः Sthûlah anuḥ, of broad jaws. विशालवदनः Viśâlavadanaḥ, broad face. पिङ्गेक्षणः Piṅgekṣaṇaḥ, of yellow eyes. अल्पात्मजः Alpâtmajaḥ, having a few sons. स्त्रीद्वेषी Strîdveṣi, having a feeling of dislike or hatred towards women. प्रियमांसकाननगः Priyamâṃsakânanagaḥ, liking meat, forests and mountains. कुप्यति Kupyati, becomes angry. अकार्ये Akârye, in unbecoming acts ; in wrong doings. चिरम् Chiram, long. क्षुत्तृष्णोदरदन्तमानसरुजा Kṣuttṛiṣhodaradantamânasarujâ, by hunger, thirst, belly, teeth and mind. सम्पीडितः Sampîḍitaḥ, afflicted ; vexed ; troubled. त्यागवान् Tyâgavân, liberal. विक्रान्तः Vikrântaḥ, powerful. स्थिरधीः Sthiradhîḥ, calm-headed ; cool-headed. सुगर्वितमना Sugarvitamanâ, respectable. मातुः विधेयः Matuḥ vidheyaḥ, obedient to one's mother. अर्कभे Arkabhe, in the sigh of Sun *i.e.*, in Leo.

5. The Moon in the Leo or Simha.

This makes the individual angry and hot tempered, his chin thick, his face broad, his eyes yellow and his offspring very few. He is a hater of women, likes to eat meat and to reside in mountains and forests; and whenever any things are done unbecoming, he gets irritated for a long time. He gets trouble with hunger and thirst; his teeth get troubled and he is also involved in some mental trouble or other. But he is unselfish and charitable, is very high-minded; his intellect is calm and steady and his prowess is great. He is very obedient and respectful to his mother.

शा०वि०—व्रीडामन्थरचारुवीक्षणगतिः स्रस्तांसबाहुः सुखी।
श्लक्ष्णः सत्यरतः कलासु निपुणः शास्त्रार्थविद्धार्मिकः ॥
मेधावी सुरतप्रियः परगृहैर्वित्तैश्च संयुज्यते ।
कन्यायां परदेशगः प्रियवचाः कन्याप्रजोऽल्पात्मजः ॥ ६ ॥

व्रीडामन्थरचारुवीक्षणगतिः: Vriḍâmantharachâruvikṣaṇagatiḥ, bashful and casting a graceful glance languidly and walking slowly. स्रस्तांसबाहुः: Srastâṃsabâhuḥ, shoulders and arms drooping, as it were. सुखी Sukhî, happy. श्लक्ष्णः: Slakṣṇaḥ, of soft body and soft speech. सत्यरतः: Satyarataḥ, truthful. कलासु Kalâsu, in fine arts, *i.e.*, dancing, music, painting, etc. निपुणः: Nipuṇaḥ, skilful. शास्त्रार्थवित् Śâstrârthavit, versed in Śâstras. धार्मिकः: Dhârmikaḥ, religious. मेधावी Medhâvî, intelligent. सुरतप्रियः: Suratapriyaḥ, lustful; passionate. परगृहैः: Paragrihaiḥ, with other's houses. वित्तैः: Vittaiḥ, wealth. Cha, and. संयुज्यते Saṃyujyate, united. कन्यायां Kanyâyâm, when Moon is in the sign Kaṇyâ or Virgo. परदेशगः: Paradeśagaḥ, living in different lands or places. प्रियवचाः: Priyavachâḥ, sweet tongued. कन्याप्रजः: Kanyâprajaḥ, having lots of daughters. अल्पात्मजः: Alpâtmajaḥ, having few sons.

6. The Moon in Kanyâ or Virgo.

This lunar position makes those born under it walk and glance at others with slowness and shyness characteristic of women, the arms and the shoulder hanging as it were loosely; the individual becomes happy, his body being soft and gentle; he is truthful, clever and skilled in various arts, *i.e.*, dancing, music and painting, versed in Śâstras and religions. The native has excellent mental powers, is fond of love intercourses, gets wealth and houses from other sources. There is likelihood of going to distant or foreign lands and the native is very sweet speaking.

शा०वि०—देवब्राह्मणसाधुपूजनरतः प्राज्ञः शुचिः स्त्रीजितः
प्रांशुश्चोन्नतनासिकः कृशचलद्गात्रोऽटनोऽर्थान्वितः ॥
हीनांगः क्रयविक्रयेषु कुशलो देवद्विनामा सरुक्
बंधूनामुपकारकृद्विरुषितस्त्यक्तस्तु तैः सप्तमे ॥ ७ ॥

देवब्राह्मणसाधुपूजनरतः Devabrâhmaṇasâdhupûjanarataḥ, devoted to Devas, Brâhmaṇas and Sâdhus or saints. प्राज्ञः Prâjñaḥ, intelligent. शुचिः Śuchiḥ, uncovetuous; pure; clean. स्त्रीजितः Strîjitaḥ, subject to the influence of wife or women. प्रांशुः च Prâṃśuḥ cha, and tall. उन्नतनासिकः Unnatanâsikaḥ, of elevated nose. कृशचलद्गात्रः Kriśachaladgâtraḥ, limbs, lean and thin. अटनः Aṭanaḥ, fond of travels. अर्थान्वितः Arthânvitaḥ, wealthy. हीनांगः Hînâṃgaḥ, of defective limbs. क्रयविक्रयेषु कुशलः Krayavikrayeṣukuśalaḥ, capable and clever in buying and selling, clever in business. देवद्विनामा Devadvinâmâ, named second time after the name of a Deva. सरुक् Saruk, sickly. बंधूनाम् Bandhûnâm, to friends and kinsmen. उपकारकृत् Upakârakṛit, doing good. विरुषितः Viruṣitaḥ, reproached; abused. त्यक्तः Tyaktaḥ, forsaken; left. Tu, but. तैः Taiḥ, by them. सप्तमे Saptame, in the 7th house, *i.e.*, when Moon is in Tulâ or Libra.

7. The Moon in Librâ or Tulâ.

The person is very devoted in worshipping the Devas, Brâhmanas, and saints, is wise, pure, uncovetuous but controlled by wife or women. He is tall; his nose is elevated. His limbs are weak and lean; he is given to travelling habits and is wealthy. He is of defective limbs, clever in buying and selling. He gets a second name in honour of some Deva. He is afflicted with maladies and is always ready to do good to his friends and kinsmen, though reproached by them and in the end forsaken by them.

मालिनी—पृथुलनयनवक्षा वृत्तजंघोरुजानुर्जनकगुरुवियुक्तः
शैशवे व्याधितश्च ॥ नरपतिकुलपूज्यः पिंगलः क्रूरचेष्टो झष-
कुलिशखगांकश्छन्नपापोऽलिजातः ॥ ८ ॥

पृथुलनयनवक्षा Prithulanayanavakṣâ, eyes and chest broad and spacious. वृत्तजंघोरुजानुः Vrittajaṅghorujânuḥ, thighs, knees, and legs circular (or round). जनकगुरुवियुक्तः Janakaguruviyuktaḥ, separated from father and religious preceptor. शैशवे Śaiśave, in early age. व्याधितः च Vyâdhitaḥ cha, and diseased; and ill. नरपतिकुलपूज्यः Narapatikulapûjyaḥ, worshipped in royal families. पिंगलः Piṅgalaḥ, yellowish;

auburn. क्रूरचेष्टः: Krûrachesṭaḥ, not straightforward; wicked. झषकुलिशखगाङ्कः: Jhaṣakuliśakhagâṃkaḥ, bearing marks of a fish, thunderbolt or bird (in hands or feet or some other limbs). छन्नपापः: Chhannapâpaḥ, secretly vicious. अलिजातः: Alijâtaḥ, born under Moon and Vṛiśchika (Scorpio).

8. The Moon in Scorpio or Vṛiśchika.

This combination makes the individual's eyes and chest wide and spacious, thighs, knees and legs round and fleshy, makes him separated from his father and religious preceptor at an early age and afflicts the native with maladies. The individual is worshipped by royal families; he is yellowish in colour. His actions are not straightforward and he bears in his body some astrological marks of a fish, thunderbolt or a bird. The individual commits vicious deed hiddenly and in great privacy.

शा०वि०—व्यादीर्घास्यशिरोधरः पितृधनस्त्यागी कविर्वीर्यवान् । वक्ता स्थूलरदश्रवोधरनसः कर्मोद्यतः शिल्पवित् ॥
कुब्जांशः कुनखी समांसलभुजः प्रागल्भ्यवान्धर्मविद् ।
बन्धुद्विट् न बलात्समैति च वशं साम्नैकसाध्योऽश्वजः ॥ ९ ॥

व्यादीर्घास्यशिरोधरः: Vyâdîrghâsyaśirodharaḥ, face and neck very long or elongated. पितृधनः: Pitṛidhanaḥ, inheriting father's property. त्यागी Tyâgî, liberal; kind. कविः: Kaviḥ, a literary author; a poet. वीर्यवान् Vîryavân, powerful. वक्ता Vaktâ, a speaker. स्थूलरदश्रवोधरनसः: Sthûlaradaśravodharanasaḥ, teeth, eyes, lips, and nose being very large. कर्मोद्यतः: Karmodyataḥ, energetic in actions. शिल्पवित् Silpavit, a sculptor; author and painter, etc. कुब्जांशः: Kubjâṃśaḥ, shoulders depressed. कुनखी Kunakhî, having bad nails. समांसलभुजः: Samâṃsalabhujaḥ, arms and hands long. प्रागल्भ्यवान् Prâgalbhavân, having genius; witty and mature. धर्मवित् Dharmaviṭ, virtuous. बन्धुद्विट् Bandhudviṭ, hating friends. न Na, not. बलात् Balât, under compulsion. समैति Samaiti, comes (under control). च Cha, and. वशं Baśam, control. साम्ना Sâmnâ, with love; with sweet words. एकसाध्यः: Ekasâdhyaḥ, practicable only. अश्वजः: Aśvajaḥ, born under the Dhanu sign.

9. The Moon in Sagittarius or Dhanu.

The individual's neck and face are very long. He inherits his father's property, is charitable and unselfish, and he is a literary author. He is of great prowess, and can talk well. His teeth, ears, lips and nose are large or thick. He is found always ready to do many works and is a good sculptor. His shoulders are low; his nails are disfigured; his arms are long; he is witty and mature in his speech and manners; religious but hater of his friends and kinsmen. He can be influenced not by force but by sweet words.

शा॰वि॰—नित्यं लालयति स्वदारतनयान् धर्मध्वजोऽधः कृशः । स्वक्षः क्षामकटिर्गृहीतवचनः सौभाग्ययुक्तोऽलसः ॥ शीतालुर्मनुजोऽटनश्च मकरे सत्वाधिकः काव्यकृल्लुब्धोऽगम्यजराङ्गनासु निरतः सन्त्यक्तलज्जोऽघृणः ॥ १० ॥

नित्यं Nityam, always. लालयति Lâlayati, caresses and cherishes. स्वदारतनयान् Svadâratanayâm, one's own wife and children. धर्मध्वजः Dharmadhvajaḥ, hypocrite; impostor in religious matters. अधःकृशः Adhaḥkṛiśaḥ, lower half of the body being lean and thin. स्वक्षः Svakṣaḥ, graceful eyes; eyes being good. क्षामकटिः Kṣâmakaṭiḥ, waist being slender. गृहीतवचनः Gṛihîtavachanaḥ, open to advice; once heard and kept in memory; very retentive; of good memory. सौभाग्ययुक्तः Saubhâgyayuktaḥ, prosperous; of good luck. अलसः Alasaḥ, idle; lethargic. शीतालुः Śîtâluḥ, unable to bear cold. मनुजः Manujaḥ, the human being. अटनः च Atanah cha, and of wandering character. मकरे Makare, under Makara sign. सत्वाधिकः Satvâdhikaḥ, strong and liberal. काव्यकृत् Kâvyakṛit, a literary author. लुब्धः Lubdhaḥ, covetous; avaricious. अगम्यजराङ्गनासु Agamyajarâmganâsu, with tabooed old women; with old women of low caste. निरतः Nirataḥ, addicted to. सन्त्यक्तलज्जः Saṃtaktyalajjaḥ, shameless; impudent. अघृणः Aghṛiṇaḥ, heartless, merciless.

10 The Moon in Makara or Capricorn.

The individual always cherishes and supports his wife and children, is an hypocrite in religion; the lower half of his body is lean and thin. His eyes are nice and graceful and his waist is slender. He is open to advice, and has a very retentive memory; he is fortunate but idle. He is unable to bear cold and is prone to travel. He is strong and liberal, and composer of literary works. He is covetous and holds illicit intercourse with tabooed old women (of low caste). He is shameless and heartless.

तोटक—करभगलः शिरालुः खरलोमशदीर्घतनुः पृथुचरणोरुपृष्ठजघनास्यकटिर्जरठः ॥ परवनितार्थपापनिरतः क्षयवृद्धियुतः प्रियकुसुमानुलेपनसुहृद्घटजोऽध्वसहः ॥ ११ ॥

करभगलः: Karabhagalaḥ, having a neck like that of a camel. शिरालुः: Sirâluḥ, nerve, vein being visible all throughout the body. खरलोमशदीर्घतनुः: Kharalomaśadirghatanuḥ, having a tall body, rough and covered with hairs. पृथुचरणोरुपृष्ठजघनास्यकटिः: Prithucharaṇorupriṣṭhajaghanâsyakaṭiḥ, having feet, thighs, back, hip, face, and waist, long and broad. जरठः: Jaraṭhaḥ, illiterate. परवनितार्थपापनिरतः: Paravanitârthapâpaniratḥ, addicted to others' wives, others' wealth and interested in the wicked deeds of others. क्षयवृद्धियुतः: Kṣayavṛiddhiyutaḥ, subject to rise and fall by turns. प्रियकुसुमानुलेपनसुहृत् Priyakusumânulepanasuhṛit, liking flowers, emollients, and friends. घटजः: Ghaṭajaḥ, born when Moon is in Kumbha or Aquarius. अध्वसहः: Adhvasahaḥ, capable to bear fatigue in long marches on roads.

11. The Moon in Aquarius or Kumbha.

The individual will have a neck like that of a camel; his nerves and veins, being very prominent and visible all throughout; his body will be hairy, hairs being rough and thick; he will be of a tall stature; his feet, thighs, back, hip, face and waist being long and broad; the native will be quite illiterate. He will hold illicit connection with others' wives and will be involved with others' wealth. He will be vicious and there will be many ups and downs in life. The native will have a liking for flowers, emollients and friends and will be able to stand the troubles of long marches on roads.

मालिनी—जलपरधनभोक्ता दारवासोऽनुरक्तः समरुचिरशरीरस्तुंगनासो बृहत्कः ॥ अभिभवति सपत्नान्स्त्रीजितश्चारुदृष्टिर्द्युतिनिधिधनभोगी पंडितश्चांत्यराशौ ॥ १२ ॥

जलपरधनभोक्ता Jalaparadhanabhoktá, enjoying others' wealth or what is obtained by selling pearls, jewels or the produce of the sea. दारवासोऽनुरक्तः: Dâravâsonuraktaḥ devoted to wife, property and clothings or dresses. समरुचिरशरीरः: Samaruchiraśarîraḥ, of fully developed limbs and fair body. तुंगनासः: Tumganâsaḥ, having a prominent nose. बृहत्कः: Brihatkaḥ, of large head. अभिभवति Abhibhavati, overpowers, सपत्नान् Sapatnân, enemies. स्त्रीजितः: Strîjitaḥ, conquered by wife or other women. चारुदृष्टिः: Châruḍriṣṭiḥ, of eyes good looking. द्युतिनिधिधनभोगी Dyutinidhidhanabhogî, one beautiful and enjoying wealth and hidden properties. पंडितः Panḍitaḥ, Pandit; a learned man. च Cha, and. अंत्यराशौ Antyarâśau, in the last sign, *i.e.*, when Moon is in the sign Mîna or Pisces.

12. The Moon in Pisces or Mîna.

The person born under this combination will earn money by the sale of pearls, jewels and other sea products; will enjoy money earned by other persons; will be fond of his wife, his property and clothings or dresses; his body will be evenly built and he will be beautiful; his nose will be long and prominent, and the native will possess a very big head. He will overpower his adversaries but he himself will be overpowered by his wife or other women. His eyes will be beautiful. He will enjoy the hidden wealth obtained accidentally and the beauty of his body. The native will also be a learned scholar.

भ्रमरविलसित—बलवति राशौ तदधिपतौ च स्वबलयुतः स्याद्यदि तुहिनांशुः। कथितफलानामविकलदाता शशिवदतोऽन्ये त्यनुपरिचिंत्याः ॥ १३ ॥

इति श्रीवराहमिहिराचार्यप्रणीते बृहज्जातके चन्द्रराशिशीलाध्यायः सप्तदशः ॥ १७ ॥

बलवति Balavati, on becoming powerful. राशौ Râśau, the sign where the Moon is during the birth time. तदधिपतौ Tadadhipatau, the ruler of the sign (above mentioned) च Cha, and. स्वबलयुतः Svabalayutaḥ, on becoming powerful. स्यात् Syât, be. यदि Yadi, if. तुहिनांशुः Tuhinâṃśuḥ, the Moon. कथितफलानाम् Kathitaphalânâm, the fruits; results above mentioned. अविकलदाता Avikaladâtâ, the full bestower. शशिवत् Śaśivat, like the results of Moon. अतः Ataḥ, from this. अन्ये Anye, with other planets than the Moon. इति Iti, thus. अनुपरिचिंत्याः Anuparichintyâḥ, should be thus considered subsequently.

13. Now the results that have been already mentioned will be fully brought into display when (1) the sign where the Moon existed during the birth time, (2) the ruler of this sign, and (3) the Moon, these three be all powerful (not

afflicted in any way) and united or aspected by benefics. Such should be considered also, while judging of the other planets and the signs to be described in the following Chapter.

Note.—(*a*) If two of the three be powerful, the results will not be so full; if one only be powerful, the results will be very feeble and if none of the three be powerful, no effects will be seen.

Thus ends the Seventeenth Chapter of the Bṛihajjâtaka on the Moon and the signs, by Śrî Varâha Mihirâchârya.

CHAPTER XVIII.

ON THE PLANETS AND THE ZODIAC.

औपछंदसिक—प्रथितश्चतुरोऽटनोऽल्पवित्तः क्रियगे त्वायुधभृद्वितुङ्गभागे । गवि वस्त्रसुगन्धपण्यजीवी वनिताद्विट् कुशलश्च गेयवाद्ये ॥ १ ॥

प्रथितः Prathitaḥ, well celebrated. चतुरः Chaturaḥ, clever; skilful; intelligent. अटनः Aṭanaḥ, walker; prone to travel; of travelling habits. अल्पवित्तः Alpavittaḥ, slightly wealthy; not so wealthy. क्रियगे Kriyage, when the Sun is in Aries. तु Tu, but. आयुधभृत् Âyudhabhṛit, earning one's livelihood by using weapons of warfare; a military man; a soldier. वितुङ्गभागे Vituṅgabhâge, not in the highly exalted degrees of Aries. गवि Gavi, in the sign Vṛiṣa; when the Sun is in Taurus. वस्त्रसुगन्धपण्यजीवी Vastrasugundhapaṇyajîvî, a cloth merchant, or perfumery, or general merchant. वनिताद्विट् Vanitâdvit, disagreeing with wife and other females. कुशलः Kuśalaḥ, well trained. गेयवाद्ये Geyavâdye, in music and singing.

1. The Sun and the sign Meṣa or Aries.

When the Sun is in that portion of Aries which is not exalted, then the individual born will become celebrated, dexterous, somewhat crafty and of wandering habits; he will possess small wealth and will earn his livelihood as a professional soldier. (But when the Sun is in the exalted portion of the sign Meṣa or Áries, then the bad results, *e.g.* very little wealth and proneness to travel, &c., will not take place; the native will get more auspicious results.) (1.)

The Sun in Taurus.

When the Sun is in the sign Vṛiṣa or Taurus, the individual born will earn his livelihood as a cloth merchant or will sell sweet scents and oils or will become a general merchant. He will dislike the company of his wife or other females and will be skilled in singing and music.

Note.—A person born with the Sun exalted in Meṣa will be very rich, will remain in a place and will have numerous armed servants, will be celebrated and able.

शा० वि०—विद्याज्योतिषवित्तवान्मिथुनगे भानौ कुलीरे स्थिते तीक्ष्णोऽस्वः परकार्यकृच्छ्रमपथक्लेशैश्च संयुज्यते । सिंहस्थे वनशैलगोकुलरतिर्वीर्यान्वितोऽज्ञः पुमान् कन्यास्थे लिपिलेख्य काव्यगणितज्ञानान्वितः स्त्रीवपुः ॥ २ ॥

विद्याज्योतिषवित्तवान् Vidyâyyotiṣavittavân, a scholar, an astrologer, and a wealthy individual. मिथुनगे Mithunage, in the sign of Mithuna. भानौ Bhânau, on the Sun being. कुलीरे Kulîre, when the Sun is in Karka. स्थिते Sthite, being situated. तीक्ष्णः Tîkṣṇaḥ, fierce; surly; hot; wrathful; passionate. अस्वः Asvaḥ, poor; indigent; without wealth. परकार्यकृत् Parakâryakṛit, servants of others; doing others' works. श्रमपथक्लेशैः Śramapathakleśaiḥ, feeling exhausted from foot journey. च Cha, and. संयुज्यते Saṃyujyate, yoked; engaged. सिंहस्थे Siṃhasthe, when the Sun is in Siṃha or Leo. वनशैलगोकुलरतिः Vanaśailagokularatiḥ, fond to live in forests, mountains, and cowsheds. वीर्यान्वितः Vîryânvitaḥ, vigorous; strong. अज्ञः Ajñaḥ, illiterate. पुमान् Pumân, the individual. कन्यास्थे Kanyâsthe, when the Sun is in Kanyâ or Virgo. लिपिलेख्यकाव्यगणितज्ञानान्वितः Lipilekhyakâvyagaṇitajñânânvitaḥ, skilled in writing, painting, literature, and mathematics (*e.g.*, astrology, &c). स्त्रीवपुः Strîvapuḥ, having bodies like females.

2. The Sun in the signs Gemini (Mithuna), Cancer (Karka), Leo (Siṃha), and Virgo (Kanyâ) respectively.

The Sun in Mithuna:—Learned (in grammar or kindred subjects), versed in astrology and wealthy.

The Sun in Karka——Fierce; hot tempered, irritable; poor; agent or manager of others; earning one's livelihood by hard toils and fatigued by long marches on roads.

The Sun in Leo——Lover of mountains and forests and cowshed; very powerful and high-minded but illiterate.

The Sun in Virgo——Writer, painter, poet, mathematician, and well up in other subjects of knowledge. But he possesses a feminine body.

शा० वि०—जातस्तौलिनि शौंडिकोऽध्वनिरतो हैरण्यको नीचकृत् क्रूरः साहसिको विषार्जितधनः शस्त्रांतगोऽलिस्थिते । सत्पूज्यो धनवान्धनुर्द्धरगते तीक्ष्णो भिषक्कारुको नीचोऽज्ञः कुवणिङ्मृगेऽल्पधनवाँल्लुब्धोऽन्यभाग्ये रतः ॥ ३ ॥

जातः Jâtaḥ, born. तौलिनि Taulini, under the Libra or Tulâ. शौण्डिकः Śauṇḍikaḥ, distiller; vintner. अध्वनिरतः Adhvaniratah, one walking and walking. हैरण्यकः Hairaṇyakaḥ, a goldsmith. नीचकृत् Nîchakṛitt, doing servile or mean works. क्रूरः Krûraḥ, cruel; mischievous; wicked. साहसिकः Śâhasikaḥ, daring. विषार्जितधनः Viṣarjitadhanaḥ, earning money by selling poisons. शस्त्रान्तगः Sastrântagaḥ, skilful in the art of warfare or handling weapons. अलिस्थिते Alisthithe, in the sign Vṛiśchika; when the Sun is in the sign Scorpio. सत्पूज्यः Satpûjyaḥ, fit for saint-like worship; fit to be respected even by the saints. धनवान् Dhanavân, wealthy. धनुर्धरगते Dhanurdharagate, in the sign Dhanu. तीक्ष्णः Tîkṣṇaḥ, fiery; keen; intelligent. भिषक् Bhiṣak, physician. कारुकः Kârukaḥ, workman; artist. नीचः Nîchaḥ, mean; vile, low. अज्ञः Ajñaḥ, illiterate. कुवणिक् Kuvaṇik, a bad merchant. मृगे Mṛige, when the Sun is in Mṛiga or Capricornus. अल्पधनवान् Alpadhanavân, slightly wealthy; somewhat rich. लुब्धः Lubdhaḥ, avaricious; covetous; greedy. अन्यभाग्यैः Anyabhâgyaiḥ, by others' fortunes. रतः Rataḥ, living by; taking advantage of.

Note.—Some read. वृथार्जितधनः Vrithârjitadhanaḥ, one whose earnings are spent in vain for "विषार्जितधनः"

3. The Sun in the signs Tulâ (Libra), Vṛiśchika (Scorpio), Dhanu (Sagittarii) and Makara (Capricorn) respectively.

The Sun in Tulâ——Distiller, vintner; always on foot on roads; a goldsmith; doing low services.

The Sun in Vṛiśchika——Cruel; adventuresome, bold; earning money by selling poisons; skilful in the art of warfare. (The result might be that his earnings may be spent in vain).

The Sun in Dhanu——Worshipped by saints, wealthy, keen, intelligent, physician and artist or sculptor.

The Sun in Makara——Vile, low, illiterate, a merchant dealing in mean articles, somewhat wealthy, avaricious and taking benefit of other's fortunes and help.

व० ति०—नीचो घटे तनयभाग्यपरिच्युतोऽस्वस्तोयोत्थपण्यविभवो बनितादृतोऽन्त्ये । नक्षत्रमानवतनुप्रतिमे विभागे लक्ष्मादिशेत्तुहिनरश्मिदिनेशयुक्ते ॥ ४ ॥

नीचः Nîchaḥ, doing low, mean works. घटे Ghaṭe, when the Sun is in Kumbha or Aquarius. तनयभाग्यपरिच्युतः Tanayabhâgyaparichutaḥ, bereft of sons and fortune. अस्वः Asvaḥ, poor; not having money. तोयोत्थपण्यविभवः Toyotthapaṇyavibhavaḥ, earning money by selling jewels, pearls or other sea-products. वणिताद्दृतः Vanitâdritaḥ, honoured by wife. अन्त्ये Antye, when the Sun is in the sign Mîna or Pisces. नक्षत्रमानवतनुप्रतिमे Nakṣatramânavatanupratime, corresponding to the portion of the body of the Zodiacal Man (Kâlapuruṣe) which the sign in question (the Sun and Moon both existing here) indicates. विभागे Vibhâge, part or portion of the body; limb. लक्ष्मा Lakṣmâ, mole or other signs; marks. आदिशेत् Adiśet, tell; to be declared. तुहिनरश्मिदिनेशयुक्ते Tuhinaraśmidineśayukte, the Sun and the Moon united in the sign.

4. The Sun in Aquarius or Kumbha.

The individual born under this combination will do deeds unsuited to his rank in life and will lose his sons and fortune. He will become poor.

The Sun in the sign Pisces or Mîna.

The individual will become fortunate in acquiring money by the sale of pearls, jewels, and other sea-products. He will be very much honoured and loved by women and will possess a mole or other marks on the part of the body corresponding to that of the Zodiacal Man indicated by the sign occupied by the Sun and Moon together.

त्रोटक—नरपतिसत्कृतोऽटनश्चमूपवणिक्सधनः क्षततनुश्चौरभूरिविषयांश्च कुजः स्वगृहे ॥ युवतिजितान्सुहृत्सु विषमान् परदाररतान् कुहकसुवेषभीरुपरुषान्सितभे जनयेत् ॥ ५ ॥

नरपतिसत्कृतः Narapatisatkritaḥ, honoured by kings. अटनः Aṭanaḥ, walker; prone to travel. चमूपवणिक्सधनः Chamupavaṇiksadhanaḥ, commander, merchant, and a wealthy man. क्षततनुः Kṣatatanuḥ, body with many scars or marks of wounds. चौरः Chauraḥ, thief. भूरिविषयान् Bhûriviṣayân, having one's mind diverted to various things; having one's senses directed to many things. Of divided attention and hence somewhat of restless mind. च Cha, and. कुजः Kûjaḥ, Mars. स्वगृहे Svagrihe, in his own houses, *i.e.*, in the 1st and 8th houses; in Aries and Vriśchika. युवतिजितान् Yuvatijitân, one subject to one's wife. सुहृत्सु Suhritsu, towards friends. विषमान् Viṣamân, disagreeing; not on favourable terms. परदाररतान् Paradâraratân, in connection with other's wives. कुहकसुवेषभीरुपरुषान् Kuhakasuveṣabhîruparuṣân, magician, fond of dressing, timid, and heartless. सितभे Sîtabhe, in the houses of Venus, *i.e.*, in Vriṣa and Tulâ, in Taurus and Libra. जनयेत् Janayet, produces.

5. Mars in Meṣa (Aries) or Vriśchika (Scorpio) (Mars' houses).

The individual born under this combination will be honoured by kings, will become the commander of an army and will be a traveller. He will become a trader and a rich person ; get in his body marks of wounds in some warfare ; will be a thief ; will possess many things and enjoy many pleasures and hence his attention will be divided.

Mars in Vṛisaḥ (Taurus) and Tulâ (Libra) (Venus' houses).

The person will become subject to the influence of women, will be on bad terms with his friends, will be in illicit intercourse with others' wives. The man will become a magician, will be fond of good shows and fine clothings, timid, and of coarse speech and no affection.

व० ति०—बौधेऽसहस्तनयवान्विसुहृत्कृतज्ञो गांधर्वयुद्धकुशलः कृपणोऽभयोऽर्थी ॥ चांद्रेऽर्थवान्सलिलयानसमर्जितस्वः प्राज्ञश्च भूमितनये विकलः खलश्च ॥ ६ ॥

बौधे Baudhe, when Mars is in the houses of Mercury, *i.e.*, in Mithuna and Kanyâ (in Gemini, and Virgo). असहः Asahaḥ, spirited and intolerant. तनयवान् Tanayavân, having lots of children. विसुहृत् Visuhṛit, wanting friends. कृतज्ञः Kritajñaḥ, grateful. गांधर्वयुद्धकुशलः: Gândharbayuddhakuśalaḥ, expert in singing and warfare. कृपणः: Kṛipaṇaḥ, miser. अभयः: Abhayaḥ, fearless. अर्थी Arthî, wanting money ; desirous of wealth. चांद्रे Chândre, when Moon is in Karka or Cancer. अर्थवान् Arthavân, wealthy. सलिलयानसमर्जितस्वः: Salilayânasamarjitasvaḥ, earning money by business of ships ,&c. प्राज्ञः: Prâjñaḥ, intelligent ; learned. च Cha, and. भूमितनये Bhûmitanaye, Mars. विकलः: Vikalaḥ, of defective limbs. खलः: Khalaḥ, wicked ; cheat ; a deceitful person.

6. Mars in Mithuna and Kanyâ (houses of Mercury).

The person will become spirited and intolerant, will get many sons, and no friends, doing good to others, and clever in music, singing, and in the knowledge of warfare. The individual will be a miser, fearless, and desirous of wealth.

Mars in Karka (Cancer) (Moon's house).

The native will become rich, will earn money by ship business and crossing seas, will be learned, will be of defective body and will turn out a wicked and deceitful person.

श्रा० वि०—निःस्वः क्लेशसहो वनांतरचरः सिंहेऽल्पदा-
रात्मजो जैवे नैकरिपुर्नरेंद्रसचिवः ख्यातोऽभयोल्पात्मजः ।
दुःखार्तो विधनोऽटनोऽनृततरतस्तीक्ष्णश्च कुंभस्थिते भौमे भूरि-
धनात्मजो मृगगते भूपोऽथवा तत्समः ॥ ७ ॥

निःस्वः Niḥsvaḥ, without any property. क्लेशसहः Kleśasahaḥ, patient; enduring; suffering patiently. वनान्तरचरः Vanântaracharaḥ, wandering in the forests. सिंहे Siṃhe, when the Mars is in Leo or Siṃha. अल्पदारात्मजः Alpadârâtmajaḥ, having a few wives and children. जैवे Jaive, in the houses of Jupiter, in Dhanu or Mîna. न एकरिपुः Na ekaripuḥ, having many enemies. नरेंद्रसचिवः Narendrasachivaḥ, royal minister. ख्यातः Khyâtaḥ, well-celebrated. अभयः Abhayaḥ, fearless. अल्पात्मजः Alpâtmajaḥ, having few children. दुःखार्तः Duḥkhârtaḥ, afflicted; troubled with pain. विधनः Vidhanaḥ, poor. अटनः Aṭanaḥ, one prone to travel; a traveller. अनृतरतः Anṛitaratah, one telling lies; a liar. तीक्ष्णः Tîkṣṇaḥ, irritable; hot; independent. च Cha, and. कुंभस्थिते Kumbhasthite, when Mars is in Kumbha or Aquarius. भौमे Bhaume, on Mars being. भूरिधनात्मजः Bhûridhanâtmajaḥ, having much riches and many children. मृगगते Mṛigagate, when Mars is in Makara or Capricorn. भूपः Bhûpaḥ, king. अथवा Athavâ, or. तत्समः Tatsamaḥ, equal to a king; like a king; king-like.

7. Mars in Siṃha (Leo), Dhanu (Sagittarius) Mîna (Pisces), Kumbha (Aquarius) and Makara (Capricornus) respectively.

Mars in Siṃha (Leo)—a person born under this combination will become poor, and enduring, a wanderer in the forests, and will possess a few wives and children.

Mars in Dhanu or Mîna—The native will get many enemies, will become a royal minister, will be well reputed, fearless and will get very few children.

Mars in Kumbha (Aquarius)—The individual born under this planetary combination will become afflicted with miseries, deprived of wealth and addicted to falsehood. He will be a traveller and of an independent temper.

Mars in Makara (Capricorn)—This combination makes the individual owner of abundance of wealth and sons, a king or like a king.

व० ति०—द्यूतर्णपानरतनास्तिकचौरनिःस्वाः कुस्त्रीककूटकृदसत्यरताः कुजर्क्षे । आचार्यभूरिसुतदारधनार्जनेष्टाः शौक्रे वदान्यगुरुभक्तिरताश्च सौम्ये ॥ ८ ॥

द्यूतर्णपानरतनास्तिकचौरनिःस्वाः Dyûtarṇapânaratanâstikachauraniḥsvâḥ, a gambler, debtor, drunkard, atheist, thief and an impoverished person. कुस्त्रीककूटकृदसत्यरताः Kustrîkakûṭakṛidasatyaratâḥ, having a debauched wife, deceitful, and arrogant and addicted to falsehood. कुजर्क्षे Kujarkṣe, when Mercury is in Mar's houses, *i.e.*, in Meṣa and Vṛiśchika. आचार्यः Âchâryaḥ, preacher; teacher; spiritual guide. भूरिसुतदारधनार्जनेष्टाः Bhûrisutadâradhanârjaneṣṭâḥ, having many children and wives and always engaged in earning money. शौक्रे Śaukre, when Mercury is in Vṛiṣa or Tulâ, Taurus or Libra. वदान्यगुरुभक्तिरताः Vadânyagurubhaktiratâḥ, generous and a devotee to one's Guru, alms-giving and a religious person attached to his spiritual guide. च Cha, and. सौम्ये Saumye, on Mercury being.

8. Mercury in Meṣa (Aries), Vṛiśchika (Scorpio), Tulâ (Libra) and Vṛiṣa (Taurus) respectively.

Mercury in Meṣa or Vṛiśchika—This combination makes the native a gambler, debtor, drunkard, atheist, thief and an impoverished person. His wife will become debauched; he will become deceitful, insolent and addicted to falsehood.

Mercury in Vṛiṣa or Tulâ—The man will become a preacher; will get many wives and children and will be already intent in earning money. He will be also liberal and very much devoted to his Gurû or spiritual preceptor.

उपेंद्रवज्रा—विकत्थनः शास्त्रकलाविदग्धः प्रियंवदः सौख्यरतस्तृतीये । जलार्जितस्वः स्वजनस्य शत्रुः शशांकजे शीतकरर्क्षयुक्ते ॥ ६ ॥

विकत्थनः Vikatthanaḥ, liar; garrulous; talkative. शास्त्रकलाविदग्धः Śastrakalâvidagdhaḥ, versed in Śâstras or religious books and in fine arts, *i.e.*, music, painting, singing, &c. प्रियंवदः Priyamvadaḥ, speaking sweet and appropriate words. सौख्यरतः Saukṣyarataḥ, fond of pleasures; ease loving. तृतीये Tritiye, when Mercury is in Mithuna or 3rd house. जलार्जितस्वः Jalârjitasvâḥ, earning money by the sale of pearls, jewels and other sea-products. स्वजनस्य शत्रुः: Svajanasya śatruḥ, enemies to one's own friends and relations. शशांकजे Śaśâṃkaje, Mercury. शीतकरर्क्षयुक्ते Śitakararkṣayukte, when in Karka sign, the sign of the Moon.

9. Mercury in Mithuna (Gemini) or Karka (Cancer.)

Mercury in Mithunà.—The individual born under this combination will talk much (ironically), will become well versed in Śâstras and fine arts, music, painting, singing, &c., will speak sweet words and will always be fond of ease and convenience.

Mercury in Karka.—The person born will earn money by the sale of jewels, pearls and other sea products and will become an enemy to his own friends and relations.

प्रहर्षिणी—स्त्रीद्वेष्यो विधनसुखात्मजोऽटनोऽज्ञः स्त्रीलोलः स्वपरिभवोऽर्कराशिगे ज्ञे । त्यागी ज्ञः प्रचुरगुणः सुखी क्षमावान् युक्तिज्ञो विगतभयश्च षष्ठराशौ ॥ १० ॥

स्त्रीद्वेष्यः Strîdveṣyaḥ, disliked by women. अविधनसुखात्मजः Vidhanasukhâtmajaḥ, deprived of money, happiness and children. अटनः Aṭanaḥ, one prone to travel; traveller; walker. अज्ञः Ajñaḥ, illiterate; ignorant. स्त्रीलोलः Strîlolaḥ, hankering after women; eagerly desirous of women. स्वपरिभवः Svaparibhavaḥ, defeated by one's own relations; suffering disgrace from one's own relations. अर्कराशिगे ज्ञे Arkarâśige jñe, when Mercury is in the Sun's sign, *i.e.*, in the sign Siṃha or Leo. त्यागी Tyâgî, generous. ज्ञः Jñaḥ, a learned scholar. प्रचुरगुणः Prachuraguṇaḥ, well and variously qualified; possessing many virtues. सुखी Sukhî, happy; living in comfort. क्षमावान् Kṣamâvân, forgiving. युक्तिज्ञः Yuktijñaḥ, knowing; reasoning; capable to make one understand through reasoning. विगतभयः च Vigatabhayaḥ cha, and fearless. षष्ठराशौ Ṣaṣṭharâśau, in the sixth sign; when Mercury is in Virgo or Kanyâ.

10. Mercurv in Siṃha (Leo) or Kanyâ (Virgo) respectively.

Mercury in Siṃha.—The person born will be disliked, rather hated by his wives or women; and will become deprived of money, happiness and children. He will be a traveller and an illiterate person. He will eagerly desire women, and suffer disgrace from his own relations.

Mercury in Kanyâ.—The person born under this combination will become unselfish, generous, a learned scholar, endowed with many qualities, happy, forgiving, will know how to convince others by reasoning and will be void of any fear.

औपच्छंदसिक—परकर्मकृदस्वशिल्पबुद्धी ऋणवान्विष्टिकरो

बुधेऽर्कजर्क्षे ॥ नृपसत्कृतपंडिताप्तवाक्यो नवमेंऽत्ये जितसेवकोंऽ-

त्यशिल्पः ॥ ११ ॥

परकर्मकृत् Parakarmakrit, doing others' works; working for other men. अस्वः Asvaḥ, poor; indigenous. शिल्पबुद्धिः Śilpabuddhiḥ, intelligent in arts; a sculptor. ऋणवान् Riṇavân, running into debt; apt to take away others' things but not to return them. विष्टिकरः Viṣṭikaraḥ, attending on others' calls for no fees. Carrying out others' orders for no fees. बुधे Budhe, Mercury. अर्कजर्क्षे Arkajarkṣe, in Saturn's sign, *i.e.*, in Makara and Kumbha; in Capricorn and Aquarius. नृपसत्कृतपंडिताप्तवाक्यः Nṛipasatkṛitapaṇḍitâptavâkyaḥ, honoured by kings; learned in sciences and laws. नवमे Navame, in the ninth sign, *i.e.*, in Dhanu or Sagittarius. अंत्ये Antye, in Mîna, the 12th sign; in Pisces, the last sign. जितसेवकः Jitasevakaḥ, an intelligent servant, serving or attending cleverly and intelligently; readily discovering the views of other people. अंत्यशिल्पः Antyaśilpaḥ, an artisan of a low order.

11. Mercury in Makara (Capricornus), Kumbha (Aquarius), Dhanu (Sagittarius) and Mîna (Pisces).

Mercury in Makara or Kumbha.—The man will be engaged in the services of others, poor, will have some tact for sculpturing, will be a debtor, and will attend on others' calls for no fees.

Mercury in Dhanu.—The native will get honours from kings, will become learned in sciences and laws.

Mercury in Mîna.—The native will be an intelligent and faithful servant or will be able to befriend other men and will readily discover the views of other people and will also be an artisan of a low order.

शा०वि०—सेनानीर्बहुवित्तदारतनयो दाता सुभृत्यः क्षमी तेजोदारगुणान्वितः सुरगुरौ ख्यातः पुमान्कौजभे ॥ कल्पांगः सधनार्थमित्रतनयस्त्यागी प्रियः शौक्रभे बौधे भूरिपरिच्छदात्मजसुहृत्साचिव्ययुक्तः सुखी ॥ १२ ॥

सेनानीः Senânîḥ, commander of an army. बहुवित्तदारतनयः Bhuvittadâratanayaḥ, having much wealth, many wives and sons. दाता Dâtâ, a generous person; a giver; donor.. सुभृत्यः Subhrityaḥ, a good and faithful servant. क्षमी Ksamî, forgiving. तेजोदारगुणान्वितः Tejodâraguṇânvitaḥ, gifted with a beautiful spirited wife and with many qualities. सुरगुरौ Suragurau, Jupiter. ख्यातः Kṣyâtaḥ, well renowned. पुमान् Pumân, man; the individual born. कौजभे Kaujabhe, in Aries and Scorpio; when Jupiter is in Meṣa and Vṛiśchika, the Mars' houses. कल्पांगः Kalpâṃgaḥ, of strong and vigorous body; free from diseases. सधनार्थमित्रतनयः Sadhanârthamitratanayaḥ, wealthy, having friends and children. त्यागी Tyâgî, a giver, generous person. प्रियः Priyaḥ, liked by all. शौक्रभे Śaukrabhe, in Venus's signs, *i. e.*, in Vṛiṣa and Tulâ. बौधे Baudhe, in Mercury's signs, *i. e.*, in Mithuna and Kanyâ; in Gemini and Virgo. भूरिपरिच्छदात्मजसुहृत् Bhûriparichchadâtmajasuhṛit, having many clothes, houses, servants, wives, sons and friends. साचिव्ययुक्तः Sâchivyayuktaḥ, a minister. सुखी Sukhî, happy; living in comfort.

12. Jupiter in Meṣa (Aries) and Vṛiśchika (Scorpio), Vṛiṣa (Taurus) and Tulâ (Libra), Mithuna (Gemini) and Kanyâ (Virgo) respectively.

Jupiter in Meṣa or Vṛiśchika.—Commander of an army, one having abundance of wealth and many wives and sons; a giver; a good and faithful servant; of a forgiving nature; having a spirited wife; eminent and endowed with many qualities.

Jupiter in Vṛiṣa and Tulâ.—The man born will possess a strong and vigorous body free from diseases, will always be in possession of wealth, will have friends and sons and will be unselfish, charitable, and liked by all.

Jupiter in Mithuna and Kanyâ.—The man will own many clothes, houses, servants, wives, sons, and friends. He will become a minister and will be happy.

शा॰वि॰—चान्द्रे रत्नसुतस्वदारविभवप्रज्ञासुखैरन्वितः ।
सिंहे स्याद्बलनायकः सुरगुरौ प्रोक्तं च यच्चन्द्रभे ॥ स्वर्क्षे माण्ड-
लिको नरेन्द्रसचिवः सेनापतिर्वा धनी ।
कुम्भे कर्कटवत् फलानि मकरे नीचोऽल्पवित्तोऽसुखी ॥ १३ ॥

चान्द्रे Chândre, when Jupiter is in Karkaṭa, the 4th sign, the sign of Moon. रत्नसुतस्वदारविभवप्रज्ञासुखैः Ratnasutasvadâravibhavaprajñâsukhaiḥ, (endowed) with jewels, sons, property, wives, prosperity, influence, intelligence, and happiness. अन्वितः Anvitaḥ, endowed; united. सिंहे Siṃhe, when Jupiter is in Siṃha or Leo. स्यात् Syât, will become. बलनायकः Balanâyakaḥ, a commander of an army. सुरगुरौ Suragurau, when Jupiter is; on Jupiter being. प्रोक्तं Proktaṃ, said. च Cha, and. यत् Yat, whatever. चन्द्रभे Chandrabhe, in Moon's signs. *i. e.*, in Karka. स्वर्क्षे Svarkṣe, in his own houses. माण्डलिकः Mâṇḍalikaḥ, head of a village (or an assemblage); ruler of a province. नरेन्द्रसचिवः Narendrasachivaḥ, minister to a king. सेनापतिः Senâpatiḥ, commander of an army. धनी Dhanî, wealthy. कुम्भे Kumbhe, when Jupiter is in Kumbha. कर्कटवत् Karkaṭavat, will be all that have been mentioned when Jupiter is in Karkaṭa or Cancer. फलानि Phalâni, fruits. मकरे Makare, when Jupiter is in Makara or Capricorn. नीचः Nîchaḥ, doing acts unbecoming to his family. अल्पवित्तः Alpavittaḥ, with little wealth. असुखी Asukhî, unhappy; afflicted with grief.

13. Jupiter in Karka (Cancer), Siṃha (Leo), Dhanu (Sagittari), Mîna (Pisces), Kumbha (Aquarius) and Makara (Capricorn) respectively.

Jupiter in Karka—The individual will be endowed with jewels, sons, wealth, property, wife, prosperity, influence, intelligence and happiness.

Jupiter in Siṃha—The individual born will become the commander of an army and will get also those mentioned under "Jupiter in Karka," *i.e.*, jewels, sons, property, wife, prosperity, influence, intelligence and happiness.

Jupiter in Dhanu or Mîna—The individual will become the head of an assemblage, or the ruler of a province, a minister to a king, a general and will be wealthy.

Jupiter in Kumbha—The individual will get jewel, sons, property, wife, prosperity, intelligence, and happiness, *i.e.*, all that have been said in the case of a person born with Moon in the sign Cancer.

Jupiter in Makara—The individual will do acts low and unbecoming, will have little wealth and will be miserable.

पुष्पिताग्रा—परयुवतिरतस्तदर्थवादैर्हृतविभवः कुलपांसनः कुजर्क्षे ॥ स्वबलमतिधनो नरेन्द्रपूज्यः स्वजनविभुः प्रथितोऽभयः सिते स्वे ॥ १४ ॥

परयुवतिरतः Parayuvatiratah̤, addicted to others' wives. तदर्थवादैः Tadarthavâdaih̤, through their influence. हृतविभवः Hṛitavibhavah̤, robbed of his properties; deprived of his wealth. कुलपांसनः Kulapâṃsanah̤, bringing disgrace to one's family; a source of family dishonour. कुजर्क्षे Kujarkṣe, in Mars' houses, *i. e.*, in Meṣa or Vṛiśchika. स्वबलमतिधनः Svabalamatidhanah̤, earning money by one's own prowess or intellect. नरेन्द्रपूज्यः Narendrapûjyah̤, honoured by kings. स्वजनविभुः Svajnavibhuh̤, a head amongst his own friends and kinsmen. प्रथितः Prathitah̤, famous. अभयः Abhayah̤, fearless. सिते Site, Venus. स्वे Sve, in her own house, *i.e.*, in Vṛiṣa and Tulâ, *i.e.*, in Taurus and Libra.

14. Venus in Meṣa, (Aries), Vṛiśchika (Scorpio), Vṛiṣa (Taurus), and Tulâ (Libra).

Venus in Meṣa or Vṛiśchika—Addicted to others' wives, losing his property through their influence, and bringing disgrace on his family.

Venus in Vṛiṣa or Tulâ—The individual will earn money by one's own prowess or intellect, will be honoured by kings, will be an head amongst his own friends and relations, will become famous and fearless.

औपच्छंदसिक—नृपकृत्यकरोऽर्थवान् कलाविन्मिथुने षष्ठगतेऽतिनीचकर्मा । रविजर्क्षगतेऽमरारिपूज्ये सुभगः स्त्रीविजितो रतः कुनार्य्याम् ॥ १५ ॥

नृपकृत्यकरः Nṛipakṛityakarah̤, a royal officer. अर्थवान् Arthavân, wealthy. कलावित् Kalâvit, versed in singing, music, &c. मिथुने Mithune, when Venus is in Mithuna or Gemini. षष्ठगते Ṣaṣṭhagate, in the sixth; when Venus is in Kanyâ. अतिनीचकर्मा Atinîchakarmâ, doing vile and hard works. रविजर्क्षगते Ravijarkṣagate, in the signs of Saturn, *i.e.*, in Makara and Kumbha. When Venus is in Capricorn and Aquarius. अमरारिपूज्ये Amarâripûjye, on Venus being in. सुभगः Subhagah̤, liked by every one. स्त्रीविजितः Strîvijitah̤, under women's subjection. रतः Ratah̤, addicted; unlawfully connected with. कुनार्य्याम् Kunâryâm, with bad lewd women.

15. Venus in Mithuna (Gemini) or Kanyâ (Virgo), Makara (Capricorn) or Kumbha (Aquarius).

Venus in Mithuna, a royal officer, wealthy and versed in music, singing, dancing, &c.

Venus in Kanyâ, doing low and hard menial services.

Venus in Makara or Kumbha, of beautiful appearance, liked by all, under the grasp of women and unlawfully connected with debauched and bad women.

शिखरिणी—द्विभार्योऽर्थीभीरुः प्रबलमदशोकश्च शशिभे हरौ योषाप्तार्थः प्रवरयुवतिर्मंदतनयः। गुणैः पूज्यः सस्वस्तुरगसहिते दानवगुरौ झषे विद्वानाढ्यो नृपजनितपूजोऽतिसुभगः॥१६॥

द्विभार्यः: Dvibhâryaḥ, having two wives. अर्थी Arthî, wanting, begging wealth. भीरुः Bhîruḥ, timid; afraid of. प्रबलमदशोकः: Prabalamadaśokaḥ, very passionate and miserable; very haughty and morose. च Cha, and. शशिभे Śaśibhe, in Karka sign, *i.e.*, when Venus is in the sign Karkaṭa or Cancer. हरौ Harau, in Siṃha; when Venus is in the sign Leo. योषाप्तार्थः: Yoṣâptârthaḥ, getting money through wife or women. प्रवरयुवतिः: Pravarayuvatiḥ, the excellent wife being exalted as the most high. मंदतनयः: Mandatanayaḥ, having few sons. गुणैः: Guṇaiḥ, owing to one's being qualified. पूज्यः: Pûjyaḥ, honoured, respected. सस्वः: Sasvaḥ, wealthy. तुरगसहिते Turagasahite, in Dhanu; when Venus is in Sagittarius. दानवगुरौ Danavagurau, Venus. झषे Jjhaṣe, in the sign Mîna; when Venus is in the sign Pisces. विद्वान् Vidvân, a learned man; a wise man; scholar. आढ्यः: Âḍhyaḥ, rich. नृपजनितपूजः: Nṛipajanitapûjaḥ, honoured by kings. अतिसुभगः: Atisubhagaḥ, very lovely; very beautiful; liked by all.

16. Venus in Karka (Cancer), Siṃha (Leo), Dhanu (Sagittarius) and Mîna (Pisces).

Venus in Karka—This combination gives two wives, makes the individual desirous of money, timid, strongly passionate and awfully miserable.

Venus in Siṃha.—The individual born under this combination will get money through wife or women, exalt his excellent wife as the most high, and will possess few sons.

Venus in Dhanu—The person will be highly honoured by many on account of various good qualities and will be wealthy.

Venus in Mîna—The native will be rich, affluent, learned, honoured by kings and will be of beautiful appearance and liked by all.

व० ति०—मूर्खोऽटनः कपटवान्विसुहृद्यमेऽजे कीटेतु बंधवधभाक् चपलोऽघृणश्च । निर्ह्रीसुखार्थतनयः स्खलितश्च लेख्ये रक्षापतिर्भवति मुख्यपतिश्च बौधे ॥ १७ ॥

मूर्खः Mûrkhaḥ, an illiterate ; a fool. अटनः Aṭanaḥ, one prone to travel ; a walker ; a traveller. कपटवान् Kapaṭavân, a cheat ; a deceitful person ; a hypocrite. विसुहृत् Visuhṛit, having no friends. यमे Yame, Saturn. अजे Aje, in Meṣa ; in Aries. कीटे Kîṭe, (when Saturn is) in Vṛiśchika or Scorpio. तु Tu, while ; but. बंधवधभाक् Bandhavadhabhâk, one who kills or binds ; an executioner or hangman or one making captives ; or one suffering imprisonment or blows. चपलः Chapalaḥ, restless ; fickle. अघृणः Aghṛiṇaḥ, heartless. च Cha, and. निर्ह्रीसुखार्थतनयः Nihrîsukhârthatanayaḥ, a shameless, miserable, poor, and sonless person. स्खलितः Skhalitaḥ, illiterate ; wanting knowledge and making mistakes. च Cha, and. लेख्ये Lekhvye, in writing ; in painting. रक्षापतिः Raksâpatiḥ, jailor. भवति Bhavati, becomes. मुख्यपतिः Mukhyapatiḥ, a chief officer ; a chief. च Cha, and. बौधे Baudhe, (when Venus is) in the houses of Mercury, *i.e.*, Mithuna or Kanyâ, *i.e.*, in Gemini or Virgo signs.

17. Saturn in Meṣa (Aries) and Vṛiśchika (Scorpion), Mithuna (Gemini) and Kanyâ (Virgo).

Saturn in Meṣa—The individual born under this combination will become an illiterate, fool, a traveller, and a deceitful person. He will be deprived of friends.

Saturn in Vṛiśchika—The individual will be concerned with acts of killing or capturing, will be fickle and heartless ; (or the individual will suffer imprisonment or receive blows.)

Saturn in Mithuna or Kanyâ—The individual will be shameless, miserable, poor, and a sonless person. The man will make mistakes in writing and painting, will be an illiterate, a jailor, or will become a chief of an assembly or a chief officer.

मंदाक्रांता—वर्ज्यस्त्रीष्टो न बहुविभवो भूरिभार्यो बृषस्थे ख्यातः स्वोच्चे गणपुरबलग्रामपूज्योऽर्थवांश्च कर्किण्यस्वो विकल दशनो मातृहीनोऽसुतोऽज्ञः सिंहेऽनार्यो विसुखतनयो विष्टिकृत्सूर्यपुत्रे ॥ १८ ॥

वर्ज्यस्त्रीष्टः Varjyastrîsṭaḥ, one practising illicit intercourses with women not fit to be approached (women of low caste). न Na, not. बहुविभवः Bahuvibhavaḥ, having much power or property. भूरिभार्यः Bhûribhâryaḥ, having several wives. वृषस्थे Vrisasthe, when Saturn is in Vrisa or Taurus. ख्यातः Khvyâtaḥ, reputed; glorious. स्वोच्चे Svochche, in Saturn's exalted sign, *i.e.*, when Saturn is in Tulâ or Libra. गणपुरबलग्रामपूज्यः Gaṇapurabalagrâmapûjyaḥ, honoured as a chief by an assemblage of persons, by the whole city, by the army, by the village. अर्थवान् Arthavân, wealthy. च Cha, and. कर्किणि Karkiṇi, (when Saturn is) in Karkaṭa or Cancer. अस्वः Asvaḥ, poor. विकलदशनः Vikaladaśanaḥ, having a few teeth. मातृहीनः Mâtṛihînaḥ, motherless; separated from his mother. असुतः Asutaḥ, sonless. अज्ञः Ajñaḥ, knowledgeless. सिंहे Simhe, (when Saturn is) in Leo. अनार्यः Anâryaḥ, one who is not an Ârya; not respectable; unworthy; mean; base. विसुखतनयः Visukhatanayaḥ, having no happiness nor any sons. विष्टिकृत् Viṣṭikrit, a bearer of burdens; a porter. सूर्यपुत्रे Sûryaputtre, on Saturn residing in.

18. Saturn in Vṛiṣa (Taurus), Tulâ (Libra), Karka (Cancer) and Siṃha (Leo).

Saturn in Vṛiṣa—Practising illicit intercourses with women of low caste not fit to be approached, not at all wealthy, having many wives.

Saturn in Tulâ—very eminent, honoured as a chief by an assemblage of persons, by the whole populace of the city, by the army, by the village, and very rich.

Saturn in Karka—Poor, having a few teeth and these defective, deprived of mother and sons; and illiterate.

Saturn in Siṃha—Illiterate and not honoured, unhappy, deprived of sons, and doing the work of a porter.

शा० वि०—स्वंतः प्रत्ययितो नरेंद्रभवने सत्पुत्रजायाधनो जीवत्क्षेत्रगतेऽर्कजे पुरबलग्रामाग्रनेताथवा। अन्यस्त्रीधनसंवृतः पुरबलग्रामाग्रणीर्मंददृक् स्वक्षेत्रे मलिनः स्थिरार्थविभवो भोक्ता च जातः पुमान् ॥ १६ ॥

स्वंत: Svantaḥ, happy in latter age ; or it may mean, having an excellent and noble death. प्रत्ययित: Pratyayitaḥ, one who is trusted; relied upon ; confided in. नरेंद्रभवने Narendrabhavane, in king's palace ; before the king's presence. सत्पुत्रजायाधन: Satputrajâyâdhanaḥ, having good sons, a good wife, and good riches. पुरबलग्रामाग्रनेता Purabalagrâmâgranetâ, the foremost leader in a town, army or village. अथवा Athavâ, or; here it does not convey any meaning. अन्यस्त्रीधनसंवृत: Anyastrîdhana-saṃvṛitaḥ, united with others' wives, with others' riches ; having in his lot these things. पुरबलग्रामाग्रणी: Purabalagrâmâgraṇîḥ, the chief leader amongst townpeople, army, or village. मंददृक् Mandadṛik, of small or defective eyes ; weak-eyed. स्वक्षेत्रे Svakṣetre, in his own signs, *i.e.*, in Makara and Kumbha ; in Capricorn or Aquarius. मलिन: Malinaḥ, dirty ; impure ; sullied ; black ; low ; vile ; base. स्थिरार्थविभव: Sthirârthavibhavaḥ, having one's riches, power and property remaining steady for a long time. भोक्ता Bhoktâ, the enjoyer. च Cha, and. जात: Jâtaḥ, born. पुमान् Pumân, the individual.

19. Saturn in Dhanu (Sagittarius), Mîna (Pisces), Makara (Capricorn) and Kumbha (Aquarius).

Saturn in Dhanu or Mîna (Jupiter's houses).—The individual born under this combination will get confidence in palaces or royal families, will have good sons, a good wife and an abundance of wealth, will become the foremost leader of a village or city people or of an army and will become happy in his old age or die an excellent and a noble death (*i.e.*, not by any accident, *e.g.*, lightning, injury, drowning, poisoning, or premature death).

Saturn in Makara and Kumbha (Saturn's houses.)—The individual will be in illicit connection with others' wives, will gain wealth of other persons, will become the chief leader amongst the village or town people, or within an army ; and will remain dirty and impure. His wealth and prosperity will remain steady and he will enjoy these things, acquired by him.

Note :—The effects will fully come to pass if the planet, the sign occupied by the planet and the ruler of such sign be all powerful ; otherwise the effects will come to pass imperfectly and if none of the three be powerful, the effects will fail. *Vide* the last verse of the preceding Chapter.

पुष्पिताग्रा–शिशिरकरसमागमेक्षणानां सदृशफलं प्रवदन्ति लग्नजातम् । फलमधिकमिदं यदत्र भावाद्भवनभनाथगुणैर्विचिन्तनीयम् ॥ २० ॥

इति श्रीबृहज्जातके राशिशीलाध्यायोऽष्टादशः ॥ १८ ॥

शिशिरकरसमागमेक्षणानां Śiśirakarasamâgamekṣaṇânâm, of "the Moon and the Zodiac" and the "aspects of the Moon." सदृशफलं Sadriśaphalam, the effects similar to what have been described. प्रवदन्ति Pravadanti, they say. लग्नजातम् Lagnajâtam, the effects when each of the twelve signs becomes the rising sign (*i.e.*, the Ascendant). फलम् Phalam, the results; the effects. अधिकं Adhikam, more; extra; more (than what are prescribed in the natures of the signs). इदं Idam, this. यत् Yat, what. अत्र Atra, in this case, *i.e.*, each sign becoming the Ascendant. भावात् Bhâvât, from the natures (of the twelve houses). भवनभनाथगुणैः Bhavanabhanâthaguṇaih, from the Bhavas (*i.e.*, 12 houses) and from their rulers according as both of them or one of them or none are powerful. विचिन्तनीयम् Vichintanîyam, to be judged; to be pondered over before giving out the judgment.

20. The effects that have been mentioned under the heading "The Moon and the Zodiac" (in the preceding Chapter) will also be the effects when that sign becomes the rising sign or the Ascendant. The results that will be mentioned in the subsequent Chapter on Aspects will also be the results when the sign (where the Moon was found and aspected by any planet) becomes also the rising sign (and aspected by the same planet). Nay—the effects here are more due to the rising sign for they extend to the 2nd, 3rd and other Bhâvas (houses). The natures of the twelve houses are also to be considered in connection with their rulers; *e.g.*, when the rising sign is strong and its ruler is also strong, then the nature of the rising sign, *i.e.*, the body, will also be perfectly strong; if the sign be strong, and the ruler a little less strong then the result will also be full; if one be strong and the other not strong, the result will be half weakened; if the two be not strong, then the result will not at all be visible (*i.e.*, the body will not be strong). And so on with other houses of wealth (2), brothers (3), friends (4), (5) sons, (6) enemies, (7) wife, &c.

Note:—The effects are declared similar owing to there being no difference between their natures in the two respective cases; and also because the famous astrologers are of this opinion.

Satyâ, the famous astrologer, writes the following when each sign becomes the Lagna or the rising sign:—

तथा च सत्यः । "मेषविलग्ने कुनखी सुरोपणो भेदकृत्स्खलितवाक्यः । पित्तानिलभूयिष्ठः कृपणोऽतिबहुव्ययश्चैव ॥ रहितो बाल्ये गुरुभिर्मंदसुतः स्वजनसहजहितकर्ता । धर्मस्थितो विदेशोपगश्च कर्मारभत्यफलम् ॥ नीचां वा पिशुनां वा विकलां लभतेऽन्यपूर्विकां भार्याम् । सहजसमान्यपि मित्राणि चास्य बंधुत्वमुपयांति ॥ शस्त्रेण वा विषैर्वा मरणं पित्तोद्भवैर्विकारैर्वा । स्वात्पक्षाज्ज्वलनाद्वा वर्षाद्दुर्गात्प्रपतनाद्वा ॥ वृषभविलग्ने स्थूलोष्ठगंडनासो महाललाटश्च । श्लेष्मानिलभूयिष्ठस्त्यागी बहुशो व्ययरतश्च ॥ कन्याप्रजोऽल्पपुत्रः पितुर्जनन्याश्च दोषकृद्बहुशः । कर्मणि सततं सक्तो विधर्मयुक्तोऽर्थभाक् चैव ॥ नित्यं कलत्रकांक्षी शस्त्रविघाती सदा स्वजनहर्ता । मृत्युः शस्त्रैः पाशैर्मृगैश्च लभतेऽन्यदेशेषु ॥ देहश्रमैर्जलैर्वा शूलैर्वाप्यटननिरसनैश्चैव । पुरुषश्चतुष्पदैर्वा बलान्वितान्मृत्युमुपयाति ॥ पूर्वविलग्ने मिथुने हीनांगः सूयतेऽधिकांगो वा । प्रियवाग्विशिष्टकर्मा मिश्रप्रकृतिर्द्विजननीकः ॥ अल्पमतिरल्पकायः सतां च महितो गुरूणां च । अल्पसहजोऽल्पचेष्टः परावमर्दी गुणयुतश्च ॥ कर्मसु बहुष्वभिरतो धर्मं साधयति न चाथ धर्मेण । प्राप्तांल्लाभान्विविधान्दोषैस्तैस्तैश्च नाशयति ॥ बह्वीः पत्नीर्लभते रोगांश्च दारुणाञ्जयति । व्यालाद्द्विपान्मृगाद्वाप्युदकाद्वा मृत्युमुपयाति ॥ कर्किणि पूर्वविलग्ने नैकाग्रो गुह्यरोगवान् भीरुः । उरसि कृताभिज्ञानः कफानिलात्मा दृढग्राही ॥ पापानहितान्भजते परस्वमपि निक्षिपद्व्ययेन सकृत् । स्वजनाहृतः स्वजनैर्विभर्त्सितो ह्यस्थिरप्रसवः ॥ तीक्ष्णं कर्म विदेशे नित्यं ह्युद्वेदितः परस्वामी । असदृशदारो रिपुनिर्जितश्च पूज्यः समूहानाम् ॥ कंठापीडाद्रज्ज्वा कफोदयादस्थिभंजनाद्भेदात् । देहच्छेदादथवा जलोदरान्मृत्युमाप्नोति ॥ सिंहविलग्ने कठिनः प्रियामिषः पैत्तिको विततनाशः । बह्वारंभकुटुंबः कृपणस्त्वथ संमतः ख्यातः ॥ सहजविषादी स्वजनस्य घातको विक्रमैः स्वकैर्युक्तः । अविषादी कर्मकरो विविधोपायैस्त्वधर्मिष्ठः ॥ भार्या बह्वीर्लभते विंयाद्विविधाः कुलैरुपेताश्च । कट्यां रुजश्च बहुशो जान्वोर्दशनेषु चाप्नोति ॥ मृत्युः शस्त्रैः पापैर्विषैश्च काष्ठैरथामयैश्चापि । मंत्रुचरैर्वा सत्वैर्बुभुक्षया ह्रासमुपयाति ॥ षष्ठविलग्ने प्रियवाक् तनुच्छविर्दीर्घकरचरणः । मिश्रप्रकृतिश्चार्याकृतिर्व्रणी चार्थवान् कृपणः । स्वजनस्येष्टः कन्याबहुप्रजो भ्रातृभिर्विरुद्धश्च । धर्मप्रियोऽल्पलाभः कर्माणि निपुणः समाचरति ॥ त्रिविधाच्चतुष्पदगणाच्छस्त्रात् पित्तोद्भवाद्रोगात् । शोकात्संपाताद्वा मृत्युं चाप्नोति पाशाद्वा ॥ सप्तमराशौ लग्ने विषमांगः सूयते विषमशीलः । कफवातिकः सुचपलो ह्रस्वग्रीवः कृतज्ञश्च ॥ अर्थान्विपुलांल्लभते व्ययेन संपूज्यते यशः प्रायः । गुरुसेवायां निरतः पितान्यजनसहजपूज्यः ॥ अध्वरुचिर्धर्मिष्ठो विनाशमायाति पीडनैः स्वैः स्वैः । मृतभार्यः कलहरुचिर्बहुशः शोकादिभिः क्लिष्टः ॥ मृत्युः ख्यातात्पुरुषात्स्वजनात्सौम्याच्चतुष्पदाद्वापि । खेदाच्च विप्रयोगादुपवासान्मार्गयोगाद्वा ॥ अष्टमराशौ लग्ने विशालरज्ज्वाननोदरः क्रूरः । पित्तप्रकृतिः पिंगेक्षणो मृदुद्रुतगतिः परस्वामी ॥ स्फीतकुटुम्बस्वजनोऽन्तकश्च बहुव्ययो बहुप्रसवः । सुखरहितो भ्रातृव्यो वृषसेवी

धर्महीनश्च ॥ भार्यानिमित्तविमुखो शत्रोरर्थांश्च ददाति बहुशश्च । स्वकुलोद्भूतांश्छत्रूंल्लभते रोगांश्च नैकविधान् ॥ गात्रच्छेदैः शत्रोर्वशं गतो बंधनैः प्रहारैश्च । रोगैर्वा पापकृतैर्ज्वलनाद्वा मृत्युमुपयाति ॥ स्थूलोष्ठदशननासा नवमे लग्ने कफानिलप्रकृतिः । मांसलगुह्योरुभुजः कुनखी कर्मोद्यतः शूरः ॥ क्षुद्रांस्त्रीचान्भजते चौर्यादनलान्नृपाच्च नष्टधनः । विज्ञानानां प्रसवो बहुपूज्यो भ्रातृघातरुचिः ॥ कर्मविदेशेष्विष्टः कुरुते चित्तानि चार्हति नृपेभ्यः । धर्मे तु मध्यममतिर्दारैश्च विरोधमुपयाति ॥ रोगान्वदने लभते चतुष्पदाच्चात्मनः समाप्नोति । मृत्युं बिलेशयाद्वा नृपाच्च बंधाज्ज्वनाद्वापि ॥ दशमविलग्ने तनुनासिकापुटो दीर्घवक्त्रकरचरणः । वाय्वात्मको मृगास्यो भीरुश्चपलोऽथ बंधनभाक् ॥ क्षुद्रकुटुंबोऽल्पधनः कृपणः कन्याप्रजो मृतस्वजनः । सहजसमृद्धः शौर्यान्नृपादरण्याच्च लब्धधनः ॥ उपवासव्रतशीलो नीचामिष्टामवाप्नुयाद् भार्याम् । बहुविग्रहोऽल्पकेशो दुर्बलजानुश्च रोगार्तः ॥ बालादनिलाच्छस्त्रान्नृपाद्द्विपात्प्रपतनाद्गजाद्वापि । पित्तोदयादजीर्णान्म्रियते वा मार्गविभ्रंष्टः एकादशे विलग्ने स्तब्धः क्रूरः कुलाग्रजः पुरुषः । पित्तानिलभूयिष्ठस्तिलपुष्पसमानमासश्च ॥ प्राप्तान्नाशयतेऽर्थान् बहुभृत्यः साध्यते व्ययैश्चापि । क्षीणः स्वगोत्रगुरुजनपरपक्षसुहृत्स्वजनशत्रुः ॥ कर्मणि पापे सक्तस्तनुश्च कांतानवाप्नुयाल्लाभान् । धर्मध्वजप्रवृत्तौ दैवतपूजश्च कारयति भार्याम् ॥ विग्रहशीलो लभते विविधान् रोगान्कफोद्भवानुरसि । म्रियते च जठररोगाद्भ्रमनात्स्त्रीणां प्रयोगाद्वा ॥ द्वादशगे प्राग्लग्ने स्थूलोष्ठो मीनदृङ् महानासः । कफवातिको महात्मा त्वग्दोषी नैकमतिचेष्टः ॥ शिष्टायव्ययभृत्यैः स्वजनस्त्रीपूजितः सहजनाथः । कर्मणि धर्मे युक्तः पित्रोपचयः सुदारश्च ॥ नीचाचारां भार्यां लभते च रिपून्सुदारुणान् क्रूरान् ॥ रोगात्सशोणितोदाप्नुयाद् भयं व्यालसिंहेभ्यः ॥ मृत्युं पुरुषैर्गणवृंदपूजितैर्गुह्यजैर्विकारैर्वा । विद्यौषधप्रयोगादुपवासान्मार्गदोषाद्वा ॥

A person, born when—

(1) Aries is the rising sign :– will have ugly fingers, will be angry, quarrelsome, not keeping to his word, of bilious and windy temperament, a miser, and will be afflicted with miseries. He will in his young age be separated from his parents and from his religious teacher, will have few children, will help his brothers and kinsmen, will be virtuous, will go abroad, and will do useless works. He will get for his partner a woman of a low caste, or a deceitful woman, or one of defective limbs, or one who was already married. His relations will be friendly. His death will occur either by weapons or by poison, or by bilious complaints, or by those persons round him, or by fire, rain or by being shut up in a prison or by fall.

(2) Taurus, the rising sign :—thick lips, large cheek, thick nose, and broad forehead ; of phlegmatic and windy temperament ; very charitable, spending very much ; will have many daughters, and a few sons ; will do wrong to his parents ; will be engaged in various acts ; will be irreligious, will be wealthy ; always liking to keep his wife near to him ; will suffer from weapons ; and will cause injury to his kinsmen.

His cause of death :—weapons, ropes, or animals ; or will die in foreign lands, or through overwork, water, or spear, want of food or exercise or through quadrupeds.

(3) Gemini, the rising sign :—of defective limbs, or of extra limbs ; sweet tongued ; doing special meritorious deeds, of a mixed temperament, will have two mothers, of small intellect, of small stature, will be a favourite of the sages and his preceptor ; will have few brothers ; not very active, will put others to pain and trouble ; will be qualified ; will be engaged in various works ; will be virtuous, will squander away his earnings, will possess several wives and will have serious diseases. Cause of death :—Snake-bite, poison, animals, or water.

(4) Cancer, the rising sign :—will be wanting in concentration, will suffer diseases of genital organs, will be timid, grateful, of phlegmatic and windy temperament ; crab-like tenacious ; will follow wicked people and his enemies ; will spend others' wealth ; will be haughty amongst his own friends and kinsmen ; reproached by his relatives, will lose his children, engaged in important works in foreign lands ; not of clear speech, a master over others ; will have an unequal match, will be defeated by his enemies, and will be honoured by many. His cause of death :—throat complaints, rope, phlegmatic complaints, the fracture of bones, cuts, or dropsy.

(5) Leo, the rising sign :—will be of a hard nature, fond of meat, of bilious temperament, will be confidential about secrets, will do many works and support his large family, will be a miser, will be liked by all, well renowned, a man of resignation, able and energetic, and will be irreligious, will have several wives from various families, will have a diseased waist, knees and teeth. His cause of death :—weapons, hurtful animals, poison, wood, diseases, aquatic animals, or starvation.

(6) Virgo, the rising sign :—will be sweet tongued, will have a beautiful body, will have long legs, of a mixed temperament, of a respectable appearance, will have wounds, will be wealthy, a miser, liked by his kinsmen, will have many daughters, will not go on well with his brothers, will like to do virtuous acts, will not earn much and will be an artisan and capable in works. His cause of death :—quadrupeds, weapons, bilious attacks, grief, fall or rope.

(7) Libra, the rising sign :—will possess odd limbs, will be of a rough nature, of phlegmatic and windy temperament, will be fickle, of short neck, grateful, will get much wealth, will be respected for his acts of charity, will serve his religious teacher devotedly, will be respected by

his father, brothers and followers, will be fond of walking, will be virtuoùs, will be troubled by his kinsmen, will lose his wife, will be quarrelsome and will suffer from grief. His cause of death :—a famous man, his kinsmen, wild quadrupeds, perspiration, separation from his dear things, fasting or the fatigue through long journey.

(8) Scorpio, the rising sign :—will have a broad face, a big belly, and a conspicuous sinew proceeding from the vertebral column; will be of a rough nature and of a bilious temperament; will have his eyes yellow; will be slowly but quickly travelling; a master over others, will support a large family, will be disliked by his relatives, will spend much, will have many children, will not live happily, will have no enemies, will lose his virtues, will take care of oxen, will be morose and surly on account of his wife, will yield nothing to his enemies, will have his own men for his enemies; will suffer from many diseases and will yield to his foes out of fear of his body being cut to pieces. His cause of death :—imprisonment, blows, bad diseases, or fire.

(9) Sagittari, the rising sign :—will have thick lips, large teeth, long nose, of phlegmatic and windy temperament, a fleshy genital organ, thighs and arms, will have ugly nails, always ready to work, a hero in battle, will work under men of low caste, will lose his wealth through thieves, fire, or the king, will be learned, will be respected by many people, will give trouble to his brothers, will work in foreign lands, will be liked by the king, will be somewhat virtuous, will quarrel with his wife, and will have a diseased face. Cause of death :—quadrupeds, snakes, the king or imprisonment.

(10) Capricorn, the rising sign :—will have a thin nose, long face, arms and legs; of windy temperament, will have a face like that of a deer (or elephant), will be timid, fickle, will suffer imprisonment; will have a small family, small wealth; will be a miser, will have daughters, will lose his kinsmen, will live in plenty, will earn riches by his prowess, or by the king or through forest; will observe fasting; will have a wife of a low caste and be attached to her, will have a large body, few hairs, weak knees, and will complain of some diseases or other. Cause of death :—children, wind, weapons, the king, poison, fall, an elephant, an increase of bile, or dyspepsia.

(11) Aquarius, the rising sign :—will be dull, cruel, the eldest in his family, of bilious and windy temperament, will have a nose shaped like the flower of the sesamum plant, will squander away his wealth, will have many servants, will be hated by his kinsmen, preceptors, enemies

and friends; will be addicted to sinful acts, will have a fine body and wealth; a religious hypocrite, will make his wife worship the Devas, will get many sacred stones, symbolical of Devas and will suffer from phlegmatic attacks affecting the chest. Cause of death:—pains in the belly; vomitting; or drugs administered by a woman.

(12) Pisces, the rising sign:—will have thick lips, fish-like eye, and long nose, of phlegmatic and windy temperament; will be a sage; will have his skin very rough, and not of one mind and of active habits, will have much income and expenditure, will be respected by his servants and wife, will be virtuous, will have a good wife, will help his father, will join a woman of low deeds and will have very bad and cruel enemies. Cause of death:—disease, corruption of the blood, snake, lion, the chiefs of parties of men; venereal diseases, drugs, fasting, or exhaustion through long journey.

Thus ends the Eighteenth Chapter on the Planets and the Zodiac by Sri Varâha Mihirâchârya of Avantika.

CHAPTER XIX.

ON ASPECTS.

शा०वि०–चंद्रे भूपबुधौ नृपोपमगुणी स्तेनोऽधनश्चाजगे निःस्वः स्तेननृमान्यभूपधनिनः प्रेष्यः कुजाद्यैर्गवि । नृस्थेऽयोव्यवहारिपार्थिवबुधाभीस्तंतुवायोऽधनो स्वर्क्षे योद्धृकविज्ञभूमिपतयोऽयोजीविदृग्रोगिणौ ॥ १ ॥

चंद्रे Chandre, on Moon (residing). भूपबुधौ Bhûpabudhau, king, a pandit or scholar. नृपोपमगुणी Nripopamaguṇî, king-like ; well-qualified. स्तेन: Stenaḥ, a thief. अधन: Adhanaḥ, poor. च Cha, and. अजगे Ajage, in the sign Meṣa or Aries. निःस्व: Niḥsvaḥ, poor. स्तेननृमान्यभूपधनिन: Stenanṛimânyabhûpadhaninaḥ, thief, honoured like a king, king, wealthy man. प्रेष्य: Preṣyah,, a servant. कुजाद्यै: Kujâdyaiḥ, aspected by the several planets, Mars, &c. successively (*i.e.*, by Mars, Mercury, Jupiter, Venus, Saturn and the Sun, successively). गवि Gavi, in the sign Vṛiṣa or Taurus. नृस्थे Nṛisthe, in the sign Mithuna or the Gemini. अयोव्यवहारिपार्थिवबुधाभि: Ayovyavahâripârthivabudhâbhiḥ, a professional soldier, king, scholar, a fearless person. तंतुवाय: Tantuvâyaḥ, a weaver. अधन: Adhanaḥ, poor. स्वर्क्षे Svarkṣe, in one's own constellation ; in Moon's own house, *i.e.*, in the sign Karka or Cancer. योद्धृकविज्ञभूमिपतय: Yoddhvakavijñabhûmipatayaḥ, a soldier, poet, scholar, king or landlord. अयोजीविदृग्रोगिणौ Ayojîvidṛigroginau, a professional soldier and one suffering from eye-disease.

1. When the Moon occupies the sign Meṣa or Aries, and if the Moon be aspected by Mars, the individual born will become a king—by Mercury, the native will become a learned scholar—by Jupiter, the native will become like a king—by Venus, the native will be endowed with many qualities—by Saturn, the native will be a thief—by Sun, the native will become poor, will have no property.

When the Moon in Vṛiṣa or Taurus is aspected by Mars, the native will become poor—by Mercury, the native will become a thief—by Jupiter, the native will get honours like a king—by Venus, the native will become a king—by Saturn, the native will become wealthy—by the Sun, the native will be engaged as a servant.

When the Moon in Mithuna or Gemini is aspected by Mars, the native will become a professional soldier or a seller of weapons—by Mercury, the native will become a king —by Jupiter, the native will become a scholar or learned man —by Venus, the native will become fearless—by Saturn, the native will become a weaver—by the Sun, the native will become poor.

When the Moon in Cancer or Karka is aspected by— Mars, the native will become a soldier—by Mercury, the native will become a poet or literary author—by Jupiter, the native will become a scholar—by Venus, the native will become a king or landlord—by Saturn, the native will become a professional soldier—by the Sun, the native will suffer from eye diseases.

Note.—All that have been said of the Moon in the several signs aspected by several planets applies also to those signs respectively when they become the Ascendant. The Moon by aspecting the several signs of the Zodiac except the sign Cancer, produces malefic effects when such signs are the rising signs.

शा० वि०—ज्योतिर्ज्ञाढ्यनरेंद्रनापितनृपक्ष्मेशा बुधाद्यैर्हरौ तद्वद्भूपचमूपनैपुणयुताः षष्ठेऽशुभैः स्त्र्याश्रयः । जूके भूपसुवर्ण-कारवणिजः शेषेक्षिते नैकृती कीटे युग्मपिता नतश्च रजको व्यंगोऽधनो भूपतिः ॥ २ ॥

ज्योतिर्ज्ञाढ्यनरेंद्रनापितनृपक्ष्मेशाः Jyotirjñâḍhyanarendranâpitanṛipakṣeśâḥ, an astrologer, a wealthy person, a king, a barber, a king, a king. बुधाद्यैः: Budhâdyaiḥ, by Mercury, (Jupiter, Venus, Saturn, Sun, Mars) successively. हरौ Harau, in Siṃha ; when the Moon is in the sign Siṃha or Leo. तद्वत् Tadvat, as before ; *i.e*, when aspected by Jupiter, Venus, Saturn, Sun, Mars. भूपचमूपनैपुण्ययुताः: Bhûpachamûpanaipuṇayutâḥ, king, commander of an army, clever and skilful. षष्ठे Ṣaṣṭhe, in the sign Kanyâ or Virgo. अशुभैः: Aśubhaiḥ, when aspected by the malefics, *i.e.*, Saturn, Sun and Mars, respectively. स्त्र्याश्रयः: Stryâśrayaḥ, one living under the shelter of women ; serving under women. जूके Jûke, when Moon is in Libra or Tulâ. भूपसुवर्णकारवणिजः: Bhûpasuvarṇakâravaṇijaḥ, a king, a goldsmith and a trader. शेषेक्षिते Śeṣekṣite, when aspected by the remaining, *i.e.*, Saturn, the Sun or Mars. नैकृती Naikṛitî, a low dishonest person ; a murderer. कीटे Kîte, when Moon is in the sign Vṛiśchika or Scorpio. युग्मपिता Yugmapitâ, father of twins; some also render, having two fathers and read द्विपित्रकः one father real and another adopted by religion. नतः च Nataḥ cha, and humble and obedient. रजकः Rajakaḥ, a washerman. व्यंगः Vyaṃgaḥ, one of defective limbs. अधनः Adhanaḥ, poor; indigent. भूपतिः Bhûpatiḥ, a king.

2. If the Moon in Siṃha (Leo) be aspected by Mercury, the native will become an astrologer; if aspected by Jupiter, wealthy; if by Venus, a king; if by Saturn, a barber; if by the Sun, a king; and if by Mars, a king.

If the Moon in Kanyâ (Virgo) be aspected by Mercury, the native will become a king; if aspected by Jupiter, the commander of an army; if by Venus, skilful in all actions; if by Saturn, the Sun or by Mars, will be under the protection of women (serving under them).

When the Moon in Tulâ (Libra) is aspected by Mercury, the native will become a king; if aspected by Jupiter, a goldsmith; if by Venus, a trader; and if by the Sun, Saturn, or Mars, an executioner, a very low dishonest person.

When the Moon in Vṛiśchika (Scorpio) is aspected by Mercury, the native will become the father of twins (or he may get two fathers one real and the other adopted by religion); if aspected by Jupiter, humble and obedient; if by Venus, a washerman; if by Saturn, defective in his limbs; if by the Sun, poor; and if by Mars, will be a king.

Note.—The above effects are also visible when the corresponding signs are the rising signs respectively.

शा० वि०—ज्ञात्युर्वीशजनाश्रयश्च तुरगे पापैः सदम्भः शठश्चात्युर्वीशनरेंद्रपंडितधनी द्रव्योन भूपो मृगे। भूपो भूपसमोऽन्यदारनिरतः शेषैश्च कुंभस्थिते हास्यज्ञो नृपतिर्बुधश्च झषगे पापश्च पापेक्षिते ॥ ३ ॥

ज्ञात्युर्वीशजनाश्रयः Jñâtyurviśajanâśrayaḥ, a supporter, or a chief protector of one's family, a king, the refuge or supporter of many persons. च Cha, and. तुरगे

Turage, when the Moon is in the sign Dhanu or Sagittarius. पापै: Pâpaiḥ, aspected by the evil planets Saturn, the Sun and Mars. सदंभ: Sadambhaḥ, arrogant, vain. शठ: Saṭhaḥ, hypocrite. च Cha, and. अत्युर्वीशनरेन्द्रपण्डितधनी द्रव्योन भूप: Aturvîśanarendra-paṇḍitadhanîdravyonabhûpaḥ, a King-Emperor, a king, a pandit, a wealthy person, poor, or a king. मृगे Mṛige, when the Moon is in Makara or Capricorn. भूप: Bhûpaḥ, a king. भूपसम: Bhûpasamaḥ, one king-like. अन्यदाररत: Anyadâraniratah, one having illicit intercourse with others' wives. शेषै: Śeṣaiḥ, by the remaining, *i.e.*, by Saturn, the Sun or Mars. च Cha, and also. कुंभस्थिते Kumbhasthite, when Moon occupies the Kumbha sign. हास्यज्ञ: Hâsyajñaḥ, one knowing how to make others laugh, how to give amusement to others; witty; sarcastic. नृपति: Nṛipatiḥ, a king. बुध: Budhaḥ, one learned; pandit. च Cha, and. झषगे Jjhaṣage, when Moon occupies the Mîna or Pisces. पाप: Pâpaḥ, vicious. च Cha, and. पापेक्षिते Pâpekṣite, aspected by the malefics, Saturn, Sun, or Mars.

3. If the Moon in Dhanu (Sagittarius) be aspected by Mercury, the native will become the chief in one's family (*i.e.*, will protect his kinsmen); if aspected by Jupiter, a king; if by Venus, the supporter of many men; if by Saturn, the Sun, or Mars, will be a hyprocrite, vain, arrogant person, not doing good to any.

When the Moon in Markara (Capricorn) is aspected by Mercury, the native will become a Mahârâjâh or the King-Emperor; when aspected by Jupiter, a king; when by Venus, a scholar; when by Saturn, a wealthy man; when by Sun, a poor man; and when by Mars, will be a king.

When the Moon in Kumbha (Aquarius) is aspected by Mercury, the native will become a king; when aspected by Jupiter, will be like a king; by Venus, in illicit intercourse with the wives of other men; by Saturn, Sun, or Mars, in illicit intercourse with others' wives.

When the Moon in Mîna (Pisces) is aspected by Mercury, the native will become witty and sarcastic; when aspected by Jupiter, will be a king; by Venus, a scholar; by Saturn, Sun, or Mars, a sinner.

Note:—The same remarks hold good when the signs are the rising signs respectively, The Moon by aspecting the several signs of the Zodiac except the sign Cancer produces malefic effects when these are the rising signs,

शा० वि०—होरेशर्क्षदलाश्रितैः शुभकरो दृष्टः शशीतद्गत-स्त्र्यंशे तत्पतिभिः सुहृद्भवनगैर्वा वीक्षितः शस्यते । यत्प्रोक्तं प्रतिराशिवीक्षणफलं तद्द्वादशांशे स्मृतं सूर्याद्यैरवलोकितेऽपि शशिनि ज्ञेयं नवांशेष्वतः ॥ ४ ॥

होरेशर्क्षदलाश्रितैः Horeśarkṣadalâśritaiḥ, by the planets residing in the half signs or horâs ruled by the lord of the half sign (horâ) where the Moon exists. शुभकरः Śubhakaraḥ, benefic; auspicious. दृष्टः Driṣṭaḥ, aspected. शशी Śaśî, the Moon. तद्गतः Tadgataḥ, situated in that horâ (half sign) (whence the planets are aspecting the Moon). त्र्यंशे Tryaṃśe, in the Dreṣkâṇas; in the Decanates. The Moon residing in any Decanate. तत्पतिभिः Tatpatibhiḥ, by the rulers of that Decanate. सुहृद्भवनगैः Suhridbhavanagaiḥ, situated in the friend's houses. वा Vâ, or. वीक्षितः Vîkṣitaḥ, aspected. शस्यते Śasyate, is said to produce good or auspicious results. यत् Yat, whatever. प्रोक्तं Proktam, is told. प्रतिराशिवीक्षणफलं Pratirâśivîkṣaṇaphalam, the fruits of each of the twelve signs, where the Moon resides, being aspected by the other planets. तत् Tat, these things; these results. द्वादशांशे Dvâdaśâṃśe, in the Dvâdaśâṃśas, (twelfth divisions of any sign) where Moon becomes situated. स्मृतं Smritam, to be remembered; are applicable. सूर्याद्यैः Sûryâdyaiḥ, by the planets Sun, &c., (Sun, Mars, Mercury, Jupiter, Venus, Saturn). अवलोकिते Avalokite, on being aspected. अपि Api, even. शशिनि Śaśini, on Moon residing (in the Navâṃśas). ज्ञेयं Jñyeyam, (now) to be known; to be described. नवांशेषु Navâṃśeṣu, in the Navâṃśas (ninth part of a sign). अतः Ataḥ, in the following verses.

4. The effects produced by the Moon occupying the solar or lunar horâ of a sign during birth time will be benefic if she be aspected by planets occupying respectively the solar or lunar horâs(1).

The effects produced by the Moon occupying any Drekkâṇa of a sign during birth time will be benefic if She be aspected by a planet that is the ruler of the above-mentioned Drekkâṇa(2).

The effects produced by the Moon occupying any sign will be benefic if She be aspected by planets occupying Moon's own or allies' houses(3).

The effects produced by the Moon occupying any sign and aspected by several planets as described above in the preceding three verses are applicable in the case when the Moon occupies any Dvâdaśâṃśa of that sign(4).

The effects produced by the Moon occupying any Navâṃśa of a sign and aspected by several planets will now be described in the following verses.

Notes.—(1) If the Moon be aspected by planets occupying horâs whose rulers are different from the rulers of the horâs occupied by her, the effects will be malefic. The same remarks apply to the rising horâ.

If the planets referred to in the verse be benefic, the results are fully auspicious; if they be malefic, the results are middling; and so on.

(2) and (3) The same remarks apply to the rising Drekkâṇa.

(4) The same remark holds with reference to the rising Dvâdaśâṃśas. If the rising Dvâdaśâṃśa be other than that of Karka, and if the rising sign be aspected by the Moon, the effects will be malefic; if the rising Dvâdaśâṃśa be that of Cancer, and if the rising sign be aspected by the Moon, the effects will be benefic

व० ति०—आरक्षिको वधरुचिः कुशलो नियुद्धे भूपोऽर्थवान् कलहकृत् क्षितिजांशसंस्थे । मूर्खोऽन्यदारानिरतः सुकविः सितांशे सत्काव्यकृत्सुखपरोऽन्यकलत्रगश्च ॥ ५ ॥

आरक्षिकः Ârakṣikaḥ, city magistrate; or police Kotwal or magistrate. वधरुचिः Vadaruchiḥ, a murderous person; executioner; one connected with the act of killing. कुशलः Kuśalaḥ, clever. नियुद्धे Niyuddhe, in wrestling; in gymnastics. भूपः Bhûpaḥ, king. अर्थवान् Arthavân, one wealthy; one rich. कलहकृत् Kalahakṛit, quarrelsome. क्षितिजांशसंस्थे Kṣityâṃśasaṃsthe, in the Mars's Navâṃśa; when Moon is situated in the Navâṃśa of Aries and Vṛiśchika, the houses of Mars. मूर्खः Mûrkhaḥ, illiterate; stupid; fool. अन्यदारानिरतः Anyadâraniratah, in illicit intercourse with others' wives. सुकविः Sukaviḥ, good poet. सितांशे Sitâṃśe, (Moon) in the Navâṃśas of Vṛiṣa and Tulâ, (Tarus and Libra). सत्काव्यकृत् Satkâvyakṛit, very good poet. सुखपरः Sukhaparaḥ, indulging in pleasures. अन्यकलत्रगः Anyakalatragaḥ, in illicit intercourse with others' wives. च Cha, and.

5. When the Moon during birth occupy the Mars' Navâṃśa in the corresponding Meṣa or Vṛiśchika portions and when She is aspected by the Sun, the individual born will become a city magistrate or kotwal; when aspected by Mars, an executioner; by Mercury, a gymnast, an athlete or a wrestler; by Jupiter, a king; by Venus, a wealthy

man ; and when by Saturn, the individual will become a quarrelsome creature. If, at the time of birth, the Moon occupy the Venus' Navâṃśa in the corresponding Tulâ or Vṛiṣa portions, and if She be aspected by the Sun, then the individual will become an illiterate fool ; by Mars, addicted to others' wives ; by Mercury, can appreciate poetry or other literary works ; by Jupiter, can compose very nice poems or other literary works ; by Venus, a sensualist ; by Saturn, will be in illicit connection with others' wives.

व० ति–बौधे हि रंगचरचौरकवींद्रमंत्री गेयज्ञशिल्पनिपुणः शशिनि स्थितेंऽशे । स्वांशेऽल्पगात्रधनलुब्धतपस्विमुख्यः स्त्रीपोप्यकृत्यनिरतश्च निरीक्ष्यमाणे ॥ ६ ॥

बौधे Baudhe, in the Navâṃśas of Mercury, *i.e.*, in the Mithuna and Kanyâ portions (Mercury's houses). हि Hi, certainly. रंगचरचौरकवींद्रमन्त्री Rangacharachaurakavindramantrî, a wrestler, a thief, a physician, a minister. गेयज्ञशिल्पनिपुणः Geyagñaśilpanipuṇaḥ, musician and clever artisan. शशिनि Śaśini, on Moon occupying. स्थिते Sthite, occupying. अंशे Aṃśe, in the Navâṃśas. स्वांशे Svâṃśe, in one's own Navâṃśa, *i.e.*, in the Karka Navâṃśa (that of the Moon). अल्पगात्रधनलुब्धतपस्विमुख्यः Alpagâtradhanalubdhatapasvimukhyaḥ, lean, avaricious, ascetic, chief. स्त्रीपोप्यकृत्यनिरतः Strîpoṣyakṛityaniratah, supported by wife; engaged in doing one's duty. च Cha, and. निरीक्ष्यमाणे Nirîkṣyamâṇe, aspected.

6. When, during birth, the Moon occupy the Mercury's Navâṃśas, *i.e.*, the corresponding Mithuna or Kanyâ portions, the native will become a wrestler, if She be also aspected by the Sun ; will be a thief, if aspected by Mars ; will be a first class poet, if aspected by Mercury ; will be a minister, if aspected by Jupiter ; a musician, if aspected by Venus ; and will be an artist, if also aspected by Saturn.

When the Moon occupy her own Navâṃśa, *i.e.*, the corresponding Karka portion, the native will be lean and thin, if she be also aspected by the Sun ; will be a miser and greedy of wealth, if the Moon be aspected by Mars ; will be an ascetic, if she be also aspected by Mercury ; will be a chief, if the Moon be also aspected by Jupiter ; will be maintained by women, if aspected by Venus; and will be attached to one's duties, if the Moon be also aspected by Saturn.

प्रहर्षिणी—सक्रोधो नरपतिसंमतो निधीशः सिंहांशे प्रभुरसुतोऽतिहिंस्रकर्मा । जावांशे प्रथितबलो रणोपदेष्टा हास्यज्ञः सचिवविकामवृद्धशीलः ॥ ७ ॥

सक्रोध: Sakrodhaḥ, angry. नरपतिसंमत: Narapatisammataḥ, endeared by the king. निधीश: Nidhîśaḥ, earning money by dealing with pearls, jewels &c. सिंहांशे Siṃhâṃśe in the Navâṃsa of Siṃha or Leo. प्रभु: Prabhuḥ, master. असुत: Asutaḥ, sonless, अतिहिंस्रकर्मा Atihiṃsrakarmâ, very mischievous; murderous. जीवांशे Jîvâṃśe, in Jupiter's Navâṃśa, *i.e.*, in the Navâṃśas of Dhanu and Mîna (Sagittari and Pisces). प्रथितबल: Prathitabalaḥ, renowned for strength. रणोपदेष्टा Raṇopadeṣṭâ, advisers in battle, how phalanxes are to be arranged, &c. हास्यज्ञ: Hâsyajraḥ, skilled in making others laugh. सचिवविकामवृद्धशील: Sachivavikâmavṛiddhaśîlaḥ, minister, eunuch, religious.

7. If, at the time of birth, the Moon be in the Siṃha's Navâṃśa, the native will become of an angry nature, if she be also aspected by the Sun; dear to kings, if aspected by Mars; master of buried treasures, if aspected by Mercury; a master whose orders are obeyed, if aspected by Jupiter; will become sonless, if aspected by Venus; will do mischievous actions, if aspected by Saturn.

If the Moon be in Jupiter's Navâṃśa in the corresponding Dhanu or Mîna portions, the native will become strong and famous if the Moon be aspected by the Sun; will know the art of warfare, if aspected by Mars; will become witty and sarcastic, if aspected by Mercury; a prime minister, if aspected by Jupiter; will become void of virility, *i.e.*, eunuch if aspected by Venus; will become religious and charitably disposed, if aspected by Saturn.

शालिनी—अल्पापत्यो दुःखितः सत्यपि स्वे मानासक्तः कर्मणि स्वेऽनुरक्तः । दुष्टस्त्रीष्टः कृपणश्चार्किभागे चंद्रे भानौ तद्वदिन्द्वादिदृष्टे ॥ ८ ॥

अल्पापत्य: Alpâpatyaḥ, having a few sons. दुःखित: Duḥkhitaḥ, sorrowful; morose; unhappy. सति अपि Sati api, though existing. स्वे Sve, riches. मानासक्त: Mânâsaktaḥ; honourable. कर्मणि Karmaṇi, in one's duties. स्वे Sve, appropriate to one's family. अनुरक्त: Anuraktaḥ, attached. दुष्टस्त्रीष्ट: Duṣṭastrîṣṭaḥ, liked by bad women. कृपण: Kripaṇaḥ, miser. च Cha, and. अर्किभागे Arkibhâge, in the Navâṃśas of Saturn, *i.e.*, in Makara and Kumbha portions. चन्द्रे Chandre, on Moon (occupying). भानौ Bhanau, pertaining to the Sun. तद्वत् Tadvat, like that (the effects of the Moon.) इन्द्वादिदृष्टे Indvâdidriṣṭe, aspected by the Moon and other planets, *i.e.*, by the Moon, Mars, Mercury, Jupiter, Venus, Saturn.

8. If, at the time of birth, the Moon occupy Saturn's Navâṃśa, *i.e.*, the corresponding Makara and Kumbha portions, the native will get few children, if she be aspected by the Sun; will become miserable and will get trouble in acquiring riches and property, if she be aspected by Mars; will become arrogant, if aspected by Mercury; will become a worthy man doing worthy acts becoming to his family, if aspected by Jupiter; will become a lewd, a debauchee, if aspected by Venus; become a miser, if aspected by Saturn.

These effects are applicable also to the then rising sign. (1) Whatever effects have been described about the Moon in several Navâṃśakas and her being aspected by the planets Sun, Mars, etc., are applicable also to the Sun being in those Navâṃśakas and his being aspected by the Moon, Mars, etc.

Remarks.—(1) The aspect of the Moon is always considered inauspicious excepting when it is directed to that of the Karka (Cancer), when it is auspicious. The same remark applies to the rising Navâṃśa as to the Moon—but if the Moon aspect the rising sign when the rising Navâṃśa is other than that of Cancer, the effects will be malefic.

व० ति०–वर्गोत्तमस्वपरगेषु शुभं यदुक्तं तत्पुष्टमध्यलघुताशुभमुत्क्रमेण । वीर्यान्वितोंऽशकपतिर्निरुणद्धि पूर्वं राशीश्वरस्य फलमंशफलं ददाति ॥ ६ ॥

इति श्रीवराहमि०बृह०दृष्टिफलाऽध्यायः एकोनविंशः ॥१६॥

वर्गोत्तमस्वपरगेषु Vargottamasvaparageṣu, in vargottamas (the most auspicious degrees specified in the 1st chapter, verse 14), in one's own Navâṃśas and in another's Navâṃśas. शुभं Śubham, auspicious; good. यत् Yat, whatever. उक्तं Uktaṃ, is told. तत् Tat, that. पुष्टमध्यलघुता Puṣṭamadhyalaghutâ, very strong or prominent, mediocre strong, and less strong. अशुभम् Aśubham, inauspicious results. उत्क्रमेण Utkrameṇa, in the reverse order. वीर्यान्वितः Vîryânvitaḥ, strong. अंशकपतिः Aṃśakapatiḥ, the Navâṃśa ruler. निरुणद्धि Niruṇaddhi, overpowers; checks; stops; prevents any results being produced. पूर्वं Pûrvam, aforesaid. राशीक्षणस्य Râśikṣaṇasya, when the signs are aspected; the aspects of the signs. फलम् Phalam, results. अंशफलम् Aṃśaphalaṃ, the results of its own Aṃśas. ददाति Dadâti, gives; bears; engenders.

9. The results that have been mentioned here due to the Moon in the several Navâṃśas being aspected by several planets in the several signs are of two kinds, auspicious and inauspicious; *e.g.*, becoming a king is auspicious and becoming an executioner is inauspicious and so on. Now when the Moon is situated in Vargottama, the most favourable position, then the auspicious results are rendered highly auspicious; when the Moon is situated in her own Navâṃśas these results are of a mediocre nature; and when the Moon is situated in another's Navâṃśas, the auspicious results are of a weak nature. As regards the inauspicious results, they are just the opposite; *i.e.*, when the Moon is situated in the Vargottama, the inauspicious results are very weak; when the Moon is in her own Navâṃśas, the inauspicious results are middling; and when the Moon is in another's Navâṃśas, the inauspicious results are highly inauspicious (1).

If the ruler of the Navâṃśa where the Moon is situated be very powerful, it stops the results aforesaid as regards the signs and manifests the results of the Navâṃśas(2).

Notes.—(1) The same remark applies to the rising sign and the Sun.

(2) The effects of the half signs, Decanates, Dvâdaśâṃśas are not stopped; only the effects of the sign are stopped; and the results of the Navâṃśas are rendered visible, if the ruler of that Navâṃśa be very strong. In case the ruler of the Navâṃśa be not strong, the results of the sign are to be predicted, if the ruler of the sign be strong; and if both are strong, both the effects of the sign as well as the Navâṃśas are to be

predicted. Of the results of the corresponding rising sign, the Moon, and the Sun, whichever is very strong, the effects of that will become visible. The Navâṃśaka effects due to the Sun being in that Navâṃśaka are not to be taken here.

Thus ends the Nineteenth Chapter on Aspects by Śri Varâha Mihirâchârya of Avantika.

CHAPTER XX.

ON THE PLANETS IN THE TWELVE HOUSES OR BHÂVAS.

मंदाक्रांता–शूरः स्तब्धो विकलनयनो निर्घृणोऽर्के तनुस्थे मेषे सस्वास्तिमिरनयनः सिंहसंस्थे निशांधः। नीचेंऽधोऽस्वः शशिगृहगते बुद्बुदाक्षः पतंगे भूरिद्रव्यो नृपहृतधनो वक्ररोगी द्वितीये ॥ १ ॥

शूरः Śûrah, a hero, a warrior, valiant man. स्तब्धः Stabdhaḥ, dull; slow at work, hard; obstinate. विकलनयनः Vikalanayanaḥ, of eyes defective. निर्घृणः Nirghriṇaḥ, heartless; cruel. अर्के Arke, on the Sun occupying. तनुस्थे Tanusthe, the Ascendant. मेषे Meṣe, the sign Meṣa or Aries. सस्वः Sasvaḥ, having riches. तिमिरनयनः Timiranayanaḥ, one having maladies incident to eyes; having eye diseases. सिंहसंस्थे Siṃhasaṃsthe, in a Leo or Siṃha. निशांधः Nśândhaḥ, blind at night; Moon-blind. नीचे Nîche, in the house detrimental to the Sun, *i. e.*, in the house Tulâ or Libra. अंधः Andhaḥ, blind. अस्वः Asvaḥ, poor. शशिगृहगते Śaśigrihagate, in the house of Moon, *i.e.*, in the sign Karka or Cancer. बुद्बुदाक्षः Budbudâkṣaḥ, with swollen eyes resembling a bubble; or having a mote in one's eyes. पतंगे Patañge, on the Sun going to. भूरिद्रव्यः Bhûridrabyaḥ, of considerable wealth. नृपहृतधनः Nripahrita-dhanaḥ, having his wealth stolen by a king. वक्ररोगी Vaktrarogî, having diseases on one's face. द्वितीये Dvitîye, in the second house from the Ascendant.

1. If, at the time of birth, the Sun occupy the Ascendant, the individual born will become a hero, a valiant warrior, slow at work, dull; will get defective eyes, and will become merciless. This is true of all the signs becoming the Ascendant save the signs Meṣa (Aries), Siṃha (Leo), Tulâ (Libra), and Karkaṭa (Cancer) when the results aforesaid will not be visible. The following will then be the results. If the Sun be in the Ascendant Meṣa, the individual born will become wealthy and his eyes will be diseased; if the Sun be in the Ascendant Siṃha, the native will become moon-blind; if the Sun be in the Ascendant Tulâ, the native will become blind and poor; if the Sun be in the Ascendant

Karka, the eyes of the native will become swollen and watery like the bubble or there will be a mote in his eye.

When the Sun is in the second house from the Ascendant, the individual will get abundance of wealth but his wealth will all be taken away by the king. He will suffer also from diseases on his face.

औपच्छंदसिक—मतिविक्रमवांस्तृतीयगेऽर्के विसुखः पीडितमानसश्चतुर्थे । असुतो धनवर्जितस्त्रिकोणे बलवाञ्छत्रुजितश्च शत्रुयाते ॥ २ ॥

मतिविक्रमवान् Mativikramavân, intelligent and chivalrous; having intellect and heroic valour. तृतीयगे Trityage, when the Sun is in the third house from the Ascendant. अर्के Arke, the Sun. विसुखः Visukhah, unhappy; afflicted with grief and mental sufferings. पीडितमानसः Piditamânasah, mentally disturbed. चतुर्थे Chaturthe, when the Sun is in the fourth house from the Ascendant. असुतः Asutah, sonless. धनवर्जितः Dhanavarjitah, void of wealth. त्रिकोणे Trikone, when the Sun is in the fifth house from the Ascendant. बलवान् Balavân, strong. शत्रुजितः Satrujitah, defeated by the enemies. शत्रुयाते Śatruyâte, when the Sun is in the sixth house from the Ascendant.

2. If, at the time of birth, the Sun occupy the third house, the native will become intelligent and powerful; in the fourth house, the native will become unhappy and mentally disturbed; in the fifth house, the native will become sonless, and deprived of money; and in the sixth house, the native will become strong but will be subjugated by his enemies.

Remarks.—शत्रुजितः is read जहृरिपुः by some astrologers. The meaning then would be, the native destroying his enemies. Satyâchârya reads षष्ठे रिपुरोगशोकघ्नः "Sasthe Ripurogaśokaghnah" meaning the Sun being in the sixth house, the enemies, diseases, and sorrows are all destroyed. But here the author has followed Yavanâchârya, the famous ancient astrologer and Śuchidhvaja.

व० ति०—स्त्रीभिर्गतः परिभवं मदगे—पतंगे स्वल्पात्मजो निधनगे विकलेक्षणश्च । धर्मे सुतार्थसुखभाक् सुखशौर्यभाक्खे लाभे प्रभूतधनवान्पतितस्तु रिःफे ॥ ३ ॥

स्त्रीभिः Stribhiḥ, by women. गतः Gataḥ, got. परिभवं Paribhavam, disgrace. मदगे Madage, when the Sun is in the seventh house from the Ascendant. पतंगे Patañge, the Sun (occupying). स्वल्पात्मजः Svalpâtmajaḥ, having few sons. निधनगे Nidhanage, in the seventh house. विकलेक्षणः Vikalekṣaṇaḥ, of defective eyes. च Cha, and. धर्मे Dharme, in the ninth house. सुतार्थसुखभाक् Sutârthasukhabhâk, having sons, wealth. and happiness. सुखशौर्यभाक् Sukhasauryabhâk, enjoying happiness and heroism. खे Khe, in the tenth house. लाभे Lâbhe, in the eleventh house. प्रभूतधनवान् Prabhûtadhanavân, considerably wealthy. पतितः Patitaḥ, fallen and ruined due to his karma. रिःफे Riḥphe, when the Sun is in the twelfth house.

N.B.—Some read. सुतार्थरहितः Sutârtharahitaḥ, devoid of sons and wealth for सुतार्थसुखभाक् in the second stanza. Thus Satyâchârya reads also.

3. If, at the time of birth, the Sun be in the seventh house from the Ascendant, the individual born will suffer disgrace at the hands of women; if the Sun be in the eighth house, the native will get a few sons and his eyes will become unsteady and defective; if the Sun be in the ninth house, the individual will get wealth, sons, and happiness; if the Sun be in the tenth house, he will become strong and happy; if in the eleventh house, he will become very wealthy; and if the Sun be in the twelfth house, he will become a fallen and ruined man.

Remarks.—Satyâchârya says the result of the ninth house is disease, poverty and deviation from the good customs and observances. Some astrologers read धर्मे सुतार्थरहितः, in the ninth house the individual is deprived of sons and wealth.

शा० वि०–मूकोन्मत्तजडान्धहीनबधिरप्रेष्याः शशाङ्कोदये । स्वर्क्षाजोच्चगते धनी बहुसुतः सस्वः कुटुम्बी धने । हिंस्रो भ्रातृगते सुखे सतनये तत्प्रोक्तभावान्वितो नैकारिर्मृदुकायवह्निमदनस्तीक्ष्णोऽलसश्चारिगे ॥ ४ ॥

मूकोन्मत्तजडान्धहीनबधिरप्रेष्याः Mûkonmattajaḍândhahînabadhirapreṣyâḥ, dumb, lunatic, stupid; blind, low and mean, deaf, or a slave doing servile works. शशाङ्कोदये Śaśâṃkodaye, on the Moon rising in the horizon or on being in any other rising signs than Meṣa, Vṛiṣa, and Karka. स्वर्क्षाजोच्चगते Svarkṣâjochhagate, when Moon is in her own house, Karka, in Meṣa or in Vṛiṣa, her exalted house. धनी Dhanî, rich. बहुसुतः Bahusutaḥ, having numerous sons. सस्वः Sasvaḥ, wealthy. कुटुम्बी Kuṭumbî, having numerous relations. धने Dhane, when Moon is in the second house from the Ascendant. हिंस्रः Hiṃsraḥ, mischievous, murderous. भ्रातृगते Bhrâṭrigate, when Moon is in the third house from the Ascendant. सुखे Sukhe, in the fourth house. सुतनये Satnaye, in the fifth house. तत्प्रोक्तभावान्वितः Tatproktabhâvânvitaḥ, having those things that are understood by their names aforesaid, *i.e.*, having happiness in the fourth and sons in the fifth house. नैकारिः Naikâriḥ, having many enemies. मृदुकायवह्निमदनः Mṛidukâyavahnimadanaḥ, of weak body, of weak appetite, of weak virility. तीक्ष्णः Tîkṣṇaḥ, hot tempered. अलसः Alasaḥ, idle, lazy. च Cha, and. अरिगे Arige, in the sixth house.

4. If, at the time of birth, the Ascendant be any sign excepting Meṣa, Vṛiṣa, and Karka, and if the Moon be in the Ascendant, the individual born will become dumb, or lunatic, stupid, blind, low, deaf or a menial slave. If the Moon be in the Ascendant Meṣa, the individual will get many sons; if in the Ascendant Vṛiṣa, will get wealth; and if in Karka Ascendant, will get wealth too. If the Moon be in the second house from the Ascendant, his family will become large; if in the third house, he will become mischievous, murderous; if in the fourth house, will be happy, will get kinsmen and houses; if in the fifth house, he will get numerous sons, intelligence and the like; if in the sixth house, the individual will get many enemies; his physical constitution will become soft and weak; his appetite will be also weak; his virility will be weak; his temper will be hot and he will spend his time idly.

शा० वि०—ईर्षुस्तीव्रमदो मदे बहुमतिर्व्याध्यर्दितश्चाष्टमे । सौभाग्यात्मजमित्रबन्धुधनभाग् धर्मस्थिते शीतगौ ॥ निष्पत्तिं समुपैति धर्मधनधीशौर्यैर्युतः कर्मगे । ख्यातो भावगुणान्वितो भवगते क्षुद्रोऽङ्गहीनो व्यये ॥ ५ ॥

ईर्षुः Îrṣyuḥ, envious; jealous. तीव्रमदः Tîvramadaḥ, very liçentious; strongly passionate. मदे Made, in the seventh house. बहुमतिः व्याध्यर्दितः Bahumatiḥ vyâdhyarditaḥ, not one-minded and afflicted with maladies. च Cha, and. अष्टमे Aṣṭame, in the eighth house. सौभाग्यात्मजमित्रबन्धुधनभाक् Saubhâgyâtmajamitrabandhudhanabhâk, enjoying happiness and prosperity, sons, friends, and relations, and wealth. धर्मस्थिते Dharmasthite, when Moon is in the 10th house from the Ascendant. शीतगौ

Śitagau, the Moon. निष्पत्तिं Nispattim, completion; success everywhere. समुपैति Samupaiti, gets. धर्मधनधीशौर्यैः Dharmadhanadhîsauryaih, with virtue, wealth, intellect and heroic valour. युतः Yutah, united. कर्मगे Karmage, in the tenth house. ख्यातः Khyâtah, reputed. भावगुणान्वितः Bhâvagunânvitah, endowed with profit and the like. भवगते Bhavagate, in the eleventh house. क्षुद्रः Ksudrah, mean; mischievous. अङ्गहीनः Angahînah, of defective limbs. व्यये Vyae, in the twelfth house.

5. If, at the time of birth, the Moon be in the seventh house from the Ascendant, the native will be jealous of other's property and will be strongly passionate; if in the eighth house, his mind will not be steady and he will be afflicted with maladies; if in the ninth house, the native will become fortunate and prosperous, will get sons, friends, relations and wealth; if the Moon be in the tenth house from the Ascendant, then the native will become successful in all his undertakings, and will be religious, wealthy, intelligent and heroic; if in the eleventh house, famous and always profiting; and if in the twelfth house, the native will be mischievous and of defective limbs.

व० ति०—लग्ने कुजे क्षततनुर्धनगे कदन्नो धर्मेऽघवान्दिनकरप्रतिमोऽन्यसंस्थः । विद्वान्धनी प्रखलपंडितमंत्र्यशत्रुर्धर्मज्ञविश्रुतगुणः परतोऽर्कवज्ज्ञे ॥ ६ ॥

लग्ने Lagne, in the Ascendant. कुजे Kuje, on Mars being. क्षततनुः Ksatatanuh, of scarred or wounded body. धनगे Dhanage, in the second house. कदन्नः Kadannah, eating very low meals and other coarse things. धर्मे Dharme, in the ninth house. अघवान् Aghavân, vicious. दिनकरप्रतिमः Dinakarapratimah, having effects like those of the Sun being in those places. अन्यसंस्थः Anyasamsthah; situated in the remaining signs (*i.e.*, 3, 4, 5, 6, 7, 8, 10, 11, 12 houses). विद्वान् Vidvân, learned. धनी Dhanî, wealthy. प्रखलपंडित मंत्र्यशत्रुः Prakhalapanditamantryaśatruh, a wicked of the first water, learned, minister, foeless person. धर्मज्ञविश्रुतगुणः Dharmajñaviśrutagunah, religious (or having a knowledge of law), renowned. परतः Paratah, in the remaining signs (9, 10, 11, 12 houses). अर्कवत् Arkavat, like those mentioned under the Sun's heading. ज्ञे Jñe, on Mercury being in.

6. If, at the time of birth, Mars be in the Ascendant, the native will get marks of wounds on his body; if Mars be in the second house from the Ascendant, the native will eat very low and coarse meals; if in the ninth house, the native will commit

sinful deeds, and if in the other houses (1), the results will be the same as mentioned under the heading of the Sun, *i.e.*, unhappy in the fourth, sonless, moneyless in the fifth, strong in the sixth, under wife's control in the seventh, few sons in the eighth, happy and strong in the tenth, wealthy in the eleventh, and fallen in the twelfth house.

Again if, at the time of birth, Mercury be in the Ascendant, the native will become a Pandit; wealthy in the second, wicked in the third, Pandit in the fourth, minister in the fifth, foeless in the sixth, virtuous and having a knowledge of law in the seventh, qualified and famous in the eighth, and like the Sun in the remaining houses, *i.e.*, getting sons, wealth, happiness in the ninth, becoming happy and powerful in the tenth, wealthy in the eleventh, and fallen in the twelfth house.

Note.—(1) That is, the 3rd, 4th, 5th, 6th, 7th, 8th, 10th, 11th, and 12th houses.

इंद्रवज्रा—विद्वान्सुवाक्यः कृपणः सुखी च धीमानशत्रुः पितृतोऽधिकश्च । नीचस्तपस्वी सधनः सलाभः खलश्च जीवे क्रमशो विलग्नात् ॥ ७ ॥

विद्वान् Vidvân, learned. सुवाक्यः Suvâkyaḥ. sweet speaking; of smooth and persuasive speech. कृपणः Kṛipaṇaḥ, miser. सुखी Sukhî, happy. च Cha, and. धीमान् Dhîmân, intelligent. अशत्रुः Aśatruḥ, foeless. पितृतः Pitṛitaḥ, than one's father. अधिकः Adhika, greater; superior. च Cha, and. नीचः Nîchaḥ, low, mean. तपस्वी Tapasvî, ascetic. सधनः Sadhanaḥ, wealthy. खलः Khalaḥ, crooked; wicked; mischievous. च Cha, and. जीवे Jîve, on Jupiter being in. क्रमशः Kramaśaḥ, one after another. विलग्नात् Vilagnât, from the Ascendant.

7. The individual born will become a Pandit, if Jupiter be in the Ascendant; sweet speaking, if Jupiter be in the second house from the Ascendant; miser in the third, happy in the fourth, intelligent in the fifth, foeless in the sixth, superior in qualities to his father in the seventh, doing low, mean acts in the eighth, ascetic and devotee in the ninth, wealthy in the tenth, profitting in the eleventh house and wicked and doing fearful deeds in the twelfth house.

चित्रता—स्मरनिपुणः सुखितश्च विलग्ने प्रियकलहोऽस्तगते सुरतेप्सुः ॥ तनयगते सुखितो भृगुपुत्रे गुरुवदतोऽन्यगृहे सधनोऽन्त्ये ॥ ८ ॥

स्मरनिपुणः Smaranipuṇaḥ, clever in love affairs. सुखितः Sukhitaḥ, happy, living in comfort. च Cha, and. विलग्ने Vilagne, in the Ascendant. प्रियकलहः Priyakalahaḥ, quarrelsome. अस्तगते Astagate, in the seventh house. सुरतेप्सुः Suratepsuḥ, desirous to cohabit. तनयगते Tanayagate, when Venus is in the fifth house. सुखितः Sukhitaḥ, happy. भृगुपुत्रे Bhṛiguputtre, on Venus being in. गुरुवत् Guruvat, like the results mentioned under Jupiter's heading. अतः Ataḥ, from this. अन्यगृहे Anyagṛihe, in the remaining houses (2, 3, 4, 6, 8, 9, 10, 11, 12 houses). सधनः Sadhanaḥ, wealthy. अंत्ये Antye, in the twelfth house, the Pisces (Mîna).

8. The individual born will become clever in love affairs and will live in comfort if Venus be in the Ascendant; will be fond of quarrelling and a sensualist, if Venus be in the seventh house; will become happy if Venus be in the fifth house. The results of the other houses are the same as those of Jupiter in those places; *i.e.*, the individual will turn out sweet speaking, if Venus be in the second house, miser in the third, happy in the fourth, foeless in the sixth, mean in the eighth, ascetic in the ninth, wealthy in the tenth, profitting in the eleventh, and wicked in the twelfth house. The only peculiarity to be noted here is when Venus is in her exalted house the sign Mîna (Pisces), the individual will become wealthy, in whichever house from the Ascendant this be placed.

Remarks:—Some read गुरुवदतस्तु भवे द्रविणी स्यात् for the latter portion of the second stanza. The meaning is the same.

शिखरिणी—अदृष्टार्थो रोगी मदनवशगोऽत्यंतमलिनः शिशुत्वे पीडार्त्तः सवितृसुतलग्नेत्यलसवाक् ॥ गुरुस्वर्चोच्चस्थे नृपतिसदृशो ग्रामपुरपः सुविद्वांश्चार्वंगो दिनकरसमोऽन्यत्र कथितः॥९॥

अदृष्टार्थः Adriṣṭârthaḥ, poor. रोगी Rogî, afflicted with maladies. मदनवशगः Madanavaśagaḥ, subject to the attraction towards the opposite sex. अत्यंतमलिनः Atyantamalinaḥ, very dirty and impure. शिशुत्वे Śiśutve, at a very early age; in childhood. पीडार्त्तः Pîḍârtaḥ, sickly; afflicted with maladies. सवितृसुतलग्ने Savitṛisutalagne, Saturn being in the Ascendant. इति Iti, thus. अलसवाक् Alasavâk, slow and dull in speech. गुरुस्वर्क्षोच्चस्थे Gurusvarksochchasthe, in the signs of Jupiter, in Saturn's own houses and exalted house; *i.e.*, in the signs Dhanu and Mîna, Makara and Kumbha, and Tulâ, *i.e.*, in 7, 9, 10, 11 and 12 signs. नृपतिसदृशः Nṛipatisadṛiśaḥ, like a king. ग्रामपुरपः Grâmapurapaḥ, head or ruler of a village or city. सुविद्वान् Suvidvân, a very learned scholar. चार्वंगः Châryamgaḥ, of beautiful body. दिनकरसमः Dinakarasamaḥ, of like results that are mentioned under the Sun's heading in those places. अन्यत्र Anyatra, in the remaining houses, *i.e.*, in (2, 3, 4, 5, 6, 7, 8, 9, 10, 11, 12 houses). कथितः Kathitaḥ, said; mentioned.

9. If, at the time of birth, Saturn be in the Ascendant in any sign excepting Tulâ, Dhanu, Makara, Kumbha, and Mîna, the native will become poor, always sickly, very lustful, very dirty and afflicted with maladies in childhood. He will be also slow and indistinct in speech. If Saturn be in the Ascendant Tulâ, Dhanu, Makara, Kumbha, or Mîna, the native will become like a king, the ruler of a city or village, a Pandit, and will be of a beautiful appearance. The results of the other houses are the same as those of the Sun, *i.e.*, the individual will become wealthy (wealth being snatched away by the king) and diseased in mouth, if Saturn be in the second house from the Ascendant; will become intelligent and powerful, if in the third; unhappy and sickly in the fourth; sonless, moneyless, in the fifth; powerful, defeated by the enemies, in the sixth; under wife's control, in the seventh; of few sons, and defective eyes, if in the eighth; will get sons, wealth, happiness in the ninth; will become happy and powerful in the tenth; will get wealth in the eleventh; and will become fallen, if in the twelfth house.

मालिनी—सुहृदरिपरकीयस्वर्क्षतुंगस्थितानां फलमनुपरि-
चिंत्यं लग्नदेहादिभावैः । समुपचयविपत्ती सौम्यपापेषु सत्यः
कथयति विपरीतं रिःफषष्ठाष्टमेषु ॥ १० ॥

सुहृदरिपरकीयस्वर्क्षतुंगस्थितानां Suhṛidariparakîyasvarkṣatuṅgasthitânâm, whether the houses occupied by the several planets are their friendly signs or inimical or neutral signs or their own houses or their exaltation signs and the like. फलम् Phalam, effects; results; fruits. अनुपरिचिंत्यं Anuparichintyam, are to be considered. लग्नदेहादिभावैः Lagnadehâdibhâvaiḥ, by the natures, temperaments of the Ascendant and other houses, *i.e.*, by the body, wealth, &c. समुपचयविपत्ती Samupachayavipattî, the increase and decrease respectively. सौम्यपापेषु Saumyapâpeṣu, on the benefics and malefics occupying. सत्यः Satyaḥ, Satyâchârya, the astrologer. विपरीतं Viparîtam, reverse. रिःफषष्ठाष्टमेषु Riḥphaṣaṣṭhâṣṭameṣu, in the 12th, 6th and 8th signs.

10. The results aforesaid in this Chapter are to be considered with respect to the natures of such houses, (body, wealth, &c.) and these are heightened or lowered according as the houses occupied by the several planets are their friendly signs or inimical or neutral signs or their own houses or their exaltation signs and the like; (*e. g.*, the friendly houses will give full auspicious results and give less inauspicious results; the inimical houses will give inauspicious results; the house of detriment will give also the inauspicious results; the indifferent houses will give both the auspicious and inauspicious results; one's own house will give fully the auspicious results and the exalted houses will give an excess of auspicious results and so on)(1).

Satyâchârya says the auspicious planets in any house increase the nature (bhâva) of that house; and the inauspicious planets in any house decrease the nature of that house, excepting the sixth, eighth, and twelfth houses; the effects here are reversed (*e.g.*, the nature of the twelfth house is expenditure; now if a benefic planet be in the twelfth house, the expenditure will be lessened and if a malefic planet be in the twelfth house, the expenditure will be increased; and so on) (2).

Notes.—(1) All this is according to Gârga.

(2) According to Satya, if a benefic planet be in the 6th house, the enemies will decrease, *i.e.*, be ruined and if a malefic planet occupy it, the enemies will increase. And so on.

अनुष्टुभ्—उच्चत्रिकोणस्वसुहृच्छत्रुनीचगृहार्कगैः ॥
शुभं संपूर्णपादोनदलपादाल्पनिष्फलम् ॥ ११ ॥
इति श्रीवराहमिहिराचार्यप्रणीते बृहज्जातके भावाऽ-
ध्यायो विंशः ॥ २० ॥

उच्चत्रिकोणस्वसुहृच्छत्रुनीचगृहार्कगैः: Uchchatrikoṇasvasuhṛichchatrunîchagṛihârkagaiḥ, situated in any of the 12 signs of exaltation, trikoṇa, own houses, friends, enemies, and ḥouses detriment. शुभं Śubham, auspicious. संपूर्णपादोनदलपादाल्पनिष्फलम् Sampûrṇapâdonadalapâdâlpaniṣphalam, fruits or results as follows :—full, three-fourth, half, one-fourth, less than one-fourth, or nothing whatsoever (as the case may be).

11. (Two kinds of results we get from the horoscopes, one auspicious and the other inauspicious). Now the auspicious results that will be given by the planets will be given fully when the planets are exalted ; when in Mûlatrikoṇa, three-fourths of its full value will be given ; when the planets are in their own houses, half will be given; when the planets are in their friends' houses, one-fourth will come to pass; and when in the enemies' houses, even less than one-fourth will be awarded ; and when the planets are descending or in their detrimental house, no auspicious results will be awarded. The malefic planets do the reverse. Thus the Descending or detrimental malefics produce bad results to the fullest extent ; the malefics in their inimical houses will produce one-fourth less bad results; in their ally's houses will give one-half less bad results; in their own houses, produce one-fourth of the full extent; and in their Trikoṇa or triangular houses less than one-fourth and when the malefics are exalted, they do not give any bad results (the evil effects will fail).

Thus ends the twentieth chapter on the influences of planets (Bhâvâdhyâya) by Śrî Varâhâchârya of Avantika.

CHAPTER XXI.

ON ÂŚRAYA YOGA.

Or on the planets and the several Vargas.

पुष्पिताग्रा—कुलसमकुलमुख्यबंधुपूज्या धनिसुखिभोगिनृपाः स्वभैकवृद्ध्या ॥ परविभवसुहृत्स्वबंधुपोष्या गणपबलेशनृपाश्च मित्रभेषु ॥ १ ॥

कुलसमकुलमुख्यबंधुपूज्याः Kulasamakulamukhyabandhupûjyâḥ, worthy of one's family, or chief in one's family, or worshipped by friends (respectively). धनिसुखिभोगिनृपाः Dhanisukhibhoginṛipâḥ, one wealthy, or happy, or epicure or a king (respectively). स्वभैकवृद्ध्या Svabhaikavṛidhyâ, when one, two, three, four, five, six or seven planets are in their own houses respectively. परविभवसुहृत्स्वबंधुपोष्या Paravibhavasuhṛitsvabandhupoṣyâ, living on another's wealth, or supported by friends, or relations, or brothers and cousins. गणपबलेशनृपाः Gaṇapabaleśanṛipâḥ, head of any assembly, or commander of an army or a king. मित्रभेषु Mitrabheṣu, in the friend's houses or signs; when one, two, three, four, five, six or seven planets are in their friends' houses respectively.

1. The individual born will get average wealth and dignity becoming to his family if one planet be found during birth time in its own house; will become the chief member in his family if two planets be found in their own houses; will become honoured by his friends and kinsmen if three planets be in their own houses; wealthy, if four planets exist; will live in comfort and be happy, if five planets exist; will possess all human enjoyments if six planets exist; will become a king, if seven planets exist respectively in their own houses. Similarly a native will be (1) a dependant and supported by other's wealth, (2) will be supported by friends, (3) will be supported by his own relations, (4) will be supported by his brothers and cousins, (5) will become the head of many people, (6) will become a general, and (7) will become a king if one, two, three, four, five, six, or seven planets occupy respectively their friends' houses.

मालिनी—जनयति नृपमेकोऽप्युच्चगो मित्रदृष्टः प्रचुरधनसमेतं मित्रयोगाच्च सिद्धम् ॥ विधनविसुखमूढव्याधितो बंधतप्तो वधदुरितसमेतः शत्रुनीचर्क्षगेषु ॥ २ ॥

जनयति Janayati, makes, produces. नृपम् Nripam, king. एकः Ekaḥ, one planet. अपि Api, even. उच्चगः Uchchagaḥ, when in its exalted position. मित्रदृष्टः Mitradṛiṣṭaḥ, aspected by an ally planet. प्रचुरधनसमेतं Prachuradhanasametam, surrounded by abundance of wealth. मित्रयोगात् Mitrayogât, on account of being accompanied by a friendly planet. च Cha, and. सिद्धम् Siddham, perfected; getting honours on all sides. विधनविसुखमूढव्याधितः Vidhanavisukhamûḍhavyâdhitaḥ, poor, unhappy, fool or diseased. बंधतप्तः Bandhataptaḥ, suffering confinement, or afflicted with many miseries. वधदुरितसमेतः Vadhaduritasametaḥ, suffering from pains of death. शत्रुनीचर्क्षगेषु Satrunîcharkṣageṣu, in an enemy's sign or in the sign of detriment.

2. If, at the birth time of a person, one planet be exalted and also aspected by a friendly planet, he will become a king; if, during birth, one planet be exalted and also accompanied by a friendly planet, the person will get abundance of wealth and will be honoured everywhere; if, during birth, one planet occupy either an inimical or a detrimental sign, the person will become poor; if two planets occupy either inimical or detrimental sign, the person will become afflicted with grief. If three planets occupy their inimical or detrimental signs, the person will become a fool. If four planets do so, the person will become afflicted with diseases; if there be five such planets, the person will suffer imprisonment; if there be such six planets the person will be a victim to much grief; and if there be seven, he will suffer the pains of death, or will incur the sin of putting one to death.

Note:—Mercury and the Sun cannot at the same time occupy their detrimental signs, *i.e.*, Pisces and Libra respectively. Seven planets cannot therefore occupy their detrimental signs at the same time. In this, as in certain other cases, already stated, the author has simply quoted the views of former writers.

उपजातिका—न कुम्भलग्नं शुभमाह सत्यो न भागभेदा-
द्यवना वदन्ति ॥ कस्यांशभेदो न तथास्ति राशेरतिप्रसंगस्त्विति
विष्णुगुप्तः ॥ ३ ॥

न Na, not. कुम्भलग्नं Kumbhalagnam, when the sign Kumbha or Aquarius becomes the Ascendant. शुभम् Śubham, auspicious. आह Âha, told. सत्यः Satyaḥ, Satyâchârya, the Astrologer. न Na, no, not; the Kumbha Lagna is not inauspicious. भागभेदात् Bhâgabhedât, due to its being divided in the Dvâdaśâmśas, *i.e.*, into the Kumbha Dvâdaśâmśa. (The Kumbha Dvâdaśâmśa becoming the Ascendant is not auspicious). कस्य Kasya, of what; of what sign (*i.e.*, of all the signs). अंशभेदः Amśabhedaḥ, division into Kumbha Dvâdaśâmśa. न Na, not (in that way). तथा Tathâ, in that way. अस्ति Asti, is. राशेः Râśeh, of whichever sign. अतिप्रसंगः Atiprasamgaḥ, unwarrantable; unsupportable. Tu, but. इति Iti, thus. विष्णुगुप्तः Visnuguptaḥ, Vishnugupta, the Astrologer.

3. Satyâchârya does not consider the Kumbha (Aquarius) Lagna (the rising sign) to be auspicious; but Yavanâchârya is of opinion that when Aquarius is the rising Dvâdaśâmśa, then it is not auspicious; (1) the whole Kumbha Lagna is not inauspicious. Against this Yavanâchârya's opinion, Viṣṇugupta says which sign has not got such sub-divisions as Aquarius Dvâdaśâmśas? Therefore the remarks of Yavanâchârya are not at all warranted.

Remarks.—(1) If the Dvâdaśâmśa of the Kumbha Lagna be inauspicious, then all the other signs, on account their being also sub-divided into Kumbha Dvâdaśâmśas, are also inauspicious. So the above remark is going rather too much beyond the mark; as beneficent effects have been ascribed to several signs.

व०ति०—यातेष्वसत्स्वसमभेषु दिनेशहोरां ख्यातो महोद्य-
मबलार्थयुतोऽतितेजाः ॥ चान्द्रीं शुभेषु युजि मार्दवकान्तिसौ-
ख्यसौभाग्यधीमधुरवाक्ययुतः प्रजातः ॥ ४ ॥

यातेषु Yâteṣu, on going into. असत्सु Asatsu, the malefics, the Sun. असमभेषु Asamabheṣu, in the odd signs. दिनेशहोरां Dineśahorâm, in the solar horâs; in the first half of the sign. ख्यातः Khyâtaḥ, celebrated. महोद्यमबलार्थयुतः Mahodyamabalârthayutaḥ, endowed with abundance of energy, strength and wealth. अतितेजाः Atitejâḥ, very powerful. चान्द्रीं Chândrîm, in the latter half of any sign. शुभेषु Śubheṣu, the benefics (going). युजि Yuji, in the even signs. मार्दवकान्तिसौख्यसौभाग्यधीमधुरवाक्ययुतः

Mârddavakântisaukhoyasaubhâgyadhîmadhuravâkyayutaḥ, endowed with mildness, lustre, intimacy, fortune, intelligence and sweet speech. प्रजात: Prajâtaḥ, the individual born.

4. When the malefic planets (*e.g.*, the Sun) occupy the first half of any odd sign (the solar horâs of odd signs) during birth time, the individual will become widely famous, energetic, strong, wealthy and very powerful. When the benefic planets occupy the first half of any even sign (the lunar horâs of even signs) the individual will become gentle and delicate in constitution ; fair in complexion ; he will make friends with many ; will be fortunate, intelligent, of sweet speech, and will be liked by all.

इंद्रवज्रा–तास्वेव होरास्वपरर्क्षगेषु ज्ञेया नराः पूर्वगणेषु मध्याः ॥ व्यत्यस्तहोराभवनास्थितेषु मर्त्या भवंत्युक्तगुणै-र्विहीनाः ॥ ५ ॥

तासु Tâsu, in those. एव Eva, thus. होरासु Horâsu, in (those) half signs or horâs. परर्क्षगेषु Pararkṣageṣu, (but) in the other planets' signs. ज्ञेया Jñyeâ, to be considered. नराः Narâḥ, persons. पूर्वगुणेषु Pûrvaguṇeṣu, in the aforesaid qualities. मध्याः Madhyâḥ, mediocre ; in a moderate degree. व्यत्यस्तहोराभवनस्थितेषु Vyatyastyahorâbhavanasthiteṣu, situated in the horâs and houses different from those mentioned before ; when both the horâs and signs are different. मर्त्याः Martyâḥ, persons. भवंति Bhavanti, become. उक्तगुणैः Uktaguṇaiḥ, of the aforesaid qualities. विहीनाः Vihînâḥ, devoid.

5. If the horâs occupied by the malefic and benefic planets be the same as mentioned above while the signs are different, (1) the person will possess the qualities that have been stated above respectively for the two Yogas in a mediocre degree ; but if both the horâs and signs be different (2), the effects will fail.

Note:—(1) *i.e.*, If the malefics be in the second half (solar horâ) of any even sign, the effects mentioned above will be reduced to half ; so the results would be, if the benefics occupy the second half (lunar horâ) of any odd sign (2). If the malefics be in the first half (lunar horâ) of any even sign, the native will be deprived of the good qualities, energy, strength, wealth, etc., mentioned above. If the benefics be in the first half (solar horâ) of any odd sign, the native will be deprived of the good qualities, gentleness, etc., mentioned above.

व०ति०—कल्याणरूपगुणमात्मसुहृद्दृकाणे चंद्रोऽन्यगस्त- दधिनाथगुणं करोति ॥ व्यालोद्यतायुधचतुश्चरणांडजेषु तीक्ष्णो- ऽतिहिंस्रगुरुतल्परतोऽटनश्च ॥ ६ ॥

कल्याणरूपगुणम् Kalyâṇarûpaguṇam, of good features and qualities. आत्मसुहृद्दृकाणे Âtmasuhriddrikâṇe, in one's own or a friend's decanate. चंद्रः Chandraḥ, Moon. अन्यगः Anyagaḥ, in the other decanates than those mentioned before. तदधिनाथगुणं Tadadhinâthaguṇam, the qualities of the ruler of the corresponding decanate. करोति Karoti, does; produces. व्यालोद्यतायुधचतुश्चरणांडजेषु Vyâlodyatâyudhachatuścharaṇâṇḍajeṣu, in the serpent decanate, armed decanate, quadruped decanate, or in the bird Drekkâṇ (successively) तीक्ष्णः Tîkṣṇaḥ, hot tempered; wicked; cruel. अतिहिंस्रगुरुतल्परतः Atihimṣragurutalparataḥ, very mischievous, murderous, addicted to one's religious preceptor's wife. अटनः Aṭanaḥ, of wandering habits. च Cha, and.

6. If the Moon occupy either her own or a friendly (1) Decanate, the native will get good appearance and good qualities; if the Moon occupy an indifferent's Decanate, the qualities also will be of a mediocre nature; if the Moon be in an enemy's Decanate, the native will not possess any good appearance or any good qualities. The native will become hot tempered, wicked or cruel, if the Moon be in the serpent Decanate; will be very mischievous, murderous, if the Moon be in the armed Decanate; will be addicted to one's religious preceptor's wife, if the Moon be in the quadruped Decanate; and will become a traveller if the Moon be in the bird Dreṣkâṇ.

Note :—(1) Friendly at the time of birth, *vide* Chap. II, stanza 18.

Remarks :—The 2nd and 3rd Karka Dreṣkâṇs, the 1st and 2nd Vriśchik Drekkâṇ and the 3rd Decanate of Mîna Dreṣkâṇa are called serpent Dreṣkâṇs. The first and third of Meṣa Dreṣkâṇa, the second and third of Mithuna, the second and third of Siṃha, the 2nd of Kanyâ, the 3rd of Tulâ, the first and third of Dhanu and the 3rd of Makara are called armed Dreṣkâṇs.

Quadruped Dreṣkâṇaṣ :—Second of Meṣa; second and third of Vriṣa; first of Karka; first, second and third of Siṃha; the third of Tulâ; the third of Vriṣchika; the first of Dhanu and the first of Makara.

Bird Dreṣkâṇaṣ :—2nd of Mithuna; 1st of Siṃha; 2nd of Tulâ; and the 1st of Kumbha. If the Drekkâṇa occupied by the Moon be of more than one character, the person will be all that have been stated for each character.

शालिनी—स्तेनो भोक्ता पंडिताढ्यो नरेन्द्रः क्लीबः शूरो विष्टिकृद्दासवृत्तिः । पापो हिंस्रोऽभीश्च वर्गोत्तमांशेष्वेषामीशा राशिवद्द्वादशांशैः ॥ ७ ॥

स्तेनः Stenaḥ, thief. भोक्ता Bhoktâ, enjoyer. पंडिताढ्यः Paṇḍitâḍhyaḥ, learned, rich. नरेन्द्रः Narendraḥ, king. क्लीबः Klîbaḥ, a eunuch ; hermaphrodite. शूरः Sûraḥ, a hero ; a valiant warrior. विष्टिकृत् Viṣṭikṛit, a porter. दासवृत्तिः Dâsavṛittiḥ, a servant. पापः Pâpaḥ, vicious. हिंस्रः Himsraḥ, mischievous ; murderous. अभीः Abhîḥ, fearless. च Cha, and. वर्गोत्तमांशेषु Vargottamâmśeṣu, in the Vargottama degrees. एषां Eṣâm, of these (*i.e.*, thief, &c.). ईशाः Îśâḥ, kings. राशिवत् Râśivaṭ, having like results as those mentioned under the heading of signs. (The Moon and the Signs). द्वादशांशैः Dvâdaśâmśaiḥ, in the rising Dvâdaśâmśas of those signs.

7. Any person born in the rising Meṣa Navâmśa (the sign Meṣa being not the Ascendant) will become a thief ; in the rising Vṛiṣa Navâmśa (the Vṛiṣa not being the Ascendant), an enjoyer ; in the rising Mithuna Navâmśa (the Mithuna not being the Ascendant), a learned Pandit ; in the rising Karka Navâmśa, wealthy ; in the rising Simha Navâmśa, a king ; in the rising Kanyâ Navâmśa, a eunuch; in the rising Tulâ Navâmśa, fond of fighting in battles ; in the rising Vṛiśchika Navâmśa, a porter ; in the rising Dhanu Navâmśa, a servant ; in the rising Makara Navâmśa, a sinner ; in the rising Kumbha Navâmśa, a mischievous person ; in the rising Mîna Navâmśa he will be fearless. Any person, born when the rising Navâmśa is at the same time a Vargottama Navâmśa, becomes the king of the respective classes of persons above mentioned, *i.e.*, any person born in the rising Meṣa Vargottamâmśa becomes the king of thieves and so on. (For the Vargottama, see verse 141, Chap I). Any persons born in any rising Dvâdaśâmśa, will get the same results as those mentioned when the Moon is in that sign.

व० ति०—जायान्वितो बलविभूषणसत्वयुक्तस्तेजोऽतिसाहसयुतश्च कुजे स्वभागे। रोगी मृतस्वयुवतिर्विषमोऽन्यदारो दुःखी परिच्छदयुतो मलिनोऽर्कपुत्रे ॥ ८ ॥

जायान्वितः Jâyânvitaḥ; will be a married man. बलविभूषणसत्वयुक्तः Balavibhûṣaṇasatvayuktaḥ, endowed with strength, ornaments, and generosity. तेजोऽतिसाहसयुतः Tejotisâhasayutaḥ, endowed with prowess (fire of energy) and bravery. च Cha, and. कुजे Kuje, on Mars occupying. स्वभागे Svabhâge, his own Triṃśâṃśaka. रोगी Rogî, diseased. मृतस्वयुवतिः Mritasvayuvatiḥ, having one's wife dying before him. विषमः Viṣamaḥ, wicked. अन्यदारः Anyadâraḥ, addicted to others' wives. दुःखी Duḥkhî, miserable. परिच्छदयुतः Parichchadayutaḥ, having dresses. मलिनः Malinaḥ, dirty. अर्कपुत्रे Arkaputre, Saturn being in his Triṃśâṃśaka.

8. If Mars occupy his own Triṃśâṃśa, the individual born will get a wife, strength, ornaments, generosity, fire of energy and bravery. If Saturn be in his own Triṃśâṃśa, the native will be afflicted with diseases; his wife will die before him; his temper will be angry; he will be addicted to others' wives; he will be miserable; will have a house, clothes, attendants and the like and will be very dirty.

Remarks:—The Triṃśâṃśa is not mentioned in the Śloka; how then is this meaning conveyed here? In the results of Venus to be said in verse 10, this Triṃśâṃśa will be noticed subsequently.

व० ति०—स्वांशे गुरौ धनयशःसुखबुद्धियुक्तास्तेजस्विपूज्यनिरुगुद्यमभोगवंतः। मेधाकलाकपटकाव्यविवादशिल्पशास्त्रार्थसाहसयुताः शशिजेऽतिमान्याः ॥ ९ ॥

स्वांशे Svâṃśe, in his own Triṃśâṃśaka. गुरौ Gurau, Jupiter. धनयशःसुखबुद्धियुक्ताः Dhanayaśahsukhabuddhiyuktâḥ, united with wealth, fame, happiness, and intellect. तेजस्वीपूज्यनिरुगुद्यमभोगवंतः Tejasvîpûjyanirugudyamabhogavantaḥ, lustrous and energetic, honourable, healthy, hopeful and enthusiastic, capable of enjoying. मेधाकलाकपटकाव्यविवादशिल्पशास्त्रार्थसाहसयुताः Medhâkalâkapaṭakâvyavivadaśilpâśastrârthasâhasayutâḥ, intelligent, artist, hypocrite, literary author, arguer, artisan, versed in Śâstras, brave. शशिजे Saśje, Mercury in his own Triṃśâṃśaka. अतिमान्याः Atimânyâḥ, very much respected.

9. If Jupiter occupy his own Triṃśâṃśa, the individual born will become wealthy, famous, happy and intelligent. He will also be lustrous and very energetic, universally

respected, healthy, always hopeful and ready to do any work and possessing all human enjoyments. If Mercury occupy his own Trimsâmsa, the native will become intelligent, artistic, hypocrite, literary author, arguer, workman (*e.g.*, carpenter, &c.) versed in Sâstras and brave. He will also be very much respected.

Remarks—By "artistic" is meant here as skilled in music, dancing, painting, etc.

मंदाक्रान्ता–स्वे त्रिंशांशे बहुसुतसुखारोग्यभाग्यार्थरूपः
शुक्रे तीक्ष्णः सुललितवपुः सुप्रकीर्णेंद्रियश्च । शूरस्तब्धौ
विषमवधकौ सद्गुणाढ्यौ सुखिज्ञौ चार्वंगेष्टौ रविशशियुतेष्वार-
पूर्वांशकेषु ॥ १० ॥

इति श्रीवराहमिहिराचार्यप्रणीते बृहज्जातके
आश्रययोगाध्याय एकविंशः ॥ २१ ॥

स्वे Sve, in one's own. त्रिंशांशे Trimśâmśe, in one's Trimśâmśa. बहुसुतसुखारोग्यभाग्यार्थरूपः Bahusutasukhârogyabhâgyârtharûpah, having many sons, living in comfort, healthy, fortunate, wealthy and of good appearance. शुक्रे Śukre, on Venus occupying. तीक्ष्णः Tîkṣṇaḥ, wicked. सुललितवपुः Sulalitavapuḥ, having a very fair and gentle body. सुप्रकीर्णेंद्रियः Suprakîrṇendriyaḥ, a sensualist, capable to hold intercourse with many women. च Cha, and. शूरस्तब्धौ Sûrastabdhau, hero; one confounded (slow at work). विषमवधकौ Viṣamabadhakau, wicked; executioner. सद्गुणाढ्यौ Sadguṇâḍhyau, well qualified, rich. सुखिज्ञौ Sukhijñau, happy, learned. चार्वंगेष्टौ Chârvamgeṣṭau, of a beautiful body, liked by all. रविशशियुतेषु Raviśaśiyuteṣu, the Sun, Moon occupying successively. आरपूर्वांशकेषु Ârapûrvâmśakeṣu, the Trimśamśakas of Mars, Saturn, Jupiter, Mercury and Venus successively.

10. If Venus occupy her own Trimśâmśa, the individual born will get numerous sons, much happiness, health, fortune, and wealth and good appearance. He will become also wicked, his body being very fair; he will be gentle and delicate and he will be a great sensualist.

If the Sun be at the time of birth in Mars' Trimśâmśa, the native will become a great hero; if the Moon be in Mars Trimśâmśa, the native will be confounded and dull. If the Sun be in Saturn's Triṃśâṃśa, the native will become wicked; and if the Moon be in Saturn's Triṃsâṃśa, the native will become an executioner. If the Sun be in Jupiter's, the native will become well-qualified; and if the Moon be there the native will become wealthy. If the Sun be in Mercury's Triṃśâmśa, the native will live in comfort and will be happy; and if there be the Moon, he will become a scholar. If the Sun be in Venus's Triṃṣâṃśa, the native will possess a beautiful body and if there be Moon, the native will become lovely and liked by all.

Thus ends the Twenty-first Chapter on Âśraya Yoga in Bṛihajjâtaka by Śrî Varâha Mihirâchârya.

CHAPTER XXII.

ON MISCELLANEOUS PLANETARY COMBINATIONS.

वैतालीय—स्वर्क्षतुङ्गमूलत्रिकोणगाः कण्टकेषु यावन्त आश्रिताः। सर्व एव तेऽन्योन्यकारकाः कर्मगस्तु तेषां विशेषतः॥१॥

स्वर्क्षतुङ्गमूलत्रिकोणगाः Svarkṣatuṅgamûlatrikoṇagâḥ, the planets residing in their own houses, or in their exalted houses, or in their mûlatrikoṇa (the primary triangular) houses. कण्टकेषु Kaṇṭakeṣu, in the four angles commencing with the Ascendant. यावन्तः Yâvantaḥ, as many as. आश्रिताः Âśritâḥ, are situated. सर्वे Sarve, all. एव Eva, certainly. ते Te, they. अन्योन्यकारकाः Anyonyakârakâḥ, Kâraka planets to each other; they being instruments of each other. कर्मगः Karmagaḥ, the planet in the tenth house from another such Karka planet. तु Tu, but. तेषां Teṣâm, of these Kâraka planets; of these angular planets. विशेषतः Viśeṣataḥ, especially reckoned.

1. The angular planets (1) (from the Ascendant) when they are in their own houses, or when they are exalted or when they are in their Mûlatrikoṇa houses are said to be the Kâraka planets to each other, *i.e.*, they become co-workers (mutually helping causes) in generating certain effects. Of these angular planets, the planet in the tenth house from another planet is reckoned as the special co-worker of that planet.

Note—(1) Planets occupying the angular or Kendra houses.

रथोद्धता—कर्कटोदयगते यथोडुपे स्वोच्चगाः कुजयमार्कसूरयः। कारका निगदिताः परस्परं लग्नगस्य सकलोऽम्बराम्बुगः॥ २॥

कर्कटोदयगते Karkaṭodayagate, the Ascendant being the Karka or Cancer. यथा Yathâ, thus; for instance. उडुपे Uḍupe, the Moon (residing). स्वोच्चगाः Svochchagâḥ, when exalted. कुजयमार्कसूरयः Kujayamârkasûrayaḥ, Mars, Saturn, the Sun, and Jupiter. कारकाः Kârakâḥ, Kâraka planets; co-workers. निगदिताः Nigaditâḥ, are said to be; are known as. परस्परं Parasparam, amongst each other. लग्नगस्य Lagnagasya, of the planet that is in the Ascendant. सकलः Sakalaḥ, all the planets. अंबरांबुगः Ambarâmbugaḥ, in the tenth and in the fourth houses.

2. Suppose, for example, the Ascendant to be the sign Karka (Cancer) occupied by the Moon and suppose Mars, Saturn, the Sun and Jupiter to occupy respectively their exalted signs, then these four planets (Mars, Saturn, the Sun and Jupiter) are known as Kâraka planets or co-workers amongst each other (1). Moreover all the planets (2) occupying the fourth or the tenth houses are Kâraka planets to the planet occupying the Ascendant (the Ascending planet is not the Kâraka of them, *i.e.*, the reverse does not hold).

Notes--(1) The following description represents the positions of the planets as stated in this verse :—*e.g.*, the fourth house Cancer at the top represents the Ascendant ; Moon and Jupiter are there ; Cancer is the exalted house of Jupiter as well as the Moon's own house. The seventh house Tulâ is Saturn's exalted house ; Mars is exalted in Makara, the 10th house and the Sun is also exalted in Meṣa, the 1st house. Moon and Jupiter are in the 4th house which is the Ascendant ; Saturn is in the 7th house ; Mars is in the 10th house and the Sun is in the 1st house which is Meṣa.

The Commentator infers from this stanza that the planets occupying their own houses, exalted and Mûlatrikoṇa signs are also mutually Kâraka planets if they occupy the angular signs from one another, though not the angular signs from the Ascendant.

All the planets whether they occupy their own signs, their exalted signs or their Mülatrikoṇa signs or not, according to the Commentator.

अनुष्टुभ्–स्वत्रिकोणोच्चगो हेतुरन्योन्यं यदि कर्मगः ।
सुहृत्तद्गुणसम्पन्नः कारकश्चापि स स्मृतः ॥ ३ ॥

स्वत्रिकोणोच्चगः Svatrikoṇochchagaḥ, the planets situated in their own houses, in their Trikoṇa houses and in the exalted houses. हेतुः Hetuḥ, the helping cause. अन्योन्यं Anyonyam, amongst each other. यदि Yadi, if. कर्मगः Karmagaḥ, when in the tenth house (from such sign). सुहृत् Suhṛit, the friendly planet. तद्गुणसम्पन्नः Tadguṇa-sampannaḥ, or the planet that is for the time being friendly. कारकः Kârakaḥ, co-worker ; the helping planet. च Cha, and. अपि Api, also. स Sa, that planet ; the planet in the tenth house. स्मृतः Smṛitaḥ, is reckoned to be.

3. If any planet occupy its own or its exalted or its Mûlatrikoṇa house (1) and moreover if it be situated in the tenth house from any other planet (also in its own, or its

exalted or its Mûlatrikoṇa house), then the first planet on account of its being friendly or the then friendly (2) is known as the Kâraka of the second planet (*i. e.*, the second is not the Kâraka of the first) (3).

Notes :—(1) But not occupying the angular houses from the Ascendant.

(2) Because it occupies the tenth house.

(3) The effects of the Kâraka planets are described in Varâha Mihira's work on Yoga Yâtrâ or marching occasions, in which it is said that when a prince loses his kingdom, he recovers it in the Antardaśa period of a Kâraka planet; again it is said that a man enjoys comfort, wealth and success when the Moon passes through the house of a Kâraka planet, or through the 2nd house from that occupied by the Sun. Also that the journey may be a successful one, it shall be commenced when the Moon occupies either of the two places mentioned above, otherwise the traveller will meet with disasters on the way.

अनुष्टुभ्–शुभं वर्गोत्तमे जन्म वेशिस्थाने च सद्ग्रहे । अ
शून्येषु च केन्द्रेषु कारकाख्यग्रहेषु च ॥ ४ ॥

शुभं Śubham, auspicious. वर्गोत्तमे Vargottame, in the Vargottama Navâṃśa. जन्म Janma, birth. वेशिस्थाने Veśisthâne, in the house second from the sign which the Sun occupied during one's birth time. च Cha, and. सद्ग्रहे Sadgrahe, on the benefic planets (*e.g.*, any one of Mercury, Jupiter, Venus) occupying. अशून्ये Aśûnyeṣu, occupied by; without any planets not existing, *i.e.*, the planet occupying even one or more of the four angles. च Cha, and. केन्द्रेषु Kendreṣu, in one or more of the angular houses. कारकाख्यग्रहेषु Kârakâkhyagraheṣu, on there being Kâraka (co-working) planets also. च Cha, and.

4. The individual, born when the rising Navâṃśa is a Vargottama one, or when the Moon occupies a Vargottama Navâṃśa, will be happy and prosperous throughout his life. Such also will be the results to one during whose birth time the 2nd house from the Sun may be occupied by benefic planets or wheneven one of the 4 angular houses (1) be occupied by planets. The results will be also happy and prosperous if during the birth time there be Kâraka (co-working) planets in the signs (2).

Notes—(1) If one of the angular houses be occupied by a planet, the person will be happy; if two or more be occupied he will be happier still.

and if the planets be benefic, the person will be exceedingly happy and prosperous.

(2) The results will be more happy, if there be more favourable combinations.

वैतालीय–मध्ये वयसः सुखप्रदाः केन्द्रस्था गुरुजन्मलग्नपाः । पृष्ठोभयकोदयर्क्षगास्त्वन्तेऽन्तः प्रथमेषु पाकदाः ॥ ५ ॥

मध्ये Madhye, while in the prime of manhood; in the middle age. वयसः Vayasaḥ, of the age; of the period of life. केन्द्रस्थाः Kendrasthâḥ, situated in any angular (cardinal) house. गुरुजन्मलग्नपाः Gurujanmalagnapâḥ, Jupiter, or the ruler of the sign occupied by the Moon during birth, or the ruler of the Ascendant during birth. पृष्ठोभयकोदयर्क्षगाः Priṣṭhobhayakodayarkṣagâḥ, when situated respectively in the signs that rise in the horizon with their backs first, in the Pisces, and in the signs that rise in the horizon with their faces in the front (when the Daśâpati is about to enter his own period of awarding fruits). तु Tu, but. अन्ते Ante, during the latter part of the Daśâ period. अन्तः Antaḥ, during the middle of the Daśâ period. प्रथमेषु Prathameṣu, during the first part of the Daśâ period. पाकदाः Pâkadâḥ, yielding results.

5. If, at the time of the birth, of a person any angular house be occupied by Jupiter, or the ruler of the sign occupied by the Moon during birth or the ruler of the Ascendant, the individual born will be happy while in his full vigour of manhood. Again, if at the commencement of a Daśâ period, the Daśâpati (the ruler of such period) happen to occupy a back rising (Priṣṭhodaya) sign, (1) he will award his results at the end of the Daśâ period. If such ruler occupy a front rising (2) (Śirodaya) sign, he will produce his effects at the beginning of his period and if the ruler occupy the double rising (3) (Śirapriṣṭhodaya) sign the effects will be felt in the middle of the Daśâ period.

Notes :—The Daśâ period is to be divided into three equal parts.

(1) The back rising signs are Meṣa, Vṛiṣa, Dhanu, Karka and Makara.

(2) The front rising signs are Mithuna, Siṃha, Kanyâ, Tulâ, Vṛiśchika, and Kumbha.

(3) The double rising signs are Mîna (see verse 10, Chapter I).

पुष्पिताग्रा—दिनकररुधिरौ प्रवेशकाले गुरुभृगुजौ भवनस्य मध्ययातौ । रविसुतशशिनौ विनिर्गमस्थौ शशितनयः फलदस्तु सर्वकालम् ॥ ६ ॥

इति श्रीवराहमिहिरविरचिते बृहज्जातके प्रकीर्णकाध्यायो द्वाविंशतितमः ॥ २२ ॥

दिनकररुधिरौ Dinakararudhirau, the Sun and Mars. प्रवेशकाले Praveśakâle, when about to enter a sign; while in the first third part of any sign. गुरुभृगुजौ Gurubhrigujau, Jupiter and Venus. भवनस्य Bhavanasya, of any house or sign. मध्ययातौ Madhyayâtau, while in the middle third of any sign. रविसुतशशिनौ Ravisutaśaśinau, Saturn and the Moon. विनिर्गमस्थौ Vinirgamasthau, while in the last third part of any sign. शशितनयः Śaśitanayaḥ, Mercury. फलदः Phaladaḥ, awarding results; produce their effects. तु Tu, but. सर्वकालम् Sarvakâlam, always; anywhere in any sign throughout his course.

6. The Sun and Mars award their respective results immediately after entering a sign (*i.e.*, while in the first 3rd part of a sign); Jupiter and Venus produce their effects when passing through the middle third of any sign; Saturn and Moon do so when passing through the last third of a sign and Mercury produces its effects throughout the sign.

Note:—The sign is supposed here to be divided into three equal parts of 10 degrees each.

Thus ends the Twenty-second Chapter on Miscellaneous Yogas by Śrî Varâha Mihirâchârya of Avantika.

CHAPTER XXIII.

ON THE CHAPTER ON EVILS.

Or on Malefic Planetary Combinations.

शा० वि०—लग्नात्पुत्रकलत्रभे शुभपतिप्राप्तेऽथवालोकिते चंद्राद्वा यदि संपदस्ति हि तयोर्ज्ञेयोऽन्यथासंभवः। पाथोनोदयगे रवौ रविसुतो मीनस्थितो दारहा पुत्रस्थानगतश्च पुत्रमरणं पुत्रोऽवनेर्यच्छति ॥ १ ॥

लग्नात् Lagnât, from the Ascendant. पुत्रकलत्रभे Putrakalatrabhe, in the fifth and seventh houses, the houses of son and wife respectively. शुभपतिप्राप्ते Subhapatiprâpte, on being occupied by auspicious rulers. अथवा Athavâ, or. आलोकिते Âlokite, being aspected by. चंद्रात् Chandrât, from the Moon. वा Vâ, or. यदि Yadi, if. संपत् Sampat, wealth; son or wife is here meant as the wealth, as the case may be. अस्ति Asti, comes. हि Hi, certainly. तयोः Tayoḥ, of them; sons or wife. ज्ञेयः Jñeyaḥ, are to be considered. अन्यथा Anyathâ, otherwise. असंभवः Asambhavâḥ, not possible; not having or possessing. पाथोनोदयगे Pâthonodayage, the sign Kanyâ being the Ascendant. रवौ Ravau, on the Sun being. रविसुतः Ravisutaḥ, Saturn. मीनस्थितः Mînasthitaḥ, in the sign Pisces (the seventh from Kanyâ). दारहा Dârahâ, killing the wife; *i. e.*, meaning the death of the wife. पुत्रस्थानगतः Putrasthânagataḥ, in the fifth house from Kanyâ, *i. e.*, in the sign Makara. च Cha, and. पुत्रमरणं Putramaraṇam, the death of the son. पुत्रः Putraḥ, the son. अवनेः Avaneḥ, of the earth. यच्छति Yachchati, gives; yields.

1. If, during the birth of a person, the fifth house from the Ascendant or from the Moon be either occupied or aspected by its ruler or any benefic planet, that man will have sons (1) as his property; and if the seventh house be so occupied or aspected, he will get a wife as his property. Otherwise (2), he will get no sons nor wife (such events can be forecast from the nature of other houses).

Again if the sign Kanyâ be the Ascendant and if the Sun be there and Saturn occupy the sign Mîna, then the person will lose his wife. Again if the sign Kanyâ be the

Ascendant and if the Sun be there and Mars occupy the sign Makara, the person will see the death of his son.

Notes.—There are twelve kinds of sons in the Hindu Law.

(1) Aurasa—The eldest legitimate son, born of the real father and mother.

(2) Kṣetraja—the offspring of a wife by a kinsman duly appointed to raise up issue to the husband.

(3) Datta—An adopted son with the consent of his natural parents.

(4) Kṛitrima—a grown-up son adopted without the consent of his nátural parents.

(5) Ádhamapravava—an adopted son of a low-caste person.

(6) Gûḍhotpanna—a son born secretly of a woman, when her husband is absent, the real father being unknown.

(7) Apaviddah—a son that is abandoned by the father or mother or by both and adopted by a stranger.

(8) Paunarbhava—a son born of a woman married again.

(9) Kânîna—the son of an unmarried woman.

(10) Sahoḍa—the son of a woman pregnant at marriage.

(11) Krîtaka—a son purchased from his natural parents.

(12) Daśîpravava—a son of a female slave.

Thus the commentary adds :—

अत्र केचिद्द्वादशप्रकारं पुत्रं वर्णयंति । औरसः, क्षेत्रजः, दत्तः, कृत्रिमः, अधमप्रभवः, गूढोत्पन्नः, अपविद्धः, पौनर्भवः, कानीनः, सहोढः, क्रीतकः, दासीप्रभव इति । तथा च सारावल्याम् । " शुभभवनमथ शुभयुतं शुभदृष्टं वा सुतर्क्षमिह येषाम् । तेषां प्रभवः पुंसां भवत्यवश्यं न विपरीतम् ॥ एकतमे गुरुवर्गे शुभराशावौरसो भवेत्पुत्रः । लग्नाच्चंद्रादथवा बलयुक्ताद्वीक्षितोऽपि वा सौम्यैः ॥ संख्या नवांशतुल्या सौम्यांशे तावती सदा दृष्टा । शुभदृष्टे तद्द्विगुणा क्लिष्टा पापांशके तथा दृष्टा ॥ सौरर्क्षे सौरगुणो बुधदृष्टो गुरुकुजार्कदृग्धीनः । क्षेत्रजपुत्रं जनयति बौधोऽपि गुणो रविजदृष्टः ॥ मांदं सुतर्क्षमिंदुं निरीक्षिते यदि शनैश्चरेण युतम् । दत्तकपुत्रोत्पत्तिः क्रीतश्च बुधस्य चैवं स्यात् ॥ सप्तमभागे कौजे सौरयुते पंचमे सदा भवने । कृत्रिमपुत्रं विंद्याच्छेषग्रहदर्शनान्मुक्ते ॥ वर्गे पंचमराशौ सौरे सूर्ये च तत्र संयुक्ते । लोहितदृष्टे वाच्यो जातश्च सुतोऽधमप्रभवः ॥ चंद्रे भौमांशगते धीस्थे मंदावलोकिते भवति । गूढोत्पत्तिर्भवेत्पुत्रः शेषग्रहदर्शनायाते ॥ सत्पुत्रः शेपग्रहदर्शनायाते ॥ तस्मिन्नेव च भौमे शनिवर्गस्थे निरीक्षिते रविणा । पुरुषस्य भवति पुत्रोऽपविद्ध इति चरकमुनिवचनात् ॥ शनिवर्गस्थे चंद्रे शनियुक्ते पंचमे सदा सौरे । शुक्ररविभ्यां दृष्टे पुत्रः पौनर्भवो भवति ॥ चूडा यदार्कसत्वात्कलादृतस्यैव पंचमे भवने । रविदृष्टेऽप्यथ सहिते कानीनः संभवति पुत्रः ॥ वर्गे रविचंद्रमसोः सुतगेहे चंद्रसूर्यसंयुक्ते । शुक्रेण दृष्टमात्रे पुत्रः कथितः सहोढश्च ॥ पापैर्बलिभिर्युक्ते पापर्क्षे पंचमे सदा राशौ । जातो पुत्रः पुरुषः सौम्यग्रहदर्शनातीते ॥ शुक्रनवांशे तस्मिन् शुक्रेण निरीक्षिते

त्वपत्यानि। दासीप्रभवानि वदेच्चंद्रेऽपि केचिदाचार्याः॥ सितशशिवर्गे धीस्थे ताभ्या दृष्टेऽथवापि संयुक्ते। प्रायेण दारिकाः स्युस्तद्राशिगणेऽपि वान्यथा पुत्राः॥" इति।

Thus the Sârâvali writes:—If in one's horoscope, the house of sons (*i. e.*, the fifth house) be an auspicious one, or if it be either occupied or aspected by a benefic planet, the individual will have one or other of the twelve kinds of sons described above.

If the son's house (*i.e.*, the fifth house) from the Ascendant or from the Moon whichever is more powerful, be an auspicious one and if it be the Varga of Jupiter or be aspected by benefic planets, the issue will be Aurasa or a legitimate son. The number of sons will be the number represented by the Navâṃśa occupied by the benefic planet in the fifth house; again if the fifth house be also aspected by benefic planets, then the sons will be double of the aforesaid number. Again, if the fifth house be occupied by malefic planets, the number of sons represented by the Navâṃśa occupied by the malefics will die; and double that number will die if the house be also aspected by malefic planets.

If the fifth house be the house of Saturn, and if it be aspected by Mercury and not by Jupiter, Mars and the Sun, the issue will be Kṣetraja and will get the qualities of Saturn; if the fifth house be that of Mercury and if it be aspected by Saturn and not by Jupiter, Mars and the Sun, the issue also will be Kṣetraja but he will possess the qualities of Mercury.

If the fifth house be that of Saturn and occupied by Saturn and if it aspects the Moon, the issue will be Dattaka; if the fifth house be of Mercury and occupied by Mercury and if it aspects the Moon, the issue will be Krîta.

If the last Navâṃśa of the fifth house be that of Mars and if there be Saturn in the fifth house and if it be not aspected by the remaining planets, the issue will be Kṛitrima.

If the fifth house be the Varga of Saturn and if the Sun be there and if it be aspected by Mars, the issue will be Adhamapravava.

If the Moon occupy the Navâṃśa of Mars in the fifth house and if it be aspected by Saturn and not by the remaining planets, the issue will be Guḍhotpatti.

If the fifth house be the Varga of Saturn and occupied by Mars and if it be aspected by the Sun, the issue will be Apaviddha. Thus says Charaka.

If the fifth house be the Varga of Saturn and occupied by Saturn and if it be aspected by Venus and the Sun, the issue will be Paunarvava.

If the fifth house be beyond the rays of the setting Sun and if it be âspected by the Sun, or if it be occupied by the Sun, the issue will be Kânina.

If the fifth house be the Varga of the Sun and the Moon and if it be occupied by the Sun and the Moon and aspected by Venus, the issue will be Sahoda.

If the fifth house be inauspicious and occupied by powerful malefics and if it be not aspected by any benefic planet and if Venus aspects the Venus Navâmśa of the fifth house, the issue will be Dâsipravava. Some read Moon, in the place of Venus aforesaid.

If the fifth house be the Varga of Venus and the Moon and if it be occupied or aspected by them, the issue will be females of the character indicated by those houses; or there will be male issues other than the twelve sorts above mentioned.

अत्र कलत्रस्थानेऽपि केचिद्विशेषं वर्णयंति। " शुक्रेंदु जीवशशिजैः सकलैस्त्रिभिश्च द्वाभ्यां कलत्रभवने च तथैकेन। एषां गृहेऽपि च गणेऽथ विलोकिते वा संति स्त्रियो भवनवर्गखगस्वभावाः॥ एवं क्रूरैर्नाशो लग्नाच्च द्राद्वदेच्चबलयोगात्। शशिरविजयोः कलत्रे भार्या पुंसां पुनर्भूः स्यात्॥ भवनाधिपांशतुल्या भवंति नार्यो निरीक्षणाद्वापि। एकैव रविकुजांशे गुरुबुधयोश्चापिजामित्रे॥ प्रायेण चंद्रसितयोर्बलसंयुक्तेऽथवापि जामित्रे। दृष्टे वा बहुपत्न्यो भवंति शुक्रे विशेषेण॥ गुरुशुक्रयोः स्ववर्णा रविकुजशशिभानुजैर्भवंत्यूनाः। शुक्रे वेश्याप्रायाश्चन्द्रेऽपि वदंति केतुमालाख्याः॥ "

Some describe in some details regarding one's wife, thus:—

If the seventh house from the Lagna or from the Moon whichever is more powerful, be occupied by Venus, Moon, Jupiter and Mercury, or by any three or any two or any one of these, or if the seventh house be the house of any of these four or if it be aspected by all or any of these, the wives will be of the characters indicated by the Vargas of the influencing planets; and if there be evil planets, the death of wives is to be forecast.

If the seventh house be occupied by the Moon and Saturn, the wife will quit the husband and marry again.

The number of wives will be the number represented by the Navâmśa occupied by the ruler of the seventh house or the number represented by the Navâmśa aspected by the ruler of the seventh house.

If Jupiter or Mercury occupy the 7th house and the Navâmśa of the Sun or Mars or if the Moon and Venus (Venus especially) be powerful or if they occupy or aspect the seventh house, the person will have several wives.

Under the influence of Jupiter and Venus, the wife will be of the same caste and rank; under the influence of the Sun, Mars, Moon or

Saturn, the wife will be of a lower rank. Under the influence of the powerful Venus or of the powerful Moon, the wife will become a prostitute. Thus the Ketumâla says.

प्रहर्षिणी—उग्रग्रहैः सितचतुरस्रसंस्थितैर्मध्यस्थिते भृगुतनयेऽथवोग्रयोः । सौम्यग्रहैरसहितसंनिरीक्षिते जायावधो दहननिपातपाशजः ॥ २ ॥

उग्रग्रहैः Ugragrahaiḥ, by the malefics, Mars, Saturn, Sun. सितचतुरस्रसंस्थितैः Sitachaturasrasaṃsthitaiḥ, situated in the fourth and eighth houses from Venus. मध्यस्थिते Madhyasthite, (if Venus be situated) between the malefics. भृगुतनये Bhrigutanaye, on Venus being. अथवा Athavâ, or. उग्रयोः Ugrayoḥ, between the malefics. सौम्यग्रहैः Saumyagrahaiḥ, by the benefic planets. असहितसंनिरीक्षिते Asahitasaṃnirîkṣite, not accompanied by nor aspected by. जायावधः Jâyâbadhaḥ, the death of the wife. दहननिपातपाशजः Dahananipâtapâśajaḥ, resulting from fire, or from fall from a height or by hanging by ropes or so.

2. The person's wife will die from fire if, during his birth time, malefic planets Mars, Saturn, or Sun be situated in the 4th and 8th houses from Venus; will die by falling (from some elevated place) if malefic planets be on both sides of Venus; or will hang herself by ropes if Venus be not accompanied nor aspected by any benefic planet. (These results will occur during the lifetime of the husband.)

Notes:—This is also the opinion of Gârgi, the famous astrologer. Some authors note here two Yogas only, which is not proper.

व० ति०—लग्नाद्व्ययारिगतयोः शशितिग्मरश्म्योः पत्न्या सहैकनयनस्य वदंति जन्म । द्यूनस्थयोर्नवमपंचमसंस्थयोर्वा शुक्रार्कयोर्विकलदारमुशंति जातम् ॥ ३ ॥

लग्नात् Lagnât, from the Ascendant. व्ययारिगतयोः Vyayârigatayoḥ, in the twelfth or sixth house. शशितिग्मरश्म्योः Śaśitigmaraśmyoḥ, the Sun and Moon. पत्न्या Patnyâ, together with his wife. सह Saha, together with. एकनयनस्य Ekanayanasya, of one-eyed beings. वदंति Vadanti, say. जन्म Janma, birth. द्यूनस्थयोः Dyunasthayoḥ, in the seventh house from the Ascendant. नवमपंचमसंस्थयोः Navamapañchamasaṃsthayoḥ, in the ninth or fifth house. वा Vâ, or. शुक्रार्कयोः Sukrârkayoḥ, Venus and the Sun. विकलदारम् Vikaladâram, of defective limbs. उशंति Uśanti, say. जातम् Jâtam, born.

3. If, during the birth time of any individual, the 6th and the 12th houses from the Ascendant be occupied, one by

the Sun and the other by the Moon, (or both the planets in either the 6th or the 12th house), the person and his wife will each have one eye only. Again the person will be deformed if Venus and the Sun (both) (1) occupy one of the three houses, the 7th, the 9th or the 5th from the Ascendant.

Note:—(1) Venus or the Sun according to some. This is opposed to Gârgî, whom the Commentator quotes. Gârgî holds the opinion of the text.

मालिनी—कोणोदये भृगुतनयेऽस्तचक्रसंधौ वंध्यापतिर्यदि न सुतर्क्षमिष्टयुक्तम् । पापग्रहैर्व्ययमदलग्नराशिसंस्थैः क्षीणे शशिन्यसुतकलत्रजन्मधीस्थे ॥ ४ ॥

कोणोदये Koṇodaye, Saturn being the Ascendant. भृगुतनये Bhṛigutanaye, Venus. अस्तचक्रसंधौ Astachakrasandhau, in the last Navâṃśas of Vṛiśchika, Karka, or Mîna as well as in the seventh house from the Ascendant. वंध्यापतिः Vandhyâpatiḥ, the husband of a barren wife. यदि Yadi, if. न Na, not. सुतर्क्षम् Sutarkṣam, the constellation indicating the son, *i.e.*, the fifth house from the Ascendant. इष्टयुक्तम् Iṣṭayuktam, occupied by a benefic planet. पापग्रहैः Pâpagrahaiḥ, by the malefic planets. व्ययमदलग्नराशिसंस्थैः Vyayamadalagnarâśisaṃsthaiḥ, in the twelfth, seventh, and the first houses; in all, two, or one of these. क्षीणे Kṣîṇe, waning. शशिनि Śaśini, Moon. असुतकलत्रजन्म Asutakalatrajanma, the birth of an individual having no son nor wife. धीस्थे Dhîsthe, in the fifth house from the Ascendant.

4. If, during the birth time of any individual, Saturn be the Ascendant (1) and if Venus occupy the Chakrasaṃdhi Navâṃśas and the 7th house from the Ascendant, the person's wife will be barren, on condition that the fifth house be not united with any benefic planet. Again, if the malefic planets occupy the 12th and the 7th houses and the Ascendant, the waning Moon occupying the 5th house, the person will have no wife nor sons.

Note:—(1) It is clear that the Ascendant must be Vṛiṣa or Kanyâ, or Makara, in which case the 7th houses will respectively be Vṛiśchika, Mîna, and Karka; and the last Navâṃśas of these three houses are known as Chakrasandhis or Ṛikṣandhis (see verse 7 san, Chapter I.)

हरिणी–असितकुजयोर्वर्गेऽस्तस्थे सिते तदवेक्षिते परयुवतिगस्तौ चेत्सेंदुस्त्रिया सह पुंश्चलः । भृगुजशशिनोरस्तेऽभार्यो नरो विसुतोऽपि वा परिणततनू नृस्त्र्योर्दृष्टौ शुभैः प्रमदापती ॥ ५ ॥

असितकुजयोः Asitakujayoḥ, of Saturn and Mars; of any one of these. वर्गे Varge, in the Varga division or in the Varga degrees. अस्तस्थे Astasthe, in the seventh house from the Ascending house; in the Descending house. सिते Site, Venus. तदवेक्षिते Tadaveksite, aspected by either Saturn or Mars. परयुवतिगः Parayuvatigaḥ, going to another's wife. तौ Tau, Saturn and Mars (united in the Descending sign). चेत् Chet, if. सेंदुः Senduḥ, united with the Moon (also). स्त्रिया Striyâ, with wife. सह Saha, together with. पुंश्चलः Pumśchalaḥ, the husband addicted with another woman and the wife addicted with another man; both the husband and wife as adulterer and harlot. भृगुजशशिनोः Bhṛigujaśaśinoḥ, of Venus and Moon (in one sign). अस्ते Aste, in the seventh house, (Saturn and Mars in the seventh from Venus and Moon). अभार्यः Abhâryaḥ, having no wife. नरः Naraḥ, the individual born. विसुतः Visutaḥ, without son. अपि Api, even; and. वा Vâ, and. परिणततनू: Pariṇatatanûḥ, old; when late in life. नृस्त्र्योः Nṛistryoḥ, the male and female planet (both in the seventh house). दृष्टौ Dṛiṣṭau, aspected by. शुभैः Śubhaiḥ, by the benefic planet. प्रमदापती Pramadâpatî, the husband of a very aged wife.

5. The individual born will be in illicit intercourse with another man's wife if, during his birth time, Venus be in the Descendant and in Saturn or Mars's Varga and also aspected by Saturn or Mars.

Both the individual and his wife will commit adultery if the Moon, Saturn and Mars be in the Descendant and Venus occupy Saturn or Mars's Varga and be also aspected by Saturn or Mars.

The person will have neither wife nor sons, if Venus and the Moon occupy a sign, Saturn and Mars being in the 7th house from the Venus and the Moon (some say from the Ascendant).

The person's wife will be an elderly woman and the man will marry late in life if when the male and female planets occupy a sign; Saturn and Mars occupy the Descendant and be aspected by benefic planets.

मंदाक्रान्ता—वंशच्छेत्ता खमदसुखगैश्चन्द्रदैत्येज्यपापैः । शिल्पी त्र्यंशे शशिसुतयुते केन्द्रसंस्थार्किदृष्टे । दास्यां जातो दितिसुतगुरौ रिःफगे सौरभागे । नीचोऽर्केन्द्वोर्मदनगतयोर्दृष्टयोः सूर्यजेन ॥ ६ ॥

वंशच्छेत्ता Vamśachhettâ, destroyer of one's race or family. खमदसुखगैः Khamadasukhagaiḥ, in the tenth, seventh and fourth houses respectively. चन्द्रदैत्येज्यपापैः Chandradaityejyapâpaiḥ, by the Moon, Venus, and the malefics (Sun, Mars or Saturn) respectively. शिल्पी Silpî, an artisan; an artificer. त्र्यंशे Tryamśe, the Decanate. शशिसुतयुते Saśisutayute, accompanied by Mercury. केन्द्रसंस्थार्किदृष्टे Kendrasamsthârkidriṣte, (the sign of the ruler of the aforesaid Decanate) aspected by Saturn in the Ascendant or in any of the other angles. दास्यां Dâsyâm, of a maidservant; of a female slave. जातः Jâtaḥ, born. दितिसुतगुरौ Ditisutagurau, on Venus being. रिःफगे Riḥphage, in the twelfth house from the Ascendant. सौरभागे Saurâbhâge, and in Saturn's Navâmśa. नीचे Nîche, engaged in low menial services, unbecoming of him. अर्केन्द्वोः Arkendvoḥ, the Sun and Moon being situated. मदनगतयोः Madanagatayoḥ, in the descending house. दृष्टयोः Driṣṭayoḥ, on being aspected by. सूर्यजेन Sûryajena, by Saturn.

6. The individual born will make his family extinct with him, if, during his birth, there be Moon in the 10th house, Venus in the 7th house and the malefic planets in the 4th house; will become an artisan and painter if during his birth Saturn be in the Ascendant or any other angular house and aspect a sign whose ruler's Decanate is occupied by Mercury; will be born of a maid-servant if Venus exist in the 12th house from the Ascendant at birth and is also in Saturn's Navâmśa; and will do menial deeds unbecoming of him if the Moon occupy the Descendant and be aspected by Saturn.

शा० वि०—पापालोकितयोः सितावनिजयोरस्तस्थयोर्वाध्यरुक् चंद्रे कर्कटवृश्चिकांशकगते पापैर्युते गुह्यरुक् । श्वित्री रिःफधनस्थयोरशुभयोश्चंद्रोदयेऽस्ते रवौ चंद्रे खेऽवनिजेऽस्तगे च विकलो यद्यर्कजो वेशिगः ॥ ७ ॥

पापालोकितयोः Pâpâlokitayoḥ, on being aspected by the malefics. सितावनिजयोः Sitâvanijayoḥ, Venus and Mars. अस्तस्थयोः Astasthayoḥ, while descending; while setting. बाह्यरुक् Vâdhyaruk, having diseases visible from outside, *e.g.*, elephantiasis and the like. चन्द्रे Chandre, on the Moon being in. कर्कटवृश्चिकांशकगते Karkaṭavriśchikâṃśakogate, in the Karka or Vriśchika Navâṃśas. पापैः Pâpaiḥ, by the malefics. युते Yuťe, united with. गुह्यरुक् Guhyaruk, having diseases not visible from outside; diseases of the genital organ. श्वित्री Śvitrî, a white leper. रिःफधनस्थयोः Riḥphhadhanasthayoḥ, in the twelfth and second houses. अशुभयोः Aśubhayoḥ, Saturn and Mars (respectively). चंद्रोदये Chandrodaye, on the Moon ascending. अस्ते रवौ Aste ravau, on the Sun descending. चन्द्रे Chandre, on the Moon being in. खे Khe, in the tenth house. अवनिजे Avanijo, on Mars being in. अस्तगे Astage, descending. च Cha, and. विकलः Vikalaḥ, defective in body. यदि Yadi, if. अर्कजः Arkajaḥ, Saturn. वेशिगः Veśigaḥ, in the second house from the Sun, called Veśi.

7. If, during birth, Venus and Mars be in the Descendant and be afflicted (aspected by malefics), the individual will be afflicted with diseases visible from outside (such as elephantiasis and the like); if the Moon be in Karka or Vriśchika Nâvâṃśa and be united with malefics, the person will be afflicted with diseases not visible from outside (such as the diseases of the genital organ and the like).

The person will be attacked with white leprosy if the Moon be in the Ascendant, Saturn in the 12th, Mars in the 2nd and the Sun in the 7th house from the Ascendant; will be deformed if the Moon be in the 10th house from the Ascendant, Mars in the 7th house from the Ascendant and Saturn in the 2nd house from the Sun.

व० ति०—अंतः शशिन्यशुभयोर्मृगगे पतंगे श्वासक्षयप्लिहकविद्रधिगुल्मभाजः । शोषी परस्परगृहांशगयो रवींद्वोः क्षेत्रेऽथवा युगपदेकगयोः कृशो वा ॥ ८ ॥

अंतः Antaḥ, occupying the middle position. शशिनि Śaśini, on the Moon occupying. अशुभयोः Aśubhayoḥ, between the malefics, Saturn and Mars. मृगगे Mrigage, in the Makara sign. पतंगे Patange, the Sun (called a bird). श्वासक्षयप्लिहकविद्रधिगुल्मभाजः Śvâsakṣayaplihakavidradhigulmabhâjaḥ, having diseases asthma, consumption, spleen, abscess, or a chronic enlargement of the spleen. शोषी Śoṣî, consumptive. परस्परगृहांशगयोः Parasparagrihâṃśagayoḥ, in each other's Navâṃśas, *i.e.*, Sun in Moon's

Navâmśa and Moon in Sun's Navâmśa. रवीन्द्वोः Ravindvoḥ, of the Sun and Moon. क्षेत्रे Kṣetre, houses. अथवा Athavâ, or. युगपत् Yugapat, at the same instant. एकगयोः Ekagayoḥ, in one sign; the Sun and Moon both in one sign, say Leo and so on. कृशः वा Kriśaḥ vâ, or lean and thin.

8. The individual born will be afflicted with asthma, consumption, spleen, abscess, or a chronic enlargement of the spleen if, during his birth, the Moon occupy a place between Saturn and Mars and the Sun occupy the sign Makara; or the person will be afflicted with pulmonary consumption if the Sun occupy the Moon's Navâmśa and the Moon occupy the Sun's Navâmśa; or the person will be reduced to a skeleton if the Sun and Moon occupy together either Karka or Simha.

व० ति०—चन्द्रेऽश्विमध्यझषकर्किमृगाजभागे कुष्ठी समन्दरुधिरे तदवेक्षिते वा। यातैस्त्रिकोणमलिकर्किवृषैर्मृगे च कुष्ठी च पापसहितैरवलोकितैर्वा ॥ ६ ॥

चन्द्रे Chandre, on Moon being in. अश्विमध्यझषकर्किमृगाजभागे Aśvimadhyajhjhaṣakarkimrigajabhâge, situated in the fifth Navâmśa (middle) of Dhanu (Sagittarius) or in the Navâmśa of Mîna, Karka, Makara and Meṣa (any of these). कुष्ठी Kuṣthî, leper. समन्दरुधिरे Samandarudhire, united with Saturn and Mars. तदवेक्षिते Tadavekṣite, aspected by Saturn and Mars. वा Vâ, or. यातैः Yâtaiḥ, on going to. त्रिकोणम् Trikoṇam, in the trikoṇa (triangular) houses; in the fifth or the ninth house from the Ascendant. अलिकर्किवृषैः Alikarkivrișaiḥ, by the signs Vriśchika, Karka and Vrișa occupying. मृगे Mrige, Capricorn, in the sign Makara. च Cha, also. कुष्ठी Kuṣṭhî, leper. च Cha, also. पापसहितैः Pâpasahitaiḥ, united with malefics, Saturn or Mars. अवलोकितैः Avalokitaiḥ, aspected by them. वा Vâ, or.

9. The individual born will be a leper if during his birth the Moon occupy the middle of Dhanu (*i.e.*, the 5th Navâmśa of Dhanu) or the Navâmśa of the signs Mîna, Karka, Makara, or Meṣa, and be either accompanied or aspected by Saturn and Mars(1). Again, the person will be a leper if during his birth the 5th or the 9th house from the Ascendant be the signs Vriśchika, Karka, Vrișa, or Makara and be either occupied or aspected by Saturn and Mars (2).

Notes:—(1) According to Yavanâchârya, if the Moon be also aspected by benefic planets at the same time, the person may not get leprosy but itches, ringworms, &c.

(2) Some read Saturn or Mars.

व० ति०-निधनारिधनव्ययस्थिता रविचन्द्रारयमा यथा तथा। बलवद्ग्रहदोषकारणैर्मनुजानां जनयन्त्यनेत्रताम् ॥ १० ॥

निधनारिधनव्ययस्थिताः Nidhanâridhanavyayasthitâḥ, situated in the houses eighth, sixth, second and twelfth. रविचन्द्रारयमाः Ravichandrârayamâḥ, the Sun, Moon, Mars, and Saturn. यथा तथा Yathâ tathâ, irrespectively situated; placed anywhere (not with any order). बलवद्ग्रहदोषकारणैः Balavadgrahadoṣakâraṇaiḥ, due to the excess of bile, phlegm, or wind, the humours of the body indicated by the most powerful of the above mentioned four planets. मनुजानां Manujânâm, of men. जनयन्ति Janayanti, produce. अनेत्रताम् Anetratâm, blindness or diseases of the eye.

10. The individual born will become blind, if during his birth, the Sun, Moon, Mars and Saturn be in the 8th, 6th, 2nd and 12th houses in any way (*i.e.*, irrespectively) and the blindness will be due to the excess of bile, phlegm, or wind whichever belongs to the most powerful of the four planets.

Note:—If the powerful planet be the Moon, blindness will be due to phlegmatic affections. If such planet be Mars, it will be caused by bilious affections; if it be the Sun, then by heat; and if it be Saturn, it will be caused by windy affections, by stones and the like.

वैतालीय-नवमायतृतीयधीयुता नच सौम्यैरशुभा निरीक्षिताः। नियमाच्छ्रवणोपघातदा रदवैकृत्यकराश्च सप्तमे ॥११॥

नवमायतृतीयधीयुता Navamâyatritîyadhîyutâ, in the ninth, eleventh, third, and fifth houses. न च सौम्यैः Na cha saumyaiḥ, and not aspected by the benefics. अशुभाः Aśubhâḥ, the malefic planets (the Sun, Moon, Mars, and Saturn). निरीक्षिताः Nirîkṣitâḥ, aspected by. नियमात् Niyamât, by causes (pertaining to the most powerful planet). श्रवणोपघातदाः Śravaṇopaghâtadâḥ, originating diseases of the ears, *i.e.*, deafness. रदवैकृत्यकराः Radavaikrityakarâḥ, originating the diseases of teeth. च Cha, and. सप्तमे Saptame, in the seventh house.

11. If, at the birth time, the malefics (the Sun, the Moon, Mars or Saturn) occupy the 9th, 11th, 3rd and 5th houses and be not aspected by benefics, the individual born will become deaf through causes indicated by the most

powerful planet; if such planets (1) be in the Descendant, the teeth of the individual will be weak and deformed.

Note:—(1) As described above, *i.e.*, occupying the 9th, 11th, 3rd and 5th houses and not aspected by benefic planets.

वैतालीय–उदयत्युडुपे सुरास्यगे सपिशाचोऽशुभयोस्त्रिकोणयोः । सोपप्लवमंडले रवावुदयस्थे नयनापवर्जितः ॥ १२ ॥

उदयति Uḍayati, on rising in the horizon. उडुपे Udupe, the Moon. सुरास्यगे Surâsyage, united with Râhu, *i. e.*, when it is a Lunar Eclipse. स Sa, the individual born. सपिशाचः Sapiśâcha, possessed by a ghost. अशुभयोः Aśubhayoḥ, on the malefics being. त्रिकोणयोः Trikoṇayoḥ, in the Trikoṇa houses. सोपप्लवमंडले Sopaplavamaṇḍale, on being eclipsed. रवौ Ravau, the Sun. उदयस्थे Udayasthe, in the Ascendant. नयनापवर्जितः Nayanâpavarjitaḥ, will be blind; will be deprived of eyes.

12. The Moon being in the Ascendant and if she be then eclipsed and if Saturn and Mars be respectively in the 5th and 9th houses from the Ascendant, the individual born will get himself possessed by ghosts. Again, if, during the birth time, the eclipsed Sun be rising and if Saturn and Mars occupy respectively the 5th and the 9th houses from the Ascendant, the person will lose his eyes.

शा० वि०–संस्पृष्टः पवनेन मंदगयुते द्यूने विलग्ने गुरौ सोन्मादोऽवनिजे स्थितेऽस्तभवने जीवे विलग्नाश्रिते । तद्वत्सूर्यसुतोदयेऽवनिसुते धर्मात्मजद्यूनगे जातो वाससहस्ररश्मितनये क्षीणे व्यये शीतगौ ॥ १३ ॥

संस्पृष्टः Samspriṣṭaḥ, attacked by; afflicted with. पवनेन Pavanena, by windy complaints, *i.e.*, gout or rheumatism. मंदगयुते Mandagayute, united with Saturn. द्यूने Dyune, in the seventh house. विलग्ने Vilagne, in the Ascendant. गुरौ Gurau, on Jupiter being. सोन्मादः Sonmâdaḥ, mad, lunatic, idiot. अवनिजे Avanije, on Mars being. स्थिते Sthite, situated. अस्तभवने Astabhavane, in the Descending house. जीवे Jîve, Jupiter. विलग्नाश्रिते Vilagnâśrite, in the Ascendant. तद्वत् Tadvat, like that; insane; unsteady. सूर्यसुतः Sûryasutaḥ, Saturn. उदये Udaye, rising. अवनिसुते Avanisute, Mars. धर्मात्मजद्यूनगे Dharmâtmajadyunage, in the ninth, fifth or seventh houses. जातः Jâtaḥ, born. वा Vâ, or. सहस्ररश्मितनये Sasahasraśmitanaye, with Saturn. क्षीणे Kṣiṇe, waning. व्यये Vyaye, in the twelfth house. शीतगौ Sîtagau, the Moon.

13. The individual born under Saturn in the Descendant, and Jupiter in the Ascendant will be afflicted with windy

complaints, gout, rheumatism, &c.; born under the Descendant Mars and the Ascendant Jupiter will become insane; born under the Ascendant Saturn and Mars in the 5th, 7th or 9th house, will become an idiot; will also become an idiot if born under the waning Moon and Saturn in the 12th house from the Ascendant.

व० ति०—राश्यंशपोष्णकरशीतकरामरेज्यैर्नीचाधिपांशकगतैररिभागगैर्वा । एभ्योऽल्पमध्यबहुभिः क्रमशः प्रसूता ज्ञेयाः स्युरभ्युपगमक्रयगर्भदासाः ॥ १४ ॥

राश्यंशपोष्णकरशीतकरामरेज्यैः Râśyaṃśapoṣṇakaraśîtakarâmarejyaiḥ, by the ruler of the Navâṃśa of the sign where the Moon is situated during birth, by the Sun, by the Moon, and by Jupiter. नीचाधिपांशकगतैः Nîchâdhipâṃśakagataiḥ, in the Navâṃśas of the rulers of their detrimental houses. अरिभागगैः Aribhâgagaiḥ, in the Navâṃśas of their enemies. वा Vâ, or. एभ्यः Ebhyaḥ, out of these planets if there be one, two, or more. अल्पमध्यबहुभिः Alpamadhyabahuviḥ, of a trivial, mediocre, and strong character respectively. क्रमशः Kramaśaḥ, successively; in seriatim. प्रसूताः Prasûtâḥ, born. ज्ञेयाः Jñeyâḥ, are to be known. स्युः Syuḥ, become. अभ्युपगमक्रयगर्भदासाः Abhyupagamakrayagarbhadâsâḥ, (1) a slave in order to get one's livelihood (if one planet be in the Navâṃśas of their detrimental houses, or in their enemies houses) (2) a slave bought for a certain amount (if two planets be such), (3) a slave of a slave in a domestic family.

14. The individual born will serve under other men for his livelihood if, during his birth, (1) the ruler of the Moon-occupied Navâṃśa, (2) the Sun, (3) the Moon, or (4) Jupiter occupy either the Navâṃśa of the ruler of his detrimental house, or any other enemy's Navâṃśa; will become a slave (purchased per money value) if two of the aforesaid planets occupy either the one Navâṃśa or the other; and if three of the aforesaid planets occupy the one Navâṃśa or the other, the person will be the slave of a slave.

हरिणी—विकृतदशनः पापैर्दृष्टे वृषाजहयोदये खलतिरशुभक्षेत्रे लग्ने हये वृषभेऽपि वा । नवमसुतगे पापैर्दृष्टे रवावदृढेक्षणो दिनकरसुते नैकव्याधिः कुजे विकलः पुमान् ॥ १५ ॥

विकृतदशनः Vikritadaśanah. of deformed teeth; having ugly teeth. पापैः Pâpâih, by the malefic planets. दृष्टे Driste, aspected by. वृषाजहयोदये Vrisâjahayodaye, the signs Vrisa, Mesa, Dhanu rising. खलितः Khalitah, baldheaded. अशुभक्षेत्रे Aśubha. kṣetre, in the inauspicious houses, *i.e.*, in those of Meṣa, Simha, Vriśchika, Makara, Kumbha; in any of these. लग्ने Lagne, becoming the Ascendant. हये Haye, in Dhanu. वृषभे Brisabhe, in the sign Vrisa. अपि वा Api vâ, or even. नवमसुतगे Navamasutage, in the ninth or fifth houses. पापैः Pâpaih, by the evil planets. दृष्टे Driste, aspected by. रवौ Ravau, the Sun. अदृढेक्षणः Adridhekṣaṇah, eyes always turning and unsteady; of useless eyes. दिनकरसुते Dinakarasute, Saturn. नैकव्याधिः Naikavyâdhih, having many diseases. कुजे Kuje, Mars. विकलः Vikalah, deformed. पुमान् Pumân, the native.

15. The individual born under the Ascendant Vriṣa, Meṣa, or Dhanu and aspected by the malefics will have ugly teeth; will be baldheaded if born under the Ascendant Meṣa, Simha, Vriśchika, Makara, Kumbha, Dhanu or Vrisa and aspected by the malefics; will be of weak sight, if born under the afflicted Sun in the 9th or 5th house from the Ascendant; will be afflicted (1) with various maladies, if born under the afflicted Saturn in the 5th or in the 9th house; and will be of defective limbs, if born under the afflicted Mars in the 5th or in the 9th house.

Note :—(1) Aspected by malefics.

पुष्पिताग्रा—व्ययसुतधनधर्मगैरसौम्यैर्भवनसमाननिबंधनं विकल्प्यम् । भुजगनिगडपाशभृद्दृकाणैर्बलवदसौम्यनिरीक्षितैश्च तद्वत् ॥ १६ ॥

व्ययसुतधनधर्मगैः Vyayasutadhanadharmagaih, in the twelfth, fifth, second, or ninth house. असौम्यैः Asaumyaih, by the evil planets. भवनसमाननिबंधनं Bhavanasamânanibandhanam, to be captured and restrained as denoted by the nature of the rising sign, *e.g.*, those born under the Ascendant Meṣa, Vriṣa, Dhanu, are confined by being bound with ropes; under Mîthuna, Kanyâ, Tulâ, Kumbha, are loaded with fetters; under Karka, Makara, Mîna, shut up in a well-guarded place without being tied, as if a bird in a cage; under Vriśchika, in a subterranean cell. विकल्प्यम् Vikalpyam, are to be thought. भुजगनिगडपाशभृत् Bhujaganigaḍapâśabhrit, suffering imprisonment of the nature denoted by Serpent Decanate and Fetter Decanate. दृकाणैः Drikâṇaih, by the ruler of the rising Decanate (under which an individual is born). बलवदसौम्यनिरीक्षितैः Balavadasaumyanirîkṣitaih, if strong and aspected by evil planets. च Cha, and. तद्वत् Tadvat, like that.

16. The individual born under the malefic planets occupying the 12th, 5th, 2nd, and 9th houses promiscuously will suffer capture and imprisonment as denoted by the nature of the rising sign (1). Again, if, during the birth time, the rising Decanate be either Serpent or Fetter Decanate (2) and if the sign (3) of its ruler be afflicted, the person will also suffer imprisonment of the nature of such sign.

Notes :—(1) If the Ascendant be Meṣa, Vṛiṣa or Dhanu, the person will be bound with ropes. If the Ascendant be Mithuna, Kanyâ, Tulâ, or Kumbha, he will be loaded with fetters. If the Ascendant be Karka, Makara, or Mîna, the person will be shut up in a fortress, but will be taken care of. If the Ascendant be Vṛiśchika, the person will be kept in a subterranean cell.

(2) The Serpent Decanates: These are the first, second and third Decanates of Karka, the 1st and 2nd of Vṛiśchika and the 3rd of Mîna.

The Fetter Decanate.—The first Decanate of Makara.

(3) That is, if the rising Decanate be the 1st Decanate of Karka, for instance, the ruler of such Decanate is the Moon whose sign is Karka. If the rising Decanate be the 2nd Decanate of Karka, its ruler is Mars whose sign is Vṛiśchika; and if it be the 3rd Decanate of Karka, the ruler of such Decanate is Jupiter, whose sign is Mîna.

हरिणी—परुषवचनोऽपस्मारार्तः क्षयी च निशापतौ सर-
वितनये वक्रालोकं गते परिवेषगे । रवियमकुजैः सौम्यादृष्टैर्नभः
स्थलमाश्रितैर्भृतकमनुजः पूर्वोद्दिष्टैर्वराधममध्यमाः ॥ १७ ॥
इति श्रीबृहज्जातकेऽनिष्टाध्यायस्त्रयोविंशः ॥ २३ ॥

परुषवचन: Paruṣavachanaḥ, using very harsh and rough words. अपस्मारार्तः: Apasmârârtaḥ, afflicted with epilepsy; having epileptic fits; dead. क्षयी Kṣyaî, consumptive. च Cha, and. निशापतौ Niśâpatau, Moon. सरवितनये Saravitanaye, Saturn. वक्रालोकं गते Vakrâlokaṃ gate, aspected by Mars. परिवेषगे Pariveṣage, with halo all round. रवियमकुजैः Raviyamakujaiḥ, by the Sun, Saturn or Mars. सौम्यादृष्टैः: Saumyâdṛiṣṭaiḥ, not aspected by any benefic. नभःस्थलम् Nabhaḥsthalam, in the tenth house; in the sky overhead. आश्रितैः: Âśritaiḥ, oocupying. भृतकःमनुजः: Bhṛitakaḥ manujaḥ, the individual born becomes a servant of another. पूर्वोद्दिष्टैः: Pûrvoddiṣṭaiḥ, by the planets aforesaid. वराधममध्यमाः: Varâdhamamadhyamâḥ, of a good, bad, or mediocre nature.

17. The individual will be using very harsh words and will be afflicted with epilepsy and with consumption if

he be born under the Moon accompanied by Saturn, and aspected by Mars and surrounded by a halo (1).

The individual born under the Sun, Saturn and Mars occupying the 10th house from the Ascendant and not being aspected by benefic planets, becomes a servant of a dignified, average, and low rank as the case may be (2).

Notes:—(1) If the Moon be united with Saturn only, the person will be a man of harsh speech; if the Moon be united with Saturn and aspected by Mars, the person will be epileptic; if the Moon be united with Saturn, aspected by Mars and there is a halo also, the person will be consumptive.

(2) If one of the three planets Sun, Saturn, and Mars occupy the 10th house, the person will be a dignified servant; if 2 planets occupy the 10th house, he will be a servant of middle rank and if 3 planets occupy the 10th house, he will be a servant of a low rank.

Thus ends the Twenty-third Chapter on Evils by Varâha Mihirâchâraya of Avantika.

CHAPTER XXIV.

ON FEMALE HOROSCOPES.

व० ति०—यद्यत्फलं नरभवे क्षममंगनानां तत्तद्वदेत्पतिषु वा सकलं विधेयम्। तासां तु भर्तृमरणं निधने वपुस्तु लग्नेंदुगं सुभगतास्तमये पतिश्च ॥ १ ॥

यद्यत् Yadyat, whatever. फलं Phalam, fruits. नरभवे Narabhavé, on the birth of a male individual क्षमं Kṣamam, possible. अंगनानां Amganânâm, in the case of females. तत्तत् Tattat, those results only. वदेत् Vadet, declare. पतिषु Patiṣu, to the husbands of females. वा Vâ, or. सकलं Sakalam, all the results (that are calculated from a female horoscope.) विधेयम् Vidheyam, are to be applied; are to be told as those of her husband. तासां Tâsâm, of the females. तु Tu, but. भर्तृमरणं Bhartṛimaraṇam, death of their husbands. निधने Nidhane, from the eighth house. वपुः Vapuḥ, about the body, the physique of the females. तु Tu, but. लग्नेंदुगं Lagnendugam, to be counted from the nature of the Ascendant and the Moon-occupied sign. सुभगता Subhagatâ, prosperity; fortune. अस्तमये Astamaye, from the seventh house. पतिः च Patiḥ cha, and the husband; *e.g.*, what the husband will be.

1. Of all the effects that are declared in the horoscopy of men, those only are applicable to women which are possible for them; the rest are applicable to their husbands. According to some, all the effects will affect the husband. The death of the husband shall be determined from the 8th house (from the Ascendant) in female horoscopes. Matters connected with the physique of a woman shall be determined from the rising sign and the sign occupied by the Moon; and matters connected with her prosperity and fortune and her husband's beauty, &c., shall be determined from the 7th house.

Notes:—Such effects as are declared in the king-making combinations, etc., are to be told with regard to the husbands; those that are declared under the Nâbhasa Yogas or Astral Combinations are applicable to both.

व० ति०—युग्मेषु लग्नशशिनोः प्रकृतिस्थिता स्त्री सच्छील-
भूषणयुता शुभदृष्टयोश्च । ओजस्थयोश्चमनुजाकृतिशीलयुक्ता
पापा च पापयुतवीक्षितयोर्गुणोना ॥ २ ॥

युग्मेषु Yugmeṣu, situated in the even signs. लग्नशशिनोः Lagnaśaśinoḥ, the Moon and the Ascendant being situated in. प्रकृतिस्थिता: Prakṛitisthitâḥ, truly feminine; womanish, mild and gentle, befitting a woman. स्त्री Strî, female. सच्छीलभूषणयुता Sachchîlabhûṣaṇayutâ, of good character and having ornaments. शुभदृष्टयोः Śubhadṛiṣṭayoḥ, aspected by benefic planets. च Cha, and. ओजस्थयोः Ojasthayoḥ, situated in the odd signs. च Cha, and. मनुजाकृतिशीलयुक्ता Manujâkṛitiśîlayuktâ, having male appearance and male characteristics. पापा Pâpâ, vicious. च Cha, and. पापयुतवीक्षितयोः Pâpayutavîkṣitayoḥ, accompanied or aspected by the malefics. गुणोना Guṇonâ, ill-qualified; having no qualifications.

2. The woman born will possess a truly feminine form and look if the Ascendant and the sign occupied by the Moon be even; will moreover be of good character and will possess ornaments (chastity and other virtues being counted among the ornaments), if the above signs be aspected by benefic planets. But if such signs be odd, the woman will get a maculine appearance and possess male characteristics; and if they be either found with or aspected by malefic planets, she will have no qualifications and become vicious.

Note :—If the conditions be partly good and partly bad, the woman will be qualified partly with the above qualifications and partly with the above disqualifications.

इंद्रवज्रा—कन्यैव दुष्टा व्रजतीह दास्यं साध्वी समाया कुच-
रित्रयुक्ता ॥ भूम्यात्मजर्क्षे क्रमशोऽशकेषु वक्रार्किजीवेंदुजभार्ग-
वानाम् ॥३॥

कन्या Kanyâ, the female born. एव Eva, thus. दुष्टा Duṣṭâ, bad; vicious, even before marriage. व्रजति Vrajati, produces; elopes with another male. इह Iha, in this Mars's house. दास्यं Dâsyam, maid-servant. साध्वी Sâdhvî, chaste. समाया Samâyâ, with Mâyâ; कुचरित्रयुक्ता Kucharitrayuktâ, of a bad character. भूम्यात्मजर्क्षे Bhûmyâtmajarkṣe, in Mars's houses, i. e., in Meṣa and Vṛiśchika. क्रमशः Kramaśaḥ, successively. अंशकेषु Aṃśakeṣu, in the Triṃśâṃśa (of Mars). वक्रार्किजीवेंदुजभार्गवानाम् Vakrârkijîvendujabhârgavânâm, of Mars, Saturn, Jupiter, Mercury, and Venus respectively.

3. The female born will become corrupt (even before marriage) if the Ascendant or the sign occupied by the Moon at the time of birth is either Meṣa or Vṛischika, and also if the rising Triṃśâṃśa or the Triṃśâṃśa occupied by the Moon be that of Mars; will be a maid-servant, if the above Triṃśâṃśa be that of Saturn; will be chaste and pure, if the above Triṃśâṃśa be that of Jupiter; will be tricky and tempting, if it be that of Mercury; will be of bad character, if it be that of Venus.

इंद्रवज्रा–दुष्टा पुनर्भूः सगुणा कलाज्ञा ख्याता गुणैश्चासुरपूजितर्क्षे ॥ स्यात्कापटी क्लीबसमा सती च बौधे गुणाढ्या प्रविकीर्णकामा ॥४॥

दुष्टा Duṣtâ, of a bad character. पुनर्भूः Punarbhûḥ, marrying a second time. सगुणा Saguṇâ, endowed with qualities. कलाज्ञा Kalâjñâ, knowing music, dancing, painting, &c. ख्याता Khayâtâ, famous. गुणैः Guṇaiḥ, on account of being humble and amiable. असुरपूजितर्क्षे Asurapûjitarkṣe, in Venuś houses, *i.e.*, in Vṛiṣa and Tulâ. स्यात् Syât, become. कापटी Kâpaṭî, hypocrite. क्लीबसमा Klîvasamâ, like eunuchs. सती Satî, chaste. च Cha, and. बौधे Baudhe, in the houses of Mercury, *i.e.*, in the houses of Mithuna or Kaṇyâ. गुणाढ्या Guṇâḍhyâ, well qualified. प्रविकीर्णकामा Pravikîrṇakâmâ, lustful; going to all persons.

4. The female born will be of a bad character if the Ascendant and the sign occupied by the Moon during birth be either Vṛiṣa or Tulâ, and also the rising Triṃśâṃśa or the Triṃśaṃśa occupied by the Moon be that of Mars; if it be that of Saturn, she will marry a second time; if of Jupiter, she will possess good and virtuous qualities; if of Mercury, she will be skilled in music and dancing; if it be that of Venus, she will be renowned for her good qualities. Again she will be wily and deceitful if the Ascendant or the Moon-occupied sign at birth be Mithuna or Kanyâ and also if the rising Triṃśâṃśa or the Triṃṣâṃśa occupied by the Moon be that of Mars; will be a hermaphrodite, if it be of Saturn; will be chaste, if of Jupiter; well qualified, if of Mercury, and she will, out of lust, commit adultery, if it be that of Venus.

शा० वि०--स्वच्छन्दा पतिघातिनी वहुगुणा शिल्पिन्यसाध्वीन्दुभे । नृाचारा कुलटार्कभे नृपवधूः पुंश्चेष्टितागम्यगा ॥ जैवेनैकगुणाल्परत्यतिगुणा विज्ञानयुक्तासती । दासी नीचरतार्किभे पतिरता दुष्टाप्रजा स्वांशकैः ॥५॥

स्वच्छन्दा Svachchhandâ, of an independent nature. पतिघातिनी Patighâtinî, slayer of one's husband. बहुगुणा Bohugunâ, diversely well qualified. शिल्पिनी Śilpinî, an artist. असाध्वी Asâdhvî, an unchaste woman. इन्दुभे Indubhe, the sign Karka (Moon being there or Karka being the Ascendant). नृाचारा Nrâchârâ, behaving like a male, having manners properly belonging to males. कुलटा Kulaṭâ, an unchaste woman. अर्कभे Arkabhe, the sign Siṃha being the Ascendant or Moon being in Siṃha. नृपवधूः Nripavadhûḥ, queen. पुंश्चेष्टिता Puṃścheṣṭitâ, having masculine natures. अगम्यगा Agamyagâ, in illicit intercourse with men not approachable. जैवे Jaive, in the signs Dhanu and Mîna (being the Ascendant or Moon being there. नैकगुणा Naikagûṇâ, of many good qualities. अल्परतिः Alparatih, satisfied after a short cohabitation. अतिगुणा Atiguṇâ, of many good qualities. विज्ञानयुक्ता Vijñânayuktâ, of wonderful knowledge. असती Asatî, an unchaste woman. दासी Dâśî, maid-servant. नीचरता Nîcharatâ, addicted to low persons. अर्किभे Arkibhe, in the houses of Saturn *i. e.* Makara and Kumbha (these being the Ascendant or the Moon being in them). पतिरता Patiratâ, devoted to her husband. दुष्टा Duṣṭâ, bad. अप्रजा Aprajâ, barren. स्वांशकैः Svâṃśakaiḥ, in Venus' own Triṃśâṃśa.

5. The female born will act freely according to her own will if the Ascendant or the Moon-occupied sign at birth be Karkaṭa and if the rising Triṃśâṃśa or the Triṃśâṃśa occupied by the Moon be that of Mars; will murder her husband if it be that of Saturn; will possess many good qualities, if of Jupiter; will be a refined artist, if of Mercury; will be unchaste, if it be of Venus.

The female born will be of a masculine nature, if the Ascendant or the Moon-occupied sign at birth be Siṃha, and if the rising Triṃśâṃśa or the Moon-occupied Triṃśâṃśa be that of Mars; will be unchaste, if of Saturn; will be a queen, if of Jupiter; will have a masculine nature, if of Mercury; will be corrupt with men unapproachable, if of Venus.

The female born will possess many good qualifications if the Ascendant or the Moon-occupied sign at birth be Dhanu or Mîna and if the rising Triṃśâṃśa or the Moon-occupied Triṁśâṃśa be that of Mars; will cohabit shortly, if of Saturn; will have many good qualities, if of Jupiter; will be a woman of knowledge, if of Mercury; unchaste, if of Venus.

The female born will be a maid-servent if the Ascendant or the Moon-occupied sign at birth be Makara or Kumbha and if the rising Triṃśâṃśa or the Moon-occupied Triṃśâṃśa be that of Mars; will join a person of low caste, if of Saturn; will be chaste, if of Jupiter; will be of bad conduct, if of Mercury; and will be barren, if of Venus.

अनुष्टुभ्-शशिलग्नसमायुक्तैः फलं त्रिंशांशकैरिदम् ॥
बलाबलविकल्पेन तयोरुक्तं विचिंतयेत् ॥६॥

शशिलग्नसमायुक्तैः Śaśilagnasamâyuktaiḥ, of the Ascendant and the sign occupied by the Moon during one's birth. फलं Phalam, effects; results. त्रिंशांशकैः Triṃśâṃśakaiḥ, of the Triṃśâṃśas (of the Ascendant or the sign occupied by the Moon during one's birth). इदम् Idam, thus (as stated above). बलाबलविकल्पेन Balâbalavikalpena, according to the superiority of strength. तयोः Tayoḥ, of these Triṃśâṃśas, *i.e.*, the rising Triṃśâṃśa and the Triṃśâṃśa occupied by the Moon. उक्तं Uktam, as stated. विचिंतयेत् Vichintayet, are to be considered.

6. Tho effects that have been described for the rising Triṃśâṃśa or those described for the Triṃśâṃśa occupied by the Moon will come to pass according as the one Triṃśâmśa or the other is the more powerful.

प्रहर्षिणी-दृक्संस्थावसितसितौ परस्परांशे शौक्रे वा यदि घटराशिसंभवोऽशः ॥ स्त्रीभिः स्त्रीमदनविषानलप्रदीप्तं संशांतिं नयति नराकृतिस्थिताभिः ॥७॥

दृक्संस्थौ Dṛiksaṃsthau, each aspecting the other. असितसितौ Asitasitau, Saturn and Venus. परस्परांशे Parasparâṃśe, each occupying the other's Navâṃśas, *i.e.*, Vṛiṣa or Tulâ. शौक्रे Saukre, on Venus's house being the Ascendant वा Vâ, or. यदि

Yadi, if. घटराशिसंभव: अंश: Ghaṭarâśisambhavaḥ Aṃśaḥ, on Kumbha Navâṃśa rising. स्त्रीभि: Strîbhiḥ, by women. स्त्रीमदनविषानलप्रदीप्तं Strîmadanaviṣânalapradîptam, female lust. संशांतिं Saṃśântim, satiety; satisfaction. नयति Nayati, brings. नराकृतिस्थिताभि: Narâkṛitisthitâbhiḥ, by an artificial male organ.

7. If, during the birth time of a female, Saturn occupy Venus' Navâṃśa and Venus occupy Saturn's Navâṃśa and if Venus and Saturn aspect each other, or, if the sign Vṛiṣa or Tulâ be the Ascendant and the rising Navâṃśa be that of the sign Kumbha, the female will satisfy her lust by the help of other women having an artificial male organ.

शा० वि०–शून्ये कापुरुषो बलेऽस्तभवने सौम्यग्रहावीक्षिते क्लीबोऽस्ते बुधमंदयोश्चरगृहे नित्यं प्रवासान्वितः ॥ उत्सृष्टा रविणा कुजेन विधवा बाल्येऽस्तराशिस्थिते कन्यैवाशुभवीक्षितेऽर्कतनये द्यूने जरां गच्छति ॥८॥

शून्ये Śûnye, on there being no planets. कापुरुष: Kâpuruṣaḥ, a coward or a blameable man. अबले Abale, becoming weak. अस्तभवने Astabhavane, in the 7th house. सौम्यग्रहावीक्षिते Saumyagrahâvikṣite, not aspected by any benefic. क्लीब: Klibaḥ, a eunuch; one impotent. अस्ते Aste, in the seventh house. बुधमंदयो: Budhamandayoḥ, Mercury or Saturn. चरगृहे Charagṛihe, in the moveable houses. नित्यं Nityam. always; very frequently. प्रवासान्वित: Pravâsânvitaḥ, living in foreign countries. उत्सृष्टा: Utsriṣṭâḥ, left by husband; divorced. रविणा Raviṇâ, when the Sun is in the seventh house. कुजेन Kujena, when Mars is in the seventh house विधवा Vidhabhâ, a widow. बाल्ये Vâlye, at a very early age. अस्तराशिस्थिते Astarâśisthite, in the descending sign. कन्या Kanyâ, the girl. एव Eva, certainly. अशुभवीक्षिते Aśubhavîkṣite, aspected by malefics. अर्कतनये Arkatanaye, on Saturn being. द्यूने Dyûne, in the seventh house. जरां Jarâm, old age. गच्छति Gachhati, gets; reaches, *i.e.*, does not marry at all; she remains ever a maid.

8. The woman will have a mean contemptible coward fellow for her husband if, during birth, there be no planets in the 7th house from the Ascendant or from the Moon-occupied sign, the 7th house itself being not aspected by any benefic planet; or her husband will be impotent, if such 7th house be occupied by Mercury or Saturn; or her husband will be living in foreign countries, if such 7th house be a moveable sign; will remain in his place, if the 7th house be a fixed

sign, and will partly be in foreign and partly in his own place if the 7th house be a common sign; or her husband will reject her, if such 7th house be occupied by the Sun; or she will become a widow while young, if it be occupied by afflicted Mars, and she will remain unmarried throughout her life, if it be occupied by afflicted Saturn (1).

Note :—(1) May be married in her old age, if Saturn be well aspected.

शा० वि०–आग्नेयैर्विधवास्तराशिसहितैर्मिश्रैः पुनर्भूर्भवेत् । क्रूरे हीनबलेऽस्तगे स्वपतिना सौम्येक्षिते प्रोज्झिता ॥ अन्योन्यांशगयोः सितावनिजयोरन्यप्रसक्ताङ्गना । द्यूने वा यदि शीतरश्मिसहितौ भर्तुस्तदानुज्ञया ॥९॥

आग्नेयैः Âgneyaiḥ, by (many) malefic planets. विधवा Vidhabhâ, a widow. अस्तराशिसहितैः Astarâśisahitaiḥ, in the seventh house. मिश्रैः Miśraiḥ, by the mixture, *i.e.*, where both the benefics and the malefics are found in the seventh house. पुनर्भूः Punarbhûḥ, a widow remarried. भवेत् Bhavet, becomes. क्रूरे Krûre, the malefics, *i.e.*, the Sun, Mars, or Saturn. हीनबले Hînabale, becoming weak. अस्तगे Astage, in the seventh house. स्वपतिना Svapatinâ, by one's own husband. सौम्येक्षिते Saumyekṣite, aspected by benefics (Mercury, Jupiter or Venus). प्रोज्झिता Projjhitâ, rejected; abandoned; forsaken. अन्योन्यांशगयोः Anyonyâṃśagayoḥ, each one in the other's Navâṃśa. सितावनिजयोः Sitâvanijayoḥ, of Venus and Mars. अन्यप्रसक्ताङ्गना Anyaprasaktâṃganâ, female addicted to another male. द्यूने Dyûne, in the seventh house. वा Vâ, or. यदि Yadi, if. शीतरश्मिसहितौ Śîtarasmisahitau, (Mars and Venus) together with the Moon. भर्तुः Bhartuḥ, of the husband. तदा Tadâ, then. अनुज्ञया Anujñayâ, by the permission.

9. The woman will become a widow if during birth the 7th house from the Ascendant or the Moon-occupied sign be occupied by several malefic planets; the woman will quit her husband and marry another if such 7th house be found with malefics as well as benefics; and if such 7th house be occupied by malefic planets, be weak, and be aspected by a benefic planet the woman will be forsaken by her husband.

If Venus and Mars be in each other's Navâṃśa, the woman will commit adultery; and if the seventh house from the Ascendant be found with the Moon, Venus as well as Mars, she will be corrupt with another person under the express order of her husband.

शालिनी—सौरारर्क्षे लग्नगे सेंदुशुक्रे मात्रा सार्द्धं बंधकी पापदृष्टे। कौजेऽस्तांशे सौरिणा व्याधियोनिश्चारुश्रोणी वल्लभा सद्ग्रहांशे ॥ १० ॥

सौरारर्क्षे Saurârarkṣe, the signs of Saturn (*i. e.*, Makara or Kumbha) or the signs of Mars (*i. e.*, Meṣa or Vriśchika). लग्नगे Lagnage, on becoming the Ascendant. सेंदुशुक्रे Sanduśukre, with Moon and Venus. मात्रा Mâtrâ, together with her mother. सार्द्धं Sârdham, with. बंधकी Bandhakî, in illicit intercourse with others. पापदृष्टे Pâpadṛiṣṭe, aspected by evil planets; afflicted. कौजे Kauje, belonging to Mars; if the setting Navâmśa be that of Mars. अस्तांशे Astâmśe, if the descending Navâmśas belong to. सौरिणा Sauriṇâ, by Saturn. व्याधियोनिः Vyâdhiyoniḥ, having diseased female organ of generation. चारुश्रोणी Châruśroṇî, of beautiful hips and organ of generation. वल्लभा Vallabhâ, dear to one's husband. सद्ग्रहांशे Sadgrahâmśe, on a benefic planet's Navâmśa descending.

10. Both the woman and her mother will be in illicit intercourse with other males if during the birth time of the woman the signs of Saturn or Mars, (*i.e.*, Makara or Kumbha or Meṣa or Vriśchika) be rising and if it be occupied by the afflicted Moon and Venus. Again the woman will have a diseased genital organ if Mars' Navâmśa be descending, with Saturn's aspect on the Descending sign; if, on the contrary, the Navâmśa of a benefic planet be descending, the woman will possess a fine genital organ and will become an agreeable wife.

मालिनी—वृद्धो मूर्खः सूर्यजर्क्षेंऽशके वा स्त्रीलोलः स्यात्क्रोधनश्चावनेये। शौक्रे कांतोऽतीवसौभाग्ययुक्तो विद्वान्भर्त्ता नैपुणज्ञश्च बौधे ॥ ११ ॥

वृद्धः Vriddhaḥ, aged; an old man. मूर्खः Mûrkhaḥ, a stupid; an illiterate or fool. सूर्यजर्क्षे Sûryajarkṣe, if the sign of Saturn (*i.e.*, Makara or Kumbha) be descending. अंशके Amśake, if the Navâmśas of Saturn be descending. वा Vâ, or. स्त्रीलोलः Strîlolaḥ, one attached to women. स्यात् Syât, will become. क्रोधनः Krodhanaḥ, one of angry temper. च Cha, and. आवनेये Âvaneye, if the sign of Mars (*i.e.*, Meṣa or Vriśchika) or its Navâmśas (be setting). शौक्रे Śaukre, if the signs of Venus, (*i.e.*, Vriṣa and Tulâ) or her Navâmśas (be setting). कांतः Kântaḥ, of a very beautiful form. अतिवसौभाग्ययुक्तः Atîvasaubhâgyayuktaḥ, very fortunate and liked by one's husband. विद्वान् Vidvân, learned. भर्ता Bhartâ, the husband. नैपुणज्ञः Naipuṇagñaḥ, clever and skilful. च Cha, and. बौधे Baudhe, if the sign of Mercury, (*i. e.*, Mithuna or Kanyâ) or its Navâṃśa be setting.

11. If, during birth, Makara or Kumbha be descending or Saturn's Navâṃśa be descending, the woman will get an old fool for her husband; if Meṣa, Vṛiśchika be descending, or Mars' Navâṃśa be descending, she will get a husband, angry but devoted to her; if Vṛiṣa or Tulâ or Venus's Navâṃśa be descending, the husband will be of good form and of good look and will be fond of his wife; if Mithuna or Kanyâ, *i.e.*, Mercury's Navâṃśa be descending, the husband will be learned, clever and skilful.

पुष्पिताग्रा–मदनवशगतो मृदुश्च चांद्रे त्रिदशगुरौ गुणवान्
जितेंद्रियश्च । अतिमृदुरतिकर्मकृच्च सौर्ये भवति गृहेऽस्तमयस्थि-
तेंऽशके वा ॥ १२ ॥

मदनवशगतः Madanavaśagataḥ, lustful; amorous; passionate. मृदुः Mriduḥ, quiet; delicate; soft; tender. च Cha, and. चांद्रे Chândre, when the Moon's sign Karka is the seventh house or when the Moon's Navâṃśa is setting. त्रिदशगुरौ Tridaśagurau, on Jupiter's sign, *i.e.*, Dhanu or Mîna descending or when Jupiter's Navâṃśa is setting. गुणवान् Guṇavân, qualified with many good parts, *e.g.*, heroism, &c. जितेंद्रियः Jitendriyaḥ, one who has controlled one's passions. च Cha, and अतिमृदुः Atimṛiduḥ, very soft. अतिकर्मकृत् Atikarmakṛit, dealing much in trade affairs; some read it as रतिकर्मकृत् and render its meaning as very licentious. च Cha, and. सौर्ये Saurye, when the Sun's sign Siṃha is descending or when its Navâṃśa is descending. भवति Bhavati, becomes. गृहे Grihe, in the house. अस्तमयस्थिते Astamayasthite, descending. अंशके Aṃśake, or the Navâṃśas. वा Vâ, or.

12. If, during birth, the Karka or Moon's Navâṃśa be descending, the husband will be very passionate but quiet; if Dhanu or Mîna or Jupiter's Navâṃśa be descending, the husband will be brave, have control over his passions and desires and will possess other virtues; if the sign Siṃha or the Sun's Navâṃśa be descending, the husband will be very mild and will do various works (!) (some take it:—will indulge in much sexual union).

Notes :—If the Descending sign be that of one planet and the descending Navâmsa be that of another planet, then the effects of that which is powerful of the two will come to pass.

(1) Some authors read Ratikarma instead of Atikarma and render the meaning as indulging much in sexual union.

व० ति०—ईर्ष्यान्विता सुखपरा शशिशुक्रलग्ने ज्ञेन्द्वोः कलासु निपुणा सुखिता गुणाढ्या । शुक्रज्ञयोस्तु रुचिरा सुभगा कलाज्ञा त्रिष्वप्यनेकवसुसौख्यगुणा शुभेषु ॥ १३ ॥

ईर्ष्यान्विता Irsyânvitâ, jealous; envious of the prosperity of other persons. सुखपरा Sukhaparâ, luxurious; loving pleasure and ease. शशिशुक्रलग्ने Sasisukralagne, Moon and Venus in the Ascendant. ज्ञेन्द्वोः Jñendvoḥ, if Mercury and Moon be in the Ascendant. कलासु Kalâsu, in fine arts, music, &c. निपुणा Nipuṇâ, skilled in; well versed in. सुखिता Sukhitâ, happy. गुणाढ्या Guṇâḍhyâ, having many qualifications. शुक्रज्ञयोः Śukrajñayoḥ, if Venus and Mercury be Ascending. तु Tu, also. रुचिरा Ruchirâ, beautiful. सुभगा Subhagâ, dear to one's husband. कलाज्ञा Kalâjñâ, versed in music, etc. त्रिषु अपि Triṣu api, when the three planets Moon, Mercury, Venus are in the Ascendant. अनेकवसुसौख्यगुणा Anekavasusaukhvyagunâ, having much wealth and many good qualities. शुभेषु Śubheṣu, the three auspicious planets, *e.g.*, Mercury, Venus, Jupiter being in the Ascendant.

13. The woman born will be envious of others' prosperity and very pleasure-loving if, during the birth, the Moon and Venus be in the Ascendant; will be skilled in the fine arts, will be in the enjoyment of comfort and will be well-qualified if the Moon and Mercury be in the Ascendant; will know music, dancing, will be dear to her husband, if Venus and Mercury be in the Ascendant; she will have vast wealth, immense comfort and numberless good qualities if Moon, Mercury and Venus all three be in the Ascendant, or if Mercury, Jupiter and Venus be in the Ascendant.

व० ति०—क्रूरेऽष्टमे विधवता निधनेश्वरोंऽशे यस्य स्थितो वयसि तस्य समे प्रदिष्टा । सत्स्वर्थगेषु मरणं स्वयमेव तस्याः कन्यालिगोहरिषु चाल्पसुतत्वमिंदो ॥ १४ ॥

क्रूरे Krûre, on a malefic planet occupying. अष्टमे Aṣtame, in the eighth house. विधवता Vidhavatâ, widowhood. निधनेश्वरः Nidhaneśvaraḥ, the ruler of the eighth house from the Ascendant. अंशे Aṃsé, in the Navâṃśas. यस्य Yasya, of whichever planet. स्थित: Sthitaḥ, situated. वयसि Vayasi, in the Antardaśâ period. तस्य Tasya, of that planet. समे Same, same ; equal (to the Antardaśâ period) or equal to the natural life period of that planet (as stated in verse 9, Chapter VIII). प्रदिष्टा Pradiṣṭâ, said. सत्सु Satsu, the benefic planets when occupying. अर्थगेषु Arthageṣu, in the second house from the Ascendant. मरणं Maraṇam, death. स्वयम् एव Svayam eva, her own (death just after her husband's death). तस्या: Tasyâḥ, her. कन्यालिगोहरिषु Kanyâligohariṣu, in the signs Kanyâ, Vṛiśchika, Vṛiṣa, or Siṃha. च Cha, and. अल्पसुतत्वं Alpasutatvam, producing very few children. इंदौ Indau, the Moon (residing in).

14. The woman will become a widow if, during her birth time, the 8th house from the Ascendant be possessed by a malefic planet and this will take place (1) in the Daśâ or Antardaśâ period of the planet whose Navâṃśa is occupied by the ruler of such 8th house (reckoned after her marriage). If the 8th house be possessed by a malefic planet and the 2nd house by a benefic planet the woman will die before her husband ; the woman will have few sons, if during her birth, the Moon be in the sign Kanyâ, Vṛiśchika, Vṛiṣa or Siṃha.

Note:—(1) Will take place so many years after her marriage as are equal to the Antardaśâ period of the planet in question.

Some Commentators are of opinion that she will become a widow after the natural life period of the planet (as stated in verse 9, Chapter VIII) whose Navâṃśa is occupied by the ruler of such 8th house, reckoned from her marriage.

शा० वि०—सौरे मध्यबले वलेन रहितैः शीतांशुशुक्रेन्दुजैः । शेषैर्वीर्यसमन्वितैः परुषिणी यद्योजराश्युद्गमः ॥ जीवारास्फुजिदैन्दवेषु बलिषु प्राग्लग्नराशौ समे । विख्याता भुवि नैकशास्त्रनिपुणा स्त्री ब्रह्मवादिन्यपि ॥ १५ ॥

सौरे Saure, Saturn. मध्यबले Madhyabale, half strong, *i.e.*, neither strong nor weak. बलेन Balena, with favourable planets and position of strength. रहितै: Rahitaiḥ, devoid of. शीतांशुशुक्रेन्दुजै: Sîtâṃśuśukrendujaiḥ, with Moon, Venus and Mercury. शेषै: Śeṣaiḥ, the Sun, Mars and Jupiter being. वीर्यसमन्वितै: Vîryasamanvitaiḥ, becoming very strong. परुषिणी Paruṣiṇî, going to many persons for the satisfaction of her passion ; or of a masculine character. यदि Yadi, if. ओजराश्युद्गम: Ojarâśyudgamaḥ, the odd signs rising in the horizon. On Meṣa, Mithuna, Siṃha, Tulâ, Dhanu, Kumbha rising. जीवारास्फुजिदैन्दवेषु Jîvârâsphujidaindaveṣu, Jupiter,

Mars, Venus, Mercury (becoming). बलिषु Baliṣu, strong. प्राग्लग्नराशौ Prâglagnarâśau, the Ascendant being. समे Same, the even signs. विख्याता Vikhvyâtâ, famous. भुवि Bhuvi, in this earth. नैकशास्त्रनिपुणा Naikaśâstranipuṇâ, knowing many Śâstras. स्त्री Strî, female born. ब्रह्मवादिनी Brahmavâdinî, versed in the science of release (Mokṣa). अपि Api, also.

15. If, during the birth time of a woman, Saturn be of mediocre strength (neither powerful nor weak), the Moon, Venus and Mercury be weak and the Sun, Mars, and Jupiter be powerful and if the Ascendant be an odd sign, the woman will enjoy many men (1).

If, during the birth time of a woman, Jupiter, Venus, Mars and Mercury be powerful and the Ascendant an even sign, the woman will be far-famed, vastly learned and the knower of Brahma Vidya (the science of Brahmajñân).

Note:—(1) or will be of a masculine character according to some.

प्रहर्षिणी–पापेऽस्ते नवमगतग्रहस्य तुल्यां प्रव्रज्यां युवतिरुपैत्यसंशयेन । उद्वाहे वरणविधौ प्रदानकाले चिंतायामपि सकलं विधेयमेतत् ॥ १६ ॥

इति श्रीवराहमिहिराचार्यप्रणीते बृहज्जातके स्त्रीजातकाऽध्यायश्चतुर्विंशः ॥ २४ ॥

पापे Pâpe, the malefic planets (being). अस्ते Aste, in the seventh house. नवमगतग्रहस्य Navamagatagrahasya, the planet also residing in the ninth house from the Ascendant. तुल्यां Tulyâm, like what have been aforesaid in the Prabrajyâdhyâya (the 15th Chapter). प्रव्रज्यां Prabrajyâm, asceticism. युवतिः Yuvatiḥ, the female born. उपैति Upaiti, gets. असंशयेन Asamśayena, no doubt; undoubtedly. उद्वाहे Udvâhe, during marriage time. वरणविधौ Varaṇavidhau, during the Sambandha period or during the time of choosing a bride. प्रदानकाले Pradânakâle, during the time of making over the girl to the bridegroom. चिंतायाम् Chintâyâm, during the time when any question is asked to get an answer. अपि Api, also. सकलं Sakalam, all. विधेयम् Vidheyam, are to be applied. एतत् Etat, these.

16. Now the woman will become an ascetic in spite of the other effects declared (1) when the 7th house from the Ascendant during the birth is occupied by a malefic planet provided there be in addition to this, some planet in the 9th house also; and the asceticism will be of the class indicated by the planet occupying such 9th house.

All that have been mentioned in this Chapter apply also to the horoscopes cast during the marriage time, promise of gift, selection of a bride and at the time of query.

Note.—(1) Other effects already described will not come to pass; asceticism will be the result.

Thus ends the Twenty-fourth Chapter on Female Horoscopes by Śrî Varâha Mihirâchârya.

CHAPTER XXV.

ON DEATH.

शा० वि०—मृत्युर्मृत्युगृहेक्षणेन बलिभिस्तद्धातुकोपोद्भव-
स्तत्संयुक्तभगात्रजो बहुभवो वीर्यान्वितैर्भूरिभिः। अग्न्यम्ब्वायुध-
जो ज्वरामयकृतस्तृट्क्षुत्कृतश्चाष्टमे सूर्याद्यैर्निधने चरादिषु
परस्वाध्वप्रदेशेष्विति ॥ १ ॥

मृत्युः Mrityuḥ, death. मृत्युगृहे Mrityugrihe, in the eighth house from the Ascendant. ईक्षणेन Ikṣaṇena, on being aspected at the time of birth. बलिभिः Balibhiḥ, by the strong planets. तद्धातुकोपोद्भवः Taddhâtukopodbhavaḥ, arising from the disaffection of the humour of the body corresponding to that planet aspecting in the eighth house. तत्संयुक्तभगात्रजः Tatsaṃyuktabhagâtragaḥ, seen in that part of the body of the native which is corresponding to the part in the Zodiacal Man indicated by the eighth house from the Ascendant. बहुभवः Bahuvabaḥ, arising from many disaffections, diseases. वीर्यान्वितैः Vîryânvitaiḥ, strong. भूरिभिः Bhûribhiḥ, by many planets. अग्न्यम्ब्वायुधजः Agnyambvâyudhajaḥ, by fire, water, and weapons. ज्वरामयकृतः Jvarâmayakritaḥ, with fever and indigestion (belly complaints). तृट्क्षुत्कृतः Tritkhutkritaḥ, from thirst and hunger. च Cha, and. अष्टमे Aṣtame, in the eighth house from the Ascendant. सूर्याद्यैः Sûryâdyaiḥ, by the Sun and other planets successively. निधने Nidhane, in the eighth house from the Ascendant. चरादिषु Charâdiṣu, in the moveable (fixed and common) houses, etc. परस्वाध्वप्रदेशेषु Parasvâdhvapradeśeṣu, in the foreign lands, in one's own country, or roadside. इति Iti, thus.

1. The eighth house from the Ascendant being at the time of birth unoccupied by any planet and at the same time being aspected by powerful planets, death comes to the native owing to the disease of the humour indicated by such strong planet (1) on the part of his body corresponding to what is indicated by the 8th house on the body of the Zodiacal Man. If there be many strong planets aspecting the eighth house, then various corresponding diseases occur on the corresponding parts of the body and death will occur. But when the eighth house is occupied by the Sun, the native will die of fire; when by the Moon, the death will

be caused by water; if occupied by Mars, death will be caused by weapons; if by Mercury, death will be caused by fever; if by Jupiter, the native will die of stomach complaints; if by Venus, he will die of thirst; and if by Saturn, he will die of starvation. If this eighth house be a cardinal sign, the native will die in foreign lands; if a fixed sign, in native lands; if a common sign, he will die on road.

Notes:—(1) The humour indicated by the Sun is bile; by the Moon, wind and phlegm; by Mercury, bile, phlegm and wind; by Jupiter, phlegm; by Venus, wind and phlegm; and by Saturn, wind.

If the strong planets be auspicious, the diseases arise out of the good works done; otherwise out of the bad works committed; if the planets be neither strong nor weak, the diseases will arise out of works partly good and partly bad.

शा०वि०—शैलाग्राभिहतस्य सूर्यकुजयोर्मृत्युः खबंधुस्थयोः कूपे मंदशशांकभूमितनयैर्बंध्वस्तकर्मस्थितैः ॥ कन्यायां स्वजनाद्धिमोष्णकरयोः पापग्रहैर्दृष्टयोः स्यातां यद्युभयोदयेऽर्कशशिनौ तोये तदा मज्जितः ॥२॥

शैलाग्राभिहतस्य Sailâgrâbhihatasya, struck with stones; on one's receiving injury from stones. सूर्यकुजयोः Sûryakujayoḥ, the Sun and Mars occupying. मृत्युः Mrityuḥ, death. खबंधुस्थयोः Khabandhusthyoḥ, in the tenth or in the fourth house from the Ascendant. कूपे Kûpe, in a well; death results by being sunk into a well. मंदशशांकभूमितनयैः Mandaśasâṃkabhûmitanayaiḥ, Saturn, Moon, or Mars. बंध्वस्तकर्मस्थितैः Bandhvastakarmasthitaiḥ, in the fourth, seventh and tenth houses respectively. कन्यायां Kanyâyâm, in the sign Kanyâ. स्वजनात् Svajanât, by one's relatives. हिमोष्णकरयोः Himoṣṇakarayoḥ, the Moon and the Sun. पापग्रहैः Pâpagrahaiḥ, by the malefics. दृष्टयोः Driṣṭayoḥ, aspected by. स्यातां Syâtâm, becomes. यदि Yadi, when. उभयोदये Ubhayodaye, on the rising of the common signs. अर्कशशिनौ Arkaśaśinau, the Sun and Moon. तोये Toye, in water. तदा Tadâ, then. मज्जितः Majjitaḥ, drowned.

2. The individual dies of wounds received from stones if, during his birth time, the 4th or the 10th house from the Ascendant be occupied by the Sun and Mars; dies by falling into a well if the 4th, 7th and 10th houses be respectively occupied by Saturn, the Moon and Mars; dies

at the hands of his own relatives, if the sign Kanyâ be occupied by the afflicted Sun and Moon; will meet with death by being drowned, if the Ascendant be a common sign and if it is occupied by the Sun and Moon.

शा०वि०—मंदे कर्कटगे जलोदरकृतो मृत्युर्मृगांके मृगे शस्त्राग्निप्रभवः शशिन्यशुभयोर्मध्ये कुजर्क्षे स्थिते ॥ कन्यायां रुधिरोत्थशोषजनितस्तद्वत्स्थिते शीतगौ सौरर्क्षे यदि तद्वदेव हिमगौ रज्ज्वग्निपातैः कृतः ॥३॥

मंदे Mande, Saturn being. कर्कटगे Karkaṭage, in the sign Karka. जलोदरकृतः Jalodarakritaḥ, due to dropsy. मृत्युः Mrityuḥ, death. मृगांके Mrigâmke, the Moon. मृगे Mrige, in the sign Makara. शस्त्राग्निप्रभवः Śastrâgniprabhavaḥ, by weapons or by fire. शशिनि Śaśini, the Moon. अशुभयोः Aśubhayoḥ, between the malefics. मध्ये Madhye, between. कुजर्क्षे Kujarkṣe, in the signs of Mars, *i.e.*, in Meṣa or Vriśchika. स्थिते Sthite, situated. कन्यायां Kanyâyâṁ, in the sign Kanyâ. रुधिरोत्थशोषजनितः Rudhirotthaśoṣajanitaḥ, by blood diseases; blood being spoilt and rendered hot. तद्वत्स्थिते Tadvatsthite, situated the same as before, *i.e.*, between two evil planets. शीतगौ Śitagau, the Moon being. सौरर्क्षे Saurarkṣe, in the signs of Saturn, Makara or Kumbha. यदि Yadi, if. तद्वत् Tadvat, the same as before, *i.e.*, situated between any two evil planets. एव Eva, thus. हिमगौ Himagau, the Moon being. रज्ज्वग्निपातैः Rajjvagnipâtaiḥ, by rope, fire, or fall (from a big place). कृतः Kritaḥ, happened.

3. The individual born will die of dropsy if the sign Karka be occupied by Saturn and the sign Makara by Moon at birth time; will die of weapons or fire if the Moon occupy the sign Meṣa or Vriśchika and be between the malefics; will die of blood diseases (blood being spoilt and hot) if the Moon occupy the sign Kanyâ and be between malefics; will die by hanging, by fire, or by falling from a height, if the Moon occupy the sign Makara or Kumbha and be between the malefics.

शा०वि०—बंधाद्धीनवमस्तयोरशुभयोः सौम्यग्रहादृष्टयोर्द्रेष्काणैश्च सपाशसर्पनिगडैश्छिद्रस्थितैर्बंधतः ॥ कन्यायामशुभान्विते ऽस्तमयगे चंद्रे सिते मेषगे सूर्ये लग्नगते च विद्धि मरणं स्त्रीहेतुकं मंदिरे ॥४॥

बंधात् Bandhât, by hanging or by being fastened or tied down. धीनवमस्तयोः Dhînavamastayoḥ, in the fifth or ninth house. अशुभयोः Aśubhayoḥ, between the two malefic planets. सौम्यग्रहादृष्टयोः Saumyagrahâdriṣṭayoḥ, not aspected by any benefic planet. द्रेष्काणैः Dreṣkâṇaiḥ, any of the Decanates in the 8th house being. च Cha, and. सपाशसर्पनिगडैः Sapâśarpanigaḍaiḥ, a serpent Drekkân or a Nigaḍa (iron fetter) Drekkân ; the second and the third Decanates of Karka, the first and the second Decanates of Vriśchika and the third Decanate of Mîna are known as Serpent Drekkân ; the first Decanate of Makara is known as Nigaḍa Drekkân. कन्यायाम् Kanyâyâm, in the sign Kanyâ. अशुभान्विते Aśubhânvite, united with malefic planet. अस्तमयगे Astamayage, descending. चंद्रे Chandre, the Moon being. सिते Site, Venus being. मेषगे Meṣage, in Meṣa. सूर्ये Sûrye, the Sun being. लग्नगते Lagnagate, in the Ascendant. च Cha, and. विद्धि Viddhi, know. मरणं Maraṇam, death. स्त्रीहेतुकं Stribetukam, caused by wife. मंदिरे Mandire, in one's own dwelling house.

4. The individual born will die of imprisonment, by hanging, or in some other state of capture, if, during birth, the 9th or 5th house be occupied by two malefic planets and if such planets be not well aspected; will die of imprisonment, if the 8th house from the Ascendant contain a serpent or fetter Decanate (1); will die in his own house by a woman if the 7th house from the Ascendant be Kanyâ occupied by the Moon and a malefic, if the Sun be in the Ascendant, and Venus in the sign Meṣa.

Notes :—(1) The second and the third Decanates of the sign Karka, the first and second Decanates of Vriśchika and the third Decanate of Mîna are known as Serpent Decanates. The first Decanate of Makara is known as fetter Decanate (Nigaḍa Decanate).

शा० वि०—शूलोद्भिन्नतनुः सुखेऽवनिसुते सूर्येऽपि वा खे यमे । सप्रक्षीणहिमांशुभिश्च युगपत्पापैस्त्रिकोणाद्यगैः ॥ बन्धुस्थे च रवौ वियत्यवनिजे क्षीणेन्दुसंवीक्षिते । काष्ठेनाभिहतः प्रयाति मरणं सूर्यात्मजेनेक्षिते ॥५॥

शूलोद्भिन्नतनुः Sûlodbhinnatanuḥ, by being hung on any stake that is meant for impaling criminals; by being pierced by a pointed weapon. सुखे Sukhe, in the fourth house from the Ascendant. अवनिसुते Avanisute, Mars being in. सूर्यः Sûryaḥ, the Sun. अपि Api, also. वा Vâ, or. खे Khe, in the tenth house. यमे Yame, Saturn being in सप्रक्षीणहिमांशुभिः Saprakṣîṇahimâṃśubhiḥ, by the Moon, when she has waned very much. च Cha, and ; also dies on stake. युगपत् Yugapat, at one and the same time. पापैः Pâpaiḥ, by the malefics. त्रिकोणाद्यगैः Trikoṇâdyagaiḥ, in the fifth, ninth, or the first house. बन्धुस्थे Bandhusthe, in the fourth house. च Cha, and ; also dies in stake. रवौ Ravau, the Sun. वियति Viyati, in the tenth house. अवनिजे Avanije, Mars. क्षीणेन्दुसंवीक्षिते Kṣiṇendusaṃvikṣite, aspected by the waning Moon. काष्ठेन Kâṣṭhena, by wood. अभिहतः Abhihataḥ, struck. प्रयाति Prayâti, goes away. मरणं Maraṇam, death. सूर्यात्मजेन Sûryâtmajena, by Saturn. ईक्षिते Ikṣite, aspected.

5. The native will meet with death by being mounted on a sharp pointed iron rod or spear if, during his birth, any of these combinations take place :—(1) if the 4th house from the Ascendant be occupied by Mars or the Sun and if the 10th house be occupied by Saturn or (2) if the Sun, Mars, Saturn and the waning Moon be in the Ascendant, the 5th and the 9th house, or (3) if the Sun occupy the 4th house and if Mars, occupying the 10th house, be aspected by the waning Moon. Again the native will die of injury received from a piece of wood if the Sun occupy the 4th house and Mars in the 10th be aspected by Saturn.

व०ति०—रन्ध्रास्पदाङ्गहिबुकैर्लगुडाहताङ्गः प्रक्षीणचन्द्ररुधिरार्किदिनेशयुक्तैः ॥ तैरेव कर्मनवमोदयपुत्रसंस्थैर्धूमाग्निबन्धनशरीरनिकुट्टनान्तः ॥६॥

रन्ध्रास्पदाङ्गहिबुकैः Randhrâspadâmgahibukaiḥ, in the eighth, tenth, first or fourth house. लगुडाहताङ्गः Laguḍâhatâmgaḥ, struck by a club. प्रक्षीणचन्द्ररुधिरार्किदिनेशयुक्तैः : Prakṣiṇachandrarudhirârkidineṣayuktaiḥ, united with waning Moon, Mars, Saturn and Sun. तैः Taiḥ, by those planets respectively. एव Eva, and. कर्मनवमोदयपुत्रसंस्थैः Karmanavamodayaputrasaṃsthaiḥ, in the tenth, ninth, first, fifth houses from the Ascendant. धूमाग्निबन्धनशरीरनिकुट्टनान्तः Dhûmâgnibandhanaśarîranikuṭṭanântaḥ, death resulting from smoke, fire, hanging or fastening, or by being struck with some wooden club.

6. The individual will die on being struck with a club or stick if, during his birth, the 8th, 10th, 1st, and 4th houses be occupied respectively by the waning Moon, Mars, Saturn and the Sun, or he will die by being smoked, by fire, by imprisonment or by blows from a club or stick if the 10th, 9th, 1st and 5th houses be occupied respectively by the waning Moon, Mars, Saturn and the Sun.

व॰ ति॰—बन्ध्वस्तकर्मसहितैः कुजसूर्यमन्दैर्निर्याणमायुधशिखिक्षितिपालकोपात् ॥ सौरेन्दुभूमितनयैः स्वसुखास्पदस्थैर्ज्ञेयः क्षतक्रिमिकृतश्च शरीरघातः ॥७॥

बन्ध्वस्तकर्मसहितैः Bandhvastakarmasahitaiḥ, in the fourth, seventh and tenth houses respectively. कुजसूर्यमन्दैः Kujasûryamandaiḥ, by Mars, Sun, and Saturn respectively. निर्याणं Niryâṇam, death. आयुधशिखिक्षितिपालकोपात् Âyudhaśikhikṣitipâlakopât, by weapons, fire, or through king's anger. सौरेन्दुभूमितनयैः Saurendubhûmitanaiḥ, by Saturn, the Moon, or Mars. स्वसुखास्पदस्थैः Svasukhâspadasthaiḥ, in the second, fourth or tenth houses respectively. ज्ञेयः Jñeyaḥ, is known. क्षतक्रिमिकृतः Kṣatakṛimikṛitaḥ, by worms growing on some injured parts of the body. च Cha, and. शरीरपातः Śarîrapâtaḥ, the going away of this body.

7. If, during birth-time, the 4th, 7th, and 10th houses be respectively occupied by Mars, the Sun, and Saturn, the person will die by being struck with weapons, being burnt in fire or by wrath of the king. If the 2nd, 4th and 10th houses be respectively occupied by Saturn, the Moon and Mars, the person will die of sores and worms.

शा॰ वि॰—खस्थेऽर्केऽवनिजे रसातलगते यानप्रपाताद्वधो । यन्त्रोत्पीडनजःकुजेऽस्तमयगे सौरेन्दुनाभ्युद्गमे ॥ विण्मध्ये रुधिरार्किशीतकिरणैर्जूकाजसौरर्क्षगैर्याते वा गलितेन्दुसूर्यरुधिरैर्व्योमास्तबंध्वाह्वयान् ॥ ८ ॥

खस्थे Khasthe, in the tenth house. अर्के Arke, the Sun. अवनिजे Avanije, Mars. रसातलगते Rasâtalagate, in the fourth house. यानप्रपातात् Yânaprapâtât, due to fall from any conveyance or vehicle, or horse or so. वधः Vadhaḥ, death. यन्त्रोत्पीडनजः Yantrotpîḍanajaḥ, on being crushed or smashed by a machine. कुजे Kuje, Mars. अस्तमयगे Astamayage, in the seventh house. सौरेन्दुना Saurendunâ, by Saturn, Moon, and Sun ; some read waning Moon for Moon. अभ्युद्गमे Abhyudgame, in the Ascendant. विण्मध्ये Viṇmadhye, in the fœces. रुधिरार्किशीतकिरणैः Rudhirârkiśîtakiraṇaiḥ, Mars, Saturn, and Moon. जूकाजसौरर्क्षगैः Jûkâjasaurarkṣagaiḥ, in the signs Tulâ, Meṣa, Makara and Kumbha. याते Yâte, on going to. वा Vâ, or. गलितेन्दुसूर्यरुधिरैः Galitendusûryarudhiraiḥ, waning Moon, the Sun and Mars. व्योमास्तबंध्वाह्वयान् Vyomâstabandhvâhvayân, to the tenth, seventh, fourth houses respectively.

8. The individual will die of a fall from horseback or any vehicle or conveyance if, during his birth, the Sun be in the 10th house and Mars be in the 4th house;

will die on being crushed by a machine, if Mars be in the 7th house and the Sun, Moon and Saturn be in the Ascendant; will die in a dirty place containing fœces if (1) the sign Tulâ be occupied by Mars, the sign Meṣa by Saturn, and the sign Makara or Kumbha by the Moon or if (2) the 10th, 7th and 4th houses be occupied by the waning Moon, the Sun and Mars respectively.

वैतालीय—वीर्यान्वितवक्रवीक्षिते क्षीणेन्दौ निधनस्थितेऽर्कजे। गुह्योद्भवरोगपीडया मृत्युः स्यात् कृमिशस्त्रदाहजः ॥९॥

वीर्यान्वितवक्रवीक्षिते Vîryânvitavakravîkṣite, aspected by powerful Mars. क्षीणेन्दौ Kṣiṇendau, on the Moon being. निधनस्थिते Nidhanasthite, in the eighth house. अर्कजे Arkaje, Saturn occupying. गुह्योद्भवरोगपीडया Guhyodbhavarogapiḍayâ, by diseases on the private parts, by piles, fistula and the like. मृत्युः Mrityuḥ, death. स्यात् Syât, will come. कृमिशस्त्रदाहजः Krimiśastradâhajaḥ, arising from worms in any abscess, or by weapons, or by fire.

9. The person will die of fistula or cinus in the anus or pudendum or some such diseases affecting the private parts, if the waning Moon be aspected by powerful Mars and if Saturn be in the 8th house; the part will be worn away by worms, or operated with the lancet or burnt.

व० ति०—अस्ते रवौ सरुधिरे निधनेऽर्कपुत्रे क्षीणे रसातलगते हिमगौ खगांतः। लग्नात्मजाष्टमतपःस्विनभौममंदचंद्रैस्तु शैलशिखराशनिकुड्यपातैः ॥ १० ॥

अस्ते Aste, descending. रवौ Ravau, the Sun. सरुधिरे Sarudhire, with Mars. निधने Nidhane, in the eighth house. अर्कपुत्रे Arkaputre, Saturn. क्षीणे Kṣiṇe, waning. रसातलगते Rasâtalagate, in the fourth house. हिमगौ Himagau, the Moon. खगांतः Khagântaḥ, death by birds. लग्नात्मजाष्टमतपःसु Lagnâtmajâṣtamatapaḥsu, in the Ascendant, fifth, eighth and ninth houses respectively. इनभौममंदचंद्रैः Inabhaumamandachandraiḥ, Sun, Mars, Saturn and Moon. तु Tu, also. शैलशिखराशनिकुड्यपातैः Śailaśikharâśanikuḍyapâtaiḥ, falling from mountain peaks, or by lightning or by the fall of houses.

10. The native will die from the attack of birds, when, during birth, the Sun together with Mars exist in the 7th house, Saturn in the 8th, and the waning Moon in the

4th house; will die from falling from a mountain top, by being struck with lightning, or by a wall tumbling over him, if the 1st, 5th, 8th, and 9th houses be found with the Sun, Mars, Saturn and the Moon respectively.

वैतालीय–द्वाविंशः कथितस्तु कारणं द्रेष्काणो निधनस्य सूरिभिः । तस्याधिपतिर्भवोऽपि वा निर्याणं स्वगुणैः प्रयच्छति ॥ ११ ॥

द्वाविंशः Dvâviṃśaḥ, the twenty-second. कथितः Kathitaḥ, said. तु Tu, but. कारणं Kâraṇam, cause. द्रेष्काणः Dreṣkâṇaḥ, Decanate. निधनस्य Nidhanasya, death's. सूरिभिः Sûribhiḥ, by the Pundits (on astrology). तस्य Tasya, of that twenty-second Decanate. अधिपतिः Adhipatiḥ, ruler. भवः Bhabaḥ, of the sign in which the twenty-second Decanate exists. अपि Api, also. वा Vâ, or. निर्याणं Niryâṇam, death. स्वगुणैः Svaguṇaiḥ, on account of its being related to that Decanate. प्रयच्छति Prayachhati, gives; produces.

11. In case the planetary combinations aforesaid do not occur in the case of any individual, look to the 22nd decanate from the rising decanate at birth time; this 22nd decanate will account for his death; thus the sages say. Death will be caused by the ruler of this 22nd decanate or by the ruler of the sign which contains this 22nd decanate, whichever is the most powerful, by water, fire or other means appropriate to this powerful ruler.

व०ति०–होरानवांशकपयुक्तसमानभूमौ योगेक्षणादिभिरतः परिकल्प्यमेतत् ॥ मोहस्तु मृत्युसमयेऽनुदितांशतुल्यः स्वेशेक्षिते द्विगुणितस्त्रिगुणः शुभैश्च ॥ १२ ॥

होरानवांशकपयुक्तसमानभूमौ Horânavâṃśakapayuktasamânabhûmau, on the place indicated by the sign where the ruler of the rising Navâṃśa resides. योगेक्षणादिभिः Yogekṣaṇâdibhiḥ, from several combinations or aspects, *i.e.*, on those places indicated by the sign of any other planet co-existing with the above mentioned ruler or those indicated by the sign of the planet aspecting the ruler of the rising Navâṃśa or those indicated by the sign of the ruler of the Navâṃśa occupied by the lord of the rising Navâṃśa. अतः Ataḥ, after this. परिकल्प्यम् Parikalpyam, are to be judged and determined. एतत् Etat, this. मोहः Mohaḥ, the period of senselessness preceding death. तु Tu, but. मृत्युसमये Mṛityusamaye, at the time of death. अनुदितांशतुल्यः Anuditâṃśatulyaḥ, lasting for a period equal to the time taken by that part of the Navâṃśa that has not yet risen above the horizon. स्वेशेक्षिते Sveśekṣite, aspected by the ruler of this rising Navâṃśa. द्विगुणितः Dviguṇitaḥ, double the above period. त्रिगुणः Triguṇaḥ, treble the above period. शुभैः Śubhaiḥ, if aspected by the benefic planets. च Cha, and.

12. Now the places where death will occur are being specified. Look to the sign where the ruler of the rising Navâṃśa exists, or the sign of any other planet that happens to co-exist with the above mentioned ruler, or the sign of the planet aspecting the ruler of the rising Navâṃśa or the sign of the ruler of the Navâṃśa occupied by the lord of the rising Navâṃśa. The places (1) indicated by these signs will be the places where death will occur. If many places are thus found, select judiciously the place of the most powerful planet. The period of unconsciousness preceding death will be the time taken by the portion of the rising Navâṃśa (2) (that has not yet risen above the horizon) to rise. If the rising Navâṃśa (3) be aspected by its ruler, such period will be twice; and if it be aspected by benefic planets, it will be three times (4) the period first stated.

Notes :—(1) Meṣa, places frequented by sheep. (2) Vṛiṣa, places frequented by oxen; Mithuna, a house; Karka, a well; Siṃha, a forest; Kanyâ, water-bank; Tulâ, market or store-house; Vṛiśchika, a hole; Dhanu, stables; Makara, watery pools and marshes; Kumbha, a house; Mîna, watery places.

(2) and (3) some take the rising sign instead of the rising Navâṃśa.

(4) Where one planet indicates two signs, there the place of the Mûlatrikoṇa sign will be the place of death. According to some the place of death is the particular portion of the house belonging to the most powerful planet, *e.g.*, the place of worship; the bath; the kitchen, &c. (*vide* 12 verse, Chap. II).

(4) If the rising sign be aspected by its ruler, and by a benefic planet, the period of unconsciousness will be six times as long.

मालिनी—दहनजलविमिश्रैर्भस्मसंक्लेदशोषैर्निधनभवनसंस्थै-
र्व्यालवर्गैर्विडन्तः । इति शवपरिणामश्चिन्तनीयो यथोक्तः पृथुवि-
रचितशास्त्राद्गत्यनूकादि चिंत्यम् ॥ १३ ॥

दहनजलविमिश्रैः: Dahanajalavimiśraiḥ, by the fiery, watery, or mixed Decanates. भस्मसंक्लेदशोषैः: Bhasmasaṃkledaśoṣaiḥ, will be burnt to ashes, or thrown in running streams, or dried up on a high barren place. निधनभवनसंस्थैः: Nidhanabhavanasaṃsthaiḥ, in the eighth house from the Ascendant. व्यालवर्गैः: Vyâlavargaiḥ, by the dogs, jackals, crows, etc. विडन्तः: Viḍantaḥ, devoured. इति Iti, thus. शवपरिणामः: Śavapariṇâmaḥ, the disposal of the dead. चिन्तनीयः: Chintanîyaḥ, is considered. यथोक्तः: Yathoktaḥ, as stated above. पृथुविरचितशास्त्रात् Prithuvirachitaśâstrât, from the Sâstras written by Pṛithu Âchârya. गति Gati, (the previous and after) lives. अनूकादि Anûkâdi, former birth; future birth, etc. चिंत्यम् Chintyam, is considered.

13. Now the disposal of the dead body is being mentioned. If, during birth time, the 22nd Decanate from the rising Decanate be fiery, the dead body will be cremated and reduced to ashes; if watery, the dead body will be thrown in a river or a pool of water ; if mixed, the body will be dried up. If the 8th house contain a Serpent Decanate, the body will be devoured by jackals, crows and the like. For a knowledge of the previous and future incarnations of any person and of the nature of such life, the reader is referred to more elaborate works on horoscopy written by Pṛithuyasâ, the son of Varâha Mihira.

Note.—A fiery Decanate is the Decanate of a malefic planet.

A watery Decanate is that of a benefic planet.

A mixed Decanate is the Decanate of a benefic planet occupied by a malefic planet as well as the Decanate of a malefic planet occupied by a benefic planet.

Serpent Decanates are already mentioned. These are the 1st and 2nd of Karka; the 1st and 2nd of Vṛischika, and the 3rd of Mîna.

मालिनी—गुरुरुडुपतिशुक्रौ सूर्यभौमौ यमज्ञौ विबुधपितृति-
रश्चो नारकीयांश्च कुर्युः । दिनकरशशिवीर्याधिष्ठितात् त्र्यंशनाथा-
त्प्रवरसमनिकृष्टास्तुंगह्रासादनूके ॥ १४ ॥

गुरुः Guruḥ, Jupiter. उडुपतिशुक्रौ Uḍupatiśukrau, the Moon and Venus. सूर्यभौमौ Sûryabhaumau, the Sun and Mars. यमज्ञौ Yamagñau, Saturn and Mercury. विबुधपितृतिरश्च: Vibudhapitṛitiraścha, from the Devaloka (region of Gods), the Pitṛiloka (region of Fathers), from the Tiryakloka (region of birds). नारकीयं Nârakîyâm, from the Hell. च Cha, and. कुर्युः Kuryuḥ, is to be reckoned. दिनकरशशिवीर्याधिष्ठितात् Dinakaraśaśiviryâdhiṣṭhitât, (from the Decanate) occupied by the stronger of the Sun and the Moon. त्र्यंशनाथात् Tryamśanâthât, from the ruler of the Decanate. प्रवरसमनिकृष्टाः Pravarasamanikṛiṣṭâḥ, of the best, middling, and worst character तुंगह्रासात् Tuṅgahrâsât, if the planet be exalted, or removed from exaltation. अनूके Anûke, as regards the former state of existence.

14. If the Decanates occupied by the Sun or the Moon whichever is powerful, be ruled by Jupiter, the individual has come from Devaloka, the land of the Devas; if ruled by Moom or Venus, the person has come from Pitṛiloka, the land of the Fathers; if ruled by Sun or Mars, the person has come from the world of lower animals; and if ruled by Saturn or Mercury, the person has come from the region of hell.

If the lord of the Decanate occupied by the Sun or the Moon, whichever is powerful, be in his exaltation, the past life was also of an exalted character; if middling, the character was also middling, and if detrimental, the character was also low.

मालिनी–गतिरपि रिपुरंध्रत्र्यंशपोऽस्तस्थितो वा गुरुरथ रिपुकेंद्रच्छिद्रगः स्वोच्चसंस्थः ॥ उदयति भवनेऽन्त्ये सौम्यभागे च मोक्षो भवति यदि बलेन प्रोज्झितास्तत्र शेषाः ॥१५॥

इति श्रीवराहमिहिराचार्यप्रणीते बृहज्जातके नैर्याणिकाऽध्यायः पंचविंशः ॥२५॥

गतिः Gatiḥ, future state of existence. अपि Api, also; even. रिपुरंध्रत्र्यंशपः Ripurandhratryamśapaḥ, from the rulers of the sixth and the eighth. अस्तस्थिताः Astasthitâḥ, in the seventh house. वा Vâ, and; this is its meaning here. गुरुः Guruḥ, Jupiter. अथ Atha, (to fill up the stanza). रिपुकेंद्रच्छिद्रगः Ripukendrachhidragaḥ, in the sixth, angular or eighth houses. स्वोच्चसंस्थः Svochchasamsthaḥ, in his exalted house; in the sign Karka. उदयति Udayati, when rising. भवने Bhavane, in the house. अन्त्ये Antye, in the twelfth; the last. सौम्यभागे Saumyabhâge, in the

Navâṃśa of a benefic planet. च Cha, and. मोक्ष: Mokṣaḥ, release from births; salvation. भवति Bhavati, comes. यदि Yadi, if. बलेन Balena, by the powerful planet. प्रोज्झिता: Projjhitâḥ, forsaken. तत्र Tatra, there (or) at the same time. शेषा: Śeṣâḥ, the other planets excepting Jupiter.

15. If there be no planets in the 6th, 7th, and 8th houses, then look to the Decanates of the 6th and the 8th houses at the moment of birth (from the rising Decanate) and find out the most powerful of the rulers of these Decanates. The person will go after death to the world indicated by this powerful planet. If there be planets in the 6th, 7th and 8th houses, then find out which is the most powerful and the person will go to the world of this most powerful planet. Again(1) if Jupiter occupy the 6th house or one of the angular houses or the 8th house and be also exalted, or (2) if the sign Mîna be rising and Jupiter occupy it and be in the Navâṃśa of a benefic planet, while the other planets are powerless, the person will obtain final release (Mokṣa) after death.

Notes :—For the worlds of the several planets, *vide* preceding verse.

The next world may also be determined from the position of the planets (as the above configuration) at the time of death as at the time of birth of a person.

Thus ends the Tewnty-fifth Chapter on Death by Śrî Varâha Mihirâchârya of Avantika.

CHAPTER XXVI.

ON LOST HOROSCOPES.

इंद्रवज्रा-आधानजन्मापरिबोधकाले सम्पृच्छतो जन्म वदे-द्विलग्नात् ॥ पूर्वापरार्द्धे भवनस्य विंद्याद्भानावुदग्दक्षिणगे प्रसूतिम् ॥१॥

आधानजन्मापरिबोधकाले Âdhânajanmâparibodhakâle, when both the time of conception and the time of birth are unknown. सम्पृच्छत: Samprichhataḥ, of the person who makes the query, or questions; of the questioning man. जन्म Janma, birth. वदेत् Vadet, one is to say; one is to infer and say. विलग्नात् Vilagnât, from the Ascendant during the time of query. पूर्वापरार्द्धे Pûrvâparârdhe, in the first fifteen degrees or in the latter fifteen degrees. भवनस्य Bhavanasya, of any sign. विंद्यात् Vindyât, know. भानौ Bhânau, the Sun being situated in. उदग्दक्षिणगे Udagdakṣiṇage, in the Northern signs (*i.e.*, in the signs Makara, Kumbha, Mîna, Meṣa, Vṛiṣa, and Mithuna; these are called the six signs beginning with Makara) or in the Southern signs (*i.e.*, in the signs Karka, Siṃha, Kanyâ, Tulâ, Vṛischika, and Dhanu; these are called the six signs beginning with Karka). प्रसूतिम् Prasûtim, birth, month of birth.

1. When both the time of conception and the time of birth are unknown, the solution (*i.e.*, the ascertaining of the time of birth) is to be effected from the Ascendant during the time of question (set seriously and clearly). If the first half of the Ascendant (first fifteen degrees) rises, the month of birth will be in the Northern Path of the Sun (in any of the six months from Makara to Mithuna); if the second half of the Ascendant rises, the month of birth is the Southern Path of the Sun (in any of the six months corresponding to those from Karka to Dhanu).

Notes:—The rising sign at the time of query is called Praśna Lagna or the Significator.

The Northern Path of the Sun is called the Uttarâyaṇa; the six months are: Mâgha (15th January-15th February); Phâlguna (15th February-15th March); Chaitra (15th March-15th April); Vaiśâkha (15th

April-15th May); Jaiṣṭha (15th May-15th June); Âṣâḍha (15th June-15th July).

The Southern Path of the Sun is called the Dakṣiṇâyana, and lasts for six months; Śrâvaṇa (15th July-15th August); Bhâdra (15th August-15th September); Âśvin (15th September-15th October); Kârtik (15th October-15th November); Agrahâyaṇa (15th November-15th December); and Pauṣa (15th December-15th January).

उपजातिका-लग्नत्रिकोणेषु गुरुस्त्रिभागैर्विकल्प्य वर्षाणि वयोनुमानात् ॥ ग्रीष्मोऽर्कलग्ने कथितास्तु शेषैरन्यायनर्तावृतु-रर्कचारात् ॥२॥

लग्नत्रिकोणेषु Lagnatrikoṇeṣu, in the Ascendant, fifth or ninth house (from the Ascendant) at the time of query successively. गुरुः Guruḥ, Jupiter (resides in). त्रिभागैः: Tribhâgaiḥ, according to the three Decanates of the Ascendant, rising at the time of query. विकल्प्य Vikalpya, considering; ascertaining. वर्षाणि Varṣâṇi, number of years; the year of birth. वयोनुमानात् Vayonumânât, judging from the appearance of the individual what is his age at present. ग्रीष्मः: Grîṣmaḥ, the summer season (comprising two months when the Sun passes through Gemini and Cancer). अर्कलग्ने Arkalagne, if the Sun (or the Sun Decanate) be in the Ascendant at the time of query. कथिताः: Kathitâḥ, said; have been mentioned (in verse 12, Chapter II). तु Tu, but. शेषैः : Śeṣaiḥ (the other seasons will be indicated) the other planets, Moon, etc., (or their Decanates rising in the horizon). अन्यायनर्तौ Anyâyanartau, in case the season (thus determined) does not correspond to the Ayaṇa (already determined). ऋतुः: Rituḥ, the seasons (each season consisting of two months) are to be determined. अर्कचारात् Arkachârât, according to the movements of the Sun.

2. First determine the sign occupied by Jupiter at the time of birth in the following way:—if the first Decanate of any sign rises in the horizon at the time of query, the sign occupied by Jupiter at birth will be the Ascendant itself at the time of query; if the second Decanate rises, Jupiter's sign will be the fifth sign from the Ascendant; and if the third Decanate rises, Jupiter's sign will be ninth sign from the Ascendant at the time of query (1). After this, judge from the appearance of the querent (whose horoscope is to be determined what his age would then be (2) and ascertain the year of his birth. The year of birth being thus determined, determine then the season (each season comprising two months)

of birth thus:—This will be the summer season (*i.e.*, when the Sun is in Taurus or Gemini) if the Sun or Mars or their Decanates rise (*i.e.*, occupy the Ascendant), at the time of query; (*i.e.*, for the other seasons, refer to verse 12, Chapter II); Sis̀ira or the winter (*i.e.*, when the Sun is in Kumbha or Makara), when Saturn or its Decanate is in the Ascendant; Vasanta or the spring (the Sun in Meṣa or Mîna) when Venus or her Decanate is in the Ascendant; Varṣâ or the monsoon (the Sun in Siṃha or Karka) when the Moon or her Decanate is in the Ascendant; S̀arat or the autumn (the Sun in Kanyâ or Tulâ) when Mercury or its Decanate is in the Ascendant; and Hemanta or the cold season (the Sun in Vṛis̀chika or Dhanuṣ) when Jupiter or his Decanate is rising (3). If the season thus determined do not correspond to the Ayana (the Sun's Northern or Southern Path) already determined, the correct season shall be determined from the instructions given in the following verse (4).

Notes:—(1) Some render the meaning thus:—If the first Decanate rises, then the age of the querent will be so many years as will be the number of signs from the Significator up to where Jupiter is situated. If the second Decanate rises, then the age will be so many years as will be the number of signs from the 5th house (from the Significator) up to the sign occupied by Jupiter. If the third Decanate rises, the age will be so many years as the number of signs from the ninth house up to the sign occupied by Jupiter.

But this is not approved by Yavanes̀wara and other Âchâryas. The position of Jupiter might be ascertained also from the rising Dvâdas̀âṃs̀a. If the rising Dvâdas̀âṃs̀a at the time of query be the first, Jupiter occupies the Pras̀na Lagna itself; Jupiter occupies the second house from the Ascendant, if the rising Dvâdas̀âṃs̀a be the second; occupies the third from the Ascendant, if the rising Dvâdas̀âṃs̀a be the third and so on.

(2) As Jupiter takes twelve years to go round the heavens, if the number of circuits passed through by Jupiter from the time of birth be known, the age of the person can be at once determined. For instance, suppose Jupiter to occupy the sign Vris̀chika at the time of query and the sign Vṛiṣa at the time of birth and suppose him to be in his 4th

circuit. The age of the person will be $3 \times 12+6$ or 42 years. The cycle of Jupiter can be determined from the appearance of the person, from a rough estimate of his age. In the instance cited above, the age of the person is either 6, or $12+6=18$ or $24+6=30$, or $36+6=42$ and so on. If, however, the cycle of Jupiter cannot be easily ascertained from the appearance of the person, the number of the cycle shall be determined from the part of body touched by a person at the time. In stanza 24 of Chapter 70 of the Brihat Samhitâ, the human body is divided into ten parts, each part corresponding to a Daśâ period of 12 years.

पादौ सगुल्फौ प्रथमं प्रदिष्टं जङ्घे द्वितीये तु सजानुवक्त्रे ॥
मेढ्रोरुमुष्काश्च ततस्तृतीयं नाभिं कटिं चेति चतुर्थमाहुः ॥
उदरं कथयन्ति पञ्चमं हृदयं षष्ठमथ स्तनान्वितः ॥
अथ सप्तममंसजत्रुणी कथयन्त्यष्टममोष्ठकन्धरे ॥
नवमन्नयने च साभ्रुणी सललाटं दशमं शिरस्तथा ॥
अशुभेष्वशुभं दशाफलचरणाद्येषु शुभेषु शोभनम् ॥

(1) Feet and ankles.
(2) Shanks and knees.
(3) The thighs and genital organ.
(4) The loins and the navel.
(5) The belly.
(6) The breast and the bosoms.
(7) The shoulders.
(8) The neck and lips.
(9) The eyes and brows.
(10) The forehead and the head.

So that if the belly be touched, it may be determined that at the time of query Jupiter is in his 5th round. So that the age of the person will be 4×12 or 48 years, *plus* the number of years taken by Jupiter to move from the sign occupied by him at the time of birth to the sign occupied by him at the time of query.

(3) If two or more planets occupy the Significator or the Ascendant at the time of query, the season of the most powerful planet will be the season of birth.

(4) Suppose the Ayaṇa determined from stanza 1 to be the Uttarâyaṇa; so that the month of birth is one between Capricorn and Gemini.

Suppose the Significator (the Praśna Lagna) to be occupied by the Moon whose season is Varṣâ (Karka and Siṃha); in such a case the season of Venus the alternative planet of the Moon, *viz.*, the Vasanta (Pisces and Aries) shall be determined as the season of birth as explained in the 3rd verse.

इंद्रवज्रा—चंद्रज्ञजीवाः परिवर्तनीयाः शुक्रारमंदैरयने विलोमे ॥ द्रेष्काणभागे प्रथमे तु पूर्वो मासोऽनुपाताच्च तिथिर्विकल्प्यः ॥३॥

चंद्रज्ञजीवाः Chandrajñajîvâḥ, the Moon, Mercury, and Jupiter. परिवर्तनीयाः Parivartanîyâḥ, are to be exchanged with. शुक्रारमंदैः Śukrâramandaiḥ, with Venus, Mars, and Saturn respectively. अयने Ayane, the half year; the Northern or Southern path of the Sun. विलोमे Vilome, when reversed; when against the natural order. द्रेष्काणभागे Dreṣkâṇabhâge, on the Decanate of the Ascendant at birth becoming. प्रथमे Prathame, the first. तु Tu, but. पूर्वः Pûrvaḥ, the first. मासः Mâsaḥ, month (of the season). अनुपातात् Anupâtât, by means of the rule of proportion. च Cha, and तिथिः Tithiḥ, a lunar day. विकल्प्यः Vikalpyaḥ, are obtained.

3. The Moon shall be exchanged with Venus, Mercury with Mars, and Jupiter with Saturn, in case the season above found do not correspond to the Ayanas as before determined. Now the season (of the two months) being determined, determine the month of birth exactly. It will be the first month of the season, if the first half of the rising Decanate rise at the time of query; and it will the be second month if the second half rise. The lunar day of birth shall then be determined from the proportion of the semi-Decanate that has risen above the horizon (1).

Notes:—(1) Make the proportion thus:—If the semi-Decanate represent the 30 days of the month, how many days of the month will be elapsed, when so much of the semi-Drekkân has risen above. A semi-Decanate is 5 degrees representing 30 days; so that 10 minutes of the rising semi-Decanate represent a lunar day. The longitude of the Lagna is to be determined first according to the rules for finding out the Lagna Sphuṭa.

इंद्रवज्रा—अत्रापि होरापटवो द्विजेंद्राः सूर्यांशतुल्यां तिथिमुद्दिशंति ॥ रात्रिद्युसंज्ञेषु विलोमजन्म भागैश्च वेलाः क्रमशो विकल्प्याः ॥४॥

अत्र अपि Atra api, even here (in ascertaining this lunar day). होरापटवः: Horâpaṭavaḥ, well-versed astrologers. द्विजेंद्राः: Dvijendrâḥ, the learned Brâhmaṇas. सूर्यांशतुल्यां Sûryâṃśatulyâm, equal to the number of degrees traversed by the Sun in any particular sign. तिथिं Tithim, the lunar day during birth. उद्दिशंति Uddiśanti, advise. रात्रिद्युसंज्ञेषु Râtridyusaṃjñeṣu, (the Ascendant at the time of query becoming) the night or the day signs. विलोमजन्म Vilomajanma, night time or day time reversedly (during the time of birth). भागैः: Bhâgaiḥ, by means of the degrees of the Ascendant (when questioned) risen above the horizon. वेलाः: Velâḥ, the exact hour of birth. क्रमशः: Kramaśaḥ, successively. विकल्प्याः Vikalpyâḥ, are to be ascertained ; are to be imagined or thought.

4. The well versed astrologers say that the lunar day during birth time will be represented by the number of degrees traversed by the Sun in any particular sign (1). If the Significator (*i.e.*, the Ascendant at the time of query) be a day sign, the birth will have occurred at night, and if it be a night sign the birth will have occured by day ; the exact time of birth, the ghaṭikâ shall be determined from the portion of the rising sign that has risen above the horizon (2).

Notes:—(1) The lunar month commences from the first lunar day of the bright fortnight. Suppose the Sun to occupy the 18th degree of the sign Makara at the time of birth. The lunar day or Tithi during birth is the 18th day, *i.e.*, 18 *minus* 15 = 3rd day of the dark fortnight.

(2) The length of the day or the night of birth being known, it is represented by the rising sign at the time of query ; and the longitude of the rising point being determined, the exact degrees of the sign that have risen above the horizon can be known. Then make the following proportion :—if the rising sign represents the length of the day (known already), what portion of the day will be represented by the portion of the sign that has already risen. When this is known, the horoscope may be cast with the help of the astronomical tables in the almanac. Thus the horoscope at the time of birth is fully determined. Suppose the length of the day found '(from the almanac, is 30 ghaṭikâs and the portion of the sign risen above is 5° or $\frac{1}{6}$th of the whole sign ; then at 5 ghatikâs from the morning, the birth has taken place.

The Commentators write also in this way :—

Multiply the number of Chaṣakâs (1 Chaṣakâ = six minutes) of the Significator that have risen above the horizon by the length of the day (or the night as the case may be) and divide by the Lagna Khaṇḍâ (in

Chaṣakâs) of that sign in that place; the quotient will give you the exact time of birth.

The following table gives the Lagna Khandâ, at the two places Benares and Srinagar, of the several signs in Chaṣakâs:—

Signs.		Benares Chaṣakâs.	Srinagar.	Signs.
Meṣa	...	200	233	Mîna
Vṛiṣa	...	240	283	Kumbha.
Mithuna	...	280	332	Makara.
Karka	...	320	352	Dhanu.
Siṃha	...	360	340	Vṛischik:
Kanyâ	...	400	348	Tulâ.

इन्द्रवज्रा—केचिच्छशांकाध्युषितान्नवांशाच्छुक्लांतसंज्ञं कथयंति मासम् ॥ लग्नत्रिकोणोत्तमवीर्ययुक्तं संप्रोच्यतेऽङ्गालभनादिभिर्वा ॥५॥

केचित् Kechit, some astrologers. शशांकाध्युषितात् Śaśâṃkâdhyuṣitât, occupied by the Moon, (at the time of query). नवांशात् Navâṃśât, from the Navâṃśa. शुक्लांतसंज्ञं Suklântasaṃjñam, (the month being) designated by the name of the Star, or asterism (in the aforesaid Navâṃśa) when the full Moon takes place. Thus if the full Moon be found with the Star Kṛittikâ or Rohinî, the month is called Kârtika after the name of the asterism Kṛittikâ; and so on. कथयंति Kathayanti, say. मासं Mâsam, the lunar month. लग्नत्रिकोणोत्तमवीर्ययुक्तं Lagnatrikoṇottamavîryayuktaṃ, the Ascendant itself; the fifth or the ninth house from the Ascendant at the time of query whichever is most powerful (being the sign occupied by the Moon at the time of birth). संप्रोच्यते Samprochyante, say. अंगालभनादिभिः Aṃgâlabhanâdibhiḥ, indicated by the part of the body touched perchance by a person at the time of query; or by other signs (*e.g.*, the sight of any creature or the hearing of sounds). वा Vâ, or.

5. Some astrologers are of opinion that the lunar month (ending in bright fortnight) of birth shall be determined from the Navâṃśa (1) occupied by the Moon at the time of query. Again the sign occupied by the Moon at the time of birth will be the Significator (the Praśna Lagna) or the 5th house or the 9th house from it whichever is most powerful. Or the sign occupied by the Moon at the time of birth will be the sign represented by that part of the body of the Zodiacal Man that may happen to be touched by a person at the time of query; or the sign may be inferred by other indications, *e.g.*, the sight of any creatures or their sounds heard will give the sign occupied by the Moon during birth (2).

Notes.--(1) The lunar month will be designated by the name of the Nakṣatra when the full Moon takes place. Thus if Kṛittikâ or Rohiṇî be the Nakṣatra in the Navâṃśa occupied by the Moon at the time of query, the month of birth will be Kârtika; if Mṛigaśirâ or Ârdrâ, it will be Mârgaśirṣa or Agrahâyaṇa; if Punarvasu or Puṣyâ, it will be Pauṣ; if Aśleṣâ or Maghâ, it will be Mâgha; if it be Pûrva Phalgunî, Uttara Phalgunî or Hastâ, it will be Phâlgun; if it be Chitrâ or Svâtî, the month will be Chaitra; if it be Viśâkhâ, Anurâdhâ, the month will be Vaisâkha; if it be Jyeṣṭhâ, the month will be Jaiṣṭha; if it be Purvâṣâḍhâ, or Uttarâṣâḍhâ, the month will be Aṣâḍha; if it be Śravaṇâ, Dhaniṣṭhâ, the month will be Śrâvaṇa; if it be Pûrva, Uttara Bhâdrapada, the month will be Bhâdra; if Revatî or Aśvinî, the month will be Âśvin.

Another way of thinking it is this :—

Suppose each Navâṃśa to be divided into 9 equal parts; then if at the time of query the place occupied by the Moon be—

	Beyond the	And within the	During birth time, the lunar month will be.
(1)	8th part of the Navâṃśa of Meṣa.	7th part of the Navâṃśa of Vṛiṣa.	Kârtika.
(2)	7th part of the Vṛiṣa Navâṃśa.	6th part of the Mithuna.	Mârgaśira
(3)	6th part of the Mithuna.	5th part of the Karka.	Pâuṣa.
(4)	5th of Karka.	4th of Siṃha.	Mâgha.
(5)	4th of Siṃha.	7th of Kanyâ.	Phâlguna
(6)	7th of Kanyâ.	6th of Tulâ.	Chaitra.
(7)	6th of Tulâ.	5th of Vṛischika.	Vaiśâkha.
(8)	5th of Vṛischika.	4th of Dhanu.	Jyaiṣṭha
(9)	4th of Dhanu.	3rd of Makara.	Âṣâḍha.
(10)	3rd of Makara.	2nd of Kumbha.	Śrâvaṇa.
(11)	2nd of Dhanu.	5th of Mina.	Bhâdra.
(12)	5th of Mina.	8th of Meṣa.	Âśvin.

(2) The sign corresponding to any creature or its sound is known from Chapter I; and the Moon will occupy such sign at the time of birth.

इंद्रवज्रा—यावान् गतः शीतकरो विलग्नाच्चंद्राद्वदेत्तावति जन्मराशिः। मीनोदये मीनयुगं प्रदिष्टं भक्ष्याहृताकाररुतैश्च चिंत्यम् ॥ ६ ॥

यावान् Yâvân, by as many signs distant. गतः Gataḥ, is situated. शीतकरः Sitakaraḥ, the Moon. विलग्नात् Vilagnât, from the Ascendant at the time of query. चंद्रात् Chandrât, from the Moon. वदेत् Vadet, say. तावति Tâvati, by so many signs distant. जन्मराशिः Janmarâśiḥ, the sign where the Moon exists during birth.

मीनोदये Mînodaye, on the rising of the sign Mîna in the horizon. मीनयुगं Mînayugam, the sign Pisces or Mîna, where the Moon exists during birth. प्रदिष्टं Pradiṣṭam, is said. भक्ष्याहृताकाररुतैः Bhakṣyâhṛitâkârarutaiḥ, by any eatables perchance brought there by any figures that may appear there, or by any sounds that may be heard at the time of query. च Cha, and. चिन्त्यम् Chintyam, should be thought of.

6. The sign where the Moon existed during birth time will be as many signs distant from the sign occupied by the Moon at the time of query as the Moon is seen distant from the Ascendant at the time of query. But if the Ascendant be Mîna, then Mîna will be the Janma Râśi (the sign occupied by the Moon during birth). Or the Janma Râśi might be found out by any articles of food perchance brought there by any forms that may come in or by any sound that may be heard at the time of query (1).

Notes.—From any eatables brought there, one can make out what creature takes that food and hence the sign.

Suppose Dhanu is the rising sign and Kumbha the sign occupied by the Moon at the time of query. From Dhanu to Kumbha are 2 signs; the 2nd sign from Kumbha is Mîna. Then Mîna will be the sign occupied by the Moon during the birth time.

इंद्रवज्रा—होरानवांशप्रतिमं विलग्नं लग्नाद्रविर्यावति च दृकाणे। तस्माद्वदेत्तावति वा विलग्नं प्रष्टुः प्रसूताविति शास्त्रमाह ॥ ७ ॥

होरानवांशप्रतिमं Horânavâṃśapratimam, distant from the sign of the ruler of the rising Navâṃśa at the time of query by as many signs as the number of the rising Navâṃśas; some take it as the sign of the ruler of the rising Navâṃśa at the time of query. विलग्नं Vilagnam, the Ascendant at birth. लग्नात् Lagnât, from the rising Decanate in the Ascendant at the time of query. रविः Raviḥ, the Sun; the Decanate occupied by the Sun. यावति Yâvati, by as many (Decanates distant). च Cha, and. दृकाणे Dṛikâṇe, Decanates. तस्मात् Tasmât, from that Ascendant at the time of query. वदेत् Vadet, say. तावति Tâvati, by the same number of signs distant. वा Vâ, or. विलग्नं Vilagnam, the Ascendant during birth. प्रष्टुः Praṣṭuḥ, of the querent. प्रसूतौ Prasûtau, during birth. इति Iti, thus. शास्त्रं Śâstram, the Śâstras. आह Âha, say.

7. The Ascendant at the time of birth will be shifted from the sign of the ruler of the rising Navâṃśa at the time of query by as many signs as the number of the rising Navâṃśas.

(1) or the birth Ascendant will be as many signs removed from the Significator (the Praśna Lagna) as the Decanate occupied by the Sun is removed from the rising Decanate at the time of query (2).

Notes (1).—Some take it:—The birth Ascendant will be the sign of the ruler of the rising Navâṃśa at the time of query. *E.g.*, supposing the rising Navâṃśa at the time of query to be that of Dhanu, the birth Ascendant will be Dhanu itself.

An example of our rendering:—Suppose the Significator is Siṃha 10°. This is the 4th Navâṃśa. The sign of its ruler is Karka. The fourth sign from Karka is Tulâ. This Tulâ is the Birth Ascendant.

(2) Suppose the rising Decanate at the time of query to be the 1st Decanate of the sign Meṣa and the Decanate occupied by the Sun at the same time to be the 3rd Decanate of Kanyâ. The number of Decanates from the one to the other is 18. Therefore the rising sign at the time of birth is the 18th sign from Meṣa; subtracting 12 from 18, it is the sixth sign from Meṣa, *i.e.*, the sign Kanyâ.

इंद्रवज्रा—जन्मादिशेल्लग्नगे वीर्यगे वा छायांगुलघ्नेर्कहते-ऽवशिष्टम् ॥ आसीनसुप्तोत्थिततिष्ठताभं जायासुखाज्ञोदयगं प्रदिष्टम् ॥ ८ ॥

जन्म Janma, birth. आदिशेत् Âdiśet, say. लग्नगे Lagnage, the longitude of the planet occupying the Significator. वीर्यगे Vîryage, the longitude of the most powerful of the planets occupying the Significator. वा Vâ, or. छायांगुलघ्ने: Chhâyâṃgulaghne, multiplied by the length in inches of the shadow of the gnomon (a twelve inch straight rod placed vertically on a horizontal surface under the Sun). अर्कहते Arkahate, divided by twelve. अवशिष्टम् Avaśiṣṭam, the remainder (from Aries or Meṣa will give the Ascendant during birth). आसीनसुप्तोत्थिततिष्ठताभं Âsînasuptotthitatiṣṭhatâbhaṃ, the Ascendant at the time of birth of the person seated, lying, rising or standing (being respectively). जायासुखाज्ञोदयगं Jâyâsukhâjñodayagam, the seventh, fourth, tenth, or the first sign from the Ascendant at the time of query. प्रदिष्टम् Pradiṣṭam, is said (to be).

8. The Birth Ascendant might be otherwise calculated thus:—Multiply the Sphuṭa (longitude) of the planet or of the most powerful planet that is found in the Significator by the length of the shadow of the gnomon (a straight rod 12″ long placed vertically on a level surface) in inches; divide

the product by twelve. The remainder will give the Birth Ascendant.

According to some, the 7th house from the Significator will be the Birth Ascendant, if the querent be seated at the time of query; it will be the 4th house, if the querent be lying at the time; it will be the 10th house if the querent be rising at the time; it will be the Significator itself if the querent be standing from his seat.

Note:—Suppose the longitude of the planet or (where there are several planets) of the most powerful planet occupying the rising sign to be one sign 0 degrees and 0 minutes; and suppose the length of the shadow to be 6 inches; the product of the two numbers is 6 signs. This divided by 12 gives as remainder 0 sign and 30 degrees. The Birth Ascendant is therefore the 1st sign from Meṣa, which is Meṣa itself.

शा०वि०—गोसिंहौ जितुमाष्टमौ क्रियतुले कन्यामृगौ च
क्रमात् संवर्ग्यो दशकाष्टसप्तविषयैः शेषाः स्वसंख्यागुणाः ॥
जीवारास्फुजिदैंदवाः प्रथमवच्छेषा ग्रहाः सौम्यवद्राशीनां नियतो
विधिर्ग्रहयुतैः कार्या च तद्वर्गणा ॥ ६ ॥

गोसिंहौ Gosiṃhau, the signs Vṛiṣa and Siṃha. जितुमाष्टमौ JitumAṣṭamau, the signs Mithuna and Vṛiśchika. क्रियतुले Kriyatule, the signs Meṣa and Tulâ. कन्यामृगौ Kanyâmṛigau, the signs Kanyâ and Makara. च Cha, and. क्रमात् Kramât, successively. संवर्ग्यः Sambargyaḥ, are to be multiplied by. दशकाष्टसप्तविषयैः Daśakâṣṭasaptaviṣayaiḥ, by ten, eight, seven and five respectively. शेषाः Seṣâḥ, the other signs not mentioned, *i.e.*, Karka, Dhanu, Kumbha and Mîna. स्वसंख्यागुणाः Svasaṃkhyâguṇâḥ, multiplied by their own numbers, *i.e.*, by 4, 9, 11, 12 respectively. जीवारास्फुजिदैंदवाः: Jîvârâsphujidaiṃdavâḥ, the multipliers of Jupiter, Mars, Venus and Mercury being. प्रथमवत् Prathamavaṭ, like the first, *i.e.*, ten, eight, seven and five. शेषाः Śeṣâḥ, the multipliers of the other planets not mentioned, *i.e.*, of the Sun, Moon, Saturn. ग्रहाः Grahâḥ, planets. सौम्यवत् Saumyavat, like that of Mercury, *i.e.*, their multiplier being five. राशीनां Râśinâm, of the rising signs at the time of query. नियतः Niyatah, always; must be always done. विधिः Vidhiḥ, the rule. ग्रहयुतैः Grahayutaiḥ, together with the planets occcupying the Significator; the Ascendant and the planets duly multiplied with their factors and the results all added. कार्या Kâryâ, to be performed. च Cha, and. तद्वर्गणा Tadvargaṇâ, their multiplication.

9. Multiply the longitude of the Significator (the Lagna Sphuṭa) by 10, if the Significator be Vṛiṣa or Siṃha;

by 8, if it be Mithuna or Vṛiśchika; by 7, if it be Meṣâ or Tulâ; by 5, if it be Kanyâ or Makara; or by the number of the remaining signs from Meṣa, if it be any of the remaining signs(1).

Again, multiply the longitude of the Significator by 10, if the planet occupying the rising sign be Jupiter; by 8, if it be Mars; by 7, if it be Venus; or by 5 if it be any of the remaining planets; if several planets occupy the rising sign, then multiply the longitude of the Significator by the factor for each of such planets. (Add up the several products and find the sum) (2).

Notes:—The following is the table of factors of the planets and signs.

Planets.	Sun.	Moon.	Mars.	Mercury.	Jupiter.	Venus.	Saturn.
Multipliers	5	5	8	5	10	7	5

Signs	1	2	3	4	5	6	7	8	9	10	11	12
Multipliers.	7	10	8	4	10	5	7	8	9	5	11	12

Now in this and the subsequent verses another method is being described, quite distinct, to find out the Janma-Nakṣatra (*i.e.*, asterism occupied by the Moon during birth) of the querent, his wife, brother son and enemy. The figures given in this stanza are Râśi Guṇakâras and Graha Guṇakâras—constant factors for each sign and each planet.

(1) *E.g.*, if Karka be the sign, it being the 4th sign from Meṣa, the factor for Karka is 4. The factor for Dhanu is 9; that for Kumbha is 11 and that for Mîna is 12.

(2) Suppose the Lagna Sphuṭa to be 10s. 10° 10′ and suppose Mars and Mercury to occupy the rising sign. Now from the Lagna Sphuṭa it is evident that the rising sign is Kumbha. The factor for Kumbha is 11; multiplying 10s. 10° 10′ by 11 we get 113s. 21° 50′. Dividing this by 12 we get as remainder 5s. 21° 50′ (A). Again the factor for Mars is 8 and that for Mercury is 5. Multiplying 10s. 10° 10′ by 8 we get 82s. 21° 20′. Dividing by 12 we get as remainder 10s. 21° 20′. Again multiplying 10s. 10° 10′ by 5 we get 51s. 20° 50′. Dividing by 12 we get 3s. 20° 50′. Adding this to 10s. 21° 20′, we get 14s. 12° 10′ (B). Adding together (A) and (B) we get 20s. 4° 0′.

व०ति०—सप्ताहतं त्रिघनभाजितशेषमृत्तं दत्त्वाथवा नव विशोध्य न वाथवास्मात् ॥ एवं कलत्रसहजात्मजशत्रुभेभ्यः प्रष्टुर्वदेदुदयराशिवशेन तेषाम् ॥ १० ॥

सप्ताहतं Saptâhatam, (the sum total in the preceding verse being) multiplied by seven. त्रिघनभाजितशेषम् Trighanabhâjitaśeṣam, the remainder after dividing by twenty-seven. ऋक्षं Rikṣam, the Nakṣatra or asterism of the native. दत्त्वा Dattvâ, adding. अथवा Athavâ, or. नव Nava, nine. विशोध्य Viśodhya, subtracting. न Na, not (adding or subtracting). वा Vâ, or. अथवा Athavâ, or. अस्मात् Asmât, from this. एवं Evam, thus; by the process described above. कलत्रसहजात्मजशत्रुभेभ्यः Kalatrasahajâtmajaśatrubhebhyaḥ, from the signs signifying wife, brothers, sons, and enemies. प्रष्टुः Praṣṭuḥ, of the querent. वदेत् Vadet, say. उदयराशिवशेन Udayarâśivaśena, from the rising sign, at the time of query. तेषाम् Teṣâm, (the Nakṣatra during birth) of the wife, brothers, sons, or enemies of the querent.

10. Multiply this sum (*i.e.*, the sum of A and B in the preceding verse) by 7 and if the Significator be a moveable sign, add 9 to the product; if a common sign, subtract 9 from the product; and if a fixed sign, leave the product as it is. Divide this sum or the difference or the product, as the case may be, by 27. The remainder will indicate the Janma-Nakṣatra or the birth asterism (occupied by the Moon from Aśvinî) of the querent during birth time. Similarly the wife, brother, son and enemy of the querent may have their Janma-Nakṣtara determined by repeating the above process to the Sphuṭa of the 7th, 3rd, 5th and 6th houses respectively from the Significator.

Notes.—The Commentator Bhaṭṭa Utpala says if the rising Decanate be the first, 9 is to be added; if it be the second, 9 is neither to be added nor to be subtracted; and if it be the third, 9 is to be subtracted from the product. Some authors say that this addition and subtraction of 9 are to be performed after multiplying the sum by 7 and dividing by 27; but these are not in vogue.

Add 6 signs to the longitude of the Significator; you get the longitude of the 7th house denoting the house of the querent's wife; and so on. Multiply the several longitudes thus obtained by the sign factors of those houses and by the factors of the planets, occupying such houses; add the products, multiply the sum by 7, add or subtract 9 if necessary, divide the sum or remainder by 27, the remainder will give the Birth-Nakṣatra (occupied by the Moon) of the person in question.

Add 2 signs to the longitude of the Significator, you get the longitude of the 3rd house denoting the house of the querent's brother.

Add 4 signs to the longitude of the Significator, you get the longitude of the 5th house denoting the house of the querent's son.

Add 5 signs to the longitude of the Significator, you get the longitude of the 6th house denoting the house of the querent's enemy.

The Janma-Nakṣatra is reckoned from the star Aśvinî.

व०ति०—वर्षर्तुमासतिथयो द्युनिशं ह्युडूनि वेलोदयर्क्षनवभागविकल्पनाः स्युः ॥ भूयो दशादिगुणिताः स्वविकल्पभक्ता वर्षादयो नवकदानविशोधनाभ्याम् ॥ ११ ॥

वर्षर्तुमासतिथयः: Varṣartumâsatithayaḥ, the year, season, month, lunar day. द्युनिशं Dyuniśam, day or night. हि Hi, certainly. उडूनि Uḍûni, the Nakṣatras or asterisms. वेलोदयर्क्षनवभागविकल्पनाः: Velodayerkṣanavabhâgavikalpanâḥ, the ghaṭika, the rising sign, the rising Navâṃśa at the time of birth. स्युः: Syuḥ, are; become. भूयः: Bhûyaḥ, again. दशादिगुणिताः: Daśâdiguṇitâḥ, multiplied by ten, eight, seven, five respectively. स्वविकल्पभक्ताः: Svavikalpabhaktâḥ, divided by their own appropriate numbers. वर्षादयः: Varṣâdayaḥ, year, etc. नवकदानविशोधनाभ्याम् Navakadânaviśodhanâbhyâm, adding or subtracting 9, if necessary, as stated above.

11. Multiply the same sum (1) by 10, 8, 7, 5; add or subtract 9, if necessary, as stated above; divide the result by their proper divisors (2); you will obtain the year, season, month, lunar day, day or night, Nakṣatra, the ghaṭikâ, the rising sign, and the rising Navâṃśa at the time of birth.

Notes.—Here is given another method to determine the year, month, day, &c., during the birth time of a person:—

(1) The sum obtained at the end of the 9th verse; *i.e.*, A+B.

(2) These and the process of division will be found explained in the next three stanzas. The appropriate number for year is 120, the highest longevity; for seasons it is 6; for month it is 2; for the fortnight it is 2; for the lunar day it is 15, for day or night it is 2; for the Nakṣatra, it is 27; for the day or night it is the number of ghaṭikâs in the day or night; for the sign, it is 12; for the horâ it is 2; for the Navâṃśa, it is 9.

अनुष्टुभ्—विज्ञेया दशकेष्वब्दा ऋतुमासास्तथैव च ॥
अष्टकेष्वपि मासार्द्धास्तिथयश्च तथा स्मृताः ॥ १२ ॥

विज्ञेयाः Vijñeyâḥ, are considered; are known. दशकेषु Daśakeṣu, in the number obtained after being multiplied by 10. अब्दाः Abdâḥ, age, *i.e.*, the number of years. Divide the product of ten by 120, the maximum life of any individual; the remainder will give the required number of years. ऋतुमासाः Ritumâsâḥ, the season and the month; divide the above result by six; the remainder will give the season; divide the same result obtained by 2, the remainder 1 will give the first month and 0 will give the second month. तथा Tathâ, similarly. एव च Eva cha, and thus. अष्टकेषु Aṣṭakeṣu, in the product of eight. अपि Api, also. मासार्धाः Masârdhâḥ, the half month. तिथयः Tithayaḥ, the lunar day. च Cha, and. तथा Tathâ, similarly. स्मृताः Smritâḥ, are remembered. Divide by 2 the number got after being multiplied by 8; the remainder 1 indicates the bright and 0 indicates the dark fortnight; and dividing by 15, the remainder will indicate the lunar day.

12. From the first of the four products of the sum by 10 (1) mentioned in the last stanza shall be determined the age (*i.e.*, number of years), season and month of birth; and from the second of the four products of the sum by 8 (2) mentioned in the last stanza shall be determined the fortnight (bright or dark) and the lunar day.

Notes.—(1) This product is the first of the four products referred to in the 11th verse (the preceding verse) with 9 added or subtracted as the case may be. Divide the quantity by 120, the remainder will give the age of the person. Divide the same quantity by 6, the remainder will give the season of birth from Śiśira (the winter season). Divide the same quantity by 2, the remainder will give the first or the second month of the season.

(2) This product is the second of the four products in the preceding verse with 9 added or subtracted, if necessary. Divide this quantity by two, the remainder will give the fortnight of birth. Divide the same quantity by 15, the remainder will give the lunar day.

अनुष्टुभ्–दिवारात्रिप्रसूतिं च नक्षत्रानयनं तथा ॥
सप्तकष्वपि वर्गेषु नित्यमेवोपलक्षयेत् ॥ १३ ॥

दिवारात्रिप्रसूतिं Divârâtriprasûtim, the day or the night birth. Dividing the product (obtained after being multiplied by seven) by 2, the remainder 1 will give the day birth, and 0 will give the night time as the birth time. नक्षत्रानयनं Nakṣatrâ-nayanam, the ascertaining of the asterism at birth time; dividing the product (obtained after being multiplied by seven) by 27, the remainder indicates the asterism from Aśvinî. तथा Tatha, similarly. सप्तकेषु Saptakeṣu, from the product of the sum by seven. अपि Api, also. वर्गेषु Vargeṣu, from the product. नित्यम् Nityam, always. एव Eva, certainly. उपलक्षयेत् Upalakṣayet, ascertain.

13. From the 3rd of the four products of the sum by 7, mentioned in the 11th stanza, you determine the day or the night birth as well the Janma-Nakṣatra (birth asterism.)

Note.—This product is the 3rd of the four products of the 11th verse, with 9 added or subtracted, if necessary. Divide the quantity by 2; the birth will have occurred by day or by night according as the remain der is one, or zero. Divide the same quantity by 27; the remainder will give the Nakṣatra from Aśvinî.

अनुष्टुभ्—वेलामथ विलग्नं च होरामंशकमेव च ॥
पंचकेषु विजानीयान्नष्टजातकसिद्धये ॥ १४ ॥

वेलाम् Velâm, the exact time in ghaṭikâs. Divide the product of five by the day measure (if the birth has taken place during the day) or by the night measure (if the birth has taken place during the night); the remainder will give the exact time in ghaṭikâs. And when the exact time of birth is found, the Ascendant, the planetary positions, the Navâṃśas would all be found out by the prescribed rules. विलग्नं Vilagnam, the Ascendant at birth. च Cha, and. होराम् Horâm, the half sign. अंशकम् Aṃśakam, the Navâṃśas. एव Eva, thus. च Cha, and. पंचकेषु Pañchakeṣu, from the product by five. विजानीयात् Vijânîyât, know. नष्टजातकसिद्धये Naṣṭajâtakasiddhaye, for reconstructing the horoscope that has been lost,

14. From the last of the four products of the sum by 5 as mentioned in the 11th verse, determine the ghaṭikâ, the Ascendant, the Horâ, and the rising Navâṃśa at the time of birth.

Note.—This product is the last of the four products in the 11th verse with 9 added or subtracted, if necessary. Divide the quantity by the number of ghaṭikâs, as obtained from an almanac in the day or night of birth as the case may be; the remainder will give the ghaṭikâ from sunrise or sunset. Divide the same quantity by 12; the remainder will give the rising sign from Meṣa. Divide the same quantity by two; the horâ of birth will be the 1st or 2nd as the remainder is 1 or 0. Divide the quantity by 9; the remainder will give the rising Navâṃśa for the first Navâṃśa of the rising sign.

आर्या—संस्कारनाममात्रा द्विगुणा छायांगुलैः समायुक्ताः ॥
शेषं त्रिनवकभक्तान्नच्तलं तद्धनिष्ठादि ॥ १५ ॥

संस्कारनाममात्रा Saṃskâranâmamâtrâ, the number of Mâtrâs in a person's name (given at the Nâmakaraṇa ceremony). द्विगुणा Dviguṇâ, doubled. छायांगुलैः Chhâyâmgulaiḥ, to the length of the shadow of the gnomon समायुक्ताः Samâyuktâḥ, added to. शेषं Seṣam, the remainder. त्रिनवकभक्तात् Trinavakabhaktât, after being divided by 27. नक्षत्रं Nakṣatram, the asterism at the time of birth. तत् Tat, that. धनिष्ठादि Dhaniṣṭhâdi, after the Dhaniṣṭhâ asterism.

15. The number of Mâtrâs (the upper part of the Nâgarî characters), in a person's name (given at the Nâmakaraṇa ceremony) being doubled and the length in inches of the shadow of the 12th gnomon at the time of query being added to the product, divide the sum by 27; the remainder will give the birth Nakṣatra from Dhaniṣṭhâ.

Note.—A short vowel sound is counted as one Mâtrâ and large vowel sound is counted as two and a consonant is counted as half a Mâtrâ.

आर्या—द्वित्रिचतुर्दशदशतिथिसप्तत्रिगुणा नवाष्ट चेंद्राद्याः।
पंचदशघ्नास्तद्दिङ्मुखान्विता भधनिष्ठादि ॥ १६ ॥

द्वित्रिचतुर्दशदशतिथिसप्तत्रिगुणाः Dvitrichaturdasadasatithisaptatriguṇâḥ, 2, 3, 14, 10, 15, 21, नवाष्ट: Navâṣṭaḥ, 9, 8. च Cha, so. इंद्राद्याः Indrâdyâḥ, the quarters East, South-east, South, South-west, West, North-West, North, North-east, respectively. पंचदशघ्नाः Pañchadasaghnâḥ, multiplied by 15. तद्दिङ्मुखान्विताः Taddiṅmukhânvitâḥ, being added to the number of persons facing the same quarter. भधनिष्ठादि Bhadhaniṣṭhâdi, the Janma-Nakṣatra of the querent from Dhaniṣṭhâ.

16. Multiply by 15 the number corresponding to the quarter of the sky, the querent turns his face at that time; add to the product the number of persons facing the same quarter then and there; divide the sum by 27. The remainder will give the Janma-Nakṣatra of the person from Dhaniṣṭhâ.

Notes.—Here is another method for determining the Birth-Nakṣatra:

आर्या—इति नष्टजातकमिदं बहुप्रकारं मया विनिर्दिष्टम् ।
ग्राह्यमतः सच्छिष्यैः परीक्ष्य यत्नाद्यथा भवति ॥ १७ ॥

इति श्रीवराहमिहिराचार्यप्रणीते बृहज्जातके नष्टजातकाध्यायः षड्विंशः ॥ २६ ॥

इति Iti, thus. नष्टजातकं Naṣṭajâtakam, about knowing again the lost horoscope. इदं Idam, this. बहुप्रकारं Bahuprakâram, in various ways. मया Mayâ, by me. विनिर्दिष्टं Vinirdiṣṭam, has been said. ग्राह्यं Grâhyam, to be taken. अतः Ataḥ, from this.

सच्छिष्यैः Sachhiṣyaiḥ, by the intelligent disciples. परीक्ष्य Parîkṣya, after carefully examining. यत्नात् Yatnât, carefully. यथा Yathâ, as. भवति Bhavati, comes out proper.

17. Thus have been described by me the different (important) methods for the reconstruction of a lost horoscope. Good and intelligent pupils should carefully examine them and then apply the method that is best for him.

Thus ends the 26th Chapter on Lost Horoscopes by Śrî Varâha Mihirâchârya of Avantika.

CHAPTER XXVII.

ON THE DECANATES OF THE ZODIAC SYMBOLISED.

वैतालीय–कट्यां सितवस्त्रवेष्टितः कृष्णः शक्त इवाभिरक्षितुम् । रौद्रः परशुं समुद्यतं धत्ते रक्तविलोचनः पुमान् ॥ १ ॥

कट्यां Katyâm, round his loins. सितवस्त्रवेष्टितः Sitavastraveṣṭitaḥ, with a white cloth. कृष्णः Kriṣṇaḥ, of a black colour. शक्तः Śaktaḥ, capable. इव Iva, as if. अभिरक्षितुम् Abhirakṣitum, to protect one from one's danger. रौद्रः Raudraḥ, of fearful look. परशुं Paraśum, an axe. समुद्यतं Samudyatam, uplifted. धत्ते Dhatte, holds. रक्तविलोचनः Raktavilochanaḥ, of red eyes. पुमान् Pumân, a man.

1. The first Decanate of the sign Aries is a man of a black colour with a white waist-band, able to protect any (seeking his refuge), of fearful look, with axe uplifted in his hand and of red eyes.

Note.—This Decanate is human, armed, and ruled by Mars.

इंद्रवजा–रक्तांवरा भूषणभक्ष्यचिंता कुंभाकृतिर्वाजिमुखी तृषार्त्ता । एकेन पादेन च मेषमध्ये द्रेष्काणरूपं यवनोपदिष्टम् ॥ २ ॥

रक्तांबरा Raktâmbarâ, wearing a red coloured cloth. भूषणभक्ष्यचिंता Bhûṣaṇabhakṣyachintâ, always thinking of ornaments and fooding. कुंभाकृतिः Kumbhâkritiḥ, looking like a water jar; some render the meaning of a pot-like belly. वाजिमुखी Vâjimukhî, of the face of a horse. तृषार्त्ता Triṣârtâ, thirsty. एकेन Ekena, having one. पादेन Pâdena, leg. च Cha, and. मेषमध्ये Meṣamadhye, the secod Decanate of Aries. द्रेष्काणरूपं Dreṣkâṇarupaṃ, the form of the Decanate. यवनोपदिष्टम् Yavanopadiṣṭam, as advised by Yavanâchârya.

2. The second Decanate of the sign Aries is a woman wearing a red coloured cloth, intent on fooding and ornaments, of a water-jar appearance, having the face of a horse, thirsty and one-legged. Thus says Yavanâchârya.

Note:—This Decanate is represented as a quadrupedand of a woman shape; the face resembles that of a bird also. The Sun is its ruler.

इंद्रवज्रा—क्रूरः कलाज्ञः कपिलः क्रियार्थी भग्नव्रतोऽ भ्युद्यतदंडहस्तः। रक्तानि वस्त्राणि बिभर्ति चंडो मेषे तृतीयः कथितस्त्रिभागः ॥ ३ ॥

क्रूरः Krûraḥ, wicked ; hot tempered. कलाज्ञः Kalâjñaḥ, versed in arts. कपिलः Kapilaḥ, having a brown colour ; of a tawny hue. क्रियार्थी Kriyârthî, wanting to do work. भग्नव्रतः Bhagnavrataḥ, of unsuccessful resolves. अभ्युद्यतदंडहस्तः Abhyudyata-daṇḍahastaḥ, holding up a staff in his hand. रक्तानि Raktâni, red coloured. वस्त्राणि Vastrâṇi, clothes. बिभर्ति Bibbharti, wears. चंडः Chaṇḍaḥ, furious ; violent. मेषे Meṣe, in Aries. तृतीयः Tṛitîyaḥ, the third Decanate. कथितः Kathitaḥ, is said. त्रिभागः Tribhâgaḥ, all the three Decanates of the sign Aries.

3. The third Decanate of Meṣa, is a man of a wicked nature, skilled in fine arts, of a tawny hue, always wanting to do some work or other, his resolves and attempts broken in the end, holding up a staff in his hand, wearing red-coloured clothes and furious. Thus all the three Decanates of Meṣa have been described.

Note:—This Decanate is human, armed, and ruled by Jupiter.

दोधक—कुंचितलूनकचा घटदेहा दग्धपटा तृषिताशनचित्ता। आभरणान्यभिवांछति नारी रूपमिदं वृषभे प्रथमस्य ॥ ४ ॥

कुंचितलूनकचा Kuñchitalûnakachâ, with curly hairs, cut and clipped. घटदेहा Ghaṭadehâ, of water jar appearance. दग्धपटा Dagdhapaṭâ, clothings partially burnt. तृषिताशनचित्ता Tṛiṣitâśanachittâ, thirsty and intent on food. आभरणानि Âbharaṇâni, ornaments. अभिवांछति Abhivâñchhati, wishes. नारी Nârî, woman. रूपम् Rûpam, form. इदं Idam, this. वृषभे Vṛiṣabhe, in the sign Vṛiṣa. प्रथमस्य Prathamasya, of the first Decanate.

4. The first Decanate of the sign Vṛiṣa is a woman of curly, cut and clipped hairs, of a water-jar apperance, dressed in clothings partially burnt, thirsty and liking food and ornaments.

Notes:—This Drekkâṇa is woman carrying fire, and is ruled by Venus.

स्वागता—क्षेत्रधान्यगृहधेनुकलाज्ञो लांगले सशकटे कुशलश्च । स्कंधमुद्वहति गोपतितुल्यं क्षुत्परोऽजवदनो मलवासा ॥ ५ ॥

क्षेत्रधान्यगृहधेनुकलाज्ञः Kṣetradhânyagṛihadhenukalâjñaḥ, knowing agriculture, how to produce and keep grains, how to do housework, how to keep cows, and skilled in music, dancing, painting and other fine arts. लांगले Lâṅgale, ploughing. सशकटे Saśakaṭe, how to drive carriages. कुशलः Kuśalaḥ, clever. च Cha, and. स्कंधम् Skandham, neck. उद्वहति Udvahati, holds. गोपतितुल्यं Gopatitulyam, like that of a bull. क्षुत्परः Kṣutparaḥ, hungry. अजवदनः Ajavadanaḥ, having the face of a ram. मलवासा Malavâsâ, dressed dirtily; shabbily dressed.

5. The 2nd Drekkâṇa of the sign Vṛiṣa is a man. He is an agriculturist, knows well how to produce and keep grains, skilled in domestic affairs, cow-keeping, in music, dancing, painting, and other fine arts. He knows ploughing, how to keep and drive carriages. His neck is raised like that of a bull. He is hungry; his face is like that of ram; and his clothes are dirty.

Note:—This Drekkâṇa is partly human and partly quadruped. Ruler—Mercury.

दोधक—द्विपसमकायः पाण्डुरदंष्ट्रः शरभसमांघ्रिः पिङ्गलमूर्तिः । अविमृगलोभव्याकुलचित्तो वृषभवनस्य प्रान्तगतोऽयम् ॥ ६ ॥

द्विपसमकायः Dvipasamakâyaḥ, of elephant-like body. पांडुरदंष्ट्रः Pâṇḍuradamṣṭraḥ, of yellowish white teeth. शरभसमांघ्रिः Śarabhasamâṃghriḥ, of camel feet. पिङ्गलमूर्तिः Piṅgalamûrtiḥ, of a tawny hue. अविमृगलोभव्याकुलचित्तः Avimṛigalobhavyâkulachittaḥ, anxious to have the famous animals of the forest. वृषभवनस्य Vṛiṣabhavanasya, of the sign Vṛiṣa. प्रान्तगतः Prântagataḥ, the third Drekkâṇa. अयम् Ayam, this.

6. The 3rd Decanate of the sign Vṛiṣa is a man, having his body like that of an elephant; his teeth are yellowish white; his feet resemble those of a camel, his colour is brown; and he is always desirous to get the big animals of the forest.

Note:—This Drekkâṇa is both human and quadruped. It is ruled by Saturn.

व० ति०—सूच्याश्रयं समभिवांछति कर्म नारी रूपा-न्विताभरणकार्यकृतादरा च । हीनप्रजोच्छ्रितभुजर्तुमती त्रिभा-गमाद्यं तृतीयभवनस्य वदन्ति तज्ज्ञाः ॥ ७ ॥

सूच्याश्रयं Sûchyâśrayam, sewing; needlework. समभिवांछति Samabhivâñchhati, likes very much. कर्म Karma, work. नारी Nârî, a woman. रूपान्विता Rûpânvitâ, graceful; good looking. आभरणकार्यकृतादरा Âbharaṇakâryakritâdarâ, fond of decorating oneself with ornaments. च Cha, and. हीनप्रजा Hînaprajâ, without any children. उच्छ्रितभुजा Uchhritabhujâ, with raised hands. ऋतुमती Ritumatî, having attained puberty, or lustful. त्रिभागं Tribhâgam, the Decanate. आद्यं Âdyam, the first. तृतीयभवनस्य Tritîyabhavanasya, of the 3rd sign, Mithuna. वदन्ति Vadanti, say. तज्ज्ञाः Tajgñâḥ, the Pundits.

7. The 1st Decanate of the sign Mithuna is a woman liking needlework; she is of good look and takes care to decorate her body with ornaments. She is destitute of any issue, with raised hands and has attained puberty and become lustful; thus say the Pundits.

Note:—This Drekkâṇa is of the shape of a woman. This is ruled by Mercury.

उपजातिका—उद्यानसंस्थः कवची धनुष्माञ्छूरोऽस्त्रधारी गरुडाननश्च । क्रीडात्मजालंकरणार्थचिंतां करोति मध्ये मिथु-नस्य राशेः ॥ ८ ॥

उद्यानसंस्थः Udyânasamsthaḥ, living in gardens. कवची Kavachi, dressed in armour. धनुष्मान् Dhanuṣmân, holding a bow in his hands. शूरः Śûraḥ, a hero. अस्त्रधारी Astradhârî, holding weapons. गरुडाननः Garuḍânanaḥ, having a face like that of a Garuḍa (the sacred bird of Viṣṇu). च Cha, and. क्रीडात्मजालंकरणार्थचिंतां Krîḍâtmajâlamkaraṇârthachintâm, thinking of sports, his sons, ornaments, and wealth. करोति Karoti, does. मध्ये Madhye, the middle third. मिथुनस्य Mithunasya, of the sign Mithuna. राशेः Râśeḥ, of the sign.

8. The 2nd Decanate of the sign Mithuna is a man living in gardens, wearing a dress of armour, holding a bow in his hand, a hero, holding weapons, ready to fight. His face (is like that of Garuḍah, the sacred Vâhana of Viṣṇu). He thinks of sports, his sons, ornaments, and wealth.

Note:—This Drekkâṇa is of the shape of a man and is armed. It is also of the shape of a bird. Venus is its ruler.

स्वागता–भूषितो वरुणवद्बहुरत्नो बद्धतूणकवचः सधनुष्कः । नृत्तवादितकलासु च विद्वान्काव्यकृन्मिथुनराश्यवसाने ॥ ९ ॥

भूषितः Bhûṣitaḥ, decorated with ornaments. वरुणवत् Varuṇavat, like Varuṇa, the god of ocean. बहुरत्नः Bahuratnaḥ, possessing many gems. बद्धतूणकवचः Baddhatûṇakavachaḥ, having a dress of armour and a quiver. सधनुष्कः Sadhanuṣkaḥ, holding a bow in his hand. नृत्तवादितकलासु Nrittavâditakalâsu, in dance, music and fine arts. च Cha, and विद्वान् Vidvân, skilled in. काव्यकृत् Kâvyakrit, a writer of poems; a literary writer. मिथुनराश्यवसाने Mithunarâśyavasâne, in the third Drekkâṇa of the sign Mithuna.

9. The 3rd Decanate of the sign Mithuna is a man well dressed with ornaments. He is like Varuṇa, the ocean deity and possesses many gems. He has got a quiver and wears a mail coat. He holds a bow in his hand. He is well versed in fine arts, music, dancing, painting, literature, etc.

Note:—This Drekkâṇa is human, armed and ruled by Saturn.

स्वागता–पत्रमूलफलभृद्द्विपकायः कानने मलयगः शरभांघ्रिः । क्रोडतुल्यवदनो हयकंठः कर्कटे प्रथमरूपमुशंति ॥१०॥

पत्रमूलफलभृत् Patramûlaphalabhrit, carrying leaves, roots and fruits. द्विपकायः Dvipakâyaḥ, of elephant-like body. कानने Kânane, in forests. मलयगः Malayagaḥ, living near Sandal trees. शरभांघ्रिः Sarabhâmghriḥ, having feet as long as those of a camel. क्रोडतुल्यवदनः Kroḍatulyavadanaḥ, his face like that of a hog. हयकंठः Hayakamṭhaḥ, having a neck like that of a horse. कर्कटे Karkaṭe, in Karka प्रथमरूपं Prathamarûpam, the form of the 1st Drekkâṇa. उशंति Uśamti, say.

10. The 1st Decanate of the sign Karka carries leaves, roots, and fruits. It has an elephant-like body, lives in a forest near Sandal trees, has feet as large as those of the camel, has a hog-like face and a horse-like neck.

Note:—This Decanate is quadruped and ruled by Moon.

इंद्रवज्रा–पद्मार्चिता मूर्द्धनि भोगियुक्ता स्त्री कर्कशारण्यगता विरौति । शाखां पलाशस्य समाश्रिता च मध्ये स्थिता कर्कटकस्य राशेः ॥ ११ ॥

पद्मार्चिता Padmârchitâ, worshipped by lotus flowers. मूर्ध्नि Mûrdhani, on her head. भोगियुक्ता Bhogiyuktâ, having a snake. स्त्री Strî, a woman. कर्कशा Karkaśâ, harsh; rough due to being of young age. अरण्यगता Araṇyagatâ, in a forest. विरौति Virouti, cries. शाखां Śâkhâm, a branch. पलाशस्य Palâśasya, of the Palâśa tree. समाश्रिता Samâśritâ, holding; leaning against. च Cha, and. मध्ये Madhye, the middle Decanate. स्थिताः Sthitâḥ, is. कर्कटस्य राशेः Karkaṭasya râśeḥ, of the sign Karka.

11. The second Decanate of the sign Karka is a woman worshipped on her head with lotus flowers, with a snake, harsh, young, crying in a forest and leaning against a branch of the Palâśa tree.

Note :—This Drekkâṇa is of the shape of a woman. The ruler is Mars. It is also called the Serpent Drekkâṇa.

वैतालीय—भार्याभरणार्थमर्णवं नौस्थो गच्छति सर्पवेष्टितः । हैमैश्च युतो विभूषणैश्चिपिटास्योऽन्त्यगतश्च कर्कटे ॥१२॥

भार्याभरणार्थं Bhâryâbharaṇârtham, for his wife's ornaments. नौस्थः Nausthaḥ, getting on a boat. गच्छति Gachhati, goes. सर्पवेष्टितः Sarpaveṣṭitaḥ, surrounded by a snake. हैमैः Haimaiḥ, made of gold. च Cha, and. युतः Yutaḥ, dressed with. विभूषणैः Vibhûṣaṇaiḥ, with ornaments. चिपिटास्यः Chipiṭâsyaḥ, of a flat face. अन्त्यगतः Antyagtaḥ, the 3rd Drekkâṇa. च Cha, and. कर्कटे Karkaṭe, in the sign Karka.

12. The third Decanate of the sign Karka is a man on a boat in the sea, going to get ornaments for his wife. He is surrounded by a snake, and dressed with golden ornaments. His face is flat.

Note :—This Drekkâṇa is known as human and also it is known as a Serpent Drekkâṇa. Jupiter is its ruler.

रथोद्धता—शाल्मलेरुपरि गृध्रजंबुकौ श्वा नरश्च मलिनांबरान्वितः । रौति मातृपितृविप्रयोजितः सिंहरूपमिदमाद्यमुच्यते ॥ १३ ॥

शाल्मलेः Śâlmaleḥ, of the Śâlmalî tree. उपरि Upari, on the top of. गृध्रजंबुकौ Gridhrajambukau, one of the shape of a vulture and a jackal. श्वा नरः Śvâ Naraḥ, like a dog and a man. मलिनांबरान्वितः Malinâmbarânvitaḥ, clothed shabbily; dirtily dressed. रौति Rauti, cries. मातृपितृविप्रयोजितः Mâtṛipitṛiviprayojitaḥ, separated from his father and mother. सिंहरूपं Simharûpam, of the form of the sign Simha. इदम् Idam, this. आद्यं Âdyam, the first Drekkâṇa. उच्यते Uchyate, is said.

13. The first Decanate of the sign Simha is of the shape of a vulture and a jackal, seated on the top of a Sâlmâlî tree. It looks also partly like a dog and partly like a man, is dressed in shabby garments and separated from its father and mother and it is crying aloud.

Note:—This Drekkâṇa is human, quadruped, and biped; and it is ruled by the Sun.

वंशस्थ—हयाकृतिः पाण्डुरमाल्यशेखरो बिभर्ति कृष्णाजिनकम्बलं नरः। दुरासदः सिंह इवात्तकार्मुको नताग्रनासो मृगराजमध्यमः॥ १४ ॥

हयाकृतिः Hayâkṛitiḥ, of the shape of a horse. पाण्डुरमाल्यशेखरः Pâṇḍuramâlyaśekharaḥ, having on his head a garland of flowers yellowish white. बिभर्ति Bibharti, holds. कृष्णाजिनकम्बलं Kṛiṣṇâjinakambalam, the skin of the black antelope and blanket. नरः Naraḥ, the man. दुरासदः Durâsadaḥ, unapproachable. सिंहः Siṃhaḥ, lion. इव Iva, like. आत्तकार्मुकः Âttakârmukaḥ, holding a bow in his hand. नताग्रनासः Natâgranâsaḥ, with a bent nose. मृगराजमध्यमः Mṛigarâjamadhyamaḥ, the second Decanate of the sign Siṃha.

14. The second Decanate of the sign Siṃha is a man of the shape of a horse, his head being encircled with a garland of yellowish white flowers. He possesses the skin of a black antelope and a blanket, and is unapproachable like a lion. He holds a bow in his hand and the tip of his nose is somewhat curved.

Note:—This Drekkâṇa is human, armed, and ruled by Jupiter.

उपजातिका—ऋक्षाननो वानरतुल्यचेष्टो बिभर्ति दंडं फलमामिषं च। कूर्ची मनुष्यः कुटिलैश्च केशैर्मृगेश्वरस्यांत्यगतस्त्रिभागः॥ १५ ॥

ऋक्षाननः Rikṣânanaḥ, having the face of a bear. वानरतुल्यचेष्टः Vânaratulyacheṣṭaḥ, his actions like those of a monkey. बिभर्ति Bibharti, holds. दंडं Daṇḍaṃ, a club. फलं Phalam, fruits. आमिषं Âmiṣam, fish and meats. च Cha, and. कूर्ची Kûrchî, with a long beard. मनुष्यः Manuṣyaḥ, a man. कुटिलैः Kuṭilaiḥ, curling. च Cha, and. केशैः Keśaiḥ, with hairs. मृगेश्वरस्य Mṛigeśvarasya, of the sign Siṃha. अन्त्यगतः Antyagataḥ, the third. त्रिभागः Tribhâgaḥ, the Decanate.

15. The third Decanate of the sign Siṃha is a man with the face of a bear, his movements resembling those of

a monkey. He holds a club in his hand, carries fruits, fishes and meats. He has got a long beard and whiskers. His hairs are curling.

Note :—This Drekkâṇa is human, quadruped and armed. Its ruler is Mars.

उपजातिका–पुष्पप्रपूर्णेन घटेन कन्या मलप्रदिग्धांबरसं-वृतांगी । वस्त्रार्थसंयोगमभीष्टमाना गुरोः कुलं वांछति कन्याकाद्यः ॥ १६ ॥

पुष्पप्रपूर्णेन Puṣpaprapûrṇena, laden with flowers. घटेन Ghaṭena, with a water-pot. कन्या Kanyâ, a virgin girl. मलप्रदिग्धांबरसंवृतांगी Malapradigdhâmbarsambṛitâṃgî, clothed very dirtily. वस्त्रार्थसंयोगमभीष्टमाना Vastrârthasaṃyogamabhîṣṭamânâ, desiring clothings and wealth. गुरोः Guroḥ, preceptors. कुलं Kulam, family; house. वांछति Vânchhati, desires. कन्याकाद्यः Kanyakâdyaḥ, the first Decanate of the sign Kanyâ.

16. The first Decanate of the sign Kanyâ is a virgin girl carrying a water-pot laden with flowers. She is clothed very dirtily and is desirous of clothings and wealth. She is going to the family of her preceptor.

Note :—This Drekkâṇa is of the shape of a woman. The ruler is Mercury.

वैतालीय–पुरुषः प्रगृहीतलेखनिः श्यामो वस्त्रशिरा व्यायय-कृत् । विपुलं च बिभर्ति कार्मुकं रोमव्याप्ततनुश्च मध्यमः ॥१७॥

पुरुषः Puruṣaḥ, a man. प्रगृहीतलेखनिः Pragṛihîtalekhaniḥ, holding a pen in his hand. श्यामः Śyâmaḥ, black. वस्त्रशिरा Vastraśirâ, with a cloth tied round his head. व्याययकृत् Vyayâyakṛit, keeping accounts of receipt and expenditure. विपुलं Vipulam, big. च Cha, and. बिभर्ति Bibharti, holds. कार्मुकं Kârmukam, bow. रोमव्याप्ततनुः Romavyâptatanuḥ, with hairs all over his body. च Cha, and. मध्यमः Madhyamaḥ, the second Decanate.

17. The second Decanate of the sign Kanyâ is a man with a pen in his hand. He is of a black colour and has a piece of cloth round his head. He is taking accounts of receipt and expenditure; holds a big bow in his hand and his body is all overgrown with hairs.

Note :—This Drekkâṇa is human, armed and ruled by Saturn.

उपजातिका–गौरी सुधौताग्रदुकूलगुप्ता समुच्छ्रिता कुंभकटच्छुहस्ता । देवालयं स्त्री प्रयता प्रवृत्ता वदंति कन्यांत्यगत त्रिभागः ॥१८॥

गौरी Gaurî, a woman of fair colour. सुधौताग्रदुकूलगुप्ता Sudhautâgradukûlaguptâ, having well wrapped her body with white silk. समुच्छ्रिता Samuchhritâ, very tall. कुंभकटच्छुहस्ता Kumbhakaṭachhuhastâ, carrying a water-jar and ladle in her hand. देवालयं Devâlayam, temple. स्त्री Strî, woman. प्रयता Prayatâ, very pure; well controlled. प्रवृत्ता Pravṛittâ, ready to go. वदंति Vadanti, say. कन्यांत्यगतः Kanyântagataḥ, the third of the sign Kanyâ. त्रिभागः Tribhâgaḥ, the Decanate.

18. The 3rd Drekkâṇ of the sign Kanyâ is a very tall woman of fair complexion, dressed in white silk so that her face is not easily seen, carrying a water-pot and ladle, pure, and proceeding to a temple.

Note:—This Drekkâṇa is of the shape of a woman. Ruler—Venus.

व० ति०–वीथ्यंतरापणगतः पुरुषस्तुलावानुन्मानमानकुशलः प्रतिमानहस्तः । भांडं विचिंतयति तस्य च मल्यमेतद्रूपं वदंति यवनाः प्रथमं तुलायाः ॥ १६ ॥

वीथ्यंतरापणगतः Vîthyantarâpaṇagataḥ, opening a shop in a market or on the roadway and seated there. पुरुषः Puruṣaḥ, man. तुलावान् Tulâvân, holding a balance (in one hand). उन्मानमानकुशलः Unmânamânakuśalaḥ, skilled in weighing and measuring. प्रतिमानहस्तः Pratimânahastaḥ, weighing articles with his hand. भांडं Bhâṇḍam, pot filled with gold or some other articles. विचिंतयति Vichintayati, thinks. तस्य च Tasya cha, and of those articles. मूल्यं Mûlyam, the price. एतद्रूपं Etadrûpam, so much. वदंति Vadanti, say. यवनाः Yavanâḥ, Yavanâchârya and others. प्रथमं तुलायाः Prathamaṃ tulâyâḥ, the first Decanate of Tulâ.

19. The first Decanate of the sign Tulâ is a man seated in a shop that he has opened in a market or on the way to market. He holds a balance in one hand and is skilled in weighing and measuring. He has got articles in his hand to be weighed or measured and is thinking that such would be their price. Thus say Yavanâchârya and other astrologers.

Note:—This Drekkâṇa is human and ruled by Venus.

त्रोटक—कलशं परिगृह्य विनिष्पतितुं समभीप्सति गृध्रमुखः पुरुषः । क्षुधितस्तृषितश्च कलत्रसुतान्मनसैति तुलाधरमध्यगतः ॥ २० ॥

कलशं Kalaśam, a pot. परिगृह्य Parigrihya, holding in his hand. विनिष्पतितुं Viniṣpatitum, to fall down. समभीप्सति Samabhîpsati, wishes. गृध्रमुखः Gridhramukhah, having his face like that of a vulture. पुरुषः Puruṣah, a man. क्षुधितः Kṣudhitah, hungry. तृषितः Triṣitah, thirsty. च Cha, and. कलत्रसुतान् Kalatrasutân, (thinking of) his wife and sons. मनसा Manasâ, by his mind. इति Iti, thus. तुलाधरमध्यगतः Tulâdharamadhyagatah, the second Decanate of Tulâ.

20. The 2nd Decanate of the sign Tulâ is a man, his face like that of a vulture with a pot in his hand. He is on the point of tumbling ahead; hungry, thirsty and intent on his wife and children.

Note :—This Drekkâṇa is human and bird. Ruler—Saturn.

वंशस्थ—विभीषयंस्तिष्ठति रत्नचित्रितो वने मृगान्कांचनतूणवर्मभृत् । फलामिषं वानररूपभृन्नरस्तुलावसाने यवनैरुदाहृतः ॥ २१ ॥

विभीषयन् Vibhîṣayan, terrifying. तिष्ठति Tiṣṭhati, lives; lies down. रत्नचित्रितः Ratnachitritah, decked with gems. वने Vane, in the forest. मृगान् Mrigân, the animals. कांचनतूणवर्मभृत् Kâmchanatûṇavarmabhrit, holding a golden quiver and wearing an armour. फलामिषं Phalâmiṣam, fruits and meat. वानररूपभृत् Vânararûpabhrit, of a monkey appearance; looking like a monkey. नरः Narah, a man. तुलावसाने Tulâvasâne, the 3rd Decanate of Tulâ. यवनैः Yavanaih, by Yavanâchârya and other astrologers. उदाहृतः Udahritah, is said.

21. The third Decanate of the sign Tulâ is a man with the appearance of a monkey adorned with gems, terrifying animals in the forest. He carries a golden quiver and wears a dress of armour. He carries also fruits and meat.

Note :—This is the human and quadruped Drekkaṇa and ruled by Mercury.

उपजातिका—वस्त्रैर्विहीनाभरणैश्च नारी महासमुद्रात्समुपैति कूलम् । स्थानच्युता सर्प्पनिबद्धपादा मनोरमा वृश्चिकराशिपूर्वः ॥ २२ ॥

वस्त्रैः Vastraiḥ, of any clothing. विहीनाभरणैः Vihînâbharaṇaiḥ, without ornaments. च Cha, and. नारी Nârî, a woman. महासमुद्रात् Mahâsamudrât, after a distant sea voyage. उपैति Upaiti, lands. कूलम् Kûlam, a shore. स्थानच्युता Sthânachyutâ, removed from her place. सर्पनिबद्धपादा Sarppanibaddhapâdâ, with snakes coiled round her legs. मनोरमा Manoramâ, beautiful. वृश्चिकराशिपूर्वः Vṛiśchikarâśipûrvaḥ, the first Decanate of the sign Scorpio.

22. The first Decanate of the sign Vṛiśchika is a woman beautiful, naked and without ornaments, removed from her own place, landed ashore after a distant sea-voyage and having snakes coiled round her legs.

Note :—This is Woman and Serpent Drekkâṇ and ruled by Mars.

दोधक—स्थानसुखान्यभिवांछति नारी भर्तृकृते भुजगावृत-
देहा । कच्छपकुंभसमानशरीरा वृश्चिकमध्यमरूपमुशंति ॥ २३ ॥

स्थानसुखानि Sthânasukhâni, the comforts of her situation. अभिवांछति Abhivânchhati, wishes. नारी Nârî, woman. भर्तृकृते Bhartṛikṛite, for the sake of her husband. भुजगावृतदेहा Bhujagâvṛitadehâ, with a serpent coiled round her body. कच्छपकुंभसमानशरीरा Kachhapakumbhasamânaśarîrâ, her body like that of a turtle or water-jar. वृश्चिकमध्यमरूपमुशंति Vṛiśchikamadhyamarûpamuśanti, the form of the second Decanate of the sign Vṛiśchika, as desired (by the sages).

23. The form of the second Decanate of the sign Vṛiśchika is a woman with a body like that of a turtle or water-jar, trying to make her situation comfortable, and coiling a serpent round her body for the sake of her husband.

Note :—This is a Woman and a Serpent Drekkan. Ruler—Jupiter.

पुष्पिताग्रा—पृथुलचिपिटकूर्मतुल्यवक्त्रः श्वमृगवराहसृगाल-
भीषकारी । अवति च मलयाकरप्रदेशं मृगपतिरंत्यगतस्य वृश्चि-
कस्य ॥ २४ ॥

पृथुलचिपिटकूर्मतुल्यवक्त्रः Pṛithulachipiṭakûrmatulyavaktraḥ, having a broad and flat face like that of a turtle. श्वमृगवराहसृगालभीषकारी Śvamṛigavarâhasṛigâlabhîṣakarî, frightening dogs, deer, jackals and boars. अवति Avati, protects. च Cha, and. मलयाकरप्रदेशं Malayâkarapradeśam, a country called Malaya mountain, where Sandal trees abound. मृगपतिः Mṛigapatiḥ, lion. अंत्यगतस्य Antyagatasya, the third Decanate. वृश्चिकस्य Vṛiśchikasya, of the sign Vṛiśchika.

24. The form of the third Decanate of the sign Vṛiśchika is a lion with a broad and a flat face like that of a turtle.

It affrights dogs, deer, jackals and wild boars and protects the country Malaya mountain that abounds in Sandal trees.

Note :—This is a Quadruped Drekkāṇ, ruled by the Moon.

इंद्रवज्रा–मनुष्यवक्त्रोऽश्वसमानकायो धनुर्विगृह्यायतमाश्रमस्थः । क्रतूपयोज्यानि तपस्विनश्च ररक्ष आद्यो धनुषस्त्रिभागः ॥ २५ ॥

मनुष्यवक्त्रः Manuṣyavaktraḥ, having the face of a man. अश्वसमानकायः Aśvasamânakâyaḥ, having the body of a horse धनुः Dhanuḥ, bow. विगृह्य Vigrihya, holding. आयतम् Âyatam, long stretched ; tight. आश्रमस्थः Âśramasthaḥ, dwelling in his hermitage. क्रतूपयोज्यानि Kratûpayojyâni, the requisites for sacrifice. तपस्विनः Tapasvinaḥ, ascetics. ररक्ष Rarakṣa, protected. आद्यः Âdyaḥ, the first. धनुषः Dhanuṣaḥ, of the sign Dhanu. त्रिभागः Tribhâgaḥ, the Decanate.

25. The form of the 1st Decanate of the sign Dhanu is a man with the body of a horse, with a long bow stretched tight in his hand, residing in his hermitage and protecting the sacrificial requisites and the ascetics thereof.

Note :—This is human and quadruped Decanate armed. Ruler—Jupiter.

उपजातिका–मनोरमा चंपकहेमवर्णा भद्रासने तिष्ठति मध्यरूपा । समुद्ररत्नानि विघट्टयंती मध्यात्रिभागो धनुषः प्रदिष्टः ॥ २६ ॥

मनोरमा Manoramâ, delightful ; delight-giving. चंपकहेमवर्णा Champakahemavarṇâ, colour being that of Champaka flower and gold. भद्रासने Bhadrâsane, seated in a posture called Bhadrâsana. तिष्ठति Tiṣṭhati, is seated. मध्यरूपा Madhyarûpâ, fairly beautiful. समुद्ररत्नानि Samudraratnâni, the sea gems. विघट्टयंती Vighaṭṭayantî, is picking up. मध्यत्रिभागः Madhyatribhâgaḥ, the second Decanate. धनुषः Dhanuṣaḥ, of the sign Dhanu. प्रदिष्टः Pradiṣṭaḥ, is said.

26. The form of the second Decanate of the sign Dhanu is a delightful woman, of a colour resembling that of Champaka flower and gold, seated in the Bhadrâsana posture, fairly beautiful and picking up the sea gems.

Note :—This is a woman Drekkâṇa, and ruled by Mars.

उपजातिका—कूर्ची नरो हाटकचंपकाभो वरासने दंडधरो निषराणः ॥ कौशेयकान्युद्वहतेऽजिनं च तृतीयरूपं नवमस्य राशेः ॥ २७ ॥

कूर्चो Kûrchî, with a long beard and whiskers. नरः Naraḥ, a man. हाटकचंपकाभः Hâṭakachampakâbhaḥ, bright as gold like Champaka flower. वरासने Varâsane, seated in Varâsana posture. दंडधरः Daṇḍadharaḥ, with a staff in hand. निषण्णः Nisaṇṇaḥ, seated. कौशेयकानि Kauśeyakâni, silken cloth; white silken dress. उद्वहते Udvahate, wears. अजिनं Ajinam, deer skin. च Cha, and. तृतीयरूपं Tritîyarûpam, the form of the third Decanate. नवमस्य राशेः Navamasya Râśeḥ, of the ninth sign Dhanu.

27. The form of the third Decanate of Dhanu is a man with long beard and whiskers. His colour is golden and of Champaka flower. He is seated in Varâsana posture with a staff in his hand and dressed in white silk and deerskin.

Note :—This is human Drekkâṇ armed and ruled by the Sun.

दोधक—रोमचितो मकरोपमदंष्ट्रः सूकरकायसमानशरीरः ॥ योक्त्रकजालकबंधनधारी रौद्रमुखो मकरप्रथमस्तु ॥ २८ ॥

रोमचितः Romachitaḥ, hairy. मकरोपमदंष्ट्रः Makaropamadamṣṭraḥ, having teeth like those of a shark. सूकरकायसमानशरीरः Sûkarakâyasamânaśarîraḥ, having a boar-like body. योक्त्रकजालकबंधनधारी Yoktrakajâlakabandhanadhârî, holding a plough and a nose string and fetters. रौद्रमुखः Raudramukhaḥ, having a horrible face. मकरप्रथमः Makaraprathamaḥ, the first Decanate of the sign Makara. तु Tu, thus.

28. The form of the first Decanate of the sign Makara is that of a man who is covered with hairs, whose teeth resemble those of a shark, whose body is like that of a boar, who carries plough and a nose string and iron fetters and whose face looks horrible.

Note :—This is a human Drekkâṇa loaded with fetters. Saturn is its ruler.

उपजातिका—कलास्वभिज्ञाब्जदलायताक्षी श्यामा विचित्राणि च मार्गमाणा ॥ विभूषणालंकृतलोहकर्णा योषा प्रदिष्टा मकरस्य मध्ये ॥ २९ ॥

कलासु Kalâsu, in fine arts. अभिज्ञा Abhijñâ, skilled. अब्जदलायताक्षी Abjadalâyatâkṣî, with eyes like the full blown petals of the lotus. श्यामा Śyâmâ, black.

विचित्राणि Vichitrâṇi, various things. च Cha, and. मार्गमाणा Mârgamâṇâ, searching after. विभूषणालंकृतलोहकर्णा Vibhûṣaṇâlaṃkṛitalohakarṇâ, decked with ornaments and wearning ear-ornaments made of iron. योषा Yoṣâ, a woman. प्रदिष्टा Pradiṣṭâ, said. मकरस्य Makarasya, of the sign Makara. मध्ये Madhye, the 2nd Decanate.

29. The form of the second Decanate of the sign Makara is a black woman skilled in fine arts, with eyes expanded like the petals of the lotus, in search of various things, and adorned with ornaments and having in her ears iron ornaments.

Note :—This is woman Drekkâṇa, ruled by Venus.

रथोद्धता–किन्नरोपमतनुः सकंबलस्तूणचापकवचैः समन्वितः ॥ कुंभमुद्वहति रत्नचित्रितं स्कंधगं मकरराशिपश्चिमः ॥३०॥

किन्नरोपमतनुः Kinnaropamatanuḥ, body of a celestial being called Kinnara. सकम्बलः Sakambalaḥ, with a blanket. तूणचापकवचैः Tûṇachâpakavachaiḥ, with a bow, quiver, and a mail armour. समन्वितः Samaṇvitaḥ, having. कुंभम् Kumbham, a water-jar. उद्वहति Udvahati, carries. रत्नचित्रितं Ratnachitṛitam, set with precious stones. स्कंधगं Skandhagam, on his shoulders. मकरराशिपश्चिमः Makararâśipaśchimaḥ, the third Decanate of the sign Capricorn.

30. The form of the third Decanate of the sign Makara is of the shape of a celestial being called Kinnara, with blanket, quiver, bow, and a mail armour, carrying on his shoulders a water-jar bedecked with precious stones.

Note :—This is human Drekkâṇa, armed and ruled by Mercury.

दोधक–स्नेहमद्यजलभोजनागमव्याकुलीकृतमनाः सकंबलः। कोशकारवसनोऽजिनान्वितो गृद्ध्रतुल्यवदनो घटादिगः ॥ ३१ ॥

स्नेहमद्यजलभोजनागमव्याकुलीकृतमनाः Snehamadyajalabhojanâgamavyâkulîkṛitamanâḥ, anxiously thinking to get oil, liquor, water, and meals. सकंबलः Sakambalaḥ, with a blanket; with an woollen garment. कोशकारवसनः Koṣakâravasanaḥ, having a silken dress. अजिनान्वितः Ajinânvitaḥ, having a deer skin. गृध्रतुल्यवदनः Gṛidhratulya-vadanaḥ, with the face of a vulture. घटादिगः Ghaṭâdigaḥ, the first Decanate of the sign Kumbha.

31. The form of the first Decanate of the sign Kumbha is a man with the face of a vulture, eagerly expecting oil, liquor, water and meals, and dressed in woollen garment, silk and the skin of a deer.

Note :—This is human Drekkâṇa, and ruled by Saturn.

वैतालीय–दग्धे शकटे सशाल्मले लोहान्याहरतेंऽगनावने ।
मलिनेन पटेन संवृता भांडैर्मूर्ध्नि गतैश्च मध्यमः ॥ ३२ ॥

दग्धे Dagdhe, burnt. शकटे Sakaṭe, in a cart. सशाल्मले Saśâlmale, with Śâlmalî wood in it. लोहानि Lohâni, iron. आहरते Âharate, collects. अंगना Angana, a woman. वने Vane, in a forest. मलिनेन Malinena, dirty. पटेन Paṭena, with garments. संवृता Samvṛitâ, wrapped. भांडैः Bhâṇḍaiḥ, pots. मूर्ध्नि Mûrdhni, on the head. गतैः Gataiḥ, having. च Cha, and. मध्यमः Madhyamaḥ, the second.

32. The form of the second Decanate of the sign Kumbha is a woman seated in a burnt cart and carrying pieces of Sâlmalî wood in it. She is collecting iron, living in a forest, and dressed in dirty garments; she carries on her head a pot (containing various utensils).

Note:—This is a woman Drekkâṇa carrying fire. Ruler—Mercury.

इंद्रवज्रा—श्यामः सरोमश्रवणः किरीटी त्वक्पत्रनिर्यासफलैर्बिभर्ति । भांडानि लोहव्यतिमिश्रितानि संचारयंत्यंतगतो घटस्य ॥ ३३ ॥

श्यामः Śyâmaḥ, black; dark सरोमश्रवणः Saromaśravaṇaḥ, with hairs in his ear. किरीटी Kirîṭî, wearing a crown. त्वक्पत्रनिर्यासफलैः Tvakpatraniryâsaphalaiḥ, with bark, leaves, gum, oil, and fruits. बिभर्ति Vibharti, carries. भांडानि Bhâṇḍâni, pots. लोहव्यतिमिश्रितानि Lohavyatimiśritâni, made of iron. संचारयन्ति Samchârayanti, is moving from place to place. अंत्यगतः Antyagataḥ, the third Drekkâṇa. घटस्य Ghaṭasya, of the sign Kumbha.

33. The form of the third Decanate of the sign Kumbha is a dark-looking man, with hairs in his ear, wearing a crown, carrying bark, leaves, gum, oil and fruits in an iron pot from place to place.

Notes:—This is human Drekkâṇa, ruled by Venus.

इंद्रवज्रा—स्रुग्भांडमुक्तामणिशंखमिश्रैर्व्याक्षिप्तहस्तः सविभूषणश्च । भार्याविभूषार्थमपां निधानं नावा प्लवत्यादिगतो झषस्य ॥ ३४ ॥

स्रुग्भांडमुक्तामणिशंखमिश्रैः Srugbhâṇḍamuktâmaṇisamkhamiśraiḥ, with the vessels of sacrificial rites, pots, pearls, gems, and conch shells. व्याक्षिप्तहस्तः Vyâkṣiptahastaḥ, carrying with his hands. सविभूषणः Savibhuṣaṇaḥ, with ornaments. च Cha, and. भार्याविभूषार्थम् Bhâryâvibhûṣârtham, to decorate his wife. अपां निधानं Apâmnidhânam, the ocean; the sea. नावा Nâvâ, by ships. प्लवति Plavati, goes. आदिगतः Âdigataḥ, the first Decanate. झषस्य Jhhaṣasya, of the sign Mîna.

34. The form of the first Decanate of the sign Mîna is a man carrying with his hands the sacrificial utensils, pots, gems, and conch shells and also ornaments. He is sailing in a ship in the sea to get ornaments, &c., for the purpose of decorating his wife.

Note:—This is human, and ruled by Jupiter.

व०ति०–अत्युच्छ्रितध्वजपताकमुपैति पोतं कूलं प्रयाति जलधेः परिवारयुक्ता । वर्णेन चम्पकमुखी प्रमदा त्रिभागो मीनस्य चैष कथितो मुनिभिर्द्वितीयः ॥ ३५ ॥

अत्युच्छ्रितध्वजपताकम् Atyuchhritadhvajapatâkam, a long flagstaff and banner. उपैति Upaiti, goes towards. पोतं Potam, boat. कूलं Kûlam, to the other shore of the sea. प्रयाति Prayâti, goes. जलधेः Jaladheḥ, of the sea. परिवारयुक्ता Parivârayuktâ, accompanied by her family. वर्णेन Varṇena, colour being. चम्पकमुखी Champakamukhî, bright as the Champaka flower. प्रमदा Pramadâ, a woman. त्रिभागः Tribhâgaḥ, the Decanate. मीनस्य Mînasya, of the sign Mîna. च Cha, and. एष Eṣa, this. कथितः Kathitaḥ, said. मुनिभिः Munibhiḥ, by the sages. द्वितीयः Dvitîyaḥ, the second.

35. Seated in a ship with a very long flagstaff and banner and sailing to the other shore with all her family members, with a face gay and bright as the Champaka flower. This is the form of the second Decanate of the sign Mîna. Thus say the sages.

Note:—This is woman Drekkâṇa, ruled by the Moon.

इंद्रवज्रा–श्वभ्रांतिके सर्पनिवेष्टितांगा वस्त्रैर्विहीनः पुरुषस्त्वटव्याम् । चौरानलव्याकुलितांतरात्मा विक्रोशतेऽत्योपगतो झषस्य ॥ ३६ ॥

इति श्रीवराहमिहिराचार्यप्रणीते बृहज्जातके द्रेष्काणस्वरूपाऽध्यायः सप्तविंशः ॥ २७ ॥

श्वभ्रांतिके Svabhrântike, standing near a burrow. सर्पनिवेष्टितांगः Sarpaniveṣṭitâmgaḥ, with a serpent coiled round his body. वस्त्रैः Vastraiḥ, clothing. विहीनः

Vihînaḥ, void of; without. पुरुषः Puruṣaḥ, a man. तु Tu, but. अटव्याम् Aṭavyâm. in a forest. चौराग्निव्याकुलितान्तरात्मा Chaurânalavyâkulitântarâtmâ, his soul being very much troubled with the fear of thieves and fire. विक्रोशते Vikrośate, weeps. अंत्योपगतः Antyopagataḥ, the third Decanate. झषस्य Jhaṣasya, of the sign Mîna.

36. A man standing naked close to a burrow in a forest, with a serpent coiled round his body; he is very much agitated in his mind, having been afraid of fire and thieves and therefore weeps.

Note:—This is a Serpent Drekkâṇa. Ruler—Mars.

Remark:—The author has stated the uses of these descriptions of the Drekkâṇas in his Yâtrâ. If the Drekkâṇa be of agreeable appearance, carrying fruits, flowers, gems, and pots and aspected by benefic planets, there will be success. If they be of hideous appearance, armed and aspected by malefic planets, there will be disgrace and failure; if they carry serpents, or fetters, there will be delirium and imprisonment. The Drekkâṇa description is also of use in tracing out thieves according to Pṛithuyaśas, the son of Varâha Mihira in his work Ṣaḍpañchaśika, a work on Horary Astrology.

Thus ends the 27th Chapter on the Drekkâṇas by Śrî Varâha Mihirâchârya.

CHAPTER XXVIII.

CONCLUSION

उपजातिका—राशिप्रभेदो ग्रहयोनिभेदो वियोनिजन्माथ निषेककालः । जन्माथ सद्यो मरणं तथायुर्दशाविपाकोऽष्टकवर्गसंज्ञः ॥ १ ॥

राशिप्रभेदः Râśiprabhedaḥ, on the Zodiacal definitions. ग्रहयोनिभेदः Grahayonibhedaḥ, on the Planetary definitions. वियोनिजन्म Viyonijanma, on Animal and Vegetable Horoscopy. अथ Atha, subsequently. निषेककालः Niṣekakâlaḥ, on conception time. जन्म अथ Janma atha, subsequently on birth. सद्यः Sadyaḥ, very early. मरणं Maraṇam, death. तथा Tathâ, thus. आयुः Âyuḥ, on the longevity. दशाविपाकः Daśâvipâkaḥ, on Daśâs and on Antardaśâs. अष्टकवर्गसंज्ञः Aṣṭakavargasamjñaḥ, on Aṣṭakavarga.

(In this my work on horoscopy I have dwelt on the following subjects :—)

1. On the Zodiacal Definitions and First Principles. 2. On the Planetary Definitions and First Principles. 3. On Animal and Vegetable Horoscopy. 4. On the Conception Time. 5. On Birth Time. 6. On Early Death. 7. On the Determination of the Length of Life. 8. On Planetary Divisions and Subdivisions of Life known as Daśâs and Antardaśâs. 9. On Aṣṭakavarga.

शालिनी—कर्माजीवो राजयोगाः खयोगाश्चांद्रायोगाद्विग्रहाद्याश्च योगाः । प्रव्रज्याथो राशिशीलानि दृष्टिर्भावस्तस्मादाश्रयोऽथ प्रकीर्णः ॥ २ ॥

कर्माजीवः Karmâjîvaḥ, on Avocation. राजयोगाः Râjayogâḥ, on the birth of kings. खयोगाः Khayogâḥ, on Heavenly planetary combinations. चांद्रायोगाः Chândrâyogâḥ, on the Moon and the Zodiac. द्विग्रहाद्याः योगाः Dvigrahâdyâḥ Yogaḥ, on the two, three, etc., Planets and the Zodiac. प्रव्रज्या Pravrajyâ, on Recluse life. अथ Atha, then. राशिशीलानि Râśiśîlâni, (a) The Moon and the Asterisms (b) The Moon and the Zodiac, (c) The planets and the Zodiac. दृष्टिः Driṣṭiḥ, on aspects. भावः Bhâvaḥ, on the influences of the Planets. तस्मात् Tasmât, thence. आश्रयः Âśravah, on the

Planets in their several Vargas. अथ Atha, then. प्रकीर्णः Prakîrṇaḥ, on miscellaneous combinations.

10. On Avocation. 11. On the Birth of Kings. 12. On Heavenly (the Astral) Combinations. 13. On the Lunar Combinations. 14. On Double (Treble, etc.) Planetary Combinations. 15. On Monastic Orders. 16. On the Moon and the Stars. 17. On the Moon and the Zodiac. 18. On the Planets and the Zodiac. 19. On Planetary Aspects. 20. On the Planetary Influences. 21. On the Planets in their several Vargas. 22. On Miscellaneous Combinations.

शालिनी–नेष्टा योगा जातकं कामिनीनां निर्याणं स्यान्नष्ट-जन्मदृक्काणः। अध्यायानां विंशतिः पंचयुक्ता जन्मन्येतद्यात्रिकं चाभिधास्ये ॥ ३ ॥

नेष्टा योगाः Neṣṭâ Yogâḥ, on malefic combinations. जातकं कामिनीनां Jâtakam kâminînâm, on female horoscopes. निर्याणं Niryâṇam, on death. स्यात् Syât, is. नष्टजन्म Naṣtajanma, on lost horoscopes. दृक्काणः Dṛikâṇaḥ, on the Decanates symbolised. अध्यायानां विंशतिः पंचयुक्ताः Adhyâyânâmviṃśatiḥpañchayuktâḥ, these twenty-five chapters. जन्मनि Janmani, on horoscopy. एतत् Etaṭ, this. यात्रिकं Yâtrikam, (I shall now give a summary of the subjects treated of in my work) on Yâtrâ. च Cha, and. अभिधास्ये Abhidhâsye, I shall now speak.

23. On Malefic Yogas. 24. On Female Horoscopes 25. On Death. 26. On the Discovery of Lost Horoscopes. 27. On the Decanates symbolised.

I shall now give a summary of the subjects treated of in my work on Yâtrâ.

उपजातिका–प्रश्नास्तिथिर्भं दिवसः क्षणश्च चंद्रो विलग्नं त्वथ लग्नभेदः। शुद्धिर्ग्रहाणामथ चापवादो विमिश्रकाख्यं तनुवेपनं च ॥ ४ ॥

प्रश्नाः Praśnâḥ, on Praśna Prabheda. तिथिः Tithiḥ, on Tithibala. भं Bhaṃ, on Nakṣatrâbhidhâna. दिवसः Divasaḥ, on Vâraphalaṃ. क्षणः च Kṣaṇaḥ cha, and on Muhûrta Nirdeśa. चंद्रः Chandraḥ, on Chandra Bala. विलग्नम् Vilagnam, on Lagna Niśchaya. तु अथ Tu atha, and then. लग्नभेदः Lagnabhedaḥ, on Lagna Bheda. शुद्धिः Śuddhiḥ, on Graha Śuddhih. ग्रहाणां अथ Grahâṇâm atha, and of Planets. च अपवादः cha Apavâdaḥ, and on Apavâda. विमिश्रकाख्यम् Vimiśrakâkhyam, on Miśraka. तनुवेपनं च Tanuvepananam cha, also on Tanuvepanaṃ.

Ch 1. Prasna Prabheda. Ch 2. Tithibala. Ch 3. Nakṣatrâbhidhâṇa. Ch 4. On Vâraphala. Ch 5. On Muhûrta Nirdeśa. Ch 6. On Chandrabala. Ch 7. On Lagna Niśchaya. Ch 8. On Lagna Bheda. Ch 9. On Graha Śuddhi. Ch 10. On Apavâda. Ch 11. On Miśraka. Ch 12. On Tanuvepanam.

उपजातिका—अतः परं गुह्यकपूजनं स्यात्स्वप्नं ततः स्नानविधिः प्रदिष्टः। यज्ञो ग्रहाणामथ निर्गमश्च क्रमाच्च दिष्टः शकुनोपदेशः ॥ ५ ॥

अतः परं Ataḥ param, after this. गुह्यकपूजनं Guhyakapûjanam, on Guhyakapûjâ. स्यात् Syât, comes. स्वप्नं Svapnam, on dreams. ततः Tataḥ, then. स्नानविधिः Snânavidhiḥ, on bath. प्रदिष्टः Pradiṣṭaḥ, written. यज्ञः ग्रहाणां अथ Yajñaḥ Grahâṇâm atha, and on Graha Yajña. निर्गमः च Nirgamaḥ, cha, and on travels. क्रमात् Kramât, in regular order. च Cha, and. दिष्टः Diṣṭaḥ, advised. शकुनोपदेशः Śakunopadeśaḥ, on Śakuna, on miscellaneous signs such as sounds, *etc.*

5. 13. On Guhyakapûjâ. 14. On Dreams. 15. On Bath. 16. On Graha Yajña. 17. On Travels. 18. On Sakuna.

उपजातिका—विवाहकालः करणं ग्रहाणां प्रोक्तं पृथक्तद्विपुलाथ शाखा। स्कंधैस्त्रिभिर्ज्योतिषसंग्रहोऽयं मया कृतो दैवविदांहिताय ॥ ६ ॥

विवाहकालः Vivâhakâlaḥ, on marriage time. करणं Karaṇan, or Graha Karaṇa, (on the planets). ग्रहाणां Grahâṇâm, of the planets. प्रोक्तम् Proktam, said. पृथक् Pṛithak, separately. तद्विपुला Tadvipulâ, dealing on which elaborately. अथ Atha, then. शाखा Śâkhâ, sub-division. स्कन्धैः Skandhaiḥ, branches. त्रिभिः Tribhiḥ, three (1) Astronomical, (2) Horoscopical, and (3) Saṃhitâ. ज्योतिषसंग्रहः Jyotiṣasaṃgrahaḥ, Jyotisha Śâstra. अयम् Ayam, this. मया Mayâ, by me, Varâha Mihirâchârya. कृतः Kritaḥ, treated of. दैवविदां Daivavidâm, for the astronomers and astrologers. हिताय Hitâya, for the benefit of.

6. 19 Vivâhakâla. 20. Grahakaraṇa (of the planets)

The last of the above subjects has been separately treated of by me in my astronomical work known as Pañchasiddhânta. Thus the three branches of the Yotiṣa Śâstra, *viz.*, Astronomy, Horoscopy and Saṃhitâ have been dwelt on by me for the benefit of the astronomers and astrologers.

मालिनी—पृथुविरचितमन्यैः शास्त्रमेतत्समस्तं तदनु लघु मयेदं तत्प्रदेशार्थमेव। कृतमिह हि समर्थं धीविषाणामलत्वे मम यदि ह यदुक्तं सज्जनैः क्षम्यतां तत् ॥ ७ ॥

पृथु Prithu, elaborately. विरचितं Virachitam, written. अन्यैः Anyaiḥ, by other ancient writers, *e.g.* Yavanâchârya and others. शास्त्रं Sâstram, this astrological treatise. एतत् Etat, this. समस्तम् Samastam, the whole. तदनु Tadanu, after them. लघु Laghu, briefly. मया Mayâ, by me. इदम् Idam, this. तत्प्रदेशार्थम् Tatpradeśârtham, to convey instructions on this subject. एव Eva, thus. कृतम् Kritam, I have tried. इह Iha, here. हि Hi, certainly. समर्थम् Samartham, able. धीविषाणामलत्वे Dhîviṣâṇâmalatve, to enlighten the minds of the intelligent. मम Mama, mine. यदि Yadi, if. ह Ha, so. यत् उक्तम् Yat uktam, what have been written. सज्जनैः Sajjanaiḥ, by the learned critics. क्षम्यतां Kṣamyatâm, ought to be forgiven. तत् Tat, those (omissions), (if any).

7. All these astrological points have been dealt with very elaborately by ancient astrologers (*e. g.*, Yavanâchârya and others). Afterwards I write briefly to enlighten the minds of the intelligent pupils on those points. If any important points be found omitted, I beg pardon of the learned critics.

व०ति०—ग्रंथस्य या प्रचरतोऽस्य विनाशमेति लेख्याद्बहुश्रुतमुखाधिगमक्रमेण ॥ यद्वा मया कुकृतमल्पमिहाकृतं वा कार्यं तदत्र विदुषा परिहृत्य रागम् ॥ ८ ॥

ग्रन्थस्य Granthasya, of this treatise. या Yâ, whatever portion. प्रचरतः Pracharataḥ, in putting it to print. अस्य Asya, of it; its. विनाशम् Vinâśam, omissions or additions. एति Eti, have taken place लेख्यात् Lekhvyât, due to the defect of the writer, &c. बहुश्रुतमुखाधिगमक्रमेण Bahuśrutamukhâdhigamakrameṇa, by duly learning from the mouths of the well-versed astrologers. यत् Yat, whatever. वा Vâ, otherwise. मया Mayâ, by me. कुकृतम् Kukritam, wrongly written. अल्पम् Alpam, imperfectly written. इह Iha, here. अकृतम् Akritam, or omitted. वा Vâ, or. कार्यम् Kâryaṃ, should be (forgiven). तत् अत्र Tat atra, these here. विदुषा Viduṣâ, by the learned Pundits. परिहृत्य Parihritya, leaving aside. रागम् Râgam, envy.

8. If any portion of the text be found omitted, due to its being wrongly written or copied, defects should be

made up by hearing duly from the well-versed astrologers. Or if I have written wrongly or insufficiently, the learned will kindly excuse me and make the necessary corrections themselves, setting aside all feelings of jealousy.

व०ति०-आदित्यदासतनयस्तदवाप्तबोधः कापित्थके सवि-तृलब्धवरप्रसादः ॥ आवंतिको मुनिमतान्यवलोक्य सम्यग्घोरां वराहमिहिरो रुचिरां चकार ॥ ९ ॥

आदित्यदासतनयः Âdityadâsatanayaḥ, the son of Âdityadâsa. तदवाप्तबोधः Tadavâptabodhaḥ, from whom he received his education. कापित्थके Kâpitthake, in the village of Kapittha. सवितृलब्धवरप्रसादः Savitṛilabdhavaraprasâdaḥ, obtaining the boon of knowledge from the Sun. आवन्तिकः Âvantikaḥ, in the province of Avantika. मुनिमतानि अवलोक्य Munimatâni avalokya, after a careful examination of the works of the ancient sages. सम्यक् Samyak, thoroughly. होरां Horâm, this astrological treatise. वराहमिहिरः Varâha Mihiraḥ, Śrî Varâha Mihirâchârya. रुचिरां Ruchiram, neatly. चकार Chakâra, has written.

9. Varâha Mihira, the son of (the Brâhmiṇ) Âditya Dâsâ, village Kapittha, from whom he received his education and enlightenment, obtained the boon of knowledge from the Sun, spent his days (in the Court of Ujjainî) in the province of Avanti and has fully written this neat work on Horoscopy after a careful examination of the works of ancient sages on the subject.

आर्या-दिनकरमुनिगुरुचरणप्रणिपातकृतप्रसादमतिनेदम् ॥ शास्त्रमुपसंगृहीतं नमोऽस्तु पूर्वप्रणेतृभ्यः ॥ १० ॥

इति वराहमिहिराचार्यप्रणीते बृहज्जातके उपसंहा-राध्यायोऽष्टाविंशः ॥ २८ ॥

दिनकरमुनिगुरुचरणप्रणिपातकृतप्रसादमतिना Dinakaramunigurucharaṇapraṇipâtakṛitaprasâdamatinâ, by the kind favour of the Sun, the sages (Vaśiṣṭha) and Âdityadâsa, all worshipped by me. इदम् Idaṃ, this (present work). शास्त्रम् Śâstram, present work. उपसंगृहीतम् Upasaṃgṛihîtam, I have been enabled to write. नमः अस्तु Namaḥ astu, salutation be. पूर्वप्रणेतृभ्यः Pûrvapraṇetṛibhyaḥ, to the ancient writers of Horoscopy.

10. By worshipping the Sun, the sages (Vaśiṣṭha and others) and the feet of my father, the Guru, I have obtained the favour of them all, and thus I have been able to write this Śâstra. Salutation to the ancient authors of this Astrological science.

Thus ends the 28th Chapter on Conclusion by Śrî Varâha Mihirâchârya of Avantika.

THE END

APPENDIX

On Mṛityu Yogas.

Human life is classed under three heads:—first, Dîrghâyu; second, Madhyâyu; third, Alpâyu. Thirty-two years (32) is the limit of Alpâyu; sixty-four (64) years is the limit of Madhyâyu; ninety-six (96) years is the limit of Dîrghâyu. One hundred and twenty (120) years is Pûrṇâyu. Some take these limits as 32, 69 and 120.

The following notes are taken from Jaiminîya Sûtras, 5th Pâda, First Adhyâya:—

I. The length of life is determined from the ruler of the Ascendant and from the ruler of the eighth house from the Ascendant.

If the ruler of the Ascendant and the ruler of the eighth house be both in moveable signs, or if one ruler be in fixed sign and another ruler be in a common sign, the Âyu or the length of life is known as Dîrghâyu.

If one of the above-mentioned rulers be in a moveable sign and the other ruler be in a fixed sign, the Âyu is known as Madhyâyu. Or, if both the rulers be in common signs, even then it is known as Madhyâyu.

If both the rulers be in fixed signs, the Âyu is known as Alpâyu; or, if one ruler be in a moveable sign and the other in a common sign, even then it is known as Alpâyu.

II. The length of life is also determined, as above, by similar considerations from the Ascendant and the Moon.

III. Similarly the length of life is determined from the Janma Lagna (the Ascendant during birth) and the Horâ Lagna.

The *Janma Lagna* is the rising sign at the time of birth. The *Horâ Lagna* is calculated thus:—Find out the number of ghaṭîkâs from the sunrise to the Iṣṭakâla or the time when birth took place. Divide the number of ghaṭikâs by 2½ (two and a half); the quotient stands for the sign. Multiply the remainder by 30 and divide the product by 2½; the quotient stands for degrees. Multiply the remainder by sixty (60) and divide the result by 2½; the quotient stands for minutes. Now if the Janma Lagna be odd, then count the signs, degrees, and minutes as above obtained onwards from the sign occupied by the Sun; and if the Janma Lagna be even, then count the signs, degrees and minutes above obtained from the Janma Lagna itself; and the result now arrived is the *Horâ Lagna*.

Now, if the three methods, above mentioned, for determining the length of life, all coincide and yield the same result, then that is, no doubt, to be accepted; if the two methods coincide and the third differ, the result arrived at by two methods should be accepted; if the three methods differ from one another, then accept what is obtained from the Janma Lagna and the Horâ Lagna. Or, if the Moon occupy the Ascendant or the seventh house from the Ascendant, then the result obtained from the Lagna and the Moon is to be accepted.

The Prastâra Chakram is given below for information:—

	Dîrghâyu.	Madhyâyu.	Alpâyu.
Lagneś, Aṣṭameś	Moveable	Moveable	Moveable
Lagna Chandra, Lagna Horâ	Moveable	Fixed	Common
Lagneś, Aṣṭameś	Fixed	Fixed	Fixed
Lagna Chandra, Lagna Horâ	Common	Moveable	Fixed
Lagneś, Aṣṭames	Common	Common	Common
Lagna Chandra, Lagna Horâ	Fixed	Common	Moveable.

The above rules will determine generally the length of life. There are some specialities; and these are not mentioned here. The reader is referred to the Jaiminiya Sûtras.

After determining the Alpâyu, Madhyâyu, or Dîrghâyu, find out next which planet is Mârakeśa or the cause of death. In the Daśâ or Antardaśâ period of such planet, death will occur.

Now, the eighth house and the third house from the Janma Lagna (Birth Ascendant) are known as Âyusthân or life-giving houses. The twelfth houses from these are known as Mârakasthân or death-causing houses. Therefore it follows that the seventh house and the second house from the Janma Lagna becomes the Mârakasthân or death-causing houses. The rulers of these Mârakasthânas are called Mârakeśas.

Of these two houses, again, the second house is stronger than the seventh; therefore, whichever malefic planets (the rulers of the third, sixth, and the eleventh houses) be found with the Mârakeśa, *i.e.*, the ruler of the second house, death will occur during their Daśâs and Antardaśâs.

And in case their Daśâ periods do not fall within the Alpâyu period, death will occur during the Daśâ periods of the ruler of the twelfth house from the Janma Lagna or of the malefic ruler (of the 3rd, 6th and 11th houses) concerned with the ruler of the 12th house. If their Daśâ periods do not come within the Alpâyu periods, then death will occur during the Daśâs of the benefic rulers concerned with the ruler of the 12th house; and if these also do not occur, death will occur during the Daśâ period of the ruler of the eighth house from the Janma Lagna.

And if all the periods mentioned above do not come at all within the-Alpâyu period, then do not take into account at all the Mârakasthânas; consider only the malefic planets (the rulers of the 3rd, 6th or 11th houses) and death will occur during their Daśâ periods.

If Saturn be the ruler of the 3rd, 6th or 11th house and if it be found with the Mârakeśa, death will occur, no doubt, during the Daśâ period of Saturn and not of any other planet.

For further particulars see the Laghu Pârâśari, Jâtakâlaṅkâra, and other authoritative treatises.

Alphabetical Index of the Verses.